Atlantic Crossings

Atlantic Crossings

Social Politics in a Progressive Age

Daniel T. Rodgers

The Belknap Press of Harvard University Press

Cambridge, Massachusetts, and London, England

Printed in the United States of America
Fourth printing, 2001

Library of Congress Cataloging-in-Publication Data

Rodgers, Daniel T.
Atlantic crossings : social politics in a progressive age / Daniel T. Rodgers.
p. cm.
Includes bibliographical references and index.
ISBN 0-674-05131-9 (alk. paper)
ISBN 0-674-00201-6 (paper)
1. United States—Social conditions.
2. United States—Economic conditions.
3. Progressivism (United States politics)
4. Europe—Social conditions.
5. Europe—Economic conditions.
6. Europe—Foreign economic relations—United States.
7. United States—Foreign economic relations—Europe.
I. Title.
HN57.R556 1998
306′.0973—dc21 98-3188

Designed by Gwen Nefsky Frankfeldt

For Peter and Dwight

Contents

Illustrations

Atlantic Crossings

Prologue

"Was there a world outside of America?" the muckraker Ray Stannard Baker tried to recollect his state of mind as an apprentice journalist in Chicago in the 1890s. "If there was, I knew next to nothing at all about it—as a reality . . . I knew something of European history—the old tyranny of kings, the absurdity of aristocracy, the futility of feudal wars—out of which America, the wonderful, had stepped proudly into the enlightenment of the Bill of Rights and the Declaration of Independence. I was a true geocentric American."[1]

In the face of a provincialism this profound, it is hard to resist a knowing smile. Every serious reader of the past instinctively knows what Baker had yet to learn: that nations lie enmeshed in each others' history. Even the most isolated of nation-states is a semipermeable container, washed over by forces originating far beyond its shores. Even the most powerful act their part within world systems beyond their full control.

If complicity in world historical forces marks all nations, it especially marks outpost nations, like the United States, which begin as other nations' imperial projects. From the earliest European settlements in North America forward, the Atlantic functioned for its newcomers less as a barrier than as a connective lifeline—a seaway for the movement of people, goods, ideas, and aspirations. A key outpost for European trade and a magnet for European capital, the eighteenth- and nineteenth-century United States cannot be understood outside the North Atlantic economy of which it was a part.

Through that trade came human beings, both slave and free, in a world system that bound the fates of four continents together. World markets in manufactured and agricultural goods shaped the landscapes of the great port cities and the interior factory towns; they made and unmade the fate of the cotton South and the western wheatlands. In a land that elevated Shakespeare, Scott, and Dickens into its literary pantheon, books and authors circulated through the North Atlantic economy as well, carrying with them fashion, taste, ideas, and, at times, the seeds of powerful social movements. The American Revolution had itself been part of a larger shift in politics that ran from Bogotá to Berlin. The antislavery movement, the labor movement, the women's movement—these, too, were transnational events. The web of global interdependencies that binds the fate of the late-twentieth-century United States to markets and aspirations around the globe is new only in its details; in the broad sense, this has been the permanent condition of American history.

But if these are facts every historian knows, history writing too often fails to follow its own best instincts. Tangled in simplistic relationships with civics education, national historical accounts absorb their surrounding nationalism. Focused on questions of national difference, historical scholarship bends to the task of specifying each nation's distinctive culture, its peculiar history, its *Sonderweg*, its exceptionalism. Since every nation's history is—in fact and by definition—distinct, the move is not without reason. At its worst, however, the result is to produce histories lopped off at precisely those junctures where the nation-state's permeability might be brought into view, where the transnational forces do their most important work. The narrative field too often shrinks back on the nation; the boundaries of the nation-state become an analytical cage.[2]

Social politics is a case in point. Of studies of progressive and New Deal politics there is no end. On the roots of the impulse to limit the social costs of aggressive, market capitalism, some of the very best American history writing has found its focus. As befits a large-order event, large-scale explanations have been employed to understand it. Thus the rise of the interventionist state in America has been traced to the shock of particularly rapid industrialization, the thin and distended nature of the mid-nineteenth-century American state and society, the status anxieties of a declining middle class, the scientistic ambitions of a new elite of experts and professionals, the social maternalism of middle-class women, the demands from below of farmers and wage workers, and the demands of industrial capitalists at the top for a more rationalized social order than capitalist competition, by itself, could create. But an unspoken "geocentrism," as Baker styled it, frames them all.

Familiar as these explanations are, they leave unstated what every contemporary who followed these issues knew: that the reconstruction of American social politics was of a part with movements of politics and ideas throughout the North Atlantic world that trade and capitalism had tied together. This was not an abstract realization, slumbering in the recesses of consciousness. Tap into the debates that swirled through the United States and industrialized Europe over the problems and miseries of "great city" life, the insecurities of wage work, the social backwardness of the countryside, or the instabilities of the market itself, and one finds oneself pulled into an intense, transnational traffic in reform ideas, policies, and legislative devices. For a moment, London's East End and New York City's Lower East Side; the "black country" of Pittsburgh, Essen, and Birmingham; and university debates and chancery discussions in Paris, Washington, London, and Berlin formed a world of common referents.

Stretching from the 1870s, when the first American students began to catch wind of the assault on laissez-faire in the late-nineteenth-century German universities, through the convulsions of the Second World War, that moment marks off a more distinctive phase in the American past than history writing has yet fully to grasp. Politics in the previous half century had marched to a more internalist drummer. The formation of a democratic nation had been early- and mid-nineteenth-century America's core political project; from Jackson's era to Lincoln's, Americans with an eye cocked on the rest of the world had reason to think themselves in the vanguard of a world democratic movement.

After 1945, when the United States found itself suddenly astride a global system of its own, the exceptionalist theme returned, full volume. In the United States of the 1990s, university-based experts on the world's ways in social politics are more numerous than ever before, but in day-to-day American political debates, their knowledge of other nations' policies carries virtually negligible weight. The strangers abroad are not us; their experience is not usable. In the terms Max Weber once applied to the early Protestants, the United States is *in* but not *of* the world it commands; its destiny and experience are, by the very nature of things, exceptional. Bill Clinton's bid for historical greatness—the national health insurance debates of 1993 and 1994—replayed the postwar, exceptionalist theme. After a perfunctory nod toward Canada, the Democrats proceeded to set aside the rest of the world's experience as inapplicable to the special political character of the United States and to concoct a health insurance system unlike any other in the world. The Republicans, in return, lambasted their effort for not being "American" enough.

In comparison, the years between the 1870s and the Second World War were indeed different. Between the democratic confidence of the early nineteenth century and the hubris of the late twentieth century, one begins to discern a moment when American politics was peculiarly open to foreign models and imported ideas—when the North Atlantic economy formed, for many strategically placed Americans, a world mart of useful and intensely interesting experiments. These were years in which city politicians in the United States could battle the pros and cons of city-owned streetcars on the basis of Glasgow's experience, when the workings of European social insurance systems were grist for highly publicized investigatory commissions, when certain model cities in England and Germany drew social progressives from around the world, when other nations' social politics, in short, were *news.*

The making of the Atlantic era in social politics hinged on a new set of institutional connections with the industrializing nations of Europe. It required new sorts of brokers to span that connection. It required, finally, an intellectual shift, a sense of complicity within historical forces larger than the United States: a suspension of confidence in the peculiar dispensation of the United States from the fate of other nations. Against the pitchmen for made-in-America-only ideas and politics, the cosmopolitan progressives fought across a hundred fronts. But in their defeats as well as their victories, in the connections they tried to forge with progressive ideas and movements elsewhere and the battles those efforts precipitated, their endeavors shaped the era more than the conventional wisdom—preoccupied with the Americanness of American progressive politics—has yet comprehended.

In part, it is these brokers' story I have tried to tell, following a portion of the threads they themselves spun out across the Atlantic. Like their stories, this too tacks back and forth across the core domain of nineteenth- and early-twentieth-century industrial capitalism. Britain and Germany were the Americans' primary models, and rivals, abroad, but their borrowings often took them still farther afield. The North Atlantic economy I have called this broader region, stretching roughly from Berlin to San Francisco.

The result is not comparative history as that term is generally understood. The crux of comparative history is difference. By masking interdependencies between nations, freezing historically contingent processes into ideal types, and laying across them a grid of social and political characteristics, the method of comparison throws a powerful light on differences.[3] No one can work in this field without amassing a debt to the best of this comparative work. In the end, however, it is the connections between the industrializing countries of the late nineteenth and early twentieth centuries—their vulnerability to the same economic forces, the closeness with which they read each others' experience and policy experiments—that makes the differences between their policy choices historically interesting. Robert Kelley's admonition still carries weight: to take seriously "the appearance of similar movements within the several countries, like the outcroppings of common strata, derived from shared intellectual and social influences."[4] Atlantic-era social politics had its origins not in its nation-state containers, not in a hypothesized "Europe" nor an equally imagined "America," but in the world between them. There are gains to be made by starting with connections.

The first aim of these pages, then, is to reconstruct a distinctive era in the American past, in which American social politics were tied to social political debates and endeavors in Europe through a web of rivalry and exchange. Still, it would be foolish to wish to escape the question of difference. Like all polities, America *was* different. Its state structure differed from those of its European rivals, its ideology swung to different poles, its structures of interests were different, its history was distinct. The difficulty in the face of so overdetermined a list of distinctions lies in specifying what difference these differences actually made.

The proposals and policies that the cosmopolitan progressives tried to carry over the Atlantic network form, for these purposes, a laboratory rare in historical studies. Each imported measure had to be disposed of, from old-age insurance to subsidized workers' housing, from city planning to rural reconstruction. Some made the crossing to the United States with relatively little difficulty. Others sank in mid passage. Still more were transformed, their "Americanization" leaving a precise and revealing trace of the forces and circumstances they had come up against. Follow these processes through, from foreign model to domestic outcome, and there are surprises as well as confirmations to be found.

Finally, a prefatory word about ideas in politics.[5] The central protagonists of these pages were rarely intellectuals, but they cared passionately about issues and ideas. To a type of political historian and political scientist, that will be enough to set in motion, at the very outset, a certain instinctual discomfort. Conventional political analysis cleaves hard to what is called outcomes analysis; its home turf is the legislative process and the heavy claims of interest and political advantage brought to bear there. This emphasis is not without ample reason. But the political process is broader than outcomes. One must also ask how issues get into the political stream itself, how problems are defined and issues framed.

The conventional wisdom settles too often for a relatively unreflective functionalism. Be the issue intolerable poverty, chaotic urban transport, or strangling monopoly, the problem itself is imagined ultimately to drive the political engine forward. Metastasizing into crisis, it forces itself by its very urgency onto the political agenda—mediated sometimes through public opinion, sometimes through interest groups, sometimes through social movements. Between the moment when the problem wedges its way into the political arena and the moment when the heavy forces of interests and politics dispose of it, those with "ideas" have a brief role to play framing alternatives and solutions. But since in the nature of things the legislative result is always different and commonly far messier than their design, those who compete merely with words and proposals are almost always chalked up among the losers.

But this is not the real world of politics. There, as John Kingdon has shrewdly observed, ideas and problems, solutions and potential crises, circulate remarkably independently through the political stream.[6] Generated from myriad sources, their futures depend on their finding one another. Just as a political idea becomes politically viable only when it is successfully attached to a sense of need and urgency, no less do problems become politically significant only when they become attached to politically imaginable solutions. The framers of solutions do not come into the act at the last minute. They are present at the moment of creation, transforming a tragic but incurable condition into a politically solvable problem and, by that very act, defining the field within which legislators and executives will ultimately maneuver.

It was this agenda-setting role of ideas that gave political consequence to the new world of transferable social experience and appropriable policy models thrown open at the end of the nineteenth century. Americans in the Progressive Era between the 1890s and the First World War did not swim in problems—not more so, at any rate, than Americans who lived through the simultaneous collapse of the economy and the post–Civil War racial settlement in the 1870s. It would be more accurate to say that they swam in a sudden abundance of solutions, a vast number of them brought over through the Atlantic connection. The existence of a large external stock of working solutions helped denaturalize the "laws" of economics. It eased policy makers past many a political impasse. Come back to the New Deal in the same way, placing it in the stream of transnational models and influences that converged on it, and it, too, takes on a new and unexpected character.

These, then, form our central questions: how an era of transatlantic social politics came into being; how it was sustained; what difference the web of transnational connections made; how much it shaped political choices; and how like and different it shows, in retrospect, the United States to have been from its closest economic counterparts. Attending to events and processes throughout the north Atlantic economy, to both near and distant contexts, to politics as well as ideas, these pages comprise an experiment in shifting the frames and boundaries of a classic American story.

Like all reframings, its aim is to make difficulties—to make it hard to view the familiar picture in old, familiar ways. Follow the lines of progressive and New Deal social politics as they spill across the nation-state's boundaries, and one begins to rediscover a largely forgotten world of transnational borrowings and imitation, adaptation and transformation. In the transatlantic progressive moment one begins to recover a phase of American history and politics we have all but lost.

1

Paris, 1900

World of Iron

Every age, even the most calculating and material, needs a symbol, and Gustave Eiffel, who knew a promotional opportunity when it came his way, was eager to provide one. A "factory chimney," critics called his tower at its birth in 1889, "gigantic and hideous." An upended illustration of the principles of railroad bridge design, it defied the scale of the city below it. The tile roofs of old Paris's neighborhoods, the mansards and boulevards of the Second Empire, even the great towers of Notre Dame (as the sketches by Eiffel's engineers pointedly showed) all shrank to Lilliputian dimensions beside this display of engineering hubris. The Eiffel Tower was an advertisement for the tradition-shattering, revolutionary possibilities of industrial technology. Little wonder that Paris's artists immediately petitioned to have it torn down.[1]

Eiffel's tower had a second purpose as well. Built for the Paris exposition of 1889, it was designed as a giant billboard for a great, temporary market of the wares of nineteenth-century industrial capitalism. The exposition's official purpose was to celebrate the centenary of the French Revolution and, in its reflected glory, the still fragile political fortunes of the Third Republic. In fact, trade—not politics—had dominated every world exposition since the iron and glass Crystal Palace Exposition in London in 1851, and the Paris exhibition was no exception. Machines and machine-made commodities of all sorts, a swarming bazaar of buyers, sellers, and admirers of the marketable fruits of capital and enterprise all crowded onto the Champ de Mars beneath the iron frame of Eiffel's tower. Call it a fair or an *exposition universelle,* what was constructed in its name was a marketplace: vendors' stalls, sellers' cries, the haggling of exchanging parties all pushed to outsized dimensions.

Eleven years later, in 1900, the French convened a still larger fair on the same site, this time to inventory the century itself. The Eiffel Tower was repainted a bright yellow for the occasion, its gas jets replaced by hundreds of new electric lights to keep it abreast of the onward rush of technological progress. On the fairground itself, a still larger stock of goods—the largest to be displayed in this fashion anywhere until the world's fairs of the 1930s—was crammed still more tightly into still more numerous galleries. The 1889 exposition, despite its planners' intentions, had been largely a French affair. This time both Germany, ostracized in 1889, and the United States were represented in force, elbowing Britain for exhibition space and prestige in their race for industrial primacy. In 1889 visitors sated with machinery had found distraction in the belly dancers in the "Streets of Cairo" and the manly heroics of Buffalo Bill's Wild West Show; in 1900, the non-European world spoke more pointedly of markets than of sexuality. From the elaborate French colonial exhibits to the rolling dioramas of the "Around the World" illusion on the Champ de Mars, one could not avoid reminders of the headlong expansion, to a global scale, of the turn-of-the-century market. From workshops throughout the world, greased with the sweat of distant workers and hauled to Paris over elaborate networks of steam transport, acre upon acre of goods came to rest in Paris.[2]

Not all the visitors who thronged the fair in the summer of 1900 would have been comfortable thinking of the exposition as merely a great department store, a Macy's of Western civilization. In their own inventory of the century, not many would have given first rank to the penetration of the market—the domain of things salable, commodifiable, exchangeable in the private contract of buyers and sellers—into ever more extensive realms of social life. Progress, refinement, and civilization demanded their due. It was in acknowledgment of these sensibilities that the functional iron frames of the exposition buildings were iced with a nervous froth of colored plaster, allegorical sculpture, and beaux arts excesses. It was for them that the showcase buildings at the exposition's entrance were given over to art, as if their marble and oils could ennoble the material core of the century's achievements.

But in hindsight, the hard, iron frame of the Eiffel Tower was the more honest symbol of the forces that converged on Paris in 1900. Raised with such pointed indifference to its surroundings, such prideful disregard for the past, what did it symbolize if not the tough, self-centered passions of the merchants, industrialists, engineers, and capital investors whose revolution in the social and technical modes of production had already left a profound mark on Western Europe and the United States? With great energy, imagination, and callousness they had turned upside down an older artisan and peasant economy, pushing back the countervailing forces of state and custom where they had blocked the way. They had served what the century's economists had called the natural laws, the iron necessities of the market. They had injected the self-striving individualism, the unsentimental calculation, the primacy of price and profit once concentrated within the limits of the town marketplace, into vast new domains of economic life. The goods laid out in such profusion on the Champ de Mars were testimony to their success.

If the Paris exposition of 1900 summed up the century, there could be no doubt what its main icon stood for: the sharp, exuberant, often liberating, and (lest we forget) painfully disruptive revolution in human relations released by the marriage of machine technology to the social ethics of the marketplace. The world of iron was the domain of industrial capitalism.

Confidence in the age of capital was the fair's official message; the new order put itself on display and pronounced the results progress. But one does not need to read far in contemporary impressions of the Paris exposition to catch a note of doubt and worry. Twice within living memory this overtly stable nexus of markets and trade had unraveled in economic crisis; in 1900 the nations of the North Atlantic economy were just working their way back to prosperity from the hard times of the mid-1890s. Still more fragile was what men and women had learned, with trepidation, to call the "social peace" between the newly massed forces of labor and capital. On both sides of the Atlantic—from the wave of strikes in France between 1880 and 1883 to the meteoric rise of the Knights of Labor in the United States in 1885 and 1886 to the great strikes of London dockworkers and Ruhr miners in 1889—the 1880s had launched a cycle of worker-employer strife whose ultimate destination no one could predict.

Henry Adams may have taken a certain pride in his morbidity, but he was not alone in asking, as he watched the fair's electric generators spinning noiselessly on their axes, "where in Hell" the new century was going. Patrick Geddes, the Scots polymath and city planner, devoted his whole summer to Paris, leading schools of visitors through the fair, trying to give them a synoptic understanding of the vast social transformations revealed there. Friedrich Naumann, struggling to launch a new social progressive party out of the failures of an older German liberalism, sent a series of newspaper letters home from Paris in which he worried about the crowding of ever more rootless folk into the cities and their diminution in the new "mass-life" on display at the fair. Jane Addams, too, found it hard to shake the recent past from her mind. Drawn to Paris as a delegate to the international women's congress and a juror for the "social economy" section of the fair, she found herself haunting the fair's working-class housing displays, hoping they might show a way out of the violent passions that had engulfed the Pullman company's model village, and, from there, all of Chicago, in 1894. To drive all these issues home, the socialist International convened in Paris in the summer of 1900. But one did not need the socialists to bring the debit side of the revolution in markets and production to mind. The very organization of the fair invited such thoughts, even as it masked them.[3]

In one section of the Paris exposition, indeed, the fair's managers gave vent to the anxieties that, beneath the surface, bourgeois confidence, permeated the world of iron. Though the social economy section was easily lost in what Geddes called this "too vast labyrinth of labyrinths," a great deal of thought and organization had gone into it. Like Eiffel's tower, its origins went back to the 1889 exposition. Then, on the Esplanade des Invalides, French economists and employers had organized a small "social economy" section, consisting of a low-cost restaurant patronized by workingmen, a reading room and conference hall, several model cottages of the sort that a handful of large French employers were beginning to build for their employees' families, a pair of pavilions devoted to profit sharing, and a modest amount of display space dedicated to public and private efforts to improve the moral and physical lot of workers. Only tangentially related to the administrative machinery of the rest of the exposition, far enough removed from the central exhibition grounds that few visitors ventured there unless in search of the French military display, the social economy section crossed the consciousness of most exposition visitors as a mere line at the end of their Paris guidebooks.[4]

At the close of the 1889 fair, the social exhibits had been entrusted to a new Paris institution, the Musée Social. Designed at first simply as a warehouse for the exposition documents, the museum soon grew into a clearinghouse for social-economic information of all sorts. Blessed with influential business and government patrons and with interests and correspondents extending over most of industrialized Europe and America, the Musée Social quickly became one of the most important international nodes for discussion of the "social question."[5]

For the 1900 exposition, the Musée Social's organizers determined to lay on a much more elaborate and centrally placed social economy display. In the meeting hall of the social economy pavilion they convened a summer of international conferences on phases of the *question sociale.* For the pavilion's display rooms, they solicited the best examples of practical social amelioration the nations of the Atlantic economy could muster. If there were in the industrialized countries social designs to compensate for the privations and pains of the market revolution, here one might hope to find their outlines.

At first glance, the sheer confusion of issues assembled under the social economy umbrella was all but overwhelming. The French tried to make order out of the whole by carving it into subsections: apprenticeship and the protection of child workers, wages and profit sharing, workers' and employers' associations, farm credit, regulation of the conditions of work, workers' housing, cooperative stores, institutions for the intellectual and moral development of workers, savings and insurance institutions, hygiene (by which they meant not only public sanitation but the public battle against intemperance, slums, and the moral contamination of poverty), poor relief, and a residual category for whatever public or private initiatives for the well-being of the citizens were left over.[6]

Even the Musée Social's spokesmen realized the untidiness of the list. Social economy was a reflex category. Political economy was the science of the augmentation of wealth, the French economist Charles Gide wrote in summing up the exhibit. The field of social economy, by contrast, embraced every effort—within the constraints of political economy itself—to temper, socialize, and mutualize the pains of the capitalist transformation. It was the science of "practical realities and possible amelioration," the science of "social peace." Social economy was, in short, the ambulance wagon of industrial capitalism. Its categories were the categories of social wreckage. In 1889 it had stood half outside the fair; in 1900 no one disputed its presence at the century's summing up, or doubted that the untidy mass of anxieties raised by the terms "social economy" and "the social question" somehow cohered.[7]

To move through the social economy exhibit hall, however, was to discover how far from unified the social economy experts were on solutions.

From nation to nation, the shifts in theme were abrupt and arresting. The Russians brought a temperance exhibit. The Italians displayed the work of cooperative savings banks. The Belgians emphasized low-cost workers' housing. Great Britain, its government distracted by the escalating military hostilities in South Africa, barely mustered an exhibit at all. On one wall of the British alcove hung a chart illustrating the growth of the consumers' cooperative movement. On the other hung one of the maps created for Charles Booth's monumental survey of poverty in London—the class relations of the city outlined, street by street, in bright washes of wealth and dark masses of poverty.[8]

In retrospect, Booth's poverty maps seem the most prescient exhibit of the display. It was the German exhibit, however, that stayed longest in visitors' minds. Even non-Germans in Paris were compelled to admit that Germany was the fair's overall victor in the contest of prestige. Germany's national pavilion boasted the exhibition's tallest tower, next to Eiffel's. The most impressive industrial exhibit was the Germans'. In deference to French sensibilities, the Germans had left their huge Krupp cannons and overt military displays at home, but their imperial ambitions were everywhere on exhibit.[9]

In the social economy building, the Germans ignored the complex French categories. In the middle of their alcove they mounted instead a large, gilded obelisk representing the benefits the imperial social insurance funds had distributed to German workers since their inauguration sixteen years earlier. Compulsory, state-administered insurance against the risks of industrial accidents, sickness, and old age was Germany's great social-political invention of the 1880s. The second prong of Bismarck's campaign to crush the German socialists, state social insurance was Bismarck's device to win over the loyalty of the urban German masses through the preemptive, top-down "socialism" of the state. In a symbolic display of imperial largesse and power, surrounded by photos of the hospitals and sanitariums its agencies administered for the welfare of German workers, the state commanded the German exhibit, without a hint of competition.

The Germans spoke on the subject of the state with peculiar authority and zeal in 1900. From the imperial art collection in the German national pavilion to the gilded obelisk in the social economy palace, the German exhibits radiated the message of government's fostering and protective hand—over culture, art, labor, and the ravages of economic misfortune. What better alternative was there to the insecurities and predations of the market but the massive, countervailing, paternal power of the state?

To move from the German exhibit to the French, however, was to realize that the state was only one of the potential counterforces to the sway of the market. Though the French had taken half the building for themselves, they mounted no clear visual feature to catch the eye. At first glance all was a confusion of charts, pamphlets, reports, and documents. Some three thousand French exhibitors had responded to the call to show off their social wares: profit-sharing firms, model employers, big businessmen, philanthropic housing companies, agricultural purchasing cooperatives, workers' cooperatives, and fraternal clubs of all sorts. The Musée Social itself was characterized by much the same eclecticism; industrial paternalists, social engineers, champions of workers' cooperatives, prominent Radical politicians, conservative social Catholics, and a few independent socialists all rubbed shoulders there.

The largest room of documents in the French display was devoted to institutions of insurance and mutual assistance: *prévoyance*. One found here no hint of German statism, though there were radical voices in French politics in 1900 pressing for a state insurance system more or less on German lines. Rather, the space overflowed with the reports of hundreds of mutual savings societies and mutual insurance societies, in which a member might exchange his weekly dues against the accidents of sickness or enfeebled old age. Although the *sociétés de secours mutuels* had been given official status and modest state subventions in 1898, voluntary mutualism was their organizing principle. By 1900, almost two million Frenchmen were enrolled in them, a figure four times the combined membership of the French labor unions. In a population of 38 million, that left gaping holes in the coverage the mutual assistance societies offered. But here, in the bazaar of social policy models on display in Paris, one found a form of public weal conceived not from the state down but from society outward.

"Solidarity" was the system's keyword. French social politics had been abuzz with it since the mid-1890s when, as premier, Léon Bourgeois had propelled it to popularity. It stood, in pointed contrast to "individualism," for every voluntary expression of mutual obligation and collective assistance. Hence the otherwise inexplicable jumble in the French display of workers' associations, employers' associations, state-assisted and private associations, provincial sports clubs cheek by jowl with powerful regional trade associations: *syndicats* all (as the legal category went), in hopeless confusion. For the advocates of solidarism, however, the profusion of associational forms was precisely the point. If the chief social cost of the age of capital was the shattering of traditional forms of association so as to leave the individual isolated and helpless before the forces of the market, then the needed counterforce was not the state but association itself.[10] To drive the point home, the exposition's organizers had given the contract for construction of the social economy building to skilled workers' cooperatives, bypassing the usual, profit-taking middlemen. Was this not, in miniature, the surest corrective to the reign of price and unchecked competition: to organize the voluntary associational power of society, modestly assisting it with state funds where necessary, fostering mutualistic social energies in whatever shape they assumed?

A visitor to the social economy building, moving on with these thoughts in mind, would not have had an easy time locating the American exhibit. Despite its economic muscle in 1900, the United States was in many ways the exposition's stepchild. It had wrangled space in the front row of national pavilions only through vigorous effort. There, wedged between competitors, the American commissioners built a plaster building made up of the usual Greco-Roman architectural borrowings. The interior, however, they fitted out with American newspapers, typewriters, stenographers for hire, a telegraph, a money exchange, and a ticker tape—everything an American businessman on vacation might need. The Americans were the nouveau riche in Paris in 1900, scrambling hard for status, more eager than any others for the shoptalk of commerce. The German pavilion radiated learning, art, and empire. The French dwelt on politics and solidarity. The American pavilion, behind its classical false front, was about business.[11]

In the social economy building, the same national themes recurred. There, too, the Americans scrambled for place. Squeezed into a tiny, twenty-seven-foot-square alcove, they crammed into their exhibition space a larger stock of material than in any display but France's itself. On hinged boards and ingenious folding cases, they hung out the nation's social wares. For the center of the room, the New York Tenement House Committee contributed a model of one of the city's most notorious slum blocks, together with a model of how much more fiercely crowded that block might become if built up to the density that the city's building code allowed. Nearby, as proof that a sense of the state was not wholly missing, was a handsome collection of the bound reports of the state and national bureaus of labor statistics. In one corner was tucked an exhibit on American Negro life, including examples of handwork made at the Tuskegee Institute and W. E. B. Du Bois's statistical display of African Americans' progress in Georgia since slavery.[12]

Arrangements for the largest body of material in the American exhibit, however, fell to a fledgling social betterment clearinghouse, the League for Social Service. Organized two years earlier, it styled itself a general clearinghouse for information concerning "everything that tends to the social betterment of humanity." Its moving spirit, William Tolman, was in many ways typical of those now forgotten figures who shaped the early years of American social politics. From the position of general agent of the New York Association for Improving the Condition of the Poor, Tolman had been drawn into the Reverend Charles Parkhurst's antivice crusade in the 1890s, and from there into Mayor William Strong's reform administration in New York City, where he had made his particular concern the provision of public baths à la Berlin and London—no slight matter to a city population jammed together, more than two thousand persons to a city block, without benefit of bathrooms. With an eye to the success of the Musée Social, the League for Social Service reached out for contacts all over the industrial world. Its board of advisers included Sidney Webb and John Burns, the two most prominent spokesmen for London's turn-of-the-century experiments in "municipal socialism"; the Irish rural reformer Horace Plunkett; Jules Siegfried, the moving spirit of the Musée Social; and Georg Zacher of the German imperial insurance office. Its *Social Progress* yearbook assembled social policy ideas from around the world. Tolman himself amassed one the largest slide collections to be found in early-twentieth-century America of European civic and industrial betterment work: English model towns, Liverpool municipal housing, Glasgow municipal parks and streetcars, Amsterdam's factory safety museum, London's public baths. Eclectic and cosmopolitan, the League reflected the fluidity, amateur hopefulness, and international reach of turn-of-the-century American social reform.[13]

For the social economy display, however, Tolman hung the walls with photos of the work of self-enlightened capitalism. The endeavors of the nation's model industrial employers were represented there: the Heinz company's spotless factory workrooms, the Cleveland Hardware company's employee restaurant, the employee housing constructed by the Westinghouse Airbrake firm, and the elaborate employee morale work of the National Cash Register Company in Dayton, Ohio. In the realm of *prévoyance* the welfare capitalist theme continued; the biggest, most eye-catching displays were those of the Prudential, Metropolitan, and Equitable life insurance companies. The normally acute reporter for *L'Exposition de Paris* never saw past the life insurance company advertisements; Charles Gide thought the American exhibit formless.[14] But the message of the American display was clearer than Gide sensed: the most promising counterforce to the injuries of industrial capitalism was the enlightened conscience of capitalism itself.

These competing national styles in social economy both framed and exaggerated the rivalries at stake. Social politics took shape everywhere as an agglomeration, its elements in still in flux. Even the Germans' paternal state was fissured with contradictory tendencies. Their emphasis on the welfare contributions of the empire notwithstanding, less than 10 percent of the total benefits distributed under the German social insurance laws by 1900 had derived from the empire itself; as for administration, the Germans had farmed it out to a maze of employers' mutuals, trade union funds, and self-governing employer-employee associations only a little less complicated than those of their rival, France.[15] The French, in their turn, may have raised the principle of mutualism to its highest pitch, but, as all the leading figures in the Musée Social knew, France cut a very poor showing behind "individualistic" Britain in its number of cooperatives, mutual aid associations, friendly societies, and workers' associations.

As for welfare capitalism, its claims were everywhere on prominent display. For all their puffery, the Americans, in fact, had considerably less to show for it than their European rivals. The French social economy exhibit was salted with reports of the employee benefit systems of the large French railways and coal mining enterprises. The Krupp firm had sent a model of its elaborate employee housing and social facilities at Essen. Among examples of model workers' housing at the fair's annex in the Bois de Vincennes, the most striking was a replica of the handsome half-timbered houses that the Lever Company, with a great deal of self-congratulatory advertising, was erecting for its skilled employees near Liverpool. The outlines of yet another social-political regime—a private, paternal welfare state, dominated by large, socially conscious employers—could hardly be missed in Paris. These were not yet systems, in short, but tendencies, rival clusters of ideas that, crisscrossing national boundaries, pressed at every legislative body's doors.

A visitor trying to grasp the outlines of social economy at the turn of the century could not ignore, finally, two more rival centers of ideas and social power, neither affixed to any nation-state. The first of these was the international socialist movement, the second the international women's movement. What role working-class–based parties would play in the framing of social politics was still far from clear in 1900. Where the barriers to socialist participation in politics had been most stringently enforced—in Germany, where the socialists, outlawed until 1890, still faced a mass of special legal prohibitions, and in Belgium, where male working-class suffrage was only seven years old in 1900—the socialists had gone a long way to construct within the shell of the official state an internal social nation of their own. The socialists' sprawling subcultures of trade unions, cooperative stores, newspapers, sports and singing societies, restaurants, breweries, bakeries, women's alliances, and mutual assistance societies of all sorts formed, in the boast of the Belgian socialist Émile Vandervelde, "a new world [that] is in the course of creation, on the edge of bourgeois society and in opposition to it." In this "great economic cooperative" lay the outlines of yet another response to the age of iron, a more egalitarian and democratic form of mutualism than the French *solidaristes* could imagine, brought into being by the autonomous labor of workers themselves.[16]

When it came to issues of legislation, however, the socialists' position was much more strained and ambivalent. Much of the growth of the socialist parties at the turn of the century stemmed from their willingness to enter local and parliamentary politics with an immediatist program of social-political reforms, overlapping at dozens of points the projects of middle-class social reformers. It was to further that immediatist project that Alexandre Millerand had consented to join a moderate reformist French government in 1899, the first socialist to occupy a seat in any modern European cabinet, and in that capacity to preside over the opening of the exposition itself. Even so much firmer a socialist as Jean Jaurès could imagine in 1903 that the transition to socialism might take place so gradually that it would be like navigators "aware of having crossed the line of a hemisphere—not that they have been able to see as they crossed it a cord stretched over the ocean warning them of their passage, but that little by little they have been led into a new hemisphere by the progress of their ship."[17]

But where middle-class social economists accepted the constraints of political economy, the raison d'être of socialism was the necessity of reconstructing relations of power and property from the ground up. Short of that, the turn-of-the-century socialists' stance toward state authority was a matter of deep, inner conflict. At the Paris meeting of the Second International, anarchists and *possibilistes*, revolutionary and reform socialists locked themselves in intense battle once more over the legitimacy of alliance with the political agencies of the bourgeoisie.

Ambivalence toward the state ran hard, indeed, through all workers' institutions in the North Atlantic economy. To the embarrassment of the organizers of the social economy section of the exposition, most European labor organizations had declined invitations to participate. The most significant exception, the American Federation of Labor (AFL), earned its grand prize in the social economy section as much for showing up as for its display. Seared by the proliferating court-ordered labor injunctions of the 1890s, the AFL had no more sympathy than its European counterparts with the notion that workers might confidently rely on legislation for their economic salvation. Labor and socialist organizations did far more than their reformist rivals to articulate the injustices of the world of iron. Within the social policy debates, however, they were to play a complicated role, never fully certain what they wanted of the state or what measure of justice, in a pinch, the state could provide.[18]

If women did not quite form a nation of their own, they too came into the debates over social politics with interests and institutions distinct from those of the middle-class men who dominated social politics' central forums. Unlike the socialists, who held their meetings at a conspicuous distance from the fairgrounds, the international women's congress met in the heart of the Paris exposition. From the first, the gender line in social reform was more fluid and permeable than the line between bourgeois social reform and reform socialism. But the accents and emphases the women's organizations brought to social politics were, nonetheless, identifiably different.

"Women's works and institutions" was the theme of the Paris women's congress. That did not preclude discussion of equal rights and equal justice, but the dominant note of the congress was women's social duties—not for self but for the elevation, protection, and education of others.[19] Women had long been the principal distributors of charity to the poor in the Anglo-American world. Over the next decade and a half, women reformers in Europe and the United States would mount successful crusades for the legal protection of women and child factory workers, minimum wage laws in the "sweated" women's trades, compensated childbirth leave for working mothers, provisions for maternity and infant medical care, milk inspection, school reform, and special state assistance for poor women heading their families alone.

Where the dominant stream in social politics took the labor relationship as its starting point, social maternalists began with the particular vulnerabilities of women, children, and families. Where the mainstream of social policy debate ran toward talk of social peace and economic justice, women's social policy debates were laced with a rhetoric of needs and protection. The two strains were not as distinct as the generation of historians who have helped rediscover the maternalist impulse in social policy development has sometimes implied. By the early twentieth century, nonetheless, observers were beginning to remark on the rise of a new *état maternel.* Standing consciously to the side of the nationalist rivalries over social politics, with an international network second only to the socialists' in extent and efficiency, social maternalists formed yet another organizing pole around which social politics might gather.[20]

In 1900 there was, then, no agreement on how an effective counterforce to the world of iron might be constructed. State paternalism, private paternalism, mutualism, socialism, maternalism: the shorthand phrases led toward different configurations of power and policies. Any social politics worthy of the name would have to find some means of integrating the claims of each: the public authority of the state, the moral force of voluntary association, the economic resources of the industrial capitalists, the democratic self-agency of the workers, and the special needs of society's dependents. What one found in Paris was not an answer. In the charts and pamphlets and photographs crammed into the social economy pavilion what one found, rather, was one of the key sites and processes through which answers would be formed.

For amid the vendors' stalls at the Paris exposition, what was this social economy section, ultimately, but a bazaar of its own kind, a world of choice, a marketplace for the exchange of social-political schemes both large and small? If its wares were ideas and experience rather than commodities, it, too, was nevertheless a place of trade. Around the common, international knot of worries contemporaries called the "social question," it assembled a world of competing solutions. It made graphic the point too easily lost in retrospect: the transnational reach of social politics. Nowhere in the North Atlantic world was social policy to be made in national isolation. Through rivalry and exchange, every one of the social policy clusters on display in Paris had taken shape, and through those processes each would change—not the least for those latecomers to Paris, the Americans.

Explaining Social Politics

Paris in 1900, amid the puffed sleeves and boiled shirts of the bourgeoisie who thronged the fair, buttoning their inner social fears under outer pride and confidence: surely this is an unlikely place from which to begin a historical examination of some of the choices that were to shape American social politics in its formative years. Better to start, one might well think, in turn-of-the-century Chicago's packing house district, where the reeking air, the overcrowded frame dwellings, and the immigrant workforce, recruited at the lowest wages the labor market would stand, were products of the same cost calculations that made marketable uses (so the packers boasted) out of every piece of a pig but its squeal. Better, perhaps, to start in a Chicago union hall, or jammed in among the angry men at one of the demonstrations of the unemployed reanimated by every downturn in the business cycle. Better, perhaps, to start in the boardrooms of one of the leading welfare capitalists, or the offices of one of the interlocking agencies they founded to press the distinctive social interests of large-scale capital on the managers of the state. Better to start with the structure of the state itself, and the mix of party hacks and bureaucrats who ran it. Still better, perhaps, to start with a conversation in a tenement in New York City's Hell's Kitchen section between a poor mother and the charity association's friendly visitor, or standing in a race-segregated line in a county relief office in the South.

On each of these sites, in fact, the leading explanations of social politics have set down their foundations. Because the transnational reframing of the history of American social politics incorporates some of the frameworks and assertions of earlier models while challenging others, it is important to pause a moment with their claims and their evolution.[21]

To the earliest historians of social politics, writing close to the archives of the key agents of social reform, the most important contexts were not far-flung but immediate. Social politics' key arena was where individual conscience came up hard against the cruelties, miseries, injustices, and inefficiencies of modern life. This was a narrative strategy that mirrored the reformers' own chosen stories. Enlightenment and publicization were the central acts in social politics. The truly difficult labor, waged inwardly against the impediments of the reformers' own time- and class-bound selves, and outwardly against the social drag of indifference and denial, was to make the immediacies of need and justice plain.[22]

The social scientists who pioneered the study of comparative social politics in the decade after World War II had little use for these local, biographical contexts. Steeped in theories of global process, their framework was boldly international. It was also, to a great extent, evolutionary—indeed, all but automatically so. As they watched social spending grow in both conservative and progressive political regimes in the 1950s and 1960s, it seemed to many of the leading postwar social scientists that the logic of surplus capital accumulation might by itself prove capable of repairing the social dislocations the capitalist revolutions in production had begun. Given expanding national incomes, their data seemed to show, social expenditures for education, welfare, and social services increased. Within the framework of this convergent, developmental law, neither the hard work of social muckraking nor, indeed, the contingencies of history and politics seemed critically essential.[23]

The assumption of steadily growing social investments was not destined to last. As the postwar welfare states came under heavy attack in Europe and North America in the hard times of the 1970s, the *politics* in social politics suddenly moved into central analytical focus. One result was that class was thrust into the very center of social-political analysis—though with profoundly mixed results.

For most of those who first put class analyses forward, the central story in social politics was an infusion of power from the bottom up. Through the social democratic parties on the European continent, the Labour Party in Britain, and the Congress of Industrial Organizations (CIO) and the New Deal left in the United States, the welfare states of the twentieth century had arisen in a great upwelling of hope and power from below. Where the working class did not have the capacity to act politically by and for itself, it had gained its way by forcing concessions from the class in power through strikes and workplace resistance, through riots and demonstrations, or through threats to destabilize the balance of parties.[24]

No sooner had this claim been made, however, than radical critics of the "social democratic explanation" of social politics turned the class relation in social policy on its head. Social politics does not flow up from the masses, they countered; more often it is imposed as a set of rescue operations from above. Its terms are those through which the ruling elites buy off challenge to their rule, distract the working class from autonomous political mobilization, and forestall a genuine democratization of the social realm. In Bismarck's Germany, social policy was the work of a Junker-dominated "feudal" elite, eager for new forms of advantage in its holding action against the forces of popular democracy. In modern nations that role is given to the men of big business and capital. Welfare capitalists, whose experiments in more enlightened wage and workplace policies have put them at a competitive disadvantage, are often key actors in this regard. But what calls the tune is the security of the dominant property regime itself. Both modern and "feudal" elites employ social policy essentially the same way: steered by the class in power, the state moves from one shoring up operation to another, distracting, neutralizing, pacifying, or preempting so as to sustain the dominant structure of power and property.[25]

Ostensibly, these new emphases on class put politics back at social politics' center. In fact, as skeptics pointed out, the political element was far weaker in both the critical and social democratic readings of social politics than it superficially appeared. By reducing the state to an agency of the class in power, class interpretations of social politics left the political realm without important historical consequence of its own. It was at this juncture that a third cluster of students of the politics of social policy entered the debate, sympathetic to the left's stress on structures but unconvinced of the captivity of the state to the economic interests arrayed around it. Their initial assertion of the state's "autonomy" from the class interests arrayed around it turned out to be a false start. What the advocates of a "state-centered" approach to social policy began more successfully to contend was that there was sufficient slippage between class interests and the processes of politics to make the latter an important arena of social policy formation in its own right. Reframed more generally as an "institutional-political process" approach to social politics, it is now characterized by close attention to the structures of politics along several dimensions: the administrative capacities (and incapacities) of the state, the composition of parties and electorates, and the structurally embedded legacies of past policy decisions.[26]

Finally, to those who have looked most closely at social policy from the recipients' end, yet another theme has seemed paramount. Up close, the agents of social policy may aid and enable, they may work modest additions of justice, but they also impose discipline. The very act of separating citizens into distinctive social categories—the poor on welfare and the "working" poor receiving merely earned income credits and food stamps, "minorities" eligible for affirmative action programs and "majorities" who are not, persons with "families" and persons who simply live together—serves to divide and survey the recipients of the state's assistance. So do the rules social politics winds around all it touches. The disciplining of mind and body that modern welfare states undertake not only shores up the leading economic interests of the state, it is claimed. It also enables the reproduction of the dominant social arrangements—be they the nuclear family, the prevailing sexual conventions, or the dominant structure of aspirations. Politics as conventionally defined is beside the point; discipline is social politics' driving motor.[27]

To each of these claims, strong evidence can be adduced. The sound and fury over the interpretation of social politics derives not from grand theories chasing too little evidence but from an abundance of evidence chasing theories too narrow to contain it. From Jacob Riis's crusade against the slums and dives of the barely regulated private housing market in 1890s New York to Florence Kelley's campaign to tame the conditions of sweatshop labor, the rhetoric of enlightenment has done unmistakable work. In the boom years that followed the Second World War, when parliamentary coalitions of every stripe proved sympathetic to social welfare needs, a good many of the teeth seemed to have been drawn from the politics of welfare. When that era unraveled, there was no mistaking the fact that welfare policies survived best in states where the parliamentary position of the working class was strongest. The history of social policy shows equally clear examples of policies forced into legislation from below (old-age pensions in Britain in 1908) and from above (workingmen's social insurance in Germany between 1883 and 1889). Governments are not only the meeting place of interests; their capacity for policy execution, their structured ways of coming to decisions, and the inertia of precedent all play unmistakable roles in social policy formation. As for the day-to-day discipline of social policy, no one who has stood in a welfare office line, or visited a free clinic's emergency room, should doubt its force or pervasiveness.

None of these explanations, then, is without a broad foundation of truth. But none by itself suffices. Need and exposure do not, by themselves, cause anything but momentary embarrassment. The automaticity of the postwar welfare state's growth was an illusion of the social scientists' modernization theories. The convergence of social political regimes, to the extent it had taken place, was not a historical given; it was *brought about* through the hard work of brokers and intermediaries. Nor are class interests simple determinates of social politics. When social democracy's political moment finally came, in Britain and Scandinavia after the Second World War, the labor parties made the most of it; but they acted largely to expand policies already in place, constructed during a period when working-class parties had only brief and marginal access to power and deeply ambivalent feelings about its exercise. Ruling elites were no clearer about their own interests. For every Bismarck in the 1880s or Gerard Swope in the 1930s, there were scores of captains of land and industry who resisted, viscerally, every act of redistributive meddling in the market. If, face to face, social policy disciplines, those who have looked closely have shown that it is also resisted, manipulated, and diverted.

No piece of social politics, in short, can claim a tidy lineage, a monocausal raison d'être, or, least of all, tidy effects. The field of social politics is too large for any one site of explanation, or single cast of characters, to command it all. Its processes, too, are multiple: compassion, outrage, exposure, publicization, agitation, mobilization, invention, lobbying, pacification, preemption, calculation, bargaining, compromise, enforcement, administration, and manipulation.

It is in this regard that one comes back to the projects and ideas on display in the social economy building in Paris. Within the skein of social politics' intertwined processes, the social economy exhibit captured only a thread. But that one was indispensable: the process Hugh Heclo once called that of "puzzling through" from problem to potential corrective. "Politics," he writes, "finds its sources not only in power but also in uncertainty," not only in command but also in "puzzlement." To those who "power" belongs the field of maneuver, decision, and administration; to those who "puzzle" belongs the shaping of agendas and alternatives.[28]

It was persons of the latter sort who most eagerly sought out the conferences and displays in the social economy hall in Paris in 1900, and whose concerns it most clearly revealed. No polity in the North Atlantic economy could do without them. Some who played the part functioned as policy drafters: Theodor Lohmann, framer of Bismarck's initial social insurance proposals; William Beveridge, the major intellectual architect of the post-1945 welfare state in Britain; the Stockholm economists of the 1930s; and the "brains trusters" who helped shape Franklin Roosevelt's instincts into New Deal practice. Around them, however, was a still larger field of discussion and debate: policy forums mounted at the border between university expertise and public politics, pressure groups, formal international congresses and informal intellectual gatherings, journals of opinion and journals of social practice. This was the field in which was produced the ideas, alternatives, and solutions that made social politics possible.

The social policy tinkerers and inventors, publicists and policy scavengers, policy experts and policy brokers who, in these ways, filled in the void between social-economic need and social-economic solutions did not *make* social politics. Without a firm institutional base either within or outside the state, they never wielded clear political power. They were disproportionately drawn from that part of the middle class made deeply uneasy by the raw power of industrial capitalism. But uncertainty about their own class position was a common fixture of their identity, and the middle class from which so many of them came proved, over and again, a fickle and unreliable supporter of the social policies they devised.

Nor were they, for the most part, state functionaries. "State-centered" analyses of social politics in this period have not adequately fathomed how indistinct the line between state and society remained throughout most of Europe and the United States, how thin the apparatus of state management was, and how reliant it was on temporary and borrowed expertise. Even for the principal architects of social politics, government service typically figured as an episode rather than a career. The chief drafters of the Social Security Act of 1935 came to the New Deal on three- to six-month loans; William Beveridge wrote his *Report* while being eased out, not for the first time, of government employment. Universities gave some of these figures a firmer niche; it was within university economics departments from Berlin to Baltimore in the 1870s and 1880s that the core intellectual terms of modern social politics were forged. But for most of this period, universities were unreliable shelters for those who strayed too deeply into controversy. From Charles Booth, a shipping line owner who made himself, via his London survey, into the world's leading authority on the ecology of urban poverty, to William Beveridge, who worked out the economics of unemployment while a settlement house resident at Toynbee Hall, to that consummate pair of autodidacts, Sidney and Beatrice Webb, a large number of the era's key figures were self-taught experts working on the intellectual margins of imperfectly professionalized fields. The transatlantic moment in social politics was in many ways an age of amateurs.

Persons of this sort did not administer social policy; nowhere did they control legislative outcomes. Their proposals were never advanced except to be battered and recast by those who possessed not policy notions but interests. Yet without their production of proposals, without their intellectual work in framing the terms of debate, social politics could not have transpired. The bourgeois reform projects of the Musée Social, the social strategies of the German monarchy, the immediate program of the reform socialists, the agenda of the American New Deal, and the social democratic welfare states of the 1940s and 1950s were all stocked with their work. Whether the political muscle to power their ideas into legislation came from above or below, the programmatic ingredients of late-nineteenth- and early-twentieth-century social politics were, to an astonishing extent, of their making.

Beginning, as they did, not with systematic understandings of society or politics but with piecemeal solutions and practical social inventions, their interests were as diffuse as the category "social economy" itself. Their vocabulary was full of large, amorphous worries: "the social question," "the labor question," "the city problem," the problems of "cooperation" and "community." Their projects spun off in clusters in ways that defy the categories of a more specialized age. But their energies were not without order. The cohering elements in their practice, essential to the chapters that follow, are worth a bit of excavation.

Asked to define so loose an entity as the "social question," a resident of early-twentieth-century New York City could have done no better than to point to the nameplates in the lobby of the United Charities Building at the corner of Twenty-Second Street and Fourth Avenue. Five blocks to the south lay Union Square, the city's great, volatile gathering point for radical and working-class politics. The big garment workers' unions were a major presence there and, by the 1930s, the city's Socialist and Communist Parties as well. Union Square was the nodal point of the city's annual May Day parade and the staging ground for the largest Depression-era demonstrations of the unemployed. The Charities Building, by contrast, was the city's meeting point for middle-class social politics.

The institutions that at one time or another were lodged in the United Charities Building were legion: Florence Kelley's National Consumers' League; the National Child Labor Committee; the National Housing Association; the New York School of Philanthropy; the Commission on the Church in Social Service of the Federal Council of Churches; the city's two largest private charitable relief agencies; the *Survey* magazine, clearinghouse for social policy news and debate of every sort; and a library used (as Franklin Roosevelt's secretary of labor remembered) by "everybody who was in social work." When these agencies outgrew their quarters, few moved more than a few blocks away. Two doors down from the United Charities Building, in 1905, was William Tolman's Institute of Social Service. A block to the north were the offices of the American Association for Labor Legislation. Less than a block to the east was the headquarters of the Russell Sage Foundation, with its funds and fingers in pies ranging from public health and tuberculosis prevention to child labor and the promotion of city playgrounds, urban social surveys, low-interest pawnshops, the condition of women's wage labor, tenement house regulation, folk schools for Appalachian mountaineers, the making of a regional plan for greater New York, and the construction of a model suburb at Forest Hills Gardens on Long Island. New York City's nexus of interlocking persons, funds, and issues was particularly extensive, but in the corresponding circles in Chicago, Madison, Frankfurt, Berlin, London, and Paris the basic picture was much the same.[29]

In the face of such earnest, eclectic endeavor, historians have too often been tempted to simplify: to see in late-nineteenth and early-twentieth-century social politics, struggling to be born, the welfare state regimes of the second half of the century. The impulse is wrong, however, and must be resisted. None of these players held the "welfare state" as an end goal. The "statism" of the welfare state, as we have seen, was no foregone conclusion. Like the French *solidaristes*, many of social politics' most active proponents imagined the state accomplishing its social purposes best by subsidizing the voluntary institutions of society: labor unions, cooperative associations, and mutual assistance societies of many sorts. "Subsidarist" systems, we shall call them, and they carried a heavy social-political burden throughout late-nineteenth- and early-twentieth-century Europe. Even when the shapers of social politics put their faith in direct government action, they were as often to imagine local governments as welfare's key agents as to reserve that role for the nation-state itself.

Just as the term "state" misrepresents, so, more subtly, does the term "welfare." For most of this period, overtones of employer or state paternalism severely limited the word. The National Civic Federation's Welfare Department occupied itself in the early years of the century with employer-provided factory lunch rooms, rest rooms, personnel bureaus, and safety devices; the contemporary German Central Office for Workers' Welfare Institutions (Centralstelle für Arbeiterwohlfahrtseinrichtigungen) cultivated precisely the same terrain. Though one can find many isolated outcroppings, the term "welfare state" did not come into currency until the end of the 1940s, as a new term in the Republican Party's attack on the remnants of the New Deal, from which it was passed on to British opponents of the Labour government's reforms, only to be accepted finally, in an act of linguistic defiance, by the British Labour Party itself in 1949–1950. In Germany, even now, the analogous term is not *Wohlfahrtsstaat* but *Sozialstaat.* The "welfare state" was not the articulated goal of its framers, but a label trailing the fact.[30]

The point is larger than a linguistic one. To clamp the preoccupations of the current welfare state regimes on the past is to narrow and distort it. In modern usage, the welfare state is, at bottom, a social insurance state, securing a measure of security against old age and sickness to its citizens. Simultaneously it is a poor relief state (particularly in American usage), grudgingly doling out relief for those who have fallen through the welfare state's security provisions into "welfare" itself. But social insurance was only a small part of a social-political agenda that sprawled, so full of open choices, across a dozen subclasses in Paris in 1900. The German Verein für Sozialpolitik, whose 143 volumes of social investigation between 1873 and 1914 form as detailed a map as we possess of the terrain of "social politics" before the First World War, studied everything from strikes and labor unions to housing and city administration, usury and credit, agricultural conditions, trade, and taxation.[31] In the United States, pursuit of the agenda of social politics will lead us to the ownership of streetcars, city planning, the risks of wage labor, wartime state "socialism," labor politics, the social reconstruction of the countryside, and the quest for "modern" housing. We will find out what social politics meant only by following the interlocking and intersecting concerns of those who engaged in it.

Still, as eclectic as these lists appear, they were not formless. However baggy the participants' key terms—*économie sociale*, the "social problem," *Sozialpolitik*—they too had bounds and meanings. Those who worked within them rarely wanted radically to change the underlying system of property; that was what Gide wanted to make clear by nestling social economy within the field of political economy proper. They groped, rather, toward what they tended to see as a middle course between the rocks of cutthroat economic individualism and the shoals of an all-coercive statism. They lived in a world of commodities and markets: highly visible markets of stalls and pushcart peddlers, crowded hiring halls, and roads lined with rural laborers waiting to see if their labor would sell that day. The progressive architects of social politics had no notion that markets could be done away with—or that the world would be the better if one tried.

But not everything belonged in the market. This was the thread that, ultimately, wove their endeavors together. Whether it was the child labor crusaders' insistence that young children be extracted from the industrial labor market, the economists' campaign to municipalize certain "natural monopolies," the city planners' attempt to mitigate the claims of price over the uses of urban land, the housing reformers' conviction that the working poor would never be adequately sheltered through the unchecked play of the urban land and building markets, the agricultural reformers' struggle to socialize the atomized conditions of rural exchange, or the social insurance experts' effort to mitigate the risks of commodified labor—in one way or another the projects returned to a common theme. Against the onward rush of commodification, the advocates or social politics tried to hold certain elements out of the market's processes, indeed to roll back those parts of the market whose social costs had proved too high. The word Gøsta Esping-Andersen has invented in another context for them—"de-commodification"—was not in their vocabulary, but it comes closer than the "welfare state" to their core concerns.[32] Around this thread, more than another, they wound the tacit logic of their schemes.

The de-commodification thread in social politics distinguishes it from the goals of another group—no less eager than social economy's partisans to employ the economic potential of the state—that saw the state fundamentally as a tool for business's promotion. Promotionalists with their eye on economic development were legion on both sides of the Atlantic. Protective tariff duties were their most important nineteenth-century construction, but one could find them wherever investment and trade made a sprinkling of tax revenues, special legal privileges, or economic stimulus attractive. Contemporary analysts, focusing on state presence more than state purposes, have sometimes confused the two projects. At times, indeed, the ambitions merged, as in the high-tariff, social protectionism of a Joseph Chamberlain or Theodore Roosevelt or the "commercial" Keynesianism of the post–World War II era. But the goals of the two projects were quite distinct. Promotionalism's aim was to thicken and expand markets. The goal of social politics was to control and constrain them.

None of this, finally, was played out in national isolation. Like the aspirations on display in Paris in 1900, social-political arguments and proposals in the late nineteenth and early twentieth centuries slid over national boundaries. The acute hunger of the era's social reformers for international information was impossible to miss. The Labor Bureau's representative to the Paris exposition, W. F. Willoughby, spent his summer seeking out his French and German counterparts at the fair's international gatherings and filling in endless schedules of information. Others filled doctoral dissertations, journal articles, and popular books with descriptions of foreign social welfare programs or experimented with graphic means to display to the public the world's steps toward the social question's solution. One could find their work at the Musée Social, at Harvard University's Social Museum (the ultimate resting place for the German state insurance display), in Edinburgh (where Geddes was perfecting the technique of the urban exposition), in Frankfurt (where a social museum and library, modeled on the Paris archetype, was soon to be established), or in Dresden (where the first major exposition devoted to modern city problems was held in 1903). In Madison, Wisconsin, John R. Commons's seminar room was soon circled by a massive chart of all the world's labor legislation—a visual reminder of the transatlantic reform network.[33]

Sustained by books, pamphlets, and travel, that network fluctuated in its strength and density between the 1870s and the 1940s, but through it flowed a vast amount of borrowing and debate. The currents ran in all directions, between the European nations as well as far beyond them. The term social policy "diffusion," by which these processes of exchange are sometimes characterized, imprisoned in a metaphor of space rather than of persons and politics, is far too bloodless too capture the phenomenon at work.[34] Through these international channels came not only models ripe for imitation but also arguments, rivalries, competition, and debate.

Nothing, to be sure, came through the transnational networks of debate and connection unaltered. Like others who worked within these networks, the Americans amended everything they reached to appropriate. Nor could it have been otherwise. From settlement houses to zoning ordinances, labor legislation to farm cooperatives, city-owned transit systems to federal old-age insurance, every imported idea and scheme was, by necessity, multiply transformed: first in consequence of the American progressives' difficulty in grasping what lay behind a veil of cultural distance and potential misperception; second as they trimmed their borrowings so as to fit their sense of American conditions and distinctiveness; and finally transformed once more as each half-borrowed scheme was bent and reshaped by the distinctive pressures of American political circumstances that came to bear on it. Our quarry is not identities but processes, not essences but geneses: an arc of transformations that was, for a moment, central to the formation of choices and politics.

This, then, is the importance of the mass of documents gathered in the shadow of the Eiffel Tower—so eclectic, outwardly confused, and international. From these and similar wells of proposals, American social progressives were to draw not only much of the distinctive language of social politics but also a disproportionate amount of their own social-political agenda. Their politics was full of borrowings. The processes of importation and adaptation, rejection and transformation so central to the Atlantic-wide reckoning with the new world of commodities profoundly shaped their own practice as well. The Americans were latecomers at Paris, outsiders looking in. But lateness imparted no immunity from the choices so graphically displayed there. How an alternative to the world of iron could be erected, strong enough to serve as an effective counterforce to the destructive excesses of market capitalism yet open enough that it could engage the democratic, voluntaristic energies of a people—that would also be theirs to puzzle through.

2

The Atlantic World

Landscapes

Two phenomena of the late nineteenth century made the North Atlantic progressive connection possible. The first was the rapidly convergent economic development of the key nations of the North Atlantic basin. Across the older, intricately varied political and cultural checkerwork of Europe and North America began to appear, in thicker and thicker concentrations, economic institutions instantly recognizable from one end of the North Atlantic region to the other. Nothing was more important for sustained trade in social policies than this dramatic expansion of the social landscapes of industrial capitalism. In a world of nation-states, economic forces were particularly aggressive trespassers and powerful centralizers of experience.

The second phenomenon was less tangible and more fragile than the first, but to the emerging transnational social-political networks it was no less fundamental. This was a new understanding of common histories and vulnerabilities. The new landscapes of fact and the intertwined landscapes of mind had equally indispensable parts to play in the Atlantic progressive connection. For social policies to be borrowable across political boundaries, there must be not only a foundation of common economic and social experience but also a recognition of underlying kinship. The polities in question must be seen to face similar needs and problems, to move within shared historic frames, and to strive toward a commonly imagined future. Relatedness is the core assumption. Where there is only comparison or culturally imagined difference there can be envy or pride in abundance, but there can be no sustained trade in social policy.

Neither of these two convergent tendencies was unopposed during the era of Atlantic social politics. Nationalism was a powerful, convulsive force in late-nineteenth- and early-twentieth-century life. The social landscapes of industrial capitalism, for all their common features, were riven with economic disparities. But enough of the real and imagined distance between the nation-states shrank in this era to make a trade in social policy possible. To the opening phase of the Americans' entry into the new networks of international exchange we will return more closely in chapter three, focusing on the currents of transatlantic economic debate in the 1870s and 1880s. But to begin examining the North Atlantic progressive connection we will do best to begin with its structures—with the reconfigurations in imagination, economics, and politics through which a new form of transnational politics came into being.

From the moment the first Europeans arrived in the North American continent, Europe had occupied a central, ineradicable place in their political imaginations, but the terms of the relationship had not always been ones of connection. From the American Revolution into the last quarter of the nineteenth century, the figures of speech that dominated the Atlantic relationship had been, to the contrary, starkly oppositional. Europe was the Old World, the continent of decadence and decay. America was new: the continent of rebirth, site of a new historical dispensation. "We have a new mould for our society, cast on principles different from any tried before," Mark Hopkins of Williams College put the mid-nineteenth-century orthodoxy. The oppositions loomed larger than life, too massive and heavily polarized to make European political experience usable.[1]

There were several ways to conceive the point. In the dominant, "republican" understanding of the relationship between European and American politics, the tyrannies of the Old World were pitted against the freedom of the New World. When seen through this lens, the ancien régime's kings and aristocrats, its standing armies and standing churches, became the European continent's very essence. Through their monopoly on governance, the aristocracies seemed to have hung the state's apparatus on the peoples of Europe like massive millstones. Overtaxed, overgoverned, rent-racked, and impoverished, the European nations groaned under the double weight of political and economic parasitism.

The genius of New World liberty, in contrast, had been to set the people's will and welfare on top. Constitutional government, democratization of office holding and suffrage, and abolition of inherited privilege down to the final, nation-wrenching overthrow of the despotism of slavery: in these Americans imagined that the torch of liberty had been passed westward to the New World republic. In these, the exceptionalist historical promise of America was engraved. When one was in this republican mood, the ocean filled the mind like a moat. J. Hector St. John de Crèvecoeur had set the tone in his description of the American promise in 1782: "No aristocratical families, no courts, no kings, no bishops, no ecclesiastical dominion, no invisible power giving to a few a very visible one; no great manufacturers employing thousands, no great refinements of luxury" but, in their place, "new laws, a new mode of living, a new social system."[2]

No nation so conceived in antonyms could, in point of fact, be very effectively emancipated from its polar opposite. The republican understanding of America depended utterly on its contrast with an imaged Europe. Those who thought within this frame sometimes imagined the United States as an island of world historical immunities, insulated from the Old World's fate and historical processes. At other times they gave the relationship a messianic turn in which the torch of liberty would ultimately return from the New World to an outworn Europe. Either way, New and Old Worlds were locked in their mutually reinforcing differences.

The republican image of Europe was not made wholly out of wish and illusion. One of the marks of an observant American traveler in rural Europe before the First World War was curiosity as to who owned it. The answer could not but stiffen the Americans' patriotic sentiments. One quarter of England and Wales in 1873 was held by only 360 owners; in the same year 350 landowners possessed fully two-thirds of all the land in Scotland.[3] From landed bases like these, the old aristocracies retained a powerful lien on politics and the state. Nowhere in late-nineteenth-century Europe, France and Switzerland excepted, did universal male suffrage rule, as it did in theory (and, in practice, for white males) in the United States. At one extreme was Belgium where, until a general strike finally forced the government's hand in 1893, less than a tenth of the adult male population was eligible to vote; even after the reforms of the 1890s, a system of plural votes for property holders and university graduates permitted the wealthiest third of the nation to outvote all the rest in parliamentary elections. Not far behind Belgium in its suffrage restrictions was Sweden, where on the eve of suffrage reform in 1909 barely a third of all adult men met the property tests for Riksdag elections.[4]

In Germany, where Reichstag elections were open to universal male suffrage, local and state elections were hedged in by such extremely high barriers that the Social Democratic Party in 1900, although it could count on a quarter of the popular Reichstag election vote, had yet successfully to elect a single delegate to the Prussian legislature. The most casual visitor to imperial Germany could not miss the massive political presence of the Junkers in the army, the higher ranks of government administration, the Prussian legislature, and the Reichstag. Victorian England was much more effectively democratized than Germany, but even in 1890, in the wake of three major suffrage reform acts, residence and property exclusions still kept four out of every ten adult males off the voting lists. Despite a century of rising bourgeois fortunes, almost half the seats in the turn-of-the-century British cabinet were still occupied by landed aristocrats.[5]

Democratic radicals in nineteenth-century Europe honed these same points of contrast and helped publicize the American promise. John Bright's image of the United States mirrored his dream for his own, emancipated England: "A free church, a free school, free land, a free vote, and a free career for the child of the humblest born in the land." Henry George's electrifying speaking tours of Britain in the 1880s, which drew crowds to hear the political and economic curse of land monopoly excoriated in an American accent, tangibly affirmed the New World's radical promise. Even Marxian socialists like the English Social Democratic Federation's H. M. Hyndman (who toured the United States in 1880) or the German Social Democratic Party's Wilhelm Liebknecht (who followed in 1886) came back impressed by the success of the American democratic experiment. James Bryce summed up the recurrent theme: "America has in some respects anticipated European nations. She is walking before them along a path which they may probably follow. She carries behind her . . . a lamp whose light helps those who come after her more than it always does herself."[6]

But if the image of their democratic future in the west riveted the imaginations of European democrats in the 1870s and 1880s, it was the Americans who polished the image to perfection. When in the middle years of the century, buoyed by curiosity, cheap steamship travel, and new reserves of disposable wealth, middle- and upper-class American tourists began to descend on Europe, their responses fell quickly into the waiting formulas. Pilgrims in search of proof of their own distinctiveness, Americans in mid-nineteenth-century Europe came back amply sated.

A case in point was Gilbert Haven's grand tour of 1862. A New England Methodist and abolitionist, Haven spent nine months abroad, progressing slowly from England via France and Germany to the Holy Land.

Like many others of his day and class, Haven designed his itinerary in homage to the books he had read and the authors he admired. From the English Lake District (bathed in Wordsworth's aura), his path led him to Scotland (full of Walter Scott and Robert Burns references), Coventry (for its Shakespeareana), London (which he recognized through Samuel Johnson's pages), Paris, Waterloo (for Wellington and Napoleon), and on through the Rhine country to Luther's Wittenberg, which he reached, fittingly, on Christmas Eve. But though Haven tried to keep his mind on the literary references, he could not. The cottages of the common English rural folk "without books or papers, or a multitude of things that have long ceased to be luxuries to our people," herded together in tortuously compacted clusters on the edges of the landlords' vast enclosures, which the common folk would never own—all this swam in Haven's imagination like a landscape out of an antislavery free-soil tract. "I felt as never before the unspeakable superiority of America," he wrote within a day of his arrival in England. Even in the Lake District, he stopped to inquire into tenant farm rents, which he thought appallingly high. "No one can conceive who has not seen it, the state of the masses of England," he wrote just before making his Channel crossing; "the social oppression is enormous."[7]

But the Continent was worse. In England, Haven had warmed to the debates over suffrage expansion; he yearned for John Bright to lead a great democratic movement committed to universal, American-style suffrage. To cross over to Napoleon III's France was to descend into open despotism. He was shocked at the sight of women engaged in hard manual labor. Even Paris did not restore his equilibrium. The city's new boulevards, built at such vast expense, seemed to Haven but a new architectural version of Vanity Fair. The emperor, he was certain, could not last: this was "royalty petting and riding the tiger of democracy which it cannot tame." On Haven went into the realm of "the second of our continental despots," Prussia, slipping through the gambling dens of Wiesbaden ("hell itself," he called them, though he had not been able to resist a confirming look) to Luther's city, where Haven's patriotism, his Protestantism, and his democratic radicalism spilled out in one last effusion. The Old World was doomed. Ultimately "the two revelations," Protestantism and democracy, "will reign together over Europe and the world. Luther and America will, under God, make all things new."[8]

The formulas of the republican encounter with Europe were a lesson in patriotism. The polarities already fixed in the mind's eye of the American travelers bent their attention toward evidence of backwardness and poverty:

the wooden clogs of the peasants, the dark country bread, the women toiling in the fields. They brought into relief the pretenses of the European monarchs: the pageants and parades, the imperial profiles Theodore Child thought ridiculously ubiquitous in late 1880s Germany, stamped on pocket handkerchiefs, embroidered on sofa cushions, carved on tobacco pipe bowls. The standing armies, so unfamiliar to Americans, were a constant affront. They "hang on the nations," George Calvert reported from Heidelberg in 1852, like "a monstrous idleness, a universal polluting scab." "My Berlin was a city of army officers, faultless in uniform and arrogant," W. E. B. Du Bois recalled of his student days in the 1890s: "a city of almost daily pageants, that pranced and caroled through the Brandenburg Gate and brought the world to a sudden salute before William, by the Grace of God. Everywhere there were soldiers, soldiers, soldiers."[9]

Emperors and soldiers were but the outer marks, these Americans thought, of a general, overbearing state power. "There the State is always the central figure," the secretary of the Connecticut Board of Education warned American students contemplating a European university education in the early 1870s. "There is always near you, or rather *over* you, the outstretched arm of resistless power." The function of the grandiose state was to repress, demoralize, and impoverish the people. Underneath the "specious proofs of princely munificence and of regal sympathy with the popular wants," he cautioned, there always ran the same desire: "to develop the loyalty of the masses, if not to repress thought and paralyze efforts for liberty."[10]

Into the twentieth century, the contrast between New World democracy and Old World tyranny continued to shape American travelers' reports of Europe. Ray Stannard Baker, on assignment for *McClure's* in Germany in 1900, was sure that no workman in the "civilized" world would trade places with the German laborer, condemned to coarse bread and low wages, taxed to support a huge and costly army, and harassed by a "cloud of officials, great and small." A decade later Booker T. Washington set off for Europe, taking as his guide and ghostwriter Robert E. Park, who had spent four years as a student in turn-of-the-century Germany. Park introduced Washington to European socialists, labor unionists, and social reformers; together they were taken on a tour of the achievements of London "municipal socialism" by John Burns, the labor radical of the 1880s who now sat in the British cabinet; they left the well-beaten tourist paths for the villages of Bohemia, Poland, and southern Italy to see the African-Americans' newest immigrant competitors at their source. But nothing dimmed the promise of

American exceptionalism for Washington. "He was an American," Park confided later, "and thought everything in America surpassed anything in Europe. He just wanted to get the dirt on them that was all, to discover for himself that the man farthest down in Europe had nothing on the man farthest down in the U.S."[11]

From a Europe so conceived, there was nothing to be learned. The American Federation of Labor's Samuel Gompers, returning to the England of his boyhood for a summer's tour in 1909, reiterated the point. "The Old World is not our world. Its social problems, its economic philosophies, its current political questions are not linked up with America . . . In the procession [of nations], America is the first."[12]

By the last decades of the nineteenth century these reassuring republican contrasts had begun to jostle more and more frequently in American minds with a rival, "aesthetic" framing of the Old World–New World relationship, whose keys were no longer oppression and liberty but culture, custom, and time. Against the slow, organic forces of Old World growth, they set the New World's raw, competitive unfinishedness. The new juxtapositions carried more unsettling political consequences than the old. But they, too, were couched in polarities of time and culture that made a common social-political ground between the continents extremely difficult to find.

It was the customs of the grand tour that most forcefully encouraged the aesthetic mood. Seeking out an imagined premodern and apolitical Europe, middle- and upper-class Americans traveling through Europe in the late nineteenth century fell quickly into the terms packaged for them in their commercial guidebooks. Above all, the grand tour was a lesson in time and antiquity. Here was a continent not only dotted with antiquities but also seeming itself to be a museum, where nature and artifice blended into a seamless, "organic" whole. Where republican tourists saw Europe as awaiting a democratic awakening, aesthetic Europe was as changeless and complete as a painting. "There looks as if there was nothing remaining to be done," William Willoughby wrote home from England in 1891. Lincoln Steffens filed the same report from Hamburg: "Everything is completed, finished, squared off,—no rough edges, no dirt and no tearing down." To some Americans, the time-wornness of Europe breathed despair and pessimism, a "deep sadness," as E. A. Ross put it, in contrast to the "rank corn and cotton optimism of the West." But the Europe the aesthetic tourist yearned to see was stable and old, as smoothly worn as the old cathedral stones themselves.[13]

Like the republican vision of Europe, the image of Europe's organic antiquity was in the mind's eye before the American travelers actually saw it. Frederick Law Olmsted, who set out on a tramp through rural England in 1850, was only five miles from Liverpool when he found what he longed to see. "There we were right in the midst of it! The country—and such a country!—green, dripping, glistening, gorgeous! We stood dumb-stricken by its loveliness." He continued, "A stone house interrupts our view in front; the road winds round it, between it and another; turns again, and there on our left is the church—the old ivy-covered, brown stone village church, with the yew-tree—we knew it at once, and the heaped-up, green, old English courtyard." He wrote again the next day: "Such a scene I had never looked upon before, and yet it was in all its parts as familiar to me as my native valley. Land of our poets! Home of our fathers! Dear old mother England! it would be strange if I were not affected at meeting thee at last face to face."[14]

Literary tropes like these helped bridge some of the imagined distance between New and Old Worlds. In cultivating their literary affinities with Europe, late-nineteenth-century Americans gained what some of them hungered desperately for: a deeper past and a relationship (as a young Alabama tourist put it in 1891) to "a greater whole." Tourists on the aesthetic grand tour moved through Europe with their noses in the leather volumes of a late-Victorian library. In Scotland during her first trip to Europe in the 1880s, Jane Addams was reading Scott; in Italy, Ruskin; in Germany, Carlyle. "I am no longer an American ghost," the young Carey Thomas wrote home from England in 1881. "I have claimed my heritage—my castles and ruins, abbeys and cathedral towns and thatched cottages, my lakes, the homes of my poets, my dramatic landscapes, my English mists, my purple heather."[15]

But even as consciousness of common cultural traditions joined the continents in the minds of late-nineteenth-century Americans, the contrast between new and old, raw and settled, forced them all the farther apart. Conventional American tourists abroad had no interest in reminders of the United States, still less in the forces of economic change disrupting the stability of their imagined Europe. Even Olmsted, sharp observer that he was, did not let the complaints of the English farmers he talked with disturb his romantic mood. John Frey of the Molders Union looked in on the slums of London's Whitechapel district, but he spared his readers the details of the big English manufacturing towns, on the grounds that all industrial towns looked alike. One sought out rural England ("unmitigated England,"

Henry James called it) in preference to commercial London, the ruins of the Rhine valley in preference to raw and pushy Berlin, cathedrals (as ripe as rindy old cheese, wrote Oliver Wendell Holmes, Sr.) in preference to parliaments. May Kenny, a young Georgia woman on the grand tour in the mid-1890s, spent her time in Paris being swept down the boulevards by carriage from one historic site to another: the Opéra, Notre Dame, the Bastille, the Pantheon. Some of her party ascended the Eiffel Tower, but she refused, in fear that its modernity would break the city's spell.[16]

Such an encounter with Europe throbbed with none of the messianic sense of world historical change that had gripped Gilbert Haven at Wittenberg. Politically, there was no missing in the aesthetic reappraisal of Europe a sharp deflation of the democratic ideal. The aesthetic travelers let the huddled cottages assume a patina of quaintness and transformed the uniforms of the soldiers into a brilliant wash of color. "For English reforms," Henry Adams wrote half mockingly of himself on his return to London, "Adams cared nothing." "He resented change. He would have kept the Pope in the Vatican and the Queen at Windsor Castle as historical monuments. He did not care to Americanize Europe. The Bastille or the Ghetto was a curiosity worth a great deal of money, if preserved; and so was a Bishop; so was Napoleon III. The tourist was the great conservative who hated novelty and adored dirt." Where in the early 1870s the anthropologist Lewis Henry Morgan could not think of the Arc de Triomphe except as a monument to despotism, a generation later John Frey thought it part of the handsomest streetscape in the world. Visiting Napoleon's tomb, Frey gave not a whisper of censure. The stages of historical progress, once marked so clearly by constitutionalism, suffrage expansion, and the abolition of slavery, fell into confusion.[17]

Such half-articulated doubts about the older democratic certainties were no mere quirk of the grand tour. Across a broad front in both the United States and fin de siècle Europe, those who once had once thought the formal structures of democracy sufficient were not as confident as they had been a quarter century before. Suffrage and constitutionalism, the liberties of trade and person: as a political program bare and alone, these had lost much of their earlier luster. By the end of the century, European radicals, stung by the rapid consolidation of American trusts and monopolies, by the eruption of popular protest in the land of formal democratic promise, and by the unnerving stench of American political corruption, had begun to recant their earlier admiration for the United States. "A quarter of a century ago the American republic was the guiding star of advanced English political thought, [but] it is not so now," William Clarke, the most favorably inclined of the early Fabians toward the United States, wrote in the mid-1890s. Of one thing Clarke was now sure, that "a mere theoretic democracy, unaccompanied by any social changes, was a delusion and a snare." The image of a democratic showcase in the west faded for European radicals. Worrying about the immigrant voter question and backpedaling hard on African-American suffrage, many Americans, too, joined the general retreat from the mid-nineteenth-century democratic verities.[18]

But if this rereading of Europe in organic rather than republican terms could not be separated from dissolution of confidence in formal constitutional democracy, it would be wrong to see in it only conservative and nostalgic political implications. For what was the middle-class American tourists' hunger for an imagined, preindustrial Old World stability except an act of recoil against the disordered, violent camping expedition that was the United States? Europe was "organic" and harmonious, the United States "anarchic"; through the one ran common customs, through the other unrelieved competitive individualism. Pushing out the older political antitheses, the dualities seated themselves at the very core of the aesthetic image of Europe.

By the end of the century, European progressives were turning the same polarities back on the United States itself. In the reports of reform-minded European visitors to the United States, the dirtiness of turn-of-the-century American cities was an insistent theme—a metaphor for governmental inadequacy and social atomization. Charles Booth's Chicago was a mass of wet mud and rubbish, old boilers and drainpipes dumped everywhere. Samuel Barnett of Toynbee Hall thought Boston more refuse-filled and pocked with more unsanitary houses than Whitechapel itself. Ramsay MacDonald, who toured the United States as a young journalist looking for book material in 1897, thought Chicago "like a demented creature, harum scarum, filthy from top to toe." "There is no order, no prevision, no common and universal plan," H. G. Wells admonished.[19]

These were the swift impressions of travelers. Arthur Shadwell, however, a particularly observant English physician, had traversed the heart of industrial Europe gathering materials for a comparative study of industrial societies by the time he reached the United States in 1903. In New York City he found himself constantly reminded of "wretched little towns in the south of Europe." The "leading notes" of the city's architecture, he wrote, were "anarchy, shabbiness, personal ostentation and public indifference." In industry, too, atop a "huge volcano" of labor-employer conflict, Shadwell reported, "it's all hurry-scurry work. Let her go! Give her hell! That's the word." Germany was thorough in its industrial methods, Britain self-satisfied. The dominant characteristics of the United States, by contrast, were "enterprise, audacity, push, restlessness, eagerness for novelty, inventiveness, emulation, and cupidity."[20]

Most of the European critics thought they knew why. Their United States was a country on the run, too busy with its private affairs to bother knitting its pieces together, tossing its cast-off goods wherever they might land, scamping public life in its drive to release individual energy. There was no larger sense of the whole to govern its ceaseless, anarchic energies. The United States, Barnett thought, was a society "with the protection of government removed." Its people had "no conception of the state as an entity, no idea of America as a whole, no national consciousness." Ramsay MacDonald concluded that "no one can conscientiously set the country down as much more than a money making and imitative nation, vitiated by an atomic conception of democratic liberty and equality." John Burns reiterated the theme: the promise of America was "circumscribed and impeded by the undue exaltation of the Unit over the Aggregate, of the Individual as against the Community, of the Monopoly as against the State." Terrific private ingenuity and overwhelming public disorder, runaway individual enterprise and aggregate chaos—this was the impression of progressive European travelers. Old World cultivation of the common life confronted the harum-scarum individualism of the New. The contrast with "organic" Europe was polar.[21]

In its emphasis on the social and the cooperative, then, the aesthetic framing of the Atlantic contrast was not without its social-political potential. But for the moment both the republican and aesthetic polarities acted as powerful restraints on any considerable social-political traffic from the Old World to the New. Within the republican framing of the Atlantic relationship, the European nations could only follow in the footsteps of American precedent. Within the aesthetic frame, the contrast between New and Old Worlds sank deep into unmovable strata of culture. So long as Europe and the United States remained arrayed in polar opposition, stuck at opposite ends of imagined time, social-political borrowing ran up against mental barriers too formidable to surmount.

The exaggerated Europes so dear to the Americans' image of themselves were not politically usable. The imagined landscapes that drew American tourists to Europe served ultimately to force the continents' imagined histories down radically separate tracks. For the transatlantic exchange in social politics to come into being, a significant number of Americans would have to find their way past the imagined landscapes of New and Old. They would have to begin to see the United States and Europe not as oceans and aeons apart but as washed over by a common, contemporaneous sea of change and disruption.

Outside the polarities of the nineteenth-century grand tour, beyond the ken of both the republican and the aesthetic tourists, engines of convergence were, in fact, hard at work. On both sides of the Atlantic a new world of coal and iron, factory towns and sprawling urban agglomerations, accumulated capital, massed wage labor, and new forms of misery was swiftly coming into being. Late-nineteenth-century Essen, Manchester, Lille, and Pittsburgh were not merely similar phenomena, not merely parallel independent developments. They were all part of the furiously expanding world market that was to cart its wares, in such profusion, to Paris in 1900.

The birthplace of this new world was Britain. From the late eighteenth century forward, with consequences that had all but swept away the social landscape of Scott and Wordsworth by the time late-nineteenth-century American tourists set out to look for it, the forces of industrial capitalism had turned the old agrarian economy upside down. The mills, machinery, and steam pumps of the new economic order were still strange and revolutionary when they burst into William Blake's consciousness in 1790s London, their "cogs tyrannic/Moving by compulsion each other." By the last third of the next century, the output of Britain's mines and factories bestrode the world. In 1870, the United Kingdom produced almost a third of the world's manufactured goods. Britain's mines produced two and a half times as much coal in 1870 as its nearest rival and almost four times as much iron ore; in cotton spindles, Britain's lead was almost five to one.[22]

Figures of this kind deeply interested contemporaries; by nationalizing the processes at work, they turned the statistics of industrial production into markers of national prestige. The nations of the North Atlantic economy vied for markets with fierce intensity, manipulating trade and tariff policies or grabbing for captive colonial markets in an effort to leapfrog past each other in industrial primacy. Still, to focus on the nation-state is to distort the fundamental forces at work. Slipping across national borders with the fluidity of quicksilver, investment capital and management and production techniques diffused through the avenues of North Atlantic trade. By the late nineteenth century, what struck those who traversed the industrial regions of the Old and New Worlds was not their difference but their extraordinary sameness.

Physically, the most important common linkage was coal. Not all the world's industrial regions sat above or close by massive coal deposits in the nineteenth century, but most did. Coal was the critical natural resource of the industrial revolution. Essential to the steam energy that powered the century, indispensable to the production of iron and steel, coal power hauled the goods, drove the machinery, cooked the food, heated the grates, and wreathed in soot the cities of Europe and America. Heavy and expensive to transport, it drew investors, enterprises, workers, and cities to it. The coal regions were furnaces not only of production but also of labor-capital conflict—home to the largest labor unions of the late nineteenth and early twentieth centuries and early sites everywhere of state economic action.

Of the four major manufacturing regions of nineteenth-century Britain, three (the fourth was London) lay atop a landscape of coal. The most important was the great textile mill and factory agglomeration of northern England. In 1901 more than a third of Britain's "great cities" of more than 100,000 persons were to be found there, within a forty-mile radius of Manchester. This was the heart of industrial England, a Dickensian world that tourists skirted as they would a leper colony. A second, almost as massive, concentration of mills and factories stretched across southern Scotland, from Glasgow to Dundee, this one, too, resting atop coal and iron deposits. It was said that coming up the River Clyde in the 1880s, one could hear the din of shipwrights' hammers before one actually saw Glasgow, shipbuilder to the nations, a capital-rich and slum-ridden hub of world trade. Britain's third major industrial region encircled Birmingham in the English midlands; the "black country," it was called, from the glare and slag of its forges. Coketown, Dickens called the new industrial city in derision. But there were Coketowns everywhere.[23]

They stretched through Belgium and northern France, across a broad seam of mineral deposits from Lille to Liège, copies in every essential regard of their English progenitors. Belgium's mines, factories, and densely packed industrial towns made it the most intensely industrialized nation of continental Europe—a region of strenuously overcrowded workers' dwellings, low wages, intensive child labor, and startlingly high illiteracy rates. Across the French border, the social landscape resumed without a break. The northern departments were the heart of industrial France, the source of most of its coal and cotton textiles, site of many of its large, paternalistic industrial enterprises, cockpit of the radical French labor movement, and, by the century's end, a stronghold of working-class socialism.[24]

To the east, the common landscape resurfaced in the lower Rhineland and the Ruhr. Capital investment came late to the Ruhr, but nowhere in

Europe between 1870 and the First World War did industrialization advance at a more furious pace. By the turn of the century the Ruhr and its surrounding ring of industrial cities—the silk-weaving center of Krefeld, Düsseldorf with its machinery works, Barmen and Elberfeld with their budding chemical industries, the coal and iron center of Dortmund, and Krupp-dominated Essen—boasted the continent's largest, most intense concentration of heavy industry. Between 1890 and 1900, German steel production, the heart of it in the Ruhr, vaulted ahead of Britain's and soon helped nose Germany past Britain in shares of world manufacturing output. Germany's headlong industrial expansion did not depend entirely on the enterprises of the lower Rhineland. Adding their weight were Silesia, with its coal and iron industries; Alsace-Lorraine; and Saxony, another Belgium of coal mines, textile mills, fiercely overcrowded housing, and (as Paul Göhre found out in the 1890s) stubbornly resentful workers. Mid-nineteenth-century American tourists had found Germany a primitive, comfortless backwater. By 1900 the industrial regions of Germany were in the teeth of an economic transformation swifter even than that of the United States itself.[25]

On the western rim of the Atlantic, tied into the same nexus of trade, primed by infusions of British capital and wholesale borrowings of British technology, the same forces ran. The existence of easily accessible water power, to be sure, gave the older industrial regions of the United States a peculiarly bucolic feel. Arthur Shadwell in 1903 thought the textile mill regions of New England, to his surprise, "rather pretty and tame." By the second half of the nineteenth century, however, the "Europeanization" of the industrial landscape was well under way. Pennsylvania, with its massive coal deposits, was the nation's economic heartland. The country's two most important manufacturing cities, New York and Philadelphia, drew on Pennsylvania mines for their swelling energy needs; the Pittsburgh district was the American Ruhr. In the Middle West, the Illinois coal fields fed another massive industrial concentration, stretching from Pittsburgh and Cleveland on the east to Milwaukee and Chicago on the west. Samuel Barnett, traversing the United States from west to east in 1890–1891, thought reaching Chicago like coming home to Manchester, with its densely packed factories and shouting advertisements. Pittsburgh reminded Beatrice Webb of a cross between backward Italy and her own English Black Country. Arthur Shadwell, too, thought Pittsburgh the familiar thing: "hell with the lid off," just like Essen and Sheffield only more so.[26]

Nor was there any missing the ferocious acceleration of industrial capitalism's advance. The United States had caught up to Britain in steel production by 1880 and in coal production by 1900. In the production of ships and textiles, Britain remained unchallenged, but in the Anglo-German-American race for overall manufacturing output, the primacy of the Americans was a settled fact by the century's end. Alarm at the American penetration of customary European markets fed a steady press diet. The "Americanization" of the world, European journalists called it. It would be fairer to think of it as the Europeanization of America. Better still, to think of it as the manifestation of market processes that sprawled everywhere across the boundary lines neatly marked by statesmen and diplomats.[27]

Coketown was the first defining element of the new world industrial capitalism made. The second was what contemporaries called, with both expansive pride and sweeping nervousness, the "great city." Great cities were not as novel as the new factory towns. Nodal points of trade and capital accumulation, they had played a critical role in the economy of early modern Europe. London had a population of more than a million in 1800, Paris 500,000, Vienna 250,000. But the multiplication of big urban centers in the last decade of the nineteenth century was, nonetheless, a startling phenomenon. From Andrew Mearns's *The Bitter Cry of Outcast London* to Jacob Riis's *How the Other Half Lives* to the strident German outcry against the *Grossstadt*, the growth of the metropolis played hard on the consciousness of turn-of-the-century social reformers throughout the North Atlantic economy.[28]

Of the proliferation of great cities—not mere towns but cities of 100,000 persons or more—the facts left no doubt. In 1871 there were eight cities in the German empire of more than 100,000 persons, accounting in total for about 5 percent of the German Empire's population. Forty years later there were forty-eight *Grossstädte*, one of which, Berlin, had passed the million mark; two in ten Germans now lived in one. There were fifteen great cities in France and forty-one in Britain and Ireland, including the giant of them all, London, swollen now to a population of 7 million. In the United States, where there had been fourteen great cities in 1870, there were fifty in 1910. Notwithstanding the massive, diluting effects of the agrarian West and South, the United States in 1890 was already as urbanized as Belgium, as measured by the percentage of its population in cities of more than 20,000. Of the seven *Millionenstädte* in the North Atlantic economy in 1890, three were located in the United States.[29]

Some of these great cities were heavy-industry complexes. The more common pattern was woven out of trade, finance, and small-scale manufacturing. London's East End, New York's Lower East Side, and their counterparts throughout the North Atlantic economy were centers of production as well as poverty, crowded hives of low-wage, irregular work for the great cities' swelling populations. From their inner commercial cores of banks and fashionable shopping districts, the great cities spread out through their dock districts, warehouses, and rail yards, on into a seemingly endless sea of sweatshops and small factories, corner stores and pawnshops, slums and cheap working-class housing, all in great unplanned confusion.

Where the industrial regions were an object lesson in vertically arrayed power, the great cities were an object lesson in contrast and motion. One must imagine nineteenth-century cities not as units but as a congeries of neighborhoods; to walk through them was to pass through a seemingly endless regress of social contradictions. Concentrations of enormous wealth lay hard by concentrations of abject poverty, splendid carriage parks by whiskey alleys, handsome shopping thoroughfares for the bourgeoisie by acres of pawn shops, pushcarts, and secondhand stores for the masses. The polarities of wealth were not new, but their visible concentration cheek by jowl in a stark urban chiaroscuro, joined only by the thin and impersonal relationships of wages and markets, was novel and, to many observers, unnerving.

The great cities' contrasts in fortune were one of their characteristic marks; another was the ceaseless motion of property and populations. The great cities were inherently unstable not only at the ever-receding point where they bled into the countryside but at their core as well, as land values and property uses shifted with the whims of markets and fashion. Contributing to this instability was the astonishing tide of persons who poured yearly into the cities, scrambling for place and shelter in an environment that never had enough to go around. Berlin, Vienna, Glasgow, and New York all presented particularly acute cases of housing famine, but no great city in the nineteenth and early twentieth centuries could be said to have adequately solved the problem of housing supply. Transportation and public health issues also pressed hard on urban authorities as they struggled to rationalize the crazy quilt of private water contractors, night-soil haulers, and horsecar lines that sprang up to meet the new urban needs. It is little wonder that the great cities should have absorbed so much of the political energy and imagination of turn-of-the-century progressives. Nowhere else was the clash between private property rights and public needs more tangibly and urgently displayed.

Well into the twentieth century, to be sure, the urban and industrial regions of Europe and the United States remained grimy, crowded islands in an agricultural sea. The townscapes of industrial capitalism broke suddenly out of the surrounding agrarian background. England, where the economic revolution had had longest to work, was a partial exception. By 1900, only 12 percent of the United Kingdom's working population still drew its livelihood from farming. Even in intensely industrialized Belgium at the same moment, a quarter of the labor force still worked in agriculture; in Germany it was a third, and in France and the United States, a little over 40 percent.[30] Beyond the core regions of industrial development stretched the broad, agrarian expanse—the Junker-dominated rye fields of Prussia and Poland; the estates of the Austro-Hungarian empire; the peasant plots of southern Europe, Ireland, and Scandinavia; the cotton fields of the deep South; and the endlessly receding plains of the trans-Mississippi West—where well over half the turn-of-the-century working population was still engaged in agriculture.

But the countryside was no more immune to the market revolution than the cities. Foreign grain began to pour into Europe in the late 1860s and 1870s—from Canada, Russia, and (most importantly) the United States—with devastating consequences for agricultural stability. In Ireland these pressures fanned long-standing tensions over religion and landownership into outright tenant revolt. And if resistance was common, flight was universal. The extreme case was Sweden, where 20 percent of the population emigrated between 1860 and 1910. Everywhere rural depopulation proceeded at a startling rate as the countryside emptied itself into the cities, leaving contemporaries struggling to find new crop mixes and marketing structures for the farm population that remained behind.[31]

By the last quarter of the nineteenth century, there were, in consequence, uprooted peasants throughout the North Atlantic economy. The cities of the United States received them in particularly massive numbers, but Europe, beneath the tourists' preoccupation with stasis and custom, was hardly less in flux. In England by the century's end, scarcely more than a quarter of the people lived in the county in which they had been born; in Berlin in 1890, four out of every five male workers between the ages of thirty and sixty had been born outside the city. There were migrants everywhere: transient Irish in English factory towns, Polish miners in the Scottish collieries, Spanish miners in the coal works of southern France, Italian textile mill operatives in the factory towns of Belgium and the Lorraine, and country folks in every city. Of Liverpool's family heads in the 1870s, a quarter were Irish-born. In the German Ruhr, over a quarter of the miners spoke Polish in 1890; in the Ruhr town of Gelsenkirchen, a third of the city's schoolchildren did so.[32]

Among the most visible consequences of these interlocked changes in markets and labor was a tremendous outpouring of new goods. Real wages rose in the North Atlantic economy over the long course of the late nineteenth and early twentieth centuries. So did the opportunities for education, the supply of books and reading matter, the range of consumable pleasures, and the avenues of mobility. Even before the spread of the automobile and household electricity, the stock of goods purchasable by common folk—from gas lighting to ready-made clothing, from a nickelodeon ticket to a tram ride to the countryside—expanded with virtually miraculous speed. Wherever the tide of cheap factory-made goods and foreign grain broke apart the old peasant and artisanal economies of agrarian society, the collision released intense human energies. Were it not that "improvement" seemed so firmly written in the material history of the nineteenth and twentieth centuries, the progressive confidence that society, too, could be improved can hardly be imagined.

But if the economic revolutions of the nineteenth century brought a flood of new goods into being, there could be no denying that they also brought new forms of misery. By a Benthamite calculus, it is not clear that the overall deficit of pain over pleasure increased, but the market revolutions powerfully reshaped both the experience and the consciousness of economic misery. The pains of rural life had been harsh and recurrent: crop failures, pestilence, disease, accident, childbirth. However these were shaped or intensified by social arrangements of property, taxation, or manorial power, they wore a certain air of naturalness and (hence) inevitability. The pains of industrial capitalism were less predictable, and their human face was less easily disguised. Both mobility and vulnerability increased with the growing commodification of labor. Without the safety of peasant plot, kin, and custom, the collapse of earning capacity in the new wage-labor market could be breathtakingly swift. Early investigators of the urban working class were fascinated with the thin line between competence and misery, and the extent to which men and women found themselves so capriciously pushed from one to the other. In these new forms of misery, the hand of human callousness, or calculation, or stupidity, or cheapness loomed at least as large as fate itself. An industrial accident, a landlord's eviction notice, a boss's intransigence over wages: these were all patently social events. Being matters of power and politics, it was hardly surprising that some men and women thought they must have social and political solutions.

The hand of conscious human action was no less manifest in the pains of great city life and—as the Populists' outcry against bank and railroad power showed—in the countryside as well. Thomas Haskell has argued that in the late nineteenth century, the causes of social problems seemed to recede, drifting away from the identifiable.[33] But over the long haul, it is fairer to say the reverse. As custom receded before the onward march of commodification, the role of human agency became more and more evident. An entire vocabulary sprang up around the term "social"—"social economics," "social politics," the "social problem," the "social question"—all in testimony to the growing consciousness of the socially constructed nature of market capitalism. Pain was old, but the pains of the wage-labor market and of great city life were different than before, and less easily accepted under the old formulas.

Finally, one need not romanticize the countryside to point out that the new world of industrial capitalism was shaken by far more overt conflict than the old. Bread riots, urban mobbings, and peasant uprisings had been a common enough feature of preindustrial societies. But whether or not middle-class progressives were right in calling the new age one of outright "industrial warfare," there is no doubt that social classes faced each other more frequently and over more deeply institutionalized hostility than before. Strikes were the most unnerving sign of the new order; bitter and violently fought on both sides, they grew in scope as the era proceeded, pulling the state more and more deeply into the role of policeman, negotiator, or military suppressor. But strikes were not external to the new regime of market relations; like the wage bargain itself, of which they were a part, strikes were institutionally essential to it. So was the incentive on both sides toward collective discipline and organization, whether through a united labor front or a solid cartel of employers. Where private rights ended and public rights began in this simmering conflict between organized labor and organized capital was an item of perpetual debate. When Charles Gide described the field of social economy as the problem of "social peace," however, both noun and adjective carried heavy freight.

Coketown and *Grossstadt*, material improvements and mounting insecurities: to stress the common lineaments of this new social order is not to deny the national peculiarities within it. In all essential regards, nonetheless, Europe and its economic frontier in the west moved through these upheavals as a single, complex unit. On both sides of the Atlantic, the outlines of this world, its modal landscapes and its key sources of discontent and conflict, were increasingly recognizable. It was a different Europe than the guidebooks let on, and a different United States than the keepers of a special American destiny wanted to admit. Underneath the political and aesthetic contrasts, there was neither Old nor New World but a common, economy-driven new-world-in-the-making.

Progressive Politics

The new Atlantic economy of the late nineteenth century was to encourage a new Atlantic-wide politics. From its first stirrings in the 1890s, the new social politics was to emerge as a powerful political force by the 1910s, with representatives in every capital in the North Atlantic world. Even the Americans, so distant from the chief centers of policy and intellectual innovation, were to be drawn in.

Those who forged the new social politics in the generation before the First World War never shared a common name. Some of them never found a consistent referential language even for themselves. William Beveridge referred to himself variously as a "Tory democrat," a "Labour imperialist," "very nearly" a socialist, and a Liberal. Frederic C. Howe, the American municipal reformer, called himself a single-taxer, a "liberal," a "reformer," and a "radical." Between national political cultures, the confusion of terms was even more pronounced. In France the pioneers of social politics styled themselves radicals, *solidaristes*, economic *interventionistes*, or simply proponents of *la réforme sociale*. In England they went under the name of "new Liberals," "new radicals," Christian socialists, Fabians, or "collectivists." In Germany, a dozen rival socio-political parties and pressure groups constructed themselves around permutations of the core term, *sozial*.[34]

One comes close to a common denominator, however, with "progressive." As a political designation it was English before it was American, born in the heated municipal politics of 1890s London before crossing to the United States in the first decade of the new century. By 1910, in the Progressive People's Party (Fortschrittliche Volkspartei) of Friedrich Naumann, Lujo Brentano, and other younger reform intellectuals, the term "progressive" had acquired social-political overtones in Germany as well.[35] It was central to the self-identity of the proponents of social politics to think of themselves as committed less to an abstract principle than to a distinctive place at history's leading edge, where the effects of the revolutions in production and exchange cut most sharply.

Radicals and reformers before them had imagined themselves at work at the cutting edge of history, of course, but they had not located the economy as the key sector of change. Since the great eighteenth-century revolutions, their core project had been to restrain not the processes of commodification but the concentrated powers of the monarchical state. The mechanics of political authority had been their particular genius: written constitutions and self-limiting governments to tie the hands of potential despots, parliamentary autonomy and popular prerogatives, expanded suffrage and more straightforward representation, broader civil immunities and explicit bills of rights.

Into the last quarter of the nineteenth century, these projects still framed party politics and political culture. France in 1870, with Napoleon III's empire in default after an ill-contrived test of military will with Prussia, was just beginning its third, still profoundly uncertain, trial of republicanism. Modern Germany, brand new in 1871, hammered together by the same Prussian armies that had toppled Napoleon III from his throne, was absorbed in constitution making and nation-state building. In Britain in 1870, where William Gladstone was beginning his second year as prime minister, the agenda of liberal politics had been stable for a quarter of a century: political democratization, free trade, Irish rights, and freedom of religious dissent. In the United States in 1870, where radicals and reformers were still absorbed in the aftershocks of secession and civil war, the political reconstitution of the nation and the terms on which liberty was to be offered to the former slaves overshadowed every other political consideration.[36]

The progressives of the late nineteenth and early twentieth centuries were not indifferent to these issues. In countries where the principle of parliamentary majoritarianism had not yet been secured (as in pre–World War I Sweden), where the suffrage was constrained by particularly high property qualifications (as in the states and cities of Germany), or where the landed aristocrats still possessed a formal veto over popular majorities (as in England before David Lloyd George forced the House of Lords to give way in the budget crisis of 1909 to 1911), the agendas of old and new reform politics could hardly be unscrambled.

But whether the shapers of the new social politics sustained the old democratic radicalism or (more commonly) borrowed selectively from it, hedging the rest round with second thoughts and qualifications, they shared a conviction that a politics focused on the redivision of state power could no longer suffice. As the authority that had once been the prerogative of courts and kings and the landowning nobility passed to the possessors of capital and captains of industry, as the key sources of power and pain became economic and social, the grand legal-political dismantling projects of the radical past faded before the need to rethink the purposes of society and the state. This was what H. G. Wells, writing from the United States in 1906, meant when he insisted that there was more political promise to be found in the ambitious metropolitan park system being laid out in Boston, or in the dynamos at Niagara that were just beginning to generate public power for the province of Ontario, than in Washington, D.C., where the "national government lies marooned, twisted up into knots, bound with safe-guards, and altogether impotently stranded." This was what progressives everywhere meant when they claimed that the mere negation of power was not enough. The focus of politics turned from constitutions to administration, from the consequences of aristocratic privilege to the contexts of everyday life. "The politics of the future," Britain's Joseph Chamberlain put the point as early as 1883, "are social politics."[37]

Piece by piece, through persistent individual and collective effort, a good deal of social-political work had by then already been done. Public limits on the conditions of mine and factory work—together with one of the key inventions of modern social politics, a paid public inspectorate to enforce them—went back in England to the early nineteenth century; limits on the rights of English property owners to rent and build as they willed for human habitation were the work of the sanitary politics of the 1840s. The local German insurance funds *(Kassen)* on which Bismarck's system would build long antedated the empire; encouragement of the *sociétés mutuels* had been a pet project of Napoleon III. Many of the key institutions of progressive politics, in short, were old. But not until the century's end did the big party- and coalition-forming issues of politics, framed by the great eighteenth-century revolutions, begin to shift toward the new axes.

The first major ruptures in the prevailing political frame proceeded opportunistically, in quick, untheoretic seizures of crises and opportunities. Bismarck, who had a visceral dislike for state interference in private wage contracts, backed crabwise into his social insurance program of the 1880s—setting the sanctity of a factory master's economic "household" aside for the prospect of disarming the outlawed socialists and rewedding the loyalties of the German working class to the state and emperor. Gladstone's Irish land reform act of 1881, abrogating contracts, removing the question of fair rent to a special state commission, and pledging state aid for a buyout of English landlords, was a similar singularity, an emergency breach of Liberal principles in an attempt to calm the seething anger of Irish tenants and drive the vexing Irish question, at last, out of politics.

By the 1890s, however, signs of broader, more lasting political realignments could be seen across the North Atlantic economy and in its outposts in Australia and New Zealand. The progressive movements of that decade—Wilhelm II's flirtation with a "social monarchy," the emergent social radicalism in France, the Liberal-labor alliance in New Zealand, and the progressive urban coalitions in Britain and the United States—differed sharply in their origins. In Germany, the "new course" of the early 1890s was the fruit of monarchical ambition. Cutting himself free from the aging Bismarck, who was no longer willing to preside over further social-political experimentation, the young new emperor set out on a path of social politics from above: gathering a corps of reformist state administrators into the Prussian chanceries, pressing on the Reichstag an agenda of industrial safety and regulatory legislation, lending his favor to the organization of a social gospel movement within the established Protestant church, intervening personally in the Ruhr miners' strike of 1889, and convening the first Europe-wide intergovernmental conference on uniform labor standards. In France, in contrast, the social politics of the 1890s grew out of middle-class, republican antecedents. Léon Bourgeois was its most prominent symbol, a leading Radical politician and cabinet member, philosopher of *solidarité*, prime mover in the Alliance d'Hygiène Sociale, and an honorary president of the Musée Social. To the long-standing republican absorption in anticlerical and constitutional politics, his Radical government of 1895–96 added for the first time an ambitious social agenda: regulation of factory employment, progressive income taxation, and public old-age pensions.[38]

In New Zealand between 1891 and 1906 a Liberal-labor alliance drew on still different ingredients. Capitalizing on the long-simmering tension between large landowners, with their sprawling sheep estates, and a land- and job-hungry urban working class, the government pushed through a sweeping program of progressive land taxes, public land leases for small holders, comprehensive factory regulation, stigma-free old-age pensions for the (morally respectable) poor, suffrage for adult women, and, for organized labor, a compulsory arbitration law—the first anywhere of its sort—extracting deadlocked wage contests from the market and placing them in the hands of specially delegated judges.[39]

New Zealand was the showcase of progressive politics in the 1890s. To Jane Addams's friend and political ally Henry Demarest Lloyd, who traveled halfway round the world to see it, New Zealand was "the political brain of the modern world"—the world's "'experiment station' of advanced legislation." Sidney Webb in 1898, shaking off his dismay at constitutionally deadlocked politics in the United States, was equally enthusiastic: "Instead of the nominal English Constitution of 1789, you have here a genuine Democracy, the people really getting what it wishes to get."[40]

Personal disappointments exaggerated the contrast, for in both Lloyd's United States and Webb's England the new progressive forces were already at work in city politics. In London between 1889 and 1907, a Progressive alliance of Liberals, labor unionists, and Fabians dramatically broadened the city's range of public services. In Glasgow, Boston, Detroit, and elsewhere in the 1890s, parallel reform coalitions locked horns with corporate streetcar and utility monopolies in a rehearsal of the techniques and political style that were soon to overflow onto the national political stage.

By the first decade of the twentieth century there was no party system within the North Atlantic economy that had not been profoundly shaken by the new social politics. In Britain, the Liberal government of 1906–1914 embarked on a flurry of legislation that, a quarter century later, still stuck in Franklin Roosevelt's mind for its daring. For the aged poor, it inaugurated an old-age pension system borrowed from New Zealand; for the crippling economic effects of sickness, a program of compulsory wage-earners' health insurance borrowed from Germany; for the most exploited of workers, a set of Australian-style wage boards empowered to establish legal minimum wages; for the sake of fiscal justice, progressive land and income taxes; for the unemployed, a German-style network of state-run employment offices; and, for workers in trades of particularly uneven labor demand, an untried experiment in pooling the risks of unemployment through state-administered insurance. The Radical coalitions that governed France between 1899 and 1914, though their failures were greater, proposed no less: progressive income taxation, public medical assistance to the elderly poor, a legally fixed maximum working day, tax subsidies for trade union unemployment benefits, public mediation of labor disputes, and—in a policy reversal that hinted at the international volatility of the new social politics—German-modeled, compulsory, old-age insurance. In timing and content, the prewar progressive movement in American politics fit, as fragment to whole, into this broader North Atlantic pattern.[41]

On both sides of the Atlantic, politicians rode the new issues to power and popularity: David Lloyd George and the young Winston Churchill in Britain, Georges Clemenceau in France, Theodore Roosevelt and Woodrow Wilson in the United States. Parties and pressure groups drew up sweeping social programs. For the rest of the twentieth century, although parties split and polarized over the new issues, no politics could be divorced from social politics.

Participants in these events knew their own affinities. On his European tour of 1911, Theodore Roosevelt talked with Wilhelm II of diplomacy, industrial progress, and systems of state old-age and accident insurance; in England he was eager to talk with the "new Liberal" David Lloyd George and with the former labor firebrand among the London Progressives, John Burns. A year later, seeking to snatch a victory of sorts from the American Progressive Party's electoral disappointments, Medill McCormick proposed that the party send himself, Roosevelt, Gifford Pinchot, George W. Perkins, and a handful of others on a trip to England, Belgium, Germany, and Switzerland "and fill the newspapers with the stuff. Meet Briand, Lloyd George, Winston Churchill, right through, but a cut to the right of the Socialists." The Kansas progressive William Allen White put the same sentiment in more radical terms: "We were parts, one of another, in the United States and Europe. Something was welding us into one social and economic whole with local political variations. It was Stubbs in Kansas, Jaurès in Paris, the Social Democrats in Germany, the Socialists in Belgium, and I should say the whole people in Holland, fighting a common cause."[42]

The progressives' success in remaking the agenda of politics was no guarantee that their solutions would prevail. Everywhere the new policies proceeded in fits and starts, in opportunities seized and opportunities closed off again. Wilhelm II's new course of 1890 was exhausted by 1894; a second wave of social-political legislation in Germany, begun in 1905 was spent by 1911. The British "new Liberals" had depleted most of their political capital well before the First World War. Léon Bourgeois's government of 1895 fell within a year; the reform ambitions of Clemenceau's government of 1906 were quickly consumed in a cascade of labor strikes.

The fragility of prewar progressive politics was partly the result of a plurality of parties competing for the same terrain. In France, social politics was by definition coalition politics, always fragile. In the prewar United States, neither of the major parties successfully cornered the market in progressive issues. In Britain as late as 1905, the Webbs were still busy "permeating" the Conservative Party, certain it was the more promising vehicle than the Liberal Party for their collectivist ambitions. In Germany, where the Social Democratic Party and socialist labor unions remained beyond the pale of imperial legitimacy—tightly policed, their members excluded from all but the most minor administrative offices—social politics at the national level ran fitfully, on one leg alone, as reformers gained the emperor's ear and then lost it to others. Everywhere, the new politics made similar enemies. Property owners' and tax payers' associations, employers' interest groups, and chambers of commerce multiplied apace. Court challenges tied the French contributory old-age insurance act in knots after 1910; in the United States, the judiciary was notorious as a graveyard for social-political initiatives. The new politics, in short, hardly thrust out the old. But between 1890 and 1914 reform politics was reconstituted in a new key and language.

The new politics was framed not only by the age's economic transformations but also by what progressives everywhere, with nervous delicacy, called the "labor question." The rise of mass working-class organization was a key feature of the times, and, like the new forms of capital, its reach was international. From the American Knights of Labor organizers canvassing for recruits in the English midlands in the 1880s to the British and American fraternal delegates trading places at their respective annual labor union gatherings to the work of Marx's successors at the Second Socialist International, there was no missing the sharply conscious international edge to labor politics. The German and Swedish Social Democratic Parties, the French and Belgian Parties Ouvriers, the English Social Democratic Federation, the American Socialist Labor Party, and the Second International itself were all founded between 1875 and 1889. A quarter of a century later, socialist parties constituted a major political challenge everywhere in the North Atlantic economy. In the United States, the socialists polled almost a million votes in 1912. In France in the last election before the First World War, one in six popular votes went to the socialists; in Germany, one in three. Even the hinterlands were not immune. In Sweden the socialist share of the popular vote went from near zero to 30 percent between 1900 and 1914; in Denmark it jumped from 14 percent to 29 percent. Only in Britain and its Australasian outposts were the socialists marginalized from politics before the First World War, and that was in no small part because Labour Parties had preempted the potential political space. "It was the sudden international emergence of mass labour and socialist movements in and after the 1880s which seemed to place numerous governments and ruling classes in essentially the same predicaments," Eric Hobsbawm writes with some exaggeration. But the point was not lost on contemporaries.[43]

Beneath the growth of socialist and labor organizations lay a still more widespread, less organized set of resentments, more worrisome in some ways to middle-class progressives in their inchoateness and volatility. Strikes and lockouts, bitterly and often violently fought on both sides, were their most visible manifestation. From the 1880s forward these erupted on a scale unknown before. The Knights of Labor's nationwide eight-hour-day strike of 1886 and the London dockworkers' and Ruhr miners' strikes of 1889 were harbingers of the massive disputes to come. Strike waves shook France and the United States in the early 1890s; the United States, France, and Germany between 1903 and 1906; and virtually all the industrialized societies between 1910 and 1913.[44] These, in turn, were fuel for labor union recruiting. Union rolls in Germany between the early 1890s and the First World War mushroomed from less than 300,000 to 2.5 million; in Britain, from 1.6 to 4.1 million; in France from 140,000 to over a million; in the United States from 400,000 (in 1897, when reliable estimates begin) to 2.6 million.[45]

In the face of these challenges, governments swung between military repression and the "soft embrace" of social-political concession. Yearning as they did for "social peace," it is not surprising that progressives swung with much the same ambivalence. Institutions of labor-capital mediation captured a good deal of progressive attention, from New Zealand–style compulsory arbitration to the personal intervention of a Roosevelt or Lloyd George in labor disputes to the network of industrial courts, conciliation bureaus, and legally mandated works committees elaborated slowly in post-1890 Germany. When mediation failed, however, progressive governments (as those of Wilson, Lloyd George, and Clemenceau were all to show) could respond as harshly as conservative ones.

It was within all these fields of force—the rapid intensification of market relations, the swelling great city populations, and the rising working-class resentments from below—that the new social politics took shape. The common social landscapes of industrial capitalism helped to knit its national strands together; so did deep, commonly shared anxieties. The internationalization of capital and labor were its preconditions. But progressive politics in the North Atlantic economy possessed its own international dynamics and institutions, and in the reconfiguring of social politics on a transnational frame, these were no less essential.

Within Europe itself, one of the most striking signs of the new transnational social politics was the phenomenon of legislation passed from one nation to another, sometimes despite acute distrust and rivalry. An early example was British-modeled factory legislation, which began to turn up in France, Germany, and elsewhere in the 1870s. A generation later, borrowings of this sort formed a crazy quilt of transnational influences and appropriations. Danish old-age pensions were imported (via New Zealand) to Britain, British industrial liability codes to France, and French subsidarism to Denmark, Holland, and Scandinavia, even as more radical French progressives turned to German-style compulsory state insurance. The noisiest of these appropriations was the British National Insurance Act of 1911, which was cheered on by Lloyd George less than three years before the war as outstripping Germany at its own social-political game.

Beneath and enabling these events lay a web of less prominent connections. One was the international conference of like-minded reformers, whether expert or amateur. Accelerated by the Paris expositions, conference organizing was one of the most striking products of the era. By the eve of the First World War, there were regularly convening international conferences on labor legislation, the welfare and protection of children, social insurance, unemployment, housing, garden cities and city planning, public baths, prisons, and the public and private relief of poverty; there were also regularly convening international conferences of factory inspectors, consumers' league organizers, city officials, trade unionists, and feminists. Each of these sustained an ongoing administrative structure, and their big, verbatim, published proceedings were essential to a well-equipped social library.[46]

Another conduit was the public or private inspection visit. England was an early magnet. Since the middle of the nineteenth century, England's freely operating agencies of working-class associationalism (labor unions, cooperatives, and friendly societies) and its broadly institutionalized collective bargaining—all anomalies in mid-nineteenth-century Europe—had drawn the attention of continental reformers. German progressives, hoping to deflect the German labor movement from revolutionary socialism, were particularly eager visitors, coming themselves and sponsoring tours of German workingmen. Other Germans came to see, and be inspired by, the new English garden cities, the municipal work of the London Progressives, or the English settlement house movement.[47]

By the turn of the century, a countercurrent of curiosity about Germany was flowing as hard in the other direction, as British progressives struggled to unravel the relationship between Germany's social policy and its striking commercial success. British manufacturers, restless under the regime of free trade, sent workers' commissions ("tariff trippers," their detractors called them) to study labor and social conditions in protectionist Germany. Others set out to investigate the social efficiency of German cities, the work of the imperial labor statistics bureau and the social insurance system, or the techniques of German trade and technical education.[48] Other lines of investigation spread farther afield. British agricultural reformers studied Denmark, and Danish reformers Ireland. The investigations of the Verein für Sozialpolitik had a cosmopolitan reach; the Musée Social sent investigators across the world.[49]

In every one of the industrializing countries, finally, there were influential publicists with a keen interest in another nation's social policy. Eased out of the New Zealand labor ministry in 1896, William Pember Reeves, the principal architect of the New Zealand labor reforms of the 1890s, ended up in London where, quickly absorbed into Fabian circles, he lectured widely on New Zealand social policy. German social-political networks were stocked with admirers of English social policy, from Max Hirsch, founder of the Hirsch-Duncker labor union movement on the lines that had inspired him in England in the 1860s, to Hermann Schulze-Delitzsch, the English cooperatives' admirer and a key figure in the German credit cooperative movement, to Lujo Brentano, the leading labor relations expert in the Verein für Sozialpolitik. On the reformist edge of German social democracy, Eduard Bernstein and Hugo Lindemann had both been deeply drawn into the enthusiasms of the London Progressives in the 1890s.[50]

A striking example of the cosmopolitan type was Britain's William Dawson. Sent to Germany as an economic journalist in the 1880s, he had found his way (as did many contemporary Americans) into Adolph Wagner's economics lectures in Berlin, where, with a convert's eagerness, he caught the early stirrings of German social politics. His first two books on Germany (on Lassalle and Bismarck, respectively) were embarrassingly effusive; his attempt to found a British journal dedicated to German-style "state socialism" failed in the early 1890s. But after these false starts, Dawson found his groove in more straightforward reportage. Between 1891 and 1914 he authored nine more books on Germany, translating its social-political developments into closely written, admiring, and influential description. After 1908 a new concern over the growth of "force worship" in contemporary Germany sobered his tone, but no one in Britain knew its social politics more intimately than he. When David Lloyd George needed an expert on German social insurance, Dawson was recruited for the task; he ended his career as principal clerk for the National Health Insurance Commission for England.[51]

Within the shifting, eclectic social-political currents of the day, the single-mindedness of Dawson's absorption with Germany was unusual. But at a lesser intensity his type was critical to the emergent progressive politics. Superimposed on the convergent economic and social forces of the age, brokers of international social politics like Dawson added to the network of ideas, ambitions, and information that made the progressive political connections possible. With their libraries of borrowable, adaptable social-political models and projects, they helped create a new hunger for knowledge of foreign political experience. That hunger, in turn, made experts out of amateurs like Dawson, and gave them sympathetic allies within the chanceries and publication outlets outside them. With these resources, they helped construct the international patterns of admiration, appropriation, rivalry, publicity, and exchange that left so distinct a mark on the new social politics.

That cosmopolitan imprint hardly made politics across the nation-states the same. The convergent tendencies of social politics played themselves out against deep structural differences in state organization and an ever-present, potentially explosive, nationalism. The progressive intellectual accomplishment was more modest: by infusing the political imagination with the convergent economic forces of the age, it drew politics across the world of iron, for the moment, into a common frame.

Coming from so far, the Americans had no automatic access to the networks and discussions taking shape in Europe. The distance that held them at arms length was, as we have seen, both physical and cultural: the practical difficulties of travel, and the oceanic dichotomies within their own minds between New World politics and Old. Slowly, however, Americans began to find their way across the barriers of both space and mind.

An early channel was through university study abroad. From a trickle in the mid 1870s to a broad, institutionally established stream in the 1890s, a generation of American students of economics and social science made their way to Germany for graduate study. They passed the itineraries of their *Wanderjahre* from hand to hand until these hardened into formula: a semester in Johannes Conrad's economics seminar in Halle, a research paper with the Verein für Sozialpolitik's leading figure, Gustav Schmoller, and, almost always, the lectures of Adolph Wagner in Berlin, where the theoretical and ethical fallacies of classical economics were laid out with passionate argument.

A more modest early node of contact was created within the Bureau of Labor. Founded as a sop to the labor vote in 1885, the bureau soon emerged as the key social investigative agency in Washington. Its first international inquiries turned on the question of comparative standards of living, to which it tended (as did parallel inquiries elsewhere) to give the answers that home-country pride demanded. But the bureau's inquiries quickly broadened. In its *Bulletin* one can read closely written, detailed accounts of the workings of Dutch poor relief; British agencies of labor conciliation; French and German company welfare policies; British city-owned public utilities; and pawnbroking, public baths, workmen's compensation legislation, child labor legislation, and factory legislation across the nations of Europe. In 1911, when the Germans recodified their social insurance legislation and the British enacted their National Insurance Act, the bureau printed both documents in full.[52]

Some of this work of translating and transcribing was murderously dull. Before the end of the century, when parallel bureaus of labor statistics began to be organized in Europe, the American desire for information could be sated only by delivering the bureau's questionnaires personally to as many foreign government officials, labor union secretaries, and employers as would take the time to fill them out. W. F. Willoughby, the bureau's senior agent abroad in 1900, yearned for nothing more deeply than to shuffle the tediousness of this work off on his younger colleague and board the next ship home. But careers and expertise were made in the experience. Willoughby parlayed his painstakingly obtained information into the first comprehensive American book on social insurance and the beginnings of a university teaching career. John Graham Brooks, the first president of the National Consumers' League, made his initial trip to Europe in the 1880s to investigate German accident insurance for the Bureau of Labor. E. R. L. Gould, founder of New York City's largest philanthropic housing company, got his start with a bureau-sponsored investigation of European public and philanthropic housing. Perhaps the most famous of the bureau's investigators was Walter Weyl, cofounder of the *New Republic*, who began his career as a social-political writer investigating the conditions of European railroad employment.[53]

An international link of a different kind ran through the social gospel movement. In every corner of the North Atlantic economy, from the early Fabian Society to the German Evangelical Social Congress to the well-placed sprinkling of Protestants in the Musée Social, progressive politics was intricately entangled with social Protestantism. W. T. Stead, who made his mark as a social evangelist and journalist on both sides of the Atlantic, was a prominent figure in the Atlantic social gospel network. Another was the Christian socialist W. D. P. Bliss, sponsor of the first American edition of the *Fabian Essays* and Tolman's collaborator at the League for Social Service. Ties between the American and German social gospel movements were never as close as those between the United States and Britain, but when the University of Chicago's Charles Henderson set out to report on the stirrings of German social Protestantism in the 1890s, the *American Journal of Sociology* made space for his reports.[54]

The settlement house movement was one of transatlantic social Protestantism's most striking productions. Here the innovators were English. From the opening of Toynbee Hall in Whitechapel at the edge of London's East End in 1884, Samuel Barnett's institution was a magnet for American visitors. Jane Addams made visits in 1887, 1888, and 1889. Stanton Coit, whose Neighborhood Guild in the Lower East Side beat Hull House by three years as the first American settlement, had apprenticed as a Toynbee Hall resident. Richard Ely and Margaret Dreier (cofounder of the English-modeled Women's Trade Union League) signed Toynbee Hall's visitors' book in 1889; Gifford Pinchot, set his name down in 1890, one of forty-two American visitors that year. Robert Woods (of Andover House, Boston), Vida Scudder (of the College Settlement in New York), Charles Zueblin (of the Northwestern University Settlement in Chicago), George Hodges (of Kingsley House, Pittsburgh), and Cornelia Foster Bradford (of Whittier House in Jersey City) all visited Toynbee Hall before setting out institutionally on their own.[55]

Inevitably, American and English settlement house developments diverged. Rooted in a woman's college network unknown in England, the American movement was much more quickly and deeply feminized than its English model. Sharing neither the Oxford cultural pretensions of Toynbee Hall (with its fine arts exhibits and reading rooms wreathed in pipe smoke) nor its residents' easy, Oxbridge-greased access to government policy making, the American settlement houses were more alert to issues of family, immigrants, and neighborhoods. But the social investigations that from the outset kept the American settlements from becoming mere charity outposts were a direct offshoot of the London original. And the American settlement house residents worked extremely hard to sustain the English connection. Hull House, Greenwich House, and Lillian Wald's Henry Street Settlement all functioned as hostelries for an astonishingly broad list of sojourning English progressives. Through Henry Street came, among others, Graham Wallas (the first man to take up residence there), Patrick Geddes, Mary Macarthur and Margaret Bondfield of the Women's Trade Union League, and the early Labour Party's Keir Hardie and Ramsay MacDonald. At Hull House, an irresistible way station for reformers from abroad, Jane Addams read Henrietta Barnett's letters aloud at dinner time. In the Chicago stockyard district's University Settlement in the late 1920s, Mary McDowell reserved a permanent place on her desk for Beatrice

Webb's autobiography; at the Chicago Commons, Graham Taylor kept Charles Booth's photograph in a prominent spot in the library.[56]

Sometimes the social Protestant connection yielded less expected results. Robert A. Woods was a young student at Andover Seminary in the late 1880s when William J. Tucker, an early social gospel teacher, picked him out to work up the subject of "social economy." Dispatching him first to New York City to investigate the relationship between socialism and trade unionism, Tucker then sent him on to England in 1890, where he settled into Toynbee Hall for a six-month stay. Barnett introduced him to the leading social gospel figures and charity experts: Charles Booth; Charles Loch of the Charity Organization Society; W. T. Stead, deep in plans for land colonies for the London poor; and Andrew Mearns, author of *The Bitter Cry of Outcast London*. But the socialists soon interested Woods more than the philanthropists, and the labor movement soon interested him most of all. William Clarke pulled Woods into the discussions of the Fabian Society, then only six years old, joined him on a tour of the northern English factory towns, and helped nurse his growing interest in the new industrial trade unionism. In London, Woods sought out the borough workingmen's clubs and the infant socialist movement. Above all the "new unionism" of unskilled London workers, still fresh from the great dockworkers' victory of 1889, inspired him. He thought the dockers' John Burns "a splendid fellow"; Burns's collaborator, Tom Mann, was "one of the finest figures in English life to-day." Woods's *English Social Movements*, summarizing these discoveries and enthusiasms in 1891, was one of the first descriptions of the "social democracy" stirring beneath the outward complaisance of late-Victorian England.[57]

Woods's lessons at the Fabian Society's hands were to form a type, an event that repetition made expected, even formulaic. Possessed of enormous skills of self-publicity, the Fabians formed something of a transatlantic network of their own. A striking number of them made the crossing themselves in the 1890s. Sidney and Beatrice Webb traversed the United States from New York to San Francisco in 1898, hunting up, among others, Albert Shaw, E. R. L. Gould, John Graham Brooks (by now "an old acquaintance"), the Bureau of Labor's Carroll Wright, Theodore Roosevelt, Woodrow Wilson (still at Princeton), and Jane Addams. In that same decade, Graham Wallas, Ramsay MacDonald, William Clarke, Enid Stacy, Percy Alden, Percival Chubb, and John W. Martin all made lecture trips to the United States.[58]

The Webbs, stunned by the "infantile" character of American politics, never repeated the event, but other Fabians forged lasting transatlantic connections. William Clarke became a close friend of Henry D. Lloyd and a regular contributor to Edwin Mead's *New England Magazine.* Graham Wallas kept in correspondence with a score of Americans and eventually became a member of the *New Republic*'s inner circle. A few prominent Fabians emigrated to the United States and, together with W. D. P. Bliss, organized a short-lived American Fabian League in New York in the mid-1890s. A handful of American progressives joined the main London society itself, among them Frances Willard of the Women's Christian Temperance Union, the feminist Charlotte Perkins Gilman, William English Walling, a key figure in the formation of the Women's Trade Union League and the early National Association for the Advancement of Colored People, and the settlement house movement's Charles Zueblin. But membership was never as important to the Fabians as simple attention. Working their American connections hard, they soon made an afternoon tea and conversation with the Webbs as fixed a goal for American progressives traveling in Europe as the cathedral towns were for the aesthetes.[59]

Yet another, gradually enlarging node of connection ran through the international conferences. Americans had cut only a minor figure in the French-dominated social economy conferences held in Paris in 1889 and 1900. Of the 1,639 members of the International Congress on Public Assistance and Private Charity in 1900, only 23 were Americans. At the International Congress for Labor Legislation, which met that same exposition summer, Willoughby of the Bureau of Labor and Harvard's John Cummings constituted the entire American presence. Over the next years, however, the American presence grew. Ten Americans were reported as attending the International Congress on Unemployment in Paris in 1910; 28 turned up in Vienna that same summer for the International Housing Congress. The International Social Insurance Congress would have held its meeting in New York in 1915 (the first international gathering of its sort in the United States) had the First World War not intervened.[60]

Journals of liberal and progressive opinion formed another channel of social-political knowledge and exchange. European letters had long been a familiar genre; it was a rare American with a yen for writing who could not find an outlet for his or her travel impressions in the local newspaper. Prominent political travelers like William Jennings Bryan set out with a journalistic contract in their pocket, returning home to bundle up their dispatches for book publication.[61] Increasingly the genre of travel impressions was joined by specially commissioned investigative pieces. Albert Shaw's *Review of Reviews*, an American offshoot of W. T. Stead's British journal of the same name, was an early, active conduit for news of European social politics. The aptly titled *World's Work* was another. So were the social gospel–linked *Outlook* (which recruited Mansfield House's Percy Alden and the "new Liberal" Robert Donald to write its British news), the *Chautauquan* (which was running a series entitled "Social Progress in Europe" by 1904–1905), and the social-work journal, the *Survey*.

The muckraking press had its cosmopolitan curiosities. *McClure's* sent Ray Stannard Baker to Germany to see what he could find in 1900. Its rival, *Everybody's Magazine*, sent Charles E. Russell around the world in 1905 in search of the most important examples of social advance. Under the title, "Soldiers of the Common Good," Russell filed articles on the municipalization work of the London County Council ("plain, bold, unqualified socialism," he reported approvingly), Swiss direct democracy, German state railroads, the Australian Labor Party, and most enthusiastically of all, the new New Zealand ("this practical Utopia of the South Seas"). Some journals made a specialty of interest in progressive currents abroad. Benjamin O. Flower's radical *Arena* was filled with reports from what he called our "foreign experiment stations abroad." The *New Republic* was launched with a sense of political kinship with the British *Nation* and shared with it a great number of common writers.[62]

Although curiosity and optimism fueled most of this work, some of the best of it flowed from defeat. Henry D. Lloyd and Frederic C. Howe, the two most able and prolific of the cosmopolitan reform journalists, turned to the task out of a sense of frustration and impasse at home. Lloyd had begun his career as a Chicago editorial writer of conventional economic opinions until the hard times of the 1870s jolted him out of accustomed tracks. He wrote an angry book on labor relations in the Illinois coal fields, made a national name for himself with an indictment of the monopoly practices of Standard Oil, and plunged deeply into Populist and labor politics. By 1896, however, shaken by the degeneration of Populism into mere free-silver politics, Lloyd had had enough. "I am weary of shoveling filth," he wrote a friend. "I think I have done my share . . . I want to begin laying a few blocks for a better social structure." He would be neither theorist nor muckraker but collector—a "salad" maker (as he was soon to put it) of "all the good ideas of Europe and Australasia." "The Utopias have been all written," he wrote in describing his new political faith two years later:

> What is especially wanted at this point of our development is a focusing into view of all the different things that are being done of, by, and for the

> people in different parts of the world and in different provinces of effort. If the American people could be roused to the point of naturalising all the reforms that have been successfully instituted . . . in town government, national socialism, and in the voluntary field of co-operation, we should have a very nearly ideal Utopia, right here and now.

It was in this mood that he set off to investigate constructive social politics abroad: the cooperative movement in Britain and on the Continent, social politics and compulsory arbitration in New Zealand, and direct democracy in Switzerland, leaving behind a book on each by the time of his death in 1903.[63]

In similar fashion, Frederic C. Howe, who succeeded Lloyd as the leading interpreter of progressive Europe to American audiences, came to his calling when mayor Tom L. Johnson's reform coalition in Cleveland, in which Howe had played a leading part, stumbled in 1909. Adrift, he too set out to discover more successful stories elsewhere. Like Lloyd, Howe turned the world into a kind of lending library of practical, tested reform notions. "I had dreams of social democracy," he remembered long afterward. "What we needed were facts. I would assemble the achievements of Germany, England, Switzerland, and Denmark, and present them as a demonstration of constructive democracy, of the kind of a society we might have if we but saw the state as an agency of service."[64]

By the decade before the First World War, these gathering streams of interest in European social politics were joined by especially commissioned investigations. The National Civic Federation, entering into the heated debate over American municipal streetcar politics in 1906, dispatched a commission of fifteen experts to observe municipal ownership at work in England and Scotland. During the American debate over industrial accident legislation between 1910 and 1913, the American Federation of Labor, the National Association of Manufacturers, and several state governments all organized rival commissions to sort through the experience of Britain and Germany for the lessons they might hold for the United States. Spurred on by the municipal reform crusade, a team of investigators from the Bureau of Municipal Research spent four to five months in Frankfurt gleaning the secrets of efficient municipal administration in 1912. The next summer at least four institutionally sponsored investigations in Europe were under way: George Price's study of European factory inspection methods for the New York garment trades' Joint Board of Sanitary Control; Raymond Fosdick's investigation of European police methods for the Rockefeller-financed Bureau of Social Hygiene; yet another investigation of

European social insurance, this one by Katharine Coman for the Progressive Party's information service; and the inquiries of the mammoth, 120-some-person moving caravan of the American Commission on Agricultural Cooperation and Rural Credit in Europe. Some of the American expeditions amounted to little more than publicly sponsored junkets. But Howe and his friend Lincoln Steffens thought the endeavor important enough to shepherd a party of eighty businessmen through Europe in 1911 on a visit arranged by the Boston Chamber of Commerce.[65]

By the eve of the First World War, socially concerned Americans could travel to Europe on one of several specially packaged tours. A City College professor of sociology offered a summer study tour for social workers in 1911, including visits to the London settlement houses, the English garden cities, Belgian cooperatives, and Paris child nurseries. The International Civic Bureau's European municipal tour of 1912 boasted an arrangements committee headed by Howe. The largest of the prewar sociological grand tours, the Institute of Educational Travel's "Civic and Social Tour" of 1914, planned an excursion of sixty-five days in Europe, guided by three economics professors, the secretary of the City Club of New York, and the executive secretary of the English Garden Cities and Town Planning Association. The itinerary included a labor arbitration court and the Imperial Insurance Office in Berlin; vocational schools in Munich; cooperatives in Copenhagen and Brussels; municipal housing in Amsterdam, Liverpool, and Ulm; the Paris and Frankfurt social museums; model workers' housing at the Krupp and Cadbury works; a Belgian reformatory colony for vagrants; an English Salvation Army colony of the unemployed; the children's hospital in Düsseldorf; public milk stations for mothers of infants in Paris, public baths in London, and public pawnshops in Brussels, all interspersed with conferences on city planning, housing, syndicalism, trade unionism, and social insurance. Tucked in amid this social earnestness were a handful of art galleries and a morning at Shakespeare's Stratford-upon-Avon.[66]

We Americans are "Losing Our Scorn for 'Abroad,'" the editors of the *Nation* wrote in summing up these trends in the summer of 1914. "Plainly, we are moving away from the attitude that no Old World idea need apply for employment here."[67]

Weave as it did the interests and experiences of American and European progressives together, bind them as it did in a common understanding of the forces at work on both sides of the Atlantic, this evolving web of connections could not erase two enduring peculiarities of the transatlantic progressive relationship. The first was the asymmetry of the exchange. The second was the mediating effects of travel.

That American progressives should have found themselves drawing so much more heavily on the experience and ideas of their European counterparts than Europeans did on theirs was no historical given. In the transatlantic radical world of the 1880s, the biggest splash of all had been made by the American radical economist Henry George. His influence on Australasian labor politics was formative; his five tours of Great Britain and Ireland in the 1880s took the islands by storm. The Fabian Society was jolted out of its initial gauzy spiritualism by George's lectures on land monopoly. In the mid-1880s, as George and his labor allies seemed to be closing in on electoral victory in New York City, even Marx's London circle was sure that the initiative had passed to the Americans. Invited by the German immigrant Socialist Labor Party in 1886 to spread the doctrines of Marxian orthodoxy in the United States, Marx's son-in-law, Edward Aveling, came back instead to lecture London audiences on George's example of a big-tent labor party. When Sidney Webb wrote in 1889 that "the present English popular Socialist movement may be said to date entirely from the circulation here of *Progress and Poverty*," it was only a modest exaggeration.[68]

Radical and progressive Europeans continued to make American pilgrimages in the decades to come and to carry social political ideas and innovations back home from the United States. Through the 1920s, the Fabian Society's *What to Read?* tracts were stocked with American as well as British titles.[69] American progressive experiments in probation and juvenile court justice, public parks and playgrounds, bureaus of labor statistics, women's suffrage, and, above all, public primary education had a lasting impact on European progressives. Politically, the promise of American-style democracy could still inspire, as the chanting crowds that mobbed Woodrow Wilson's arrival in Europe in late 1918 so dramatically showed.

Lay this list alongside the list of initiatives moving in the other direction, however, and there is no missing the stark trade imbalance on the American side. From settlement houses to zoning ordinances, labor legislation to farm cooperatives, city-owned transit systems to social insurance, the list of social-political experiments drawn westward from the European nations to the United States outstrips by severalfold the corresponding movement in the opposite direction. The transatlantic progressive connection was no one-way street, but in the period from 1870 to 1940 nothing defined it for American participants more than its massive asymmetry.

One of the painful signs of this imbalance was a marked contraction of

European progressive interest in American politics. Where American attention to British progressive politics was "coherent and continuous," Kenneth Morgan writes of this period, the influences in the other direction were "intermittent and partial at best."[70] The Marxian disillusionment with American politics is well known. The Webbs' came early. Both were driven hard by theory.

Alfred Zimmern's seven-month pilgrimage in search of progressive America in 1911 and 1912 was more telling and more poignant. Fresh from studying civic republicanism in ancient Athens, Zimmern arrived in the United States fired with ideals of civic political culture, both ancient and modern. He worked hard to locate the centers of political vitality in the New World. In New York he looked in at the United Charities Building, hunted up the city's leading socialists, lunched with Theodore Roosevelt, and attended a mass meeting of protest and remembrance for the 146 garment workers who, locked in the Triangle Shirtwaist Company's loft, had been killed in a factory fire. He observed an election and poked his head into a Lower East Side public school where immigrant children saluting the flag "really made me feel that America was a land of freedom." "The East Side is in a way a terrible slum, but it is different from an English slum because the people there are vigorous, hopeful, and happy," he wrote. After a swing through the South, where he tried to hunt up W. E. B. Du Bois, he made his way to Madison, Wisconsin. "The State has been practically governed by the University," he wrote eagerly. "Broadly speaking . . . the economics students here are lawmakers . . . and every question is threshed out in class before it is threshed out by the legislature." With John Commons at the university ("a sort of American Sidney Webb," Zimmern thought him) and Charles McCarthy at the Legislative Reference Library in the statehouse, a true science of politics seemed to have been put into effect.[71]

"Lots of new ideas," Zimmern wrote his sister, "which may be applied at home." But from there on, progressive America unraveled for him. The more he talked with Americans, the thinner his confidence wore. The raw, unmitigated capitalism of Chicago unnerved him. The U.S. Steel Corporation's model city, Gary, Indiana, seemed to him a monstrous "fortress." Six months after he began, he wrote home: "I have long ago given up looking at America as the land of progress. The only question left in my mind is how many years it's behind England. I think it's somewhere in the eighties and not going our pace at that."[72]

By the time Zimmern picked it up, the metaphor of American behindhandedness was already a hardened trope among European progressives.

Sometimes it was used as a general rhetoric of dismissal, as when E. R. Pease of the Fabian Society concluded, on reading John Graham Brooks's latest account of labor relations in the United States, that "in the things that pertain to man as a social and intellectual being, America is decades, if not centuries, behind us." Sometimes it was employed more precisely. Thus in labor legislation the British Labourite J. R. Clynes put the United States twenty years behind Britain in 1909; in trade union development, fifteen years. Either way, it was hard for Americans to miss the sense abroad that politically and socially the United States exhibited a case of arrested national development.[73]

The cumulative weight of judgments like these could not but reinforce the Americans' sense of outsiderness, their place as junior partners in the Atlantic exchange. To that sense of marginality, the second enduring factor of the Atlantic progressive exchange added its weight. That was the physical distance of the American participants from the new social-political network's centers. The Americans had been latecomers at the Paris exposition in 1900, scrambling for place and information. It was inherent in the geography of their relationship that the Americans were repeatedly to encounter European social politics, letters of introduction in hand, as if on a brief surveying expedition into a distant land.

Coming from so far, the Americans rarely saw things in the building stage. The word "finished" runs through their accounts like a thread. They came in search of practical accomplishments, from a polity that often seemed to them full of rag ends and unfinished business. The emphasis on the built rather than the process of building often obscured the politics of European social policy making. Few of the American progressives in Germany had a fully adequate sense of the terrific political tensions within Wilhelmine Germany—or, later, within Weimar politics. They made an idol of John Burns long after Burns had diminished to an old, played-out volcano. The experience of coming to social-political Europe as foragers for tested, usable devices led them to emphasize the advantages of the devices they were keen to bring back, rather than the sorts of coalitions responsible for putting them in place. It accentuated their tendency to think of politics in terms of invention and rational design—a conception that set them up, more than once, for cruel disappointment.

The fact that they came from so far, and were continually surprised at what they found, likewise encouraged in the American social travelers' minds the sense of behindhandedness that was already so striking a feature of European progressive assessments of the United States. Late-nineteenth-century American travelers in Europe, as we have seen, had tended toward metaphors not of lag but of dichotomy. American students in late-nineteenth-century Germany sketched the German nation as Janus-faced: both modern and reactionary. Henry Lloyd never quite settled the balance between humility and hubris. "We have much to learn from Europe," he wrote Frank Parsons in a patriotic moment, "but we are going to reciprocate by teaching them more reform in some coming quarter of an hour than they ever guessed in all their history."[74]

In seizing the metaphor of lag, however, a certain number of Americans began to find, at last, a route past the polar types and exaggerations that had dominated the language of Atlantic contrast. By the decade before the First World War, the new terms had settled deep in the rhetoric and self-consciousness of many American progressives. "Shall we always . . . 'stand by the roadside and see the procession go by?'" Wisconsin's Charles McCarthy wrote after his own first pilgrimage to progressive Europe. "Shall we always hear the returning travelers' tales of the improvements throughout the world with a provincial and smug spirit and be foolish enough to believe that we can learn nothing, while right in our midst are problems which have confronted every nation at some time in its history?" The relationship of New and Old Worlds metamorphosed into a long-distance race down the ways of progress. The United States was not worlds apart in time or space from the leading nations of Europe. A laggard, "more and more a camp follower among the great peoples of the earth" (as a writer in *Arena* put it), it was simply behind.[75]

Given the density of connections and influences joining social politics throughout the North Atlantic economy, given the multiple faces of the "social question" and the avenues of approach to it, the notion that the world's polities might be imagined as a long line of runners, strung out, one behind another, in a footrace toward progress, was every bit as strained and artificial as the rival metaphors it supplanted. It was inherent in the rapidity with which social-political devices and ambitions had begun to circulate that the particular mix of ingredients was everywhere unstable. Rivals diverged down separate lines of endeavor and leapfrogged past each other.

But the image of a race helped point progress in a clear direction and gave American progressives an added sense of urgency. "The greatest nation on earth slowly crawls into the rear of the humanitarian procession," Charles Henderson charged in a comparison of American and European methods in child welfare. Frederic Howe's Ohio ally Brand Whitlock echoed the formula: while the "new" Old World was learning democracy, "the old new world was and is paltering and hesitating over municipal problems which Europe solved a generation ago." A delegate to the International Association for Labor Legislation meeting in Zurich in 1912 admitted that it had been "a little trying to the nerves of an American to see that the United States is put in a category with rather backward countries." But the sense of being emissaries from a backward land clarified the Americans' task; theirs was to catch up with the "progressive" nations of the world, to borrow, adapt, and bend the work of others to the circumstances of the United States.[76]

The metaphor of laggards and leaders also helped to shield American progressives from the charges of political utopianism their antagonists were poised to hurl at them. It made their idealism hard-headed and practical. "Many persons think that the progressive movement proposes to usher in the millennium by legislation," Benjamin De Witt wrote in 1915. "Nothing could be farther from the minds of the men and women who call themselves progressive. What they propose to do is to bring the United States abreast of Germany and other European countries in the matter of remedial legislation." To catch up to the "civilized" nations of the world was a running progressive theme. Seconding Theodore Roosevelt's nomination at the Progressive Party convention of 1912, Jane Addams made the point official: "The new party has become the American exponent of a world-wide movement toward juster social conditions, a movement which the United States, lagging behind other great nations, has been unaccountably slow to embody in political action." If the rhetoric left its users vulnerable to the accusation that their schemes were un-American, unsuited to the special political genius of the United States, it had its countervailing advantages. Cosmopolitan American progressives took the gulf between Old World and New World political cultures and labored to transform it into a lag in time, a gap to be overcome.[77]

Strained as these refigurings of the Atlantic relationship were, they were not wholly wrong. They were not wrong in their depiction of American society as raw with antagonisms, desperately in need of new agencies of control and coherence. Nor were they wrong in their insistence on the common economic and social forces beneath the societies the world markets were making, or the political possibilities of piggybacking on other nations' social-political experiences. Even the theme of lag, though in their frustration American progressives sometimes exaggerated it, held a grain of truth. Pioneering in political democracy, the Americans had let the economics of marketplace capitalism run their course, and now they found the attention of their one-time European admirers elsewhere—on the social tasks of democracy.

"We are no longer the sole guardians of the Ark of the Covenant," Walter Weyl opened his *The New Democracy* in 1912. "Europe does not learn at our feet the facile lessons of democracy . . . Foreign observers describe our institutions with a galling lack of enthusiasm." He added: "Today the tables are turned. America no longer teaches democracy to an expectant world, but herself goes to school to Europe and Australia . . . Our students of political and industrial democracy repair to the antipodes, to England, Belgium, France, to semi-feudal Germany . . . Why has the tortoise Europe outdistanced the hare?"[78]

That sentiment—that momentary emancipation from the "geocentricity" around them—was one of the American progressives' key achievements. Nations that lag are nations that can connect. Underneath the nationalism of the age, the suspicion that the world might have passed the Americans by was, in its own right, a heroic accomplishment. It shaped American politics through the New Deal in far more ways than historians have yet fathomed. Against the inward-turning counterforces, these nagging doubts about the self-sufficiency of American politics could hardly be expected to win an easy victory. Even in the realm of the imagination, there were no clear-cut triumphs. But over the oceanic distance between New World and Old, American progressives began slowly to discern—where kings and cathedrals had once dominated the imaginative landscape—models and allies, reservoirs of potentially usable experience, the unexpected outlines of a progressive Europe.

3

Twilight of Laissez-Faire

Natural Acts and Social Desires

The first line of extended American contact with European social politics was distinctly an affair of the mind. It ran not through parties or parliaments, through investigative commissions or Fabian Society contacts, but through the seminars and lecture halls of late-nineteenth-century Germany. Its characteristic mark was a language of economic values: a quarrel with the ethical core of the new world of iron that its partisans called a quarrel with laissez-faire.

Like so many later threads of the Atlantic progressive connection, the German university connection began modestly, even haphazardly. Nonetheless, between the mid-1870s, when the first Americans began to find their way to Germany for postgraduate education in economics, and the student migration's peak in the late 1890s, a generation of young progressive intellectuals found themselves endeavoring to work out their political and economic commitments in a foreign tongue, in the shadow of an immensely broad and active state, and in a political culture steeped in quarrel over the self-acting, self-regulating market. Coming home to build and staff many of the key agencies of American progressive reform, they left the marks of their German encounter across a broad spectrum of social-political endeavor.

The first institutional link to be built to the new social politics in

Europe, the German university connection was, by the same token, the first to be disavowed. Reentering a cauldron of academic and political controversy in the United States, the young, German-trained American progressive intellectuals of the 1870s and 1880s slowly learned the advantages of selective memory. Ducking the smears of un-Americanism hurled their way, they came to insist that their social politics was a pure, native product. Their ideas came out of the prairies of Illinois and "the free air of the Mississippi Valley," Richard T. Ely wrote for his generation—though, in his case, the point was particularly disingenuous; they sprang from no foreign source but directly from the traditions and economic realities of America itself.[1] Whatever impulse there might have been for deeper reflection was snuffed out by revulsion at Germany's precipitation of war in 1914. Their volumes of closely penned student lecture notes—Schmoller on *Nationalökonomie*, Treitschke on politics, Wagner on *Finanzwissenschaft*, Gneist on Prussian constitutional and administrative law—were left to sink slowly into archival dust.[2]

But the German university connection had, in truth, lasting historical consequences—not only for the sleepy American colleges that it transformed but also for transatlantic social politics itself. It knocked the provincial blinkers off a cadre of young Americans and gave them a lasting sense of participation in an international movement of intellectual and political reform. It fired them with policy-making ambitions and new, borrowed models of public influence. Above all, the German university connection formed the context in which a generation of young progressive intellectuals were to work their way past the most formidable intellectual obstacle to social politics throughout the North Atlantic economy: the structure of ideas that proclaimed the folly—still more, the unnaturalness—of the very effort.

"Laissez-faire" was the critics' name for that system of ideas. "English economics" was the German phrase for it, with a nod to how profoundly its prestige depended on Britain's rise to world economic domination in the middle years of the nineteenth century. It did not mean, as it was often later said, a state that served merely as an idle night watchman. Even at the high tide of the laissez-faire economists' influence in 1850s and 1860s, the British state had its hand in an extensive array of matters, not only military and imperial but social and economic as well. Britain's legal limitations on the work of women and children, its mine and factory inspectorates, its sanitary regulations, and its provisions for assistance to the poor were, for all their glaring inadequacies, more extensively developed at the middle of the nineteenth century than anywhere else in the North Atlantic economy. The maxim at the heart of classical economic liberalism—that the sphere of individual liberty ran as far as, but no farther than, the point at which it collided with someone else's liberty—was, in practice, capable of sustaining a state watchman of considerable vigor.[3]

But if historians bent on finding an era of perfect governmental quiescence have failed to locate it, the age of laissez-faire was no mere retrospective construction of its critics. Whatever else laissez-faire meant, it meant devolving primary responsibility for economic well-being from politics to markets, from considerations of state to myriad private desires. This was the kernel of Adam Smith's argument that national wealth was more surely promoted by private exchanges than by the inherently bungled operations of the mercantilist state. This was why repeal of British protective duties on grain in 1846, pitched as a battle between "free" and artificially administered trade, loomed so large in the symbolic history of laissez-faire. The "classical" economists did a great deal more than simply shift the mantle of prestige from public authority to private competition, from the state to the self-interested labors of traders, manufacturers, and entrepreneurs. But there can be no doubt that classical economics lent a special privilege to the activities, and the sphere of action, of those who organized the competitive markets in goods and labor.

The work of private ambition and desire was not simply more efficient than the efforts of the state; more fundamental still was the insistence that actions of private trade and bargaining were more "natural." Like the devolution of economic responsibilities from state to trader and entrepreneur, the point was far-reaching. It facilitated a shift in the rhetoric of economics from the language of policy to the language of scientific law. Still more, it elevated the haggling, fractious competition of economic action into a higher abstraction, the market, stripped it of its relationship to other social activities, and reimagined it as a special realm of natural, autonomous, and automatically self-regulating processes. Within the sphere of production and trade, forces of equilibrium were continually at work; it was only from "outside" that the self-acting forces of individual desire were at risk of derangement.

The naturalness of private, self-interested economic action was a conviction open to endless variation. One heard it in Adam Smith's case for a "system of natural liberty." One heard it in William Pitt's concern in 1795 that state action could only "impede" and "derange" the processes by which prices, wages, and trade "always find their own level." Ninety years later, when John Graham Brooks pasted into his scrapbook a jibe at his social economy lectures, that it was "Nature," not the sentimental desires of laborers or reformers, that "has got to be consulted first" in economic questions, the point had lost none of its force.[4]

None of the propagandists of laissez-faire took the nature-artifice distinction to exclude every form of state or social regulation. John Stuart Mill's assertion that he did "not know of any single practical rule [of political economy] that must be applicable in all cases" could equally well have been made by Smith himself. The force of classical economics was more subtle than its dogmas—those "simple tales, by aid of which an intelligent governess might make clear to the children nestling around her where lies economic truth," as Alfred Marshall would deride them. It drew up not so much a rule as a circle of special privilege around the behaviors of the market. Within was the realm of nature and "freedom of the trade"; outside lay politics and society. External forces might regulate, intervene, or interfere, sometimes beneficially, more often simply to impede the production of wealth. Either way, within the intellectual system of laissez-faire, the action came as an intrusion into the special sphere of economic processes. Laissez-faire was not about absolutes but about the burden of proof, and it stacked that burden massively against state economic action. Even John Stuart Mill, for all his flexibility of mind, never abandoned the essential point: "*Laisser-faire*, in short, should be the general practice: every departure from it, unless required by some great good, is a certain evil."[5]

Had the principle of the self-acting economy rested on its logic alone, it would have been formidable enough. It was buttressed, however, by an ethos of the freely acting self, whose force ran deep in the moral culture of the nineteenth-century bourgeoisie. If the freely chosen act was the moral act, then the realm of "free" trade and exchange held more than economic utility; it was the realm of moral growth. The point moralized the hard, sometimes fatalistic lessons of classical economics and wrapped its suspicion of the state in an ethical embrace. It set self-help and self-reliance on one side of the moral scale; the smothering "tutelage" and infantilizing "leading strings" of the "intervening" state on the other. Economic "paternalism" did not merely bungle its practical tasks; it inhibited the moral growth of those whose hands it held. Collective political action and individual moral action tended toward a zero-sum pair. The worth of private market actions was elevated from economic law to social ethos.

All this that the term "laissez-faire" bundled together—a wide-ranging suspicion of the clumsiness of state action, a subtle denaturalization of economic actors other than the private self, and an intellectual reconstitution of the jostling, cry-filled, early-modern marketplace from an arena of suspicion to an arena of self-equilibrating, moral freedom—constituted an intellectual system of no mean force and consequence. Buoyed by the miracle of British economic growth, it spread as far as British goods and prestige would carry it.

As a cultural outpost of Britain, the United States received the new economic lessons early and forcefully. Across the mid-nineteenth-century Atlantic, from cultural metropolis to cultural province, packaged in textbook, didactic story, sermon, syllogism, and political maxim, whole libraries of simplified summations of British economic science moved. No more than their British counterparts did nineteenth-century Americans swallow whole the practical corollaries of laissez-faire. With the great British revolution in trade policy, nineteenth-century American Congresses refused to fall into step. From 1816 onward the protective tariff was a fixture of American trade policy and a point of firm (though fiercely contested) conviction for the manufacturers whose markets it sheltered. In the first half of the century, when investment capital in the United States was scarce, state funds and credit guarantees underwrote a great deal of early investment in canals and railroads. Nineteenth-century American economics was an economics of underdevelopment. There was rarely a moment when entrepreneurs did not look, with an eager eye, on the state as a promotional partner.[6]

Popular understandings of political economy were still more complicated. Even at the height of the classical economists' transatlantic prestige, the economic presence of the state in American state and local statute books, as William Novak has recently reemphasized, never disappeared. The mid-nineteenth-century law record is filled with nuisance laws, trade licensing statutes, fire regulations, measures to protect against commercial fraud and extortion, measures to regulate noxious trades, and measures to promote public morals. Some of this economic legislation was old, remnants of the broad economic and licensing powers of the well-governed seventeenth- and eighteenth-century state before the classical economists' dismantling project had gotten under way. Other parts were new, like the slowly thickening corpus of state and municipal public health legislation. Many of these measures carried tangible costs for property owners; others functioned primarily as symbolic legislation, fitfully enforced, if indeed they were written so as to be effectively enforced at all. Like legislation everywhere in the North Atlantic economy, American legislation swung fitfully back and forth between general welfare considerations and the new, self-limiting ideology of the "naturally" working market. The clearest test of the power of the laissez-faire ethos lay not in the statute-book exceptions but in the realm of conviction—in the rendering of public economic action as an "intervention" in the realm of "natural" economic law and economic "freedom."[7]

To these convictions, the peculiar organization of nineteenth-century American intellectual life lent important reinforcement. Nowhere else in the North Atlantic economy did the denominational college hold so large a sway, with its governing boards of clergymen and business donors, its pedagogical reliance on quizzes, recitations, and the laborious cramming of textbook material, and its philosophical commitment to the comprehensive logic of knowledge, spiraling up to the college president's own capstone course in moral philosophy.

One consequence was a structural commitment to the simplified and the out of date. At Harvard and Columbia, where Edmund James and Richard Ely learned economics in the mid-1870s, the subject was still taught from Millicent Fawcett's *Political Economy for Beginners*, intended (as she herself wrote) for "boys' and girls' schools." Within the American economics professoriate of the early 1870s, one could find clergymen, editors, moral philosophers, and men of affairs, but, except for Yale's Francis A. Walker, hardly one whose scholarly contribution had gone significantly beyond textbook repackaging of British economic authority. Beyond the colleges, where debate was wider, a journalist-entrepreneur like Henry C. Carey could try to work tariff protectionism into a more comprehensive social economics. But the collegiate system gave Carey no students and no institutional base.[8]

It was for all these reasons that, even in a nation that set aside free trade as an English luxury, that lavished subsidies on railroads and war veterans, that carved out scores of crucial exceptions from the rule of laissez-faire, the creed itself took hold in the middle years of the nineteenth century and flourished. Albert Shaw, who knew something of practical as well as university economics in the 1880s, was certain that "the so-called English political economy [had] no such doctrinaire devotees in the mother country as in America" and no such syllogism-wracked literature. Francis Walker's judgment is the most memorable: "While *Laissez-Faire* was asserted, in great breadth, in England," none of the English economists held it "with such strictness as was given to it in the United States. Here it was not made the test of economic orthodoxy, merely. It was used to decide whether a man were an economist at all."[9]

The same economic doctrines moved into continental Europe in the same era. In France, their embrace was swift and enthusiastic; conservatives, social Catholics, and a small cluster of maverick "social economists" harbored their doubts, but in the intellectual academy and the mainstream reviews, the "optimistic" school, as Charles Gide was to call it, swept economic thinking before it.[10] In Germany, where resistance was considerably stiffer, Adam Smith's ideas could be heard in the universities as early as the 1790s. The great liberalizing reforms of the early-nineteenth-century Prussian state bureaucracy—dismantlement of the guilds' monopolies on trade and dissolution of the peasants' ties to the land—drew authority from the British example. But it was in the years between 1848 and 1866, in what James Sheehan calls "the great age of free trade and freedom of enterprise" in Germany, that the precepts of British political economy penetrated most deeply—into the liberal parties, the universities, and elements of the state bureaucracy. All this went hand in hand with an intense interest in the English institutions of voluntary self-help and bourgeois habit formation: friendly societies, workingmen's associations, and cooperative enterprises. Even the young Gustav Schmoller, who was to spearhead the attack on English economics in the 1870s, was still certain of the imported orthodoxies in 1864. "Self-help and self-responsibility," he professed in his first published contribution to the "labor question," "are the only cures for our time."[11]

But precisely because laissez-faire came to the German states over more sharply contrasting policy traditions than elsewhere in Europe or North America, the reaction against it was strongest and swiftest there. As early as 1840, Friedrich List had tried to demonstrate that British-style free trade could only widen the gap between advanced nations and developing nations like Germany, or the United States, where List had spent eight years in exile. Elaborated on over the next generation, List's attempt to unmask the economic interests veiled behind the English economists' doctrine of natural law formed a rallying point for German opposition. Laissez-faire was no natural, universal science, it was objected. It was the ideology of British export manufacturers: "Manchester economics," a cotton spinners' creed.

The revolt of the younger German economists was tangled from the beginning in a yearning for a distinctive German course through the upheavals of industrial capitalism. By 1872, *Manchestertum*'s critics had formed a rival economic organization of their own, the Verein für Sozialpolitik, stocked with younger economics professors and pledged to combat the "tyranny" of the English economic doctrines. "We are convinced that the unchecked reign of partially antagonistic and unequal individual interests cannot guarantee the common welfare," the Verein's founding call read. State intervention was not an emergency makeshift, not a necessary evil, but "fulfillment of one of the highest tasks of our time and nation."[12]

The insurgent economists did not carry everything before them. They had barely been organized before they were smeared with a polemical nickname: *Kathedersozialisten*, "professorial socialists." By 1874, the rising star among Prussian historians, Heinrich von Treitschke, had added his peculiarly strident voice to the attack, charging *Manchestertum*'s critics with piping the tune for the revolutionary socialism of the masses. In Berlin the next year, young Henry Farnam's eye was caught by a bookstore window display that laid out Treitschke's attack, "Socialism and Its Patrons," side by side with Schmoller's response. From the moment the first American economics students set foot in Germany in the mid-1870s, even before the official break with the era of free trade in 1878 to 1881—when Bismarck turned to protectionism, outlawed the socialists, cleared the British-leaning officials out of the bureaucracy, and set his course toward the state social insurance legislation of the 1880s—economic discussion in Germany was roiled as no other in Europe in furious debate, with laissez-faire at its polemical center.[13]

The 1870s were, indeed, a decade of doubts and strain among economists throughout the North Atlantic economy. In France in the late 1870s, the institutionalization of economics as a regular part of university law faculties unexpectedly brought onto the scene a corps of young, legally trained economists, far less indebted than their journalist predecessors to the laissez-faire orthodoxies. Most of the French-language publicists of the new school, with their ear cocked toward Germany, were institutionally still on the margins. Émile de Laveleye taught at Liège in the 1870s and Gide at provincial Montpellier, but even the Paris law faculty included a prominent and controversial economic *interventioniste* by the decade's end.[14]

In Britain, a quieter retreat from the certainties of classical economics had begun still earlier. Without the institutional reconfiguration that took place in 1870s France or the sense of social crisis so vivid in 1870s Germany, British economic revisionism had little of the polemical ferocity of its continental cousins. Still, no acute reader of the intellectual signs of the times, from J. E. Cairnes's and Stanley Jevons's first published dissents of the early 1870s through Arnold Toynbee's ethically charged lectures on the industrial revolution in 1881–82, could miss the fact that classical economics was awash in considerable doubt in its native land. The evolving editions of

John Stuart Mill's *Principles of Political Economy*, with their accumulating qualifications, told the same story.[15]

In this context of international disenchantment, the rigidities of textbook economics in the United States could hardly have been long sustained. There, too, the economic reverses and violent labor disputes of the 1870s pressed hard on the certainties of classical economics. Through the *Nation*'s intermittent jibes at the *Kathedersozialisten*, through the pages of the British reviews, or the revisionism of their own Francis Walker, American economics students in the 1870s could not but sense reverberations of the intellectual turmoil across the Atlantic.[16] The strains of industrial capitalism's headlong development in America were not to be denied. In the twilight of laissez-faire, they could not have remained at high noon.

As it was, however, the transition in economic ideas ran through channels as international as late-nineteenth-century economic life itself. First made in the outwash of British political economy, nineteenth-century American economics was remade via a sharp German detour. From a culture saturated with simplified redactions of the laissez-faire creed, a generation of American students found themselves unexpectedly shunted into the nation where, above all others in Europe, classical economics lay most heavily under siege. From a polity distinctly weak in state administrative structures and controls, they found themselves spectators of the most wide-reaching state culture in Europe. In its contrasts and initial disorientations, in the sensation it provoked of stepping suddenly out of the political-intellectual backwaters into a modern city of the mind, the experience set the mold for the social-political travelers who would follow. To be transported suddenly out of the "neat, clean syllogisms" of American textbook economics into a sea of controversies was at once exhilarating and troubling.[17] The encounter could not but set off a messy eruption of heterodox ideas, neither German nor native, but born out of the meeting of the two.

No one consciously designed the German university connection in economics or, still less, anticipated its importance. Several of those who were to exert the widest influence on American economics landed in Germany with other subjects altogether on their mind. Richard T. Ely intended to follow a course of philosophical study when he arrived in Halle in 1877. Only on discovering that his chosen philosopher had retired was he steered by another young American in Halle, Simon Patten, into Johannes Conrad's economics seminar. Patten, for that matter, had also arrived with philosophical ambitions before being pulled into Conrad's circle by yet another young American in Halle, Edmund J. James.[18]

Even at the height of the connection, the German universities never monopolized American study abroad. In the 1890s Charles Beard made his way to Oxford to be swept up in that university's distinctive brand of Christian social economics. Others sought out, after 1895, the new, Fabian-founded London School of Economics; Edith Abbott, arriving just in time to hear the Webbs begin their campaign to "break up" the English poor law, was among them. Still others found their way to the Sorbonne or the École libre des sciences politiques in Paris.[19] But the German universities possessed powerful structural attractions. Unlike the warren of closed, gentry-dominated, and expensive colleges that made up Oxford and Cambridge, the German universities were open, public institutions. Unlike the French universities, absorbed in the professional production of lawyers, physicians, and *lycée* instructors, the intellectual reach of the German universities was as broad as nineteenth-century scholarship itself. So cheap were their fees that in 1889 it was estimated that the cost of a year in Germany, transatlantic travel included, was fully a third less than a year's study at Cornell, Harvard, or Johns Hopkins. In philosophy, history, philology, and theology the international fame of German scholarship had attracted American students since the early years of the century. Into these preexisting tracks and advantages the first American economics students fell in the 1870s.[20]

Once established, the alumni of the German connection worked hard to sustain the system they knew. From the University of Pennsylvania's Wharton School of Finance and Economy, Edmund J. James sent a stream of graduate students back to Conrad's seminar in Halle where, by the early 1890s, ten to fifteen Americans were regularly to be found. James helped fill the Wharton School faculty with German-trained economists: Simon Patten, Roland P. Falkner, Samuel M. Lindsay, Leo S. Rowe, Henry R. Seager, Emory R. Johnson, and Joseph F. Johnson. Columbia was another center of German-trained economists, and it, too, regularly sent graduate students to Germany to cap their economics studies.[21]

American students in late-nineteenth-century Germany quickly constructed subcultures of their own for the exchange of aid and advice. Sent to Halle by James and Patten in 1891, Samuel McCune Lindsay, timid and uncertain about his plans, found lodging with Emory Johnson, who had just arrived from Ely's seminar at Johns Hopkins. Another Johns Hopkins student, Henry Seager, nursed Lindsay through his first illness and urged him on toward the University of Vienna. When Lindsay undertook an extended study tour through Italy he traveled with Leo Rowe, a Wharton student like himself. In Berlin where, sooner or later, the vast majority ended up, Mary Kingsbury in 1895 and 1896 found herself in the middle of a circle of

American students that included Walter Weyl (who would be one of the cofounders of the *New Republic*), Emily Greene Balch (later a professor of economics at Wellesley and a prominent figure in the international women's networks), Robert A. Woods (now of the South End Settlement in Boston), and Franklin H. Dixon (soon to become a Dartmouth professor and expert on railway legislation).[22]

Women like Balch and Kingsbury were rare in the German university connection. Not until 1890 were women admitted, even as auditors, into the Prussian universities. Before then the handful of American women who sought out a German postgraduate education struggled to make special arrangements in the more open universities of southern Germany or, like Florence Kelley or M. Carey Thomas, gave up Germany for Zurich, where a woman could earn a degree. Years after the fact Alice Hamilton still remembered the ordeal her sister underwent at the University of Munich in the mid-1890s. Unable to agree on how properly to segregate her, the faculty finally landed on the expedient of seating her at the lecturer's right hand, where she faced, with intense, daily embarrassment, a sea of male German faces. Alice Hamilton herself remembered being run into the gutters by male German students, marching, arms linked, down the sidewalk. The main international contacts for progressive women were to run through channels farther from Germany: the Toynbee Hall connection, the international women's suffrage movement, or the broad network of international women's conferences.[23]

If the German university connection was a largely male experience, for those young men interested in social questions in the late nineteenth century, Germany was an intellectual mecca and a key station on an increasingly well-traveled career path. By the end of the 1890s the numbers of Americans in German economics courses had begun to diminish as the cost of a German education rose against the cost of study at the new American graduate schools, as the German universities grew more crowded and more nationalistic, and as the German revolt in economics grew less novel. But not before a major transfer of ambitions and ideas had been accomplished. Of the initial 6 officers of the American Economic Association in 1885, 5 had studied in Germany; of its first 26 presidents, at least 20 had done so. In 1906, when Yale's Henry Farnam polled what he took to be the 116 leading economists and sociologists in the United States and Canada, 59 had spent a student year or more in Germany.[24]

The backgrounds of the Americans were predictable—northern-state Protestants were the modal type, many of them sliding into academic careers after false starts toward the ministry—but not so uniform as to preclude a wide range of reactions to their years of study. Germany itself, shifting under the American students' feet, was hardly the same from the beginning of the student migration to the end. But despite the diversity and change, certain patterns endured.

The most personal reaction was a sense of release: "a certain joyous expansion," as Ely remembered it. The phrase reappears over and again in the surviving memoirs—an unexpected note for a society historians have characterized as among the stiffest in late-nineteenth-century Europe. The rigidities of German *Bürgertum* were not lost on the Americans. The rituals of university enrollment seemed a ridiculous exercise in bureaucratic formality. To M. Carey Thomas, Germany was a strange culture of too little soap, exaggerated manners, and ludicrous emperor worship. But despite the soldiers, the bureaucrats, the boorish maleness of the students, and the *Verbotens*, Germany was liberating nonetheless.[25]

In part the sense of liberation came—as it would to progressive travelers long afterward—from leaving the familiar behind. W. E. B. Du Bois, who fell in love across the racial bar, felt particularly profoundly the release from "those iron bands that bound me at home." Others felt the fetters of culture slip in different ways. The letters Samuel McCune Lindsay and his parents exchanged boil over with controversy over the beer hall question, Lindsay's increasing readiness to spend money on concert and theater tickets, and, above all, his announcement that his family's teetotalism was not worth the price of social isolation. Mother, father, and sister were dispatched across the Atlantic to chaperon him through the moral temptations of Europe. He, in turn, struggled to convert them to a less "narrow" form of family life, less constrained by the dogmas of the *Sunday School Times*.[26]

If escape from piety and prejudice figured prominently in incidents like these, there was a deeper, more political aspect to the Americans' sense of release: a quality they began to call "sociability." Like parched souls, American students in late-nineteenth-century Germany sought out the public leisure of the German bourgeoisie: the concert halls and outdoor musicals, the parks, the strange and alluring atmosphere of the open-air beer gardens. "They are a social animal truly and far more so than the Americans," Lincoln Steffens wrote. Others, pasting their scrapbooks full of concert tickets, tacitly echoed the conclusion. It was not simply the Germans' capacity for enjoyment but the publicness and sociality of their leisure, in comparison with the more private patterns the Americans knew, that astonished.[27]

Indeed, the "social idea" struck the American students at every turn. Like their surprise at a culture of public enjoyment, this, too, would become a recurrent trope among American progressive travelers in Europe. In Germany the thread of the social seemed to ascend unbroken from the open-air concerts through the university lecture halls up to the very state itself. Even philosophy concentrators wrote with a sense of nervous, excited discovery about a wholly new class of social problems that pressed on their consciousness in Germany. Germany taught Americans "a more serious conception of the interlacing interests of Society," Garrett Droppers remembered long afterward.[28]

Some of this sociological instruction was the work of the Social Democrats. None of the late-nineteenth-century American students had seen a broad-based working-class socialist movement before; in one way or another, many them endeavored to take its measure. Henry C. Adams, who reached Berlin in the fall of 1878, just as debate over an official ban on socialist political activity was cresting, read as much of the socialists' literature as he could acquire, locking the pamphlets in his trunk lest the maidservant report his purchases to the police. Mary Kingsbury not only read Kant and frequented the opera but also sought out Liebknecht's oratory; at the end of her stay she and Emily Balch set off for London to observe the International Socialist Trade Union Congress and hear Jean Jaurès, Sidney and Beatrice Webb, and Keir Hardie speak. Where the line against Social Democratic Party adherents was rigidly enforced in university appointments, however, the German professors were perforce not Social Democrats, and neither were their American students. With the relaxation of the antisocialist laws, Johannes Conrad sent Samuel Lindsay to observe a Social Democratic Party convention, but he took care to assure himself that Lindsay not been intellectually infected. Du Bois moved around the edges of the German socialist movement, but it was the Verein für Sozialpolitik he joined, not the Social Democratic Party. Only Florence Kelley, who found herself in a circle of émigré Russian and German radicals in Zurich, actually threw in her lot with working-class socialism.[29]

Far more important to American students than the Social Democrats were the social ambitions of the late-nineteenth-century German state. "German logic, which never stops until the very last consequences are drawn," Du Bois concluded in the 1890s, "has . . . gone from political to social unity—from the idea of the State as the great military guardian of the physical boundaries, to the idea of the State as the guardian and leader of the social and industrial interests of the people." It was not working-class pressure that had reshaped state policy, he thought, but the reverse: the German workers were socialist "because the German professors have preached socialism, German popular leaders have deified it, and the German state has practiced it, until all German reform movements take on a more or less socialistic form." The careful distinctions the American students brought with them between state and society, between spheres of public and private action, blurred. As for the animus against state intervention to which Americans were accustomed, the German polity seemed to have no trace of it at all. The state seemed to pervade everything, without regard to the lines defended, like so many crucial barricades, at home. One saw it in the new state railroads and state insurance schemes, the soldiers in the streets, the clean, publicly swept city streets, the bureaucrats and regulations, and the policeman seated in full, conspicuous view at every labor union gathering and political meeting to ward off insult to the emperor.[30]

Finally, there were the professors. Their polemics against English economics eventually wore thin on the Americans' ears. But being public servants themselves, engaged in the construction of an economics with the "social" and the state explicitly brought back in, the professors cut a powerful figure in late-nineteenth-century Germany. Emancipated from the routines of American college pedagogy, they seemed to the Americans to be endowed with astonishing public authority. They lectured not only to university degree candidates. Their special weekly lectures, open to all, where they gave their views on public questions of the day, were highly visible public events, especially in Berlin. The leading German professors served in the upper houses of the state diets, where the universities had special representation. Their seminars, way stations to higher government service, were heavily salted with lawyers and state officials. They managed their own (often contentious) journals, pursued research, wrangled publicly over public issues, grasped hard for political influence, and stocked the government bureaus with loyal students. American college professors, with their easy access to editorial columns and reviews, had not been without authority of their own, but to students fresh from the narrow pieties of the late-nineteenth-century American colleges, the German professors' public status seemed astonishingly firm and deep.[31]

The Americans burnished the contrast in academic cultures, on their part, through the teachers they sought out. Lujo Brentano, the most English of the central figures in the Verein für Sozialpolitik, attracted few American economics students. Max Weber, despite a good deal of crossover into the sister social sciences, attracted none at all; institutionally insecure and preoccupied with different questions than the furor over laissez-faire, he cut no recognizable figure whatever in their consciousness. In the Germany within Germany that the American students made for themselves, the central figures were the men of Berlin who, between them, fanned the quarrel with laissez-faire most publicly: Adolph Wagner and, after 1882, Gustav Schmoller. The one was a theorist full of ethical furor, the other a man of history and piecemeal reform. In their contrasting ways, however, each preached an economics in which the state was inextricably implicit: a social instrument no less natural, or dispensable, or external to economic life, or inherently prone to derange and bungle than the market itself. In Farnam's poll, no other German teachers came close in remembered influence.[32]

The one who cut the broadest swath, personally and intellectually, was Wagner. Though marginalized by historians, who have consigned him to that politically and conceptually disquieting space where right and left can no longer easily be distinguished, his figure loomed for the Americans largest of all. "One of the great economists of his age," Ely would still remark of him in the 1930s. Wagner's stormy intellectual life bore witness to the transformative social force of capital in 1860s and 1870s Germany. He had begun his academic career at the Handelsakademie in Vienna where, as he remembered it, twin columns to Columbus and Adam Smith had presided over the institution and the spirit of its instruction. Wagner's own teaching followed the mold. In his first encounter with working-class socialism in a public meeting in Freiburg in 1869, he took the offensive by introducing a set of preemptive resolutions endorsing self-help, the sanctity of private property, and the principle of the limited state.[33]

From this beginning, however, he found he could not let the socialists' critique go. Moving to Berlin in 1870, into a city swelling with new wealth and real estate speculators, exacerbated his discontent. "One thing is unmistakable," he wrote his brother within a month: "everything turns on a reform of the idea of property." By the fall of 1872 he was lecturing to four hundred students a week on the labor question, going "pretty broadly, criticizing the basic juridical principles of our economic order: personal freedom, private property." "Read some Marx, Lassalle, even Bebel," he urged his brother. Whatever else the socialists had done, they had "completely broken up the fog of pink-tinted optimism, with which the dominant British school in economics had for so long shrouded every evil."[34]

By 1873 Wagner was certain that 95 percent of social democratic theory was correct; but rather than be a Social Democrat, he emerged from his intense reckoning with Marx a peculiar kind of Tory socialist. His "Address on the Social Question," given in 1871, was an impassioned plea for the voluntary restriction of egoism and self-interest on the part of the rich. The ethical, prophetic element remained a dominant note in Wagner's teaching; it reminded English observers of Ruskin in a "gruffer, harsher tone." Garrett Droppers, who arrived in Berlin from Harvard in 1888, remembered being struck with the "thinness" of American economic teaching in comparison to what Wagner offered. "German teaching inspires more fervor—gives one somewhat a spiritual sense of the true destiny of man." In Berlin, Droppers had found economics "more saturated with the spirit of social helpfulness, a higher sense of the dignity and functions of the State, an enthusiasm for the welfare of society. It was to me a new experience and I have never forgotten or lost it."[35]

What distinguished Wagner as an economist, however, was not simply his scorn for self-interest as the mainspring of economics, nor his rage at the myth of the natural harmonies of free competition, nor even his contention, rare among the *Kathedersozialisten*, that the legal privileges of property had to be rethought, down to their social core. It was the extent to which Wagner looked to state absorption of economic activity as the key to the remoralization of economic life. By the 1880s he was urging the extension of state enterprise into railroads, canals, banking, insurance, utilities, mining, and housing. To drive the land speculators out of the cities, he urged the public assumption of all urban land titles. To counter capitalism's tendency to grind wages to subsistence minima, he urged a legal limit on profits and an openly redistributive tax policy. "State socialism," he was calling it by the 1880s. Its goal, without the "craziness" and "criminality" of revolutionary socialism, was to lead the economy "more and more out of private into public organizational forms."[36]

To the textbook notion that the German reaction to classical economics was dominated by historical methods, Wagner's career is an important corrective. Like Marx and David Ricardo, from whom he drew so freely, Wagner taught economics as a science. Ultimately it gelled into an economic law that bore his name. A precise inversion of classical economists' project of state dismantlement, it held that the advance of civilization meant an automatic, ever widening range of state control and enterprise.

Had Wagner succeeded, as he dearly wished to, in catching the emperor's private ear, he might have made a career as a court economist. Failing that, he plunged into agitational politics. From the Verein für Sozialpolitik, whose caution soon disgusted him, he veered first into the

Christian-Social Workers' Party, Adolf Stoecker's effort to mobilize a mass political movement on prochurch, proemperor, anticapitalist, and anti-Semitic foundations. In the brief springtime of the "social monarchy" after 1890, he played a leading role in organizing the Evangelical Social Congress. Though Wagner ended up in the Junkers' Conservative Party, he was never a Junker primitivist. He dismissed Bismarck's antisocialist legislation as "pitiable," and he defended workers' claims to a far higher share of the national income. In the 1890s he barely escaped unseating after bringing the case for miners' bargaining rights into the Ruhr, where the coal masters would have none of it. His blend of ethical seriousness and demagoguery, his hatred of the plutocracy and insistence on the "social" idea, defy easy pigeonholing. But a version of market-substituting, income-redistributing social politics could not be missed in his teaching. He was the model of the professor immersed in agitational politics: the economist as secular preacher of the coming "social" age.[37]

Gustav Schmoller was, in contrast, a man of exquisitely judicious bearing. His dissent from the economics of "individual egoism," no less deep than Wagner's, grew not out of Marx but out of history. Against the search for a timeless science, with which Adam Smith's successors had saddled economics, he defended the need to think historically, contextually, and empirically about economic policy. No one played a larger part in driving home to American students the historical relativity of all economic doctrines. Through the academic journal he edited and the papers that flowed from his seminar, historical economics became virtually synonymous with Schmoller's name.[38]

History, however, did not provide Schmoller with his lasting fulcrum. As an instrument with which to unhinge the concept of the market's timeless "naturalness," historical economics posed a powerful critique to the classical doctrines. But not even Schmoller could make history a viable intellectual substitute for economic theory. By the 1890s, sensing the historical school was becoming swamped in ever-expanding, formless empirical results, the brightest American students were already seeking out Schmoller's rival marginalists in Vienna instead.[39]

Schmoller's lasting influence was, like Wagner's, as a man of the state. But where Wagner was *Kathedersozialismus*' public preacher, Schmoller was its model policy consultant. Within a year of his call from Strasbourg to the University of Berlin in 1882, he had formed a small Political Science Society of Berlin professors and highly placed government officials to discuss current legislation: a model of the arts of academic permeation. He turned his close ties to the Prussian Ministry of Education into a position as the most powerful "professor-maker" in late-nineteenth-century Germany; by the turn of the century, despite the emperor's efforts to dilute Schmoller's influence, economics chairs and government offices throughout Germany were filled with his pupils.[40]

Of all the institutions Schmoller dominated, the Verein für Sozialpolitik was the most important. The idea for the Verein was born at a meeting under Schmoller's roof. It was Schmoller who was asked to deliver the opening address at Eisenach in 1872; from 1890 until his death in 1917 he chaired the association and, despite the grumblings of some of the younger members, virtually embodied it. Like Schmoller, the Verein played its cards with both skill and caution. From the first, it attracted virtually all the bright younger German economists, together with a sizable number of highly placed civil servants, journalists, civic-minded men of affairs, and a handful of enlightened employers. After the collapse of the Economic Congress in 1885, the Verein served as the only professional economics association in late-nineteenth-century Germany. But it was not merely a professional association. From its beginning as the organizational rallying point for laissez-faire's critics, its purpose was policy influence.[41]

In its search for means, the Verein tacked with time and occasions. For the first several years the annual meetings consisted of forums designed to bring the views of employers, professors, and journalists to bear on the "most urgent phases of the social question." The meetings culminated in general debate and a straw vote on the issues of the day, which was widely reported in the press. Bismarck's sudden policy reversals after 1878 threw the Verein into confusion. After a disastrously divisive debate on Bismarck's new tariff proposals in 1879, the straw polls were abolished. Abandoning the labor question for safer issues of agricultural policy in the 1880s, the Verein let Bismarck's social insurance legislation go by with only feeble debate. Reemboldened in the 1890s, the Verein experimented with summer vacation courses in social economics for state officials, university students, and clergymen. A more enduring mode of influence came through its monographic investigations. By the late 1880s, following an agenda set by the Verein's governing circle of academic economists, the association had become a factory of social fact-finding and was cautiously and professionally building the empirical rationale for the socially active state, while leaving mobilization of public opinion to other organizations.[42]

The Verein's most successful sphere, however, was permeation of the debates among the higher, policy-making state officials. Figures like Frankfurt's mayor Franz Adickes, the Prussian finance minister Johannes Miquel, Freiherr von Berlepsch, the Prussian minister of commerce during the "new course" of the early 1890s, and Ernst Engel, director of the Prussian Statistical Bureau, were welcomed into the association's ranks. Through its selection of issues for investigation and debate, the Verein's leadership bid to set the terms for practical social policy formulation.

The result was a deeply cautious course, disputed from within and attacked from without. Even in its early years, the Verein had not thought it prudent to invite workers' representatives to its panels on the labor question. By setting social policy apart in a realm separate from constitutional policy, the Verein evaded the issues of democratization that were pressing hard on the German constitutional structures. Even within its chosen sphere, the Verein's weight was never a match for that of the larger, tangible interests bearing down on imperial politics. The German reform economists, caught between their state status and the obligation to uphold the state that came with it, proud of their state influence yet fearful that they might lose influence altogether by showing the least hint of disloyalty, were considerably less powerful figures than the Americans took them to be. Nonetheless, decades before the equivalent would appear in Britain or the United States, they had created what was to be one of the critical institutions of progressive social politics: an institutional nexus of professors and state officials, academic learning and practical policy making.

Over this fusion of university expertise and the bureaucratic state, Schmoller presided with deep conviction. Born into a family of civil servants, he imbibed from birth the traditions and self-image of the higher state bureaucracy. Over the dark and bloody ground of competition and egoism, he thought the servants of the state had stood apart from selfish interests—as protectors of the masses from the class domination of the wealthy, as the "one neutral element in the class conflict." If Schmoller's resulting conclusions were narrower than Wagner's, they were, in the German imperial context, ambitious enough. Against the resistance of Bismarck and the German industrialists, he was a persistent champion of workers' protective legislation. When the trust question came to a head in German politics, his suggestion was to carve out a place for representatives of the state on the boards of the largest cartels and to impose on them a heavy excess-profits tax. Where Wagner proposed to subsume large sectors of the market into state administration and to force, through taxation, a measure of income redistribution, Schmoller saw the state in juridical, bureaucratic terms, as a neutral arbiter, limiting and redressing the injuries of the market, "standing above egotistical class interests" and setting their limits.[43]

In seeking out these men and these arguments, the American students in Germany could not fail to have their economic certainties temporarily shaken. The experience of relinquishing, often painfully, what E. Benjamin Andrews called "the absoluteness of theory" pervades their memories. From Schmoller they all absorbed a lesson in the historicity of economic dogmas. Emily Balch and Edmund J. James returned home to teach Wagner's law of the ever-widening social functions of the state. Others remembered, years later, Wagner's moral "earnestness" and his stress on the "social idea."[44]

And yet, like Germany itself, the Berlin economists were troubling teachers. Their nationalist barbs at Anglo-American culture, their dismissal of the United States as the land of consummate interest politics, and their "contempt of everything American," as one student remembered it, disturbed their American students.[45] Most troubling of all was their scorn for democracy and their uncritical public reverence for the authority of the emperor and the state. In the first flush of excitement at the pageantry of state power, American students sometimes gave in to a borrowed patriotism. Du Bois came home to declare that "if there ever existed a race of divinely appointed kings," he was sure it was the Hohenzollerns. Samuel Lindsay's first deliberate act in Germany, on hearing martial music in a Hamburg beer garden, was to leap up on a table, wave his hat, and yell with the others. Few of the American students did not harbor their own doubts about abstract democracy. Ely thought Berlin's restrictions on the municipal suffrage would be a boon for New York City.[46]

But most of the American students were repelled by Bismarck's iron hand and by the show of military uniforms in the streets, the Reichstag, and the court entourage. James thought Bismarck had done Germany a "great wrong" in retarding the growth of self-government. E. R. A. Seligman thought the antisocialist campaign had reduced the nation "almost into the condition of vassals." The best any of the American students would say of Bismarck's social insurance scheme in the 1880s was Ely's comment that it was intensely "interesting." English-speaking persons, John H. Gray warned in 1890, did not understand how closely linked the social insurance proposals were to the regime's measures of repression.[47]

In one way or another, finally, all Americans studying in Germany brushed up against the excesses of state power. It "made the blood of the American and English students boil" to see police recorders take up their posts at political meetings, Mary Kingsbury remembered. "I did not find it pleasant to be obliged to show a passport before a hotel proprietor would be willing to assign me a room," Henry C. Adams wrote with barely suppressed fury long afterward: "It was a disagreeable necessity imposed upon me that I should look into each morning's paper under the list of books *verboten,* to see which ones in my possession next should be put under lock and key."[48]

Germany did not inspire imitation. The struggle to isolate, both conceptually and practically, the usable from the false threads—a task that was to bedevil every progressive traveler in Europe—was a fixture of the transatlantic progressive connection from the first. Rather, their German years set the Americans, sometimes furiously, to thinking. The most complete diary of a German sojourn is the one Henry C. Adams kept in Berlin in 1878–79, and its pages squirm with convictions in flux. Adams was no innocent abroad in the late 1870s. From Grinnell College he had gone on to study at Andover Theological Seminary and the new Johns Hopkins University. He had heard Francis Walker lecture on economics and studied the tramp labor problem himself in the hard times of the mid-1870s. He already possessed a Hopkins Ph.D. by the time he arrived in Wagner's seminar in Berlin.[49]

Nothing in Adams's preparation, however, prefigured the sharp, agitated economic questioning that erupts in the diary entries from his first months in Berlin. He threw himself into study of the socialist question, confessing that his work there "has given me a foothold again on Political Economy." He worried over the issue of "laissez-faire." He set to work on a scheme to limit individual accumulation, though he could not follow all its implications through to his satisfaction. "The problem is to restrict free competition, but how?" he wondered. A week after his first Christmas abroad, Adams's vocation was muddled, his religious ideas in tumult, and his mood agitated.

> I only know that English economy has served . . . and is serving as an opiate to the consciences of men who are trampling their fellow man in the dust. The slavery question is not yet worked out. If it was right for Christ to take the cloak away which covered the sins of men, it is right for me to do the same for that which makes mere men think their own acts of injustice are not their acts but the outworking of laws beyond human

> control. Nothing in the economic world is beyond the control of men and men must waken up to the controlling of these laws.

The piety, idealism, and ethical turmoil, Adams had brought with him. The mark of the German encounter was their displacement into the frame and language of *Manchestertum*'s German critics: laissez-faire, the system of "free competition," "English economy."[50]

Germany disturbed; that was its essence. Simon Patten came home eager to "help in the transformation of American civilization from an English to a German basis." Adams, in a burst of patriotic fervor, pledged himself "to work that [America] may never come to be like Europe."[51] Among persons who entered with so many mixed feelings into such agitated waters, one should look for no simple transfer of ideas or aspirations. The Americans moved not into a school of economic thought but into a society that heaved with debate over the social question. But the spectacle of a nation playing so fast and loose with the truisms of laissez-faire, whose lecture halls rang with denunciations of the textbook laws of economics, could not fail to jolt the Americans who saw it. Their German sojourn loosed the young Americans from ethical rigidities; it offered them new models for an academic career; it unhinged the intellectual edifice of laissez-faire, if not beyond reconstruction then beyond uncritical reiteration. As in all journeys, however, the baggage ultimately had to be brought home.

Professing Economics

The first act of the German-trained American students, as they began to take up professorships of their own in the 1880s, was a rush to re-create the forms of academic life into which they had been initiated abroad. Into the curricula they shoved the defining marks of German university scholarship: lecture, seminar, research paper, monograph, scholarly journal, graduate education, and the Ph.D. degree. From Germany, too, they brought back identifiable marks of content. They began to sprinkle the catalog offerings with new courses—social politics, social economics, public finance (Wagner's special province), the problems of labor and capital—and ventilated the old textbook pedagogy with new readings. In his introductory courses, Ely assigned Walker and Laveleye; for advanced students in economics (who would find German "indispensable," he warned) he recommended

Wagner, Schmoller, Knies, Roscher, and Gustav Schönberg's new, collectively compiled *Handbook of Political Economy* ("one of the best economic treatises—if not the best—ever written," Ely called it). In his first years of teaching, Henry C. Adams led students through a history of economics running from the mercantilists and classical English economists, through the "Revolt against English Political Economy," to the "newest Germany economy."[52]

J. Franklin Jameson, who heard Ely lecture in the early 1880s, complained acerbically that Ely "fought his man of straw, the *a priori* economist over again, and demolished him much as usual." Ely's was "a narrow little mind," Jameson thought, "steeped in German prejudices." But the latter charge missed the mark. Of so many mixed minds about Germany, none of Ely's cohort came back Germanophiles. Only a handful kept up lasting German connections or sustained a serious interest in the development of German politics. Rather, they came back with ideals (which occasionally, in a referential kind of shorthand, they conflated with Germany itself) and, still more, a sense of enlistment in an international movement in ideas. Ely assigned students to report on the latest controversies in the (London) *Economist* and the (Paris) *Journal des économistes* as well as the *Preussische Jahrbücher* and *Conrads Jahrbücher für Nationalökonomie*. The book review columns of the academic journals Ely's cohort launched breathed the same cosmopolitan atmosphere. In the *Political Science Quarterly*, which served as the combined outlet for Columbia University's political science and economics faculties, almost half the books reviewed between its founding in 1886 and 1890 were foreign language titles, about evenly split between French and German, with a smattering of Italian as well. Whatever else it did, the German university experience radically broadened the Americans' intellectual culture.[53]

Mere curricular and classroom influence, however, was not their goal; what the intellectual leaders among the German-trained economists wanted was a social politics of their own. Those in the cohort of American students whom the German assault on laissez-faire had taken most by surprise came back in the late 1870s and early 1880s with not only massive doubts about laissez-faire but also sweeping, still inchoate visions of radical change. Albion Small taught students his "abomination of laissez-faire." "This younger political economy," Ely wrote in 1884, "no longer permits [economic] science to be used as a tool in the hands of the greedy and the avaricious for keeping down and oppressing the laboring classes. It does not acknowledge *laissez-faire* as an excuse for doing nothing while people starve, nor allow the all-sufficiency of competition as a plea for grinding the poor." The difficulty lay in finding a program and a public platform.[54]

How deeply that first cohort yearned for popular influence and authority comparable to that they had seen in their teachers abroad can hardly be exaggerated. They threw themselves into university extension course lectures on the problems of the day: the labor question, Henry George's theories, labor legislation, monopolies, and socialism. They wrote for popular outlets. Several reached out for labor union contacts. By the middle of the decade, Ely, the boldest of his generation, was deep into studies of working-class socialist and labor movements, producing alarmingly sympathetic pieces of scholarship, as his critics saw them. Read a labor paper, he urged Americans of conscience in 1886, the year the Knights of Labor mushroomed into a major social movement, join a labor union, "put your shoulder to the wheel, help them to move their load." Within a year Edmund J. James, whose prudence normally far outran Ely's, had signed on as the "labor reform" editor of Joseph Cook's intense, shortlived social gospel magazine, *Our Day*. When George E. McNeill's Knights of Labor–sponsored *The Labor Movement: The Problem of To-day* was published in 1887, the opening three historical chapters on the social upheavals of the industrial revolution and the efficacy of labor organization were written by James—the only academic voice in a chorus of labor and radical opinion. Adams, too, made labor contacts. These actions were not precisely the equivalent of Adolph Wagner's plunge into working-class politics in Berlin, but in their ethico-economic intensity and political incaution, they were very close.[55]

The content of their alternative to laissez-faire was harder to pin down than the intensity of the young, German-trained economists' anger and their hunger for the broadest possible influence. Whatever else, they would not be top-down statists; their German and American experiences both reinforced the point. Rather, through the mid-1880s, the most prominent of them labored to promote a transformation of values deep and thorough enough to hollow out the system of competitive and individualistic economics at its ethical core. Ely, Adams, and Seligman all took up the cooperative idea—not as an exercise in self-help but as an alternative to the commodification of labor. Seligman, whose wealthy German-Jewish family connections gave him the most cosmopolitan background of the group, moved from a thesis on the medieval guilds to an intensely admiring study of the prophets of English Christian cooperative socialism. Ely plunged into correspondence with the leading British cooperators and set his students to investigating cooperation's traditions and possibilities in the

United States. His own *French and German Socialism in Modern Times*, published in 1883, ended not with the *Kathedersozialisten* but, like Seligman's work, with the Christian socialist program of Kingsley and Maurice.[56]

Adams was no less keenly interested in means of superseding the existing wage system. By 1884 he thought he had found an answer in the notion of vesting workers with "proprietary" rights in the firms whose labor they supplied—perhaps through some form of enforceable job tenure, perhaps through a combination of comanagement and profit-sharing devices. Whatever the details, it would be "a forerunner, I sometimes hope, of a reform in property and social rights that will forbid this old world to know itself."[57]

"Socialism" the insurgent economists began to call this general transvaluation of values in the 1880s. The usage was a British borrowing, not a Marxian one. Particularly where social Christianity intersected with Oxford Idealism, the term "socialism" could be heard in that decade in all sorts of unexpected British quarters. One found it in Mill's reconsiderations on "socialism" in 1879, in Samuel Barnett's program of social reforms packaged as "practicable socialism" in 1883, in Joseph Chamberlain's readiness to call "every kindly act of legislation" a kind of "socialism." Most famous was the reported (and never quite denied) concession of Gladstone's chief lieutenant in the House of Commons in the late 1880s: "We are all socialists now."[58]

A certain deliberate vagueness inhered in all these progressive uses of the term "socialism," an indefiniteness that drew from the well of displaced religious sentiments that young insurgent American economists knew so well. Their socialism was not class centered or state centered but, at heart, ethical. "Socialism" was the antonym of competitive individualism: an extension of the "social" idea that had struck them abroad. Socialism meant revolt against the "each one for himself" doctrine in economics, Ely explained. It meant, Seligman wrote, a wider scope for the "forces which tend to weld society together, [and] to render the idea of self subservient to that of the common weal."[59]

Through this intellectual route the German-trained economists made their way back, in the end, to the role of legislation and the state. They had absorbed too much history to imagine that the state stood radically apart from society. Seizing a phrase from Wagner, Ely had begun to argue by 1884 that the state was simply another form of cooperative association: a "compulsory cooperative community" with no less ethical and spiritual force behind it than the church or the family. James, whose German sympathies merged with high-tariff family tradition, was ready to declare the state "one of the most important, if not, indeed, the most important factor in the economic evolution of society itself." Even Adams, more suspicious of state power than the others, wrote: "Whether 'state,' or 'nation,' or 'society,' the fundamental thought is the same. The thing itself brought to view is an organic growth, and not a mechanical arrangement." The state was not an arrangement apart from society—an unnatural, extraneous, intervening force. Ely put it most directly: government "is the agency through which we must work."[60]

In 1885 and 1886 this tumult of German-triggered, American-exacerbated heresies and aspirations came to a head in a context that insured it would produce far more than ripples in a collegiate teapot. The immediate event was a startling rise in labor organization; heartened by a series of unusually successful strikes in 1884 and 1885, recruits by the hundreds of thousands began to pour into the Knights of Labor in the first sustained, national labor drive in the nation's history. In the legislatures, the issue of monopoly power was rising to a head. Compounding the tumult was Henry George, at the high point of his influence in 1886. Publicly and privately all the younger economists sparred with George's simplified and radicalized recasting of classical economics—by which the full blame for economic misery was made to fall on the villainy of rent—even as they envied George's ability to win masses of converts.[61]

The organizational vehicle the German-trained economists devised was an American version of the Verein für Sozialpolitik: the American Economic Association. The initial impetus for the project came from James and Patten. As students, both men had heard Johannes Conrad lecture on the Verein's work and urge its example on his American listeners. In 1884, after a second trip to Germany, James did his best to comply. From the title of the draft James and Patten circulated for a "Society for the Study of National Economy," with its transparent anglicization of the standard German term for economics, *Nationalökonomie*, to its statement of positions on the leading issues of the day, drawn up so that it should have "as definite a program as the Verein für Sozialpolitik," there was no missing the borrowed German model or ambition.[62]

Canvassing all the newly returned German university economics students for recruits, Ely and Seligman called an organizational meeting in September 1885, at which the problem of a common platform was subjected to intense discussion. Adams, James, and Ely all worried lest the association brand them with the *Kathedersozialisten* label or appear to commit them to dismissing English economics in toto. Adams was not alone in insisting that "the German view of social relations," in which all relations culminated in the state, was not theirs. Ely's suggestion that they place on record their agreement that "the doctrine of laissez-faire is unsafe in politics and unsound in morals" was stronger language than the majority was ready to accept.[63]

But from the opening line of the platform—"We regard the state as an agency whose positive assistance is one of the indispensable conditions of human progress"—no one could doubt the association's determination to be a rallying point for the critics of laissez-faire. Even had we not Ely's private statement that "the idea of the A.E.A. is to accomplish in America what the Verein für Socialpolitik has done in Germany" or the echoes of Schmoller at Eisenach in Ely's opening address, the association's eagerness for lay members of influence and weight, its assignment of topics for investigation, and its initial determination to produce policy proposals for debate all signaled its intimate links to the German quarrel with *Manchestertum*. When the association reached out for honorary members in 1887, Laveleye, Wagner, Knies, and Roscher were among the first to be embraced.[64]

Sensing the controversy in the winds, the editors of the journal *Science* asked James to arrange a series of articles explaining the insurgency in economics. Seligman wrote the opening piece, on economic method, in which he insisted on the historical relativity of all economic doctrines, the "absolute right of property" included. James defended the central importance of the state, not as an accidental or external economic factor but as "the 'great silent partner' in every business enterprise." Ely heralded the new ethical element in economics. ("Open your Mill, your Schönberg, your Wagner, your economic magazines, and you readily discern that the course of economic thought is largely, perhaps mainly, directed to what *ought* to be.") Adams wrote on the relationship between law and property. Columbia's Richmond Mayo Smith, who had learned his economics in Berlin and Heidelberg in the mid-1870s, concluded with a defense of statistical and empirical method.[65]

Theirs was not a simple offshoot of German economics, the writers all insisted. But no one could miss the new, cosmopolitan threads woven through their revolt; Schmoller's historical method, Knies's and Wagner's ethical vision, a whiff (through James) of Wagner's law of ever-increasing state functions, a hint (through Adams and Seligman) of Wagner's call to rethink the conventions of property ownership down to the core.

The established economics professors erupted in anger. Yale's Arthur T. Hadley, no simple advocate of laissez-faire, who confessed to having learned a thing or two in Wagner's seminar in his time, retorted that no one could dismiss, by mere will, "the rigidity of economic laws." "The danger of believing that economic laws can be interfered with by human effort is ten times greater than the danger of an extreme belief in *laissez-faire*." The point of economics, Hadley insisted, was the discovery of the inexorable limits of human will—that bad currency drives out good, or that reckless marriages and too many children meant starvation wages. Political economy "says to the legislator, 'Thus far shalt thou go, and no farther.' It does not say, 'Such and such legislation will produce the best results'; but it says 'Beyond certain limits, all legislation fails.'"[66] The insurgents responded with the point on which, like a fulcrum, all the rest turned: that to accept economics as a system of immutable laws of nature was to give in to fatalism and despair.

The *Science* exchange of 1886 brought together most of the elements of the new insurgency in economics: contestation over the root metaphors of classical economics, the younger economists' eagerness for the public arena and the public ear, their moral seriousness, their deep and angry quarrel with "laissez-faire," and their tense and intricate relations with their German teachers. Elsewhere Adams in that year was writing of an "overthrow of the wages system"—a sea change in economic relations whose result "will constitute a social revolution"; James was mocking "the old song about the supreme sacredness of private property"; and Seligman was writing of the chasm between the haves and the have-nots as the "paramount question of political economy to-day." The English academic debate over economic doctrines in the mid-1880s, more isolated from German influences, was in comparison merely a polite tea party. Strung somewhere between economics and exhortation, the young insurgents of the American Economic Association were in full cry against the notion of the naturally working market.[67]

For this level of revolt, the American colleges and universities of the 1880s were not prepared to be a nursery. The margin of freedom in the United States was not narrower than that in imperial Germany, with its rigid bars against Social Democratic influence. But in the United States, where the insurgency in economic doctrines ran up against a structure of university finances and authority dominated by businessmen donors, the room for maneuver was, in its own way, extremely narrow. In late-nineteenth-century Germany the established forces drew their most heavily defended line at insult to the state; in the United States the more critical line was insult to property. Property was no small matter anywhere in the North Atlantic economy, to be sure, as evidenced by the presence of the Saar's leading coal and iron magnate at the polemical head of the attack on the *Kathedersozialisten* in the 1890s. But in the United States, where state structures were so much weaker and the business class monopolized positions of status without serious competition from a landed aristocracy, the American critics of laissez-faire were far more isolated and vulnerable. The status of the German professors was not the Americans' to take, despite the trappings of research and scholarship they had labored so hard to set in place.

In part, the fragility of the American insurgents' circumstances was, like so many of the contrasts in the North Atlantic economy, the product of institutional timing. In Germany, the state and its universities were older than industrial capitalism, and their authority predated it. In the United States, where everything was new—the nature of the post–Civil War state, class relations, capital organization, and labor organization—questions of property redistribution cut closer to the bone. In a polity where so much of the infrastructure of public life (libraries, parks, church edifices, and universities) came as gifts from wealthy businessmen, the authority wielded by the German professoriate could not be easily transferred. That was what the University of Michigan president James B. Angell meant when he reminded Henry C. Adams that the range of academic freedom permissible in Germany could not possibly be expected in the United States. Not only were ideas differently arranged in the United States than in Germany—so was power.[68]

Adams was one of the first to discover this for himself. Not yet having obtained a secure faculty berth, his teaching was split in 1886 between half-time positions at the University of Michigan and Cornell. From the outset of the latter appointment, Cornell's acting president had worried that Adams lacked the "realism that comes from conversation with . . . any one of a hundred New York bankers." When in the spring of 1886, in response to Adams's request for a permanent Michigan appointment, President Angell asked for a formal statement of Adams's views on private property, inheritance, and "state socialism," Adams had responded boldly: "The final right of control over all productive agencies lies with society, and a proprietor should always be regarded as an agent who manages for a principal. The question, therefore, as to how far men should be permitted to control productive agents as though they had a final right in them, is wholly a question of expediency, that can be answered only by experiment and the common sense of men."[69]

In August, however, Adams made the mistake of mounting the same critique of the "sacredness" of property (together with some sympathetic remarks on the recent Knights of Labor rail strike) at a public gathering at Cornell's engineering school, with one of the university's principal benefactors on the speakers' platform. The presiding faculty member, R. H. Thurston, sprang to the rebuttal. Those at the top of economic enterprises as wide-reaching as the rail corporations "are always the strong, brave, far-seeing, wise, and prudent, the enterprising and energetic," he declared. They could brook no dictation by strikers or anarchists who had lost out in the competitive struggle. To protest against the prevailing rate of wages was futile, for it was not men who set these conditions, it was the "all-compelling law" of nature, trade, and God.[70]

All the economic pieties of the day came tumbling out of Thurston's long, extemporaneous response. The Cornell trustees, concluding that Adams's ideas were "subversive of the social order," contented themselves with terminating his appointment. Desperate to hold on to his Michigan appointment, Adams sent Angell an abject retraction of his past eight years' work, professing that his ideas had been unhinged ever since he had first come upon socialist arguments in Berlin. In a last fling of self-respect, he could not resist suggesting that Angell himself take a look at Toynbee's *The Industrial Revolution.* But by then his humiliation had been accomplished.[71]

Adams's treatment was a painful lesson for the German-trained economists in the special circumstances of economic debate in late-nineteenth-century America. The 1890s were littered with similar academic heresy cases; most involved economists, and, as Mary Furner has shown, the trustees rarely lost. Even James, who rose to the pinnacle of the Wharton School's faculty leadership and salary structure, was eventually forced out by a new provost, himself a major university donor. Still young and scrambling hard for secure positions in the 1880s, the German-trained economists struggled to reconstruct their social politics on less vulnerable lines. Reluctantly, the American Economic Association let overt policy formulation go. After both James's committee on transportation and Adams's committee on public finance failed to agree on policy proposals, the association jettisoned its standing committees on public questions. Where the Verein für Sozialpolitik found its niche in selecting a few of the leading social-economic controversies of the day for intensive empirical investigation and debate, the American association meetings soon relapsed into a miscellany of scattered, individual contributions. By 1888, desperate for the strength of numbers, the association had already quietly abandoned its statement of principles.[72]

Rhetorically, too, the German-trained economists beat a retreat from the prophetic language of the 1880s—part Wagner, part Ruskin, part social gospel Protestantism. The fundamental nature of the wage relationship, which had preoccupied Adams, Ely, and Seligman in the early 1880s, was eased out of the sphere of professional economic discourse. Talk of appropriating the language of "socialism" from the socialists vanished like morning mist. With outlets to the popular magazines and a core of loyal students, Ely hung on longer than the rest. Forced out of the secretaryship of the American Economic Association in 1892 when he proposed holding the association's annual meeting at the great camp meeting of Methodist earnestness at Chautauqua, he moved through a succession of social gospel alternatives to the AEA. But when burned in his own academic heresy trial in 1894, even Ely beat a retreat.

The reverses of the decade were not so severe as to dissolve the dream of effecting—beyond any piecemeal work of policy recommendation—deeper changes in economic values. On both sides of the Atlantic, visions of moderating and reconstructing the individualism of the day were integral to the progressive project. Whether the notion of the "social" was dressed in the language of solidarism or Fabianism or the German professors' "ethical" economics, all progressives took for granted that its antithesis was not this or that specific arrangement of law or custom but an ethos of private desires. Progressive politics would always run on the dual tracks of the prophetic and the particular. But as the dream of a cooperative community, ascending all the way to the socially active state, foundered in the class tensions of the 1880s, the first generation to have learned its economics in the context of the German quarrel with laissez-faire scrambled for less vulnerable ground. As they worked their way, painfully, toward more carefully defined measures and less vulnerable positions, Schmoller's model came, out of Wagner's shadow, into its own.

The first of the insurgent economists' precautionary measures took them back to their own most worried knot in the German connection: the problem of delimiting the reach of the state. Between their own social politics and the open-ended state language of their German teachers, they could not avoid the necessity of building a firmer, safer wall. As it turned out, it was Adams who had already supplied it in a paper delivered five months before his world fell in upon him. Although Ely's talk of the "God-given" agency of the state had never been his, Adams had, in his own way, been trying to slip around the conceptual lines between artificial and natural economic actors that divided the state from the realm of economic "freedom." Now in "Principles That Should Control the Interference of the States in Industries," Adams came back to the laissez-faire economists' rhetoric of lines and distinctions.

Of the state's legitimate realms of action, Adams emphasized two. The first were measures that set a floor beneath the "plane of competitive action," lest market dynamics drive the ethical level down to that of the most unscrupulous competitors; factory legislation, it had been called in England since the beginning of the century. The second involved enterprises that were "from their very nature monopolies"—in which the costs of creating a rival, duplicate facility gave so disadvantageous a return to late investors that competition inevitably failed. Railroads were an obvious example of a "natural monopoly" of this sort; city utilities were another. In realms like these, where the market inherently failed, Adams thought some form of public control inescapable—whether through public franchises, price regulation, the establishment of a competitive state enterprise, or creation of an outright publicly owned monopoly.[73]

The keepers of the decade's economy orthodoxies were not assuaged. "The views which underlie modern socialism are here put in their strongest shape, with a moderation which makes them all the more insidious," the *Independent*'s reviewer protested of Adams's essay. But the German-trained economists seized on Adams's distinctions with alacrity; between noninterference and the vortex of the German state, it gave them a theoretical point on which to stand. Adams himself had been far less clear about its practical consequences, even before adding, prior to letting the paper go to the American Economic Association for publication, a nervous declaration that the entire argument sprang wholly out of the "individualistic" point of view.[74] Seligman, seizing (for the moment) the cautious end of the Adams's essay, urged that Adams's work was "proof of the fact that abandonment of *laissez faire* does not connote socialism or anything materially approaching socialism." Ely chose the more radical moral in Adams's argument; within a year of absorbing Adams's natural monopoly argument, he was calling for public assumption of railroads, telegraphs, streetcar lines, and city electric, gas-, and waterworks—if not immediately, at least slowly and inexorably. James, deep in a fight to prevent Philadelphia's municipal gasworks from being auctioned off to private interests, readily absorbed the same point. The urban utility fights of the next two decades, critically important watersheds in the genesis of popular progressive politics, were all tightly wound around the "natural monopoly" argument. Still later, the New Deal's Fair Labor Standards Act and the Tennessee Valley Authority still remained within the ambit of Adams's concerns.[75]

If Adams's essay helped to frame and focus the insurgents' views of the state, however, there remained the problem of constructing a firmer strategic base than the prophetic, political pulpits of the 1880s. In this pinch, Schmoller's more cautious model of expert influence grew in attractiveness. When James again took up the project of an American Verein für Sozialpolitik in 1889, his design was this time more faithful to the original. The purpose of his new, ambitiously named American Academy of Political and Social Science was, like the Verein's, not outright policy formation but debate. Following an agenda set by its faculty organizers, it brought professors and Philadelphia men of affairs under a common roof for discussion of topical public issues. From the first, the academy's models were rarely far from sight. The early numbers of its *Annals* found room for long, translated extracts from Schmoller, Gustav Cohn, Achille Loria in Siena, Eugen Böhm-Bawerk in Vienna, and Paul de Rousiers in Paris. Leo Rowe reported on the meetings of the Société d'économie sociale, Willoughby on the Musée Social, Robert C. Brooks on the German cities' congress, and John Gray on the meetings of the Verein itself. In one regular department, Leo Rowe kept track of the newest international ideas in city government reform; Samuel Lindsay did the same for general social-reform news.[76] In 1902, under the editorship of yet another alumnus of the German university connection, Emory Johnson, the *Annals* finally found its lasting format, a variation of the scheme the Verein für Sozialpolitik's *Schriften* had used in the 1870s. Each issue brought a symposium of expert opinion to bear on a pressing, policy issue of the day: municipal ownership and franchises, industrial conciliation and arbitration, housing, child labor, business regulation, penology, trade and tariffs.

Expert policy counsel, in fact, turned out to be the ground on which laissez-faire's professorial critics regrouped and refashioned a position of influence. By the end of the century, the students of the first German-trained economists were working hard to establish new forms of authority by colonizing the social space between university professorships and expert government service. Their efforts came to define a central structural element of American progressive politics. Emory Johnson himself took his

Berlin-burnished expertise in transportation policy to a lectureship at the Wharton School and a seat on the Isthmanian Canal Commission. His colleague Roland Falkner served as staff statistician to the Senate Finance Committee during its tariff deliberations of the early 1890s. Adna F. Weber went from graduate study in Berlin to deputy directorship of the New York Bureau of Labor Statistics, which soon developed into something of a clearinghouse for European social policy ideas. The model career in this regard was B. Henry Meyer's. Meyer had studied with Schmoller and Wagner in Berlin in 1894–1895, imbibing from Wagner an idea of expanded state functions and from Schmoller an animus against deductive economic theory. On his return, he turned his knowledge of the Prussian railway system into a professorship at the University of Wisconsin, a major role in drafting Wisconsin's railroad commission bill, the commission's first chairmanship, and, from 1911 to 1939, a seat on the federal Interstate Commerce Commission.[77]

In time the generation of the 1880s, too, learned the new roles. Seligman became the country's leading expert on progressive taxation—though not, he emphasized, on Wagner's explicitly redistributionist principles. Adams, while quietly teaching classes in labor organization and social and industrial reforms, found his niche of policy influence, at last, as chief statistician of the new Interstate Commerce Commission, where he carefully advanced the case for technically competent oversight of rates and working conditions. Even Ely, after his brush with the University of Wisconsin regents in 1894, learned the arts of inside, expert policy permeation, immersing himself in issues of land economics.[78]

So familiar did this route to influence become that in time the transition from exhortation to expert, university-based authority came to seem like a natural progression. Inherent in the social processes of professionalization, it seemed to need no explanation. But this system of authority, too, was half borrowed, a conjunction of domestic politics and the transatlantic progressive connection. Nothing compelled reliance on university faculty for policy-making expertise. Nothing, for that matter, compelled political reliance on experts at all. The apparatus of the British state was not in the hands of experts but of Oxford and Cambridge amateurs. The London ministries drew their senior civil service and policy-making staff from general education courses and privileged backgrounds, sorting the candidates through a system of competitive examinations to which policy expertise was, by design, irrelevant. Among those who cracked this mold, well-connected, freelance intellectuals were considerably more common than university dons. The same was true of membership on the royal commissions of inquiry.[79]

The model of requiring training in economics or public law for higher civil service positions, like the practice of professors tacking back and forth between lecture hall and government panel, was German, founded on the peculiarly tight connections between the German universities and the German state. The public inquiry commission was one of its modal forms. University economists were fixtures on state commissions; even a figure as relatively marginal as Max Weber in the 1890s was appointed to the Bundesrat's inquiry commission on stock and commodity exchanges.[80]

The German-trained American economists of the 1890s brought this example back and labored, with considerable effect, to graft it onto to the more diffuse structures of American state power. From the Senate inquiry into the relations between labor and capital, which was run essentially out of Senator Henry Blair's back pocket in 1883, to the Industrial Commission of 1898 to 1902, with its massive stack of expert-prepared reports, to the Commission on Industrial Relations of 1912 to 1915, with John R. Commons of the University of Wisconsin as one of its key members and a full-time staff of social economists in its service, the development of the modern public investigative commission encapsulates the rise of the professor to the status of expert policy adviser. The advisory boards of the new social policy pressure groups—the American Association for Labor Legislation, the National Consumers' League, and the National Child Labor Committee, all stocked with graduates of the German university exchange—told the same story. In 1908, at the high point of the Progressive-era collaboration between university-based experts and progressive state administration, forty-one University of Wisconsin faculty members occupied seats on at least one official state commission. Within a year after a change of administration in 1914, the professors had been cleaned out to the last appointee. Still, infiltration of the state apparatus proved a surer road toward influence than the public, prophetic ambitions of the Adams's generation.[81]

Out of their first exposure to the superheated German assault on Manchester economics, in short, American veterans of the German university connection began to find for themselves a measure of power and an institutional place for their new sense of the state. Piece by piece they began to help fashion the elements of an American social politics. By the end of the century they had done a great deal to ease economic discourse past the moral-economic syllogisms of their youth. If they had not erased the privileged "naturalness" of the market, they had done a vast amount to naturalize the agencies of public action and control. The great controversy between the classical and historical schools, Adna F. Weber was sure by the turn of the century, had "long since settled itself" in eclectic blends and compromises. The bright lines between state and economy dissolved into expedient and practical considerations—hotly contested still, but stripped of an earlier generation's metaphysics.[82]

But of all the consequences of the events that, undesigned, had shunted a generation of young, politically ambitious intellectuals through the universities of late-nineteenth-century Germany, the most important was the most obvious: it impressed a lasting intellectual cosmopolitanism on those who passed through it. It made them conscious citizens of a Euro-American world of social-political endeavor.

The German university connection opened the transatlantic "moment" in American social politics. Into the American context its alumni brought a sense of enormous release from the tightly bounded intellectual worlds of their youth—not the least the tightly, syllogistically packaged intellectual paradigms of laissez-faire. They brought back new political ambitions and models of authority. They brought back an acute sense of a missing "social" strand in American politics and a new sense, as unnerving as it was attractive, of the social possibilities of the state. Their paths, together with the paths of those they taught and influenced, will crisscross all the later chapters of this story.

But as their experience showed, the Atlantic connection was to be no simple diffusion of ideas, no abstract transit of intellectual categories, no peaceful pleasure cruise. The tense and troubled reckoning of the German-trained Americans with what they heard and saw abroad, and the collision of their new social politics with economic structures at home, were built into the dynamics at work. In a world of nations, transatlantic social politics was, from the outset, full of traps and dangers. The exhilaration and the strains that were to endure in transatlantic social politics were both compacted in its opening moment.

4

The Self-Owned City

The Collectivism of Urban Life

The struggle over economic doctrines that began in the 1880s first came to a political head in the "great cities" of the 1890s. So accustomed are modern readers to thinking of nation-states as the key actors in social politics that the point is worth pausing over. Yet where the rhetoric of "urban crisis" in late-twentieth-century America reverberates with despair, a century ago the city stood at the vital center of transatlantic progressive imaginations. If conscious public action can rescue today's cities from the juggernaut of social and economic forces bearing down on them, it is now commonly said, it will take the will and resources of the national government to make it happen. But to an earlier generation of urban progressives on both sides of the Atlantic, the formula was just the reverse. If the nation was to be reformed, it would be by first seizing the social possibilities of the cities.

The urban "moment" in the history of American progressive politics, sliced thin enough to be sandwiched between the Populist revolt and Theodore Roosevelt's reformation of the presidency, has not gone unnoticed. But its international dynamics and dimensions have barely begun to be reckoned with. Whether for Fabians in 1890s London, left liberals in 1890s Frankfurt, or progressives in Cleveland and Chicago, the great cities formed key sites of social-political mobilization, experiment, and controversy. To shape urban social politics, there was no system builder to rival a

Henry George or an Adolph Wagner. Its theory, though not lacking for publicists, remained inchoate and implicit. Its common coins were the mundane, material utilities of urban life: water, streets, trolley cars, public baths, gasworks, and housing. But in battles over who should control these goods and services, in dreams of liberating the city from predatory commercial interests into its own social consciousness, the transatlantic revolt against laissez-faire was put to its first common test.

The links between the great cities and social politics were many. Where the primary business of nation-states was with armies and empires, public welfare lay in the domain of local government. Poor relief was located there, as were most of the systems of mutual assistance and support. To their inherited political responsibilities, moreover, the great cities brought considerable resources. Young, ambitious social-political reformers made their way to London, Paris, Chicago, Berlin, or New York, drawn by the same force that drew peasants, politicians, entrepreneurs, and artisans to the cities. The social settlements took root there; the universities (Oxford and Cambridge excepted) were urban creatures. Most of those who staffed the progressive pressure groups and public agencies on both sides of the Atlantic were, perforce, city dwellers. The popular press and the big agencies of working-class mobilization were headquartered there as well—potential allies, should the middle-class reformers need or want them.

Most important, the great cities' very structure incorporated some of the key problematics of progressive politics. Social fragmentation was the first and most obvious of these. Not even in the grimmest coal districts were the class divisions of industrial capitalism more visibly set out for view. "What is true of London, is true of Manchester, Birmingham, Leeds, is true of all great towns," Friedrich Engels wrote in 1844. "Everywhere barbarous indifference, hard egotism on the one hand, and nameless misery on the other, everywhere social warfare, every man's house in a state of siege, everywhere reciprocal plundering under the protection of the law."[1] The charge exaggerated, but there could no be doubt that the great cities put the competitive, fragmented face of industrial capitalism on particularly intense display. Vertically the great cities disaggregated into interests and classes; horizontally they split into agglomerations of sharply differentiated neighborhoods. One moved between them as through a series of sudden scene changes, as if the backdrops and stage furniture were suddenly whirled away and contrasting sets dropped incongruously in their place. The great cities were distended collections of contrasting subcities: a financial district here, mansion district there, tenderloin sections, factory towns, a concentration of warehouses and department stores, middle-class suburbs, and vast working-class regions subdivided by turn into neighborhood and ethnic territories. Mid-nineteenth-century London and Paris had not even a facade of local self-government to hold the whole together, lest the class conflicts of the city once more spark a tinderbox of revolution.

Most unnerving of all was the massing of the cities' working poor. Into the cheapest housing districts flowed those among the tide of displaced rural folk who, failing to find a secure foothold in the city's factories, offices, or warehouses, ended up in the great urban market for irregular, unskilled labor. They turned New York City's Five Points district in the shadow of City Hall, London's Whitechapel in the sprawling East End, and the inner courtyards of tenement Berlin into turn-of-the-century metaphors for wretchedness. The writer Jack London, arriving in England in 1902, had no idea where the East End was to be found, but he knew he had to see it, just as progressive Europeans in New York City knew they had to see the plutocratic palaces of upper Fifth Avenue. Amassed capital and concentrated poverty, gluttonous displays of wealth and abject misery: the city concentrated both in what urban writers delicately called the "sunshine and shadow" of urban life.[2]

And yet, though a place of fractures and fragments, the city was at the same time an enormous collectivity. On that point, Engels missed the mark. If quiet, daily warfare was inextricable from great city life, so, no less, were its systems of interdependence. Brought into the city through far-flung markets in goods and labor, sorted into neighborhoods by markets in land and shelter, sustained by armies of shopkeepers, peddlers, teamsters, and middlemen, city dwellers lived in a web of mutual dependency that was at once extraordinarily powerful and barely visible. Nowhere outside the great cities did the necessities of shelter and sustenance hinge as fully on invisible suppliers. The "private city," as Sam Bass Warner calls it, creature of a myriad private decisions, was, in fact, a vast network of mutually dependent relations.[3]

Despite itself, the formless capitalist collectivism of the city forced collective considerations into political consciousness. The most pressing of the great cities' urgencies was health. Much of the history of social politics' formation might, indeed, be written as the story of the battle for a concept of public health, rooted not only in personal discipline and hygiene but also in the social environments of labor and shelter. To the traditional health risks of old age, childbirth, and accident, the cities added the risks of concentrated, interdependent living—much of it, like water-borne microbes, invisible to the amateur eye. It was the great, shocking sanitary investigations spearheaded by Edwin Chadwick in Britain in the 1840s that first pinpointed the ecological causes of urban disease and showed the far-reaching public consequences of a polluted well, an alleyway of standing sewage, or the airless warrens of an inner courtyard. By the private calculus of their owners, none was worth the costs of improvement. The sanitary investigations thus offered not only a medical lesson in the health risks of concentrated populations; they also offered an economic lesson in the hidden social injuries of self-regarding commercial acts.[4]

In Britain first, then elsewhere, propelled by sanitary science, cholera epidemics, and a mounting fear of the moral contagion of the "slum," nineteenth-century political authorities began to move toward tighter regulation of the private city through more systematic bylaws and building codes, sanitary ordinances, and dwelling inspections. More momentously, city authorities began to move toward the provision of goods that had hitherto been accepted as in the domain of private supply. Water was the first. When the sanitary movement began in Britain in the 1840s, waterworks throughout the North Atlantic economy were virtually all private, profit-making undertakings. Under the prod of epidemic and contagion, however, city governments began to invest more and more heavily in public systems of water supply. From simple piping operations, the cities' expanding populations pushed city governments on to the construction of widely flung systems of reservoirs, aqueducts, mains, and filtration plants. By the end of the century, water supply had grown into an immense public economic undertaking. While the average capitalization of Britain's fifty largest industrial firms in 1905 was 4.4 million pounds, Birmingham's water system was capitalized at close to 8 million pounds and London's new Metropolitan Water Board at almost 47 million pounds.[5] Even by the sparest, night-watchman conception of public safety, the interdependencies of great city living could be an engine of collectivism on a startling scale.

But if a city could and should sell water to ensure the adequacy and purity that private water companies failed to maintain, what else should it supply? Should it light its streets for the safety of its inhabitants, build parks and playgrounds for their bodily health and recuperation, build schools and libraries to protect against popular ignorance, rebellion, and misrule? Should it own the city's cemeteries and slaughterhouses to guard their neighbors' health? Should it own public baths, when, as Jane Addams claimed in 1892, there were not more than three bathtubs within the one-third square mile surrounding Hull House? Or milk pasteurization stations and milk depots, to make sure infants' milk was not watered? Or hospitals and outpatient dispensaries?[6] Should it sweep the streets and cart away the city's daily mass of refuse? Should it condemn dwellings unfit for habitation, and, once these were pulled down, erect new, decently built, sanitarily sound housing in their place? Should it construct streetcar lines to allow its unhealthily concentrated populations, jammed by necessity within walking distance of their place of work, to disperse to healthier, suburban areas? What should a city regulate? What should it trust to the market's incentives? What should it franchise? What should it own and operate? The unplanned collectivism of city life forced all these issues, unhinged older assumptions, and blurred the lines between private and public obligations.

"Functional expansion" of city governments' tasks is the sociological term for the phenomenon, but this figure of speech should not mislead. Wherever municipal authorities turned, their added tasks brought them directly into conflict with established private entrepreneurs. None of the new domains of municipal supply was unoccupied. Mid-nineteenth-century cities swarmed with commercial water suppliers, carters, private refuse haulers, landlords and property investors, sellers of watered milk, jerry-builders, streetcar companies, street sweeping contractors, franchise holders of all sorts, and purchasable city officials who, in selling the city's commercial possibilities, collaborated in its commodification. Even sewage brought cities up against a swarm of commercial operators large and small who dealt for profit in the city's excrement: cesspool drainers, sewage farmers, manure dealers, or the nightly army of women who, for a pittance, toted the contents of well-to-do Berliners' chamber pots to the River Spree. Municipalization, even of the most menial necessities of urban living, entailed no simple expansion of services. When cities assumed the tasks of supply, they cut into the business of private suppliers.

Municipalization meant, in short, a diminution of the market, a transformation of goods from private to public. On the one side lay goods and services priced by market rules and open to private entrepreneurial initiative; on the other, public goods, socially priced if directly priced at all. In time, the middle ground was to be filled by an array of hybrids that blurred the early distinction: quasi-private goods, commercially initiated but publicly regulated, or quasi-public goods, publicly specified but commercially supplied. But for turn-of-the-century urban progressives, the choice of what lay in and outside the market's realm was stark and politically momentous. Though their opponents sometimes branded them "collectivists," the progressives did not collectivize great city life. That was the accomplishment of the city's market makers in goods and labor, its entrepreneurs and (by the century's end) its monopolists. The progressives' project was different: to try to realize the implicit collectivism of the city on conscious and public lines.

Broad powers were not new to the cities of the Atlantic world. The social and economic competence of medieval and early modern cities had been large and untheoretical. Municipal corporations lodged the sick and provided for the poor; owned markets, docks, and common land; regulated prices and wages; warded the streets; and meted out justice. Into the modern era, remnants of these powers endured in an occasional public market, city hospital, poor farm, or city stone quarry. But challenged from without by the centralizing appetites of the nation-states, and hollowed out from within by demands for an ever-widening sphere for entrepreneurial liberty, the economic functions of cities slowly shrank down to a much more limited compass.

In the middle third of the nineteenth century, at the height of urban privatization, the range of municipal action varied considerably across the North Atlantic economy, but the trend of policies and ideas was general. When the great cities' needs for water, sanitation, light, and transportation began to outrun the competence of traditional household technologies, those who took up the slack everywhere were private venture capitalists. Water, when it did not come from private wells in the private-utility city, flowed through the pipes of commercial suppliers; garbage and refuse collection was the terrain of small entrepreneurs; gas for street lighting was purchased from private gasworks; electricity, when it entered the cities from the Edison and Siemens patent factories in the 1880s, was big business from the very outset; transportation was the work of myriad commercial carters and porters, cab and omnibus drivers, streetcar and steam railroad companies.[7]

Between urban consumers and the cities' commercial suppliers, however, friction was endemic. Growing at every edge, cities were eager for technological improvements and expanded services. Having sunk their capital into a piping system or a horse-drawn street railway line, private investors in city services wanted above all to nurse their existing investments for all the return they would yield. Private water suppliers, reluctant to undertake expensive investments in reservoirs, aqueducts, or cleaner water sources, clashed repeatedly with city councils over the adequacy and quality of supply. London, where as late as 1899 the city's private water companies treated the city to regular summer water famines, was a particularly notorious example.[8] City councils and private gas companies quarreled over prices and revenues. In a scenario replayed from Toronto and New York to Glasgow, Munich, and Cologne, city councils and the private holders of streetcar franchises locked horns over the commercial companies' unwillingness to extend lines and service beyond the city's dense, inner core, where returns on invested capital were highest.

Nothing promoted capital's productivity more effectively than a monopoly position. To secure a monopoly, private utility investors moved with a daring that their reluctance to invest in expensive technological improvements belied. Where the scale of investment was particularly high, as in gas and streetcar systems, investors labored with special zeal to forestall the organization of rival enterprises—purchasing and pocketing franchises they had no intention of fulfilling, setting one of government's several hands against the other, bribing public officials, or simply buying up competitors faster than advocates of competition could create a market. In these regards, the adjective "natural" in the "natural monopoly" arguments of the insurgent economists was misleading. Commercial utility companies *made* their monopolies with all the financial and political resources at their disposal and reaped from them profits as handsome as the late nineteenth century offered.[9]

Structural conflicts over prices, profits, and supply formed one part of the background to late-nineteenth-century utility politics; the other was the deeply set aversion of urban property owners to increased taxation. So long as the city was understood as an unnatural tax incubus—an expense to be minimized in the budgets of its private, individual constituents—pressures toward public parsimony were built into urban politics. Everywhere proposals for new public investments met contest and delay. The foremost sanitarian of the era, Edwin Chadwick, was in perpetual political trouble in his own England; his landmark Public Health Act of 1848 operated for only six years before Chadwick's critics crippled it with amendments and exiled Chadwick, for good, from public office. Between 1873, when cholera, sweeping through Hamburg, made clear the inadequacy of that city's water supply, and 1890, when the city council finally agreed to invest in water filtration technology, lay, as Richard Evans has shown, years of bureaucratic footdragging and the dogged resistance of the city's Property Owners Association. The private-utility city was sustained not only by the interests of its commercial suppliers but also by a powerful, tax-averse ideology.[10]

The first breaks in this pattern came with water and sewage. Spurred by the pioneering English sanitarians, English municipal authorities took the lead in the 1850s in the conversion of water from a private to a public good, gradually buying out their commercial waterworks and investing in new systems of city-administered supply. By 1879, almost half of England's urban sanitary areas were supplied with public water; by 1903, on the eve of London's conversion to public water supply, public investments in water supply outweighed private investment almost two to one.[11] In themselves, water mains for city fountains and hydrants did not put water directly into the dwellings of most urban folk. Public bathhouses for the working class came closer. Made a permissible expense for English cities in an act of 1846, there were thirteen municipal bathhouses in London eight years later; by the 1890s, the biggest of them boasted laundries, cafés, and public lecture halls in addition to shower baths and swimming pools.[12]

But more plentiful and cleaner city water did not, paradoxically, produce more health. As water poured into cesspools, vaults, and privies, collecting in pools and the overtaxed creeks and ravines that passed for sewers, the undrained, overwatered late-nineteenth-century city became its own environmental hazard. On the heels of public water then came, against taxpayer resistance, still greater investments in drains and sewers—not only sewers to flush the cities' streets of slops and horse droppings (like the big, tourist-visited sewers of Napoleon III's Paris) but also, through one of Chadwick's technological breakthroughs, water-flushed sanitary sewage systems that, linked to household "water closets," slowly began to drive the night-soil haulers and cesspool emptiers out of business.[13]

The chain of interlinked events that led from public water to public sewerage investments, and then (when drains still did not bring health) to even more distant water supplies and new filtration techniques, was one of several paths down which ambitious city governments found themselves propelled toward wider spheres of action. Some of the linkages were technological, as in the ever-moving front of the battle with waterborne disease. Some were organizational and financial, as administrative competence acquired in a city waterworks or city gas lighting plant tempted city councils to look outward to new sources of action or revenue. Another dynamic of expanding supply flew on the wings of metaphor, as the sanitary battle against the epidemiological miasma of the undrained city metamorphosed into a campaign against the moral and social "miasma" of the city's slums and cheap lodging districts.[14] Histrionic often enough, and cruel to those shoved aside in the slum clearance campaigns or hustled out into the night by tenement inspectors ticketing for overcrowded sleeping rooms, the campaign against the slums and "rookeries" represented, nonetheless, the beginnings of a broader conception of urban social costs. Once the boundaries of the city enterprise began to move outward, all these factors formed powerful accelerators.

The most celebrated late-nineteenth-century illustration of municipal enterprise was Joseph Chamberlain's Birmingham. Almost none of the steps the English city took in the 1870s was in itself new. It was Chamberlain's grasp of the potential interrelations between the new fields of municipal enterprise, his zeal to do everything at once, and the shrewdness of his public investments that made Birmingham a byword for late-nineteenth-century civic activism. Wreathed in the smoke of its factories and workshops, as popular prints of the period depict it, Birmingham was hardly a model city when Chamberlain assumed the mayor's seat in 1873. Its death rate was said to be the highest of any great city on the island, its commercially piped water was inadequately supplied, its sewers were badly overtaxed, and its city council, frightened by the impending cost of repairs, was hunkered down on the maxim of public frugality.[15]

Chamberlain, a machined-goods manufacturer accustomed to larger spheres of action than the small businessmen and shopkeepers who had long dominated Birmingham's city council, proposed to break the impasse over sewage, health, and taxes by pushing the city into direct utility supply. Birmingham's commercial gas suppliers, who had been fattening on the easy terms of their franchise, were his first target. Within a year, the city had bought them out and was plowing the profits from its commercial gas sales into civic improvements. From that beginning, the rest quickly followed. With the income secured from the municipalization of gas supply, the city purchased and expanded Birmingham's waterworks and began to invest in overdue sewage and sanitary improvements. Seizing on an act permitting public condemnation of unsanitary dwellings, Chamberlain led the city into an ambitious reconstruction of city land values. Forty-three acres of cheap housing near the city's core were torn down, their residents scattered, and a brassy new commercial street was run through in their place, paid for by profits on the resale of abutting land to commercial building investors. By 1890, Chamberlain himself having moved on to national politics, Birmingham boasted not only of its public gas revenues and the air of prosperity on the new Corporation Street, but also of new public baths, a public art school and art museum, a new set of city parks, model sewers and a new city sewage farm, and one of Britain's most expensive city halls, wreathed in mosaics and allegorical statuary: a monument to Birmingham's commercial "civicism."[16]

Aggressive, commercial civic-mindedness was the hallmark of Birmingham's municipal revival, and it went together with a quiet ratcheting upward of power in the city. By the end of the 1870s the tax-conscious shopkeepers had lost their hold on Birmingham's city council to wealthier men like Chamberlain himself, accustomed to bolder capital investments. Manufacturers stocked the city's gas and improvements committees where they kept a sharp eye on the city's commercial advantages. Where there were no clear civic profits to be made, their interest fell off sharply. Against Birmingham's block upon block of "back-to-back" working-class housing, the city council made little headway; as late as 1900, almost a quarter of the city's dwellings were still without sanitary sewer connections. Little wonder, then, that the radical economist R. H. Tawney should dismiss Chamberlain-style "municipal trading" (as municipal assumption of income-producing activities was officially known) as a project by and for its business backers: "Clearly there are no germs of a revolution here."[17]

But in a less dramatic key, there were. Chamberlain himself bragged that the city had broken out of "pedantic adherence to the supposedly fixed principles of political economy" that set off, in rigid opposition, the realm of market action and the boundaries of legitimate public work.[18] From a kind of limited watch-and-ward association of the city's property holders, the city had been transformed into a major economic enterprise. Birmingham's citizen-capitalists had hardly set out to alter class relations in the city; the slums, which regrouped beyond Corporation Street, endured. Birmingham's political lesson worked on a different plane: that a city might itself successfully extract public returns from the markets its presence created.

By the turn of the century one could find Birminghams, in this sense, across most of the North Atlantic economy. The great exception was France, where cities, kept under extremely tight rein by state officials and without the independent capacity to contract debts, were all but precluded from experiments in municipal ownership. But in England, Scotland, and Germany, the decades on either side of the turn of the century were marked by an extraordinary efflorescence of municipal enterprises.[19]

By the nineties Birmingham's lead in municipal undertakings had been usurped by Glasgow, the great, gray, ship- and machinery-making economic capital of industrial Scotland. Public health called the tune in Glasgow more than public profits. After repeated quarrels with commercial gas suppliers over adequacy of service, the city had municipalized the city's gas supply in 1869, five years before Birmingham; where Birmingham's city council kept gas charges high and poured the profits into the city treasury, Glasgow cut gas prices in half and loaned out free gas stoves to ease the city's pall of coal smoke and encourage more hygienic cooking. Heir to the appallingly overcrowded, dark, stone tenements that were urban Scotland's curse, Glasgow city authorities not only tore down slum housing but also (in a move Birmingham's city councillors resisted) began to build public replacement housing in its stead. When electricity-generating and telephonic technology came to Scotland, the city embarked on the municipal supply of both.[20]

It was streetcars, however, that made Glasgow's municipal ambitions world famous. Although several cities in Britain owned their own underlying track system, no other city of comparable size had undertaken a city-owned street railway system. In 1894, out of patience with the private franchiser's refusal to expand service beyond Glasgow's profitable inner core and determined to find means to disperse its overcrowded inner-city population, the city undertook to run the cars itself. The private franchiser, retreating to omnibuses, and the city streetcar committee ran in head-to-head competition for months, until the private company retired in defeat.

German cities, although they were more broadly empowered than English or Scottish cities, had begun the nineteenth century far behind them with regard to public health. Berlin was notoriously filthy; as late as 1872, Chadwick was certain that you could identify traveling Berliners by the distinctive stench clinging to their clothing. Hamburg excepted, modern water and sewer works did not come to the major German cities until the 1870s. Over the next decades, however, municipal investments in water, sanitation, and gas supply began to rise sharply throughout the German empire—fueled by new commercial and industrial wealth and intercity rivalry. By 1889, half the gasworks in the German empire were municipally owned; a decade later, encouraged by these results, German cities were moving aggressively into the purchase of electrical power plants at a pace unmatched in Europe.[21] In the areas where commercial companies held the field (as in the streetcars) German city officials began driving harder and more precise bargains. The agreement the Berlin authorities reached with the city's franchised streetcar operator in the late 1890s prescribed not only payment of a percentage of the gross passenger receipts to the city and technical improvements at the city's direction but also maximum hours for streetcar employees, maximum fares, and the provision of special, cheap, wage earners' tickets.[22] Visitors to turn-of-the-century Berlin marveled at the transformation of the technically deficient and "execrably" dirty city of the past into a model of public cleanliness and efficiency—the home "*par excellence*" of "the modern application of sanitary science to public administration," as the *American Monthly Review of Reviews* put it.[23]

As in Britain, however, the showcase cities were the smaller ones, farther away from the complex pressures of court and imperial politics. What Birmingham and Glasgow were to the United Kingdom, Frankfurt and Düsseldorf were to Germany. Under Mayor Franz Adickes between 1891 and 1912, Frankfurt embarked on a construction program of broad new streets and parks; a modern sewage plant and incinerator; city baths, lavatories, and swimming pools; and a new civic university set on a new, Vienna-style Ringstrasse. On the city's eastern rim, it launched an ambitious revenue-producing city harbor on the Main, surrounded by a city-platted district of factories and workers' housing. It established a city-run employment bureau that was widely imitated in Germany. It bought out its streetcar franchisers, expanded service with cheap fares for wage earners, and constructed a city-owned electrical plant to facilitate electrification of the system. To ease the housing pressures on the old city, it undertook an aggressive suburban annexation policy, extended city loans to philanthropic associations for the construction of peripheral low-cost housing along the new city streetcar lines, and developed the first city zoning ordinance in Germany. Düsseldorf was a close rival, with its big, scientifically planned, city-owned harbor; city mortgage and savings banks; labor exchange and arbitration courts; and city-owned pawn shops, hospitals and sanitaria, cemeteries, slaughterhouse, public reading rooms, theater, and symphony orchestra. Frederic Howe, who studied the city closely, was sure that Düsseldorf "owns more things and does more things for its people" than any city in the world.[24]

"Municipal socialism," Chamberlain called the phenomenon approvingly in 1891, when the term "socialism" carried its broadest meaning in the English-speaking world. If this was socialism, however, it was the socialism of the business classes. Virtually everywhere, as in Birmingham, the lead in the expansion of city enterprises was taken by local businessmen. Though labor union officials were not uncommon on British city councils, uncontested elections, very long tenure in office, and long, unpaid, midday meetings all severely limited the influence even of the labor aristocracy of skill and property. Glasgow's city council did not seat its first bloc of labor representatives until 1898. A small minority in a structure that went a long way toward isolating British city governments from popular politics, labor councillors never called the tune for prewar municipal "socialism."[25]

As for the working-class electorate, Albert Shaw's conclusion in the mid-1890s that "the slums do not vote" in Britain was not precisely true. The Fabian Society's Graham Wallas, running for the London school board in 1894, was deeply chagrined in the pollings' last hour to see the kinds of voters his canvassers had roped in, men and women "with broken straw hats, pallid faces, and untidy hair, . . . dazed and bewildered, having been snatched away in carriages or motors from the making of match-boxes, or button-holes, or cheap furniture, or from the public house, or, since it was a Saturday evening, from bed. Most of them seemed to be trying, in the unfamiliar surroundings, to be sure of the name for which, as they had been reminded at the door, they were to vote." But hemmed in by residency restrictions and the requirement that one's taxes be paid up at election time, the slums did not vote in great numbers. Experts thought the cumulative effect of such restrictions was to eliminate between 25 percent and 40 percent of adult men from the cities' suffrage rolls. Politically the cities belonged to the business classes, their new public economic enterprises included.[26]

In Germany, the structures of exclusion stood still higher and firmer. Municipal suffrage requirements varied from state to state in imperial Germany, but in none did city politics approach even the imperfect state of British municipal democratization. The key was a set of extremely high property hurdles. In Hamburg in 1904, only 29 percent of the those eligible to vote in Reichstag elections had the necessary property to vote for the local city council; in Frankfurt by 1914, even after inflation had eroded the property bar, no more than 50 percent qualified. Throughout the Prussian heart of the empire, half the seats on city councils were reserved for house owners. Compounding the matter in Prussia was a three-class voting rule in municipal elections. Structuring of the electorate under the three-class system began with the division of the tax roll into three parts. Starting from the highest tax contributor and moving downward, those who together paid the first third of the city's taxes were grouped in the first class of city voters; those who paid the second third belonged to the second class, the rest to the third class. To each class went the right to elect one-third of the city council. The result was an extraordinary concentration of plutocratic power at the top, and a highly effective barrier to popular pressure from the bottom. In Berlin, first- and second-class voters together constituted just 3 percent of the city electorate. In Essen in the early 1890s, Albert Shaw watched the one first-class voter to appear at the polls single-handedly elect a third of the city council.[27]

Despite these odds, the Social Democrats made considerable inroads into German city politics in the decade before the First World War. In Frankfurt in 1912 they held one-third of the city council seats, and in Berlin they had almost as large a share. Structurally, however, there were powerful limits to their influence on policy. By the last quarter of the nineteenth century, German city administration rested in the hands of an extraordinarily strong, professional bureaucracy. University trained, life-tenured *Oberbürgermeister*, like Düsseldorf's Wilhelm Marx and Frankfurt's Franz Adickes, who had worked their up from a public law or economics degree through directorships of city departments, magistracies, and mayors' seats in smaller towns, played a leading role in German city politics—a buffer against sheer wealth and sheer numbers alike. As for the extracouncil committees charged with oversight of poor relief, education, and the like, their seats went overwhelmingly to business and professional men. German cities, in short, were in the hands of persons very like the businessmen who dominated British city governments—though with a stronger technical and administrative element.[28]

The great cities' working-class dwellers were of a deeply mixed mind about business-style municipal trading. Years of mistrust accumulated between city authorities and the cities' laboring folk did not incline local working-class majorities to fall unthinkingly into step with the cities' new projects. For most city dwellers in the late nineteenth and early twentieth centuries, as Hamish Fraser writes of Glasgow, city government was a stern and distant presence.

> The local state was the police, which in a city like Glasgow had, because of largely Highland recruitment, some of the characteristics of an alien, occupying force. The local state was the magistrate in the burgh courts handing out sentences to the drunk and disorderly, to the vagrant, to the dilatory ratepayer, and issuing warrants for the evictions of tenants. The local state was the sanitary officials raiding the ticketed houses between midnight and five in the morning in a hopeless effort to curb overcrowding or reprimanding tenants for failing to keep clean the common stairs and closets . . . The local state was the new town hall, undoubtedly magnificent but on land gained at the cost of clearing the homes of the poor. The local state was the parochial board which treated the poor, in need or in sick-

> ness, with a parsimonious disregard for basic needs . . . The local state was the belt-happy teacher or the truancy officer of the school board that made education compulsory but not free. None of these manifestations of urban authority was likely to endear it to the many of the working class.[29]

To this general animus, Marxian socialists added still greater mistrust. Compared with the grand project of appropriating the means of production from the bourgeoisie, seizure of a waterworks here or a sewer line there could not but seem pitifully inadequate. Not until 1893 did the German Social Democratic Party drop its ban on party participation in city elections. The next decade brought a flurry of intense debate over municipal issues within the party, culminating in 1904 in a program of municipal demands; but its centerpiece was not utility politics but democratization and more equitable taxation. Once elected to city councils, socialists pushed hardest for traditional labor issues: model working conditions for city employees, work relief for the unemployed, labor courts to adjudicate wage earners' grievances, and more generous relief for the poor.[30] In France, where the elections of 1896 swept socialist majorities into some 150 municipal councils, the goals of working-class socialism came closer to home: work relief for the out-of-work, funds for the assistance of striking workers' families, homes for workers injured in the course of their trade, more generous and less humiliating assistance to the poor, and school meals and day nurseries for poor children. This was a politics of the cooperative, social family rather than the politics of public enterprise.[31] Between the businessmen's "municipal trading" and the workers' "municipal socialism" stretched a chasm in expectations.

But the idea of the city's owning its own infrastructure, extending outward its goods and even its heavy-handed services, was protean enough in its political implications that it was not surprising that the lines of class should on occasion blur. The amorphousness of the municipalization idea and the anticommercial animus within its business ethos gave municipal ownership an appeal broad enough to cross the normally segmented boundaries of city life. In this lay the significance of London "Progressivism"—during its heyday in the 1890s the most closely watched experiment in municipal politics in the North Atlantic economy.

European's largest urban agglomeration, late-nineteenth-century London was, politically, hardly a city at all. Lacking any effective citywide government until 1889, public authority devolved on a maze of subdivided and overlapping bodies. London's police force was directed by the central government's Home Office; responsibility for streets and local sanitation was parceled out to local vestry boards; large-scale public works was the business of an appointed Metropolitan Board of Works.[32] London's commercial interests profited heavily from this fragmentation of public authority. London was one of the last of the great cities in Britain, almost thirty years after Birmingham, to take water supply into its own hands. In the city of 1889, the key utilities—transport, gas, electricity, and water—were all private undertakings.

When, in that year, Parliament authorized the formation of London's first citywide, elected governing body—the London County Council (LCC)—long-buried political ambitions rose quickly to the surface. The council's Progressive majority was essentially a Liberal Party association under another name; more than half the Progressive council members were business and professional men. But the Progressive councillors also included a handful of women and, by 1892, a radical backbench of socialists and workingmen. At the labor minority's head was John Burns, leader of the London dockers' great strike victory of 1889, who had burst into London politics only a few years before, haranguing crowds of unemployed workers under a flaming red flag. The Fabian Society, still new and casting about for a program and political venue, sent a half dozen members to the council in 1892, including Sidney Webb.[33]

Determined to follow in the steps of the northern municipalizers, the Progressive majority quickly voted to municipalize London's water supply, gasworks, electric supply, docks, and streetcars. Mimicking Birmingham with its Corporation Street, the council cut its own brand-new commercial street through a region of cheap shops and houses at Kingsway. Where the Metropolitan Board of Works had razed slums, leaving the resettlement to private builders and philanthropic housing associations, the council built and leased some of the most innovative working-class housing in prewar Europe. It built pocket parks in the city's working-class boroughs, complete with bandstands and free concerts for the moral elevation and uplift of the people—staging 1,200 summer concerts in the 1907 season alone. It invested in trade and technical education. Its staff inspected everything from music hall lyrics to smoke nuisances. Parliament, which never lifted its thumb far from London's administration, stymied the Progressives' ambitions for gas, electricity, and dock management, and shunted water supply off to an independent public body. But by 1905 there were city-operated tramcars buzzing down London's streets and city steam ferries—their "LCC" logo painted so boldly that no one could mistake it—plying the Thames.

For Burns and the labor minority, the LCC's crowning achievement was to organize its own public works force, bypassing the "rings" of small contractors who had traditionally bid, often in collusion, on city work. Burns had chosen a seat the Drainage Committee in 1889 on the grounds that it employed more city workers than any other. When the decision to circumvent the construction contractors was made, he thought it "the biggest thing yet done for Collectivism." With as many as 3,000 city construction employees at work, Burns's was no idle notion; together with a small army of clerks, inspectors, transport workers, and schoolteachers, they made the LCC the city's single largest employer at the turn of the century.[34]

Where Burns pushed the issue of labor standards, the Fabians extended the municipalization idea to a still broader array of goods and services. One by one, they added to the list of candidates for municipalization: city-owned bakeries and slaughterhouses; municipally issued fire insurance; and outright municipalization of milk distribution, markets, hospitals, and the liquor trade.[35] Around municipal trading, the LCC radicals wove a utopian aura of possibilities. With Sidney Webb talking of providing streetcars as free as public libraries, with John Burns proposing to organize the docks as a great labor collective and to drive the sweatshops out of business with municipal clothing factories, and with radicals hinting of widening the sphere of public enterprise, from the city outward, until the economy itself should be socialized, the crowded political tent of municipal ownership had grown broad indeed.

The municipal trading idea could not be radicalized indefinitely, however, without accumulating formidable enemies. By 1900, after a decade of London Progressivism, opponents were beginning to find the means of conservative counterorganization. The antimunicipalization revolt took a multitude of organizational forms—the Association for the Protection of Property Owners, the Middle Class Defence Association, the Liberty and Property Defence League—and had a wealth of financial resources, not the least of which was heavy support from the commercial electric utility companies. Together these groups engineered parliamentary investigations of municipal trading in 1900 and 1903. Pointing with alarm to the rising tax rates and debt levels in the nation's cities, they seized on every loose thread in the talk of "municipal socialism" and did their best to split off the small-propertied, middle-class ratepayer from the municipal trading alliance.[36]

Class was the conservatives' card. "Ratepayers! It's Your Money *WE* Want," a cartoon municipal socialist declared in a Conservative election poster in 1907. With his stubby, working-class finger thrust out toward the public, jaw unshaved, and top hat askew, the figure was the conservatives' very image of labor-based soak-the-middle-class politics. Sidney Webb had satirized the conservative view years before:

> The Individualist City Councillor will walk along the municipal pavement, lit by municipal gas and cleansed by municipal brooms with municipal water, and seeing by the municipal clock in the municipal market, that he is too early to meet his children coming from the municipal school hard by the county lunatic asylum and municipal hospital, will use the national telegraph system to tell them not to walk through the municipal park but to come by the municipal tramway, to meet him in the municipal reading room, by the municipal art gallery, museum and library, where he intends to consult some of the national publications in order prepare his next speech in the municipal town-hall . . . "Socialism, sir," he will say, "don't waste the time of a practical man by your fantastic absurdities. Self-help, sir, individual self-help, that's what's made our city what it is."

In 1907, the foes of municipal trading swept the Progressives out of LCC control. With great fanfare, their Conservative successors abolished direct public construction work, brought the contractors back in to bid on city construction jobs, and sold off the steam ferries.[37]

Like most administrative revolutions, the revolution in municipal services fell short of its ambitions. London's patchwork of public and private operations endured; not until the 1940s would the city's gasworks finally fall into public hands. The politics of municipal supply was always to hang on relatively narrow balances. But for the all the controversies and reverses, a major shift in the supply of city services had been accomplished. By the eve of the First World War, more than 80 percent of the water sold in the United Kingdom, some 60 percent of the electricity, and 37 percent of the gas was municipally supplied; 80 percent of streetcar riders rode on city-owned tramways. In Germany the trend toward municipal utility supply was equally unmistakable. In 1908 and 1909, when the controversy over municipal trading was at its height in the United States, Frederic Howe surveyed the extent of municipal operations in the fifty largest cities in Germany and Great Britain.[38] Some of those that reported possessing gas or electricity plants produced power only for their own street lighting or streetcars; some owned their streetcar systems but leased them out to private operators. But the results were telling, nonetheless:

Cities owning their own:	*No. in Germany*	*No. in Great Britain*
Water supply	48	39
Gas supply	50	21
Electricity supply	42	44
Streetcars	23	42
Public baths	48	49
Markets	50	44
Slaughterhouses	43	23

Investing boldly in public works, urban business-class progressives had engineered a major shift in the line between city and private enterprise. They had established for turn-of-the-century cities a new set of collective tasks, which, spinning out from concerns with public health, defied determinate limits. Long before the "welfare state" was more than a cloud on the sky of the nation-state, they began to elaborate a network of locally administered public services and socially priced goods. They had, however tentatively, experimented with cross-class political alliances. To American progressives, their work could not but be a goad and a model.

Cities on a Hill

Swept up in the common forces of the North Atlantic economy, the cities of the United States had been no exception to the larger urban patterns of the nineteenth century. There, too, the city's public, administrative core was surrounded by a broad periphery of contract, franchise, and purchase; there, too, the boundary between public and commercial supply was contested and constantly moving. As economic actors, American city governments had considerable historical experience. With a booster's zeal for the assets that might alchemize a country crossroads into another Cincinnati or Chicago, nineteenth-century American city governments had invested heavily, often well past the point of financial prudence, in transportation facilities—not only in public roads and bridges but in commercial and mixed public-private transportation ventures as well. In Georgia between 1831 and 1860, half the capital for railroad investment came from local and state governments; Pennsylvania local governments in the 1840s and 1850s sank some fourteen million dollars in railroad company stocks, Philadelphia itself investing almost ten million dollars. Cincinnati owned outright a city rail line to its southern markets.[39]

In the wake of the depression of the 1870s, when the bottom fell out of many of these investments, several states moved to erect higher hurdles to local debt contraction, but none put an iron ring around a city's range of potential action. American municipal reformers may have envied the relative fiscal autonomy of German cities, but their own constitutional capacity was far broader than that of French city governments. To the close and continuing authority of the English central authorities over local policy decisions and investments, or the Prussian monopolization of local police powers in the hands of central state administrators, there were no American counterparts.

Neither tradition nor legal capacity precluded movement, in step with European cities, into the new urban technologies. Following the British lead, late-nineteenth-century American cities invested heavily in public water and sewer facilities. Of the thirty-eight great cities in turn-of-the-century America, all but eight owned their own waterworks—a fraction little different from Britain's. All but two—Baltimore, which still limped along with cesspools, and New Orleans, where the city sewers were a private, commercial business—possessed modern, publicly constructed sewers.[40]

Beyond water and sewer operations, national patterns in public investment began to diverge more sharply. European visitors to the United States cursed the wretched state of American city streets. Mile upon mile they ran, through mires of mud and refuse and sinkholes of rotting wooden paving blocks—though in fairness to the urban governments authorities that struggled to grade and pave and clean the streets of each day's new mountain of manure and garbage, it must be acknowledged that there were many more miles of urban streets in the United States than in the more compactly settled cities of Europe. In other public investments, however, American cities led the world. Into public schools, overcrowded and understaffed though they often were, late-nineteenth-century American cities poured huge resources of wealth. Parks, beginning with the laying out of New York City's Central Park in the late 1850s, were yet another public triumph in the United States; they drew a stream of European admirers, the London County Council's parks committee's chair among them. By the end of the century, American cities were aggressively buying up large rings of surrounding parkland—carriage parks, to be sure, green, urban lungs far more heavily used by the better off than the poor, but a major investment in public amenities nonetheless. Public city playgrounds were an American social invention. When the municipalization movement began to gather steam in Europe, then, American cities were no strangers to large-scale undertakings.[41]

From the first, there were Americans who followed the growth abroad of city-owned services with closely informed interest. Many were veterans of the German university connection. Richard Ely, interested since his student years in German municipal administration, came back from a swing through urban Germany and Britain in the late 1880s to advocate a wide-ranging program of municipal services. Joining European practice with Henry C. Adams's "natural" monopoly arguments, Ely was soon calling for outright municipalization of city utilities across a very broad front.[42] In Philadelphia in the mid-1880s, Edmund J. James, armed with the balance sheet of German and British municipal gas operations, had thrown himself into the fight to wrest the city's gasworks back into direct public management. Later, as streetcars came into the eye of American urban politics, James fired off from Paris and Berlin a barrage of model franchise arrangements.[43]

The first American systematically to cultivate the Atlantic connection in progressive municipal politics, though he himself had not studied in Germany, was one of Ely's students, Albert Shaw. Coming as a young Iowa journalist to graduate study at Johns Hopkins in the early 1880s, Shaw had been assigned by Ely to write about communitarian socialism and, later, midwestern cooperatives. From Baltimore he returned to the Midwest and the day-to-day politics of franchise, sanitation, and city governance as an editorial writer for the *Minneapolis Tribune.* Out of patience with the "laissez-faire bugbear," as he derided it, he signed on with the American Economic Association as an early lay member. When one of his undergraduate teachers, Jesse Macy, urged Shaw to join him on a ramble through Britain, "to go through the country notebook in hand and take a sort of photograph of the present political and social conditions of England," he had demurred. But a year later, in 1888, pulled by the tide that tugged at all of Ely's pupils, he set off on his own sociological tour of Britain and the Continent. The trip introduced Shaw to the British journalist and reformer William T. Stead, who within two years tapped Shaw to become editor of an American edition of Stead's *Review of Reviews* and, in that capacity, despite the strains between the flamboyant Stead and his much more cautious American partner, to serve as a conduit between British and American reform journalism. In the shorter run, Shaw came back fired with the enthusiasms of a municipal reformer. Three more trips ensued in quick succession, followed by a stream of newspaper and magazine pieces that culminated in 1895 in his two-volume *Municipal Government in Great Britain* and *Municipal Government in Continental Europe*.[44]

Shaw approached European cities with the instincts of a public health reformer, an enormous appetite for facts, and a certain willingness to suspend his doubts. "It is a flattering picture that I draw," he wrote to Stead on the eve of his books' publication; "but I hold solidly to the doctrine that my task in all these matters is not to find out the faults of foreign people and foreign systems, but to find out their merits in order that we may profit by their wisdom and be stimulated by their good performances."[45] In the classic questions of municipal political science—the checks and balances of power, the limits and distribution of responsibilities, all the questions of constitutional political mechanics that since Madison's day had occupied so much of American political attention—Shaw was not fundamentally interested. For its businesslike straightforwardness and simplicity, British town governance, in which committees of elected councillors ran the city with a minimum of internal structural checks and balances, struck his sympathy strongly. But the "mechanism of municipal government is a secondary matter." Altogether too much attention in the United States, Shaw objected, "has been devoted to the structure and mechanism, and, so far as the cities are concerned, they keep changing it perpetually. They are forever overhauling, repairing, or reconstructing the house, without seeming to have many attractive or inspiring uses for which they are eager to make the house ready."[46]

Where the American cities tied themselves in knots of theory, most European cities lived straightforwardly in the realm of praxis. In the most practical, businesslike way, "without either accepting or rejecting any theory as to the proper functions of the state or the municipal corporation," Shaw wrote approvingly, picking the Chamberlainite language out of the air, European cities were adding function upon function for their citizens' well-being. Whether it was the new Ringstrasse in Vienna, the great sewers in Paris, municipal gas and streetcars in Glasgow, slum clearance and rehousing in London, sanitary science in Berlin, or the broad attentiveness of German cities to the general welfare, their "municipal collectivism" turned straightforwardly on the "welfare" of their citizens and the tasks of "municipal housekeeping."[47]

It was essential to the parallels Shaw was intent on driving home that city conditions on both sides of the Atlantic were "similar in all their essential characteristics." The best in Europe, notwithstanding the aesthetic tourists' fascination with the past, was new.

> Fifty years ago [in England] there were no underground sewers; there were no public water supplies; there was no street lighting worthy of the name; there were no street railways nor other systems of municipal transit beyond a few omnibuses and carriages; there were no well-paved streets; there was no system of street cleansing; there were no municipal arrangements for domestic scavenging or the disposition of the waste accumulations of overcrowded towns; there were no building regulations which protected the working classes against overcrowding under horribly unsanitary conditions; there were no measures for the prevention of the spread of epidemic diseases; there were no public fire departments; there was no public system of education; there was no municipal control of the liquor traffic or of other evils which are now subject to strict municipal supervision and control; there were practically no such things as municipal parks or playgrounds; there were, of course, no public libraries and reading-rooms; infinitely farther from any man's conception were free public baths or municipal laundries for the tenement districts—or any one of a dozen other kinds of municipal provision for the health, comfort, and protection of urban populations that are now made a part of the marvelously expanded municipal activity of great and prosperous British communities.

The key to the success of the European cities was their possession of precisely the traits Americans so often imagined as peculiarly their own: practicality, efficiency, ambition, modernity.[48]

Shaw's resolution of urban political science into pure action did not land on altogether sympathetic ears. Since the floodgates had been thrown open to adult male suffrage in the 1820s and 1830s, generations of "good government" urban reformers had struggled to check, balance, dilute, or negate the potential for popular abuses of power in the American city. The editors of the *Century*, though they gave Shaw a prominent forum in the early 1890s, never fully understood his point. Fighting hard for civil service reform, they construed Shaw to mean that the secret to the success of a government like Glasgow's was its exclusion of the floating voters and its delegation of city affairs to the businesslike management of businessmen. Harry Pratt Judson, reviewing Shaw's *Municipal Government in Great Britain,* concluded that the gulf between British business-class rule and American popular governance was so vast as to vitiate any comparison at all: "The question whether it is or not good policy for the community to undertake further duties for the general welfare, is simply not a question at all under existing [American] conditions. It is a waste of time to discuss it." Corruption, the stink of Tammany Hall and of a hundred lesser party machines, dogged discussions of municipal functions in the United States from the beginning.[49]

But Shaw's articles and books, published just as the European municipalization movement was heating up, their data still novel and arresting, enjoyed far more influence than normally falls to the work of a young writer. Moving to New York City, where a businessmen's project for a city-financed Manhattan subway was gathering force, Shaw's reports gained an eager hearing. When the subway question was put to a citywide vote in 1894, Shaw's retelling of Glasgow's story in the press and in the uptown reform clubs, together with the downtown organizational work of the settlement houses, single-taxers, and labor unions, brought one of municipal transit ownership's earliest American victories.[50]

Others in the same pinch formed a ready audience for Shaw's European reportage. Detroit's mayor Hazen Pingree, deep in a fight with the city's streetcar franchisers over fares and service in the early 1890s, soaked up Shaw's reports. So, under similar circumstances, did San Francisco's mayor James D. Phelan. When in 1893 the University of Wisconsin chose municipal ownership of city utilities as the subject of its annual student debate, the winning, municipal ownership side stocked its brief heavily with quotations from Adams, James, Ely—and Shaw. Ely himself put the case for municipal utility ownership succinctly in 1890: "Read Dr. Shaw . . . on Glasgow."[51]

Shaw's books formed one of several nodes of connection between European and American municipal progressives in the 1890s. Another was to be found in Boston under Josiah Quincy's mayorship from 1895 to 1900. Young and politically ambitious, wealthy enough to have traveled widely in Europe, Quincy was an early admirer of English factory legislation and English municipal administration. Elected as a "silk-stocking" Democrat, he plunged his administration into a broad program of city services consciously modeled on European precedents. Like the London Progressives, he experimented with the direct employment of city labor, bypassing subcontractors to raise the standards of labor on city work. Like the Glasgow municipalizers, he tangled with the city's gas and streetcar companies. Quincy's heart, however, lay in cultivating the city's social and recreational possibilities, in an effort to recreate the sociability that since the first student encounters with Germany had struck Americans so strongly in Europe. Taking as his special adviser Robert Woods, whose *English Social Movements*, full of the early stirrings of London Progressivism, had come out only four years earlier, Quincy built public baths and swimming pools, gymnasia, parks, and playgrounds throughout Boston. He arranged, European style, for free civic concerts and art exhibits.[52]

All this made Quincy, in Shaw's eyes, the "foremost" practical expert in municipal administration in America at the end of the century. The London Progressives, too, took Quincy as one of their own. The Fabian John Martin thought Quincy's Boston the nearest thing to what Birmingham had been in the 1870s and Glasgow in the early 1890s. Sidney and Beatrice Webb, touring the United States in 1898 with an acerbic dislike of most of the Americans they met and contempt for the "infantile" complexity of American municipal administration, thought Quincy's work among the best to be found in America. When Quincy left office in 1900 after a falling out with his city council over rising city debts and contractors' complaints against direct city employment, he returned the Webbs' compliment by undertaking a lecturing stint at the Fabians' new London School of Economics.[53]

A larger node of European-influenced municipal ambitions was to be found in turn-of-the-century New York City. A half dozen London Progressives, including John Burns himself, turned up there on lecture tours in the 1890s, eager to tout London's experience. Percival Chubb of the original Fabian group lectured back to back with Albert Shaw on "The Lessons of London" in 1894; John Martin, soon to emigrate to the city as director of the League for Political Education, gave a five-part lecture series on the London example in 1898–99. William Tolman, then general agent of the Association for Improving the Condition of the Poor, was a city presence, with his bulging boxes of lantern slides from Glasgow, London, and Paris and his fingers in a broad array of political and reform pies. In 1891 the association had constructed a "People's Bath" on the Lower East Side, where landlords packed in tenants so thickly that only 2 in 100 families in the blocks surveyed by Bureau of Labor investigators possessed a bathroom; and Tolman had come away from the work inspired with a passion for English-style city baths.[54] Most forceful of all was William Randolph Hearst, who bought his way into the city's newspaper market in 1895. Sensing well before the muckraking magazines a future in monopoly bashing, he soon set his *Evening Journal*'s headlines ablaze with denunciations of the city's utility franchisers, praise for the advantages of municipal ownership, and illustration of Glasgow's and Birmingham's success at it.[55]

With its party machines and often flagrant municipal corruption, New York City in the 1890s was no stranger to sporadic eruptions of "good government" reform. Businessmen were municipal reform politics' stock promoters, normally speaking in the language of financial retrenchment, nonpartisanship, moral vigilance, and (as in the case of the Tilden commission of 1875 to 1877, which recommended limiting the suffrage in great cities to substantial property holders) deep antipathy to democratic politics. It had been the political boss's role to think of the city as a democratic bundle of services: a business enterprise of goods to be provided, charities to be bestowed, and profits to be reaped. Through the nineties the opposing, good-government formulas held. William Strong and Seth Low, the Citizens' Union mayors who cracked Tammany's lock on the office in the year 1895 to 1897 and again in 1901 to 1903, respectively, were men of wealth and culture, dedicated to cheaper, more honest, and more efficient city management.

But encouraged by the transatlantic comparisons, there rose a steadily mounting counterpressure toward a more "positive," European-style program. The Strong administration clamped down hard on Sunday liquor sales, but it also, less expectedly, poured new money into school construction, cleaner streets, and—thanks to Tolman's work on a special mayor's committee—public baths modeled on London's example.[56] Convinced that a "civic renaissance" was in the making, the businessman-dominated Reform Club launched a new journal in 1897, *Municipal Affairs*, which plunged quickly into discussions of public art, public health, city tax reform, housing, municipal utility ownership, and "municipal socialism" itself—all illustrated with abundant European examples. For its December 1898 number, the editor, Milo Maltbie, surveyed the Atlantic urban world from San Francisco to Budapest to prove the universal trend toward expanding municipal "functions."[57]

When the Citizens' Union regrouped for the 1897 mayoral election, its program included not only public baths and lavatories but also a new city lodging house for the homeless; more small parks, schools, and recreational river piers; and tighter franchises for the city utilities. It was hardly a program to cause ripples in London, but it moved the *New York Times* to complain of municipalization "fads that the half baked have picked up from Prof. ELY and other Socialistic writers." Four years later, the reformers had added an eight-hour day on all city contracts, a "judicious increase" in direct employment on city works, and city ownership of water, electric, and gas supplies: a program as "enlightened and progressive," they pointedly claimed, as that of Paris, London, Berlin, Glasgow, or Birmingham. Uptown in the campaign of 1901, Seth Low's handlers talked of corruption, prostitution, and financial retrenchment. Campaigning downtown for working-class votes, they talked of the London County Council's city-built housing for the working class, sewage farms as in Berlin, public bathing houses as in Göttingen, city savings banks and pawnshops as everywhere in urban Germany, municipal gas and electric plants, perhaps even London's pay tea and cocoa machines heated by municipal street lamps.[58]

The cocoa machines never materialized, nor did the public housing, nor the municipal pawn shops. But Low swallowed his objections to municipal utility ownership enough to petition the legislature for the city's right to build a lighting plant for its own streets and public buildings and, even as he cut taxes, poured new money into public schools. Not until the La Guardia administration would the uptown program of efficient city management and the downtown program of expanded public services fuse. But by the end of the nineties, as in Chamberlain's Birmingham two decades earlier, the program of "good government" reform had begun to find a new key.

Elsewhere, battles along the corrupt and contested rim of city franchise and purchase worked similar effects with less obvious foreign mediation. In Detroit between 1890 and 1897 Hazen Pingree, a Chamberlain-like figure who had been drafted from his shoe manufacturing company by local businessmen to run as a Republican candidate for mayor, crusaded to reclaim the city's streets, in quick step, from the shoddy contractors who had laid them out, then from the toll-road companies that charged for them, and finally from the commercial streetcar companies that tore them up and profited on their use. Two years of contesting with the streetcar franchisers over improvements and rates turned Pingree into the country's most outspoken mayoral advocate of municipal utility ownership. In Toledo, manufacturer Samuel M. Jones, as mayor, pushed hard against a resistant city council for city-owned gas and electric plants. In Cleveland, yet a third businessman-reformer, Mayor Tom Johnson, a streetcar monopolist himself before a reading of George's *Progress and Poverty* knocked his intellectual props out from under him, plunged aggressively into utility politics between 1901 and 1909. His successor, Newton Baker, expanded the city's electric lighting plant, sold city ice cream in the city parks, ran two municipal dance halls, and marketed low-cost fish caught from a Park Department tugboat.[59]

If municipal progressive politics in the Midwest owed less to European examples than did urban progressives in New York or Boston, however, the transatlantic affinities were not lost on the midwestern municipalizers. Johnson made a pilgrimage to Glasgow before his death in 1910. Brand Whitlock, Jones's successor in Toledo, did the same in 1912, eager to see "the most wonderfully governed city, that is, from our standpoint of democracy, in the English speaking world." We are "paltering and hesitating over municipal problems which Europe solved a generation ago," Whitlock fumed. But "we are so cocky over here that we won't learn anything from the experience."[60]

The man who best linked all these impulses together was one of Tom Johnson's key political allies, Frederic C. Howe. As a Johns Hopkins student, Howe had come under Ely's influence and, still more, the spell of Albert Shaw, whom Ely had brought to Johns Hopkins in the fall of 1889 to lecture on European cities. Shaw's pictures of cities, "cities that owned things and did things for people," Howe later recalled, fired his first political enthusiasms. He set off to see them himself in the spring and summer of 1891, attending lectures at the University of Berlin and soaking up what he could of European political culture. Moving on to New York City, doctorate in hand, Howe turned to journalism for a while, enrolled in a law school, and briefly joined a civic crusade to put the city's saloons under the watch and ward of upright citizens like himself.[61]

Abandoning New York City for a Cleveland law career, Howe could not let social issues go. He moved into a settlement house and joined the Cleveland Charity Organization Society as a trustee and "friendly visitor," bringing advice and sympathy to the city's poor, only to conclude from his efforts that charity was a futile business. He became caught up in a proposal for a Cleveland civic center along the grand, formal lines of Baron Haussmann's Paris; he became secretary of the businessmen's Municipal Association, fighting corruption in streetcar franchises. On the basis of his civic-center vision and his commitment to civil service reform, he won election to the Cleveland City Council in 1901. Pulled between political ambitions and visions of apolitical, civic unity, Howe groped his way toward an urban politics with the confusions and ambivalence typical of turn-of-the-century middle-class civic reform.

His real political awakening, he later claimed, came through the single tax idea. Entering Cleveland politics at the beginning of Tom Johnson's mayoral administration, Howe discovered in Johnson a reformer of an altogether different type than he had known before: an expansive and magnetic personality, a streetcar capitalist who had turned on his own kind, and, above all, a disciple of Henry George. Single-taxers like Johnson were far from rare in the municipal ownership ranks. The Fabians had drunk deeply of George's idea of the "unearned increment," absorbing far more from George than they had from Marx. Whatever the simplicities of George's idea of rent, his indictment of those who fattened on wealth they did not create themselves—from the rising price of land in a thriving city or the swelling value of a streetcar franchise in an economically enterprising town—carried considerable moral-economic power. Where Henry C. Adams's "natural monopoly" argument narrowed the sphere of legitimate public intervention to a precise, technically determinable core of enterprises, George's vision was ethically broader and more readily grasped. Recapturing the socially created value of the city's streets and franchises meant confiscating the franchisers' unearned profit; practically, it meant municipalization. Through this logical chain, the municipal ownership movement was to be heavily stocked with single-taxers. Brand Whitlock, the muckraker Lincoln Steffens, and Tom Johnson were Henry George disciples, and so—through Johnson—was Howe.

For most of the next decade Howe and Johnson fought the streetcar franchise fight in Cleveland, first in a pitched battle for cheaper fares and then—when the streetcar companies resisted—in a long, ultimately failing campaign for municipal ownership. The crusade both clarified Howe's politics and reawakened the pictures Shaw had implanted years before. In 1905 he arranged for a commission from the U.S. Bureau of Labor to study municipal ownership in Europe, hunting down Sidney Webb and tramping through London's working-class wards with John Burns. In 1909 he was in Europe again. The next year, after Johnson's death, Howe moved to New York City to launch a career as a writer on municipal issues with a special eye on Europe. The upshot by 1915 was five books and a sheaf of well-placed magazine articles, all designed to bring progressive urban Europe to American consciousness.[62]

"There is a yeast in Europe, not unlike that of the French Revolution," Howe was sure. Following the now well-traveled route to Glasgow, Birmingham, and London, Howe looked for it first in Britain. *The British City*, a book he dedicated to Johnson, glowed with praise for British municipal trading. But viewed through the disenchantments of his single-tax contacts,

Howe's Britain was a good deal less attractive than Shaw's had been. Howe hated the House of Lords and the land-based hierarchy it represented. "Great Britain is a land speculators' paradise," he cautioned, a nation of tenants under the thumb of a reactionary landlord class. Even his admiration for British-style municipal trading dimmed as the movement lost momentum to the ratepayers' counterassault. "The British city thinks through its purse," Howe wrote with some disillusionment in 1913; its eye was always on the tax rate.[63]

By 1910 Howe's affections had turned to the German cities. There, he wrote, one found not merely cities victorious over the utility interests that had broken and defeated Tom Johnson, but "organic" cities, possessed of "communal self-consciousness." American cities were a mere "accident, a railway, water, or industrial accident." The German city, in contrast, was an "organized, living thing with a big and far-seeing programme." With no artificial limit to its activities, it touched its citizens' weal in "countless" ways. In praising German municipal life, Howe did not mean, any more than Shaw had meant, to single out its political structures. Neither the British nor the German cities relied on the rigid civil service rules Howe himself had once thought the key to municipal honesty. Suffrage exclusion—common throughout European—did not distinguish progressive European cities from reactionary ones. The answer to municipal corruption did not lie in political structure at all. "We think of forms; they, of activities." Obsessed with constitutional forms, he wrote, the Americans had managed only to "adjust everything for dead-lock, for delay, for conflict."[64]

It was the scope of municipal undertakings—civic activity in itself—that was the key. Grant a city home rule, let it begin to do big things, and it would attract to its service big, farsighted men no longer willing to leave urban politics to the petty grafters and bosses. The private city would never be anything but a plaything of private interests, but let a city's activities begin to touch its citizens' lives at a multitude of points, and there would arise a new civic loyalty, a "city sense," a new collective sensibility.

In hindsight it is easy to puncture the illusory elements in Howe's images of European cities, shining on a hill of hope and longing. In Germany, in particular, where Howe had fewer inside informants, his visual sense of the city led him to mistake organic city architecture for an organic civic life. The politics running hard just under the surface of German urban administration he barely acknowledged. Staggered, like Shaw, by the activities of European cities, he missed the checks on their autonomy, differently constituted than in the United States but in their own way no less powerful.

He did not take it as his task to pry into the question of precisely whom the European cities' activities served. In Germany, city businessmen "do not legislate in the interests of their class, as they do in America," he wrote, with far more willingness to suspend critical judgment than he should have had; "that is one of the anomalies of Germany, for I know of no other country in the world in which this is true."[65] By its nature the transatlantic progressive connection ran toward ideal types and polarities. Yearning so hard for an antithesis to exaggerated American individualism, the participants' chances for misperception were, from the beginning, enormous.

The problem affected every intermediary—Eduard Bernstein in 1890s London as much Howe in Berlin twenty years later. From the barest facts upward, everything was necessarily filtered through screens of conviction and expectation. Sylvester Baxter of the Boston public parks movement thought Berlin a "most thoroughly republican city." Ely claimed German cities were "republican with an aristocratic tendency." Robert Brooks, on a Cornell University traveling fellowship in Germany in 1899, wrote back, in disgust at wishful thinking of Baxter's sort, that German city governments were elitist and politicized to the core. Many of those who first saw Glasgow through Albert Shaw's eyes were not prepared for the gloomy stone city they themselves found. Brand Whitlock, coming to see a form of civic life that "had existed in my mind only as theory, or as the tales of wonders from afar," found himself shaken by Glasgow's unexpected poverty. The city's slums—"stairs, damp and greasy, the evil odor of poverty everywhere, . . . and squalor, hopelessness, despair all about"—appalled him.[66]

What riveted the attention of most American admirers of European city life, however, were the absences: "No offensive bill boards; no heaps of offal and rubbish, no long stretches of untidy vacancy held for speculation in the midst of the city; no tumble-down tenements; no ragged, inebriate pedestrians," the National Municipal League's president William D. Foulke wrote of Frankfurt in 1911.[67] No wretchedly paved streets and packed streetcars, no corrupt city bosses, no waste, no lawlessness, no anarchy. The "not"s multiplied as the European cities took shape in reverse of the American cities to which the reformers could not avoid contrasting them. Everything played into these judgments, from the width and paving of the streets and the comparative hideousness of the advertisements to the political convictions of the observers. The reflections and mirrors, the inner eye always focused on America while the outer eye saw Europe: all of this affected judgments.

But admirers of European civic life like Howe were not politically naive. Howe knew the difference between the Junkers and the forces expanding, as he put it, like molten lava below the crust—even if, for his purposes, he chose to elide party divisions as unimportant. He was under no illusion that the European cities moving rapidly into new realms of provision and collective enterprise were democratic in the American understanding of the term. The word portraits of handsome city baths and well-run municipal streetcars in which writers like Howe invested so much were more than travelogue prose. They were part of a struggle to socialize the language of democracy—to balance its rhetoric of rights and privileges with a new rhetoric of services, outcomes, and results. In their stress on cities that *did* things, they tried to forge a language of democratic, civic action rather than mere democratic forms. The German city, Howe admitted, in almost the same words Boston's Josiah Quincy had used sixteen years earlier, was not democratic in its administrative structure; but it was "democratic, even socialistic, in its services."[68]

If Howe was less naive about politics than he later chose to portray himself, neither was his talk of redemption through a new "city sense" so gauzy as to preclude its employment by others struggling to unlock the same political riddles. His language reappeared again and again among municipal progressives. "Our cities are to be saved by the development of the collective idea," Samuel M. Jones argued. Leo S. Rowe echoed the point: The need of the hour was a new civic "loyalty," a more public conception of civic life than the private American metropolis fostered. Glasgow's streetcars, London's steam ferries, Frankfurt's public parks and pawnshops, all melded into a vision of an organic polity in which the economic divisions of capitalism were reintegrated by new forms of public enterprise and consciousness. Unlike the nation, the city was small enough, and tangible enough, to carry such a vision. The dream of the self-owned city—of cities ambitious enough to operate their own public services, keeping their own goose of civic-generated profits, drawing the love and loyalty of their citizens with the profusion of things they did—was a dream of no mean power.[69]

One did not have to go to Europe, of course, to be caught up in the municipalizers' vision. So long as cities owned or provided anything, from the simplest police functions outward, it took neither theory nor transatlantic consciousness to imagine adding, piecemeal, to the sphere of municipal goods and functions. Like many political ideas, municipal ownership was a concept one could reach from a wide variety of starting places—a program capable of repeated invention and multiple simultaneous discovery.[70] What the European precedents did was to give American urban progressives a set of working, practical examples. Without the European connection, the vision of the self-owned city debouched into abstract economic arguments. "Experience, experience, experience, has been the *sine qua non*" of British municipal socialism, not theory, Milo Maltbie wrote in 1900. The importance of Europe lay in the possibility that on its borrowed, accumulated experience the Americans could leapfrog over economic abstractions, over the problem of defining, with surveyors' precision, the boundary of the public sphere, and seize on praxis itself. It was this that made Birmingham, Glasgow, London, Frankfurt, or Berlin, in Howe's words, an "experiment-station for us all."[71]

Among advanced urban progressives in the early-twentieth-century United States, it is hard to exaggerate the ambitions bound up in these half-imported visions of cities free of their swarms of contractors, grafters, entrepreneurs, and franchisers, of cities conscious of their own administration and directing their own fate. Or to exaggerate their sense of affinity with events across the Atlantic. That the American issue might be thought to turn, even for a moment, on the experience of Glasgow streetcars—this was the primary event. "You know that one of the best governed cities in the world is the great Scotch city of Glasgow," Woodrow Wilson casually told a crowd in Fall River, Massachusetts, in the campaign of 1912. "They are 'way ahead of us," Lincoln Steffens wrote of the European municipalizers. "Liberals and radicals all of them, they are in harness and down to the details."[72] The American municipal progressives' challenge was to see what could be done with their transatlantic enthusiasms where the political structures, whose importance they minimized, were so differently organized.

The test came with streetcars, and it brought an unsettling outcome. That locus, it is clear in hindsight, mattered more than it appeared at the time. Had the municipal ownership movement gathered force in the United States a decade or two earlier, gas supply, with its easy city profits, might have been the axis on which the public ownership issue turned, as it was in Britain and Germany. Later, in the 1920s and 1930s, the key fights were to be over regional distribution of electrical power.

Both gas and electricity were contested ground in the Progressive years as well. The first was a basic consumer good in the gas-lit city of the early twentieth century; its pricing was a perennially controversial issue. Charles Evans Hughes and Louis Brandeis were both catapulted into politics by crusades to drive down the charges of vastly overcapitalized urban gas monopolies. But experience with municipal gasworks in the 1870s and 1880s had been meager. Philadelphia, which had undertaken municipal gas operation in 1887, the only late-nineteenth-century American city of any size to have done so, had leased its gasworks back to a private operating firm by 1897 amid a cacophony of charges that the one operator had been as corrupt and unsatisfactory as the other.[73] By the first decade of the twentieth century, with competition from electricity threatening to erode the easy revenues of municipal gas operation, city councils were wary of new investments in a potentially declining technology. The moment Chamberlain had seized in Birmingham had passed, and the Americans had missed it. As for electricity, its moment was yet to come. Municipal electric power plants to light the city's streets and office buildings were a not uncommon investment, but so long as household electricity was a luxury of the well-to-do, electricity supply would support no broad municipal political base.

Streetcars, just entering a phase of extraordinary expansion in the 1890s, were a different matter. Streetcars were potentially everyone's utility. The urban dwellers' automobile in the pre-auto city, they were the key determinant of a city's spatial growth, the wage earners' means of escape for a Sunday's outing, and perhaps even the means to a modest house in the suburbs, if streetcar prices could be driven low enough. On transit issues the fiercest battles of early-twentieth-century urban politics were to be waged; on them the sharpest hopes of the European-inspired municipal reformers were to be pinned.

Nowhere in the late-nineteenth-century American city had the imbalance between private market forces and public direction been clearer than in transit politics. Hungry for services, cities had granted transit franchises with a free hand and little reflection; when franchisers failed to provide adequate service, city councils simply franchised more competitors. Chicago city authorities issued licenses to ninety-eight streetcar enterprises between 1884 and 1895, most them paper enterprises constructed purely for their speculative value. The results were crazy quilts of horse-drawn and cable-powered streetcar lines, few of which returned any revenue to their city, in a system whose benefit was its costlessness to urban taxpayers and whose drawback was its chaotic planlessness and wretched service.[74]

By the mid-1880s, some cities had begun to drive harder bargains with their streetcar companies, imposing a maximum fare, a tax on gross receipts, or a tax on the cars run. But in the main, few restrictions governed the granting of franchises. Capitalization was at the whim of the private investors, who watered their stock with the zeal of desert farmers. Franchises were typically long-term; as late as 1899 one-third of the nation's extant transportation franchises were grants in perpetuity. Public supervision of operations was unknown. Route planning was left to private initiative and competition; in the resulting free-for-all of competing lines all trying to put the maximum number of cars into service on the most lucrative routes, streetcar "blockades" piled up to gridlock downtown Boston and the Chicago Loop, as angry rival drivers jostled for place on the jointly used tracks.

What upset this system in the 1890s was capital and electrification. Out of the transit chaos of the 1880s they made order—indeed, monopolies. In Milwaukee between 1890 and 1893, a syndicate headed by Henry Villard reduced the city's streetcar operators from six to one, a consolidated utility corporation that, for good measure, absorbed all the city's electric power production facilities as well. Tom Johnson, not yet converted to reform politics, had put together a unified streetcar monopoly in Detroit by 1897. Charles Yerkes did the same for streetcars running north and west of Chicago's Loop. The last remaining independent streetcar line operating in Manhattan was gobbled up in 1900 by the city's new traction syndicate. In the twenty largest American cities in 1902, according to historian Charles Cheape, there were transit monopolies in all but four.[75]

In part the wave of streetcar consolidations reflected the underlying economic trends of the late 1890s. The same combination of aggressive financial capital and depression-weakened operators that created monopolies in tinplate, bicycles, farm machinery, and steel made utility monopolies as well. The new frequency of the word "consolidated" in utility company titles told a part of the tale: New York City's Consolidated Gas Company; Baltimore's Consolidated Gas, Electric Light and Power Company; Chicago's Consolidated Traction Company. Electrification compounded these market forces by suddenly ratcheting up the capital required for effective competition. Between 1888, when the first electric-powered streetcar system was put into operation, and 1900, when the transition from horse and cable to electric power was virtually complete, electricity revolutionized both operations and finance. It pushed streetcar systems out beyond the cities' edges, where the real money was to be made by purchasing cheap land ahead of the companies' closely held expansion plans and selling off building lots in the new trolley-served suburbs at enormous profit. Electrification brought service to far more passengers. It squeezed out competition. Together the interlocked technical and financial transformations of the 1890s put powerful weight behind the economists' notion that, in city utilities, only monopolies could ultimately survive.

The monopoly position of the new streetcar enterprises, the unprecedented scale of their finances and profits, their dependence on city franchises for the use of the public streets, and their day-to-day entanglement in politics and influence peddling ensured that the ambitions of the streetcar financiers would collide with those of the new urban reformers. Pushed by the arrogance of the streetcar companies and by public demand, reform mayors tangled with the traction companies over standards of safety and service, more adequate returns to the city treasury, labor practices, and fares cheap enough to democratize city transit. Not even Pingree, crusading for cheap three-cent fares in Detroit, initially imagined municipal streetcar ownership as anything other than a negotiating point in the struggle for advantage over the traction monopolists; municipal streetcar operation was a threat of last resort.[76] As the number of working European examples multiplied, however, the abstract bargaining chip soon became a practical demand.

An early test came in New York City. In the early 1890s a broad political coalition of city groups, frustrated with the inadequacies of the city's transportation system and the failure of private capital investors to come forward with workable expansion proposals, succeeded in establishing a public transit commission authorized to lay out, finance, and own a city subway—though not to build or operate it. The city's Chamber of Commerce took the lead, stocking the commission with its own merchant-citizens, but the proposal also found support in the city's labor unions and settlement houses. A citywide referendum on the issue in 1894 passed by a vote of almost three to one.[77] Laid out by the Rapid Transit Commission's chief engineer on designs honed by an inspection tour of the best London and Paris had to offer, twenty-one miles of publicly owned subway, second in size only to London's private underground rail system, were in operation by 1904. But city ownership of the underlying track did not turn out the same results in the United States as it had in Europe. Within a year the lessee had swallowed up its only potential rival, Manhattan's consolidated streetcar holding company. Possessed of a near perfect, publicly financed monopoly over rapid transit on the island of Manhattan, and spurning the commission's proposals for further expansion, the company proceeded to draw in, in the words of its head, August Belmont, "remarkable" profits.[78]

In Chicago, where the rapacity of the traction capitalists was bolder still, urban progressives did not tarry with halfway notions of ownership. Charles Yerkes, the man Theodore Dreiser took as the type for his lead character in *The Financier*, was the precipitating figure. In 1897, with Chicago traction franchises soon to expire, he had tried to ease a bill through the Illinois legislature that at a stroke would have extended all utility franchises in the state for 100 years. Public outcry scotched Yerkes's plan, but not his substitute measure, which raised the permissible franchise length in Illinois from twenty to fifty years. Before Yerkes's act was repealed, a gang of Chicago councilmen, seeing a pot of gold for themselves in the act, had organized a dummy electric utility company, granted it a fifty-year franchise, and cheerfully sold out the privilege to other investors, to their own considerable profit.[79] Profit was, indeed, the name of the utility business in Chicago. In the 1890s the city's two principal streetcar companies had paid out 27 percent to 29 percent of their gross receipts in dividends.[80] Yerkes, having bled the assets of his operating companies into his various holding and construction firms, soon bowed out of Chicago, but not before his chicanery and monopoly ambitions had pushed Glasgow's example of simple, straightforward, city streetcar operation into the eye of city politics.

Elected mayor on a straight-out "Immediate Municipal Ownership" platform in 1905, Edward Dunne seized the point the machine politicians (who knew a familiar and profitable system when they had one) had been reluctant to endorse. A well-to-do Irish-American lawyer, a friend of Jane Addams (whom he appointed to the city school board) and Clarence Darrow (whom he made his transit policy adviser), Dunne knew a good deal about European civic politics. He had traveled to Europe to see municipal ownership in action in 1900, and he routinely filled his speeches with the facts and figures of its success. His campaign won endorsement from the city's labor federation, the city's Hearst-owned papers, and many of the city's advanced progressives. On Tom Johnson's advice, he brought the general manager of the Glasgow municipal streetcar system to Chicago to lay his blessings on the construction of a new system of low-cost city-operated streetcar lines. Three successive referenda on the issue between 1904 and 1906 yielded substantial majorities for the municipal ownership side, though the last one fell short of the two-thirds majority constitutionally required to actually put the idea into motion.[81]

The years in which Dunne's municipal ownership movement crested in Chicago, 1905 and 1906, were pivotal for the national movement as well. William Jennings Bryan, the Democratic Party's perennial presidential candidate, came back from a round-the-world trip enthusiastic about the idea of municipal ownership. The Hearst newspaper chain, riding high on its working-class sympathies and its savage exposure of monopoly power, pushed the cause with all its formidable strength. In New York City, Hearst himself chose 1905 in which to run for mayor on a broad municipal ownership ticket. With a tide of working-class support, Hearst's Municipal Ownership League came within an eyelash of winning the election; had the Tammany machine not counted the ballots, it almost certainly would have prevailed. In Cleveland, Tom Johnson was struggling to organize a low-cost, people's streetcar line to compete with the city's private, monopoly operators. In the face of these events, municipal ownership's opponents redoubled their efforts to stem what an alarmed critic called the "great socialistic agitation [now] upon us."[82]

All of this coincided with the apogee of muckraking journalism and found reinforcement in it. *McClure's Magazine* and its competitors were awash in stories of urban graft and corruption, in a race to bring to light the hidden alliances between businessmen seeking favors and government officials selling them that Lincoln Steffens popularized, in grafters' slang, as "boodle."[83] Historians have begun to call this form of popular, progressive city politics "civic populism," and, as in London in the 1890s, public utility ownership was at its very core.

In these circumstances, it was only to be expected that an array of halfway compromises would be hastily thrown against the municipal ownership tide. The inquiry commission was one of these. By September 1905, the National Civic Federation had organized what was to be a repeated Progressive-era construction, a fact-finding commission, assigned to comb both sides of the Atlantic for experience and information. The National Civic Federation's strategy of carefully balancing the membership of its Commission on Public Ownership between private utility company executives and outspoken proponents of municipal ownership, like Ely's students Edward Bemis and John R. Commons, ensured against surprises. Commons thought the commission's tour through a sea of English teas and formal presentations in the summer of 1906 a waste of time, and he jumped ship to spend a week on his own, closeted with the Glasgow street railways committee. But in an argument about domestic policy formation that turned so fundamentally on experience abroad, the commissioners took their work with considerably seriousness.[84]

To the acute disappointment of Commons and others, the commission's effort to compare the costs and returns of public and private utility operation failed, a victim not only of the inability of the commission's members to agree on the meaning of the immense amount of British data it gathered, but, still more, of the refusal of American utility firms to open their books to comparative inspection. But the recommendations of the commission's majority, published in 1907, were not unfavorable to municipal ownership. The commission took no sides on the wisdom of municipal ownership in any city's particular circumstances. But, with three of its four utility company executives in dissent, the commission did insist that the competitive principle by itself had signally failed in the city utility business, and it recommended that cities be legally free to embark on municipal ownership if their voters so chose.[85]

The more effective compromises were structural. Louis Brandeis touted a sliding-scale scheme, borrowed from the terms of London's gas franchise, linking permissible utility company dividends to reductions in utility rates. Others pressed for tighter franchise terms. But the most important effect of the municipal ownership furor was to resuscitate the regulatory commission device and shove it into the political breach. Adopted to deal with railroad rate complaints in both late-nineteenth-century Britain and the United States, regulatory commissions had languished in America with court-crippled powers and very little effect. In the circumstances, however, the familiarity of the idea counted for more than its effectiveness; and its ability to be quickly adapted to the new turn of events counted for more than either.[86]

Policy "inertia" or "path dependency," political scientists call the phenomenon. In fact, what occurred between 1905 and 1907 was that a policy device of proven impotence, revived under the pressures for quick and decisive action, jumped its accustomed path to become suddenly an answer to a far broader array of problems than ever imagined before. In 1906, under fierce pressures to respond to railroad amalgamation, Congress had tried to breathe new life into the moribund Interstate Commerce Commission. The year before, Wisconsin's Robert La Follette had tried to make good on his promise to tame the state railroad corporations through the same device. Now in 1907 in the face of the transit crisis, La Follette asked John Commons to draft a measure extending at a stroke the oversight of the Railroad Commission to all the utility corporations operating in the state: water, electricity, gas, telephones, railroads, and streetcars. When Charles Evans Hughes, edging out Hearst in the New York governor's race in 1906, cast about for a way quickly to defuse Hearst's municipal ownership issue, he found his answer in the Wisconsin scheme: a small, statewide, expert-staffed public utilities commission, empowered to approve rates, oversee capital offerings, and set minimum standards of safety and service. Instituted in Wisconsin and New York in 1907, the utilities commission idea quickly swept the state houses; by the end of 1914 all but three states had jumped on the legislative bandwagon.[87]

Not the least of the political assets of the commission idea was that the utility companies so quickly saw its advantages. Commission regulation promised simultaneously to defuse the drive for municipal utility ownership and to extract franchise bargaining from the superheated political corridors of city hall to a more distant, safer, state venue. In Illinois in 1913, among the principal bankrollers of the successful drive for a state public utilities commission was the electric utility monopolist Samuel Insull. The National Electric Light Association touted the idea among its constituent companies as giving them "the greatest freedom from local and political influences." In Alabama, after a new Birmingham city charter in 1911 mandated a voters' referendum on all newly opened franchise questions, the utility corporations scrambled quickly to get a public utilities commission act through the legislature; a key portion of the supplementary statute of 1920 was drafted by the Birmingham Railway, Light, and Power Company's chief attorney.[88]

Where the central issues in utility politics could be framed as moral issues of profiteering and malfeasance (as the muckrakers were wont to frame them), however, the regulatory commission idea had an appeal that extended far beyond the directly affected interests. The promise of the idea was multiple: private ownership softened by public oversight; reasonable, guaranteed returns for investors; and publicly mandated standards of service for customers. By 1912 the Washington state supreme court had concluded that the idea had "solved" the problem of public utilities; it had given the public "every advantage of ownership without assuming its burdens."[89]

Resuscitated by the chain of events that had begun in Glasgow, the regulatory commission solution deflected the municipal ownership campaign; it interrupted its momentum, preempted a good deal of its political capital, and scattered some of its key allies, but it did not extinguish it. Commons, who wrote a public ownership clause into the Wisconsin bill, never thought the commission device more than a halfway measure. In Chicago and New York, the new commissions soon came under intense attack for their toothlessness and their usurpation of local policy-making authority. Some of the initial appointees to the regulatory commissions—the Reform Club's Milo Maltbie in New York among them—gave full return on the promise of public-spirited expertise, but the rapidity with which party hacks and former utility company executives began to show up as utility commission appointees quickly made it clear that the public utilities problem had not really been solved at all. The issue still agitated the mayors' conventions. On the Progressive Party's left wing, there were figures passionately committed to the municipal ownership idea—including Harold Ickes, who would later serve as public works "czar" in Franklin Roosevelt's cabinet. A Public Ownership League of America, with Frederic Howe, Edward Dunne, and Jane Addams among its vice presidents, busied itself with agitational work.[90]

The materials of streetcar "civic populism," in short, still lay at hand. Charles Beard in 1912 thought the municipal ownership movement had never been stronger, with San Francisco's inauguration in that year of a short, city-owned streetcar line in competition with private operators; with the Cleveland voters' endorsement of a city plant for the general distribution of electricity, and Ontario cities doing just that across the border; with a socialist administration in Milwaukee talking (like the London radicals) of direct city public work and (like French municipal socialists) of free medical service for the poor. In Detroit in 1922, Pingree's successors bought out the city's private streetcar lines. Three years later, New York reformers, with Governor Al Smith's blessing, began construction of a new subway line to be operated directly by the city. The Independent line, the city named it: independent of the traction monopolies.[91]

Still, measured against the British and German parallels, the outcome of the long, earnest fight for municipal utility ownership in pre–World War I America could not but be disappointing. Of the sixty-nine "great cities" in the United States in the mid-1920s, all but nine owned their own waterworks. Nearly three quarters owned public markets. But only four—Detroit, San Francisco, Seattle, and New York—owned or operated their own transit lines. Only three "great cities"—Omaha, Richmond, and Duluth—maintained municipal gasworks. Nine operated electrical lighting or power plants. Of the total streetcar trackage in the country, public operators ran less than 2 percent of it; public power plants generated barely 5 percent of the nation's total electric power output; public gasworks produced only 1 percent of the nation's supply. In comparison with Britain and Germany, which had set the pace, it was an embarrassingly meager showing.[92]

So intense the dream and the efforts to realize it; so many Atlantic parallels and so strong a sense of transatlantic affinity. Why did it come to so much less than the American municipal progressives had anticipated?

Timing and scale hold part of the answer. Starting late on the municipalization project, American urban progressives began with streetcars. But to start, without the benefit of accumulated administrative experience, with electrified streetcar systems was to begin at the top of a steep pyramid of difficulty. After a decade of electrification, turn-of-the-century urban transit systems dwarfed in scale and complexity city water- or gasworks; this was especially true in the United States, where transit companies' earlier electrification and their investments in outlying development land (a practice disallowed elsewhere) made them far larger than their European counterparts. Chicago's streetcar system, as critics of Edward Dunne's reliance on Glasgow's experience were quick to emphasize, was the largest in the world. Even Boston, with a population a little more than half that of Glasgow at the turn of the century, was served by three times the amount of Glasgow's track, over which twice the number of Glasgow's daily passengers were hauled each day.[93] Systems as large as these would have been extremely expensive for cities to purchase at the cost of their physical property alone; at the wildly overcapitalized values their companies claimed, the debt load their purchase entailed threatened to swamp city budgets altogether. Sequence mattered. Having missed the moment of most advantageous gas municipalization, American cities began farther up the hill of administrative difficulty; missing out on streetcar municipalization, they laid up still further liabilities.

Other hindrances flowed from the law. No blanket prohibition, as in France, kept American cities from the development of municipally owned enterprises. Most courts and legislatures, after a sharp, brief legal tussle, soon agreed that services dependent on the use of city streets or dependent on city-issued franchises were services that city governments themselves could directly undertake. Constitutional limits on the levels of debt that cities could contract posed a more significant barrier, though these proved amendable, particularly for "productive" enterprises promising a profit on the city's investment. It was not the law's rigidity but the double front on which the system of constitutional adjudication required the reformers to campaign that exacted the largest costs in resources and energy. Where everything, down to the finest details of a purchase agreement or a regulatory measure, went through the political system twice—first through the processes of government as normally conceived, and then, all over again, through the courts, where the property rights of investors were certain of a particularly solicitous hearing—the American system guaranteed greater delays and obstacles than progressives faced abroad.[94]

But the primary obstacle on which the municipal ownership movement faltered was the one on which Edward Dunne's attempt to take advantage of Glasgow's prestige and experience stumbled: corruption. The general manager of the Glasgow municipal streetcar system, whom Dunne brought with great fanfare to lay his blessings on a new city-owned streetcar system for Chicago, left no doubt of his dismay at the shoddy service and outdated equipment the city's private transport companies supplied. But taken aback at the stench of political corruption hovering over Chicago, he was unwilling to recommend municipalization except as an extreme resort.[95] Acutely embarrassed at the collapse of the expected endorsement, Dunne pocketed the report. But suppression of the report did not suppress the underlying issue. To city property owners' concerns over rates and taxes, to the resentments of those small businessmen who flourished on the city's margin of contract—to all those forces on which the Progressives' opponents had capitalized in London—corruption added a burden so large as to tip the balance. Tweed's looting of the New York treasury, the appetites of the so-called gray wolves on the Chicago city council, the quieter but no less systematic corruption of Philadelphia's Republican machine—these formed the background chorus to the municipal ownership debate. Indeed, they overwhelmed it.

The ability of urban party machines to sell off the city's privileges, piece by lucrative piece, was an old story by the turn of the century when the muckrakers got hold of it. Already a generation of elite and middle-class good-government reformers had struggled to correct it. Measures to limit and control the prerogatives of popularly elected officials were their stock in trade, many of them drawn from European precedents: civil service commissions along English lines (though in England, city governments were outside civil service rules), state supervisory commissions modeled on the British Local Government Board, professional city managers in imitation of the German *Oberbürgermeister*, or European-style suffrage restrictions to return the city to its property holders.[96]

The good-government reformers were not entirely wrong in assuming that the incompletely democratized British and German cities were more honestly governed than their own. On scandals, to be sure, the Americans had no exclusive patent; one had helped bring down the London County Council's predecessor, the Metropolitan Board of Works, in 1889. When it came to city corruption, "Englishmen are not in the position of throwing many stones," the British investigator Arthur Shadwell cautioned in 1906. Saloon keepers, real estate dealers, landlords, and contractors—all with licenses and favors to earn—were a common fixture on British municipal councils; men with interests at stake in city policies were not shy about privatizing representative politics.[97] Nonetheless, urban corruption in late-nineteenth-century Britain and Germany was quieter, more polite, more often an exchange of favors and advantages than hard cash. And less democratic. In this, too, timing carried deep and pervasive consequences. Where modern systems of urban government came into place before the democratization of urban politics—as was patently true in the German case and largely true of the English and Scottish cases as well—the situation was fundamentally different than in the United States. There the early rise of a white, male democracy created a system more porous to those who saw city office as a field for private profits and more inclined to treat public positions as a short-term investment, whose profits were to be taken as quickly as possible.

It was the experience of democratized corruption that ultimately made the expert regulatory commission idea so attractive—beyond its handiness and familiarity, beyond the utility companies' sub-rosa promotion of it, beyond the dynamics of a legislative fad. Even after the experts had been pushed out and the utilities had learned to cozy up so close to the regulators that it was not always easy to tell them apart, the aura of commission impartiality remained. The promise of the commission idea, in the words of the University of Wisconsin's B. Henry Meyer, was "to take the utilities out of politics" through agencies of control that yoked the objectivity of science and the neutrality of the law.[98] Conversely it was the specter of another Tweed or "gashouse ring," with access to cash flows and payroll-padding opportunities on a scale undreamed of before, that was the most potent weapon of municipal ownership's opponents. As long as the issue before the Chicago voters turned on dissatisfaction with private streetcar management, observers pointed out, Dunne's municipal ownership crusade had swept the city. The more real the possibility of outright public streetcar operation appeared, however, the more the doubts grew, and the narrower Dunne's majorities became.

In the face of the corruption issue, some of municipal ownership's academic champions quietly began to decamp. At the American Economic Association's discussion of utility issues in December 1905, only Howe and the Reform Club's Milo Maltbie gave the municipal ownership program a clear endorsement. Albert Shaw took shelter in evasion. "We are in a seething process of experiment from one end of the country to the other," he reported; he wished every experiment well but would endorse none. Ely, who had carried the torch for public ownership for so long, had already crossed over to join the movement's critics. Ely's detractors chalked up his change of mind to the influence of the new corporate sponsors of his research; he himself worried about the issues of corruption and administrative capacity.[99] As for the civic-minded businessmen who were, in the European context, municipal ownership's core constituency, their alarm at the prospect of the city's infrastructure falling into the hands of party hacks and bosses was intense indeed. Under these circumstances it was no wonder that respectable, middle-class sentiment came down on the side of halfway measures: public ownership of streetcar track but not of the cars themselves, sliding-scale pricing formulas, or private enterprise under regulatory commission oversight.

Measured against these fears and experiences, the eagerness of a Howe, a Dunne, or a Johnson not to tarry with civil service reform but to start by expanding the range of public goods and city enterprises could not but draw charges of naïveté. Howe's insistence that cities that engaged in bigger affairs would automatically draw bigger, more substantial, and more honest men into city administration to manage them had, in the American context, a certain air of unreality—whatever the case in Birmingham and Glasgow. The appeal to a renewed "city sense" springing out of civic enterprise itself left the municipalizers' project vulnerable to charges of soft-headedness—their reams of comparative cost data and stories of German municipal efficiency notwithstanding.

In fact, the answer the municipal ownership advocates gave to the problem of corruption was not as naive as it appeared. Though public discussion of corruption tended to blur distinctions in a miasma of general rottenness, the structures of corruption are complex and varied. In turn-of-the-century American cities, they took at least two distinct forms: corruption at the periphery and corruption in the ranks.

Corruption at the periphery occurs where governments and private suppliers meet. That line, where governments give out economic opportunities to private bidders through contracts, sales, or franchises, has always been extraordinarily fertile ground for the dishonestly won advantage. Corruption at the periphery occurs in the form of bribery, rebating, extortion, and payoffs. The usual good of exchange is simple cash, though employment of friends or political endorsements can be exchanged as well. As in the case of the twenty-two aldermen who (as Charles Edward Russell told the story) sold their votes on a lucrative, lower Broadway streetcar franchise in 1884 for a cool $20,000 apiece, those purchased are those who possess votes or influence.[100] But the primary beneficiaries of corruption at the periphery are the purchasers: businessmen who see a crooked way to a good deal.

Corruption in the ranks, by contrast, takes place within a city government's own workforce, to the benefit of the bosses and politicians and those indebted to them. Occasionally corruption in the ranks involves outright embezzlement, though this rarely goes uncaught. Its more normal forms are padded payrolls, nepotism and spoilsmanship in hiring, and inefficient work. Sometimes cash is exchanged. Bribery was a common enough way into a city job at the turn of the century; compulsory contributions from city job holders were the standard means by which party campaign chests were filled. But other goods are exchanged as frequently, or more so, than cash: jobs, easy work, or block voting on election day. Some nations tried to address this last issue by imposing suffrage restrictions on public employees. In Germany, employees of the state railroads were disenfranchised outright. In Victoria, Australia, government employees were excluded from regular elections and given instead independent parliamentary representation—for the more open pleading of their interests.[101]

The relationship between corruption at the core and corruption at the periphery, however, is more complicated than these devices reveal. The paradox in urban corruption is that shrinkage of one of these two opportunities for corruption expands the other. Diminish the things a city owns and manages and you reduce the potential for corruption in the ranks—but only at the expense of expanding the opportunities for corruption along a swollen periphery of private supply.

Both kinds of corruption were endemic in American cities. City political machines did not hesitate to exploit the expansion of city services for their pound of patronage. City waterworks and sanitation departments, police forces and fire departments, health inspectorates and public bath departments were all used—often blatantly—as patronage favors and engines of political loyalty. If Lincoln Steffens and his fellow muckrakers were right, however, the rankest and most costly corruption in turn-of-the-century American cities took place at the periphery. Where aggressive private capital and city officials interested in capitalizing on their offices met, the opportunities for corruption were truly prodigious—as the Yerkes affair, and scores like it, demonstrated. Municipal ownership advocates like Howe and Steffens were not wrong in thinking that corruption along the franchise periphery was the greater of the city's evils. But in the context of the muckrakers' personalization of urban politics and their editors' eagerness for a circulation booster as effective as the exposure of a flamboyantly venal party boss, the municipalizers' argumentative task was not an easy one. Fear of yet more corruption in the open, porous, democratized American city kept the domain of American city activities small—and allowed the ripest opportunities for corruption to grow all the larger.

Was the crux of the matter then porosity itself? Did the early democratization of politics and office holding in the American city—despite its imperfections, despite its strenuously defended barriers of race and gender—make the transition to an urban social politics all the harder? None of the municipal progressives put the matter that way to themselves. That their ambitions might have faltered on a matter of historically mislayered developments was a conclusion they resisted. The self-owned city in their minds was democracy's realization. From the formal shell of an arithmetical democracy, they saw cities evolving into living organs of democratic functions. That was the direction of history's arrow: from passivity to action, from forms to services, from unconscious to conscious realization of the underlying interdependencies of urban life. It was what Shaw meant when he stressed municipal "housekeeping"; it was at the heart of Howe's admiration for cities that *did* things—boldly, collectively, publicly, with an expectation of common returns. Democracy found its upshot not in a remote regulatory commission, not even in an election, but in the everyday running of Glasgow's streetcars and London's ferries.

American municipal progressives rarely admitted that the broad range of services they admired in European cities might have been dependent on the European city elites' success in staving off formal democracy so long. But the very strenuousness of their assertion of kinship between the two democracies—the democracy of form and the democracy of act—suggested that they knew the moral of European civic enterprise was double-edged. Was the European experience proof that more ambitious city endeavors would foster a more honest civic spirit? Or, to the contrary, did the transatlantic contrasts in political structure only underline the folly of embarking, in the political context of the United States, on European-style municipal trading? Did the democratization of office in the American cities preclude the democratization of services? Was the way to the self-owned city to be barred by the least anticipated of obstacles, that a polity could democratize too early, that it could hollow out and privatize the agencies of the state too powerfully?

The quarrels and controversies of 1905 to 1907 answered none of these quandaries conclusively. The municipalizers had not missed their mark by a large margin. The vision of the self-owned city, extending experimentally outward into new realms of public goods and public supply, still hung in the balance on the eve of the First World War. Propelled by the electric power controversies of the 1920s, it would resurface again, powerfully, in the political imagination of the New Dealers.

Malleability was intrinsic to the municipal ownership idea. It was a device which could be used by public health reformers, by civic businessmen like those whom Shaw and Howe wooed so hard, and, on still other occasions, by the cities' big, popular, working-class majorities. Like so many progressive projects, municipalization was a piecemeal reform, weak in theory. Recognizing the de facto collectivism of city life, it represented not an overthrow of the market but a selective encroachment on that part of it whose public character seemed most evident—even to the utility corporations that were busily absorbing the term "public service" into their titles.

Municipalization was the first important Atlantic-wide progressive project. In borrowed experience and transnational example, in a shared language of germs and sewage, gas prices and streetcar fares, municipalizers across the North Atlantic economy began to construct a modest, alternative social economy to that of the thoroughly commercial city. But as the furor over streetcars and corruption showed, the municipalization movement was also a political lesson in the dramatic importance of timing, and of the cumulative effects of small differences. In the transition from democratic forms to democratic functions that the progressives so longed to achieve, both of these factors were, in the end, to matter profoundly.

5

Civic Ambitions

Private Property, Public Designs

The city of the progressives' political imagination was at once verb and image: an expression of intense, public activity and a picture in the mind. Frederic Howe could still remember, years later, his "architectonic vision of what a city might be . . . It was a unit, a thing with a mind, with a conscious purpose, seeing far in advance of the present and taking precautions for the future." From his first exposure to Albert Shaw's lectures at Johns Hopkins, he wrote, "I studied cities as one might study art; I was interested in curbs, in sewers, in sky-lines."[1]

Art and sewers: one stumbles momentarily over the juxtaposition, hunting for one's bearings among categories time has pried apart. It was central to the progressive temperament, however, to see social politics in terms of form as well as function. That the core values of a society should be written in its street designs and public buildings, its shelters and its cityscapes, was a conviction deep in progressive culture on both sides of the Atlantic. The cities in the mind's eye of progressives materialized in civic centers and zoning maps as fully as in public waterworks and streetcars. "Beauty" was their passion, Howe remembered. But it was not beauty that fired their passions per se as much as the possibility of conscious design: of impressing publicly chosen order on the city's immense, diffuse market in land, location, and building style. From the first stirring of the city planning idea, through the community building projects of New Dealers and European social democrats, the vision of communities that not only owned their basic infrastructure but also shaped their own design was a powerful presence in progressive social politics. The Atlantic connection that energized the one also energized the other.

In some ways, the progressives' absorption in city forms was a function of travel. With so little time to lose, the visitor's eye is a reader of forms and surfaces. Like thousands of pilgrims on the aesthetic grand tour before them, trying to decipher inner worlds of culture in the outer signs of art, the progressives were eager students of forms. It was a rare American progressive in Europe who did not dwell hungrily on facades and streetscapes as if the secrets of each nation's political culture could be discerned in them. The extraordinary breadth of Berlin's streets and the assiduousness with which the city authorities maintained their cleanliness spoke in exaggerated tones to the Americans of German efficiency and civic consciousness. Vienna *was* its monumental Ringstrasse, just as Paris was its boulevards, and New York its strange, towered skyline. Each city had its distinctive building patterns to be read: the solid phalanx of four- and five-story tenements pressed out to the very edges of Berlin; the mile upon mile of narrow streets and speculator-built housing in England, welded to the framework of the sanitary bylaws; the high, stone tenements of urban Scotland; the triple-decker frame houses elbowing their neighbors for space in Boston; the tenement canyons of New York.

Europeans read American cities with equal avidity. H. G. Wells thought Manhattan's skyscrapers the mark of a city in the grip of "soulless gigantic forces." Charles Booth, to the contrary, thought they spoke to the continent's magnificent energy. As progressives throughout the Atlantic economy rummaged more and more actively through each others' experiences and inventions, there were visitors everywhere, eagerly reading city forms for their underlying social meaning.[2]

Contradictory though the results might be, these efforts were hardly foolish. The surfaces sometimes misled—nowhere more acutely than in Berlin, where the slums, elsewhere on open display, were secreted away within the inner warrens of the city blocks. But to the extent that a city's forms and buildings, streetscapes and skylines, parks and dwellings, exposed the outlines of the underlying forces of land and shelter in the city, the eye did not mislead. The row house of a Birmingham working-class family, twelve feet wide, with a narrow strip of lot behind it, high fenced and too dark for living things to grow, was different from a small, free-standing

Chicago frame house straggling along a muddy street, strong with the smell of cheap, unseasoned wood. And each was different, in turn, from an alley dwelling in Washington, or a share of an airshaft in a Manhattan tenement, or a tightly cramped two-room, kitchen-and-*Stube* apartment in Berlin. The insistent, endless rectilinearity of the streets of Manhattan, Chicago, and a thousand lesser American places was different from the grand *allées* of Paris or the crooked warrens of a German city's inner core. And each of these differences reflected different mixtures of property, law, and politics.

All three of these elements profoundly shaped the city's outer form. The underlying ownership of landed property and building capital might be diffuse or tightly concentrated. The legal underpinnings of the urban land market might be geared to quick and easy property exchange or to intricate Chinese boxes of tenantry. The public interest in the city's spatial growth might be consciously expressed or abdicated to the market's myriad determinants of price and advantage. More than architecture, it was these elements of the market—or, in M. J. Daunton's more precise terms, of the reigning "property culture"—that gave cities their basic form.[3]

Whatever else a city in the North Atlantic economy might be, it was everywhere a great, churning, legally sustained market in land and shelter. In the imagination, real property may speak of stability, but nowhere else did real property change hands faster, or partake so deeply of commodification, than in the turn-of-the-century capitalist city. With its swelling, mobile populations, the great city was an enormously successful engine for real estate speculation. Parceled and priced for sale, leased for rent, or held for the quick, quixotic turn in use patterns that might suddenly multiply its value, land was a marketable commodity. So, for all the same reasons, was shelter. From the prevailing heights and densities of buildings to the city street patterns, the modal dwelling space for a wage earner's family, or the vacant lots that—left bare by speculators looking for the main chance—lent a distinctive gap-toothed appearance to American cities, the rights and power of property lay open to be read in the city's form.

Even to imagine that this confluence of private forces might be "planned" was to make a political claim audacious in its moment. Upon that ambition a striking number of progressives converged. Milo Maltbie, a central player in the New York City streetcar battles, took his first official city position as secretary to a commission to investigate European city design. Frederic Howe was a lifetime enthusiast of city planning. His close friend Lincoln Steffens was toying in 1909 with "the biggest piece of work I ever attempted"—the establishment of a "new calling, that of city manager or municipal architect." Florence Kelley, whose National Consumers' League was at the forefront of the fight for better labor conditions for working women, helped organize one of the first city planning exhibits in the United States. The *Survey*, collector of so many social-political ideals, opened its pages from the start to the city planning idea. The Russell Sage Foundation, the financial mainstay of social welfare causes in the period just before the First World War, poured almost half its endowment into the building of a model suburb along English lines, Forest Hills Gardens, on Long Island.[4]

These same concerns with city space, shelter, and design agitated every nation in the North Atlantic economy. From the first international congress on workers' housing, convened on the Paris exposition grounds in 1889, housing congresses were a regular international event. The showplaces of pre–World War I city planning drew social reformers like magnets: Port Sunlight, Bournville, Letchworth, and Hampstead in England; Frankfurt, Ulm, Hellerau, and the Krupp settlements in Essen in Germany. So did the most ambitious of the international city planning exhibits and congresses, the largest of which drew some two thousand persons to Vienna in 1910. Through these forums, social and legislative devices circulated with extraordinary speed: model housing designs and model housing legislation, street layout and zoning schemes, schemes for the control of land speculation, and devices to shape the development of outlying land.[5]

This network was already largely formed by the time the Americans entered it in the decade before the First World War. Once again they were latecomers. Partly as a result, partly because they could never wholly drive the aesthetics of the grand tour, with its landscapes of seamless unity, from the image of Europe in their mind, the disorder of their own cities, when seen afresh in transatlantic context, was often acutely embarrassing. A commercial "accident," Howe called the typical American city, in a progressive trope of many variations; one found in it "no sense of unity, of permanence, of the rights of the whole community." Walter Weyl, fresh from a tour of the new garden cities of England, echoed the point: what was the American city, but a "jumble . . . left to the clash of egotistical interests?"—an "overgrown, anarchic" Babylon. It was not necessary, Leo S. Rowe protested, "that the city should be a monotonous succession of narrow and depressing thoroughfares, that every available space should be covered with flaring signs, that at every street corner there should be a saloon, and that every individual should be permitted to give free range to his fancy in the erection of dwellings."[6]

In fact, turn-of-the-century London flared with as many advertisements as New York. The street facades in Wilhelmine Berlin, overbearing in ornament and bourgeois pride, were no less pushy, in their own way, than the smokestacks of Chicago. The capitalist city manifested everywhere its family resemblances. But the Americans were not wrong in thinking the forces of commodification ran particularly hard and particularly unchecked in their own cities. Seeing Paris, or even London, in the context of their quarrel with the privatized city, American progressives could not but notice the points of contrast. They took the European experiments in city planning as evidence of social design, of a market steered and directed toward public ends. "Planning," a key word in 1930s social politics, was brought into the American political vocabulary, via Europe, through the city planning idea. *Städtebau* (literally, "city building") had been its original name. Rebaptized in Britain as "town planning," it stood for a network of controls over land and building, the addition of a visible, public hand to the invisible one of price and market transactions. It promised a new collective control over city design and destiny; it promised new standards of shelter. It promised to put brick and mortar on the civic reformers' "city sense." "We are beginning to see the city as a conscious, living organism which the architect and engineer, . . . the administrator and the dreamer, can build and plan for the comfort, convenience, and happiness of people," Howe wrote. "In a big way, city planning is the first conscious recognition of the unity of society."[7]

With these visions and ambitions in mind, American progressives were an eager conduit for European notions of collective city design. One by one, across the Atlantic progressive network, they brought home a kit of planning tools, some to lie unused; others to be eagerly taken up; and still others to be transformed. The marks of these importations are still visible on the American urban landscape—in the borrowed classicism of public buildings erected with so much civic zeal in the mid-1890s and afterward; in urban parkways, like Philadelphia's Fairmount (now Benjamin Franklin) Parkway, cut according to the pattern of Baron Haussmann's Paris; in zoning ordinances imported from Germany that flourished, in altered form, like starlings in a new land. Hunt assiduously enough, and you can find a dozen frame houses still standing in Lowell, Massachusetts, the fruits of the first movement for publicly assisted housing in the United States, constructed out of pieces of English garden city design, New Zealand precedents, and home-grown labor politics.

The progressives' ambitions—salted away for the opportunities the war and the Depression would give them—ran farther still. No other planners in the North Atlantic economy devised bolder civic blueprints than the Americans between the 1890s and the eve of the First World War; nowhere else was the planning of cities pushed with such evangelical zeal. The self-conscious city, owning its essential services, steering the play of forces in the urban land market, its eye on the shelter needs of its inhabitants, its pride vested in its civic buildings and public spaces—for a moment, all this seemed of a piece to advanced progressives on both sides of the Atlantic.

Every modern urban agglomeration has some degree of planning, if only in the orderly management of a platting and real estate registry. Where unified landownership and a desire for political advertisement conjoined—in Penn's Philadelphia, L'Enfant's District of Columbia, or any of the urban showplaces of princely power in early modern Europe—the designs might be elaborate indeed. In the United States, however, the plan that had eclipsed them all by the midnineteenth century was the grid. New York City's rectilinear street plan of 1811, pushed through the East River marshes up to the very top of Manhattan, with calculated indifference to the terrain, established the model. Along this open-ended grid, it was left to private investors, speculative builders, buyers, and improvers to erect whatever they hoped the future might ratify or the market would bear. Planning boards and zoning ordinances were unknown; before the 1880s not even building codes inhibited individual prerogative in filling in the grid's blank spaces. Laid out in the surveyor's office with a ruler, grid planning facilitated maximum speed and efficiency in land sales. As the British town planner Raymond Unwin observed, the grid fit cities where land uses were in perpetual flux, where a residential street one day might be commercial block or a warehouse district the next.[8]

The grid was, in all these ways, the physical analogue of the laissez-faire economy: a legal and social contrivance for maximizing opportunities for exchange that easily turned "natural" in the mind. The grid was quick; it facilitated without controlling; it was the perfect plan for the capitalist city. It gave nineteenth-century American cities a form more definite and more transparent of their underlying economies than the older, accretive shapes of their European counterparts. But it was not public design except at the most elementary level. Outside of rarities like Olmsted's Central Park in New York, it generated cities strong in private spaces but weak in public ones. Neither practically nor symbolically did it satisfy the progressives' gathering vision of the city as a collective household. Just as the impulse toward civic unity drew American progressives to Glasgow's streetcars and

London's ferry boats, that impulse drew others to the tools of urban design being forged in the great cities of Europe.

Their first stop was Paris. As a model of a modern great city harnessed to a centralized design, no late-nineteenth-century city outshone it. "The handsomest city on the earth," Lewis Henry Morgan called Paris in 1871; "it makes a prodigious impression upon a stranger." It was not old Paris Morgan had in mind, its crowded, jumbled streets interrupted here and there with arenas for royal display, but the new one that had been laid so boldly over the fabric of the early city. In the middle decades of the nineteenth century, under the prodding of Napoleon III and the direction of Georges Haussmann, Paris had been reconstructed with an audacity, expense, and lavishness of public symbolism unmatched anywhere in the North Atlantic economy.[9]

Haussmann, to whom the practical work of rebuilding Paris fell, was a versatile planner for whom the city was never simply its street pattern. As Paris's prefect, he oversaw the construction of miles of new sewers and the completion of an aqueduct system capable of finally emancipating the city's water supply from the Seine. But the heart of Second Empire Paris was in its streets. Between 1853 and 1869 Haussmann oversaw the cutting of a dozen broad new avenues through the jumbled street pattern of old Paris. Virtually all the medieval buildings on the Île de la Cité were torn down but Notre Dame itself, and replaced with massive government structures. The Place de l'Étoile was elaborated with diagonal avenues that converged with geometrical obsession on that symbol of Napoleonic ambitions, the Arc de Triomphe.

Where he had a choice, Haussmann preferred cutting new streets to widening existing ones. The cost of purchasing inner lots was less than the cost of acquiring existing street frontage. More important, in the newly platted avenues Haussmann and Napoleon III found a tabula rasa for the new street vistas that were to give Second Empire Paris its distinctive character. To ensure that investors in the newly created street frontage lots contributed to the public spaces on display, Haussmann imposed both a uniform cornice height and common horizontal window and balcony lines. The results were block-long street facades that tugged the eye toward the vista's culminating point in a public square or monument.

The grand diagonal avenues with which Haussmann labored to centralize Paris were extravagantly expensive. State loans and subventions paid for a portion of the work, but the more extensive potential resource, as Haussmann quickly realized, was the land market itself. By buying lots cheap, driving the new streets through, and selling the new building lots dear, he created something akin to a perpetual motion machine for urban public works. If the scheme had expediency to commend it, it had a certain justice as well. Who better to finance the public expense of street building than those who suddenly found themselves in possession of parcels of land ideal for the construction of expensive shops and luxury apartments?

The boom in land values in Haussmannized Paris was a textbook example of socially generated price advantage: the "unearned increment," in the terms Henry George made current. In recouping it, Haussmann was assisted by a condemnation act that permitted city authorities to condemn more land than actually needed for the street cutting itself. "Excess condemnation," as the technique was later named in the United States, empowered Paris authorities to condemn and purchase a swath of land a building lot deep along the newly planned streets and sell it (with strict architectural controls) to private bidders at whatever the market would bear, using the returns to finance the improvement itself. Not even excess condemnation, however, was as plump a goose as Haussmann needed; by 1870, his budget spiraling out of control, he had become too great a liability for Napoleon III to bear. But not before the combination of public compulsion and private, speculative investment had constructed the century's single most powerful physical representation of the planned, recentralized city.

The messages to be read in the new streets of Paris were from the outset multivalent. The new city was clearly more efficient than the old. The new diagonal avenues greatly eased the flow of traffic and the distribution of goods. If the new streets promised trade, however, they also promised pacification. Not by chance were so many of the street cuttings concentrated in the old radical, working-class sections of Paris, where the barricades had gone up so often before; nor was it by chance that Haussmann set down barracks along the most strategically placed of them for the better deployment of city troops. "The man on horseback," Lewis Mumford wrote with no love of Haussmann's Paris, "had taken possession of the city."[10] The new streets merged the city and the parade ground; they created an environment for display, for marching soldiers, for whirling carriages. They were an engine of massive population displacement, above all for the city's laboring poor. They were a public works project on a monumental scale, drawing construction workers to the capital in such large numbers that conservatives feared their presence would undo all the regime's social palliatives.

Within these deeply mixed messages, Paris's visitors struggled to discern the city's core meaning. Mid-nineteenth-century American travelers, as we have seen, often shivered in recoil from Haussmann's work. To Albert Shaw in the mid-1890s, on the other hand, Paris was the most inspiring city on the continent, dedicated to teaching "the world a lesson of order, system, and logic, of emancipation and iconoclasm." Brand Whitlock, who was smitten by Haussmann's work in 1912, marveled at Haussmann's triumph over "the hideous anarchy and accident" that oppressed American cities.[11] Haussmann's city had intruded deeply into the urban land market in the name—however false and imperial—of the public weal. That much was visible to the eye. The question the city was to raise in all those who fell in love with it was how a comparable harmony of design, an equivalent control of the land and building markets, could be contrived without an empire's autocracy and pretense.

Given the multivalence of Haussmann's work, it is not surprising that each nation in the North Atlantic economy borrowed from it a different thread. Berlin's authorities seized on its monumental possibilities. From James Hobrecht's extension plan of 1862 onward, a neobaroque capital to rival Paris grew up around the older inner city, its extravagantly broad streets, monumental squares, and diagonal avenues quickly built up with ranks of speculator-built apartments. A different sort of Haussmannization came to Britain, this one focused on slums and sanitation. On the pattern of Birmingham's Corporation Street, British city authorities cored out poor and working-class neighborhoods for new commercial streets, recouping the cost through excess condemnation and resale of the new building lots. In London between 1872 and 1884 alone, a small city of the poor (as many as 20,000 persons, in Gareth Stedman Jones's estimate) was displaced by street clearances. Like the poor in Haussmann's Paris, they spilled over into adjacent neighborhoods, quickly overloading their capacity, to form moving slums of quicksilver fluidity. While German authorities focused on street design at the moving edge of city development, English city councils focused on demolition in the inner core. When Haussmann's Paris finally came to the United States and cut across the land-office grids, it was to take on still different meanings.[12]

The first elements of Paris-inspired city aesthetics arrived in American cities in the late 1880s in bits and pieces: columns, statuary, triumphal arches, and other fragments of the grand tour brought home for domestication. Between 1888 and 1901, given the task of improving Frederick Law Olmsted's informal Prospect Park in Brooklyn, the architectural firm of

McKim, Mead, and White rebuilt it with classical colonnades, centrally focused vistas, and a triumphal arch topped with horses and winged riders—straight out of Paris and Berlin. Charles Mulford Robinson, sent by *Harper's* magazine in 1899 to gather material on European methods of urban beautification, came back to promote investment in European-style public squares and streetscapes, fountains and public sculpture, artistically wrought lampposts and ornamented street signs—and on that undisguisedly imitative aesthetic, to build a career as one of the most successful city planning consultants in the country.[13]

The triumph of Europe-inspired civic architecture was the famous "White City" constructed for the Chicago world's fair of 1893. Daniel Burnham, the Chicago architect who orchestrated the White City project, had yet to see Europe outside of picture books. He let the fair's prestigious East Coast architectural firms set the aesthetic agenda. With Paris on their minds, they gathered their central buildings in a court of honor explicitly reminiscent of the Paris exposition of 1889, pledged themselves to architectural harmony, a common cornice line and a common white exterior, and constructed one of the most compelling icons of the turn of the century.[14]

A fair is only a fair; the temporary plaster facades erected in Chicago came down as quickly as they had gone up. But they left behind—in their centrally organized vistas, their clustered public buildings, and their startling unity of style—an aesthetic language for the civic unity that turn-of-the-century civic progressives valued so dearly. When in 1901 the architectural profession persuaded the federal government to take the design of Washington, D.C., in hand, to exhume L'Enfant's plan of 1791 from layers of subsequent commercial development, railroad invasion, and shifts in taste, the task was given to the principals of the Chicago fair. One of Burnham's first acts as chair of the consulting committee was to suggest a tour through Europe. If there was anything incongruous in the ensuing spectacle of an official American commission charged with the design of the nation's chief civic symbol jaunting through the great capitals of Europe, photographing everything and poring over the map of Washington, D.C., to debate where and how the appropriated elements could be successfully transplanted, contemporaries no longer noticed it.[15]

Of all Burnham's city designs, his Washington plan was the only one to be substantially realized, but his commercial city designs, where he had no underlying classical pattern to build on, were more revealing and important. Brought by Tom Johnson to Cleveland to find some architectural means of refocusing the tremendous centrifugal private energies of the capitalist city, Burnham proposed razing a commercially faltering waterfront section just northeast of the city's business core and building it over with a vast court of neoclassical public buildings—courthouse, library, city hall, federal office building, public auditorium, and unified railroad passenger station—in a design half borrowed from the Place de la Concorde, half from the White City's central courtyard. Frederic Howe, who rallied Cleveland's civic-minded businessmen to the project, remembered it years later as an inspiring, tactile representation of progressive "city sense." The streetcar fight was the Cleveland progressives' central battle, he wrote at the time, but it was the civic center project "that has brought all classes most closely together." Commissioned on the strength of his Cleveland work to draw up a general plan for San Francisco in 1905, Burnham proposed to join parks and scenic boulevards with a Cleveland-style monumental civic center, this time set at the focal point of a network of grand, new diagonal avenues whose Parisian derivation was pronounced and unmistakable.[16]

Grandest of all the city plans was Burnham's 1909 plan for the rebuilding of his own Chicago. No city had been more thoroughly shaped by its commercial enterprises. Chicago's downtown Loop, which Burnham's architectural firm had helped pack with steel-frame commercial buildings, was caught in a noose of elevated tracks and encircling rail yards. The Chicago River was a promoters' jumble of coal and rail yards, docks, derricks, and small factories. Beyond the Loop to the south and west were miles of speculator-built working-class housing, unpaved streets, factories, packing plants, steel mills, and yet more rail yards. Burnham took on the map of Chicago as if every piece of it were moldable by conscious design. He proposed to push the rail yards back into the suburbs, fill in the railroad-overrun lakeshore with miles of parkland and lagoon, and embellish the resulting Grant Park with museums and libraries. For the Loop he proposed ambitious street widenings, and for the rest of the city a new set of diagonal arteries cut through the grid and surrounded by a ring road where old fortifications might have been, had Chicago been Paris or Vienna on a colossal scale. At the focal point of this forcefully centralized street system, on cheap land in the immigrant-populated west side within a block and a half of Jane Addams's Hull House, he drew in a civic center, a version of the central building at the Chicago fair, pumped up with a dome that (by one of the plan's renderings) was to stand some thirty stories above street level.[17]

Trying to read the symbolic meanings in Burnham's Chicago plan leads one as quickly as Haussmann's Paris designs into deeply mixed messages. On the one hand, Burnham's scheme was that of a metropolis radically at odds with the commercial, hog-butchering, steel-driving city at the hub of the nation's rail network. His drawings shifted the center of the city bodily out of the commercial Loop and turned the eye from commerce to civics. In a city that had exploited its natural resources to the hilt for the sake of profit, Burnham proposed to repossess virtually the entire lakefront as public space. He overlaid the grid street pattern, which had allowed Chicago's real estate operators to expand their business unhindered across the prairie, with diagonal boulevards that funneled, with a centripetal symmetry more insistent than Haussmann had ever dreamed of, into a government center. The Brobdingnagian size of the center's dome derived from the need to establish a symbol of civics big enough to overshadow the skyscrapers of the city's commercial core. Burnham's artist accentuated the point, not entirely for drawing's ease, by rendering the Chicago skyline as a single homogeneous plane of roofs pierced by the immense dome of the civic center. In a city noisome with political corruption, the grandest building of them all—the St. Peter's of the new Chicago—was to be the city hall.

If an anticommercial strain was deep in this visionary representation of civic virtue, the circumstances of the plan were anything but anticommercial. Unlike the case in Cleveland, where Burnham had been appointed an official city adviser, the Chicago city plan was the property of the private Commercial Club, which financed and publicized it. Burnham, in the language of an architect accustomed to selling taste to clients, emphasized the intricate link between beauty, tourism, and commerce. His business backers needed little coaxing. With the right plan, they wrote, "Chicago is destined to become the center of the modern world." To push for realization of Burnham's scheme, they hired a public relations man (the "Chief of all Pushers," they boasted) who, together with a committee of 328 "leading citizens," blanketed the city with publicity. The Chicago Plan Commission prepared a two-reel promotional movie, a $15,000 slide show, a school textbook (which was required eighth-grade reading in the city schools from 1912 into the early 1920s), and a model sermon for ministers. To every property owner and substantial rent payer it distributed a pamphlet outlining the plan's advantages. The mere possession of a plan was an extraordinary commercial coup, a brilliant advertisement for the city and its future.[18]

Amid these ambivalent messages with regard to commerce, Burnham himself chose to stress the essentials of "order" and "unity," the need to see the city "as an organic whole." The civic center, "the keystone of the arch" of the entire plan, was to be "a monument to the spirit of civic unity."[19] Unity inspired civic progressives like Johnson and Howe to their own dreams of prairie Parises, in the hope that a rearrangement of the city streets and common spaces might spur a renaissance of public consciousness and public life. Their yearnings endowed their transatlantic models with a coherence well beyond what they possessed in fact. Haussmann never published a comprehensive plan for Paris, in deference, perhaps, to the hornets' nest of opposition he had already stirred up. Most British city councils, working piecemeal from project to project, never had an overarching plan at all. In progressive America, in contrast, city plans multiplied like toadstools. Between 1907 and 1916, over one hundred cities made or commissioned "comprehensive" plans, including half the nation's fifty largest cities.[20] In their very act of discovery and embrace, the Americans centralized what they appropriated.

In grasping for stakes so high, it is not surprising that the Paris-inspired city planners realized only a tiny fraction of their paper schemes. Few of the new city planning commissions had more than admonitory, advisory powers; the city plan, American style, was an aspirational document, not a legal one. In Cleveland's civic center and Chicago's Grant Park one can still see on display the progressive vision of public city spaces. But almost none of the Paris-inspired diagonal avenues laid out over the real property grid got beyond the drawing boards. New York's planning commission of 1904 to 1907 devoted itself to an unworkable scheme of étoiles and monumental bridge approaches, almost all of which were stillborn.[21] The same fate befell the civic focal point of Burnham's Chicago plan. The spot where the civic center's massive dome was to have been reared, abandoned by investors who saw the commercial future of the city beckoning north of the river, is now the site of a sprawling interstate highway interchange.

The problem of realizing the comprehensive city plans so boldly put forward in the first two decades of the century lay not simply in the symbolic conflict between the civic and the commercial city. It also lay in finding the legal and financial means to inject Haussmann-style intervention into the fabric of property rights in urban America. It was telling in this regard that the last chapter of Burnham's Chicago plan should have been given over to a long discussion of the problems of implementation, appended by a Chicago lawyer.

From the Paris and Birmingham examples, the obvious device was excess condemnation and recoupment of costs through the sale of improved building lots. Philadelphia's ferociously expensive Fairmount Parkway project was begun in this way. But for the most part, state courts refused to uphold excess condemnation statutes against the challenge that they constituted a compulsory taking of property from one set of owners for the benefit of others. Financing major street cuttings out of general revenues would have meant running up against the same debt limits that bedeviled the municipal ownership forces. Even had these been broken through, tax financing risked political resistance from voters who lived far from the improved districts, and who were unlikely to miss the fact that the primary beneficiaries of their boulevard taxes would be those who bet most shrewdly in the land market. In Reading, Pennsylvania, in 1910, a working-class majority rejected a businessmen's city plan on precisely these grounds. For the purchase of park lands, American states had discovered how to stretch the system of special assessments by which abutting property owners were taxed for street improvements. By creating special tax districts encompassing whole neighborhoods that were held to benefit from the construction of the parks, Kansas City financed virtually the entire cost of a ring of new carriage parks between 1900 and 1915. But the benefits of street cutting and public squares were hard to displace onto an assessment district larger than that of the abutting owners, who could hardly be expected to have their property sliced up and to pay for the loss at the same time. In the contest between property rights and planning, the odds were loaded differently in the United States than in Paris. The city that had been mortgaged to private land investments was not, in practice, easily remade as a symbol of civic unity.[22]

It is just as well that so few of the Haussmann-inspired designs came to fruition. With their excessive centralizing tendencies, their étoiles and converging diagonals destined to be overwhelmed by automobile traffic, they were better symbols of their backers' hunger for civic unity than mechanisms that could achieve it. Burnham-style city planning was architecture for the eye, obsessed with symmetry and symbolism. It barely touched the private city of vested property rights and speculative land investments. Indeed, it was the promise that planning would redound to every property owner's benefit in heightened values that helped draw businessmen to the Haussmann-derived schemes. But the unabashedly European aesthetic of Burnham-style city planning—its vestment of business boosterism and progressive hunger for civic unity in a Parisian design that, not long before, had seemed an affront to republican principles—was a sign of how quickly the Atlantic divide was now being spanned.

Beyond the city-beautiful movement's beloved Paris, there were understandings of city planning that cut much more deeply into the underlying markets in land and shelter than Burnham's—or even Haussmann's. In these developments German cities led the way. In part, their inventiveness derived from the special intensity with which land and housing pressures bore down on late-nineteenth-century urban Germany. Unlike American cities, which sprawled raggedly at every rim, German cities piled up their populations like moated camps. Beyond their historic walls, some German cities were ringed by tiny peasant plots, morseled over the generations, difficult to consolidate into parcels salable for building purposes. Others, Berlin being the most notorious in this regard, were girdled by the holdings of large speculative land companies, which had everything to gain by holding up the price of outlying land until it could be economically developed to the full five-story limit of the city building ordinance. Combined with urban growth rates higher than anywhere else in late-nineteenth-century Europe, these barriers to expansion put extraordinary pressure on land and housing prices in urban Germany.[23]

The results were city densities unmatched anywhere else in the North Atlantic economy. In London just before the First World War an average of eight persons lived in every residential building; in Philadelphia the figure was five; in Chicago, nine; in tenement-filled Manhattan, twenty. For the thirty-three major German cities, the median number of persons per residential building was twenty-one. If these were the outward signs of cities built to their borders with walkup apartment buildings—*Mietskasernen*, or "rental barracks," their German critics called them—the inner experience was one of fierce competition for air and space. In Hamburg in 1905, almost half the city population was housed in dwelling units of two or fewer rooms each. In much more fortunately situated Frankfurt, about a third of the city's population was so housed. In Berlin, where the overcrowding was fiercest, three quarters of the population—adults, children, and lodgers—were crammed into such dwellings.[24] Given these circumstances, it is little wonder that the question of adequate working-class housing had played so central a role in German debates over the social question since Adolph Wagner and others had taken it up in the 1870s.

Had need alone sufficed to politicize urban land and housing issues, the center of the reform movement would have been in Berlin. "The most compact city in Europe," the British planner Patrick Abercrombie called Berlin in 1914: "as she grows she does not struggle out with small roads and peddling suburban houses, but slowly pushes her wide town streets and colossal tenement blocks over the open country, turning it at one stroke into a full-blown city."[25] American visitors, puzzled by the apparent absence of American- and British-style spatial segregation, by a system that crammed middle class and poor together in massive apartment blocks—the affluent in flats lining the avenues, the less well off in the back courtyards, the poor under the eaves and in the darkest inner rooms—sometimes had difficulty sensing the intensity of the population and economic forces at work in the German capital. In contrast to London's easily visible poor, "poverty is guarded in Berlin, secret, hidden" reported Madge Jenison, one of the few Americans bold enough to tunnel into the inner warrens of the *Mietskasernen* to find it.[26] But nowhere in Europe were densities higher. On the eve of the First World War, the number of persons per inhabited building in Berlin was seventy-six, three and a half times the comparable figure for Manhattan. Aggressive policing had by then closed many of the cellar and attic dwellings of the 1870s. But by the official standard of overcrowding—which it took more than four persons per heatable room to exceed—some 600,000 Berliners were said to live in overfilled dwellings in 1912.[27]

If a future modeled on Berlin haunted German progressives, the prime laboratories for land and building policy were smaller, less fiercely pressured German cities, where the progressive policy groups had more room to maneuver. Some of those drawn to urban land issues were *Kathedersozialisten* like Wagner, or Schmoller's student Rudolf Eberstadt; others were German single-taxers, organized by the mid-1880s into a League for Land Reform; still others, like Albert Südekum and Hugo Lindemann, were key figures in the German municipal socialist movement. Among the movement for urban land and housing reform's most important figures, finally, were the centrist mayors who, with public health liabilities on their mind, were simultaneously nudging their municipalities into new realms of public goods and supply.[28]

Such a broad and amorphous coalition rallied, by necessity, to a grab bag of measures: tighter official inspection for sanitary standards and overcrowding, reform of tenant-landlord law, and (as we shall see) expansion of the supply of cheap, sound, working-class housing. It was the noose of speculative outlying land values, however, that shaped the boldest measures. The clearest way out of the shelter dilemma, as many saw it, was for cities to preempt the market in undeveloped suburban land, link it to the urban job market by the new, electrified city streetcar systems, and promote its development for low-density and low-cost housing. This was a vision of the city diffused across the landscape—more "natural" in its form than the tenement city, which, as many Germans saw it, flourished only in an artificial hothouse of legal and economic contingencies. German land reformers envied the English small house, the attached dwelling with its tiny garden plot, the profligate space of the rowhouse suburb.[29] By the early twentieth century they had developed a new set of planning techniques and market interventions to try to realize that vision.[30]

The most straightforward of the new tools was municipal land purchase. German cities, which had been net sellers of land in the earlier part of the century, began to buy back large amounts of undeveloped land within and outside their borders to direct urban development. Encouraged by a Prussian decree on the housing question in 1901, the purchase of extensive municipal land reserves ahead of the speculative developers soon acquired considerable momentum. The leader in this movement was Ulm, which by 1911 owned an astonishing 80 percent of the land within its limits, some of which it had begun to develop with small single-family houses for sale to its inhabitants (with the city reserving the right to repurchase). Frankfurt, which owned slightly more than half its underlying land in 1906, extended long-term leases to building societies pledged to the construction of low-cost workers' housing on the city's rim.[31]

Where a maze of peasant plots cut up the surrounding land into slivers unusable for building, even commercial developers could be thwarted by the resistance a handful of landowners waiting until the price rose extravagantly enough for their liking. The solution promoted by Frankfurt's Franz Adickes empowered city officials to buy out recalcitrant landowners at judicially assessed prices when the majority of their neighbors were willing to sell, combine the plots into usable building parcels, and sell the replatted land. Blocked in the Prussian legislature, which whittled Adickes's bill down to a special act for Frankfurt, this power to expropriate the most stubborn of small plot owners had more symbolic than practical weight. But as a statement of the collective rights of the city vis-à-vis the speculative rights of landowners, Lex Adickes (as it was known) deserved the wide publicity it received.[32]

More generally applicable was a tax on speculative land values. Popularized by Adolph Wagner, promoted by the German single-taxers, and encouraged by the animus against speculation that ran particularly hard in late-nineteenth-century German political culture, the idea quickly gained momentum after the turn of the century. Frankfurt in 1904 and Cologne in 1905 were the first cities to levy progressive taxes on land transfers through measures designed to collect up to a quarter of the unearned increment in price inflation and (as Adickes saw it) to undercut the barrier of land speculation on the city's rim. By 1911, when the empire itself undertook a two-year trial of a capital gains tax on urban land, more than 650 German municipalities, eager for new revenue sources and happy to let the tax incidence fall on speculative land profits, had followed suit.[33]

The final tool in this kit of new German measures was zoning. The idea of establishing distinctive building regulations for different districts of a city had not been unknown in late-nineteenth-century Germany. The typical beneficiaries were urban Germany's wealthiest citizens, for whom the building codes often laid out a distinct, class-segregated villa preserve, protected by special building-height limits from the outward march of the multistory tenement. The onion-skin model of the city, tapering in population density as one moved outward from the inner medieval warrens through the *Mietskasernen* districts to the low-density rim, had its clear attractions for the German bourgeoisie, many of whom were eager to escape the tradition of mixed-class living. Frankfurt's zoning ordinance of 1891, the first to cover an entire city with zones of differentiated building regulations, included such villa preserves. Adickes, its prime mover, defended the zoning act differently, however, and not disingenuously, as a means to limit the price expectations of outlying landowners. By enforcing lower densities at the city's rim, Frankfurt's city council hoped to encourage cheaper and more cheaply priced suburban construction. To reinforce the point, Frankfurt's zoning ordinance set aside outlying zones for low-density workers' housing; Berlin's zoning ordinance, adopted the next year, did the same.[34]

As an elaboration of the city's building code, zoning had legal teeth and practical consequences far beyond the paper aspirations of American city plans. At its most ambitious, zoning was a device to map out in advance of the price system the shape of the city's development: steering industrial development into districts convenient to rail yards and harbors; reserving zones for cheap, small, workers' houses convenient to jobs and transport; overlaying the dreams of speculative landowners with publicly articulated design.

None of the new measures dramatically altered the land and shelter relations in Wilhelmine Germany. Blocked from aggressive annexation and land purchase policies by imperial officials who hated the socialist majority in their own capital, Berlin remained locked in its fiercely overcrowded stone forms. The efforts of housing reformers to obtain passage of a Germany-wide housing law shattered against the resistance of the householders' and property owners' lobbies. Though symbolically important, the unearned increment tax never amounted to more than a trickle within the prewar German cities' revenue streams; in Berlin in 1910, less than 4 percent of the city's revenues derived from it. Even in his own Frankfurt, Adickes's interventions in the land market triggered strenuous opposition from the property owners' associations.[35] Still, limited as the planning measures were, the German interventions into the workings of the urban land market had created a set of potentially borrowable tools with which to try to build cities different from both the privatized metropolis and Haussmann's parade ground on the Seine.

In Britain, city planning ambitions initially took a quite different direction than in turn-of-the-century Germany. Outside Scotland, where high land prices and low wages allowed the multistory tenement to flourish, British cities were built to a lower, broader scale. Where German cities pushed their multistory *Mietskasernen* out to the edge of the developed land, the outer rim of British cities distended in a sprawling expanse of two-story row houses set on narrow, relentlessly uniform streets and attenuated lots, all rigidly cut, after 1877, to the sanitary minimums of the Local Government Board's model bylaws. To offset the sameness and repetition, one block of houses might sprout bow windows, another mock-Tudor timbers set in plaster, another imitation Swiss scrollwork on the overhanging eaves, Tiffany glass windows, pseudo-Grecian wooden pillars, fancy ridges of colored roof tile, or gaily painted trim—in a riot of builders' handbook styles desperately seeking to establish a sense of place through marketable facades. The shape of urban England, a compromise between custom and inventiveness, legal rigidity and private investment calculations, was not the free result of market choices. But neither, by the same token, was it planned.[36]

The first of those to try their hand at designs shaped to visions larger than public health minima were paternalistic manufacturers. At Port Sunlight outside Liverpool in 1888, soap manufacturer William Lever laid the groundwork for a much-photographed company village of half-timbered, heavily ornamented, clustered dwellings. More sober was the employees' village George Cadbury built in the shadow of his Bournville cocoa works, where streets of plain-fronted double and quadruple houses converged on the schools, stores, and Quaker meetinghouse that Cadbury set in the town's central green. Vision played no small role in these designs, helped by the manufacturers' outright ownership of the land to be developed. But not the less advantageous were the advertising possibilities of the picturesque company village and the usefulness of attractive housing in retaining the skilled labor elite that employers needed.[37] Analogues to these British company villages were to be found throughout the North Atlantic economy: in Essen, where Krupp-sponsored Margarethenhöhe was the high-water mark of prewar German workers' housing design; in Pullman, Illinois; or Vandergrift, Pennsylvania—all joined by a highly self-conscious exchange of techniques and designs.

Economically and socially bolder was Ebenezer Howard's pioneer garden city at Letchworth. Launched in 1903, with backing from some of Britain's leading model employers, Letchworth was an experiment in single tax economics, comprehensive town planning, and an environment more attractive than either isolated country living or the pressures of great city life. A utopian socialist of the cooperative commonwealth stripe, Howard was particularly concerned to capture the new town's unearned increment for its collective use. Raymond Unwin, Letchworth's principal architect, was a Fabian socialist inspired by the aesthetics of German medieval towns. A hybrid of planning, vision, and its own speculative ambitions (one of the first sights to greet visitors disembarking at Letchworth's rail platform was the venture's land office, flags flying), the town Howard and Unwin collaborated to construct gained instant international recognition as a model of progressive design in both form and economics. Letchworth's development, Walter Weyl observed,

> is not the rank and noxious growth of wild cities, stretching out fortuitously in miles of jerry-built houses towards the cheaper land or the more necessitous land-owner . . . It is not the modern factory town, with a towering smoke-stack for a capital, surrounded by drab quadrangles of monotonous houses . . . It is not structureless, not unpremeditated. It is not a city at once congested and dispersed, with unsightly bald spaces surrounded by hoardings, and with workshops, saloons and residences huddled promiscuously.

The garden city was the city planned, "an organic, a synthetic city."[38]

In 1905 Toynbee Hall's Henrietta Barnett recruited Unwin for a parallel experiment in mixed-class suburban design on the London rim. With his Hampstead Garden Suburb, Unwin created a stunning village of meandering streets borrowed from the little towns of southern Germany, with squares and cul-de-sacs curving in on themselves to create neighborhood spaces, and subtle architectural disguises for the village's underlying class differentiations. Among prewar urban reformers in Europe and America, the English ventures in philanthropic village design—Hampstead, Letchworth, Bournville, and Port Sunlight—were among the most widely known visual icons of the day: blueprints for the resocialized city.[39]

If these tiny islands in the sea of speculator-built housing were to become less rare, however, broader public powers would be needed. It was at this juncture that British progressives awoke to the city planning techniques coming out of Germany. The initial work of publicizing the new German planning measures fell to a wealthy, well-traveled Manchester urban reformer, Thomas Horsfall. His *The Improvement of the Dwellings and Surroundings of the People: The Example of Germany*, published in 1904, was hardly a book at all but a sack stuffed with translated German reports and statutes. Prodded by John Nettlefold, chairman of the Birmingham city council's housing committee, that city quickly dispatched a delegation to investigate German planning at the source. Nettlefold himself soon steered a bill into Parliament that would have empowered British municipal authorities to purchase cheap outlying land ahead of the developers (as the Germans could), plan it in coordination with transportation systems, and lease much of it (on the Frankfurt model) to limited-divided building societies.[40]

Blocked at the Local Government Board, Nettlefold's proposal was transmuted from a land purchase scheme to a set of planning powers. Under the provisions of the planning section of the Housing and Town Planning Act of 1909, English local authorities still could not engage in general land purchases, but they were authorized to develop detailed development plans for specific, unbuilt areas about to experience intensive development and, with the approval of the Local Government Board, to enforce those plans with the power of law. Only a handful of cities, Nettlefold's Birmingham in the lead, had filed extension plans by the outbreak of the First World War. British town planning authorities could work only piecemeal, on designated portions of the urban rim. But there they could lay out streets and reserve public spaces (setting the cost against the abutting property owners), cluster neighborhoods, establish industrial and commercial districts, and specify (ahead of development) density limits and, in special cases, even lot lines. Thomas Adams, who went from the manager's office at Letchworth to the new post of town planning adviser at the Local Government Board, exaggerated when he tried to convince Americans that the town planning act had done everything needed.[41] But in its breach of customary land ownership rights and prerogatives, in its vesting of an element of foresight in the city itself, the act had done a good deal.

By the time Burnham's Chicago plan was completed, European city planners had, in short, constructed a set of legal and administrative tools that cut sharply into urban land and property structures. Between the German architects of *Städtebau* and the British garden city designers there was already a vigorous interchange of techniques and visions. Haussmann's techniques, as we have seen, were world famous. The meetings of the *Congrès international des habitations à bon marché* drew reformers from across Europe and the United States. That American progressives, coming from city land markets as volatile as any in the North Atlantic economy, would be caught up in these debates and ambitions was, by now, a given. Hoping to gain a measure of control over city design, some of them would reach out eagerly for the new international kit of techniques. What was less certain in 1909—though the Chicago plan's legal consultant was perhaps better placed than most to have predicted it—was whether these efforts would be enough to move city planning in America from its symbolic and visual agenda to deeper social purposes. That, in turn, would depend on which of the imported tools could survive the Atlantic crossing with its edge intact.

"City Planning in Justice to the Working Population"

Absorbed in their borrowed streetscapes and civic centers and the economic ambitions of their business patrons, the leading architects in the American city-beautiful movement barely noticed, at first, the new directions city planning had taken in Europe. The work of injecting a deeper social politics into city design fell, instead, to a circle of social workers and settlement house residents in that cauldron of overbuilding, lower Manhattan. Like their German counterparts, their primary interest was not in symbols but in land values and shelter, particularly as they bore down on the cities' working class.

The animating figure in this group was Florence Kelley, who had moved from Chicago's Hull House to New York City in 1899 to head the staff of the National Consumers' League. Following her investigations of women's working conditions into the factories and garment lofts of lower Manhattan, Kelley was appalled at the fierce overcrowding of the working-class sections of New York, the closely packed tenement districts still foreign to Chicago, and the new, dark urban canyons. By 1907 she had gathered a set of like-minded coworkers into a Committee on Congestion of Population in New York: Lillian Wald of the Henry Street Settlement;

Edward T. Devine of the New York Charity Organization Society; John Martin, the émigré municipal socialist; Paul Kellogg of the *Survey;* George Ford, a young architect and Greenwich House resident; Mary Kingsbury Simkhovitch of the Greenwich House settlement, who was to carry all these concerns into the public housing movement of the 1930s; and, soon, Frederic Howe. Within a year they had hired as executive secretary Benjamin Marsh, whose experience included a stint in Simon Patten's courses at the University of Pennsylvania, an investigation of begging and vagrancy in Europe and America, a Greenwich House residency, and strong single tax convictions.[42]

The Congestion Committee immediately dispatched Marsh to Europe to attend the International Housing Congress in London in the summer of 1907 and to glean policy suggestions where he could. Marsh came back with rafts of material drawn from Horsfall and Nettlefold and an enthusiasm for what he unembarrassedly called the "foreign system of city planning." In the spring of 1908, Marsh and the committee mounted a consciousness-raising "congestion exhibit" in Manhattan. Its eye-catching pieces were representations of the overcrowded city: a life-size tableau of a tenement sweat shop, its twelve-by-twelve foot floor covered at night with mattresses and sleeping workers; a three-dimensional map of Manhattan and Brooklyn population densities; slum photos; charts of death and disease rates; diagrams documenting the concentration of Manhattan land ownership; and a pair of cubes, specially prepared by Marsh, showing the increase in Manhattan land values since the 1620s. If American conditions held center stage, however, on the walls the committee hung hints of the way out: plans and photos of Bournville and Port Sunlight, Frankfurt and Cologne's zoning maps, and photos of a cooperative working-class apartment house in Berlin. The borrowed solutions did not make the congestion problem seem more intense, but in making it potentially solvable, in snatching the problem of the overfilled city away from the status of mere fate or nature, the borrowed measures made congestion political.[43]

The next summer Marsh was off to gather material in Europe again, the fruits of which he turned into a book, *An Introduction to City Planning* (1909), the first clear description of German city planning measures to reach American readers. In the spring of 1909, the committee organized yet another exhibit, this time in Washington, D.C., showered the United States Senate with German city planning materials, and convened the nation's first conference on city planning problems.[44]

Pressed by Marsh and the Congestion Committee, by Howe at the

People's Institute in New York, and by European missionaries of the new city planning techniques, the Americans' learning curve was steep. Raymond Unwin, Thomas Adams, Henry Vivien, and E. G. Culpin from the British garden city movement, Albert Südekum of *Kommunale Praxis*, and Werner Hegemann, organizer of the Berlin city planning exposition of 1910, all undertook American lecture tours between 1910 and 1913 to popularize the social-political aspects of city planning. When the journal *Charities and the Commons* ran a symposium of expert commentary on city planning in 1908, edited by Charles Robinson and heavy with civic center enthusiasms and Paris illustrations, Marsh's "City Planning in Justice to the Working Population," with its radical economic concerns and its strange kit bag of German property controls, stuck out like a rude voice at an aesthetes' tea party. Six years later, when the *Annals of the American Academy of Political and Social Science* convened a parallel symposium, the English and German techniques were common rhetorical coin.[45]

The open questions were of ends and means. To the Congestion Committee, the overriding imperative was to ease the forces crowding wage earners and their families ever more closely into lower Manhattan's tenements at ever higher aggregate rents. That meant breaking up the concentration of factories and sweatshops on the lower tip of the island and dispersing industry in smaller nodes across the city. Florence Kelley thought the sharpest tool for the purpose was municipal land purchase, to allow planners to fashion districts for industry and low-density workers' housing at the city rim. By 1910, she and Mary Simkhovitch were deep into a still more ambitious scheme—this one closer to Howard's ideas than Adickes's—to counter the population tide flowing into Manhattan with a statewide program of industrial decentralization, dispersed model towns, and rural economic revitalization.[46]

Others in the Congestion Committee circle pressed for occupancy laws along British and German lines, limiting the number of persons a given tenement volume could hold. John Martin thought the key to population dispersal lay in the development of public rapid transit, with European-style cheap fares for wage earners. The Russell Sage Foundation, worried that suburban land development would only exacerbate the problem without higher design standards than the whim of speculative ambition, found its key in the British garden city. In 1910, with architect Grosvenor Atterbury playing Raymond Unwin's role, the foundation began construction of a model suburb along the Long Island Railroad, the streets of which, curving gently upward from its Unwinesque village gate, left no doubt about its

Hampstead origins. Amid the anarchic play of economic forces in the suburban land market, Forest Hills Gardens was to be, in Atterbury's words, an oasis of social and aesthetic "collectivism."[47] Benjamin Marsh's answer lay in taxing land values to capture the landlord's unearned increment, better and cheaper transportation, and zoning as German cities had practiced it.[48] By 1912, Marsh's refusal to bend his increasingly single-minded commitment to land taxation had cost him his Congestion Committee position and his place in the city planning movement that his German reports had done so much to inaugurate. The other schemes withered, but zoning endured.

Indeed, where the other German and British importations faltered, zoning thrived in the United States—but only with political help from sources quite different from the Congestion Committee. For Marsh and Kelley, zoning's promise lay in factory dispersal. By 1910, with that in mind, the Congestion Committee had successfully maneuvered a fairly faithful copy of German zoning practices through the New York legislature (though not past Governor Hughes's veto), setting aside special areas for dispersed factory development along the city's transportation arteries and limiting the outward march of the five-story tenement.

But like every policy import, once extracted from its original economic and political setting, zoning proved an enormously malleable device, open to a multitude of purposes and possessors. When the Congestion Committee's zoning proposal failed, those who came to its rescue were New Yorkers of a very different political stripe: merchants in the city's upscale Fifth Avenue district, whose primary goal was to keep the garment shops, which were creeping up Fifth Avenue as manufacturers tried to obtain cheaper access to their merchant buyers, in the lower parts of the island, where they belonged. Broadcasting tales of their prime customers being shouldered off Fifth Avenue's sidewalks by crowds of immigrant garment workers on their lunch break, the merchants' association struck on the idea of establishing a special zone in which the height for new buildings would be set high enough for a proper retail shop but too low to be economical for rent to garment manufacturers. When this project stalled, the Fifth Avenue merchants took a simpler and more effective path, boycotting goods made within the zone they now unilaterally declared off-limits for garment manufacture, and persuading the city's major lenders to refuse loans for garment loft construction in the area. But the pushing and hauling among zoning's potential appropriators had already begun.[49]

The group that finally effected the nation's first German-derived zoning law, in 1916, was different still: a set of civic-minded New York businessmen and lawyers associated with the City Club. For them the key issue was not population density in lower Manhattan, or Fifth Avenue's crowded sidewalks, but the onward march of office skyscrapers. Having finally overcome the transit monopoly's resistance to the extension of the city's subway system, the City Club group feared the capacity of the new lines would be quickly consumed (and the city's heavy construction subsidy wasted) if Manhattan landowners were not prevented from immediately crowding the island's core with still larger office buildings. In this pinch, the German idea of differential building limits, thrown into the debate by Marsh and the Fifth Avenue merchants, had an obvious attraction. Edward Bassett of the new utilities regulatory commission for New York, who remembered being "taken off my feet" by the Düsseldorf city planning exhibit in 1908, was appointed chair of a special city commission on the heights of city buildings. George B. Ford of the Congestion Committee was the commission's secretary. Frank B. Williams, chair of the City Club's city planning committee, was appointed European investigator. Dispatched to Germany, Williams returned with a sheaf of detailed zoning ordinance maps and specifications, grist for yet another public exhibition of American and European planning techniques, mounted in the fall of 1913.[50]

Supported by a city reform administration and a state enabling act, and worked out in detail by yet another city commission, the resulting zoning ordinance of 1916 was a milestone for those who had helped bring the techniques of *Städtebau* to the United States. The first comprehensive zoning plan in the country, New York City's was no mere paper plan, like Burnham's for Chicago, nor was it a limited British-style extension scheme. It covered the entire city, German-style, with a map of differentiated use and building districts. But having been drawn with the help of lawyers hypersensitive to the property rights of city landowners, the resulting scheme rested its hand on property's developmental possibilities with extraordinary delicacy. Fearing challenge in the courts, the drafters constructed a set of building volume limits capacious enough to have accommodated virtually every existing large building in Manhattan—and hence (as the commission was at pains to make clear) virtually every downtown property owner's imaginable anticipated return. With modest architectural ingenuity, developers soon found ways to push the height of new Manhattan skyscrapers far beyond the seventeen to twenty stories the commission had thought the "economic limit" for tall buildings under the zoning act.

Though the City Club group talked boldly of the end of the skyscraper age, their delicately drafted ordinance barely touched on speculative downtown values at all.[51]

Where the 1916 act's teeth were sharper was in its second innovation: the establishment of outlying districts exclusively for residential use. This was not the German model, but Williams, for one, had no love for the pattern of mixed stores and residences typical of even the villa sections of German cities. The legal precedents for exclusive residential zoning were already in place in the courts, set there through successful California drives to clean certain "nuisances" out of residential districts, by which California voters meant, in the first instance and with explicitly racial intent, Chinese-owned shops and laundries. With a flourish of photos depicting factories "invading" residential blocks, advertisement-covered stores "invading" brownstone rows, and apartment houses "invading" neighborhoods of single-family houses, the New York City commission's final report brought the Congestion Committee's campaign for a city zoning law to a successful culmination—but only by inverting its underlying purposes. To give the "invasion" image effect, the New York State zoning law vested the power to initiate an exclusive residential district not in the city, but in each street's existing property owners. Zoning's mission was no longer to disperse overcrowded, overfactoried lower Manhattan so that its working population could breathe. Zoning's task was to keep lower Manhattan in its place.[52]

Transformations of this sort were not peculiar to the United States. Throughout the North Atlantic economy the new land-use planning devices, hedged with timidity and qualifications, had struck an exceedingly cautious, fragile balance between public power and private property rights. Everywhere the compromisers struggled with a common consideration: how to restrain the land and shelter markets from generating the most socially costly of their potential outcomes without, in the process, crippling their underlying energy. Zoning's possibilities were not yet closed in 1916. But as it came through its first American test, there was no mistaking the tilting of the borrowed device toward property's prerogatives. Frank B. Williams in 1916 was sure that zoning's prime selling point was that it would not merely stabilize but augment land values. By the 1920s, the tenet that every property owner came out a winner from a well-designed zoning plan was a fixed part of zoning's orthodoxy.[53]

The Atlantic crossing, in short, remade zoning. A device invented to curb property's speculative advantages, it flourished in the United States as a realtor's asset. Extracted from the rest of *Städtebau*'s tools, zoning in

America was for property's promotion. "As for zoning," one of its critics lamented in 1920, when the U.S. Commerce Department's big push for the adoption of zoning ordinances was barely under way:

> it has risen, or fallen, from a means toward city beautification to the position of chief stabilizer of real estate values. Its present most insistent advocate is the real estate mortgage broker, who would like to lift his securities into the realm of comparative safety-of-principle enjoyed by preferred industrials. A long way, all this, from the half head, half heart crusade against the slum, with which housing reform began.[54]

A long way, indeed, from visions of exerting conscious direction over development on the city's rim. A long way from Letchworth's "organic" form or the model working-class housing at Bournville. Longer still from the notion that the tools of *Städtebau* might finally free urban dwellers from the vise of overcrowded, shoddy, and unsanitary dwellings, and the grip of the land speculator.

The missing ingredient, of course, was housing. Visions of boulevards and Haussmannized streetscapes crossed the Atlantic to merge with native boosterism. The idea of the zoning map struck a multitude of chords. For paper plans, elastic categories, advertisements for growth, the Americans had a marked weakness. But when it came to the bottom line of the urban land question, the provision of shelter, their resistance to public means ran deep.

To be sure, none of the nations in the North Atlantic economy injected public funds into the provision of shelter without marked reluctance. The instinct of urban reformers everywhere was to leave housing to private initiative. Defenders of the market's automatic operation put their faith in the invisible hand of profit. Those with a more realistic sense of the difficulty of constructing housing cheap enough for the urban working class, yet at a margin tempting enough for private investors, looked instead to limited-profit private undertakings: quasi-philanthropic housing companies willing to build cheap sanitary housing at limited profit, or cooperative associations of workers themselves.

The most important site of housing philanthropy was London. Since the middle of the century, capital investors content with 5 percent returns on their investments and a margin on their conscience had dotted London with model dwellings for the working class. At least thirty model housing companies were at work in London in the late nineteenth century—one of the biggest of them, the Peabody Trust, the midcentury benefaction of an American businessman. When slum clearance began in earnest in Britain in the last quarter of the century, local authorities took it for granted that the limited-dividend housing companies would shoulder the rehousing work—purchasing sections of the condemned and cleared land from the city authorities and rebuilding it with low-cost, sanitary tenements.

By the end of the century the philanthropic housing companies' efforts were an inescapable presence in the London landscape: high, alien-looking apartment blocks built, for economy's sake, on a tenement scale that broadcast their institutional character, their renters hedged round by stringent behavioral qualifications and requirements. C. F. G. Masterman ridiculed the most stringently economical of them, the Peabody buildings, as "block dwellings of the style known as the Later Desolate." Yet even the Peabody's fierce economies of construction were no match for the accumulating need. The London authorities, required at the outset to compensate owners according to the rent their old jammed and unhealthy dwellings had pulled in, found themselves unable to sell the cleared tracts to the limited-dividend housing companies except at massive losses; few of the philanthropic housing companies, in turn, succeeded in rebuilding at rents that the evicted—even had they not been long dispersed elsewhere—could have afforded. Even the provision of low-cost government loans did not make up the difference. Some 123,000 persons lived in the dwellings of the London limited-dividend housing companies in 1905; still, building had not kept pace with the combination of clearances and population growth in working-class London.[55]

It was the accumulating crisis over slums, slum clearance, and rehousing that accounted for the resulting anomaly: that late-nineteenth-century Britain, where the tenets of classical economics still had considerable political purchase, should have been the first nation in the North Atlantic economy to shift from market and quasi-market housing to outright public construction. After twenty years of clearance work and little success in finding investors willing to construct low-cost replacement housing, Glasgow's city council backed into the expedient of municipal replacement housing in 1889. A year later, the Housing of the Working Classes Act extended to local authorities the power to borrow from the Public Works Board for the construction of wage earners' housing. In Birmingham, despite a particularly vicious heritage of cheap, back-to-back housing, Nettlefold and his fellow councilors effectively resisted this last phase of municipal trading. But other cities used the legislation aggressively; before the First World

War, municipal authorities in Liverpool and Glasgow each built more than two thousand units of low-cost housing.[56]

The showplace of municipal housing was London. Between 1889 and 1907, the Progressive-dominated London County Council gave municipal housing a utopian spin and energy all its own. The first of the London County Council projects—loose clusters of five- and six-story apartment blocks, far taller than their surroundings—did not depart radically from the philanthropic housing companies' patterns, though the LCC architects equipped them with more generous inner space, a more generous architectural imagination, and sometimes grouped them around a school, playground, bandstand, or small common green. Frustrated by the intractable economics of slum rebuilding, however, the LCC Progressives began to turn their ambitions to cheaper land on London's suburban rim. At Tooting to the south and Tottenham to the north, along lines of the newly municipalized tram system, they began the more audacious experiment of municipally built suburban workers' housing. Constructed as conventional, narrow row houses on narrow bylaw streets, the suburban projects had none of the institutional character that the economies of multistory building imposed on the innercity projects. What gave away their public character was the LCC architects' insistence on more generous standards of amenities and inner space, and the long horizontal lines—still striking when one comes on them—with which, in defiance of the speculative builders' pseudoindividualizing style, they tried to bind the units together in clusters and neighborhood solidarities.[57]

London's suburban projects were built too well, they cut too close to the potential market share of private builders, and they returned too little to the pockets of slum property owners to be universally popular. When the Conservatives gained ascendance on the council in 1907, they put an end to the suburban projects and turned back to the Sisyphean labors of slum clearance. Nevertheless, by the eve of the war public authorities in greater London had added some 15,000 housing units to the city's stock of low-cost housing.[58]

Municipal housing by itself did not solve the riddle of providing decent shelter where incomes were indecently low. The dwellings built under the Housing of the Working Classes Act were for the skilled and the steadily employed, not for the truly poor. All together, less than 5 percent of the housing built in England between 1890 and 1914 was local government housing; even in Glasgow, the new municipal houses amounted to barely 1 percent of the whole.[59] Most working-class families in early-twentieth-century Britain, like working-class families elsewhere, lived in other people's cast-off, crowded housing. But however contested the issues remained on the eve of the war, British authorities had added the provision of decent working-class housing to the list of a city's social tasks.

Less aggressive in slum clearance campaigns than Britain, cities elsewhere in Europe followed a different course toward housing policy. Since the late 1880s it had been clear everywhere that the markets and the philanthropists, alone or in concert, were no match for the great cities' need for cheap housing. In Germany the Verein für Sozialpolitik took up the housing question for investigation in 1885 and 1886; the Société française des habitations à bon marché dated from 1889. Their answer was not public housing, however, as in Britain, but a marriage of public funds and voluntary endeavor.

Belgium (in 1889) and France (in 1894) took the lead at the national level with the establishment of state banks to extend cheap public loans to noncommercial builders of sound workers' housing. In France, the Musée Social's Jules Siegfried was the measure's prime mover. In the minds of its promoters, the so-called *loi Siegfried* represented a carefully drawn middle way between illusions of market competence and the "path of State socialism" (as Siegfried himself put it), down which the British seemed to have blundered with their housing act of 1890. Like so many aspects of "subsidarist" social policy, the French act was stronger in principle than in execution. Local authorities dragged their feet until the subsidies were substantially raised. But the French scheme, widely imitated, quickly became orthodoxy at the international housing congresses.[60]

In Germany, despite the empire's exaggerated reputation for centralization and efficiency, no coherent policy akin to the French statute of 1894 was adopted. The turning point came, rather, in 1890, when a provision slipped quietly through the Reichstag enabling managers of the state's new regional social insurance funds to invest at their discretion in nonprofit and limited-profit working-class building associations. These rapidly accumulating public reserves, made available at a percentage point or so below the market rate, quickly became an engine, unmatched elsewhere, of public investment in nonmarket housing. By the late 1890s one could see the act's fruits in new sorts of model tenements built around large, open courtyards and equipped with playgrounds, reading rooms and meeting halls, kindergartens, libraries, and laundry rooms—the ingredients, however strong the paternal hand, of community.[61]

Many of the recipients of the subsidized housing credits in Germany were British-style limited dividend companies that drew on the conscience of accomplished accumulation. Others, given the peculiar closeness of state and society in Germany, were hard to distinguish from politically insulated public authorities. The most aggressive and successful of the limited dividend associations, Frankfurt's Aktienbaugesellschaft für kleine Wohnungen, had been founded by mayor and Verein für Sozialpolitik member Johannes Miquel. Granted extensive city credits and leases on cheap city land especially purchased for the purpose along its new streetcar corridors, the association and its sister organizations had constructed an astonishing 7.2 percent of the city's total housing stock by the eve of the First World War.[62]

Still larger were the German cooperative building societies that flourished under the post-1890 housing subsidies, some socialist or trade union in origin, others the product of philanthropic initiative. Unlike the artisans' building cooperatives in Britain organized to finance private house construction, the German building co-ops pooled the small weekly dues of a large number of working-class members, invested the funds in the construction of cooperative tenements, and rewarded members with a chance at an apartment. By 1914 the co-ops had built some 21,000 housing units in Germany, almost as many as British public authorities had constructed over the same period.[63]

As in France and Britain, the German results were terrifically uneven. Efforts to enact an empirewide housing standards law failed to breach the resistance of the Prussian authorities, leaving a patchwork of weak inspection powers. In the Rhineland, where labor pressure was particularly strong and social Catholicism gave that pressure a certain leverage with the business classes, the regional insurance boards invested up to half their funds in working-class housing. Berlin's regional insurance board, under the grip of the property holders' associations and the real estate lobby, invested only 7 percent. Düsseldorf experimented with direct municipal housing, British-style; Ulm and Frankfurt, with land purchases for low-cost housing. The vast majority of German cities, on the other hand, did neither.[64] As in Britain, publicly assisted housing was for skilled workers and the lower middle class; the poor had to make do elsewhere. Nowhere in Europe did progressives call the housing problem solved. But one way or another in the generation after 1890, housing had entered the field of social politics.

All these European housing endeavors were closely followed by American progressives. The limited-dividend housing company came early to the

United States as a conscious British importation. Most major northeastern cities boasted one or more philanthropic housing company by the turn of the century, though none—not even in New York City, the movement's center—approached the scale of the London enterprises. Housing surveys, limited slum clearance powers, and housing construction codes all successfully made the Atlantic crossing. The new measures for public housing investment were closely watched as well. The French law of 1894 had vocal American backers. Dozens of American investigators trooped through the London municipal housing projects, the favored ones with John Burns himself as their guide; the city's working-class housing developments quickly became an obligatory way station on the sociological grand tour. Still other American progressives turned up at the international housing congresses held in Paris (1900), Düsseldorf (1902), London (1907), and Vienna (1910).[65]

The most elaborate of the American investigations was a study tour of the newest British housing work, organized by the National Housing Association in the summer of 1914. Modeled in miniature on the National Civic Federation's municipal ownership commission of 1906, the seven-person committee, headed by the association's field secretary, John Ihlder, spent two weeks inquiring into every aspect of British housing, public and private. At Letchworth, Ebenezer Howard lectured them on garden city principles. In London they sought out John Burns, Thomas Adams, Sidney Webb, Raymond Unwin, and the leading figures in the London County Council's architectural office. They toured the East End slums, the Peabody buildings, the LCC projects in the East End and on the London rim, Hampstead, and the first showpiece of London extension planning under the 1909 act. In Birmingham, Liverpool, and Manchester they followed much the same itinerary: slums, "normal" houses, the new public and private improvements, conversations with ordinary tenants, and interviews with the leading housing and planning figures.

Ihlder, who assiduously took notes on rents, costs, and tenant composition, was impressed with much of what he saw. British slums were not as bad as the worst of American housing, he concluded, despite the "mean, monotonous streets," the "fearful land overcrowding," and the ubiquitous high-fenced backyard. Sanitary regulations, in place longer than in the United States, had more effectively accomplished their work. He approved of the broad powers of condemnation vested in British local governments. He liked what he saw of the pioneering efforts undertaken under the 1909 town planning act, though not as well as the broader, less discretionary work of zoning. But from the first, Ihlder's mind was on the question of finances. Letchworth was pretty, he quickly concluded, but by strict accounting principles it was a philanthropic project that did not pay. By the time he reached Manchester, he had concluded that municipal housing did not pay either. Virtually all the model housing was beyond the reach of the ordinary wage earner. Where it was not was the result of public subsidy: transfer payments disguised as reform. The "great question," Ihlder wrote on his return, was whether British cities were "not laying up trouble for the future in letting dwellings at less than an economic rent." Beyond that line, and that preoccupation, he refused to go.[66]

Like other Americans before and after them, the members of the National Housing Association party tended to find what they thought they would find and miss what failed to fit their preconceptions. Patrick Geddes, the Scots polymath and city planner, took Ihlder on a tour of the old city of Dublin, trying to get him to see the virtues of the organic medieval city, buried under later capitalist land overcrowding. But Ihlder could not see the old closes and crooked, narrow courts other than with the eye of a horrified sanitation inspector. Emily Dinwiddie, supervisor of Trinity Church's tenements in New York City, came back sure that the Peabody Trust's private tenant management—like her own—was far superior to municipal housing management. Edward Bassett, who joined the party for a while, thought the best thing in London was its cheap transportation system and its efforts toward zoning. The group's final report commended the 1909 town planning act, cities' slum clearance powers, and philanthropic housing. But the garden cities, they concluded, did not serve the working class. Thomas Adams's concern with land speculation drew in them no responding chord. As for municipal housing, they decided, it was not for America.[67]

The skeptical verdict of the National Housing Association delegation could not have come as a surprise. Its parent organization was a single-note reform lobby; finding that note early, it worked strenuously to keep other tunes from confusing the housing question. The New York State Tenement House Law of 1901 had been the association's crowning triumph—a borrowed, tightened, and overdue variant of English building regulations that outlawed the worst of prevailing building practices (rooms without windows, toilet pits in the yards) and, more consequentially, ratcheted up the standards of sanitary design for all new apartment construction. Regulation of new construction was the key: careful investigation of existing conditions, stringent building laws, and ceaseless effort to ensure their enforcement. "Don't let your city become a city of tenements," ran the catechism of the National Housing Association in 1910:

> Don't build a model tenement until you have secured a model housing law . . .
>
> Don't permit the growth of new slums. Prevention is better than cure . . .
>
> Don't tolerate cellar dwellings . . .
>
> Don't permit houses unfit for human habitation to be occupied . . .
>
> Don't tolerate the lodger evil . . .
>
> Don't urge the municipal ownership and operation of tenement houses . . .
>
> Don't confuse the fields of public and private effort.[68]

Lawrence Veiller, the abrasive, self-confident charity worker behind the "don'ts," who (with Russell Sage Foundation support) had constructed the National Housing Association, was not averse to all European imports in the housing field. His own Tenement House Law owed a deep and conscious debt to the English sanitarians. A forceful presence at city planning meetings, he signed on to zoning early; the section of the New York state act authorizing cities to ban multifamily apartments from their limits was Veiller's work. He was a frequent traveler in Europe and a faithful attendant at the international housing congresses, though he stubbornly resisted their conclusions. The exceptionalist theme in Veiller's arguments grew only stronger with the challenges of young claimants to his leadership: "In housing reform we need especially to beware of importations from across the sea . . . not because they are from across the sea, but because the conditions which exist in the old-world countries are so totally different from those which prevail in America." In the end, Veiller's hatred of the tenement brooked no distractions from the main point: the policing of the building industry. Model housing, changes in taxation, or improvements in transportation belonged, he argued, to the "post-graduate" phase of the housing problem. Faced with impure milk, one did not exhaust one's resources in establishing a model dairy; one weeded the rotten milk out of the milk supply. The former was the task of private resources; the latter task, alone, was within the public sphere.[69]

All this might have been beside the point had it not been for the way in which Veiller's crusade against the tenement house, as the first strong claimant in the field of progressive housing reform, limited the intellectual and organizational space that remained for others. This phenomenon of preemption had its analogues on both sides of the Atlantic. Seizing leadership of the British town planning movement early, the small, talented circle Howard and Unwin gathered around them dominated planning policy in Britain for decades, from the opening years of the century through the Labour Party's Letchworth-inspired New Towns program of the 1940s. Coming first on the housing reform scene in France, the *solidaristes* held reform to subsidarist principles well after France's rivals had given them up as ineffective. "Styles" in national reform policy, these are sometimes called, though the phenomenon is made out of much fiercer competition for intellectual and financial resources than "custom" or "taste" implies. Coming early and aggressively into the housing question, Veiller's circle and its animosity to state housing support had long-term consequences.

This was still more the case because the bottom line to which Ihlder came back over and over in Britain—that housing at rents below cost worked an economic and moral injury—was widely shared in American progressive circles. The Philadelphia housing reformer Carol Aronovici, by 1914 a convert to the continental European innovations in housing, was one of Veiller's sharpest critics. But after a look at the expensive architectural quaintness of Port Sunlight, he, too, could not resist concluding that "in American terms" the crucial question to be asked of British housing work was, "Does it pay?" "The garden city movement must be translated into terms of return on investment, if it is to become world-wide and remain faithful to its spirit of practical democracy."[70]

That investments must pay; that public investments, in particular, should not become a cover for mere transfer payments—all this lay deep in the fabric of progressive assumptions. Gas and streetcar municipalizers talked of capturing profits for the public weal, not of social subsidies. Parks and city plans were sold on the grounds that they enhanced everyone's property. Zoning advocates made the same claim. In the United States more than elsewhere, progressive politics was nested within the surrounding capitalist frame.

Against these institutional and social forces, countervoices were few. The model housing companies were, for the most part, fearful of public subsidies. Benjamin Marsh, with his eye, as always, on land values, wrote off municipal housing as a mere wage depressant. Settlement house workers, keen on opening up inner-city "lungs" for air and light with pocket parks and playgrounds, resisted inner-city rebuilding.

As for the city planners, they quickly cut themselves off from the housing question altogether. Charles M. Robinson's admission in the early years of the craze for city plans, that housing was a "sociological" issue occupying a sphere altogether different than that of civic art, was a sensitive finger in the wind. The National Conference on City Planning, born in the Congestion Committee's 1909 city planning exhibit in Washington, had dropped the housing question out of its debates altogether by its fourth meeting in 1912, as traffic, transportation, streets, and civic aesthetics crowded shelter to the margins. The "interrelation of housing and town planning . . . is not at all understood in America," George B. Ford objected in 1910 in a paper on the relationship of the "social" to the "architectural" in city planning. Raymond Unwin and Thomas Adams, attending the National Conference on City Planning the next year, complained that the architects and landscape designers drawn into the city planning profession in America had made no start at all on housing matters. But they spoke out to no avail. Beyond Massachusetts, where a labor-sponsored provision in the state's city planning statute of 1913 required local authorities to look especially to the "proper housing of the people," only the rare city plan included even a cursory investigation of housing needs. Zoning flourished precisely as it shed all connections to the promotion of working-class housing. Planning was public; housing in the United States was a private matter.[71]

In the circumstances, the social politics of shelter made only tiny inroads in the decade before the First World War. In 1908 a President's Homes Commission appointed to investigate the housing problem in the District of Columbia recommended the extension of public credits (as in Europe) to nonmarket builders of working-class housing. Headed by a director of the city's leading limited-dividend housing company, whose work had recently come to a halt for lack of capital funds, the recommendation carried institutional weight, but nothing came of it. Though it was extensively discussed, the subsidarist principle in housing did not make the Atlantic crossing to pre–World War I America.[72]

A more sustained campaign was waged in Massachusetts, with the support of the state's labor organizations. The Homestead Commission, created by an act of the state legislature in 1911 to investigate means of assisting "mechanics, factory employees, laborers, and others" to acquire small houses in the suburbs, might have been expected to talk its way to inconclusion—as its predecessor had done two years before. Under the influence of the transnational housing debates, however, and the prodding of its secretary, Henry Sterling, a key figure in the state labor movement, it moved into much more decisive action. The Homestead Commission's name harked back to frontier land policies, but the substance of its discussions was European and Australasian housing policy, of which Sterling was an eager student. "Nowhere in the world has the problem of providing homes for workingmen been solved by the private initiative of landowners and builders alone," Sterling had concluded by 1913. "No country is relying entirely on private capital—whether employed in the ordinary way for profit, or in the semi-philanthropic method of some of the garden villages, or in cooperative enterprises—to solve the problem of housing the people." Clinging to that illusion, Sterling charged, left the United States far "behind other leading civilized nations."[73]

When the commission's proposal to use unclaimed funds in the state's savings banks for the building of working-class housing failed to clear the courts, Sterling helped obtain a constitutional amendment allowing for direct state housing construction. Despite the commission's dissenting member's worry that it was "opposed to the natural law of supply and demand and of trade," a fifty-house demonstration project was under way on the outskirts of Lowell's mill district by 1917. Its designer, Arthur Comey, was a young Harvard graduate and an admirer of the English cooperative housing experiments at Letchworth, Ealing, and Hampstead. Comey envisioned a planned community of houses with playgrounds, community buildings, gardens, and a social center, all set on streets curved in the best city-planning style and cooperatively owned to reap the unearned increment in land inflation to the community's benefit. Comey's cooperative ownership idea lost out to Sterling's preference for a New Zealand–style individual purchase program. The crippling blow to the commission's work, however, was the skyrocketing inflation brought on by the war. In 1919, with costs rising faster than the available capital and with Sterling's interests deflected by war labor work, the state pulled out of the housing business, leaving behind a dozen frame houses on an orphaned elbow of a street.[74]

In socialist Milwaukee, the prewar agitation in favor of European-style housing experiments bore its most substantial fruit. With the city as a major stockholder, a Garden Homes Corporation was established in 1920 to develop a tract of inexpensive suburban homes for working-class families. The financial method was borrowed from Germany, and the cooperative ownership scheme was appropriated from Britain, both picked up by the city housing commission's chair on a six-months study tour in 1911. Werner Hegemann of the Berlin and Düsseldorf cities expositions helped lay out the site. Its street names honored its ancestry: Hampstead, Letchworth, Bournville, and Port Sunlight Way. By the 1920s, however, Milwaukee socialism's crest had passed. Two years after they moved in, the Garden Homes cotenants voted to terminate the development's cooperative features and sell off the houses to their individual occupants.[75]

That was the sum total of municipally assisted housing in early-twentieth-century America: Lowell's twelve houses and a hundred odd more in Milwaukee. In Cleveland, a prewar housing assistance initiative fizzled without any result at all. In Britain, by contrast, public authorities had built almost 24,000 units by 1914; in Berlin the total constructed by publicly assisted, noncommercial associations came to 11,000, and in Frankfurt to 5,500; even Paris, with its much more limited public investments, claimed 2,500 units. Edith Elmer Wood, whose lessons in the politics of shelter began in 1913 with her discovery of the President's Homes Commission report on European housing policies, remembered with some bitterness the prevailing mood: "Municipal housing or municipal slum clearance, or any form of government aid (including loans at cost) were taboo and anathema. They were un-American. They were something pertaining to the effete monarchies of Europe. It was extremely bad form even to mention them."[76]

Their noses pressed against the glass of other nations' experience, American civic progressives brought home, one by one, devices for more deliberate, conscious city building: the distinctive outlines of Second Empire Paris, the tools of *Städtebau*, even the British and continental European experiments in the social politics of shelter. In the decade before the First World War, the learning had gone on extremely quickly and the optimism was intense. Coming late to the discussions and techniques being generated abroad did not discourage the American civic progressives; it gave them the chance to stand on the shoulders of the "civilized" world's experience. Even crusty Lawrence Veiller was sure that the slum "is now doomed." With the successful transit of zoning from Germany to the United States, he wrote in 1916, "we are going to revolutionize conditions in a generation."[77]

But the Atlantic progressive connection functioned as a highly selective membrane, strikingly permeable in some areas, all but impenetrable in others. Proposals passed across its boundaries as if through a complicated array of grids and filters. Precedents were not merely exchanged; they were sifted, winnowed, extracted from context, blocked, transformed, and exaggerated. Monumental street plans and zoning made it through to prewar America; public assistance for cheap, decent housing did not. What silent, selective machinery was at work?

The simplest answer, misleading in its very obviousness, is need.

American cities, the argument goes, sites of enormous, rapid shifts in land use and value, needed the coherence of a zoning map and improved street design. Ugly in their utilitarian devotion to business enterprise, and lacking the counterweight of royal and aristocratic wealth, American cities also sorely needed the parks and ornaments that planners prescribed. Blessed with a housing industry more quickly responsive to population pressures than was the case in other countries, the United States simply did not need public investment in housing.

This functionalist argument has a beguiling appeal, but as a historical explanation it collapses almost immediately. Pressures on German housing were considerably less intense in 1890, when the German housing reform movement finally began to gain practical force, than they had been in the frantic *Gründerjahre* of the 1870s, when squatters camped at Berlin's gates. British urban death rates were lower in the 1890s, when the cry for housing reform rose to a peak, than they had been a half century earlier. Standards of urban housing were demonstrably worse in the United States in 1910 than in 1930, when a European-style publicly assisted housing movement finally got under way. Need, to make the obvious point, is subjective, political, time-dependent, and cultural.[78]

Measured against contemporary standards in housing, American conditions were certainly grim enough to have encouraged more active intervention into the land and shelter markets. The horror case was New York City where the multistory tenement, the object of housing reformers' ire everywhere in the North Atlantic economy, had its base. New York's tenement houses—crammed together like packing boxes in the Lower East Side, and now spilling over into Brooklyn and the Bronx; dark and airless save what little ventilation seeped down through the narrow light shafts; jammed with family members and the extra lodgers needed to carry the rent—were as bad as any housing in the North Atlantic community. Werner Hegemann, who knew Berlin intimately and hated its tenements, thought lower Manhattan contained "the worst conditions the world has ever seen." Comparing London's slums with Manhattan's, John Ihlder was sure Manhattan's were by far the more scandalous.[79]

New York City, to be sure, was in a class by itself. Its aggregate ratio of persons to inhabited structures was twenty to one in 1900. In Chicago, by contrast, the ratio was only nine to one, and in most American cities it was less than seven. Beyond greater New York City and its New Jersey suburbs, beyond Chicago, St. Louis, Cincinnati, and the major cities of New England, the rented, single-family, detached, double or row house was the

American norm. Working-class housing was less cramped in the United States, as a rule, than in Britain, and vastly less so than in Germany. In terms of the amenities of toilets and baths, it was considerably better.[80]

But the limited reach of the New York–style tenement block did not guarantee housing elsewhere of the sort turn-of-the-century Americans thought decent. Jane Addams's Chicago was a wilderness of mud, overflowing cesspools, and cheap frame buildings. Washington's back-alley slums were a bitter contrast to the new monumental pretensions of the capital. When, in the wake of the New York Charity Organization Society's Tenement House Exhibit in 1900, the idea of housing surveys spread, citizens' groups rushed to write similar exposés of housing conditions in other American cities.[81] Housing in the United States was bad enough to spur a vigorous movement of exposure and alarm. What that nerve, when touched, did not do was integrate housing provision into a public design.

If need was not the secret engine, sorting out the successful from the unsuccessful imports in the Atlantic exchange, neither can any other single factor be made to play that role. Where a historical problem is big enough to matter, causation is invariably multiple, the factors intertwined and interdependent.

In the American case, where accustomed rights of property were so sharply at stake, interests and ideology played heavily into the selectivity of the exchange. So did the now familiar issues of timing, inertia, precedent, and preemption. So also did the social configuration of capital. Where noblesse oblige ran far behind the impulses of accumulation and display, there were policy consequences. Like their counterparts elsewhere, American industrialists were willing enough to invest in company housing, especially where the remote location of their plants or the need for especially skilled workers emphasized the benefits. But general funds for philanthropic housing were, relative to national wealth, acutely scarce in the United States. There was no lobby for limited-profit housing in the United States comparable to the Société française des habitations à bon marché, no limited-dividend housing company on the scale of Frankfurt's Aktienbaugesellschaft für kleine Wohnungen. The Garden City Association of America, founded contemporaneously with its German and French counterparts by a combination of social gospel ministers, city planners, and investors in Long Island land and railroad stock, evaporated in the financial panic of 1907; the Russell Sage Foundation's Forest Hills Gardens project, a victim of the same inflationary pressure that sabotaged the Massachusetts state experiment in Lowell, ended at a substantial loss.[82] As for pressures from below, they fractured all too quickly in the ethnically and racially divided cities of the United States. On issues of streetcars and industrial accident compensation, labor organizations could be mobilized. But for most working-class Americans, housing remained lodged on the private side of the unspoken public-private divide.

The impact of none of these factors, however, should be exaggerated. Where the majority of urban families in the United States (as in Europe) rented their shelter from someone else, the ideology of private property was far less widely diffused than it would be a half century later. Landlords had no extensive political assets—certainly not in comparison with the utility monopolies. Organized labor's preoccupations were elsewhere, closer to the point of production. But when put to a vote in 1915, Massachusetts's constitutional amendment authorizing state credits for housing swept the electorate three to one.[83]

European progressives put their finger on a different spot: the peculiarities of the law in the United States. "The practically cast-iron Constitution," Thomas Adams called it, and it hemmed in American urban reformers in ways no progressives elsewhere experienced.[84] In city utility affairs, the courts' insistence on having the final word in valuation decisions had been an obstacle, though not a decisive one, to the municipalizers' ambitions. Where the issues cut closer to private property's prerogatives, however, the courts moved into the field in ways that left their mark over all the issues of land, shelter, and urban design. Excess condemnation, aesthetic restrictions à la Haussmann's Paris, German-style acquisition of public land on the city's rim, British-style extension planning, and (not the least) investment of public funds in housing all collided with constitutional law in the early-twentieth century United States. Of all the filtering machinery at work, the law's force was particularly unmistakable.

In the sorting house of the law, two governing principles stood out. The first was that property could be taken out of private hands by government agencies only with full compensation and only for a genuinely "public use." The second was that any simple transfer of property from one citizen to another was, on the face of it, beyond the legitimate powers of government. In practice both principles were as porous as they were, in theory, simple. They did not so much preclude legislation as filter it through grids of principles, politics, and assumptions of political economy. In contrast to Germany, where cities' rights to compel unwilling owners to sell their land were quite narrowly confined, the American courts came early to the conclusion that not only did public streets and public buildings satisfy the "public use" criteria but so did extensive carriage parks, and they allowed cities to condemn and tax as they chose in order to support them. Tax levies for public supply of water, gas, streetcars, and electricity were likewise relatively easily folded into the "public use" doctrine.[85]

The rule against redistributionist legislation was, in practice, still more flexibly executed, though its porosity was less often acknowledged. Most of what governments do under their taxing and spending powers is, in one way or another, to take property from some citizens and, for reasons judged to be just (or at least expedient), give it to others. The pensioning of northern Civil War veterans (with what seemed to its critics extravagant largesse) and the steep tariff protection accorded domestic manufacturers—the twin linchpins of late-nineteenth-century Republican Party policy—were operations of this sort. So were poor relief and railroad company subsidies. And so, in principle, was any form of use, density, or building-volume zoning that allowed the owner of property A a more lucrative set of possible employments for his property than the owner of property B, who might be equally worthy but whose land happened to lie in a different section of the city.

If the public use and antiredistributionist doctrines gave early-twentieth-century courts grounds to block legislation that violated their sensitivity to real property owners' rights and immunities, the doctrine of governments' overriding power to preserve the public health and safety gave the courts grounds virtually as generous for reversal. The "police powers" doctrine, as it was called, was the counterweight to strict property rights adjudication. As the legal expression of the interdependencies of city health and living conditions, the police powers were as deeply in flux in the early twentieth century as public policy itself.[86]

Whichever card the judges chose to deal out of their stack of mutually contradictory principles, their decisions were not final. Most legal judgments stopped at the highest state courts—not so far from the sphere of politics as to be beyond overriding by state constitutional amendment. Constitutional law was not a "cast-iron" restraint but an extra hurdle, not a simple barricade to reform (though in their frustration the progressives frequently saw it that way) so much as a highly self-conscious sorting apparatus. It let some pieces of legislation through, vetoed others, encumbered still others with fatal costs and qualifications, and shaped every piece of imagined legislation according to predictions of the justices' action.

In this context, excess condemnation was the first of the imported city planning measures to come before the bar, and the first to shatter. The fiscal engine of Haussmann's Paris and of city street recentralization throughout Europe, the technique hinged on a city's right to condemn more land than a new street would actually use, recouping the street-making cost from the sale of the replatted sites. To Paris-inspired city planners, no legal power was more essential than this. Of the staggering $24 million cost of the London County Council's Kingsway project, as the story was told and retold in American city planning circles, $20 million had come back to public hands from the rise in abutting land values. As early as 1903, a special committee of the Massachusetts legislature was in France and Britain gathering information on excess condemnation law and practice. Hypercautiously the legislature responded with a statute so narrowly fashioned as to be virtually without effect, limiting excess condemnation powers to remnant lots too small for building purposes. When the legislature attempted to expand the act, the state supreme court disallowed it on the grounds that the state's eminent domain powers could not be used to take from unwilling owners property that would ultimately end up again in private hands—regardless of the benefits the city might gain in more handsome streetscapes, improved traffic patterns, or commercial revival. Over the next decade, the city planning movement's lawyers struggled to devise excess condemnation statutes more acceptable to the courts. The National Municipal League published a model statute. A special New York City committee on taxation, with E. R. A. Seligman, Frederic Howe, and Delos Wilcox among its members, recommended another. But even with the help of state constitutional amendments, at the end of the 1920s the resulting schemes were so hedged with limitations as to make excess condemnation a virtual dead letter.[87]

Haussmannization's second legal leg, aesthetic regulation, came more quickly and decisively to the same fate. It had not been its boulevards per se that had given Paris its Second Empire style; the enforcement of a common building height and aesthetic line on the investors who rebuilt in the wake of Haussmann's engineers was what had created the order, the sense of a coherent city whole, that bowled over Americans in Paris. But in the United States, the courts were clear, the public had no overriding power to impose its sense of taste and beauty on property owners—not without paying owners the difference between what they might have built and what the planners wanted. On the outdoor advertisement issue that preoccupied so many city planners, the courts likewise held with the property owners. Advertising, the courts admitted, might be offensive to good taste; screaming for attention at the edges of a city park or square, it might even diminish the city's investment in public space. But to claim that it did tangible injury to the public weal was to indulge (as a New York court in 1909 put it) in a judgment purely "aesthetic" and "sentimental." The British Advertisement Regulation Act of 1907 could not be propelled across the Atlantic. In the face of these court-imposed compensation costs, all the "push" of Burnham's businessman backers could hardly dent the pattern of the private city.[88]

On the margins of city growth, to which the more "sociological" of the planners looked so hopefully, the courts loaded equally crippling encumbrances on the transatlantic policy borrowings. No court allowed cities to engaged in general land purchases ahead of private speculators on the German model that Florence Kelley had thought so promising. Cities might accept general grants of land given to them, but the power to spend tax revenues for the creation of a land bank for future but not yet specified uses could not get past the public use doctrine.[89]

The regulatory powers of the British town planning act of 1909 seemed to the American city planning movement's lawyers more closely within reach. The details of the act generated vigorous discussion among city planners, but here, too, the courts were firm that private compensation came before most public ends. The issue came to a head in its simplest form, in a quarrel over street platting. No power was more fundamental on the urban rim than the power to lay out streets in advance of actually building them, and no court in the United States begrudged it to cities. The catch came when an owner of outlying property decided, for private purposes, to build across the path of a projected street. Every court outside of Pennsylvania held that the building could not later be condemned for street making without the owner's being paid in full for its value. In a contest between a tangible building and a paper street (which might always be altered or indeed never built, tying up for years an owner's use of his property), the courts' verdict went to property. Blocked from imitating either the German or the British approaches to control of undeveloped land, American city planners found an alternative device in the power to register subdivision plans. But their power to disapprove—a reactive one, in any event—carried, through the 1920s, little practical consequence. In the absence of legal authority to say what should go where on the unbuilt urban rim, the city planning commissions that spread so rapidly after 1907 were all but toothless enterprises.[90]

As for housing, the courts both bent and resisted. Where the question turned directly on sanitary nuisances, the courts were willing to coerce property owners into line without mandated compensation. They accepted

Veiller's crusade against the airless tenement room and the common yard toilet as a legitimate extension of the police powers. When in 1904 the New York City real estate owners brought forward Katie Moeschen, the hard-pressed owner (so they said) of a twenty-family tenement building, to challenge the right of the city to require installation of indoor water closets without compensating poor owners like Moeschen for the cost it inflicted, the New York courts threw out the claim. California's gathering movement toward exclusion of "nuisances" (brickyards, dance halls, and, not the least, Chinese laundrymen) from special residential districts was upheld by the same police powers. But when it came to compensation for property judged so unsanitary as to require destruction, the courts returned to property's claims. In Britain, frustration at the costs of slum clearance and outrage at the ability of slum property owners to turn a profit by so badly ruining their property that the public health authorities were left with no choice but to buy it out from them, drove the lawmakers to whittle away at the level of allowable compensation. By 1890, though practice lagged behind, the letter of the law allowed owners of buildings incapable of being made fit for habitation no more than the value of the lot and any salvageable building materials. In the United States, by contrast, the courts were far more reluctant to set landlords' claims aside.[91]

As for publicly funded housing, only state constitutional amendments could reverse the courts' objections. To tax some frugal, temperate, industrious wage earners so that some others—perhaps not so frugal or industrious—could live in better housing, was simply to redistribute wealth among the state's citizenry, the Massachusetts court had decided in 1912. Enjoyable only by the persons who lived in it, not accessible by the public (like a park or city street), housing was in most court jurisdictions through the 1920s not a taxable, public use at all but a private matter.[92]

Of all the imported city planning devices, only zoning successfully squeezed through the courts. Encouraged at the Commerce Department and eagerly embraced by local real estate interests, more than four hundred cities had enacted zoning ordinances by 1925 (more than double the number with comprehensive city plans) and over nine hundred had done so by 1930. That it should have been zoning that slipped through the law's grid of property defenses remains, years later, something of a surprise. Zoning discriminated between holders of similar property. For public benefits as distant and as intangible as many of the public uses that littered the courtroom floors, zoning was capable of taking a considerable bite out of a speculative landowner's imagined profits. Opposing lawyers condemned it as an "arbitrary" interference in the natural flow of land investment, vague and whimsical in its underlying principles, reflective merely of the "momentary taste" of zoning boards and city officials. Even Veiller, one of residential use zoning's strongest partisans, thought zoning on "very shaky" constitutional ground in 1917. Then, beginning with the Massachusetts supreme court in 1920, the courts suddenly began to uphold sweeping zoning regulations: residential use districts that barred every form of commercial enterprise, that excluded apartment houses, that regulated the placement of garages on one's private lot, that set down at a stroke the legal structure of the modern, class-segregated bedroom suburb.[93]

The U.S. Supreme Court decision that in 1926 ratified this legal change of mind was so laconically expressed as to preclude reading the justices' mind. The district court had held for the plaintiff's property rights, accepting the plaintiff's claim that, having bought property with an eye to industrial development, imposition of a residential use restriction had tangibly injured its value. The brief the Supreme Court tacitly accepted, presented by the principal author of the Commerce Department's model zoning act, said almost nothing about public purposes—and still less about speculative property rights or democratically determined design. Frederic Howe's city that "thought" through its planning decisions was hardly in evidence. Refurbishing the metaphors of "invasion," it focused on the impending "blight," destabilization, demoralization, and depreciating values that the plaintiff's industrial development might bring. The right to defend one's property from the injury of neighboring property owners was old, established law. Zoning ensured nothing more or less. It slipped through the sorting machinery of the law wearing the guise not of a public power but a private one.[94]

The justices' fears for property's accustomed rights were no mere illusion. The new techniques of city planning hardly threatened property itself; like other progressive inventions, they worked on the market economy's edges and margins. But there the shears of ambition were sharp enough. As one of those enrolled under the city planning movement's banner put it at a Boston conference in 1910: "Slums, unsanitary dwellings, lack of parks and playgrounds, absence of needed recreation facilities, the lack of a comprehensive and rational system of rapid transit, the blighting of the landscape with factories or atrocious advertising"—all these were inexplicable except in terms of the "insane individualism" of American municipalities and "the failure of the citizens to assert their ownership of the city."[95] If only in the play of competing metaphors of "ownership," the courts saw an intensely serious contest; they had no intention of being sideline or dispassionate players.

To Europeans, the spectacle seemed quite extraordinary. The weight of judicial decision making in the formation of public policy in the United States was a constant source of dismay. Beatrice Webb thought the greatest gift to the Americans would be "an occasional Sidney Webb to invent ways of dodging their silly constitutions." It was standard among British progressives to contrast the turn-of-the-century United States, where politics seemed to have come to a standstill in the rust and friction of its constitutional machinery, with the frontier inventiveness of the nations of Australasia, which were engaged in policy experiments "with perfect disregard for precedent and authority." H. G. Wells came away from Washington, D.C., sure that the Americans possessed "the feeblest, least accessible, and most inefficient central government of any civilized nation in the world west of Russia"—"marooned, twisted into knots, bound with safe-guards, and altogether impotently stranded" by its constitutional limitations. "America is pure eighteenth century," Well's wrote. "They took the economic conventions that were modern and progressive at the end of the eighteenth century and stamped them into the Constitution as if they meant to stamp them there for all time."[96]

Wells was wrong on the theme of anachronism. Aggressive constitutional adjudication, far more intensely exercised in the early twentieth century than ever before, was as new as progressive politics itself. And structurally aggressive court review was far closer to the practices of their own polities than European progressives recognized. In British and German cities, as the progressives themselves knew, property was loaded with special political assets. Municipal government functioned in large part as property's special organ—there for the competing ambitions of large and small property owners, for long- and short-run property interests, to work out their compromises. Urban politics in Europe gave ownership a special vote. In the more open, democratic politics of the late-nineteenth-century United States, where the formal legislative prerogatives of property had been abandoned, the courts moved to narrow the difference between the United States and Europe. They became for the United States what the three-class voting system was for Prussia and ratepayers' suffrage was for Britain. In a nation of tenanted cities, the courts in the United States formed a special house for property—the more rigid and doctrinaire for being merely its agent and representative.

In these circumstances, it was no wonder that the American city planning movement should have been so peculiarly weighted down with lawyers. Or that from Marsh (on the radical side) to Veiller (on the conservative), it found itself compressed so tightly by the prerogatives of property in the law. Outwardly the most peculiarly American of political institutions, but playing the most "European" of political roles, the courts squeezed and narrowed visions of the organic city down to those that rubbed least on the interests of real property owners.

In the unexpected exigencies of the First World War, and again in the Depression of the 1930s, the legal dikes would partially give way. Laid up against the future, the prewar visions of more consciously ordered cities remained, more generous in their symbols of public life, less possessed by private property. It was no accident that found Raymond Unwin lobbying in 1930s Washington for a public housing program, or Edith Wood (two books on European housing politics behind her) putting her hand to that program's creation. In the meantime, the transatlantic exchange had done a small but decisive measure of work. If the results were terrifically uneven, unevenness characterized the politics of urban form and shelter in every prewar nation. Even in America, there was no missing the underlying family resemblance.

In Burnham's Chicago on the eve of the First World War, a new Grant Park was in the making, a sliver of formal Parisian design on a strip of waterfront reclaimed from a railroad freightyard. Behind it the city itself pushed outward in a maze of private designs, subdividers' notions of profit and beauty, developer-built streets and speculative housing, streetcar company investments, lucky and unlucky guesses on the motions of the land market, and ambitious paper plans. Which of these would prevail would depend on politics, on the future of the Atlantic progressive exchange, and, not the least, on how distinctly the judges would continue to construe the claims of profit and property of which, in the United States, they had become such peculiarly solicitous arbiters.

Sociological Trip to Europe

Would you like to take tea with the London Commissioner of Prisons, hear about penal methods and visit typical prisons? Would you enjoy going as special guest to world-famous settlements and meeting their leaders, to a large industrial plant, and to government departments to learn about Old Age Pensions and Unemployment Insurance? How about a visit to a Welsh coal mine, a housing scheme, a cooperative organization? Such are the unusual contacts afforded, many of them by personal invitation to the leader. The party goes to England, Holland, Belgium, Germany, Switzerland and France. There is plenty of sightseeing including the Shakespeare country, the Hague, a journey up the Rhine, days among the lakes and mountains of Switzerland, a visit to the battlefields of France.

For details write to the leader,

Dr. R. B. Stevens, Professor of Sociology,
Elmira College Elmira, New York

The Sociological Grand Tour. The genre of the social and civic tour was already twenty years old by the time this notice appeared in the *Survey* in December 1931. (*Survey* 66 [1931]: 69)

Civicism on Display. A late-nineteenth-century artist's depiction of Joseph Chamberlain's Birmingham, England, shows the new city hall and civic art gallery in the center, the neo-Roman city concert hall, and the Gothic spire of the Chamberlain Memorial. The city's new Corporation Street is beyond the city hall, obscured in this print by the smoke of great city industrial prosperity. (Author's collection)

Municipal "Socialism"

(a) A celebration of the running of the first electrified streetcar on the city-owned lines in Manchester, England, in 1901. (Local Studies Unit, Manchester Central Library, Manchester, England)

(b) The "Municipal Improvement Trolley Car" in Harrisburg, Pennsylvania, in 1901. The city reformers' campaign for modern water and sewer facilities and riverfront parks and playgrounds was spearheaded by Mira Lloyd Dock, who had spent the summer of 1899 in intensive study of parks, civic improvements, and public forestry methods in England and Germany. (Charles Zueblin, *A Decade of Civic Development*, 1905)

The Beaux Arts City

(a) Brooklyn, 1903. On the left is the entry column to Prospect Park, in the rear at right the Soldiers and Sailors Monument constructed between 1892 and 1898 on Grand Army Plaza. In this homage to Civil War nationalism, the monument's base was copied from Paris, the horses and winged riders from Berlin's Brandenburg Gate. (Museum of the City of New York)

(b) Brooklyn Bridge Plaza, as proposed by the New York City Improvement Commission of 1907. This superimposition of a Paris étoile on Brooklyn's street grid was never actually built, but construction of Philadelphia's still grander, Haussmann-derived street cutting project, Fairmount Parkway, had just begun. (New York City Improvement Commission, *Report*, 1907)

MONROE
MADISON
WASHINGTON
RANDOLPH
LAKE STREET
SOUTH WATER STREET
AVENUE
STREET

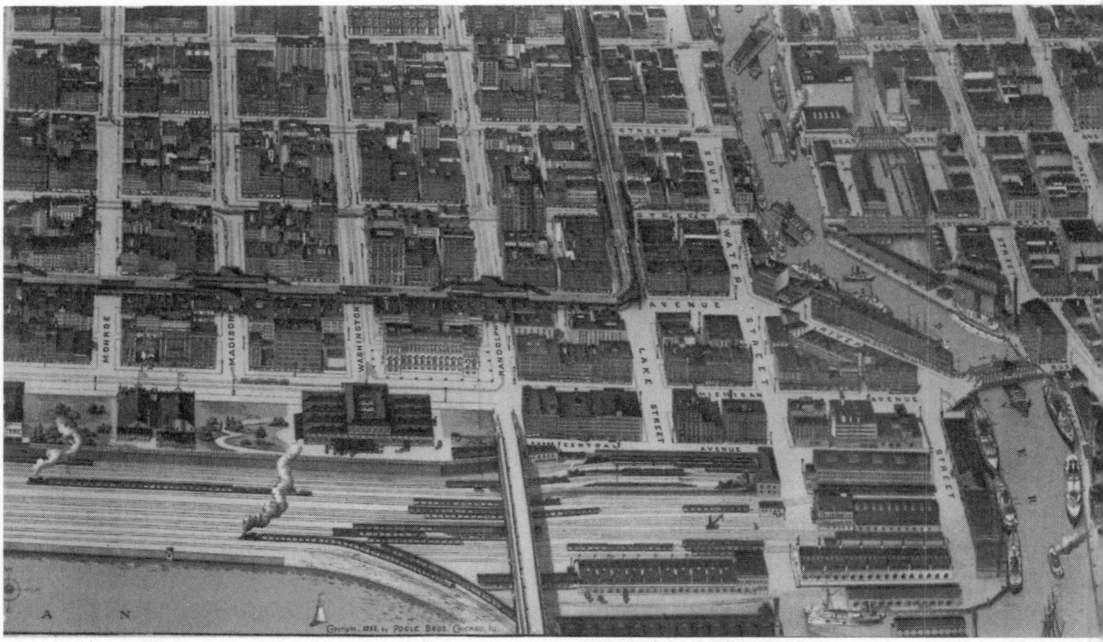

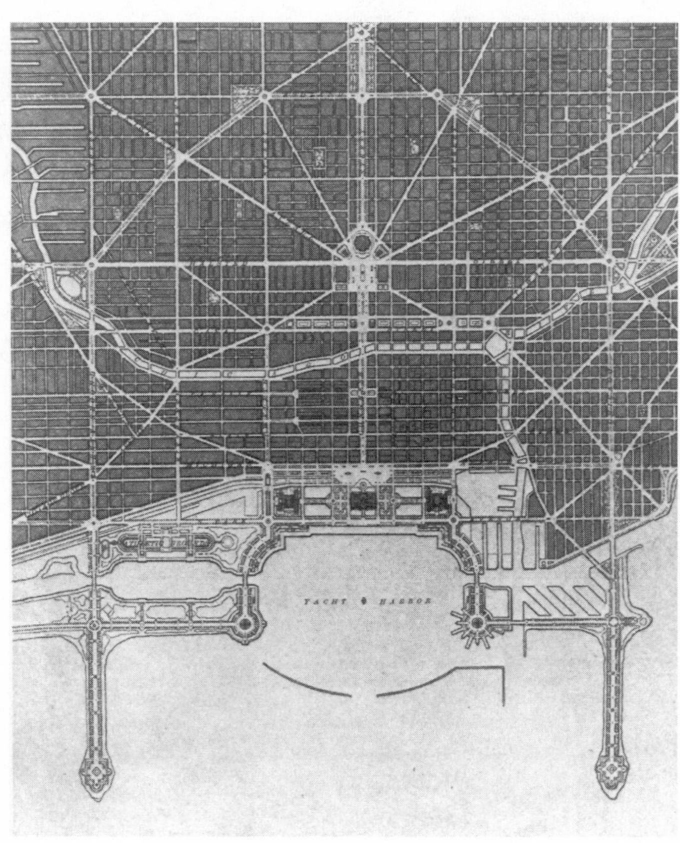

YACHT HARBOR

The City Commercial and the City Beautiful

(a—opposite page, top) A section from the Poole Brothers' panoramic view of Chicago's business district, 1898. This was the commercial city as its late-nineteenth-century business boosters imagined it, its design mortgaged to private investments in river docks and barges, streetcars, elevated trains, commercial office buildings, and railroad freight yards. (Geography and Map Division, Library of Congress)

(b—opposite page, bottom) Chicago re-envisioned as a European capital in Daniel Burnham's plan of 1909. Grant Park is in the foreground; the diagonal boulevards that Burnham proposed to cut across the city's street grid converge on the site of his imagined civic center. (Commercial Club of Chicago, *The Plan of Chicago* [1909], courtesy Princeton Architectural Press)

(c—above) An artist's rendering of the Chicago Civic Center, from the Chicago Plan of 1909. In its colossal scale and beaux arts design, this was the visual manifestation of the turn-of-the-century progressives' dream of the public city, re-centered and re-socialized. (Commercial Club of Chicago, *The Plan of Chicago* [1909], courtesy Princeton Architectural Press)

The Philanthropic Tenement

(a) Philanthropic housing in Brooklyn, as photographed by Jacob Riis in the 1890s. Riverside Tenement carried over many of its design elements from London's philanthropic housing companies. (Museum of the City of New York)

(b) London County Council working-class housing. Constructed between 1902 and 1905, the Bourne Estate was designed to house Londoners displaced by the Kingsway street-cutting project. (London Metropolitan Archives)

The high cost of urban land left its mark on the height and scale of every effort to raise the standards of inner-city housing. But the mutual exchange of designs and aspirations is equally unmistakable, particularly in the efforts to bring light and ventilation, common space, playgrounds, and public amenities to working-class shelter.

6

The Wage Earners' Risks

Workingmen's Insurance

In the debates over social politics, sprawling as they did from factory legislation to monopoly power, from public health to transit politics, from city plans to city housing, the absence of a central place for poverty cannot but come as a surprise to modern readers. Today in the United States, social-political controversy spirals down relentlessly on poverty and public assistance for the poor. The emotional center of contemporary social politics is "welfare," but it is a concept of welfare narrower than any known in the past. "Welfare" in modern America means not the common weal but poor relief; the "welfare state" is the modern poor-law state.

In fact, none of the so-called welfare states constructed before the last third of the twentieth century was focused on the poor. From Bismarck's to Beveridge's, their target population was the working class, those who worked with their hands for wages, not the destitute with no work at all. The distinctive concern of the North Atlantic economy's progressives was not to patch and mend the lives of the poor: it was the struggle to find effective means to keep those who were not abjectly poor, who still possessed work and wages, from being precipitated into poverty's abyss.

This is not to deny the presence of poverty in the progressive imagination. At the Paris exposition of 1889, the social economy section had included no special place for poverty or poor relief—though there had been categories devoted to the workers' wages, mutual assistance associations, work accidents, and the economic intervention of the state. In 1900, however, a new subsection on "public charities" was added. Smaller than the class devoted to *prévoyance*, more than five hundred exhibitors nevertheless competed in it; that summer's meeting of the International Congress on Public Assistance and Private Charity drew more than one thousand persons to its discussions.[1] From Jacob Riis in New York City to Charles Booth in London, every nation in the North Atlantic economy had its sociological investigators of the modern, great city's poor. But poverty, bare and alone, was not the issue. To limit the socially self-destructive effects of morally unhindered capitalism, to extract from those markets the tasks they had demonstrably bungled, to counterbalance the markets' atomizing social effects with a countercalculus of the public weal: these were the tasks of social politics. Poverty was but a thread in the social question's tangles.

Far more pressing in the debates of the day was the condition of labor. And that was not only because the working class was so much larger than the abjectly poor and its political loyalties much more vital to the nation-states, and not only because the standing warfare between capital and labor was so much more dramatic a threat to the social peace than the more muted, simmering resentments of the truly poor. It was also because the poor formed in the progressives' mind virtually another country.

No one, to be sure, could miss the nation of the poor. Where the countryside tended to mask its poverty, the great cities concentrated it, flaunting economic misery even as they cordoned it off. The two nations theme was a commonplace in a dozen different languages: upper crust and netherworld, obscenely rich and desperately poor.

Like all nations, these two had, in truth, many points of intersection. Beggars occupied one of them—a conspicuous sight in virtually every great city. Organized philanthropy occupied a second and larger juncture. From hospital outpatient departments (the medical recourse everywhere of the very poor) to endowed medical dispensaries, soup kitchens and homeless shelters, crèches, homes for abandoned children or fallen women, charity schools, provident loan banks, parish poor funds, and private relief bureaus, the scope of philanthropic activities was considerable in turn-of-the-century cities.[2]

For the poorest, finally, there was public relief. In France, where the Catholic church and its charities, still established and semipublic, assumed the primary burden of charitable relief, maintenance of public *bureaux de bienfaisance* did not become obligatory for local governments until the mid-1890s.[3] Virtually everywhere else in the North Atlantic economy, however, the public's responsibility to keep the poor from outright starvation was fixed in the law. Public, tax-supported poor relief was old, not new—rooted in conceptions of collective welfare that stretched deep into the preindustrial past.

Public poor relief was most highly developed in England. Out of the Elizabethan structure of tax-supported parish poor relief had emerged by the middle of the nineteenth century an elaborate, secularized system of local poor law authorities and institutions. Mandated to keep the poor from outright starvation while spending as frugally as possible, poor-law boards operated through a complicated system of deterrents and entitlements. To those with a particularly strong moral claim on relief, the boards could offer straightforward relief in money or in kind—"out of [the] doors" of the poorhouse, it was called. To the rest, they offered a choice between the workhouse and no relief at all. Grim and dreaded as the workhouses were, they collected a wide variety of the very poor: families in temporary distress, old men (or, more rarely, women) without the props of family support, alcoholics on the skids, dependent family members put in by exhausted relatives. There were 123,000 "indoor paupers" living in workhouses in England and Wales in 1850, together with another 886,000 "outdoor" recipients of public poor relief—amounting in all to almost 6 percent of the total population. Designed to deter the poor from asking for relief, but constrained to support those who did, it was a morally complicated and expensive system, and its tax burden helped give poor relief politics in Britain an intensity matched nowhere else.[4]

The legal structure of English poor relief crossed early to the United States, where it was absorbed into state law and local practice. In the United States, even more than in England, poor relief was a system full of holes, made wider as the poor were pushed and drained from the countryside into the cities. Conceived as a system of local supports for a village's own native poor, the legal structure made few concessions for the transient poor that the more extended and volatile labor markets called forth. Local poor-law authorities in the United States often exhausted themselves in struggles to displace responsibility for poor relief onto other communities, packing off their unwanted poor to the localities they had left. But inadequate as the system was, the principle of responsibility for the most helpless of the poor was legally fixed and older by far than the new social politics of the transatlantic progressive connection.[5]

In France public responsibility for the poor gradually expanded in the late nineteenth century, as radicals claimed for the state a portion of the charitable territory of the Church; virtually everywhere else, however, public responsibility for the poor contracted. As the massing of the poor in the cities accelerated—immigrants and strangers all, far from village supports—and as the economization of social relations proceeded, the impulse of public authorities to whittle down the cost of poor relief intensified. Local authorities moved, sometimes with dramatic speed, toward higher deterrents to application, stricter restrictions on public funds, and tighter forms of behavioral control. An early, much imitated step in more systematic scrutiny of the poor was taken in the industrial town of Elberfeld in the German Rhineland in 1853. After previous unsuccessful attempts at economization, Elberfeld's city authorities decided to entrust distribution of the city's poor relief funds to 150 unpaid, respectable burghers, each charged with watch and ward over the poor in his immediate neighborhood. The Elberfeld system, as it became known, spread rapidly through Germany in the 1870s and 1880s, thanks to its reputation for reducing poor relief costs. Berlin alone boasted more than two thousand unpaid "honorary" poor relievers who made regular rounds of home visits.[6]

From Germany the Elberfeld system spread to England and the United States under the banner of "charity organization." The first charity organization society was founded in London in 1869; its first American offshoot was started in Buffalo in 1877, by a former volunteer for the parent London society. Recruiting women, not men, as "friendly visitors" to the poor, the personnel of the American and English charity organization societies were not (as in Germany) public authorities, nor did they distribute public relief funds. They took it as their mission to control and systematize private charity by establishing between (sentimental) givers and (perhaps unworthy) recipients a systematic scrutiny of each individual case. The second plank in the charity organization program, however, was public and political: to remove public authorities from the business of home-based "outdoor" poor relief altogether.

The charity reformers' campaign to confine public poor relief to poor house inmates did not fully succeed in either England or America. In England, the elderly poor retained an important hold on the sympathy of poor-law boards, But the results were nevertheless dramatic enough. Between 1870 and 1878, the percentage of recipients of public poor relief in the population of England and Wales was reduced by more than one-third, almost all of it through cutbacks in "outdoor" public relief. In the United

States, advocates of "scientific charity" succeeded in many instances in cutting off outdoor relief altogether. The city of Brooklyn gave home-based assistance to 38,170 persons in 1870; in 1880, it gave none. Philadelphia by 1879 could make the same boast. Of the twenty-one American cities with populations over 200,000 in 1900, the charity organization society leaders reported with pride, ten gave "practically no public out-relief" and two more gave "very little."[7]

More generous, if fitful, reserves of public obligation remained. In the depression years of the 1890s, American city officials cooperated in the advertisement of special, privately raised relief funds, opened the police stations to the homeless in winter, or (less often) endeavored to shrink the ranks of the unemployed through emergency public works projects. Where urban political mores had not yet fallen to the charity reformers' campaigns, cities still distributed fuel or food from public funds to a fraction of the poor.[8]

But the older traditions of public sympathy and obligation were clearly fraying under the new preoccupations with public efficiency and private demoralization. The idea that misguided generosity only multiplied demand was a central tenet of the charity organization societies. It was a maxim most progressives shared as well. The Webbs believed it implicitly. In the treatment of poverty "the moral factor is the supreme issue," they were sure: the "demoralization of character and the slackening of personal effort that result from the unnecessary spreading of indiscriminate, unconditional and gratuitous provision."[9] Deterrents and inspections were both mobilized to these tasks. To ensure that the poor not assume that relief came to them by right, most countries made elimination from the voting rolls a condition of public poor relief. The poor were not beyond the sympathies of a generous poor-law board, an emergency relief committee, or local socialist majorities (as in France after 1896). But to most middle-class social reformers, including most of those groping toward new forms of social policy, the poor were citizens of a distant country, socially and psychically apart from the nation the transatlantic progressives had in mind.

It should come as no surprise, then, that progressive imaginations so often ran toward schemes of isolating the poor—siphoning them off into some better, more tightly controlled environment, where they could be reformed and the city relieved of their disturbing presence. There is a remarkable passage in the first volume of Charles Booth's *Life and Labour of the People in London*, just following his first statistical attempt to estimate the size and character of the city's poor. The heart of the matter, for Booth, was not the loafers and semicriminals at the bottom of London's class structure (Class A, he called them); effective curtailment of almsgiving would, he thought, eliminate them. Nor did the key issue lie with the working poor (Class C), hanging on to poorly paid but fairly regular jobs. It was the class in between, the surplus labor reserve of London, never regularly employed, that formed the problem. Why not, Booth suggested, take them all—11 percent of East London's population, by Booth's calculation—enroll them as wards of the state, transport them in family units to wherever land and supplies were cheap, and set them to work in a segregated state economy, a kind of giant, diversified poor farm? This was "socialism," Booth admitted, though no more socialistic in theory than the English Poor Law itself. "In taking charge of the lives of the incapable, State Socialism finds its proper work." The best of those in Class B would work their way out; the rest would be drained from the city as one would drain a great swamp in a reclamation system of human dikes and channels.[10]

Booth's paper vision (which he soon left behind) was current enough for others to put into practical measures. In Germany, where suppression of beggary and the "work-shy" was carried on with a particular severity, social reformers established a network of some two dozen voluntary rural labor colonies for the isolation and moral regeneration of the poor. Holland, too, had a network of both voluntary and penal farm colonies, which, though they failed to make a dent in urban poverty, siphoned off a fraction of the village poor into a regime of strictly supervised farm labor and (for those who stuck it out) sponsored homesteads.[11] With a fanfare all its own, the Salvation Army brought a similar scheme to Britain, where the idea of exporting the city's poor to the countryside mixed with imperial notions of dispersing them throughout the empire. In the sharp unemployment crisis of 1903 to 1905, even the British left threw its weight behind the labor colony idea. George Lansbury, the "wild young man" on London's central body for the unemployed, as William Beveridge remembered him, who helped subvert the legal restrictions on outdoor poor relief in one of East London's key working-class districts, urged rural colonization of the poor with missionary intensity. Sidney and Beatrice Webb, skeptical of the growing talk of state-administered out-of-work insurance in 1909, countered with a version of Booth's proposal: a labor colony, systematically engineered for behavioral reformation, to drain off the city's excess labor reserve.[12]

Political amorphousness was not the least of the labor colony idea's assets. Lansbury imagined labor colonies of the unemployed as the germ of a new form of cooperative social life. The Webbs' anti-utopian imaginations ran toward discipline, through a spartan regime of labor, gymnastics, drill, plain alcohol-free meals, and technical education. At the farthest extreme from Lansbury was the largest labor colony of them all, Belgium's vast Merxplas colony. A state penal colony, it housed more than five thousand beggars, vagrants, and petty criminals in 1910 in a complex of workshops, farms, and dormitories laid out with military precision on 3,000 acres of the land in northern Belgium. Here, as elsewhere, work was the essential regime, but without hope of redemption. By 1910, the Merxplas authorities had concluded that the class consigned to it was beyond reformation, and they had turned to a policy of simple isolation. Cut off from alcohol and women (for here, as elsewhere, labor colony inmates were overwhelmingly male), removed from the handouts of falsely sentimental givers or tax-supported relief, removed from the means of reproduction, the vagrant poor would slowly disappear. Merxplas was an extreme case. But what gave all the competing labor colony schemes weight was the logic of isolating the poor: for quarantine, for environmental and behavioral reform, or for political regeneration.[13]

American progressives fell in with these intellectual currents as readily as their European counterparts. Harvard's pioneer teacher of social problems, Francis G. Peabody, sought out both the Dutch and German labor colonies in the 1890s and found much to praise. So did John Graham Brooks. The principle of the Dutch penal colonies, Peabody admitted in 1894, was "socialism," but it was a socialism "that goes far beyond the familiar talk of socialism"—a socialism not of claims against the state, but of the state's claims on the individual to be "in some way and degree, by his mind or his hands or both, a contributor to the great welfare." If state labor colonies were "socialism, let us make the most of it," Peabody wrote. "It is also the hope of stable civilization and the secret of judicious charity."[14]

Indeed it was a reform socialist and lawyer, Edmond Kelly, who came closest to effectively realizing the poor colony idea in the United States. After having his interest in isolating the vagrant, tramping, begging poor piqued by the British Departmental Committee on Vagrancy's report on continental labor colonies in 1906, Kelly had visited the Merxplas complex, but it was the smaller, Swiss farm colonies that caught his imagination. Enlisting the support of both Alfred E. Smith and the charity reform establishment, he successfully pushed an act through the New York state assembly in 1911 modeled on the Swiss example. Cut out of the state's appropriations bill, Kelly's labor colony for the vagrant poor never came to be. But even Jane Addams in 1913 was certain that penal farm colonies were "in line with the development in all other philanthropy" and integral to any serious assault on unemployment.[15]

The very poor were another nation: outsiders, to one degree or another, in the social reformers' imaginations. Social politics did not start with them. Even the line of debate that eventuated in social insurance did not begin with consideration of the poor. The crucial class in that debate was the working class, suspended above Booth's poverty line by fragile economic threads. As progressives saw it, their task was not to abolish poverty but to diminish the likelihood that the many standing at poverty's brink would be pushed in by an ill turn of fortune. Social insurance—workingmen's insurance, as it was called at its birth—was as distinctly for the working class as the workhouse, the labor colony, and the bourgeois friendly visitors were for the nation of the poor.

Poverty policies turned on the effective administration of relief. At the heart of the social insurance idea was a different and more modern concept: risk. It turned on the possibility of spreading the quixotic turns of fate over broader, public communities. Social insurance was not a program of isolation. Like the market society whose rents and injuries it endeavored to repair, social insurance's keys were complicity and interdependence.

Insurance against the risks of labor was not, in the first instance, an invention of the state but of workers themselves. Throughout the North Atlantic economy, miners and factory workers, shop mates, tavern mates, and neighbors banded together to mutualize the economic risks endemic to wage labor. Sickness, accident, joblessness, the enfeeblement of old age, or the death of a wage earner: these were the workers' primary risks in labor markets without sick pay, accident compensation, pension funds, or, for most wage earners, the barest margin of job security. Their terror lay in the way in which each of these events could, without warning, snip a family's income like a thread. Unexpected and catastrophic, these life-course disasters were to wage earners what fire risk was to the uninsured merchant. It was little wonder that workers tried to cushion themselves from fate with a multitude of pools and mutual associations.

The most primitive forms of workers' mutual insurance clubs were hard to distinguish from lotteries or betting pools. Work mates would contribute to a common fund at the year's start from which death or sick payments could be drawn, the surplus (if any) to be divided up among the rest at the year's end. "Slate clubs" they were called in Britain, after the slates that hung on pub walls, chalked with the members' accounts. The number of local clubs of this sort—tied to a saloon, a church, or a workplace—is lost beyond counting. Unstable and actuarially unsound, a cross between a gambling club and a mutual assistance fraternity, they were ubiquitous throughout the domain of wage labor.

Into local associations of this sort, larger interests intruded. On the Continent, the key player was the state. In Germany, where bits and pieces of guild mutualism had outlasted the dismantling efforts of the economic liberals, quasi-public workers' welfare institutions survived in a number of archaic forms. In the mines, a focus of special state interest everywhere in continental Europe, traditional miners' *Knappschaften*, which had been allowed to decay as an impediment to free trade, were revived by a Prussian act of 1854, this time as legally defined, compulsory benefits funds, pooling miners' and employers' contributions into jointly administered provident funds against mining accidents, sickness, or death. Outside the notoriously high-risk enterprise of mining, compulsory benefits funds were much rarer. Side by side with a maze of journeymen's, trade, and fraternal associations, however, locally administered *Hilfskassen* endured, quasi-public benefits funds that collected workers' voluntary contributions against the risk of sickness. The Prussian act of 1845, which cut the last legal props from beneath the artisan guilds, simultaneously gave municipalities the power to make *Kassen* membership compulsory for certain classes of workers. Relatively few industrial workers were covered under this provision, but the possibility kept the line between private risk and the public weal fluid and indistinct in Germany.[16]

In France, *sociétés de secours mutuels* had a quasi-official character of a different sort than the German *Kassen.* Reorganized in an act of 1852, these local societies were required to register with the state, enlist local notables in their leadership, and, in return for a state-guaranteed rate of interest, deposit most of their assets in a central, state-administered fund. The bourgeois patrons recruited as honorary members under the act contributed heavily to the societies' prestige and income. After 1898 so did public, tax-levied subsidies, as the state itself increasingly absorbed the burdens of patronage. To this mix, in a gesture of imperial social politics, Napoleon III added special state banks to which citizens could turn for disability insurance and old age annuities at favorable rates.[17]

In Britain the most aggressive players in the field of working-class mutualism were not the agencies of the state but fraternal and commercial entrepreneurs. Franchising out the actuarial security of mass membership, national organizations absorbed local risk pools into more highly organized networks of membership, ritual, and support. There were almost 24,000 friendly societies (as mutual assistance associations were officially called) registered by the state in Britain and Ireland in 1900. Of their 5 million members, however, one-third belonged to the four largest affiliated societies. Sickness insurance was their stock-in-trade: sick pay to help tide members over during days lost from work and the services of a doctor under contract to the society. Dues in the friendly societies were steep enough to put them out of the reach of most common laborers, but among skilled workers friendly society membership was a key source of security and respect.[18]

More aggressive still were the commercial insurance companies. In Germany and France, insurance companies catering to the working class were slow to develop. In Britain, on the other hand, the so-called collecting societies, mail-order associations such as the Royal Liver or the Royal London, which traded in benefits pure and simple without any pretense of local management, had surpassed their noncommercial rivals in membership by the turn of the century. They, in turn, could barely hold a candle to the outright commercial insurance companies specializing in cheap policies for the masses. "Industrial insurance" companies they were called, named for their targeted market among the industrial wage-earning classes. On paydays, armies of their agents fanned across working-class neighborhoods to collect the weekly penny premiums. "With a bowler hat on the back of his head, a straight-steel pen behind his ear, and a bottle of Stephen's Blue-Black Ink in his waistcoat pocket," as Bentley B. Gilbert describes him, the insurance collector was a fixture in working-class neighborhoods, and the instantly recognizable butt of music hall satire. Critics charged—with reason—that only a pitifully small fraction of the sums collected came back in benefits. Trading in death policies that rarely exceeded $100 in value, commercial insurance for the masses was not life insurance but burial insurance: a hedge against the humiliations of a pauper's interment. All these limitations notwithstanding, the industrial insurance companies grew vigorously in the soil of working-class insecurity. They claimed 20 million policies on their books by 1900, in addition to the six million policies held by the collecting societies.[19]

One must imagine, then, the North Atlantic economy as crisscrossed with benefits pools and insurance institutions: regulated and unregulated, commercial and fraternal, actuarially primitive or highly systematized. The resulting system was both a fixture of everyday life and inadequate to it, far-flung and full of holes. No other organizations set down deeper roots in the working class. In Britain, where the labor unions claimed three million members in 1911, the officially registered friendly societies (exclusive of the collecting societies and the industrial insurance companies) claimed six million—the memberships, to be sure, multiple and overlapping. In aggregate that meant one registered friendly society membership for every eight persons, adult and child alike. In France at the time, the four million adult members claimed by the *sociétés de secours mutuels* amounted to one person in ten in the total population.[20]

In the United States, in the absence of even the most rudimentary official registration, the magnitude and economic importance of workers' mutual assistance propels one quickly into guesswork. Clearly the system was extensive, considerably more so than the surviving small town Odd Fellows' or Woodmen's meeting hall, paint peeling and roof askew, begins to hint. Every working-class neighborhood possessed its clubs and lodges. In the steel town of Homestead, Pennsylvania, in 1908, Margaret Byington counted notices for fifty fraternal society meetings within a single week. In Chicago's Italian neighborhoods, the parades of the mutual benefit societies, accompanied by banners and fife and drum, were a regular Sunday event, the members "celebrating their achievement in having surrounded themselves by at least a thin wall of protection against disaster," as Jane Addams put it. W. E. B. Du Bois estimated fraternal and mutual aid association membership among black Philadelphians in the 1890s at a third of the city's black adult male population. In Michigan City, Indiana, an industrial city of 15,000 persons at the turn of the century, there were twenty-six fraternal lodges, almost all of them wage-earner dominated, not counting the parish-based Catholic and Lutheran mutual aid societies. In Manhattan's Lower East Side, a hive of mutualism, there were almost two thousand.[21]

More precise estimates of membership are considerably more hazardous. In 1891, the Connecticut Bureau of Labor Statistics counted 386 mutual benefit societies in the state, enrolling 127,000 persons—a density (in the heart of the industrial Northeast) of one membership to every six state residents, slightly higher than the one in seven ratio Seebohm Rowntree found in York, England, eight years later. By the early part of the twentieth century, estimates ran higher still. In California in 1915 the fraternal associations—from the Native Sons of the Golden West and the Improved Order of Red Men to the Orden der Hermanns Sohne and the B'nai B'rith—counted a member for every five inhabitants of the state. In Massachusetts in 1914 the fraternal associations claimed a member for nearly every two state residents. Constructed in this way, the figures clearly exaggerated the mutual assistance societies' presence in working-class life. Cut the membership figures by half—the fraction most contemporary experts agreed reflected the proportion recruited from outside the working class; discount them by half again to correct for the multiple memberships with which men doubled or tripled their chances against fate. Still, what remains is a structure of working-class mutual assistance associations clearly comparable to that of contemporary Europe.[22]

Where the institutions of mutual assistance in the United States were weak was not in numbers but in their social and political fragmentation. In Britain and in the France the friendly societies and mutual assistance societies played a vigorous public part in the social policy debates; in Germany, the *Kassen* and the voluntary *Vereine* formed the axis on which Bismarck's social policy was compelled to turn. The quiescence of their American counterparts, in contrast, is striking. With the exception of the Fraternal Order of the Eagles' drive for publicly financed old-age pensions in the 1920s, the best established of the fraternal lodges retreated from public policy behind veils of status-enhancing ritual. As for the smaller parish-, workplace-, or neighborhood-based lodges, sick clubs, and funeral pools, there the internal divisions of the immigrant working class took a heavy toll. The most effective organizing bases for workers' risk pooling in America—language, creed, race, and ethnic distinction—splintered in the very act of mutualizing. On these ethnically and racially fragmented foundations, no public policy was going to be easily erected.

Under the circumstances, the American branches of the "industrial insurance" industry grew luxuriantly. By 1911 they had 24.7 million policies in force in the United States, three times the fraternal associations' combined membership and virtually the monetary equivalent of the contemporary German state insurance system.[23] Voluntary institutions of working-class mutualism spread as well, wherever work and wages were insecure. But uncounted and politically invisible, unrecognized by public registration and unsupported by the state, without a corps of bourgeois patrons, and internally fragmented, the voluntary associations did not thicken as nodes of public policy formation or administration in the United States.

On neither side of the Atlantic did the institutions of voluntary risk hedging insure participants against more than a fraction of the calamities working-class families knew the future held in store. Sick pay and (especially in the United States) funeral costs were the most common benefits.

With steeper dues, some mutual assistance associations provided the services of a contract doctor or, more rarely, survivors' insurance. Beyond this core the covered risks diminished dramatically. Only the best organized of the skilled workers' unions provided benefits against unemployment. Except for employees of a few of the largest corporations, retirement pensions were a luxury for the business class.

Gender narrowed these limitations still more sharply. Nowhere did the risks covered by the mutual assistance societies include those that women workers might have added to the list: pregnancy, childbirth, and the demands of infant care, all capable of snuffing out a woman's wage-earning power overnight. Workingmen's insurance was insurance for male wage earners. The fraternal associations reinforced the point by playing as hard on rituals of male solidarity as on insurance features; the slate clubs had their home in the male preserve of the pubs. Only as the targets of the insurance collectors' weekly visits did women play a significant role in the structure of voluntary insurance. Women, for whom wage earning typically occupied a relatively brief, compressed fraction of their work lives, patched together systems of mutual support in less formally defined ways, differently structured than the men's combination of social club and betting pool. Neither the institutions of voluntary risk pooling nor the state systems that in time complemented them were, on the whole, for them.[24]

Circumscribed but ubiquitous, insurance was a fact of working-class life. A ragged system for the best paid of skilled wage workers, its effectiveness eroded sharply as one descended the wage gradient. It was not for women. Nowhere did it purchase a true safety net: real insurance that "the thin wall of protection against disaster" would not crumble around a working-class family, leaving it dependent on the generosity of private charity or subject to the poor law's rigors. Tattered cloak that it was, however, everyday mutualism was a living demonstration of the ways in which the most acute of wage earners' calamities might be hedged with the law of averages.

The birthplace of something different—social insurance, it was being called by American observers by 1910—was Germany. Social insurance departed from voluntary mutuality in two critical ways, both of which pushed outward the boundaries of risk and complicity. The first, and most important, was that it compelled employers into the wage workers' risk pools. Where work consumed all but a thin margin of wage workers' lives, accidents, sickness, old-age enfeeblement, and loss of employment were not merely the workers' risks; they were industry's responsibility as well. Social insurance socialized the concept of industrial risk, reconceiving the strains of industrial work as charges against those who held the power to set its conditions.

Social insurance's second innovation was to make the risk pools compulsory for wage earners as well. This was in part to solidify the actuarially unstable, constantly reformulated voluntary associations, in part to extend their provisions deeper into the ranks of ordinary wage earners, and, most of all, to lessen the pressure on the relief agencies from those who kept tumbling through the voluntary system's rents and holes. Workers' risk pools began as a kind of solidaristic gambling match with fate. In social insurance a more public theme emerges: the just distribution among wage earners, employers, and the tax-shouldering public of the social costs generated by private wage bargains.

Relatively little of this was clear when the problem of workers' insurance began to be debated in late-nineteenth-century Germany. No one, least of all Bismarck, envisioned the state as the giant insurance company it came to be. From its birth in Germany in the 1880s to its unexpected appropriation by the British Liberal government in 1911 and its adoption still later by the New Dealers, social insurance's history was that of a series of impasses and improvisations.

In Germany, the nodes on which these improvisations grew were the *Kassen* and the *Knappschaften.* In theory binding on masters and journeymen alike, they kept a model of compulsory risk pooling alive in mid-nineteenth-century Germany. When the "labor question" came to a head in the economic collapse of the mid-1870s, with beggars and tramps at every city gate, it is not surprising that the idea of reinvigorating the *Kassen* should have attracted many of the critics of *Manchestertum.* The Verein für Sozialpolitik debated the issue at length in 1874. Only a minority, however, Adolph Wagner among them, lobbied for compulsory, public *Kassen.* The majority preferred to require wage earners to insure themselves against the risks of catastrophic income loss, leaving them free to do so through whatever pooling associations they chose. Years later, Gustav Schmoller still thought the compulsory legislation of the 1880s too precipitous; Lujo Brentano opposed it at the time altogether. But it was clear as early as the 1870s that some combination of public compulsion with the *Kassen*'s institutional form was within the reach of social policy.[25]

None of this initial policy-framing labor was Bismarck's work, as the standard accounts regularly misconstrue it. When, as chancellor of the new German empire, he turned his attention from foreign to domestic policy in the mid-1870s, insurance was barely on his agenda. His published memoirs omitted the famous social insurance legislation of the 1880s altogether. Obsessed by the rising socialist vote, the key issue for Bismarck was not labor's risks but working-class political loyalty, which he forced to a crisis by suppressing virtually all socialist activity in 1878. With the urgency of a full-blown legitimacy crisis, however, that act precipitated a search for policies with which to buy back the affections of the working class for the established social order and the state.[26]

Bismarck's instincts went not to insurance but to imperial provision. To the idea of wage earners' contributions to the state benefit funds he was never sympathetic: "If the worker must pay, the effect on him is lost." Industrial accident provision, as he first imagined it, would have been paid for entirely by employers and the Reich itself. He vetoed his chief social policy adviser's suggestion that private insurance companies be permitted to underwrite employers' accident liability risks on the grounds that it would intrude profit and commerce into a realm of social provision he hoped to carve out for the empire. Socialism from below was to be countered by social provision from above, the creation of a gift relationship that would convince radicalism's potential recruits that the most powerful agency for their welfare was the empire itself.[27]

It was the Reichstag's refusal to accept the taxes Bismarck's initial proposals entailed that, in the deliberately precipitated crisis, produced something else: a trio of compulsory insurance acts. The first to pass the Reichstag, the sickness insurance law of 1883, co-opted and extended the existing *Hilfskassen* by making membership in an approved sickness fund compulsory for certain classes of industrial wage workers and adding compulsory employer taxes to the funds' resources. The accident insurance law of 1884 supplanted the existing liability laws with a legally fixed scale of compensatory payments for industrial accidents, administered through a network of compulsory, quasi-public, employers' mutual associations. The last of the three workers' insurance acts was a compulsory old-age and invalidity insurance act, which pooled workers' dues, employers' levies, and token imperial subsidies into a pension fund for disabled wage earners and for long-term wage earners who survived beyond the age of seventy. Only here did Bismarck succeed in forcing the principle closest to his heart past the objections of his advisers and the resistance of the Reichstag. Even so, of the aggregate funds collected by the compulsory insurance institutions by 1903, only 7 percent had come from the state itself; 47 percent had been paid in through employer taxes, 46 percent by wage workers themselves.[28]

Born in compromise, in a collision of Bismarck's will and Reichstag resistance, social insurance began in an untidy confusion of inertia and improvisation. The sickness insurance act of 1883 entrusted sick benefits to a bewilderingly complex array of established and newly constructed *Kassen*, most of them financed at a ratio of two to one by wage earners and their employers. By 1909 there were more than 23,000 of them providing sick pay and medical treatment through contracted doctors, none with precisely the same benefits. The costs of industrial accident insurance, on the other hand, were set wholly on employers and administered through quasi-public employers' pools. Yet a third administrative apparatus was specially created for the old-age insurance funds, where employers' and workers' contributions were this time matched one to one.

Administratively splintered and incomplete, the German system nevertheless grew, adding on classes of the population beyond the industrial wage-earner core of the 1880s. The sickness insurance law had doubled at a stroke the number of German workers enrolled in registered mutual assistance societies to about 40 percent of all wage earners; by 1914, now extended to include farm and domestic labor, virtually all German wage earners were covered by the sickness and accident insurance legislation. Salaried workers were added to the insurance system in 1911—with a separate administrative apparatus and especially advantageous benefits. Sickness benefits for wage earners' family dependents were common in many of the *Kassen* by the turn of the century; survivors' benefits for orphans and for widows unable to work were added in 1911.

A preemptive strike against working-class socialism that its critics called the epitome of socialism itself, the German system was not only administratively confused but also contradictory in its tendencies. Parsimony was a prominent element. From the beginning, support levels were set deliberately low. Sick pay covered on average no more than 50 to 60 percent of a workers' regular wage. In the case of work accidents, employer-financed compensation payments did not begin until a worker had already lost thirteen weeks of work, and then compensation payments were made at the discretion of appeals boards, whose judgments ran heavily in employers' favor. Retirement on old-age insurance payments was, by design, out of the question. Contributions under the old-age insurance act were collected from all, but mandated to be paid out only to those who had contributed for a full thirty years, in a system that was never extensive and never popular among the German working class.[29]

These restrictions, all designed to sustain the normal goad of hunger to work, went hand in hand, however, with other, unpredicted generosities. Under the incentives of the accident insurance system, German employers invested in safety devices and regulations at a rate matched by employers nowhere else in the North Atlantic economy. In need of investment outlets, administrators of the accumulating insurance reserves had begun by the century's end to pour resources into public amenities—hospitals, sanitariums, public baths, water and sewer systems, and low-cost housing—in ways that left a profound mark on German society.

Power relations within the workers' insurance system were similarly Janus-faced. Designed to buttress the centralized state, the German insurance acts devolved authority onto an untidy mass of subsidiary bodies. Social Democrats had opposed the legislation of the 1880s, intended as it was to bury working-class radicalism under the largesse of the paternally compassionate state. But in the provision of the sickness insurance act that allotted wage earners (in accordance with their contributions ratio) two-thirds of the votes in the sickness insurance funds' administration, the socialists soon found an organizational base second only to the labor unions. Socialist majorities controlled many of the largest urban sickness funds by the turn of the century, to the distress of the doctors they employed and of imperial officials. By then Social Democratic deputies in the Reichstag were beginning regularly to cast their votes in the social insurance system's favor; when it was threatened with dismantlement from the right in the late 1920s, they embraced it as if it had been, all along, their own.[30]

To the last of the workers' principal risks, that of unemployment, German state insurance officials never devised a workable solution. In default of imperial legislation—which stalled on cost considerations after 1906—unemployment relief was left to the cities to provide as they chose. By 1910 most major German cities had established public labor exchanges: city-subsidized hiring halls to which out-of-work employees could repair to try to find advertised employment. Borrowing from Belgian and French examples, a number of German cities experimented with city subsidies for trade union out-of-work funds, in an effort to ease the seasonal demands on the agencies of relief.[31]

The key element in the German departure of the 1880s had not been French-style subvention of this sort, however, but the principle of compulsion. Welfare states on the German model, whatever else they did, would henceforth sort their citizens into risk pools, extract special taxes from them, and pool those with equivalent taxes on the employers, who held the cards in the determination of working conditions. They would socialize a portion of the risks of labor, not so that the abjectly poor could be assisted, but to make it less likely that the expected hazards of a working life would push the regularly employed wage earner either into the arms of political radicalism or onto the tax-financed rolls for poor relief.

In politics, as in fashion, novelty is never a guarantee of imitation. Coinciding with the heating up of international debate over the "social question," the German innovations of 1883 to 1889 were assured a broad hearing. At international gatherings over the next two decades, social insurance's German architects lobbied hard for converts. But with the exception of neighboring Austria, none fell quickly in line. Outside the local customs, state ambitions, and legitimacy crisis in which it had been born, compulsory wage earners' risk insurance was no simple institution to transplant. Intellectually it had powerful competitors, as the social-political rivalry on display in Paris in 1900 made clear. The propaganda efforts of the German imperial insurance office notwithstanding, there was not much reason at the turn of the century to expect that the practice of compulsory social insurance would soon break out of its central European birthplace.

Of the rival systems for dealing with the risks of labor, the most obvious was tighter supervision of the workplaces whose hazards and intensity, long hours, unguarded machinery, and air clogged with lint or coal dust were the cause of so many of the workers' risks to begin with. This was the course Germans to Bismarck's left preferred to the ambulance-chasing efforts of workingmen's insurance. At the first international congress on labor legislation, assembled in Berlin in 1890 in the brief springtime of political reform following Bismarck's ouster, labor protection standards dominated the agenda; through the First World War, they absorbed a vast amount of reform energy throughout the North Atlantic economy. Labor protection legislation was everywhere, to be sure, exceedingly difficult work. Employers' resistance to publicly prescribed working standards and intrusive factory inspections was strong, and each step was doggedly resisted.[32] Still more strenuously resisted was the idea of a legal minimum wage below which a day's labor returned not a living but only a deficit on a workers' physical vitality. In 1900 minimum wage statues applicable to certain "sweated" trades were to be found only in two provinces of Australia, where fear that Asian workers would otherwise drive out Euro-Australian workers had played an essential part in their enactment. Politically difficult as all these measures might be to achieve, however, their logic had an effective straightforwardness.

A third alternative was neither to insure nor prevent but, rather, to foster the existing systems of mutual insurance, preserving their voluntary character but deepening their impact through public subsidies. The leading late-nineteenth-century example of this joining of tax funds to collective self-help was France, where local sickness insurance societies, employer pension funds, and, after 1905, national trade union out-of-work funds were all subsidized in this way. Relatively simple to administer and relatively unchallenging to existing interests and organizations, elevated to a general principle by Catholic and Protestant social progressives, "subsidarist" systems like these spread rapidly across continental Europe. In Sweden, Denmark, Belgium, Italy, and Switzerland, voluntary sickness funds drew state subventions on the French model; in Belgium, Norway, and Denmark, and in many of the leading cities of Germany, Switzerland, and Italy, trade union out-of-work funds did so as well.

Policies of publicly subsidized but not publicly compelled mutualism did not pretend to weave a safety net below every laborer. By design the improvident—and, in practice, the unskilled and ill-paid—fell through the system's yawning fissures. The issue of comprehensiveness had begun to rattle confidence in subsidarist principles by the early years of the twentieth century. In France, advanced progressives were full of second thoughts with regard to state compulsion. By 1901 even Léon Bourgeois had signed on to the principle of compulsory, state-administered insurance against the poverty of old age—a kind of German annex, as it were, to the home-grown institutions and solidarist ethos of *mutualité.* French progressives finally set an old-age insurance act to that effect on the statute books in 1910, but it was deeply unpopular with workers. Gutted by the courts, which refused to uphold the principle of compulsory wage reductions, it was an embarrassing political failure. Subsidarist social politics was shot through with practical gaps and extravagant ethical expectations. But it was not, on its face, any less coherent than the jerry-built structures of German compulsion. On the eve of the First World War, no other system was more widespread.[33]

Finally, challenging all of these schemes was the notion of simple public grants to citizens whose need was not of their own making. This line of reasoning did not begin with the notion of risk. On the part of the working class and the poor, it began with a sense of right; on the part of the middle class and the state officialdom, it began with certain embarrassments in the administration of the poor laws. As poor-law authorities tightened up supervision and control of the poor toward the end of the century, there grew out of the very intensity of their efforts a countermovement to extract certain classes of public assistance recipients, less to be blamed for their straits than the rest, and set off for them a less demeaning system of support. In Britain, with this in mind, the sick poor had been allowed to use the medical services of the poor-law unions after 1885 without forfeiting their voting rights. In France, a web of special provisions reached out toward the sick and disabled poor; another offered poor mothers and infants free prenatal and obstetrical care, partial compensation for lost wages during state-mandated maternity leave, and subsidies for large families, in what amounted to the most highly developed "maternal" welfare state in the North Atlantic economy before the First World War.[34]

Most troubling of all, however, were the elderly poor, enfeebled by a lifetime of work and skidding downward, through no fault of their own, into more menial, less regular work and steadily diminishing pay. The era's most widely observed experiment in special provisions for the aged poor was Denmark's. By an act of 1891, local Danish authorities were empowered to grant nondisqualifying relief to elderly poor petitioners who had, until then, lived decent, morally inoffensive lives. In practice the act created a separate system of modest, noncontributory, old-age "pensions" for those who were needy, sober, and had kept themselves off the poor relief rolls the ten years previously. New Zealand adopted a similarly constructed old-age pension system for the respectable (and non-Asiatic) poor seven years later. Yearly character examinations before a local justice were required, but Henry D. Lloyd, who recorded one such New Zealand old-age pension examination in detail in 1900, thought only one in ten applicants was rejected, most commonly for family desertion or frequent drunkenness. Pensions and relief "without the [politically disqualifying] effects of the poor law" were not wholly free from the intrusiveness of public relief. Demanding no contribution from their recipients—other than a lifetime of hard work—they were not in the least a form of insurance. But in isolating old age, infirmity, motherhood, or sickness as special categories, as circumstances not fully within a person's control, these provisions tacitly acknowledged what working-class families had known all along by experience: the unwilled risks of labor.[35]

Here, then, were four rival means to address the abyss under every wage earner's feet: compulsory state-administered social insurance, legally stipulated minima of wages or workplace conditions, publicly subsidized schemes of voluntary mutualism, and pensions for the blameless poor. In competition with each other or in combinations, with differing backers and constituencies, they swirled through the international policy gatherings, the pages of the leading reviews, and the parliaments.

It was in Britain, between 1906 and 1911, that the choice between these policies came most clearly to a head. The Liberal government of those years was to Britain what the Theodore Roosevelt and Woodrow Wilson administrations, rolled into one, were to the United States. Coming into office with little preformed program except a fragile yet politically indispensable alliance with labor, a fear that Britain was falling behind in the race for national social "efficiency," and a sense that the heritage of Gladstonian Liberalism had been played out, the "new Liberals" became eager policy borrowers, scavengers across the boundaries of national political cultures. Between 1906 and 1911 they brought into Britain minimum wage legislation, old-age pensions, public employment exchanges, school meals for the children of the poor, medical attention for schoolchildren, and progressive land and income taxation—all with considerable show of their foreign precedents. In the end, against all predictions, they imported German-modeled social insurance as well.[36]

Of the social issues that pressed on the new government, old-age poverty touched the broadest nerve. With one out of every five persons over age sixty-five in turn-of-the-century England and Wales receiving poor relief, the political potential of the issue could hardly be missed.[37] Ever sensitive to the winds of politics, Joseph Chamberlain had engineered the appointment of a Royal Commission on the Aged Poor in 1893, on which he urged a system modeled on Louis Napoleon's innovation of 1850: tax-subsidized old-age annuities purchasable through the post office.

The more dramatic proposal came from another member of the Royal Commission, Charles Booth: universal, tax-financed payments of five shillings a week to every British citizen over sixty-five, regardless of means, excluding only those who had recently drawn on poor relief. Booth's proposal was a product of the peculiar mixture of iconoclasm and moralism familiar from his labor colony scheme. As he first announced his idea in 1891, it was not to soften the poor law but to tighten it up so as to eliminate home-based "outdoor" poor relief altogether. If one took the aged off the relief rolls, eliminating over a third of the poor law's recipients at a stroke, one would not only drastically reduce the size of the poor law machinery; by eliminating those with the strongest hold on public sympathy, Booth argued, one would also prune the categories of the poor down to its bottom residue of misfits, inebriates, beggars, and the weak of character—fit for either institutional confinement or abandonment to their fate. Booth's proposal to unlink old-age pensions from income tests derived from no commitment to old-age support as a right; its rationale lay, rather, in his dislike of state intrusion and his hatred of the shamming he was sure all means or morals tests promoted.[38]

However idiosyncratically Booth had broached it, the idea of universal five-shilling-a-week old-age pensions quickly drew a powerful tide of support. By 1902 the trade unions, the cooperatives, a number of influential progressives (Toynbee Hall's Samuel Barnett and Bournville's George Cadbury among them) had signed on. So had the friendly societies, torn between fear of losing some of their domain to the state and the financial pinch they had begun to feel from the rising numbers of the elderly drawing on their medical benefits. When the Liberal government entered office in 1906, proposals for universal noncontributory old-age pensions rolled out of the back benches with the aspirations of working-class Britain behind them.

"It is time we did something that appealed straight to the people," David Lloyd George wrote apropos old-age pensions. Fiscal considerations, however, dictated something more complicated. Seizing on the Danish and New Zealand precedents, the government deflected Booth's universal old-age pension idea into their more circumscribed mold: tax-financed, noncontributory pensions for the poor who could pass a test of character and were over age seventy. The result, in historian Pat Thane's words, was a system "for the very old, the very poor, and the very respectable." In this form, with only the charity organization societies in opposition, the act easily slipped through Parliament in 1908.[39]

Most remarkable in the old-age pension debates was the almost universal dismissal of the German alternative of compulsory old-age *insurance*. For all its severe limitations, the British old-age pension act was, to be sure, considerably more generous than the German scheme of 1889. Granting pensions to persons rather than to wage earners, the British act did not discriminate (as the German did) between the work careers typical of men and women. Under the British scheme, old-age benefits were higher than under the German, they came without payments by the recipient, and from the first they reached at least three times as many persons.[40] But even as a point of reference the German system had barely entered the British debates. An isolated member of Parliament gave favorable mention to the social insurance principle, only to have Charles Masterman, speaking for the government, reject it as "a system of regulation and a system of regimentation . . . utterly alien to the tradition of this country." Prime Minister Herbert Asquith sustained the point. Built on "the pillars of inquisition and compulsion," compulsory social insurance was "altogether inadmissable" in England.[41]

This was not the first time British policy makers had dismissed the precedents of German social insurance. During the British debates over accident liability legislation in the late 1890s, though all sides had mined the reports of the German state insurance office for data on accident costs and incidence, no influential British political figure had taken the idea of German-style state-administered accident insurance seriously. The British response to the unemployment distress of 1903 to 1905 was an act authorizing local committees to establish emergency public works and a flurry of interest in labor colonies. The contemporary German debate over the possibilities of insuring against unemployment barely touched British ears at all.

And yet by 1911 the government had pushed through a social insurance program that was as bold (Lloyd George insisted), as comprehensive, and more generous than Germany's itself. Among the factors that conspired to produce this reversal on the principle of compulsory social insurance, not the least was the transnational progressive network. Worked hard by business admirers of German tariff policy, given urgency by newspaper alarm over German economic and imperial competition, the project of uncovering the secrets of German social progress suddenly acquired political weight.[42]

William Beveridge was one of the new policy intellectuals for whom these events momentarily gave an entry. He had gone from Oxford to Toynbee Hall as subwarden in 1903, with the ambition of developing "an authoritative opinion on the problems of city life." Samuel Barnett, shaken by demonstrations among the East End unemployed, pushed Beveridge toward the formation of more sensible, "nonphilanthropic" policies of relief, and Beveridge, eager for the assignment, soon found himself at the center of policy debate as a member of the central London emergency unemployment board. From that experience, and from Charles Booth's studies of London dock labor and Percy Alden's reports on the operation of the German municipal labor exchanges, Beveridge quickly concluded that the key to reducing unemployment was to shrink the number of underemployed workers the markets kept in reserve. A system of efficient, state-administered labor exchanges was his device. In August 1907, Beveridge visited Germany for himself, coming back not only with his labor exchange idea more firmly fixed but with a new, less anticipated respect for the German institutions of social insurance as well. Unlike the "free gift" of a pension, Beveridge wrote, the German scheme "sets up the State as a comprehensive organism to which the individual belongs and in which he, under compulsion if need be, plays his part." Old-age pensions, Beveridge objected, were a throwback to the day of the ladies bountiful; it was in insurance that one found a principle in harmony with the "growing complexity and interdependence of industrial life."[43]

More immediately influential than Beveridge's German discoveries was Lloyd George's whirlwind visit to Germany as chancellor of the exchequer right after the passage of the old-age pensions act in the summer of 1908. A day's visit to the Imperial Insurance Office in Berlin could not have done much more than reinforce an inchoate vision of German efficiency. But Lloyd George's praise of the "elaborate and wonderful machinery" of German relief and insurance, offered in an interview the day of his return, went considerably deeper than polite rhetoric. At the same time, partly under Beveridge's influence, the new thirty-four-year-old president of the Board of Trade, Winston Churchill, had begun to tout something like the German commitment to "social organization" as the key to the Liberal Party's political future. "Underneath, though not in substitution for, the immense disjointed fabric of social safeguards and insurance which has grown up by itself in England there must be spread—at a lower level—a sort of Germanized network of State intervention and regulation," Churchill wrote Herbert Asquith in March 1908. By the end of that year, Churchill's program had swollen to include labor exchanges, a greatly expanded public works program, poor-law reform, closer state railroad control, extended compulsory education—and compulsory unemployment and sickness insurance. "I say," he urged the prime minister, "thrust a big slice of Bismarckianism over the whole underside of our industrial system, and await the consequences, whatever they may be, with a good conscience."[44]

Political ambition, an eagerness for new ideas and dramatic gestures, an interest in Germany whetted by rivalry and ambition—to these factors must be added the one Bismarck's opponents had emphasized. Social insurance, with its employers' and beneficiaries' taxes, was far cheaper than straight-out public provision of work or relief. When the ambitions of the government came up against the Gordian knot of finances in 1908–1909, the intrusive machinery of social insurance began to seem far less important than its fiscal advantages. Many of the civil servant experts were not enthusiastic. But in the impasse over revenues the cabinet reversed itself, reaching out for exogenous policy proposals, even from alien Germany.

By late 1908 Lloyd George was committed to some form of sickness insurance. Pressed by a renewed employment crisis and the radicals' "work for all" demand, the cabinet soon endorsed the untried notion of unemployment insurance as well. The next year saw the successful passage of a labor exchanges act, drafted at the Board of Trade by William Beveridge. When Lloyd George introduced the government bill for compulsory wage earners' sickness and unemployment insurance, he dismissed his advisers' suggestion to shorten the speech by omitting its references to Germany. "I would rather get up and tell them what the rates are to the employer and employed in Germany, and that my scheme does not charge so much, and does more, and then sit down without having made a speech, than leave that out."[45]

Different contexts, different outcomes. Harassed though he was by political antagonists, Bismarck had faced no concerted opposition from existing insurance institutions. The German institutions of voluntary mutualism were local; the German commercial insurance industry was in its infancy in the 1880s. Neither of these was the case in early-twentieth-century Britain. Lloyd George took it for granted that sickness insurance would have to co-opt the friendly societies rather than supplant them. The initial drafts of the sickness insurance section of the National Insurance Act assumed that employer, employee, and state contributions would be deposited into the benefits fund of the friendly society or trade union of the worker's choice. Distrust of state inroads into their business, however, and fear of being saddled with unwanted members made the friendly societies reluctant and difficult recruits to the scheme.[46]

Into this breach, the industrial insurance companies moved with alacrity. The commercial insurance companies succeeded in eliminating statutory provision for widows' and orphans' benefits, which would have directly competed with their own business. More important, they managed to modify the act—originally drafted to limit the administration of sickness insurance only to nonprofit, democratically managed associations—so as to allow the commercial companies to spin off their own nonprofit adjuncts for the purpose. The advantage to the companies, of course, was a foot in the door for the sale of burial insurance, and the commercial insurance industry pushed its way in with all the resources at its disposal. Within a year and a half of the British act's passage, 40 percent of those registered under the act were in the insurance companies' and collecting societies' satellite associations and another 23 percent were in friendly societies without local branches, managed by central offices or by the agents themselves.[47]

In the territorial combat between interest groups, doctors were not to be left out. Fully half the general practitioners in Britain worked under a friendly society contract on the eve of the National Insurance Act, chafing at the contractual terms of their livelihood. They lobbied successfully to strip the approved societies of the power to contract directly with doctors, instead allowing beneficiaries to choose their own physician from a panel approved by local health committees, which the doctors hoped to dominate. The unemployment section of the National Insurance Act also bent, though less dramatically, to the structure of established interests. Unemployment insurance coverage was limited, for the most part, to wage earners in seven highly cyclical trades. Alongside the insurance provisions of the bill, labor unions got a modest subvention to their general out-of-work funds, balanced against subventions for employers in the covered trades who managed to lessen the fluctuations in their labor needs.

As in Germany, in short, compulsory social insurance constructed at a stroke a vast new field of competition into which the existing interests—political and commercial—rushed to shoulder their way. The irony was that in Germany, the institutions of compulsory sickness insurance soon formed an island of social democracy within a heavy-handed imperial state; in much more fully democratized Britain, the field of compulsory sickness insurance quickly became the playing field of top-heavy, economic interests.

The British compromises did not please everyone. The Trades Union Congress was sharply split, its left wing opposed to any scheme of compulsory insurance that bit into workers' wages. By 1913 the Labour Party was calling for repeal of the sickness insurance section of the act and its reestablishment on a noncontributory basis. The Webbs excoriated what Beatrice Webb called "Lloyd George's rotten scheme of sickness insurance" on the grounds that it patched but did not prevent. Their rival program was much more thoroughgoing: an expanded public health service to nip environmentally borne diseases at the source, a national wage minimum, countercyclical public works expenses, and, for the residue of poverty that remained, a regimen of training establishments, labor colonies, discipline, and enforced temperance. Even Lloyd George wrote in a memorandum in 1911: "Insurance necessarily a temporary expedient. At no distant date hope State will acknowledge full responsibility in the matter of making provision for sickness breakdown and unemployment."[48]

The National Insurance Act of 1911 was not a product, like the Old Age Pensions Act, of long-brewing ferment from below; it entailed no seismic shift in political culture. Born at the top of the policy-making apparatus, it was the product of a particular conjuncture of ideas, ambitions, impasses, and opportunities. Nonetheless it represented a small but important shift in thinking about the risks of labor. Beatrice Webb, who had not assisted in Booth's London surveys of the poor without feeling its lasting effects, worried about the moral impact of the law's "unconditional" and "automatic" benefits. Winston Churchill's response to this moral objection spoke the new rhetoric of industrial risk: "I do not like mixing up moralities and mathematics." Exemplary character had never given a wage earner a guarantee against the whimsical turns of the labor market. The point of the act was to build a "new foundation of averages" in place of "the old foundation of chance."[49]

What the British National Insurance Act showed, even more, was that at a moment of political impasse, when social ambitions ran ahead of traditional institutional means, the policy makers and legislators could be induced to look beyond local traditions, with results that the entrenched interest groups could bend, even deform, but not wholly resist. In the British reversal on social insurance, the policy rivalry and exchange within the North Atlantic economy had borne dramatic fruit. But if in Britain, why not in the United States?

Fields of Interest

In the United States there was no shortage of interest in all the foreign experiments in mitigating the risks of wage labor. Workers' protective statutes were a particular case in point. Americans had already borrowed a good many British measures of this sort, and a fair amount of existing legislation—however longer in symbolism it was than in enforcement—was already to be found in the statute books. With the rapid elaboration of labor-protective statutes in Europe in the 1890s, however, the American states had not kept pace. On this point those who knew both sides of the North Atlantic economy were of a common mind. France had adopted major new pieces of factory legislation in 1892 and 1900, Germany in 1891 in the wake of Bismarck's dismissal, and Britain in 1901. In comparison, Arthur Shadwell in 1903 thought the Americans barely had an effective factory legislation system at all. John Graham Brooks echoed this judgment the same year: "In no country of the first rank is this legislation so weak as in the United States." Regionally spotty and ineffectually enforced, workplace regulation was a hook with which the parties often fished for working-class votes; but to those who knew what was being done in Europe, turn-of-the-century American workers' lives seemed barely touched by protective legislation.[50]

In the vantage of this legislative lag, one of the key pressure groups in the Atlantic progressive connection, the American Association for Labor Legislation (AALL), set down its foundations. The league's parent organization, the International Association for Labor Legislation, had been founded by leading French, Belgian, and German social economists in 1900 to press for uniform labor protection statutes. Limitation of night work for women factory laborers and elimination of phosphorus poisoning in industry were its first two projects. A German affiliate, the Gesellschaft für Sozialreform, was founded in 1901, with Gustav Schmoller, Adolph Wagner, and Lujo Brentano signatories to its organizing call. There were soon parallel national affiliates in France and Britain and a small central office in Geneva.

In 1905 two of Schmoller's former students, Yale's Henry Farnam and the New York Bureau of Labor Statistics' Adna F. Weber, took advantage of the American Economic Association's annual meeting to organize an American "section" of the international association. Richard T. Ely was named the organization's president and John R. Commons its first executive secretary; from the beginning, the board of the AALL was stocked with German-trained progressive economists. The association took its initial work as "mainly educational": above all, dissemination of an English-language version of the international association's *Bulletin*. A veritable "manual of progressive legislation," the executive committee called it; some of this legislation was "so far ahead of anything that we have done in this country, that it should receive very wide notice." When the AALL moved into active lobbying, its first campaign, for tighter safety standards in the deadly phosphorus-tip match industry, flowed straight out of the politics of lag and the mother association's precedents.[51]

More political and, for the moment, more effective than the AALL's professors in the fight for tighter factory legislation was a circle of women gathered around Florence Kelley at the National Consumers' League. The Consumers' League had also begun as a European import, though in this case the American offshoot soon outshone its London parent. The American association began life as a kind of genteel boycott association among

New York City women alarmed at the wages and desperately long hours of women department store clerks. By the time Florence Kelley was recruited as its executive secretary in 1899, the league had already branched out into a crusade to raise labor standards in the women's undergarment trade by affixing its "white label" to goods made in shops that met its standards for wages, work hours, and safety. For its honorific posts, it drew heavily on veterans of the German academic connection: John Graham Brooks, Richard Ely, Samuel M. Lindsay, Henry C. Adams, Charles R. Henderson, and E. R. A. Seligman, among others. But its organizational energy came from its women: Maud Nathan, a prominent figure in international women's circles; Greenwich House's Mary Kingsbury Simkhovitch; the sisters Pauline and Josephine Goldmark; and Florence Kelley.[52]

Before leaving Chicago for New York, Kelley had crossed swords with legislators and courts as Illinois's first chief factory inspector, and she helped propel the league from consumer pressure tactics to political action. By 1902, the league had spun off a separate lobbying agency to press the child labor issue, with Lindsay as its first executive secretary. Recruiting the Goldmarks' brother-in-law Louis D. Brandeis in the effort, the league undertook a carefully orchestrated legal defense campaign on behalf of state statutes limiting the maximum number of hours women wage earners could be compelled to work.[53]

In contrast to the American Association for Labor Legislation, the National Consumers' League did not wear its international connections on its sleeve. The league's core rhetoric was the rhetoric of exposure and muckraking. Its investigators poked their noses into airless sweatshops and steam-saturated laundries, canneries, and the city street trades. They collected masses of data on women's wages, budgets, health, employment, and living standards. But the league's international consciousness was never far from view. Reversing the dominant currents in the transatlantic progressive connection, the league soon began to spin off European sister organizations of its own; by 1910 there were league-inspired affiliates in France, Belgium, Germany, and Switzerland.[54]

A still more striking sign of the league's international reach was to be found in the "sociological" briefs prepared under Josephine Goldmark's direction for the league's hours-of-labor cases. Hardly sociological in any modern sense of the term, the briefs assembled no clear experimental evidence and mounted no very coherent argument. Their giveaway was in their running title: "The World's Experience upon Which Legislation Limiting the Hours of Labor for Women Is Based." Growing in size from the *Muller v. Oregon* brief's hundred-page supplement in 1908 to the thousand pages appended to the *Bunting v. Oregon* brief of 1915, the ever-expanding supplement amounted to a great rummaging through the world's literature on health, fatigue, and working-hours legislation, as if the contents of a great cosmopolitan bank of file drawers had been tipped bodily into a legal argument.[55]

In the case of the legislation Kelley herself ultimately thought the most fundamental—minimum wage legislation—the league's international appropriations were direct and unabashed. News of the Australian experiment in wage minima made its way to the United States through several conduits. Some heard it through the special reports of the U.S. Bureau of Labor; others, like John A. Ryan, through social Catholic circles, or from the Australian journalist Alice Henry, who, coming to the United States in 1906 for a lecture tour on a broad array of women's issues, stayed on as the National Women's Trade Union League's editor and staff expert on the Australian labor experiments.[56] Kelley herself was converted to the idea at the international consumers' league congress in Geneva in 1908, where representatives of the British National Anti-Sweating League, on the verge of the parliamentary victory that was to bring Australian-style minimum wage legislation to Britain in 1909, pressed the measure vigorously on the delegates.[57]

The model minimum wage bill the Consumers' League staff drafted the next year set no across-the-board wage minimum as American legislation after 1938 would do. Rather, faithful to its Australian and British antecedents, it authorized the appointment of special wage boards in those "sweated" trades where employers were suspected to have driven wages below the minimum necessary for health and physical survival. Each wage board's task was to undertake a systematic investigation of wages, profits, and labor in its targeted industry; should it conclude that redress was necessary, it could prescribe a legal wage minimum. Kelley, drawn to the bill's provision for the systematic taking of workers' testimony, saw it not only as an economic safeguard but also as an embryonic form of workers' representation in industry.

The cumulative impact of these interlinked campaigns for wage and workplace regulation was profound. Between the Consumers' League's victory in *Muller v. Oregon* in 1908, which cleared the constitutional way for legislation restricting the hours of women wage earners, and the American entry into the First World War, thirty-nine states enacted women's working hours legislation, nineteen of them for the first time. The stack of new child labor statutes enacted in the same period—thirty in 1911 alone, culminating in a federal child labor law in 1916—was still larger. The minimum wage movement ran afoul of much more formidable resistance in the courts, despite a Consumers' League brief crammed with Australasian and British data; but not before nine states had signed on to variations of the league's model bill in a rush in 1912 and 1913.[58]

In the United States as in Europe, the campaign for protective labor legislation was a curious amalgam of efforts, on the one hand, to eliminate certain of the most dangerous risks of the workplace and, on the other, leaving the dangers in place, to make sure that only adult men were exposed to them. From the beginnings of the protective labor legislation movement, the assumption that women and child workers belonged in a separate, particularly helpless category of workers had been central. But where in Europe men were gradually drawn into the protective tent erected for women workers, in the United States gender proved a formidable constitutional sticking point. The American minimum wage statutes that, in contrast to both their British and Australian precedents, and to Kelley's personal distress, cut adult men out of coverage altogether were a striking case in point.[59] So was the difficulty the league encountered in its efforts to extend the precedent of its hours-of-labor cases beyond women wage earners. Skewing everything toward women's and children's special vulnerabilities and, hence, their special claims under the police powers' protection, constitutional politics pressed gender into the very core of workers' protective legislation in the United States.

A parallel feminization of European precedents marked the transit to the United States of yet another policy device: public pensions for the blameless poor. Nothing hinted at this outcome when, in response to British debates over the treatment of the elderly poor, the old-age pension issue began to be discussed seriously in the United States soon after the turn of the century. Strenuously resisted by the charities establishment, which thought indiscriminate pensions, without case-by-case scrutiny and management, were profoundly misguided, the movement for old-age pensions gathered its strongest support, as in Britain, from the labor movement. Put on the ballot in a half dozen Massachusetts cities and towns in 1915, the proposal drew overwhelming majorities; in the mill town of Lawrence and among Brockton shoeworkers, the vote ran four to one in its favor. But on the official commissions, the idea barely made any headway at all.[60]

In the debate over pensions for the elderly poor, an occasional voice raised the specter of recent experience with pensions for Union veterans of the Civil War. A camel that, having gotten its nose in the tent of congressional politics, quickly threatened to fill the tent with its whole self, the veterans' pensions precedent was in no good repute in the early twentieth century, as Theda Skocpol has reemphasized. A relatively modest system of disability pensions for wounded Union Army soldiers had been thrown open after 1890 to virtually every surviving Union veteran, at an expense over almost ten times the military pension system in contemporary, soldier-saturated Germany.[61]

But most of the state commissions convened to consider the issue of old-age poverty mustered objections they thought considerably more pressing than the veterans' pension precedent. Far more important were the constitutional difficulties of easing blanket grants to the elderly poor past the "public purpose" doctrine in state constitutional law (a chancy matter, Frank Goodnow thought, as the Pennsylvania courts would show in the 1920s), the mechanisms of finance, and, above all, the perceived threat to the morals of the poor should relief come, even to the elderly, without its tithe of humiliation. Not until 1917, with a flourish of quotations from David Lloyd George and Sidney Webb, did a prominent state commission (the third to convene on the subject in Massachusetts) endorse the principle of noncontributory old-age pensions—and then only to fail to agree on an equitable means of finance. The Massachusetts Commission on Old Age of 1910 had dismissed the idea as "unwise" and "un-American," a blow to individual initiative that would "strike directly at [the] mainspring of social progress." It was only in the 1920s—and in numbers only after the crash of 1929—that states began cautiously to place a few of the elderly poor in the category of public pensioners.[62]

In the United States, blamelessness was to be affixed elsewhere: not to the poverty of old age but to the poverty of widowed motherhood. At the same moment that an American movement for old-age pensions was grinding to a political standstill, a maternalized version of the idea of extracting the most virtuous of the poor from the severities of the poor law swept through the American state legislatures. The "mothers' pension" movement, as it was called, turned on the economic crisis of widowhood and, as Skocpol and others have shown, the political muscle of middle-class, progressive women. The resulting state acts empowered counties to establish a separate, nondemeaning category of grants for widowed or deserted wives with children who passed means and morals tests. Lobbied hard by women's groups, legislatures in every state but nine put mothers' pension statutes on their books between 1911 and 1919.[63] Despite the foot-dragging and blatant racial discrimination of county authorities who kept the programs far smaller than the effective need, the acts helped carve out a special category of the blameless poor. In contrast to France, where fears of population decline gave maternalist social policy a civic and political spin, the guiding tropes of the mothers' pension movement were sentiment and women's weakness. Pitched in a rhetoric of maternal duty and family integrity, the statutes possessed a cultural logic powerful enough, for the moment, to knock the counterrhetoric of self-reliance off its feet. The mothers' pension acts acknowledged, in terms British policy makers were just beginning seriously to discuss, the special economic risks of a woman's life course. By the First World War, leading British feminists were working hard to introduce the principles of the American mothers' pension acts into British social legislation.[64]

In all these ways, the currents of contemporary debate over wages, risks, and welfare swept through the United States. Flowing back on occasion to influence European social policy development, they left a broad legislative trail in their wake. Factory legislation, minimum wage statutes, and pensions for the blameless poor, contained by gender boundaries though they were, were all absorbed into the American polity. The tougher issue was social insurance.

On this subject, too, the demand for knowledge was quick to form. Carroll D. Wright, U.S. commissioner of labor and ex officio the United States' correspondent to most of the international congresses on workers' welfare in the 1880s and 1890s, organized the first investigations. In 1891 he commissioned John Graham Brooks, already a seasoned European investigator, to gather materials for a special report on German compulsory social insurance. A Europe wide report on workingmen's insurance followed in 1898 by William F. Willoughby of Wright's staff. Under Wright's successor, a team of investigators fanned out over Europe and the United States to gather materials for a still more comprehensive investigation of workers' insurance, this one filling three bulging volumes with statutes and data.[65]

But the authors of the first investigations came back with no brief for German-style compulsory insurance. Brooks, who cautiously balanced the German achievements in safety and workers' health against the unpopularity of the recently instituted old-age insurance act, made no recommendations. Willoughby much preferred what he saw in France. The French *sociétés de secours mutuels*, with their enlisted local notables and public subsidies, were too foreign to recommend their imitation in the United States, but a state old-age insurance bank seemed to Willoughby a useful and importable device. A variant of the idea won the endorsement of Louis Brandeis and others in the wake of the life insurance company scandals of 1905. After several years of agitation, Wisconsin progressives actually established a state life insurance fund in 1911, though without agents or advertisement it did not find many takers.[66]

Compulsory insurance, however, was another matter. Without compulsion, the principles of social insurance were unattainable. With it, in the minds of most of the Americans active in the early policy debates, the project was politically inadmissible. Willoughby dismissed compulsory social insurance as resting "upon principles of state action foreign to American thought." Farnam insisted on the fundamental distinction between labor protection legislation, on the one hand, and devices for outright economic redistribution, on the other, among which compulsory social insurance, he was sure, was properly numbered. The blue-ribbon United States Industrial Commission of 1898 to 1902, which took the entire terrain of labor-capital relations as its field, simply did not discuss it.[67]

Among the scattered voices in the United States more favorable to German-style social insurance, the most active, ironically enough, were those of the socialists. When, in late 1908, the chair of the Minnesota Employees' Compensation Commission wrote to the leaders of organized labor requesting information on workingmen's insurance, it was the Socialist Party's Eugene Debs who steered him to the standard German works. The Socialist Party's national platform had included a social insurance plank since its organization in 1900. In 1916, though the Progressive Party had by then stolen the Socialists' social insurance agenda, it was the Lower East Side's Socialist congressman, Meyer London, who forced the first congressional hearing on a national program of unemployment, sickness, and old-age insurance. The historical irony was hard to escape. Social insurance, the crowning achievement of Bismarck's antisocialist project of the 1880s, its wage checkoffs still deeply controversial among European wage earners, was reframed in America as a socialist demand.[68]

The most prominent figure in the socialists' appropriation of social insurance was a physician-turned-statistician, Isaac Rubinow. The son of a wealthy textile merchant who had been forced out of Russia in 1893, Rubinow had been introduced to Lower East Side distress as a young doctor in the late 1890s. When, after a year or two of practice, he heard E. R. A. Seligman lecture on German compulsory workmen's insurance, the idea stuck. Indeed, for the next two decades it became, Rubinow's passion. Between 1904 and 1919, while supporting himself as a government and insurance company statistician, Rubinow amassed a reputation as the most knowledgeable expert on compulsory social insurance in the United States. He codirected the Bureau of Labor's exhaustive study of European social insurance in 1908 to 1911, authored the most important book on the subject to be published before the New Deal, helped shape the American Medical Association's brief opening toward state health insurance in 1916–1917 as secretary of the AMA's social insurance committee, and served as the principal expert adviser to the California Social Insurance Commission, whose campaign for state health insurance, of all the pre-1920 social insurance efforts, came closest to victory.[69]

Rubinow was all the while a socialist, and, in the ironies of intrasocialist politics, a trenchant critic of mere reformism. Where others often packaged social insurance as merely a complicated scheme for compulsory savings, Rubinow took no pains to deny the element of income redistribution. "It is useless . . . to deny that social insurance is class legislation." It was a "social guarantee" against the special mishaps of wage labor, "a social provision for the inevitable future poverty of the laborer," given by that part of society capable of covering its own risks by private means to the larger part of society, which was not.[70]

As befitted terrain marked since Bismarck's day by incongruous alliances, Rubinow's counterpart in academic circles was a figure of a very different sort. Charles R. Henderson had served almost twenty years as a Baptist minister before being brought to Rockefeller's new University of Chicago in 1892 as its chaplain and (incidentally) professor of ecclesiastical sociology. Henderson had held orthodox charity organization society views on poverty before moving to Chicago; but a restless intellect and a ceaseless civic do-goodism, so unembarrassedly worn that it made his university colleagues wince, was to move him far from that starting point. Between the late 1890s and his death in 1915 he served at one time or another as president of the international prison reform association, the National Conference of Charities and Corrections, and the Chicago United Charities; as a member of the Chicago Vice Commission; and as secretary of the Mayor's Commission on Unemployment—all the while an energetic collector of European reform ideas.[71]

A year's leave to complete his Ph.D. degree in Germany in the mid-1890s introduced Henderson to German social economics. "The Germans are far in advance of us in what they call 'social politics,' a term which

Americans find difficult even to understand," he was soon certain. Social insurance was but a thread in social politics' skein, but by 1906 Henderson was in vigorous pursuit of it. At the request of the German Imperial Insurance Office, he wrote an early account of workingmen's voluntary insurance in the United States. From his German travels, he reported on methods of poor relief, child welfare, and, most forcefully of all, social insurance. Unlike Rubinow, Henderson was no Marxist; in another context Henderson would have been a *solidariste* or a *Kathedersozialist.* His idea of social insurance culminated in "cooperation" and "national solidarity" rather than Rubinow's class justice. What united the two was a certain social idealism, a deep intellectual restlessness, and Germany.[72]

Despite the work by such pioneers as Rubinow and Henderson, most Americans remained unconvinced by the social insurance idea. The American labor unions, like most of their counterparts elsewhere, were deeply opposed to any added levies on workers' wages. French workers in 1910 had sabotaged the government's compulsory old-age insurance measure on precisely those grounds by refusing to purchase the required insurance stamps. The social policy experts were skeptical. The National Conference of Charities and Corrections, the nation's leading collection of experts on poverty and social welfare, appointed a committee to study workingmen's insurance in 1902. But when the committee finally reported back, four years later, it found itself unable to agree on anything but empty phrases. Florence Kelley spoke up for German-style compulsory insurance; John Graham Brooks, with sensibilities far closer to the majority, cautioned that the idea needed far more testing. In 1907, in an effort to energize the American Association for Labor Legislation, Henry Rogers Seager outlined a comprehensive social legislation program that began with the risks of labor: accidents, illness, invalidity and old age, premature death, and unemployment. But for none of them did he recommend compulsory insurance. English-style old-age pensions, French-style subsidies for sickness-insurance clubs, state supplements to trade union unemployment benefit funds—Seager thought all these were more promising than the German alternative.[73]

The socialists were too weak, the unions were opposed to wage deductions, and the professors were too profoundly ambivalent to kindle much excitement for social insurance. The consumers' leagues and women's clubs were too aware of the inadequacy of the insurance principle to the risks of women's work lives, their time spent as wage laborers being too brief and at wages too low to accumulate significant benefits.[74] Those who specialized in the treatment of the poor, while less adamantly opposed to contributory social insurance than to straight-out public "pensions," were too deeply preoccupied with discriminating between real and feigned needs—in all that was to become professional casework—to be much interested.

Nothing in this mix of hesitations foreshadowed the intense American debates over social insurance that took place between 1911 and 1919. As in Britain, it would take a sense of crisis, a social problem beyond the reach of traditional policy expedients, to send a motley collection of persons, swallowing their doubts about German statism, scurrying for alternatives. In Britain the trigger had been the Liberal Party's need for an affordable opening to the left. In the United States the trigger event was the crisis of the injured worker.

Like most crises, the work accident crisis was not new when it burst into the headlines in the first decade of the twentieth century. Though statistics on industrial accidents do not predate the crisis years, there is no doubt that the tale they told of machinery, speed, callousness, and profit was an old one. Made public at the height of muckraking, in a political climate already steeped in anger at corporate arrogance and corruption, the industrial accident statistics made a deep impression—as well they might have. In pre–World War I America, the investigations revealed, one-tenth of all railroad workers were injured on the job each year. In mining, iron and steel making, logging, and the machinery-driven trades, the risks were no better.[75]

The problem was endemic to all the industrial economies. Work accidents had been the first of the risks of labor to arouse Bismarck's concern; in Britain, Joseph Chamberlain, sensing the political potential in the work injury issue, had led the movement for industrial liability reform in the 1890s. But the figures left little doubt that workplace deaths and injuries in the United States proceeded at a pace unmatched elsewhere. The accident rate on American railroads at the turn of the century was five times that in either Britain or Germany; in the coal mines, the fatal accident rate was more than two and a half times the British figure and half again as large as the Prussian.[76] Some of the difference was due to the larger proportion of immigrants in the American industrial workforce; through the babble of tongues in American mines and factories, the tricks for survival were not always translated quickly enough to save a greenhorn's skin. But turn-of-the-century observers of the unprotected machinery, the rudimentary safety measures, the absence of any legal definition of dangerous trades, the indifference to industrial diseases, and the callous attitudes of employers toward their workforce thought they saw a peculiar harshness in American industrial capitalism. "Too much safety appliance robs the . . . employee of a responsibility which he ought to learn to bear," the *Wall Street Journal* editorialized, as if in confirmation, in 1910.[77]

Accidents, however, did not make the industrial accident crisis. The precipitant of the crisis was a breakdown in the legal machinery of compensation. Of compensation, to be sure, there had not been much. The legal defenses protecting employers from workers' injury suits still gave employers a considerable immunity in the state courts, as they had for half a century. For an accident caused by a fellow worker (who failed to do his part in the intense, dangerous work of tapping a blast furnace, for example) employers had no legal obligation in courts where the "fellow servant" principle still applied. Nor were employers liable for injury to a worker who knew (and hence could be assumed to have factored into his wage bargain) the risks of the job, or who himself contributed even a piece of the responsibility.

The problem was that as each of these legal escape clauses became increasingly remote from the realities of industrial work, juries and legislatures became increasingly reluctant to accept them. Only a fraction of injured workers or their families received compensation of any sort from their employers in the first years of the twentieth century. In the Pittsburgh steel mills in 1906 and 1907, 25 percent of the families of workers killed on the job received no compensation whatever; another 32 percent received awards of not more than $100, burial money only. Action in the courts was expensive and risky. Only 15 out of every 100 accidents were brought to claim in the courts in Illinois, out of which 7 judgments ran in the employers' favor. But if this was a system radically stacked against the injured, the escalating number of cases and—still more—the generous judgments juries had begun to award to a lucky few put extraordinary strain on both the courts and the companies. In the state of Washington in 1910, half the state courts' time was spent on work-injury cases. To meet the rising costs in legal fees and awards, employers' accident insurance premiums had tripled since 1905.[78]

Here, then, was a crisis that pressed hard on no single interest but on a multitude of interests—an impasse designed for innovation, even if the scramble for solutions made odd alliances and bedfellows. Some of the railroad corporations had addressed the issue by establishing company relief departments. Financed almost entirely with wage deductions, and requiring a waiver of the worker's right to court action as a condition of eligibility, company relief funds extracted an extremely high price for the meager compensation they provided.[79] For their part, the labor unions pressed hard for elimination of the employers' common-law defenses.

The more radical idea was to charge the full cost of work accident compensation against employers as a legally mandated cost of business, substituting prescribed compensation awards for the expensive, hit-or-miss system of litigation. This was the scheme Joseph Chamberlain had championed in Britain in the 1890s. His Workmen's Compensation Act of 1897 applied the principle of publicly fixed compensation schedules only to a few of the most dangerous trades, but broader variants soon spread to France, Denmark, and Italy. As late as 1902, Adna Weber had despaired of the "almost complete ignorance" of the principle in the United States, but already there was a stock of precedents lying in reserve against the American need for them.[80]

It was fitting that the most forceful early champion of workmen's compensation legislation in the United States was Theodore Roosevelt, so like Chamberlain in his politics of national efficiency, his tribunate style, and his agenda of Tory social reform. By mid-1907, a year after Britain's new Liberal government had expanded Chamberlain's act to cover virtually all wage earners, President Roosevelt had made the workmen's compensation principle his own. "It is humiliating that at European international congresses on accidents the United States should be singled out as the most belated among the nations in respect of employers' liability legislation," he declared in his annual message of 1908.[81]

By the end of that year the Russell Sage Foundation, the big-business dominated National Civic Federation, and the newspapers were all suddenly deep in discussion of the merits of workmen's compensation. The unions were initially resistant, fearful of losing the right of suit, but with the exception of the railroad brotherhoods, whose success before the courts had been unusually good, they soon shifted their struggle from one of principle to practical details. Employers seized on the compensation idea, partly in hopes of escaping the escalating expenses of litigation, partly in hopes of pulling the teeth of union organization by attending to one of labor's deepest grievances. Pressed from so many sides, the legislatures joined the cause. The first carefully drafted workmen's compensation law was enacted in New York in 1910; by 1913, twenty-one more states had jumped on the legislative bandwagon.[82]

A legislative pace this fast could be produced only by a good deal of imitation. It was the discovery of a ready-made solution with a history of success behind it that made the rapid multiplication of workmen's compensation acts possible. In this context the English precedents were indispensable. The New York Commission on Employers' Liability, with Henry Seager and Crystal Eastman, the Pittsburgh Survey's work accident expert, among its members, built its recommendations on the British act of 1897. So did the National Civic Federation, which saturated the state legislatures with copies of its model bill early in 1911.[83]

The British workmen's compensation act was not social insurance, as Chamberlain had been at pains to make clear. Like the German act of 1884, the British act imposed the costs of accident compensation wholly on employers. But where the German act had gathered employers into compulsory, quasi-public mutual associations to spread the risks of the trade and encourage industrial safety measures, the British statute mandated the pooling of neither risks nor funds. It left firms free to hedge their compensation obligations however they chose: through private casualty insurance companies, through voluntary employers' mutual associations, or through their own reserve funds. Statutorily fixed accident compensation and social insurance were two distinct and separable principles.

Given the rapid course of the debates and the multitude of constituencies to please, however, it was not surprising that some Americans should have looked past the British example to Germany, and in so doing come to a new assessment of the social insurance legacy of the 1880s. The Russell Sage Foundation, sensing the issue in the winds in 1908, tapped the manager of the United Hebrew Charities in New York City, Lee K. Frankel, to go over the ground earlier explored by Brooks and Willoughby. Frankel, in turn, recruited a New York City actuary and Social Reform Club member, Miles M. Dawson, who had once drafted an English-model workmen's compensation bill for the New York state legislature. After a summer inspection tour in Europe and participation in the International Congress on Social Insurance in Rome, where the French and Italian delegates were deep in second thoughts on the merits of subsidarism, both men came back touched with admiration for the German system. The elaborate safety and preventive work of the employers' mutuals, in particular, seemed to them beyond comparison. Before their report was completed, Frankel was hired away by the Metropolitan Life Insurance Company. But Dawson, that "crazy actuary," as the National Civic Federation's executive secretary was to call him in fury, remained an insistent defender of the German system and, buttressed by experience on the staff of Charles Evans Hughes's investigation of life insurance fraud in 1905 and 1906, an outspoken critic of commercial industrial accident insurance firms.[84]

The other leading American advocate of German-style compulsory accident insurance in the early debates was the representative of the state employers' federation on the Minnesota Employees' Compensation Commission, George M. Gillette—though for wholly different reasons than Dawson. What attracted Gillette to the German scheme was his impression that employees contributed to the accident insurance fund. In principle Gillette was wrong, but in practice, given the requirement that injured German workers had to exhaust their sickness benefits before coming onto the accident insurance system's books, he was not entirely mistaken. The National Association of Manufacturers, far to the right of the National Civic Federation, dispatched two of its leading figures to Germany in 1910, where they were feted by the Imperial Insurance Office's officials, plied with information, and came to Gillette's conclusion. They quickly put the weight of the manufacturers' association behind their own version of the German model: compulsory industrial accident insurance, jointly funded by employer and wage-earner levies.[85]

German industrial accident insurance was not simply whatever one said it was. But in the fluid politics of borrowing, the mix of appropriators was striking. From the *Survey* on the left to the National Association of Manufacturers on the right, a disparate chorus of voices had begun to praise the superiority of the German solution.

As the issues moved from pamphlets into statutes, the axis on which the contests turned was not to be the question of workers' contributions, for which the legislatures showed little appetite. The key issue was who would be allowed to occupy the field of enterprise that the new workmen's compensation statutes were constructing. To ensure a meaningful system of compensation, someone would have to guarantee that even small employers could stand the potential cost that a ruinous accident might entail. With a keen eye for the advantage of publicly made markets, the commercial casualty insurance companies were eager for the job, but in many regards their track record was not encouraging. Experience under the British acts had shown that the casualty insurance companies were far less inclined to defend their profit margins by encouraging accident reduction measures in the workplace (as the German employers' mutuals did) than by contesting compensation claims in the courts. Overhead and commission costs were high. Where workmen's compensation statutes made insurance coverage mandatory, the commercial insurance companies showed no compunction in taking the premiums of their captive clientele as high as the market would bear.[86]

Among progressives uneasy with privatization of the workmen's compensation insurance field, the German scheme of compulsory employers' mutuals did not make much headway; only in Massachusetts did a drafting commission take it seriously. The more straightforward alternative was the establishment of state-administered employers' insurance—in the form either of a state monopoly, on the lines Norwegian appropriators of the German scheme had pioneered in 1895, or a competitive public insurance office, as in New Zealand after 1900. On these borrowed templates, the first American public industrial accident insurance funds were quickly constructed. Ohio and Washington had systems in place by 1911. Two years later the Ohio fund was made compulsory for most employers. The act, drafted by the state mineworkers' union president, William Green, drew not only labor's backing but also virtually unanimous support from the state's industrial employers, who had watched New York insurance companies jack up rates two- to fivefold on the passage of that state's British-style workmen's compensation act in 1910.[87]

In California between 1911 and 1913, the state industrial accident commission took it upon itself to steer through the legislature a public insurance fund—"borrowed" from New Zealand, the commission's chair later reported, but "dressed in garments better suited for the industrial and political situation in California." In New York in 1913, labor's representatives lost a fight to establish a state monopoly industrial accident insurance fund, though not before insurance company agents and negligence lawyers, descending eight hundred strong on Albany, had been galvanized into preventive action.[88]

All told, of the twenty-two states enacting workmen's compensation laws between 1910 and 1913, one third established either compulsory state funds or (as in the compromise that finally quelled the contest in New York) elective state funds designed to compete with private underwriters. After 1913, heroic counterpressure from the insurance companies turned back the tide. By 1919, when the creation of new state funds ceased, private companies had staked out 60 percent of the workmen's compensation insurance market, the state funds 22 percent, employers' mutuals the rest. But in the rupture in everyday alliances and ideas produced by the work injury battle, social insurance had found its American entry point.[89]

In this chain of crises, impasses, borrowings, and improvisations the core event was the speed with which minds were changing. During the initial New York State deliberations on workmen's compensation in 1909, Crystal Eastman thought the labor representatives "did not know what we were talking about." When the first workmen's compensation commissions convened in 1909 and 1910, though hunger for even elementary information about the European systems was keen, interest in German-modeled schemes of public, compulsory social insurance was but a hand against the sky.[90] The workmen's compensation debates introduced Americans to the idea of public insurance against wage earners' risks; it kindled in a motley and surprisingly large number of Americans an interest in the German imperial insurance system. When in the middle of these controversies the British National Insurance Act burst on the scene in the summer of 1911, it broadened and accelerated a process already in motion.

Louis Brandeis was a particularly sensitive barometer for the Atlantic reach of Lloyd George's proposals. In 1908 Brandeis had still been thinking of individual old-age annuities, cheaply purchased through savings banks, as the most important project in the social welfare field. When in June 1911 he addressed the National Conference of Charities and Corrections, however, it was to call for "comprehensive" social insurance against sickness, accident, invalidity, unemployment, and old age. This was "the road to social efficiency," he urged, the "same path" along which Germany, France, and now England were hastening. Within a year, Theodore Roosevelt had joined the cause. His Progressive Party wrote the promise of comprehensive social insurance, "adapted to American use," into its 1912 platform.[91]

The most striking example of the flux of ideas, however, was to be found in the American Association for Labor Legislation. Given its early focus on industrial health and diseases, the AALL had been quickly drawn into the workmen's injury debates. The issue dominated its meetings from 1908 through 1912, but prevention was the core motif, not compensation or insurance. When (in what proved an aberrant court decision) the New York Court of Appeals invalidated the state's 1910 workmen's compensation statute, the New York State Federation of Labor took the lead in pressing for a constitutional amendment broad enough to legitimate not only workmen's compensation legislation but tax-financed old-age pensions, invalidity insurance, and sickness insurance as well. Henry Rogers Seager, his mind changed by the British act of 1911, signed on. "I think we can be certain this country is going to follow the countries of Europe," he was sure. "It is in the air." But the AALL itself preferred a narrower, more cautious strategy.[92]

Not until early 1913, buffeted by the amendment controversy, did the association finally appoint a committee on social insurance with Seager, Charles Henderson, Isaac Rubinow, and Miles Dawson among its members. At its conference that summer, billed as the First National Conference on Social Insurance, speakers canvassed the suddenly expanding field of issues: state funds versus private carriers for workmen's compensation risks, pensions versus contributory insurance in the support of old age, sickness insurance, unemployment insurance, and mothers' pensions. Within another year, recasting its agenda around this new core, the AALL had remade itself as the most active and important social insurance lobby in the United States.[93]

Under Henderson's prodding and the savage impact of the recession of 1913 to 1915, the association turned first to the issue of unemployment. As ready-made answers, the British labor exchanges act of 1909 and unemployment insurance scheme of 1911 quickly became the beginning and end of expert American opinion on unemployment. By 1914 the AALL had endorsed a program of public employment exchanges, countercyclical public works programs, inducements to employers to regularize their hiring patterns, and unemployment insurance—virtually a mirror of the British scheme—and was stoking the issue with conferences and publicity. The New York City Mayor's Committee on Unemployment endorsed the program at Seager's urging in early 1916. By the end of that year, William M. Leiserson, who had left John Commons's seminars for a career in labor economics, was certain that the basic frame of an unemployment policy was so clear on both sides of the Atlantic as to be no longer worth discussing.[94]

By 1915, however, with Henderson's death, the AALL had rechanneled its priorities toward health insurance and was working hard to propel a model sick pay and health benefits bill through the state houses. Actuarially, sickness posed a far easier problem to address than the unpredictable oscillations of employment. Unlike unemployment insurance, which had yet to be put to an extended practical test, health insurance had more than a quarter century's experience behind it. Unlike public old-age support, on which insurance and pension principles split the experts down the middle, the conversion of the British to German-style compulsory health insurance had created a workable consensus on means and principles.

John B. Andrews, another former Commons student and now the AALL's executive secretary, described the AALL's model health insurance bill as a blend of "the best possible points of the British and German systems." In fact, as drafted by Rubinow, Seager, and Joseph Chamberlain of the New York Legislative Drafting Fund, it was mostly German. Its essential elements were sick pay and medical treatment for low-income wage earners and their dependents. A modest benefit against the costs of childbirth was included, despite Florence Kelley's fear that it might encourage husbands to cash it in by getting their wives pregnant. On the assumption that work-related strains and diseases were the primary cause of wage earners' ill health, the benefits were to be half financed from employers' contributions, half from contributions of the employees, with the administration of each local fund to be jointly controlled by both, as in Germany. The boldest American departure was provision of a funeral benefit—a direct assault on the territory of the industrial insurance companies—which was included in a bid to convince wage earners that with the sum they pressed into the insurance collector's hand each week they could buy their burial benefits and sickness insurance too.[95]

Launched in late 1915, the AALL-sponsored health insurance campaign grew with extraordinary speed over the course of the succeeding months. In 1916 and 1917, health insurance bills were introduced in eighteen state legislatures. Two special state commissions reported on health insurance in 1917; the Massachusetts commission's members split evenly over the AALL proposal, the California commission endorsed a variant that absorbed the fraternal associations and unions, British-style, into administration of the benefits. A dozen national unions and state labor federations signed on to the principle of compulsory wage earners' health insurance. The state doctors' associations and the American Medical Association's committee on social insurance concentrated not on opposing state medical insurance but, as in Britain, on cutting the doctors into the proposed insurance administration.[96]

The AALL, the organization at the center of all these campaigns, was never large. At its peak in 1914, it counted some 3,600 members. Not until 1910 did it find the funds to send its own delegates to the parent meetings of the International Association for Labor Legislation in Europe; two years earlier, the association had had to co-opt Florence Kelley and Maud Nathan, already on their way to the international consumers' league congress. Heavily stocked with academic economists, its key board members virtually an alumni reunion from the German university connection, the AALL had had virtually no experience in politics before being drawn into the brawl over workmen's compensation in New York in 1912 and 1913. Unlike its French and German counterparts, it drew in no prominent political figures to play the part of Alexandre Millerand in the French section of the Association internationale pour la protection légale des travailleurs or the former Prussian commerce minister Freiherr von Berlepsch in the Gesellschaft für Sozialreform. Though it boasted a sprinkling of labor union leaders among its honorary vice presidents, to the broad, institutional labor union affiliations of the German association there was no American parallel.[97]

In the face of these compounded disadvantages, the AALL made its power out of other nations' precedents. The model bill was the association's primary political tool, all the more powerful in an era when social-political legislation was still new and initiative in its drafting was still extragovernmental business. In the earliest stages of debate over social insurance, in a field stocked with amateurs and weak in information, with unions, employers' federations, and government investigators all scrambling to make sense of the experience of social insurance abroad, the AALL capitalized on the politics of borrowed knowledge for all it was worth.

In fact, from the first tentative discussions of workmen's compensation in 1907 to the eve of American entry into the First World War, the movement of ideas was momentous. In late 1916 the California Social Insurance Commission polled the members of the American Economic Association and the social workers' National Conference of Charities and Corrections on the new issues. Although only a fifth of the members replied, two-thirds of those who did endorsed compulsory social insurance for the United States, with health insurance as the first step. The *Survey* now published a regular department devoted to social insurance news. Edward T. Devine, the most influential charity organization figure of the day, had thought social insurance unnecessary in 1909. By 1913 he was talking of the justice of imposing on industry through social insurance "the full cost of its product, the cost in human lives and in physical vigor."[98]

The new turn of the debate, the new political viability of discussions of social insurance, the fluent converse about European systems of labor exchanges and sick benefits, the eagerness of a political breeze tester like Theodore Roosevelt to ride the winds of Lloyd George–style politics, and the shift of mind on the issue of compulsion all marked a dramatic change in opinion since the National Conference of Charities and Corrections' inconclusive discussions of 1902. Local dynamics drove hard in this change: the scrappy and inadequate systems of American working-class security, the peculiarly callous operations of industrial capitalism in the United States, and the new tribunate style of Theodore Roosevelt's presidency. But without the Atlantic connection, the event would have been inconceivable.

Remarkable as the intellectual and political transformation was, however, it did not bring social insurance to the United States—at least, for the moment. By the end of 1913 the counterlobbying of the casualty insurance companies had drained the momentum from the movement for state workmen's compensation insurance funds. The short campaign for unemployment policies modeled on the British acts of 1909 and 1911 sputtered out with war-induced prosperity. Unemployment insurance, distrusted by organized labor and nowhere tested by extensive experience, did not successfully tempt any state legislature. Compulsory old-age insurance was stalled without a Charles Booth or David Lloyd George to break the deadlock. Health insurance came closest to fruition. It still hung in the balance at the American entry into the war in the spring of 1917. Rubinow, not without reason, was sure that its success was only a matter of time. But in an era of quick legislative fads, where workmen's compensation acts, mothers' pension statutes, and labor regulation acts had passed in the course of months from state to state, there was no missing the fact that social insurance had met considerably deeper resistance.

Social policy historians, wanting more than prewar legislatures gave, have come back repeatedly to the limits of the first American social insurance campaign, hunting through its failures for structures and materials distinctive to the United States. The premise—positing a general "European" success and American failure—is much more rickety than is usually acknowledged. Social insurance was only one of the many, competing measures circulating within the North Atlantic economy at the outbreak of the war in 1914. In Belgium, Italy, Denmark, Canada, New Zealand, and Australia there were social policy initiatives in abundance but none that yet had the distinctive characteristics of social insurance. Sweden's first experiment in social insurance, a broadly written old-age insurance statute, was a year old at the outbreak of the war; in France, with the collapse of the 1910 old-age insurance act, the experiment in a German-inspired course in social policy lay in a shambles. Britain's system, born in a wholly unanticipated conjuncture of events, had barely been set in practical motion. Within this web of connections and contingencies, the American difference was not so much categorical (a markedly weak state, an ideology peculiarly skewed against considerations of collective welfare and the like) as it was a matter of common ingredients stacked in a different order (as in the case of city politics), or mixed in different proportions (as in the legal-political powers of property).

Of the exceptionalist explanations, least satisfying are the arguments that posit a special "American idea" inhibitive to the adoption of social insurance.[99] Not that ideology failed to matter. In the United States, as elsewhere, social insurance was fought with every ounce of ideological energy at its opponents' disposal. Social insurance was "un-American"; it was "paternalism run mad"; it was a new form of "wage slavery"; it was a "hole in the dike" protecting individual freedom "from the mad waters of socialism." The British act of 1911 threatened "to destroy the virile elements of the English character," the National Civic Federation investigators concluded in 1914; it warred upon "manly sentiments," it entailed "an insidious undermining of working-class honor."[100]

But there was nothing in the American debates that had not figured in the equally polarized rhetorical contests in Germany in the 1880s and in Britain after 1908. That social insurance was "paternalistic"; that the hand of compulsion, even when it mandated a virtuous act such as savings, emptied that act of its moral element; that assurance of benefits without regard to individual fault and circumstance, no matter how modest the guarantee, could only weaken character; that public intervention in the realm of risk prevention could come only at the expense of family responsibility and solidarity; that the cost of compulsory insurance schemes in terms of the regimentation they exacted was not worth the candle—all these arguments, though they were often packaged as "the American point of view," had fallen as quickly from the tongues of Bismarck's opponents and from Lloyd George's. Not even the "made in Germany" charge was a liability peculiar to American social insurance proponents, given its currency among social insurance's critics in Britain and France.

To all these arguments there was an answer that resonated everywhere in the North Atlantic economy. "Vast industrial nations are pitted against one another in a struggle for existence that has not ceased to be terrific because it happens now to be carried on thru [sic] commercial operations instead of thru bloodshed," the *Independent* wrote in endorsing the British social insurance departure of 1911. "Such nations must bring and keep their working populations up to a standard efficiency or go to the wall." One might call the program one of "social efficiency," as Brandeis did, or "national solidarity," like Henderson; "social organisation" or "national efficiency," like Churchill and Beveridge; or "solidarism," like the French progressives. Its mark was a concern with national vigor, with efficient development of human resources, with conservation of "the human wreckage," as Theodore Roosevelt put it, "which a scrap-heap system of industrialism" had brought about. This was the hard, calculating side of the social insurance argument. There was a soft side, too, in the hope that social insurance might be a step toward the hoped-for, never-realized reign of "social peace." From both vantage points, the abstract moral individualism of an earlier era, the "fetishism of self help," as Rubinow called it, could seem thin and narrow indeed. Those who would try to measure the relative ideological weight of these arguments in the countries through which the social insurance debates swirled with their borrowed terms and common polarities have an impossible job cut out for them.[101]

That is not to dismiss the force of ideology, only to begin to specify where it carried distinctive force in the United States. The most obvious place was in the timing of the social insurance campaign and the war. In 1911 Lloyd George could still refer to Germany in terms of rivalry and respect. Theodore Roosevelt's campaign speeches in 1912 were larded with the same sentiments. These strains of envy and admiration did not, as we shall see, wholly evaporate in the war. But in politics, where nothing matters like timing, the window between the American discovery of German-style social insurance in 1911 and 1912 and the outbreak of the war in the summer of 1914 was extremely small. Health insurance, in which the German influences were undisguised, was particularly vulnerable. Within months of the framing of the AALL's model health insurance bill late in 1915, "made in Germany" charges were being thrown against it like hand grenades. After the U.S. declaration of war in 1917, one could not raise the issue of health insurance without opponents conjuring up a spiked helmet in rebuttal.[102] The very explicitness of the American borrowings, the theme of backwardness that social insurance proponents favored, their arguments from preexisting European experience, all became potential liabilities after 1917.

Ideology also counted for a good deal within the inner circles of the American Federation of Labor. Distrust of state intervention in the wage bargain still ran deep there, sustained by too many strike-breaking court injunctions and an enduring Victorian faith in working-class "manliness." Samuel Gompers, the AFL's perpetual president, had been an early recruit to the workmen's compensation movement. But compulsory insurance schemes for wage earners, with their tax on the wage earners' incomes, their restrictions on a worker's choice, their machinery of registration and regulation, and the "unmanning" they implied, were anathema to Gompers and his allies in the AFL's tight leadership cadre. Never comfortably allied with the professor-dominated American Association for Labor Legislation, Gompers resigned his honorary AALL vice presidency in 1915. The next year he crashed Meyer London's hearings on workingmen's insurance to bait London and Rubinow as socialists and denounce social insurance itself as having been incubated in a socialist hatchery.[103]

Gompers no more spoke for organized labor as a whole than did the state labor federations, which took the lead in setting social insurance before the legislatures. In these mixed and ambivalent feelings toward compulsory social insurance, there was nothing distinctive about labor organizations in the United States. Nowhere in the North Atlantic economy before 1914 were labor organizations either the authors of social insurance schemes or a significant political force in their adoption. If the unions eventually signed on to measures that had their origins in chancellery offices or middle-class reform associations, it was never without resistance and objection. The principle of wage earners' levies—indispensable to the social insurance concept—was uniformly resisted by the labor organizations. State unemployment insurance was particularly unpopular, distrusted as a means of forcing skilled workers to accept unskilled work and feared as a strike-breaking instrument. Old-age insurance, extracting levies for an old age a worker might never see, had been fertile ground for resentment from the outset in 1889. In Germany and in Britain, social insurance took shape expressly as an antidote to labor's own, distinctly different, social-political program: noncontributory old-age pensions, labor union recognition, and public works for the unemployed.

Still, nowhere outside the United States did the nominal chieftain of the leading national labor federation cozy up as closely as Gompers did on the social insurance issue to big-business barons of the sort who dominated the National Civic Federation, or with such a show of ideological conviction. To those trying to read the political tides, like Woodrow Wilson, with his accumulating political debts to labor, the intellectual rigidities of the AFL's small leadership circle carried peculiarly heavy consequences.

If timing and position made a critical difference in the ideological debates, there was also a more submerged difference that involved immigrants and race. Establishment of the minimum benefits standards integral to social insurance required agreement that uniform minimum standards could, in fact, be set. To many of those who were vying to shape the policy and politics of early-twentieth-century America, this was not so clear. The National Civic Federation's committee on foreign inquiry worried aloud how an American insurance system could possibly be designed where "there are three distinct levels of poverty—the level of the white native born, that of the immigrants, and that of the colored race—each associated with its own level of wages, opportunity, and industrial education. Could any national insurance Act possibly be adapted to these incongruous social elements?" P. T. Sherman, the National Civic Federation's leading authority on industrial accident liability, took it for granted that workmen's compensation benefits should be lower for immigrant wage earners than for citizens, by perhaps as much as half. Common benefits standards carried no mean social implications in the racially divided South; in California, with its unquenched anti-Chinese and anti-Japanese sentiments; or in northern industrial cities, with their immigrant "racial" types—all of which were inhibitory to action.[104]

In these precisely locatable ways, ideological materials common throughout the North Atlantic economy were given a distinctive spin in the United States. But the most important difference lay elsewhere: in the constituted field of interests. Whether in Bismarck's Germany, Lloyd George's Britain, or the progressives' United States, the niches social insurance's proponents sought to occupy were nowhere empty. From the most haphazard of slate clubs upward, they were already filled with claimants. As time went on, those who occupied these positions grew better and better organized, extracted deeper and deeper concessions, and resisted incursions more and more effectively.

The drafters of the German statutes of the 1880s—working in a context of a politically radical but weakly organized labor movement, employer interests without highly developed organizational expression, *Kassen* without political clout, and an insurance industry in its infancy—had advantages that were never to be repeated. It was not the strength of the German state per se, extemporizing an administrative structure out of a motley collection of quasi-public agencies, that fundamentally accounted for social insurance's success as much as it was the small scale and fragmentation of the preexisting occupants.

Lloyd George, in contrast, faced a much more intensely developed field of interests: a highly organized and politically effective labor movement, a self-conscious medical profession, and an insurance field deeply stocked with claimants, profit making and fraternal alike, all defensive of their terrain. It was these differences that forced co-optation of the doctors, the friendly societies, and, ultimately, the industrial insurance companies into the administration of health insurance in 1911, just as they encouraged co-optation of labor unions into the administration of unemployment insurance. Coming into being after a good deal of the territory had been colonized by other bodies, the British insurance measure absorbed the earlier organizations into its structures.

In the United States the array of established interests was different once more: labor was relatively weak and internally divided, the voluntary insurance fraternities were so timid as to be politically invisible, the doctors were more independent, big business was much more effectively organized, and the commercial insurance companies were extraordinarily skillful and aggressive. The differences were not total; they had to do not with the presence or absence of any single factor but with the general constitution of the terrain in which the proponents of social insurance proposed to establish a public presence. Still, nothing, in the end, mattered more than this.

Business to begin with. Bismarck and Lloyd George had both drawn on the support of individual, paternalistic employers, unafraid of blurring the lines between private and state paternalism. Neither had faced a nationally organized employers' federation. In Britain, the Employers' Parliamentary Association was formed in the immediate aftermath of the National Insurance Act of 1911, precisely to remedy the limited business influence the act's drafting had revealed. The British equivalents of the National Association of Manufacturers and the National Civic Federation in the United States—the British Manufacturers' Association and the Federation of British Industries—were not formed until the First World War. In the United States, on the other hand, employers' political organizations preceded the social insurance debates, and they played their hand strongly within them. The National Civic Federation, committed to a strategy of social peace and a measure of union cooperation, made workmen's compensation legislation one of its prime causes and signal victories. But further down that line the federation was unwilling to go. The federation was deeply opposed to the state workmen's compensation insurance funds. As for social insurance generally, the federation's staff had concluded by 1912 that the idea was "very dangerous." The labor-business delegation it sent in 1914 to investigate the new British health insurance system reported it bankrupt, both fiscally and morally; against a parallel experiment in the United States, the federation was a powerful and prominent campaigner.[105]

It is tempting to suppose that big business mounted its opposition to ward off public interference in tasks it had assumed itself. But that was hardly the case. Company health plans offered meager protection in the United States before 1917, and employer-established old-age pensions were so rare that in a survey of Massachusetts employers, only 4 firms out of 362 provided them. But terrain may be as vigorously held prospectively, as by a land speculator waiting for the opportune moment to build, as it may be held actually. Employee benefits systems did not amount to much in the pre–World War I United States, but they were enough to make employers deeply jealous of rival claimants to the field.[106]

Like employers, doctors occupied a place in the field of interests that was different in the United States than elsewhere. In Germany, the late-nineteenth-century professionalization of medicine developed within the structures of an established public health insurance system; contract *Kassen* work was expected and indispensable to a beginning doctor's livelihood. In turn-of-the-century Britain, contract work for a friendly society was almost as deep a fixture in British doctors' lives. This did not neutralize the doctors' aggressiveness in negotiations over the National Insurance Act any more than it prevented doctors' strikes over *Kassen* regulations in Wilhelmine Germany. In both countries, however, doctors' politics, framed within the experience of contract work, focused on leveraging administrative authority out of the expanding state. In the United States, in contrast, independent, proprietary medical practice was the rule and contract medicine was rare. By 1917 locally organized doctors, rebelling against the medical association leadership's bid for authority within an impending health insurance system, had stampeded into furious opposition to contract work, and to public contracts in particular. Here too, under the "made in Germany" charges, lay a field of enterprise to protect.[107]

Of all the lobbyists, however, there was no mistaking the preeminence of the commercial insurance companies. With their army of agents in every city and town, they lobbied with every force at their command to claim each new legally constructed insurance territory. It was they who pried open the Massachusetts workmen's compensation system for private insurance companies in 1911, against the recommendation of the state commission. Ohio's enactment of a state monopoly workmen's compensation fund in 1913 set the industry back on its heels for a moment, but its response was to ensure that no other leading industrial state should stray down the Ohio path. The Workmen's Compensation Publicity Bureau, an industry lobbying group, blanketed policy makers with arguments against state insurance funds between 1913 and 1929. The Insurance Economics Society of America did the same after 1916, in opposition to the AALL's health insurance campaign. While business interests were spread over a multitude of issues and doctors were initially divided, the insurance companies spoke with concentrated voice and fervor.

Insurance company hostility to the social insurance cause, was, to be sure, exacerbated by the reciprocal enmity of the reformers themselves. Tarred by revelations of financial chicanery in the life insurance industry in 1905, by the casualty insurance companies' obstructionist role in the workmen's compensation debates, and by exposure of the "industrial insurance" companies' staggering overhead costs, the insurance companies were in no good repute among progressive reformers. Under the circumstances, the AALL had no sympathy with the compromise that had cut the commercial insurance companies into health insurance legislation in Britain. The cheap funeral benefit the AALL incorporated into its model health insurance bill was explicitly designed to undercut the commercial companies' working-class business. When the Great Eastern Casualty Company told its agents that the New York health insurance bill of 1916 spelled "the end of all Insurance Companies and Agents and to you personally the complete wrecking of the business and connections you have spent a lifetime building and the loss of your bread and butter," this was hyperbole, but within it was also a kernel of truth.[108]

Outright opposition was not, however, the insurance industry's only tactical response. Two companies, the Metropolitan and the Prudential, dominated the sale of mass "industrial" insurance policies in early-twentieth-century America; together they claimed some 80 percent of the market.[109] The larger of them, the Metropolitan, with more than ten million policies in force in 1910, had not amassed its terrain without keeping a sharp eye out for competitors. Only when the number of policyholders had doubled (to a staggering total of one Metropolitan policy for every five persons in the country), the company warned its agents, would they feel safe from the threat of state insurance. In the meantime, the Metropolitan set about to preempt the field. In 1909 it hired away Lee Frankel, still in the midst of his investigation of European wage earners' insurance for the Russell Sage Foundation, to manage its new "welfare department" and to prove social insurance superfluous.

The company's announcement that it was now finished with profit motivation, that with Frankel's appointment it had plunged "into the current of the world's thought" was largely puffery. But Frankel did lead the Metropolitan aggressively into territory the insurance industry until then had ignored. Under his guidance the company distributed millions of public health pamphlets: on tuberculosis prevention, on child health, even *A Day in the Life of a Fly*, which its agents handed to their client housewives along with a free fly swatter. In cooperation with Lillian Wald of the Henry Street Settlement, it contracted visiting nurse services for its policyholders in cases where, at the agent's discretion, health services seemed a prudent investment against an early death and a premature cashing in of a policy. More slowly, the company began experimenting with employers' group insurance policies—group life insurance to begin with, followed, more hesitantly, by group health insurance policies. Through it all Frankel remained an ambiguous public figure, opposed on practical grounds to state social insurance ventures but unwilling to condemn them in principle. Frederick Hoffman of the Prudential, who had axes to sharpen of his own, thought him "exceedingly dangerous, . . . still what he has always been—a social reformer, and not an insurance man." A less critical observer might have said that Frankel represented the preemptive energies of welfare capitalism at their most humane and vigorous.[110]

Where the Metropolitan took the high road of preemptive action, Hoffman's Prudential took the low road of obstruction. In that development Hoffman himself was a complex and intriguing figure. From selling industrial insurance policies in working-class neighborhoods in and around Boston, he had moved to a Virginia insurance agency in the early 1890s. A man steeped in the racial "science" of the day, Hoffman nonetheless had the wit to sense a virtually untapped life insurance market in black southerners, ignored by the big commercial companies as actuarial unknowns. Hoffman threw himself into the problem of constructing serviceable mortality tables, scouring graveyards for life expectancy data. His work caught the eye of the president of the Prudential, John F. Dryden, who soon took Hoffman on as investigative statistician, intellectual in residence, adviser to the president, and the Prudential's ambassador to the academic world. Hoffman was an active member of the American Economic Association, the National Conference of Charities and Corrections, the American Public Health Association, the International Tuberculosis Association, the National Civic Federation, and, as a matter of course, the AALL. When the AALL appointed him to its Committee on Social Insurance in 1913, he crowed that it was he who had been chosen, not Frankel.[111]

But Hoffman was too much an "insurance man" to see in social insurance anything but a market competitor. His first exposure to the social insurance debates had come in 1900, when the Prudential sent him to Paris to install the company's prize-winning display at the exposition, and he kept a pessimistic eye thereafter on the "danger" signals he saw abroad. The incorporation of the insurance companies into the British health insurance system he thought inherently unstable. Sooner or later the government would tack a funeral benefit onto its health insurance scheme—a few pennies a week would do it—and that would be the death of the high-overhead industrial insurance business. Germany in 1912 seemed to him alive with schemes for public burial services and burial insurance, which he had no doubt could undercut his company's policies with vastly cheaper rates. In weekly letters, he bombarded his chief with proposals for preemptive action along the Metropolitan's lines: extension of the company into the unplowed field of commercial health insurance, employment of company doctors for policyholders' treatment, investment of company funds in low-cost housing—anything to shore up the public reputation of the company against the "menace" on the march abroad.[112]

The role the Prudential cut out for Hoffman, however, was not Frankel's. On the AALL social insurance committee, he became the company's mole. The workmen's compensation issue found him not far from the center of AALL opinion; casualty insurance was not part of the Prudential's business, and he made no brief for it in the workmen's compensation debates. On legislation against women's night work or hazardous working conditions, he and the association were fully in accord. But the first murmurs of interest in health insurance were a different matter. "My own position is, of course, one of absolute neutrality," he wrote Dryden after the first meeting of the AALL's social insurance committee, "but of sufficient tolerance so as not to give offense and arouse the suspicion that I am too strongly influenced by my connection with The Prudential." Outmaneuvering Dawson and Rubinow (the most "dangerous" men on the committee, he thought), Hoffman took credit for blocking the drafting of any resolutions at the AALL's social insurance conference in 1913. During the framing of the association's model health insurance bill, he dragged his feet, obstructed, pressed in vain for company initiatives in the medical insurance field, and informed his employers—more and more certain that public health insurance was "distinctly pernicious and a menace to our interests."[113]

Then in 1916, with the Prudential's blessing, he resigned from the committee to take the company's fight into the open. A blizzard of publications and news releases followed, denying the need for health insurance in the United States in a flourish of comparative health and mortality tables, denouncing the AALL's publicity work as an "outrageous fabric of falsehood," debunking the British insurance act, dismissing the European precedents as proof only that you can "flim-flam anybody if you have been to Germany." The Prudential saturated the state capitals with his pamphlets. John R. Commons, in frustration, protested that all the anti–health insurance literature "originated from one source: all of the ammunition, all of the facts and statistics that you may come across, no matter who gives them to you will be found to go back to the Prudential Insurance Co. of America, and to Mr. Frederick L. Hoffman."[114]

Had the war not intervened with its made-for-order arguments against German borrowings, had President Wilson played a Rooseveltian part, as some in his administration urged, Hoffman's endeavors might have turned out differently. Had the fraternal associations and the mutual benefit societies, above all, been made of stronger, less divided stuff; had they tried, as in Britain, to ally themselves with the state to squeeze out their commercial rivals or, as in France, to operate as subsidiary agents of the state, the industrial insurance companies might have had more competition. Industrial insurance was no more strongly developed in the United States than in Britain; the ties between sister firms in London and New York were intimate. But in the putative homeland of voluntary associations, the weakness of the mutual benefit associations was striking, and their fragmented and timid occupation of their terrain gave the industrial insurance companies enormous advantages. As it was, between the Metropolitan's high road and the Prudential's low one, between the rank-and-file doctors' revolt, business resistance, and the insurance agents' mobilization, the advocates of social insurance could not prevail. Not, at least for the moment.

The configuration of interests is never fixed. Technological change and shifts in markets and in public policy create and destroy fields of enterprise. With each refiguring of the terrain the scramble for occupancy is renewed. Shall it be a field for profit or for noncommercial activity, for large business or small, nation-state or local government, private bodies or public ones? Laggard nations have certain advantages in these choices: the condition of being behindhand shifts much of the cost of experiment and mistake onto the early players. By the time the latecomers arrive, the positions are clearer, the techniques prepackaged and refined, the experience of others appropriatable. That is what allows laggards, in certain circumstances, to leapfrog over their competitors by cashing in on the advantages of delay. The ability of nineteenth-century American and German manufacturers to surpass their British rivals by pouring borrowed techniques into newer plants is a case in point. In the realm of social politics, the British ability to borrow from Danish and German experience so as to leapfrog past Germany in social welfare provision in the years 1908 to 1911 is another. Late-blooming competitiveness, as Lloyd George demonstrated, is a position of no mean strength.

But if laggard nations have striking advantages, the risk of delay is the risk of precluded options. When the moment of choice arrives, the territory of action may already have been preempted. The fences may already be in the ground, and the occupants—no matter how well or poorly they are performing their tasks—may be extremely difficult to move. If the Lloyd George government could plan with a boldness beyond Bismarck's ken, it was, by the same dynamic, required to compromise more heavily with already entrenched interests. In the United States, where the social insurance movement's experts capitalized on their behindhandedness by scouring Europe for its lessons and inspiration, the field was too thick with claimants for proponents of social insurance to make easy headway at all. In the realm of city services and the urban land and shelter markets, where commercial utility suppliers and real estate investors had colonized the terrain aggressively and early, much the same had been true. The disadvantage of political behindhandedness is that when the issue finally gets on the agenda of political choice, the moment for effective decision may already have passed.

In the decade before World War I, one could not miss the extraordinarily rapid broadening of the social-political agenda in the United States. Ambitions had changed more than legislation, however, and legislation more than the array of interests itself. Incorporation of workmen's compensation acts into the polity had not been an effective wedge for either British- or German-style social insurance. Once the crisis over work accidents and employers' liability had been resolved, the rest remained much as it had been before: the poor a distant country, the wage earners' risks only marginally smaller, the safety net between working-class families and outright poverty still full of gaping holes. The liabilities of behindhandedness seemed destined to outrun its advantages—unless the war should change the field of interests; unless the war should make the United States still more like Europe.

7

War Collectivism

Europe, 1914

In the summer of 1913 Paul Kellogg of the *Survey* was hunting, as usual, for contributors and ideas. Under his management the *Survey* had evolved in a decade from a house organ of the charity organization movement to a general clearinghouse of progressive social reforms, extending its coverage into more and more corners of the growing social policy agenda, from labor legislation and social insurance to slums and city planning. But this time Kellogg was thinking not thematically but geographically. He wrote to a dozen important figures in the transatlantic progressive connection—from John Burns, to Hampstead's and Toynbee Hall's Henrietta Barnett, the "new Liberal" economist J. A. Hobson, the Irish land reformer Horace Plunkett, the socialist Keir Hardie, and the ubiquitous Sidney Webb—soliciting contributions to the magazine for the coming year. To all of them he extended the same invitation: to give Americans "their 'marching orders' from the older civilization to the new; things to forfend against, things to strive for."[1]

In many ways the gesture encapsulated the transatlantic moment in American social politics: its cosmopolitanism, its optimism, its sense of the United States as at the margins of an international conversation hard to hear but important to understand. "Foraging on the frontier," Kellogg called for his style of social welfare journalism, and his hunting ground was unabashedly transatlantic. He himself was proof of the power of the Atlantic progressive connection to transform even a provincial midwesterner. He had grown up in Kalamazoo, Michigan, where his father had failed in the lumber business and he himself had failed to sustain a lasting passion for small-city newspaper work. Coming east to study at Columbia University and the New York Summer School of Philanthropy in 1901, he had listened to E. R. A. Seligman, Frank J. Goodnow, and Samuel M. Lindsay (German university students all), to Lee Frankel of the United Hebrew Charities, and to the New York Charity Organization Society's Edward T. Devine, who hired Kellogg as his journal's assistant editor. The Russell Sage Foundation, down the hall from the *Survey*'s office, tapped Kellogg in 1907 to direct the first American analogue to Charles Booth's London work, the Pittsburgh social survey.[2]

A year later Kellogg was in Europe, trying to sort out the significance of the material his team of investigators had found in Pittsburgh. Joining up with Pauline Goldmark of the National Consumers' League staff and Benjamin Marsh, who was busy collecting materials for the New York City Congestion Committee, Kellogg sought out interviews with John Burns and Samuel Barnett, looked in at Letchworth, inspected one of the model cooperative tenements in Berlin, and tried to puzzle through the contrast between the massive paternalism of Krupp-dominated Essen and the reckless methods of Pittsburgh, where the toll of maimed and crippled workers was for the first time being systematically counted by the Pittsburgh Survey's staff. Pulled from his Michigan roots into an international arena of reform, by 1913 Kellogg was, in short, a citizen of the progressive world, with as keen a sense as any for whatever was forward looking and new.[3]

And yet twelve months before Europe dissolved into war, Kellogg seemed to have had not the least presentiment of the collapse. The Old World, he wrote, marched ahead of the new. None of Kellogg's European contacts, to be sure, had had a much clearer reading of the future. "War fell upon us late in the summer of 1914 as a terrible surprise," J. A. Hobson was to write in retrospect. "Hardly anybody had believed in its coming."[4] No one at the time had missed the intensifying national rivalries, the furious armaments race, or the increasingly belligerent tone of international diplomacy. But competition, as so openly displayed in Paris in 1900, had not precluded ever more active appropriations of each others' social-political inventions. Rivalry was inherent in transatlantic politics, energizing the international flow of strategies and ideas. More than two hundred international conferences of every sort were scheduled for 1914.[5] Up to and beyond the very eve of the war declarations, the contacts that Americans had cultivated in Europe were still deep in their prewar plans and ambitions. Hobson had good reason to call the war "the surprise of 1914."

The summer of 1914, in fact, found American progressives strung out all over Europe, foraging for what many of them hoped would be their future. The National Housing Association's study group sailed for England in July 1914. The Chicago Railway Terminal Commission, with Burnham's unfinished agenda in mind, dispatched an immense delegation to Europe to investigate integrated city rail facilities. Walter Lippmann was in England that same summer, drumming up contributors to the new progressive journal, the *New Republic.* A National Civic Federation committee to investigate European schemes of health insurance was in England, poised to cross over to Germany in early August. The most ambitious delegation of them all, the Civic and Social Tour of the Institute of Educational Travel, was making its way across progressive Europe on a sixty-eight-day itinerary that covered everything from German social insurance to Frankfurt zoning, the Merxplas tramp colony, the Musée Social, the London County Council's municipal trams and housing experiments, and the English garden cities. "Municipal and Social Science in the best governed communities of the Old World is half a century ahead of American practice," the tour's promotional brochure began. "In every line of practical economics, sociology and civic art, Europe has something to teach us." To emphasize the point, Charles Booth was in the United States in the summer of 1914, discussing minimum wage boards over lunch with Theodore Roosevelt.[6]

Throughout this social politics of motion, throughout the American civic and social tour organizers' nervous sense of backwardness, their eclectic interests, and their peddlerlike notion of filling their pack with social policies and mechanisms, as if they could be carried from one context to another, runs a common theme. From the American university students' delight at European "sociability" through each piecemeal effort to decommodify a streetcar line here or a laborers' risk there, the goals of most of those in the Atlantic progressive network were elements of a stronger collective life: "solidarity," a "civic sense," "society."

Of all the Americans looking for these ingredients in Europe in the summer of 1914, the most interesting was Randolph Bourne—in part because he began with social politics so far from his mind. More an aesthete than a progressive on the eve of the war, Bourne's war writing, which was to mark him as one of the most talented and passionate writers on the progressive left, was still in his future. When he was awarded Columbia University's annual Gilder Traveling Fellowship in 1913, there was no reason to think he would end up, like a well-shepherded member of the Institute of Educational Travel's tour, reporting to the fellowship's trustees on the "extraordinary" municipal slaughterhouse in Dresden or the "miracle of scientific resource and economy" to be seen in the municipal garbage disposal works at Furth.[7]

Civic ideals were not altogether absent from Bourne's consciousness. Earlier that year he had published a study of class relations in the New Jersey suburb of his youth: a passive, immigrant working class at the bottom, as Bourne saw it, a ruling class watching hawkishly for its economic interests at the top, and his own middle class squeezed in between. A miniature of America itself, its leading characteristic was its "un-social-mindedness"—its utter lack of "community" sentiment. But Bourne had not proposed a comparative study of community structures to the Gilder committee. His friend Van Wyck Brooks, in England in 1914, recalled that "half the Harvard I had known turned up sooner or later in Piccadilly Circus." For Bourne, too, the grand tour held its appeal.[8]

Baedeker in hand and aesthetic sentiments foremost, Bourne began with a whirlwind tour through the Continent's art galleries and cathedrals. In Paris he interrupted his tour long enough to buy a copy of Jaurès's *L'Humanité*, but the self-consciously radical gesture barely slowed the pace of his aesthetic pilgrimage. Crossing to England, he sought out a Welsh author, whose books he knew, for what promised to be a winter's discussion of Freud, until his host sent him packing for London.

In London Bourne's political tone picked up, but it was not an admiring one. "We get a very much idealized picture of England from sentimentalists like F. C. Howe with their picture of England advancing to State Socialism by rapid strides," he grumbled in his letters. The England he himself saw was suffocating in unctuousness. Toynbee Hall, with its Oxford pretenses set prissily in the slums, "is one of the most marvelous demonstrations of the futility of the English mind that I know." Sidney Webb he thought a study in gradualist complaisance, discoursing "with the patient air of a man expounding arithmetic to backward children"; he was sure that subterranean corruption could be found all through Webb's vaunted municipal ownership ventures. The English women's suffrage movement electrified him, but virtually nothing else did. The Liberal Party's social program seemed to have spent its energy and coherence, the Fabians to hobble along in half steps, the middle class to be oblivious to the class warfare exploding around it. "England is one succession of fearful strikes, and our fond theory of the triumph of orderly trade-unionism slowly levering the working class to a position of comfort and influence is daily knocked into a cocked hat . . . We might be in 1813 instead of 1913 . . . It is difficult to see that capitalism has been one whit weakened by all the struggle."[9]

Paris, in contrast, delighted him, in part perhaps because, having little conversational French at first, he engaged Paris through his eyes rather than through an earful of Webbsian social arithmetic. He made the acquaintance of a "sociological English woman" who took him to lectures, model tenements, and garden suburbs. He fell in love. He sought out the picturesque vestiges of pre-Haussmannized Paris.[10]

But it was the social architecture of village Europe that pulled hardest on Bourne's imagination. He was later to write of Hampstead's collective physical presence, its "overlapping and culminating roofs" sweeping down to the surrounding heath like "the entering wedge of a new civilization"—"an experimental laboratory . . . in cooperative living." He saw the same threads in Europe's surviving medieval villages. To stand in an old marketplace, with its town and hall and church tower, was to receive "an overwhelming sense of social cohesion; this place is not merely a spot where produce is bought and sold, but the centre of a community, with a tenacious interwoven life of its own, ministering to all its members and sufficient unto itself." The streets themselves testified "to some deep-seated social sensitiveness to communal beauty and civil design."[11]

Others had said as much without sensing the progressive possibilities in the phrases. By the time Bourne reached Germany in July 1914, however, the social cohesion of the imagined past and the political community of the imaginable future had merged in Bourne's mind into a full-blown social politics. With rumors of war in his ears, he raced through modern and medieval Germany—the old cities of Rothenburg and Nördlingen, the new workingmen's garden suburbs, Ulm's municipal housing, the Nuremberg public baths—with his eye on civic forms. He was headed for Norway and Sweden, "where they have so many advanced social laws and institutions," and then to the International Socialist Congress in Vienna in August. He was still in Berlin when war was announced, and he dashed for a night train for the border.[12]

Bourne's brief immersion in Germany left him with deeply divided reactions. He hated the militarism, materialism, and pushiness of imperial Germany. "There is something in the soul of the people which I can't make articulate, but which I know I don't like," he wrote from Dresden. Although he admired the boldness of the newest German architecture and professed himself "enthusiastic about their municipal science," he would be happy, he wrote his mother, if he never saw Germany again. And yet within a year Bourne was contrasting the flowering of "social" and "public" forms in Germany with the "ragtag chaos" of America. Measured against the "chaotic savagery" of the United States—the "endless chaos of straggling towns which seemed not so much towns as disgorged fragments of communities"—German cities were "models of civic art and design." They were "undemocratic in political form, yet ultrademocratic in policy and spirit," giving their citizens "what they really wanted, far more truly than our democracies seem to be able to secure." To explain the German cities' secret, Bourne fell back on Frederic Howe's term of an inner "social sense."[13]

Into 1915, against his editors' growing impatience, Bourne kept up the contrast between "our individualistic democracy, which we have proved in America leads only to plutocracy," and "a genuine social democracy" like Germany's. "The German really seems to believe that the diffused beauty and welfare of the community is superior to any individual interest or consideration," he argued. "Where except in Germany does one find . . . that diffused prosperity, that absence of slum districts, that neatness of town, village and countryside, as if some great, invisible, communal hand were continually repairing, cleansing, and garnishing?" Where else did the "Great State," as H. G. Wells had championed it, come so close to realization?[14]

Bourne admitted that the Great State, as the Germans had realized it, had its harsh and ruthless aspects. Within another two years, having seen the hand of the American war state come down with brutal force on those who did not fall in line, Bourne would turn his whole energy to a critique of state power. But for the moment Bourne was not so much talking about politics, or even about Germany, as about ideals. It was not merely German municipal efficiency or medieval beauty out of which he built, in his mind's eye, his polar antitype across the Rhine. It was, still more, his longing for a social system that had found its way out of the snare of private imperatives. Unlike Howe, Bourne was not sure one could get the civic sense without the militarism and nationalism of Wilhelmine Germany. More tough-minded than the Civic and Social Tour's organizers, he was much less certain than they that one could take any single piece of social machinery out of its cultural frame. He did not want to import Germany to the United States, even in selective bits and pieces. He wanted, rather, to hold up his imagined medieval towns and his mentally constructed Germany as affronts and embarrassments to his own frowzy, antisocial political culture. Before they attacked the Germans' version of the community ideal, let his countrymen invent something better.

In retrospect, Bourne was to write, his travels in 1914 had been like the "toddlings of an innocent child about the edge of a volcano's crater." He had seen what "an innocent mind might see and feel in Europe, this year of last breathless hush before the explosion."[15] He had also felt the force that drew so many American progressives into the Atlantic connection, both before and after 1914. In the landscape of coherence they half saw and half imagined, unity was the key: a common, public sense, with institutions and visual forms matched to it. None of the Americans anticipated that they, too, caught up in the European explosion, would slip over the crater's rim and get their own fill of unity.

When the lava burst forth in August 1914, most American progressives experienced the war's onset with acute bewilderment and dismay. None of the events had been expected, least of all the utter breakdown of international mediation and the galvanizing nationalism that swept over Berlin, London, Vienna, and Paris. Their attention to the deep layers of history had misled them, the editors of the *New Republic* concluded a year later. "We studied comparative government, we knew the outlines of the labor movements and the extension of suffrage in the various countries . . . We persistently thought of democracy, universal suffrage, equal rights, social legislation as benevolent diseases which were spreading through one after another of the nations of Europe." Economic and social forces propelled the march of history, not the atavistic forces of nationalism. "We preferred only to see the nations strung along a straight line of democratic progress and straining all in the same direction."[16]

To watch the nations in the very vanguard of social politics descend into war was acutely wrenching for American progressives. "The wheels of the clock have so completely stopped in Europe, and this civilization that I have been admiring so much seems so palpably about to be torn to shreds that I do not even want to think about Europe until the war is over and life is running again," Bourne wrote at the end of August. The progressive journalist Ray Stannard Baker confided in his notebook that "since this war began, it seems to me I've been more unsettled in my own mind than ever before in my life. Every solid thing seems to have gone into the melting pot."[17]

In the furious opening months of the war, the collapse of the progressive social agenda seemed at first absolute and universal. "Who is talking in England today about national insurance, woman suffrage, or the breaking of the land monopoly?" John Haynes Holmes asked in the *Survey* a month after the invasion of Belgium. "Where is the campaign for franchise reform in Germany? Who cares about co-operation in Belgium, or syndicalism in France, or socialism anywhere? . . . Who in these United States is thinking at this moment of recreation centers, improved housing, or the minimum wage? Who is going to fight the battle for widows' pensions, push the campaign against child labor, or study exhaustively the problem of unemployment?" Who, in short, "cares a fig about the social movement?"[18]

In the face of this dismay, American progressives scrambled to figure out how they had misread the signs of history. As in most moments of intellectual crisis, the imperative was not to shift the foundations of their understanding but to rearrange the least number of pieces necessary to contain the one that had exploded in their faces. The simplest intellectual strategy was to divide Germany into two cohabiting nations, progressive and reactionary. The line had been common enough in the prewar writings of Howe and others. The progressives' Germany had always been described as a liberal, urban-based node inside an atavistic, Junker-ridden, Prussian-dominated empire. The progressive admirers of German civic life had not been wrong about the promise of that inner Germany, many now concluded. But they had tragically misjudged its ability to crack its encasing political shell. In the progressive reviews there was a rush to blame the war on the "medievalism" of the Junkers, the European monarchs, and the "war lords."[19]

The conceptual dilemma fell particularly hard on the German-trained American professors. For many, the "two Germanys" argument provided an escape from dismay. But the apparently ferocious unity of the German people made this line difficult to hold. The failure of the German socialists and progressives to oppose the war, the efflorescence of military symbols, and the unity of resolve and purpose that filtered through the firsthand reports all complicated the effort to bifurcate Germany into its modern and atavistic parts. More painful still was the open letter of October 1914 signed by some one hundred leading German intellectuals, justifying the Belgian invasion and insisting that the causes of sword and mind, German military fortunes and German intellectual culture, were indivisibly the same. Its signers included Gustav Schmoller, Johannes Conrad, Friedrich Naumann, even Lujo Brentano—the cream of the German university establishment.[20]

Where admiration for Germany ran strongest, the result was a deeply painful reckoning with this betrayal of the teachers. Two years into the war, Simon Patten was still struggling to find defenses for a Germanophile's faith. "The new German philosophy" had been "religion with me," Patten professed; over against the "English" ideal of self-interest, it taught the values of social activity and the "social pulse." Henry Farnam, who had been poised to take up an exchange professorship in Berlin, wrote in agony that his German friends must be "under the influence of a terrible obsession." Albion Small, who spread his private despair over a convoluted twenty-eight-page lead editorial in the *American Journal of Sociology* in September 1917, could only conclude that the cliché of a Germany gone mad was not a figure of speech but a medical certainty. As American public opinion closed ranks against Germany, few of the German-trained professors held out as long as Small or Patten. Ely, in a much more agile about-face, had been beating the drums of war preparation for months. But the progressive journalists' groping for psychological explanations in the opening months of the war, as they professed their bewilderment at the "madhouse" in Europe, the eruption of "unreason," and the atavistic reversion to savagery, betrayed the same dynamics.[21]

Still other American progressives gradually worked their way toward economic explanations for the war. Frederic Howe, whose catalog of German social advances, *Socialized Germany*, published in the fall of 1915, seemed to speak to reviewers in the archaic language of a vanished epoch, had by 1916 pinned the madness, single-tax style, on economic privilege.[22] But none of these explanations satisfactorily answered the enigma of the war—the two Germanys argument because the evidence was against it, the insanity argument because it was itself psychologically so clearly tormented, the economic explanation because few of the progressives had an economic understanding of the path to war deep enough to sustain the case.

Ultimately what rescued the progressives from their confusion was not an answer to the riddle of the war's origins. It was an evasion of the question through hope: a growing sense that the war might not have derailed the progressive course of history, however terrible the detour through which it was whirling its passengers. Some of this was reflexive optimism of the sort that came with the progressive territory. Even Bourne in September 1914 was writing in a rare Panglossian moment that "while the clock of the world has stopped, we can learn many useful things, and at least look forward to the momentous readjustment." But the sense that the war might bring about some of the goals that peace had failed to effect was not made only out of naïveté. As the Germans' ability to sustain the massive war mobilization of August 1914 was stretched out over months, long beyond the predictions of its own general staff, as the German war economy continued to crank out the massive material needs of a war lavish in its demand for shells, fuel, arms, and soldiers, there were those who thought there was, once more, a German lesson to be learned.

Theodore Roosevelt, at the head of the American military preparedness campaign in 1916, could not resist professing that "this country has more to learn from Germany than from any other nation—and this as regards fealty to non-utilitarian ideals, no less than as regards the essentials of social and industrial efficiency, of that species of socialized governmental action which is absolutely necessary for individual protection and general well-being under the conditions of modern industrialism." The most strenuous defense of Germany along these lines came from *Pearson's Magazine*, through the influence of the maverick socialist Alan Benson. "Bet your bottom dollar that German efficiency is not founded on the 'every man for himself' idea," Benson wrote. "Germany has gone further in accepting and applying the doctrine of socialism . . . than has any other nation." The proof was not to be hunted up in Marx; it was patent in Germany's military success.[23]

In the early months of the war it was equally common to attribute England's faltering war machinery to precisely the opposite traits: to habits too individualistic and an economy too deeply hobbled by its laissez-faire past. As the months wore on, however, England, too, was recast as socialized by the imperatives of the war. Much of this was the work of English progressives who deluged their American correspondents with the sorts of reports they wanted themselves to believe and the Americans wanted to hear. The *New Republic* was a particularly important outlet for this stream of reportage, stocked as it was with English correspondents, including J. A. Hobson, H. G. Wells, Graham Wallas, Harold Laski, Norman Angell, and Alfred Zimmern. In the *New Republic*'s first year of publication, 1914–15, Charles Forcey has estimated that more than a quarter of its contributed pieces came through its British connections. None of these contributors gave an uncritical account of British war mobilization, but as reports filtered through of the efforts to rationalize the wartime labor market and mobilize industrial production, the impression of a sea change in British social policy, far more radical even than the legislation of 1906 to 1911, began to take hold. British social workers heralded the "intense unity" that had swept over Britain since the outbreak of the war. "England really being disciplined!" the American journalist Ray Stannard Baker wrote in August 1915.

"At a single stroke a condition has been created beyond the dreams of socialism for many years to come."[24]

Not all progressives were reassured that the war's social lining was real—or, if it was real, that it was worth the awful, unceasing carnage. Progressive women were much more often skeptical of the notion of the socializing effects of the war than their male counterparts, so often desperately eager for a visit to the front. Alice Hamilton, in Germany on a futile peace mission in 1915, wrote of her shock at seeing Albert Südekum, the socialist civic reformer whom she had met at Hull House two years before, in the uniform of a German army officer. Madeleine Doty, traveling on the same errand, saw Europe as a continent of cripples. Black-clad widows in mourning, an "unceasing" parade of gray ambulances, cities bereft of young men, and, in Berlin, the antiwar socialists in furtive, fearful meetings: this, not social unity, was what impressed her.[25]

Socialist intellectuals had their own quite different reasons to be skeptical of the talk of the "war socialism" transforming Europe. They had long insisted on the chasm separating "socialism" from "state socialism": the difference between a system in which ownership lodged in the masses and one in which crucial parts of the economic structure merely lodged in the state. At the juncture where socialist and progressive ideas met, however, even these distinctions tended to melt in the heat of the war.

William English Walling's peculiarly strained reckoning with the growing talk of "war socialism" was a case in point. Enlisting in the Socialist Party in 1910 after participating in a decade of progressive causes, Walling had become a particularly vigilant defender of the difference between real and bogus collectivism. Against every scheme of socialist reformism—the Milwaukeeans' dreams of a socialist city, the Fabian schemes of municipal ownership, the cooperative commonwealth of the Belgian socialists—he had raised the "state socialism" charge. The proper phrase for Germany, Walling retorted to Howe, was not "socialized" but "governmentalized"—or, more accurately still, "class-organized" through a Junker-dominated state. Control was the key. To think that public ownership in a capitalist state entailed any essential change so long as capital remained in the saddle was "stupid."[26]

But in the unexpected transformations of the war, the line between socialism and state socialism began to blur for Walling. In 1914 he had published a more orthodox account of state socialism, setting it in a sequence of historical stages from capitalism to "socialism proper," each an "absolutely indispensable preparation" for its successor. The question now for socialists was whether the wartime economic mobilization represented an advance or a retreat along that historical line. Through 1915 and 1916, as the patriotism that was to bring him into strident collision with his own party grew, Walling edged toward greater and greater optimism about "war socialism." "Mere nationalization," he warned was not socialism. He worried that war was being used as a club to hammer the labor movement. By 1918, however, Walling was arguing that the war had bettered the chances of a truly democratic collectivism by "100 or perhaps 1,000 percent."[27]

If a maverick socialist like Walling could set aside the distinction between state socialism and the real thing, the progressives found the passage to war collectivism still easier. In early 1915 the *New Republic*'s editors were still cautioning their readers that the "landslide into collectivism" abroad was merely a rush into "state socialism"—an autocratic sham of socialism "without any of its reality." "Collectivism introduced by command is a very different thing from the collectivism of a radical democracy." Still, in the contrast between the war-fostered social organization of the European war powers and what the *New Republic*'s editors were characterizing by the fall of 1915 as "our present method of foozling with unemployment, sickness, age, and infancy," it was hard to resist the conclusion that war collectivism was good enough.[28]

Slowly the notion of laggardness was revived, the arrow of history restraightened. How much longer would the United States "hang back in the nineteenth-century industrial chaos?" the *New Republic*'s editors complained in late 1916. "As compared with the other great states of the world," Walter Lippmann wrote in a *New Republic* editorial in March 1917,

> the United States to-day is in point of organization one of the most backward and intellectually the most timid. Whatever else the war has done, it has at least taught England and Germany and Canada and France that large-scale operations can be planned and executed, that modern nations must think in very large sums of money, that the old scruples and dogmas of legalism and laissez-faire are old men's bogeys . . . In their severest trials the progressive nations have discovered that the old unorganized, competitive profiteering is unsound and wasteful . . . But the United States trundles along without nationalized railroads or shipping, its mineral resources unsocialized, its water power exploited, its fundamental industries whipped into competition, its food distribution a muddle, its educational

system starved, its labor half organized, badly organized, and unrecognized in the structure of society.[29]

Christopher Lasch has characterized the prewar progressives as circling restlessly around the centers of power, distressed by inaction, psychologically incapable of the neutralist stance that the war might well have entailed.[30] But the flame around which they flew, mothlike, was not power in and of itself; it was the example of the war-socialized nations of Europe. Woodrow Wilson did not offer American progressives simply an idealistic set of war aims in 1917. He offered them, after years of frustrating political labor, an experiment in the possibilities of the war-collectivized state.

Many of the leading progressives seized the offer in a mood that shimmered with hope. "We stand at the threshold of a collectivism which is greater than any as yet planned by a socialist party," Walter Lippmann wrote within a month of the American declaration of war. "Private property . . . has already lost its sanctity," John Dewey declared in the New York *World.* The progressive journalist William Allen White gloated that same summer that "the back of the profit system is broken." This sense of momentous change was essential to the progressives' understanding of the war. The war represented a historical passage; none of the industrial nations would revert to their prewar individualism when the crisis had passed, Howe had written as early as 1915.[31]

This reading of European events, this faith in the social possibilities of the war, required many progressives temporarily to set aside their decentralist instincts. Their fascination with the city, the community, or the publicly strengthened institutions of mutuality was momentarily swept aside by the notion of the nation-state itself hitched to the common good. There were progressives who balked at the leap and were left in painful isolation. By the fall of 1917, Bourne had seen enough to write bitterly of the "riveting of a semi-military State-socialism on the country."[32] The problem of democratic control would soon come back, heightened by the war experience, and send certain of the progressives hunting for a firmer democratic basis—this one bottomed not on classless notions of civic unity but on a British-style alliance with the working class. To both capture and democratize the machinery of war collectivism—that was the progressive hope and challenge.

For the moment, however, the advent of wartime social controls was momentous enough. Neva Deardoff of the Philadelphia Bureau of Municipal Research attended the social science associations' annual meetings in December 1917. Through them all, she reported in triumph, ran a common theme: "Laissez-Faire is dead! Long live social control!"[33]

Across the Atlantic world, the wartime transformation in political economy was, indeed, far-reaching. Everywhere old rules were set at odds, warring social parties brought into state-sponsored harness, the market drastically narrowed, and the realm of things public dramatically swollen. The point sometimes made, however, that war is public welfare's best friend and prime historical promoter, will not stand examination.[34] It was not war in and of itself but the economization of the struggle that mattered. Had victory been as swift as in the Franco-Prussian War, whose outcome the German war planners had hoped to replicate, the conflict would barely have left a mark on social politics at all. As the forces bogged down, it was the transformation of a war of mobility into a war of production and matériel that made the difference. By the fall 1914, the French army command was calling for the production of 100,000 artillery shells a day; by early 1918, with the troops still mired in the trenches, the army was demanding 278,000 a day. The extravagant production needs of the war forced the belligerent governments deeper and deeper into economic controls, the organization of goods and labor, and, finally—to hold the production machinery in gear—social amelioration.[35]

The organization of supply came first. German states had been buying up their railroad systems since the military utility of state ownership had become clear in 1870. In Britain and France the privately owned rail systems were placed under government management within days of the war's declaration. Coal, food, and shipping were also sooner or later brought within state control as the planners wrestled with the problem of allocation. A command economy of one sort or another evolved in the critical war-goods sectors, quickly in Germany, more hesitantly in Britain and France, to ensure the inflow of raw materials and the priority of war production. None of the nation-states had a bureaucracy in place equipped for the task. In the absence of an existing state apparatus, businessmen flocked to Berlin, Paris, London, and Washington to staff the war economic corporations and war production boards, to command themselves through state authority. The systems of economic control, jerry-built at the war's outbreak, were often considerably less efficient than the facade of war systematization acknowledged. Within the war economy councils, the businessmen-bureaucrats bargained with as keen an eye for their own interests as they had ever displayed in the market. Everywhere, despite the wartime excess profit taxes, the war suppliers' profits soared. The economic controls, even the temporary nationalization of mines and railroads, left the bedrock structures of ownership, investment, and profit intact. But in none of the belligerent nations did the conviction long survive that markets alone could be counted on for the efficiency, concentration of purpose, and production that the emergency required.

Organizing labor proved a much more difficult matter than the organization of supply. A peace pact with the labor organizations was clearly essential if war production was to be sustained. Germany and France relied on informal social contracts—*Burgfrieden*, *union sacrée*—forged in the first rush of war patriotism. In Britain, after shortfalls in munitions production reached crisis proportions in early 1915, the government won not only a formal no-strike pledge for the war's duration but a rollback in union work rules. In the United States, a pact with the American Federation of Labor was sealed at the very outset.

Although the price for labor peace varied, everywhere it included formal recognition of labor's place in the basic organizational fabric of the war nations in a way unimaginable before 1914. In France, the wartime coalition brought socialists into the government in late 1914 for the first time since the Millerand controversy. In Britain, by the next spring, organized labor had gained its first formal foothold in the cabinet and institutional representation on the major war industry boards. In the United States, the AFL's Samuel Gompers—archcritic of governmental paternalism—was given a seat at the pinnacle of an elaborate organizational chart of advisory and management bodies, most of which had at least token labor representation. By the summer of 1917, with Gompers ensconced in the Advisory Commission of the Council of National Defense, with socialist Albert Thomas directing French war production, and with the Labour Party's Arthur Henderson seated in the new five-member British war cabinet, outwardly the political transformation was startling indeed. Even in Germany, where the socialists were not invited into the cabinet until the last days of the war, in a desperate move to soften the conditions of peace, the socialist unions were quietly incorporated de facto into the agencies of labor administration.

The symbolism of a seat at the table was one face of the war labor policies; the other was a rapid elaboration of institutions of labor bargaining and mediation. The war made wage disputes public and publicly arbitrable as never before. In Britain, where union-management bargaining had been widely accepted before the war, government arbitration of the process increased dramatically after 1915. Where labor organization was weak or cumbersome, the government threw its authority behind the organization of joint employer-employee works councils—Whitley Councils, they were called—to streamline the existing grievance machinery, to arrest the devolution of authority into the hands of radical union shop stewards, and, above all, to promote closer point-of-production cooperation. In the United States, where formal union recognition had been much rarer than in Britain, the government was soon mandating labor-management negotiations throughout the war industries, if not with unions, then with shop committees or company employees' associations. In Germany, where collective bargaining had been weakest of all, both government and industry ultimately gave in to labor demands for elected works committees, a concession to trade unionism in all but the name.

The problem of sustaining the labor peace was that it was inherently unstable. As wartime inflation eroded wages, as the insatiable demand for soldiers shortened the labor supply and heightened the power of those left on the production lines, the need for pacification was continuous. To try to control and rationalize the flow of manpower, the German government had turned to an outright labor draft by the end 1916. In Britain an equally unpopular system of "leaving certificates," designed to dampen labor turnover in the war industries, drew from the same imperatives. Partly in defense against these and other wartime controls, partly because of labor's newly protected status, union membership swelled during the war. In Germany, where the armies drained a particularly large fraction of the workforce to the front, union membership grew only 14 percent between 1913 and the end of 1918. In Britain it rose by half, in the United States (between 1916 and the end of 1918) by a quarter. In France by the war's end, membership in the Confédération Générale du Travail had reached almost twice its prewar level. Strikes, which had virtually evaporated in the first months of the war, resumed in 1915; in France, Germany, and Britain they reached crisis proportions by 1917. All this made the terms of industrial peace unstable and in need of constant renegotiation.[36]

Repression was an obvious choice. Where workplace restlessness crossed into radical politics, whether among timber workers in the American Northwest or among Scots machinists on the Clyde, governments did not hesitate to use the emergency powers they had seized for themselves at the war's outset. In France, the socialist ministers walked out of the governing coalition in the war's third year as the *union sacrée* broke under the pressures of the conflict. But elsewhere, to hold the early war unity together, concessions that had been strongly resisted in peacetime began to be thrown into the breach of the fragile labor peace. Minimum-wage and maximum-hours orders spread by government fiat. The unpopularly high age of eligibility for the state old-age insurance system in Germany was lowered from seventy to sixty-five. More dramatic still was the kaiser's announcement, in the midst of the German strike upheaval of 1917, that the three-class Prussian voting system, one of the very foundation stones of prewar German politics, would be up for renegotiation at the war's end.

The same dynamic that put German political relations on the bargaining table also promoted political concessions to women as they moved in large numbers into wartime production jobs. In Britain the suffrage act of 1918, which finally opened the suffrage to all adult males, extended the vote to more than one-third of all adult women as well. In the United States, Woodrow Wilson's endorsement of the women's suffrage amendment drew on the same war dynamics. In the war's unexpectedly drawn out and unstable circumstances, the governments' focus on production was capable of extraordinary work.[37]

Not the least, the war brought the progressives out of the contested margins of social politics to staff the proliferating social agencies of the war state. In 1914 John Haynes Holmes had despaired that it would be "years" before the voice of the social worker would again be heard in the land.[38] In fact, the social workers were everywhere recruited to shore up the social peace. The welfare section of the British Munitions Ministry under Seebohm Rowntree was stocked with social progressives. Even the Prussian war ministry in the early years of the war recruited its labor experts from the Gesellschaft für Sozialreform.

In the United States, the social progressives were brought en masse into government and quasi-government service. The army's need for experts on hygiene, morale, and welfare absorbed many of them. Others were recruited as labor relations experts, mediators, industrial welfare specialists, or labor standards constructors. Much of the National Consumers' League staff was drafted to oversee the treatment of the new wartime women workers. Hull House's Grace Abbott directed the War Labor Policies Board's enforcement of the wartime child labor code. Josephine Goldmark served the Council of National Defense as an expert on fatigue; her sister Pauline Goldmark was tapped to be manager of the Railroad Administration's special section for women workers. Florence Kelley herself sat on the War Department's Board of Control of Labor Standards. The Russell Sage

Foundation's Mary Van Kleeck became head of the Labor Department's Women in Industry division. Henry Seager signed on as secretary to the Shipbuilding Labor Adjustment Board. Lee Frankel and the U.S. Children's Bureau's Julia Lathrop joined forces in drafting the government's war-risk insurance act—a voluntary federal soldiers' and sailors' life and disability insurance program, designed in deliberate contrast to the Civil War pension system and widely heralded as a breakthrough for the principle of social insurance.[39]

In this ramifying network of social and economic concessions and controls, the question of who controlled the wartime collectivism could not be wholly suppressed. That markets would not suffice for the war emergency was clear, but where economic power was now to lodge varied from nation to nation. In Germany the army, fearful of letting policy issues loose in the Reichstag, ultimately gathered most of the critical authority to itself. In Britain the state authorities carved out an unusually large autonomous domain; the Munitions Ministry's vast, Lloyd George–constructed empire of directly owned and managed machinery and munitions works was without parallel elsewhere. In France and the United States, direction of the war economy devolved most heavily on business itself, either through committees of executives on emergency loan or through the war-encouraged cartels. What R. H. Tawney later wrote of the British war economy was true everywhere: "for all its magnitude and complexity, it was almost entirely an improvisation." That fact glued the wartime economic administrations, to a very great extent, to the preexisting structures of economics, ownership, and power.[40]

But if the mix of state, army, and business elements differed between the war collectivist economies, the family resemblances were far the more striking. Their common features were not simply an automatic response to the war's needs; even in the midst of war, their likenesses were built on a sifting and borrowing each other's designs. In the early, bungled months of the war, the British press trumpeted the German model of sweeping economic mobilization. Keenly interested in German organization, David Lloyd George, moving from the Munitions Ministry to the prime minister's office in late 1916, brought a great deal of it to bear in a flurry of centralizing reforms: emergency coal nationalization, a new Food Ministry, extension of shipping controls, and a slimmed-down war cabinet. The British, in turn, pressured the French war economy managers into tighter controls.

Coming latest into the war and capitalizing heavily on the advantages of their laggardness, the Americans moved into the grooves and precedents of the other belligerents with extraordinary speed. The British had resisted conscription until sixteen months into the war; the United States had a conscription act in place within six weeks. Aware of the chaos that had resulted from the British experiment with voluntary cooperation among shippers, the Wilson government embarked on construction of a state-owned emergency shipping fleet even before the war declaration. Where the British war government waited ten months before formally inviting labor in, Gompers's place had been set for months when the war began. In railroads, the Americans hesitated almost nine months, until the bottlenecks became acute, before creating a British-style Railroad Administration; the National War Labor Board's arbitration machinery was not fully mobilized until the war was a year old. But the basic structures of the war economy—the War Industries Board, the Shipping Board, the emergency Food and Fuel Administrations, emergency war taxes, and the creation of a labor seat at the planning tables—were all in place within six months.

During their three years on the sidelines of the war, the Americans had followed the mistakes and difficulties of British labor policy particularly closely. The Labor Department published an immense compilation of British war labor orders in 1917, and American progressives interested in labor standards had quizzed British visitors on the effects of the rollback of work rules in the war industries.[41] Impressed by the apparent links between labor exhaustion in the first months of the war and widespread labor unrest, the Wilson administration, rejecting the British precedent, pledged itself to maintain prewar labor standards. Rather than extracting a legally binding no-strike pledge from the unions, which seemed in Britain by 1917 only to have fueled an epidemic of wildcat strikes, the Wilson administration settled for a voluntary no-strike pledge and a wartime federal mediation service.

In all these ways, absorption of the experience of the European belligerents dramatically foreshortened the Americans' learning time and accelerated their rush into a war collectivism of their own. That was the logic behind a phenomenon that otherwise would seem merely ironic: that the United States, of all the nations in the North Atlantic economy the most resistant to state undertakings, was in the war emergency the swiftest to assume them. That speed—that leap into an organized war economy where others had blundered their way without road maps—accentuated, in turn, the American progressives' sense of being catapulted by the war into a new world where the old shibboleths no longer carried force.

The progressives' sense of leapfrogging over peacetime obstacles was particularly strong on the housing policy front. War workers' housing, to be sure, was only a minor facet of the mammoth war economy; compared with the progressives who were drawn into labor policy, the numbers engaged in the war housing work were never large. But resistance to state-assisted housing before 1917 had been, as we have seen, particularly adamant. If the wartime transatlantic connection could alter this, there was no telling what the energies collectively focused by the war might accomplish.[42]

From the outset of the war it was clear that the war planners would have to manage a crisis in war workers' housing. Recruits began to move by the thousands into the shipyards and the war munitions plants in the summer of 1917, like a swollen river shifting out of its peacetime bed. In the shipyard city of Chester, Pennsylvania, the National Housing Association's investigators estimated there were 40,000 more persons crammed into the city's housing stock by 1918 than there had been four years before. So rapid a population movement could not but throw the housing markets into chaos; but nothing in simple need itself dictated the form a solution would take.[43]

The most straightforward expedient was to let the market take care of itself, jacking up rents, raising the profit margin on lodgers, encouraging overcrowding, and generally making do. Beyond this, at the first level of intervention, was the makeshift solution of temporarily billeting workers with local families. Improved transportation by special trains or jitneys from population centers large enough to absorb the new industrial recruits was another possibility, though fear that workers would become exhausted by the long commuting journey weighed against it. The most obvious solution was the erection of temporary barracks built as cheaply and as quickly as possible, preferably by the industrial contractors themselves, with government loans if necessary, or, as a last resort, by direct government agency. Temporary shelter as quick and impermanent as an army camp: had it not been for the British example, that would certainly have been the American way in war housing.

In Britain, however, the emergency war housing needs arose in the context of different precedents and a different political setting. There, too, the first expedient had been temporary barracks housing. At the royal arsenal at Woolwich in southeast London, where the employment rolls had swelled from 11,000 on the eve of the war to 74,000 by 1917, and at wholly new industrial towns, like Gretna on the Scottish border, where a Munitions Ministry explosives works of 11,000 employees sprang out of the moors, there was no alternative to barracks housing: row on row of low frame structures arrayed in military formation. Britain's timber shortage soon moved the planners toward the permanency of concrete block construction. But it was Britain's prewar experience with municipal housing that tipped the balance from temporary housing to permanent additions to the nation's housing stock. By 1915, the government had committed itself to a massive, wartime workers housing program built to the best garden city and factory village designs. With Raymond Unwin in the lead, the garden city architects moved as a group into the staff of a massive war housing effort, this time with the nation-state as their patron.[44]

Barracks building did not cease after 1915, but the garden city designers used the war's concentration of authority to bring a new scale and community vision to public housing design. The narrow, bylaw streets within which the LCC suburban rim designers had had to work were abandoned. At Woolwich, a village of some 1,300 houses for skilled arsenal workers was constructed around a central green in as picturesque a suburb as was to be built in twentieth-century England. At Gretna, Unwin folded the war barracks of 1915 into a village of gently curved streets and generously allotted community facilities. In their four years of work, the Munitions Ministry architects erected some 10,000 permanent dwellings, as many as the London County Council had built in the previous quarter century.

Heavily censored for fear of sabotage, reports of the munitions workers' housing only gradually began to filter in to the United States. The key to the transmission was the recently installed editor of the *Journal of the American Institute of Architects*. A lushly formatted arbiter of architectural taste, the *Journal* was the flagship of architectural elitism. What induced its managers to hire Charles H. Whitaker, a charming cosmopolite, single-taxer, and William Morris–style socialist is still not clear, nor is it clear how he hung on as editor as long as he did amid the controversies he provoked. By the fall of 1917, in any event, he had begun to fill the *Journal* with reports on British war workers' housing. Printing what he could get through the censors, he dispatched New York City architect Frederick Ackerman to bring back still more.[45]

Ackerman proved an inspired reporter. His articles breathed a heady compound of economic radicalism and war optimism. "To actually see this," he was writing from Gretna by October: "to know that it was a reality; to witness an enormous industrial community in which law, order and arrangement prevailed; to see no slums and to realize that in this community there would be no slums; to sense the balance which it is possible to maintain between intensive industry and the normal life of a worker—is to feel a thrill such as one seldom experiences." The munitions towns were a living example of what the state could do when it acted in its "full power," extricating itself from the dogmas of "super-individual rights and the rights of property." He had seen more than houses in wartime England, Ackerman wrote: "It has been my privilege to have had a glimpse down the vistas . . . opened to the future."[46]

It was not the hand of the state in itself or the aesthetics of the designs that inspired this outburst on the Scottish moors. Ackerman resisted the picturesque charms of Woolwich, disappointed by its sparse public facilities. It was in Unwin's visually more simple but socially more generous plans for Gretna and Eastriggs that Ackerman thought he saw the future: in clubhouses, civic institutes, schools, churches, dental clinics, public cinemas, communal laundries, and the spirit "of social and industrial integration."[47]

At the *Journal*, Whitaker mustered Ackerman's reports and photos into a full-throated campaign for a parallel housing program in the United States. Edith Wood was recruited to describe the European systems of public housing loans, Richard S. Childs to explain the British schemes to circumvent speculation, and Sidney Webb to praise the coming partnership of government and architect, while Whitaker himself wrote of the transvaluation of values that was palpable in the war-torn air.[48] Ackerman, for his part, tirelessly promoted what he had seen in lectures and lantern slides:

> Now is the time, as never before, when we must scrutinize our ultra-individualistic tendencies, our relative lack of accomplishment along broad social lines of cooperative undertakings, our trembling fear of governmental control, and, above all, our materialistic aims. For these tendencies, unless overcome, will inhibit us absolutely from keeping pace with those nations whose suffering and loss have been much greater than our own, but who, through the integrated effort resulting from the war, have learned to realize something of the meaning of social democracy.[49]

Edith Wood was later to claim that "the Ackerman articles were what prevented our war housing from taking the form of temporary wooden barracks."[50] Her judgment may have exaggerated Ackerman's role but not the force of the British precedent. In the circumstances of acute skilled labor shortages and staggering turnover rates, it was the concreteness, the "finishedness" of the British example, compounded by an exaggerated sense that good housing alone had stabilized British war labor, that carried the day.

By the spring of 1918, a parallel program was under way in the United States. Speed was war's imperative, and speed, in turn, gave an advantage to those with a working knowledge of the British prototype. Ackerman himself, largely on the basis of his *Journal* reportage, was named chief architect to the Emergency Fleet Corporation. Arthur C. Comey, designer of the Massachusetts Homestead Commission's development at Lowell, became a district architect for the United States Housing Corporation. John Nolen, Unwin's closest American correspondent, designed for both agencies.

None of the American war housing developments was an English copy. More often than their British counterparts, the American planners laid down centralized and symmetrical designs focused on civic center sites, as if visual unity might in itself help dampen the "hot chaos" of their America. As for the individual houses, bungalows, neocolonial imitations, pseudo-farm cottages, and neo-Georgian blocks all had their partisans. But in Waterbury, Connecticut; Newport News, Virginia; Eddystone, Pennsylvania; and elsewhere, streetscapes pulled straight out of Unwin's *Town Planning in Practice* or memories of Letchworth and Hampstead—row houses, massed together under long, sheltering roofs, humped and punctuated in the German fashion that British garden city designers had so admired—formed unmistakable pointers to the transatlantic origins of the endeavor.[51]

The war housing program had barely gotten into gear before the armistice cut it short in November 1918. In the speed with which the program had been launched and the planners' confidence in its direction, war workers' housing was, nevertheless, a particularly striking example of the resources inherent in policy borrowing. In less than ten months, the Emergency Fleet Corporation and the United States Housing Corporation built half again as much permanent housing as the British Munitions Ministry had constructed in four years of war. Measured against the surrounding sea of speculator-built housing, even that, to be sure, was but a drop. It was not the structures in themselves that made the war housing program seem momentous; it was not even the fact of state ownership—for unlike the case in England, where reversion to local government authorities had been mandated from the first, the postwar disposition of the war housing in the United States was anything but clear; nor was it the community facilities—still paper plans in the rush to get housing foundations into the ground. It was the sense of a political culture cracking and reforming under the war's strain.

Elsewhere, too, in 1917 and 1918, confidence in the war's socializing effect was hard to resist, as engineers like Herbert Hoover and professors like Harry Garfield moved in to organized the nation's food and fuel supplies, as a coherent federally managed rail system began to form out of the prewar financial buccaneering, as the War Risk Insurance Bureau turned out government insurance policies by the thousand, as labor and management undertook to bargain under the eye of neutral government experts.

May 1918 found the president of the Rockefeller Foundation in Britain, surveying with "tremendous enthusiasm" Gretna's structures and welfare enterprises. How so "splendid" an enterprise could be translated into peacetime terms, how its collective accomplishment could be realized without the top-down, emergency powers of the war state, George Vincent was not sure. But the vision was clear. "We have been in this great war; we have been fused together as never before in our history by this sense of community interest . . . We cannot go back to the old idea of scramble and conflict and individual struggle and mere group rivalry . . . This war must never permit us to go back again to the old individualism of the early days."[52]

Society "More or Less Molten"

To make the transitory permanent; to secure for the peace the collectivist spirit and institutions of the war: these were the challenges the emergency war measures posed to progressives on both sides of the Atlantic. The word that soon shaped itself around those aspirations was "reconstruction." From its origins in France in discussions of the physical reconstruction of the war-devastated northeast, it soon swelled into a general term for postwar planning. When the British war government organized a committee in the spring of 1916 to anticipate postwar problems, the name Reconstruction Committee stuck to it from the first. From Britain, where reconstruction ambitions soon infected virtually every corner of domestic political debate, they were to cross the Atlantic to the United States.

In Britain, politics and morale played hard in reconstruction talk. As the Belgian war atrocity stories began to lose the force they had commanded in 1914 and 1915, as the armies bogged down in a conflict without apparent end, and as, in the growing war weariness, the labor movement began to pick up the call for a negotiated peace, Lloyd George put the idea of a war fought not merely for victory but for the postwar transformation of the victors at the very center of the politics of promise. By the last years of the war, that gesture toward a better world for the common British soldier and munitions worker came to be an indispensable means of bolstering public morale. "There is no doubt at all that the present war . . . presents an opportunity for reconstruction of industrial and social conditions of this country such as has never been presented in the life of, probably, the world," Lloyd George told a Labour Party delegation with calculated hyperbole in March 1917. "The whole state of society is more or less molten and you can stamp upon that molten mass almost anything so long as you do it with firmness and determination."[53]

In fact, not one but two reconstruction movements swelled in Britain in the last years of the war, one within the official ministries, the other in the labor rank and file. The vehicle of the first was the Ministry of Reconstruction, organized in the summer of 1917 with the task (as the cabinet put it) not of "rebuilding society as it was before the war, but of moulding a better world out of the social and economic conditions which have come into being during the war." Its committees were stocked with prominent progressives: Beatrice Webb, J. H. Whitley (of the factory works councils scheme), Seebohm Rowntree (at the head of the Munitions Ministry's welfare work), Alfred Zimmern, Patrick Geddes, Raymond Unwin, and the expert on Germany, William Dawson. Together they pushed energetically for translation of the war's social and economic lessons into the postwar peace. The labor relations experts pressed for institutionalization of the emergency joint labor-management committees in a full-blown, permanent consultative structure, ascending from the shop floor to a joint economic council at the top, so as to sustain the "cooperation of all classes, established by the war." Beatrice Webb, as she had since 1909, pushed for replacement of the Poor Law by a broad new Ministry of Public Health. The garden city group urged expansion of the wartime housing efforts into a large-scale, nationally funded, peacetime housing program. Labor colony advocates and social insurance experts worried about the problems of postwar unemployment. The economists put their expertise to schemes of gradual demobilization and decontrol so as to soften the readjustment to a peacetime economy. Above all to be guarded against was a return to "the deadly doctrine of *laisser faire, laisser passer*," William Dawson wrote, summing up the lesson of the expert reconstruction debate in terms that went back to the German lecture halls of the 1880s. This was not the sum total of the agenda British progressives had carried into the war, but the connections were unmistakable.[54]

In the ranks of British labor, in contrast, the reconstruction talk of 1917 to 1919 proceeded against an experience of sharp wartime discontinuities. The emergency rollback in work rules, the "dilution" of skill as craft workers had to make place for newcomers, the war profiteering and ascending cost of living, and the co-optation of labor union leaders by the war government—all these factors eroded the patriotic mood of the early months and led to an eruption of angry wildcat strikes by 1917. The next year there were still more workers on strike, and in 1919—in a strike wave that rolled across the entire North Atlantic economy—there were more strikers than at any time ever before.

The war not only mobilized labor in Britain but radicalized it as well. In the prewar debates over social politics, the labor organizations had played a distant, ambiguous part, distrustful of state measures and fearful of diluting the core trade union issues that were their raison d'être. The British Labour Party itself, launched in defense against a series of court reversals of union rights to strike and picket, was still not much more than a creature of its constituent trade unions in 1914. Now, with the war's politicization of economic and social relations, labor's political ambitions expanded like a giant balloon.

Part of British labor's transformation worked on the plane of international affairs. By late 1917, disillusioned with a war of too few victories and patently unequal sacrifices, the Labour Party was moving rapidly toward the idea of a labor-brokered, negotiated peace. Reports from Russia of workers' soviets gathering the powers of the state into their own hands were a heady catalyst. But ultimately it was the war collectivism itself that most strongly shaped labor's new direction. Blurring the carefully defended lines between economics and politics, absorbing the markets in the control of the nominally democratic state, sliding underneath the old structures of ownership the potential agencies of joint, perhaps even democratic, control, the British war experience mapped a world almost as new as anything taking shape in Russia. Along with traditional wages and hours conflicts, erupting faster than the labor relations experts could extinguish them in 1918–19, there was no missing the new importance of industrial control. The question being raised more and more insistently in labor gatherings was not merely how to sustain the war's partial abrogation of capital's prerogatives, but how to democratize the structures of industry itself.

On the means to that end there was no agreement, only a sense of enormous possibilities suspended in an unstable political moment. At labor meetings, advocates of a dozen different varieties of workers' control hunted for recruits. The mines were full of talk of permanent nationalization, managed, as the Miners' Federation's secretary imagined it, through a joint council of workers and technical experts. The railway workers were talking of squeezing the prewar managers out altogether and vesting control in a board split between representatives of workers and the public. Guild socialists like G. D. H. Cole dreamed of "dishing the state" and building a point-of-production based economic democracy on its ruins. Shop steward radicals were talking of the establishment of British soviets.[55]

The rival utopias in the air swept the Labour Party along with them. The party's famous reconstruction document of early 1918, *Labour and the New Social Order*, was never quite the foundation text American progressives took it to be. Both its primary authors had been men on the party's margins throughout most of the war—Ramsay MacDonald isolated by his war pacifism, Sidney Webb self-marginalized by his never well disguised contempt for the dullness of the labor leadership. But to the broader world, *Labour and the New Social Order* carried an inspirational, rhetorical magic that set it altogether apart from the official reconstruction documents. The old order, the old individualistic system of capitalist production—indeed the whole "civilization" erected on its basis—was dead, it declared: a casualty of the war. No amount of reconstruction "patchwork" would bring it back. In its place, Labour proposed to build "a new social order, based not on fighting but on fraternity; not on the competitive struggle for the means of bare life, but on a deliberately planned co-operation in production and distribution for the benefit of all who participate by hand or by brain."[56]

Of the four "pillars" of the new social order, two were distinctly Webbsian ideas: a one-time massive "levy" on capital so that the common folk would not be stuck with the costs of the war, and a "universal national minimum," the Webbs' catchphrase for a guaranteed floor under work, wages, health, and working standards. The third was the old radical share-the-wealth slogan: "the surplus for the common good." The last, pitched in the terms erupting from the pithead and shop floor, was "the democratic control of industry"—immediately through the nationalization of Britain's railways, mines, and electrical supply, and, more generally, through "the widest possible participation in power, both economic and political, which is characteristic of democracy." The new social order, Webb and MacDonald promised, would not be one based, like the old, on narrow "class" interests; it would be "a common house," dedicated to the "common good," home for "every grade and section of producers by hand or by brain."[57]

Reduced to specifics, the reconstruction platform the Labour Party actually adopted in June 1918 looked a lot more like a committee-made assemblage of pieces than a "house" or a "social order." The metaphors were pruned back. Webb's talk of universal minima, too reminiscent of the poorhouse for most of the delegates, was set aside for a more orthodox wages-and-hours plank. But the party platform also pledged that labor would not be content with postwar "patchwork."[58] As for the promise to be a party of "hand and brain," the party made good by opening up membership not simply to its constituent unions and pressure groups but to individuals as well. Radicalized by the war, the consumers' cooperatives were already rapidly moving into a de facto labor alliance.[59]

In all these ways, in organizing and politicizing the economy, the war galvanized the working class, firing its imagination with reconstruction visions far more molten than Lloyd George had any intent of accepting. When the radical American journalist Mary Heaton Vorse reached Britain in November 1918, she found that

> wherever you went, whether in the London Workers' Committee, or in the Federation of Women Workers, this talk of a new England was forever with you. You could not for a moment get out of earshot of this demand. Talk flowed up and down England. It swept into the homes of working people, through the shop committees and the workers' committees, from the Guild Socialists, to the trade unions, and to the Women's Co-operative Guild, over to the study classes of the Welsh miners. There was everywhere a ferment, everywhere a demand for a new world.[60]

In the inevitable collision of ambitions that ensued in 1919, strikes set the pace. The British government's carefully laid plans for gradual demobilization of the army so as to dovetail men with jobs and avert the massive unemployment the Reconstruction Ministry planners feared would otherwise result, were scotched after a massive soldiers' demonstration in January. A shutdown of the mines in February was averted only by appointment of a special commission of inquiry—half its members nominated by the mine owners, half (Sidney Webb and R. H. Tawney among them) by the Miners' Federation. That spring the commission conducted an extraordinary public trial of the relative merits of private ownership and permanent nationalization, in full view and with a stream of rival witnesses. An equally unprecedented gesture was the summoning of a nationwide Industrial Conference in February, a massive gathering of some six hundred business, labor, and government representatives—a kind of economic parliament in embryo, it seemed to some of the guild socialists—to try to work out the terms of a postwar social contract for industry.[61] But none of this stopped the strikes from escalating or new recruits (almost a million and a half in 1919 alone) from rushing into the unions.

Under these combined pressures, the government turned all the more to the politics of rewards. An emergency unemployment benefit was piggybacked onto the existing unemployment insurance scheme to tide soldiers past the initial strains of demobilization. Land in the empire was promised to returned soldiers who wanted to farm it. Most important, a pledge to replace the slums with decent housing was catapulted to the fore of the reconstruction agenda and pushed through on generous financial terms that (like those of the unemployment benefit) the government planners would later regret. Publicly Lloyd George talked about houses: homes "fit for heroes" with gardens, baths, perhaps even a parlor. Privately he talked about revolution. Even if the housing program should "cost a hundred million pounds, what was that compared to the stability of the state?" he urged the cabinet.[62]

The disposition of the war-nationalized industries was a far harder nut to crack. Labor was committed to permanent nationalization, businessmen to immediate restoration of the antebellum status quo, the government planners uncertain and divided. In early 1920, Arthur Greenwood, formerly of the Reconstruction Committee staff, still thought that nationalization of coal and the liquor trade was imminent and railroads, shipping, and banking not far off.[63] But the forces moving in the other direction were stronger: the specter of Bolshevism, which Lloyd George had begun to manipulate with increasing calculation and skill; the Conservative drift at the polls; and the eagerness of investors and businessmen to get industry in shape for the international competition they anticipated at the war's end. Rejecting the coal commission's narrow decision for nationalization, the government offered instead a scheme of regionally reorganized coal companies, with union representation on their boards of directors. A similar measure was proposed for the railroads. Step by step, the rest of the war economic controls were dismantled. The key war economy departments, mere shells of their wartime selves to be sure, were finally dismantled in 1921. The hopes of the Industrial Conference's planners for a permanent labor-management council fell apart in 1921 with labor's withdrawal.[64]

By the time miners finally struck in earnest in 1921, with the economy sliding into recession and employers cutting wages and payrolls, it was too late to reverse the trend of events. The utopian mood of the war, the heady sense of embarking on an "entirely new epoch," as William Dawson had put it, of building the materials of war collectivism into a "new social order," was spent. "What this Government will not do," the new prime minister, Stanley Baldwin, announced, "is to attempt to control the industries of the country."[65]

But it had been a bumpy road down, and for all Baldwin's talk of restoration, it left British social politics permanently changed. The emergency unemployment benefits of 1920 were to remain a key fixture of postwar Britain into the Depression of the 1930s. The wartime housing program endured as well (despite periodic Conservative shutdowns), slowly spreading across the landscape a new Britain of public, working-class "council" houses. Not the least, the war's transformation of labor politics endured, not only in the pent up anger that would fuel the General Strike of 1926 but, still more, in the war's propulsion of the Labour Party past labor's long-standing suspicion of the do-gooding state into the mainstream of British social politics.

The details were English, but, in the last regard, the trend was general. Whether in Germany, where the Social Democrats had unexpectedly inherited the state they had so long distrusted, or in France, where they remained on the margins of governmental power, the boundaries between social-democratic and progressive politics had been profoundly changed by the war. Throughout Europe, labor politics was now alive with talk not only of works councils and joint control, but also of social insurance, housing, planning, and economic regulation—all the issues of "bourgeois" social politics from which orthodox socialists had once kept their distance. In this respect the war's experiment in emergency economic collectivism, the jerry-built structures of the social peace, the heady talk of reconstruction, even the punctured utopias of 1919, all had lasting consequences.

On the western rim of the North Atlantic economy, the same arc and fall of end-of-the-war hopes occurred. In the United States as in Europe, reconstruction ambitions burst out of the war to collide with a war-radicalized labor movement and with employers eager to bring the state of industry back as quickly as possible to prewar conditions of "normalcy." The specifics were American, but the setting, consciousness, and influences were, to a marked extent, international.

The key model abroad was Britain. Wartime and postwar Germany were hidden behind a fog of propaganda; French reportage was overwhelmed by military events. American progressives followed British reconstruction news, however, with intense interest. The *Survey* began printing summaries of the British Reconstruction Ministry reports as soon as it could obtain them. The Whitley commission's proposal for a broad array of joint worker-management councils, dovetailing as it did with the intensifying need for labor adjustment machinery and vague, morale-aimed talk of bringing the war ideals of democracy into industry, attracted widespread American attention. The *New Republic* commissioned a description of the British scheme in the fall of 1917, pointing up the contrast between the Whitley idea and "the smouldering hostility" that characterized labor relations at home. "They are far ahead of America," the editors could not resist adding—though by the end of 1918, with the imposition of more than a hundred Whitley-inspired shop committees throughout the American war industries, the war labor arbitrators had done a good deal to narrow the gap.[66]

Of all the British reconstruction proposals, *Labour and the New Social Order* made the biggest American splash. Billing it as "probably the most mature and carefully formulated programme ever put forth by a responsible political party," the *New Republic* ran it in full as a special supplement. The *Survey*, having missed the boat in February 1918, printed the entire text of the Labour Party's reconstruction platform in August. The United Mine Workers' *Journal* republished *Labour and the New Social Order;* the California State Federation of Labor copied large portions of it into its resolutions in the fall of 1918. In the White House, President Wilson's secretary, Joseph Tumulty, made sure the president saw a copy; when Wilson began inserting mention of the coming "political and economic reconstruction" into his speeches that spring, Tumulty urged him to be still bolder. California progressive Meyer Lissner wrote Theodore Roosevelt that it was "the most inspiring and suggestive piece of political writing published in many a year." The *New Statesman*'s conclusion that "after the arrival . . . of *Labour and the New Social Order*, there seemed to be hardly a club or association, college, church, or forum, at least in the Eastern and Middle Western States, which had not been stimulated to enquire into what organized Labour in Great Britain was thinking and planning," had its self-serving side. But it harbored a germ of truth.[67]

Why the American progressives should have plucked *Labour and the New Social Order* out of the haystack of British wartime manifestos and vested in it so many hopes of their own is not altogether easily explained. The document's commitment to an outright socialist program, pledged to the "elimination" of private capitalists from the control of industry and nationalization of much of it, was no asset in American progressive circles.

Herbert Croly had promised contributors at the *New Republic*'s launching that the journal would be "radical without being socialist." Kellogg's settlement house and social work audience was not, in the standard political sense, radical at all. Among those unmoved by *Labour and the New Social Order* was Theodore Roosevelt, who retorted to Lissner that its "five to ten percent pure communism" contaminated it in the way a drop of sewage polluted a spring. The *New Republic*'s worries that the "timidities and tepidity of American progressivism" would stand in the way of taking the manifesto's true measure were not ungrounded.[68]

Where American progressives were straining so hard to believe in the war's transforming effects, however, Webb's and MacDonald's decision to subordinate details to metaphors of historical transfiguration gave *Labour and the New Social Order* a major advantage over its grayer, official rivals. The British document promised what American progressives most wanted to hear: reaffirmation that the old order was played out—"beyond repair," as the *New Republic*'s editors put it—and that the war's social gains could not be turned back. The transatlantic progressive connection had never been a particularly finely tuned instrument for party distinctions. Blending in with the general reconstruction talk, *Labour and the New Social Order* offered American progressives what they half scorned and half adored in Wilson: a vauntingly idealistic promise of a new society. From 1918 on, talk of a "new social order" in the wake of the war was ubiquitous in American progressive assessments of the conflict. "Capitalism will not come back unchallenged and uncontrolled," the *Survey* was certain by fall. "The new social order is coming," Will Durant wrote in the *Dial* in June 1918, "and that is all there is to it."[69]

This absorption of the terms of British political debate, carried across the progressive Atlantic connection, helps explain why by late 191[illegible]—barely more than a year into the war, with only a tiny fraction of the sacrifices the war had exacted in Britain, with the labor peace and the early patriotic mood still intact, with no urgent need (as yet) to shore up flagging war morale with postwar promises, and with business turning out war goods at a rate that seemed to evidence anything but the collapse of capitalism—the United States should have been awash in reconstruction plans, more than even Britain itself. Wilson offered the phenomenon no leadership. When the first British reconstruction committee reports began to filter across the Atlantic, Wilson told proponents of reconstruction planning for the United States that it was too early to consider such measures. When the armistice suddenly came, in November 1918, he told reconstruction committee proponents that it was far too late. In the first months after publication of *Labour and the New Social Order*, he had talked abstractly of the coming reconstruction, but by his annual message to Congress in December 1918 he had backed to down to simple "readjustment." Even here, with his mind absorbed in international affairs, he had little to recommend. "I have no confident judgment of my own," he told the Congress. "The process of return to a peace footing . . . promises to outrun any inquiry that may be instituted and any aid that may be offered. It will not be easy to direct it any better than it will direct itself."[70]

Unguided from the top, the reconstruction enthusiasm seemed to burst from the pores of society itself, fueled by its half-borrowed idealism, clothed in half-borrowed language. By armistice, Frank Walsh wrote, the United States was in the teeth of "a perfect hurricane of reconstruction conferences and plans, projected by every group imaginable, highbrow, reactionary, labor and every other hand." Between November 1918 and mid-1919, the American Federation of Labor, the U.S. Chamber of Commerce, the Federal Council of Churches, the National Catholic War Council, the Women's Trade Union League, social workers, farmers, and state federations of labor all cobbled together reconstruction programs. Six states established official Reconstruction Commissions. The *Dial* boasted a reconstruction program of its own, coordinated by John Dewey, Helen Marot, and Thorstein Veblen. William Jennings Bryan's *Commoner* published a reconstruction program as well. The *Survey*, which had been reprinting British reconstruction reports in a special reconstruction pamphlet series since the fall of 1918, now dedicated the first number of each month to reconstruction issues. At the *Journal of the American Institute of Architects*, in the borrowed rhetoric of British guild socialism, Charles H. Whitaker was calling for an architecture and a social order "beyond industrialism." The pro-war socialists launched a wholly new journal in January entitled *Reconstruction: A Herald of the New Time*. There were "twenty different kinds of heaven being offered in the streets in 1919," Lewis Mumford later remembered the moment. The *New Republic*'s editors unconsciously fell back on Lloyd George's phrases: "Our society today is as fluid as molten iron; it can be run into any mold."[71]

Into the new reconstruction vessels a lot of old wine was poured; but the quickness with which American progressives beat their way to England in early 1919—as if their own future were to be found there—was a particularly striking sign of the international reach of the reconstruction movement. As early as July the *Survey*'s special English correspondent, Arthur

Gleason, was objecting to "the nuisance of shoals of American commissions of investigation, committees, special delegates, who, in succession, trample the same green grass till it is pulpy." Jane Addams, Walter Weyl, and Gleason himself all turned up at the coal commission hearings in early 1919. The *Nation*'s Oswald Garrison Villard sailed for England after the armistice. So did Hull House veterans Julia Lathrop and Grace Abbott, to investigate child welfare measures for the U.S. Children's Bureau; Charles H. Whitaker, as a special Department of Labor agent studying guild socialism in the British building trades; Mary McDowell, to look at British public housing; and the AALL's John B. Andrews, for a first-hand look at British experience with public health insurance. The U.S. Department of Labor, the National Civic Federation, and the National Industrial Conference Board all sent rival delegations of employers to study British industrial relations. The National Civic Federation dispatched yet another delegation to try to settle the health insurance issue.[72]

No more than before the war did the investigators agree on what there was to be found, or how it should bear on policy at home. The employer group organized by the U.S. secretary of labor in January reported that union-based collective bargaining worked in Britain; indeed, beneath the "seething unrest," it was the most hopeful force tending toward stability. The National Civic Federation's delegation, which sailed in February, concluded that there was nothing to be learned from Britain at all. The National Industrial Conference Board's delegation in March reported that Britain was on the road toward outright Bolshevism, with the employers caving in to demands for joint control and the government lacking the political will to resist the rising tide of labor. A whole vocabulary of "catchwords and slogans, such as 'nationalization,' 'collective bargaining,' 'democratization of industry,' of wide appeal but of vague and uncertain import" had been released, it reported—"protean phrases" that, "especially at this time of violent agitation, or widespread discontent, both industrial and political, are particularly dangerous."[73]

In this bedlam of conflicting ambitions and rival utopias, in the ubiquitous reconstruction talk of a "new era," a "new order," a "new world, whose doors the war is breaking open," the imported British elements played only a part.[74] The collectivist experience of the war, the messianic strain in American progressive politics, the fad that, for the moment, tied the tag of "reconstruction" around every interest group's agenda, all figured in the event. But just as the war was an international event, so, overflowing the nation-state containers, was the international outwash of postwar ambitions.

In the riot of American reconstruction plans broached in the first six months after the armistice, no thread was more common than the hope of carrying over into the peace one or another aspect of the war economy. The social workers in November called for perpetuation of the wartime public employment service, completion of the war housing projects, and elaboration of the soldiers' and sailors' insurance into a full-scale social insurance system. Church groups were eager to extend the wartime minimum wage idea and expand the machinery of industrial peace that the war labor adjusters had put in place. The civic reformers in the National Municipal League recommended preserving the core functions of the War Industries Board to "hold the ground we have gained during the war." More surprising, still, was the league's recommendation that the war-nationalized railroads and telegraph and telephone services remain in federal hands, or if they were returned to private investors, that this be done only after the "speculative and anti-social features of the private ownership of the past" had been removed. The California progressive Hiram Johnson thought it was "no longer debatable" that the railroads should stay in the government's possession.[75]

In the Wilson administration there were some who shared the belief that the emergency collectivism of the war could not simply be dismantled. After the Republican electoral victory in November 1918, Joseph Tumulty had quickly backed down from his earlier suggestion for permanent public administration of the railroads, but in its place he pressed on Wilson a program very like Lloyd George's: old-age pensions, health insurance, a federal minimum wage and maximum hours act, a government housing program, "control" of basic raw materials, federal recognition of the right of collective bargaining, permanent federal disputes machinery along the lines of the War Labor Board, maintenance of the federal employment service, and a national industrial conference, based on the British model, to work out improved industrial relations—perhaps on lines "similar to the Whitley programme." "The real antidote for Bolshevism is social reconstruction," he wrote in an echo of Lloyd George's idiom. Wilson's postmaster general went public with a plan for permanent government ownership of the telegraph and telephone systems. William McAdoo at the Railroad Administration proposed a five-year extension of federal railway management. Harry Garfield of the Fuel Administration proposed establishment of a peacetime fuel commission composed of labor, operator, and public representatives, to mediate disputes in the coal industry.[76]

As strong as these parallels between British and American reconstruction ambitions ran, however, there were critical differences. Some of them started at the top, with Wilson. Between his wartime leadership and Lloyd George's there been much in common. In British parlance, both were "lib-lab" politicians: progressives with broad labor backing. Reelected in 1916 with active AFL support, Wilson had gone into the war with what was as close to a formal labor alliance as any American president had had before him.[77] But Wilson chose to preside over his labor-progressive alliance in every regard except in his own mind. Where other American progressives discovered, via Britain, a new interest in labor politics, where Lloyd George labored to buy working-class voters back into the Liberal coalition, postwar policy making bought out the universalistic, classless progressive rhetoric in Wilson.

Lloyd George tried to ride the reconstruction whirlwind for his own advantage; Wilson, in contrast, both feared it and disdained to go near it, eschewing Lloyd George's politics of postwar social promises for a project of extraordinary international reconstruction abroad and something close to abdication at home. Had Theodore Roosevelt presided over the war government, as he had lusted so painfully to do, the train of events might have turned out differently; but Wilson, distracted and in Paris for the first six months of 1919, could not shake his sense of having presided over a temporary wartime aberration, the more quickly dismantled the better.

Thus, leaderless at the top and without well-rooted state structures to maintain them, the war collectivist agencies began melting away almost overnight. Harry Laidler of the Intercollegiate Socialist Society visited Washington in January 1919, his head full of reconstruction schemes. The first friend he talked to in the administration told him differently: "There ain't going to be no reconstruction." Outside of Franklin Lane's Interior Department, where staffers were deep in plans for a massive soldier resettlement program on federal reclamation land, the war agencies were packing up as fast as possible.[78] The War Labor Board recommended its own dissolution in early December. Most work on the war housing projects ceased with the armistice. The finished projects were sold off, at a loss, to private investors and the rest abandoned. The Food and Fuel Administrations were dissolved in June. The railroads remained in government control until early 1920, but McAdoo himself had returned to a more lucrative job in private industry within two months of the armistice. The war had not lasted long enough to create a sense of its own normalcy or a cadre of managers committed to its operations. The administrators on wartime loan decamped for their business undertakings; the desks were barely in place when their occupants began to empty out. Under the circumstances, no amount of extragovernmental reconstruction ferment could stem the collapse of the emergency government agencies of the war.[79]

Ultimately it was not the progressives' paper plans but labor that brought the Wilson administration back into action. Emboldened by wartime collective bargaining, radicalized by events abroad, organized labor began the year in a militantly optimistic mood. As in Britain, issues of workers' control spilled out of the wartime politicization of the economy. The United Mine Workers, some of its key leaders caught up by the British example, called for nationalization of the coal industry, labor comanagement of coal operations, and independent labor politics. The railroad unions, in a widely circulated plan drafted by labor lawyer Glenn Plumb, proposed nationalization of the railroads and their operation by a tripartite labor, management, and public board. Nationalization planks were a dime a dozen in state labor federation resolves. The miner's and railroad workers' unions made motions toward a strike alliance in explicit imitation of the British "triple alliance" of miners, dockers, and railway workers. Gompers and the AFL's craft-union leadership labored hard against the tide, dragging their feet on the creation of an AFL reconstruction committee, insisting on the superiority of old-fashioned trade unionism to the new-style talk of labor comanagement, and explaining to anyone who would listen that British labor's new political departure wouldn't last long. But even the AFL was swept up by the expectations of 1919, bolting from Gompers's leadership at its 1920 convention to endorse the Plumb Plan.[80]

Still closer to the ground, the twelve months after the armistice brought a cascade of strikes, more intense than in any previous period in the nation's history. There were ground-shaking industrial battles in coal, textiles, clothing, shipping, and steel, for pay raises and shorter hours, for normalization of the emergency gains the war administrators had awarded, and for conversion of the emergency representation systems of the war into outright union bargaining rights. All told, some four million workers walked out in 1919. In only one other year of the twentieth century, 1946, were there to be more.

Where in the face of similar forces Lloyd George promised, blustered, and maneuvered, it was not until the fall of 1919, after almost a year of strikes, that the Wilson administration moved to shore up the broken social peace. In the face of a walkout in the steel industry, the administration called a special Industrial Conference, an explicit reenactment of the conference that in February had papered over labor relations in Britain. The conference brought some sixty employers, AFL-nominated union representatives, and administration-chosen representatives of the public to Washington, D.C., in early October. Wilson gave the conference no agenda, assuming that the wartime cooperation of interests would somehow naturally be reestablished. But where the British conferees kept at it for almost two and a half years, the American conference broke utterly apart after two weeks. The AFL delegates, intent on capitalizing on the temporary gains of the war, insisted on the principle of union-based collective bargaining. The employers were adamant on their right to bargain with whichever employees' representatives they chose to recognize. The "public" group, stocked with welfare capitalists, proposed a form of Whitleyism. The common ground of bargaining and negotiation that British labor unionists and employers had gradually cleared over the course of the late nineteenth century was not to be located in the United States. Everything came down to the question of the labor unions' place at the tables of the peacetime economy, and broke upon it.[81]

In the impasse, labor walked out. A second conference of "public" representatives, hastily convened to pick up the pieces, proposed a system of labor dispute mediation boards akin to the British Industrial Courts Act of 1919.[82] By then, however, the miners had joined the steelworkers on strike. The Wilson administration, reactivating the wartime coal controls it had been so eager to dismantle, suppressed the coal strike with as sweeping an injunction as the prewar courts had ever delivered. The repressive legal machinery built during the war was turned with a vengeance against alien labor radicals. In these repolarized circumstances, the agencies of public labor mediation, borrowed for the emergency from Europe, collapsed. The tripartite Railroad Labor Board, established in 1920 to rule on wages and working conditions, fell apart a year later when its management and public representatives combined to abrogate the railroad shop workers' union agreements. The most widely publicized American innovation in labor arbitration machinery, the Kansas Court of Industrial Relations, launched (its author boasted) as a "complete departure" from foreign principles, began by declaring strikes, boycotts, picketing, and work stoppages illegal under every circumstance, in all the state's essential industries.[83]

With the collapse of effective public machinery, the initiative fell back on employers. Even before the failure of the Industrial Conference, they had begun to gear up a new "open shop" drive to roll back the war-generated growth of unions. The prestige of Whitleyism, shorn of the relations to organized labor that the Whitley commission had given it in Britain, and the rhetoric of "industrial democracy" were appropriated for an "American plan" of company-controlled employee representation systems. Under the employers' counteroffensive, the wartime organizing drive in steel collapsed, and the nationalization movement slowly fizzled out in coal. The railroad unions, faced with a bill in Congress that would have stripped them of their right to strike, were forced from the high ground of the Plumb Plan. By 1923 union membership had fallen by almost one-third from its postwar high-water mark, under the combined pressures of the employers' counteroffensive and the postwar recession, which had set in a serious way by the end of 1920.[84]

Finally, to the forces of reaction the "red scare" lent its weight with peculiarly American ferocity. Just as the contagion of revolutionary ideas was worldwide in the years from 1917 to 1920, so was the frightened reaction to it. Lloyd George had begun to play hard on fears of Bolshevism in late 1919, fuming about the "small but active body of men who wrought tirelessly and insidiously to exploit the labour organizations of this country for subversive ends." By the end of 1920, with threat of a general strike in the air, Lloyd George had won an emergency powers act of extraordinary scope from Parliament that when the threatened general strike finally came in 1926, gave the government all the suppressive power it needed.[85]

On the western edge of the North Atlantic economy, the Americans might have been expected to have been shaken far less by the revolutions in eastern and central Europe. But with its immigrant working class, which not even the reddest Scots machinist could match as a lightening rod for conservative political anxieties, American politics was, in fact, shaken far more. In 1919's eruption of antiforeign and antiradical feeling, progressive projects that too plainly showed their foreign borrowings suddenly found themselves extremely vulnerable. The New York State legislature's committee on seditious activities spread its label of "pacifist and defeatist organizations" over the *Survey*, the *Nation*, the radical unions, and the settlement house crowd. The *New York Times* attacked the Plumb Plan as "a very large step toward the principles of Lenin and Trotzky." Walter Lippmann wrote in anger in November 1919: "At this moment the man who in domestic policy stands about where Theodore Roosevelt stood in 1912 and in foreign affairs where Woodrow Wilson stood when he first landed in Paris, and in his doctrine of toleration where John Milton stood two and a half centuries ago, is certain, absolutely certain to be called pacifist, pro-German and Bolshevist."[86]

Health insurance, where heavy economic interests were already arrayed in opposition, was among the conspicuous casualties. At the outbreak of the war, health insurance's advocates had quickly scrambled to stave off accusations of "Prussianism" by shifting their precedents from Germany to allied Britain. But against addition of the "Bolshevist" tag to the "made in Germany" propaganda and the branding of health insurance as a form of socialistic "state medicine," the gesture barely made a dent. The AALL kept up its health insurance campaign through 1921, beating in vain, as John Andrews put it, against the "tide of extreme reaction that set in with the armistice." Rubinow had abandoned the fight in late 1919 to direct a medical mission in Palestine.[87]

So intense the hopes, so sharp the fall. Differences in preexisting norms for labor-capital relations, the differing play of the Bolshevist card, different state structures, and different leadership at the top all made the downward arc in the United States steeper than in Britain. Yet even in America the end of the war did not mark a simple return to the status quo ante. Like swirls of mud and gravel from a receding flood, the war's collectivist experiments left a jumble of residues. The hallmark of 1920s labor relations, the formalized company representation plan, was a direct war legacy. Herbert Hoover brought his war experience with state-facilitated business cooperation into the core of the Republican Party project of the 1920s. Still later, memories of the wartime collectivist economy would play a key part in the New Deal. The trajectory from wartime collectivist utopianism, through exaggerated reconstruction promise, down to some heavily compromised residual effect was international. Even those who had insisted all along that the Americans stood providentially apart were pulled into a variant on this international postwar dynamic, as into the war itself, by the transatlantic connections.

Of the international residues of the war, one more remains to be examined. For some American progressives in 1918 there had been more to *Labour and the New Social Order* than simply a generalized promise of economic and social reconstruction. In the workers "of hand and brain" formula, they saw the announcement of a radically new kind of political party: a labor party, speaking the language of idealism and the common good, with room for intellectuals like Webb and MacDonald within it; or, to reverse the terms, an intellectual party empowered by the mass strength of working-class voters. "The indispensable political task of liberal America in the near future," the *New Republic*'s editors wrote to lead off their republication of *Labour and the New Social Order*, "is that of promoting the organization of American workers for the comparable exercise of political power . . . on a programme, the more radical the better, of constitutional agitation."[88]

The idea of a political union of brain and muscle workers was, by and large, new to American progressives. On a number of issues—the municipalization fights and the workmen's compensation movement among them—progressive reformers had labored in a common yoke with labor union leaders. But it had not been an easy alliance, hindered on the one side by a scarcely veiled contempt for the narrow group interests of the labor leadership and on the other by labor unionists' sense that the progressives had more of their heart in social peace (and in their own status as expert arbiters of that peace) than in the tangible, material claims of workers. In this sense the war marked a shift, tentative and incomplete, in the progressives' relationship to the working class, an offer of alliance on terms that anticipated and helped prepare the way for the New Deal. To these visions of a new-style labor-progressive alliance there were several roads. But one of the broadest and most important for Americans ran through England.

As with so many other Atlantic connections, the American progressives discovered a usable political model in the British Labour Party not all at once but in bits and pieces. The *New Republic*'s discovery of it was helped by the magazine's English contributors, many of whom were themselves in the process of shifting their footing from the Liberal Party toward Labour under the pressure of wartime events.[89] The *Nation*'s conversion ran, in contrast, through war doubts. The *Nation*'s owner and editor, Oswald Garrison Villard, had been no economic radical at the war's outset. He had groped his way through the election of 1912 looking for a candidate who would take the country back to the paths of Grover Cleveland; he had chided the prewar *Survey* for its excessive sympathy toward labor. But Villard's wartime pacifism brought the *Nation* up hard against the censoring hand of the state, brought a new cast of radicals into the *Nation*'s staff, and threw Villard himself into contact with the antiwar British left. When the British Labour Party, restless with a seemingly endless war, patched up its relationship with its antiwar minority and published an appeal for articulated peace aims in December 1917, the event made a deep impression on Villard. Traveling to England in the weeks after the armistice, Villard sought out the architects of the British workingmen's "people's peace," Ramsay MacDonald (Villard's political "ideal") and the "saintly" George Lansbury. By 1919, his prewar attitudes toward labor transformed, Villard was eager for a political realignment at home that would be capable of bringing the democratic forces of intellect and labor together in a British-style alliance.[90]

Among the progressive editors, Paul Kellogg came closest of all to sensing the British ferment at its source. Eager to see the relief and social work of the American Red Cross in France, he had sailed to Europe in the summer of 1917. Unlike Villard, Kellogg was not a pacifist; he had resigned from the American Union against Militarism after the American war declaration, lest foreign policy differences tear his subscribers apart. But there is no missing Kellogg's distress at the war's brutalities and his anxiety that the catastrophe should pay off in compensatory social gains. Shaken by what he saw in France and hungry for more inspiring labor than the Red Cross's Band-Aid work, he was "desperately lonely" in Europe, he recalled. Crossing to England in January 1918, he attended the Nottingham conference of the Labour Party and was, to his surprise, swept away by the war aims debate. Here, Kellogg thought, was Woodrow Wilson's idealism, Wilson's dream of a democratic and nonimperialistic peace, spoken in the accents of ordinary British workingmen. The British labor movement, he wrote Felix Frankfurter in the spring, was "the freest force in all Europe today, and the one most to be counted upon in paralleling the free statesmanship of the President." The real Wilsonians, Ray Stannard Baker concluded from his own British trip that same year, and in much the same tone, were not in the governments but in the working class; "the Labor party to-day is about the best thing in British public life."[91]

Labour and the New Social Order did not at first inspire Kellogg. Its nationalization planks were, he was sure, already out of touch with grassroots labor's desire to devolve and democratize economic control. From this starting point, however, Kellogg quickly moved to a deeper admiration for labor's domestic program. The British labor movement is "different at once from the old-time trade unionism or from the old-time class conscious socialism," he was writing by April 1918. It was a movement "organic" and "democratic," dedicated to carrying over the "communal features of wartime nationalism" without the war's regimentation and invasion of individual liberty.[92]

Kellogg's rapidly widening admiration for the British labor movement was encouraged by the man who guided him through England in early 1918 and eventually became the *Survey*'s ambassador to the British labor movement, Arthur Gleason. Gleason's was as pure an example as the times afforded of the fervor the war could inspire and how quickly that inspiration could be displaced onto labor when the war governments failed to mirror it. A quiet, intense, and intensely idealistic journalist who had gone from Yale into New York magazine work as a writer of fancy "prose poems," Gleason was in England working up a set of literary sketches of English life when the war broke out in 1914. Rushing to the front as an ambulance unit volunteer, he was immediately caught up in the Allied war cause. He testified on German war crimes before Britain's official Atrocities Committee, beat the drums for war in the American magazines, and, when the first American soldiers finally reached Europe, lectured them on war aims. His *Inside the British Isles*, published serially in the New York *Tribune* in 1917, was a glowing description of Britain's economic and social galvanization by the war, designed to stoke the interventionist cause among progressives at home.[93]

The Labour Party was on the side-lines of war-socialized Britain, as Gleason saw in early 1917. "It would be flattering to write that it is by labor that the constructive thinking is being done, but it would be untrue." The labor movement's turmoil he likened to "the muddle of a helpless creature caught unawares in a tidal wave;" its leadership was without a constructive program or a synthetic plan of reconstruction, its rank and file "uneducated" and "unimaginative." Gleason's contacts with labor issues in early 1917 came through Seebohm Rowntree and the welfare industrialists; his political heroes were Alfred Zimmern of the Reconstruction Committee and the social imperialists in the *Round Table* circle. From this perspective British labor seemed barely to have begun to think the issues out.[94]

By the time Kellogg reached England in early 1918, however, Gleason's idealism was rapidly being displaced onto the British labor movement in a translation of political ambitions that would take him deep into the movement for workers' control. The awakening of the British Labour Party from its trade union preoccupations at the end of 1917, its reorganization as a genuine political party, not merely a political committee of allied unions, and its appropriation of the rhetoric of democracy from a government mired in the war's mechanics all helped move Gleason into the Labour Party's orbit. In the face of the war state's swelling appetite for power, labor's project of devolved yet socialized control sounded a powerfully clarifying note for Gleason.

Enlisted as the *Survey*'s special correspondent on British social politics, Gleason worked his new material into a second book, *British Labor and the War*, jointly written with Paul Kellogg—a compound of Kellogg's yearning for a democratic, people's peace and Gleason's growing interest in the terms of industrial democracy.[95] By early 1919, with a *Survey* stipend in his pocket, Gleason was back in England again as the journal's correspondent to the new world in the making. He hunted up Rowntree once more and dutifully sent back an article on the Whitley councils, but the real news, he was sure, was in the shop stewards' movement, the miners' case for nationalization, and the burgeoning forces for workers' control. "The Government activities in Housing, Land Settlement, Emigration, Education, can not be compared" with the grassroots stirrings of labor, "because they are schemes and programs, not a movement of human beings," he wrote Kellogg. Even Sidney Webb, with his dreams of efficiently organized power disbursed through disinterested public administrators, barely knew which way the tide was running.[96]

By mid-1919 Gleason was sure that history's drift was toward some kind of socialism from below, coal pit and factory centered, a "revolution without philosophy," inchoate and instinctive. "Whitehall bureaucracy is mitigated by local government, just as State Socialism is mitigated by workers' control. As executive power grows, devolute it. It is the British balance . . . Step by step, piece-meal, detailed, but workable. No tidy French finalities, no doctrinaire Philosophies, no German centralization of machinery." And no American "hysteria." He tried again to describe the tidal movement he sensed: "functional representation, industrial unionism, producers' share in control, pluralistic sovereignties . . . The whole recent impulse and forward thrust of labor is in it."[97]

All this Gleason poured back to the *Survey* offices during the heady months of mid-1919. Under intense pressure from the older social work establishment, Kellogg cut back Gleason's articles severely, though always with apology. On Gleason's proposal that the *Survey* and *New Republic* cooperate in establishing a permanent publishing outlet for the British labor movement in the United States, Kellogg temporized. But in fact, by the end of 1918, the two men had already pulled the *Survey* into an unabashed alliance with the "new England" in the making from below.

Part of what drew Americans like Villard, Kellogg, and Gleason to the British labor movement was their ability to see in it what was much harder for them to see in the strange faces and accents of the immigrant-dominated labor movement at home: a working class with an idealistic heart and, still more, a thinking head. Set against Samuel Gompers's fulminations against "intellectuals" who meddled in the labor movement, set against Gompers's cresting feud with the AALL over social insurance, or set against what progressives saw as labor's insistence on trade union time-serving as the key qualification for Labor Department appointments, the open invitation in *Labour and the New Social Order* to workers of hand *and* brain was, in its own right, electrifying.

Eager for evidence of a labor movement that was not only thinking but also willing to take its thinking from others, the Americans hunted up every scrap of evidence of British working-class intellectualism they could find. The Labour Party's Fabian Society connection, the leading presence in the party of journalists like MacDonald and Lansbury, the coal miners' choice of an Oxford don as one of their representatives on the coal commission, and the ability of pure "brain workers" like Sidney Webb or G. D. H. Cole to work their way into the movement's inner circles all played into this account.

Out of the same impulses, they fell eagerly on the labor movement's educational arm, the Workers' Educational Association. Ray Stannard Baker, on meeting Albert Mansbridge, the cooperative-society clerk who had founded the association, was desperate to bring him back to the United States. Mansbridge's alliance of Oxford tutors (with Alfred Zimmern, G. D. H. Cole, and R. H. Tawney among the veterans), public funds, and intellectually starved skilled workers, all brought together for a year's study of economic and labor issues, seemed to many American progressives to represent everything that was absent in the strained and distrustful relations between workers and intellectuals in America. American representations of the British labor movement after 1918 regularly described it as a house built on four pillars: the unions, the parliamentary Labour Party, the cooperative movement, and the workers' education movement. No matter that by any realistic head count the last pillar was a mere toothpick in comparison to the others. Baker wrote that the "unity of workmen and scholars" was one of the most inspiring things to be found in wartime Britain; Gleason was to teach two classes at the Labour College, the Workers' Educational Association's more radical rival, in the winter of 1919.[98]

Talking about Britain, they were all thinking about America, of course. The subject might be British labor, but the core text was Gompers, Wilson, and the future of progressive politics in the United States. In that context the struggle to shape the meaning of British labor politics could not but open up political fissures at home. Kellogg had barely returned from Britain in the spring of 1918 before Gompers challenged him to a public debate before a stridently prowar National Civic Federation audience. William English Walling, speaking for the prowar minority socialists, smeared

Kellogg's reporting as "pro-German pacifist propaganda." To the cheers and delight of the listening businessmen, Gompers lambasted the "officious intelligentsia," the *Survey–New Republic*–Sidney Webb crowd, who thought they knew what American workers wanted better than they themselves did.[99]

Gompers and Walling were already deep in an effort—precisely at cross purposes to Kellogg, Baker, and Gleason's—to remold the British labor movement in their own image of pure-and-simple trade unionism and straight-out war patriotism. Gompers had, in fact, already picked from the British Trades Union Congress's margins the man to do it: the General Federation of Trade Unions' William Appleton, an antisocialist believer in manly self-help after Gompers's own heart. Eager to stem the talk abroad of a negotiated peace, the Wilson administration had sponsored a delegation of American Federation of Labor leaders to try to bolster the war resolve of like-minded trade unionists in England and France in the spring of 1918. In July, it bankrolled a mission of Walling's prowar socialist colleagues to lobby socialist leaders abroad. In September a delegation, including Gompers himself, was dispatched to an inter-Allied labor conference in London. Gompers, the *Labour Leader* reported, planted himself in the center of the hall—hat on his head, smoking one cigar after another—as a one-man dike against any compromise with socialism or the central European labor movements. The AFL delegation, Beatrice Webb wrote, "asserted and re-asserted that the war—at any rate since they entered it—has been a war between Democracy and Disinterestedness, on the one hand, and Autocracy and Lust of Power on the other. Whenever this thesis was controverted the Americans repeated their credo—more slowly, more loudly, and alas at greater length."[100]

The fight over British labor politics was a fight both to control and to represent it. It was inspired precisely by the contrast between the dogmas of Samuel Gompers and the far more fluid, decentralized, "organic" labor movement that Kellogg, Gleason, and the others sensed was in motion in Britain in 1918 and 1919. Not all those Americans who called themselves progressive in 1918 or 1919 rallied to the vision of a labor alliance on British lines. Those for whom winning the war overshadowed the chimerical talk of democratic reconstruction at home, those for whom any concession to class interests violated their vision of a classless common good, remained unmoved. Without the war's disruptions and labor unrest, without the temporary politicizing of every economic and industrial relation within the swollen sphere of the war state so as to bring those relations to an unexpectedly heightened democratic test, the events across the Atlantic would have moved few American progressives at all. But in the context of the moment, Britain was the bridge across which some American progressives began to move from a middle-class politics of expertise and influence to the notion of a democratic social-political alliance as broad as labor itself.

How to bring home the half-borrowed, half-imagined model was, as always, the most difficult question. Some of the American progressives who undertook to forge a movement along the British Labour Party's lines went so far as to enlist themselves in the labor organizations. Through their effort, the role of labor intellectual, more familiar in Europe than in the United States, began slowly to be filled out in the United States. Frederic Howe, whose prewar reports on Europe had radiated a classless faith in the politics of the common good, was a striking example. As immigration commissioner for the Port of New York, Howe had come up hard against the powers of the war state. Forced out in the end, after he tarried too long in deporting yet one more catch of alien radicals, he abandoned middle-class social politics to throw in his lot with the railroad unions as publicist for the Plumb Plan. Benjamin Marsh, once the Congestion Committee's secretary, turned up as head of another railroad union–sponsored operation, the People's Reconstruction League.[101]

Arthur Gleason turned his steps in the same direction. Returning home from an England "all . . . tired out" at the end of 1919, he found an outlet for a while in the *Freeman*, where he plumped for an occupationally based industrial parliament to be built alongside Congress's hollow shell. At the Bureau of Industrial Research, he worked on coal issues, trying to raise the American debate to the level of the British coal hearings. He helped the mineworkers revive the case for coal nationalization as the expert member on the union's Nationalization Research Committee in 1921–22. He was a member of the board of Brookwood Labor College, founded in 1921 as an American counterpart to the labor college movement in England. When later that year progressive labor unionists combined to construct an American offshoot of the Workers' Educational Association, Gleason served on its founding committee as well.[102]

To most American progressives inspired by the labor party idea, however, exhortation came more naturally than these examples of cross-class permeation. The labor party they had in mind was not the cloth-capped troops of the Trades Union Congress, or even a workers' education class deep in the study of economic history, but a manifesto with truth and numbers behind it: cross-class but not class conscious. Inspired by *Labour and the New Social Order*, they too easily mistook it for the Labour Party itself. "Thousands of American liberals who heretofore rather scorned trade unionism are asking 'How can we get in touch with Labor?'" the single-tax *Public* noted in the spring of 1918 with no intended irony, for the *Public* was among those pushing the question most urgently.[103]

The progressives' opening move came with a "Call to Americans" addressed to all workers "of hand or brain" and published in the *Survey*, the *Nation*, the *New Republic*, and the *Dial* in March 1919. Supporters of the "Call" included Howe, the *New Republic*'s Herbert Croly and Walter Weyl, the *Nation*'s Oswald Garrison Villard, the *Freeman*'s Albert Jay Nock, the single-taxers Amos Pinchot and George L. Record, the social gospeler John Haynes Holmes, Greenwich House's Mary Simkhovitch, Northwestern University Settlement's Charles Zueblin, the feminist Charlotte Perkins Gilman, the municipal socialist Carl D. Thompson, and such die-hard veterans of the 1912 Progressive Party as J. A. H. Hopkins—all loosely organized, for the purposes, as the Committee of 48.[104]

But the chasms of class were not to be vaulted by a manifesto alone. The mainline labor organizations, pressed closer and closer to the wall on the union recognition issue as labor struggles escalated in 1919, were uninterested in diluting their own project with the vaguer aspirations of the Committee of 48's middle-class intellectuals. In the face of labor's default, the committee turned its sights to the Independent Labor Party, organized by the Chicago Federation of Labor in late 1918. As weightless in its own way as the Committee of 48, the Independent Labor Party, with its British-borrowed name, signed up several hundred local union affiliates and constructed a platform of progressive planks: democratic control of industry, public ownership of public utilities, complete equality for women, a capital tax on war profits, social insurance, and full restoration of free speech rights. Measured against the progressives' idealized notion of the British union between Sidney Webb's brain and the Trades Union Congress's brawn, however, the results could not but disappoint. There was no controlling vision behind the platform, Charles Merz lamented in the *New Republic:* "There is no attempt, in it, to build the structure of a new social order, as the British Labor Party built."[105]

Eager to do the thinking where so much brain work was needed, the Committee of 48 timed its 1920 meeting to coincide with the Labor Party's convention in Chicago. But between the 48ers' steering committee, on which those promoting a straight-out single-tax line now carried the upper hand, and the labor representatives meeting across town, there was precious little convergence of ideas. The committee's leadership held out for a classless workers' party, committed simply to public ownership of public utilities; the labor unionists demanded a workers' party committed to unionization rights and democratic industrial control. With the negotiators locked in struggle, the Committee of 48's rank and file bolted to the labor convention—marching in to the Labor Party's convention hall singing "Onward, Christian Soldiers" as the Progressive Party convention delegates had in 1912—where their influence quickly dissipated.[106]

The progressives sang "Onward, Christian Soldiers" once again at the nominating convention of the Conference for Progressive Political Action in 1924. This time the initiative for a political alliance of hand and brain came, following more conventional European lines, from the labor unions, and this time the consequences were much greater. In this revival of the Progressive Party name, the railroad workers' unions took the lead. They had done particularly well under state economic management in the war, but by early 1922, with the Railroad Labor Board in collapse, the return of the sweeping antistrike injunction, and a series of court judgments hostile to union organizing rights, they were eager to try independent political action. The brain workers, once again, were willing. Oswald Garrison Villard signed on as the conference's assistant treasurer, Frederic Howe as its secretary, Benjamin Marsh as one of its field organizers. The socialists, depleted by the fissures of 1917, enlisted with enthusiasm. So, with explicit reference to the British example, did the *New Republic* and the *Nation*. Jane Addams, Paul Kellogg, W. E. B. Du Bois, John Dewey, John R. Commons, Rexford Tugwell, Felix Frankfurter, and Paul Douglas, among others, all lent their support. When Robert La Follette accepted the conference's nomination for the presidential race in 1924, even the AFL formally enlisted.[107]

With its labor union base and middle-class superstructure, the Progressive Party of 1924 was the closest thing on the American scene yet to the British Labour Party model. La Follette's 17 percent of the vote in 1924 was twice the maximum the Populists had achieved in a presidential election and two and a half times the best Eugene Debs had mustered at the Socialist Party's height. No other third party until the very end of the century would exceed it. Under a parliamentary system, the Progressives of 1924 might have built a significant congressional beachhead, a firm staging ground for elections to come.

But this time it was the unions that were wary of labor party politics—and still more so, of their progressive allies. Even before November, as an outright La Follette victory began to seem increasingly unlikely and as the Coolidge administration hastened to mend some of its labor fences, the railroad brotherhoods began to edge back toward more familiar brokerage politics. The habit of seeing politics as a marketplace in which labor did best by holding its ultimate allegiances to itself and peddling its wares, election by election, to whichever party bid the highest was hard to set aside. The trainmen's union, eager not to exhaust all its political assets in one spending spree, retreated to neutrality. The United Mine Workers, where John Lewis had unseated the radicals of 1919, threw its support to Coolidge. The AFL's endorsement paid little tangible return.

Encouraged nonetheless by the La Follette vote, the socialists and the progressive intellectuals were eager to put the Conference for Progressive Political Action on a permanent basis. But the unions cut their losses and withdrew. When a de facto labor party was finally to be accreted to the regional and ethnic coalitions within the Democratic Party after 1936, the labor organizations would have no formal, constituent place within it. The British Labour Party model, idealized and intellectualized in its very appropriation, could not be made to stick in the United States. Atlantic progressive politics was full of misaligned connections of this sort, their timing just far enough off to make a critical, structural difference.

If what remained in the war's ebb tide was at the level of aspiration, however, we should not be too quick to sell it short. "Many there were," Harry Laidler wrote in late 1919, "who felt that the Government at Washington was destined to lead America right into the collectivist state—a collectivism not without its . . . bureaucracy and its generous support, through interest on government bonds, of an army of former stockholders, but an industrial order, nevertheless, far removed from Spencerian individualism."[108] The illusions are easily identified in hindsight. Progressives inspired by the war's collectivist experiments wrongly presumed that the extraordinarily rapid policy learning of 1917 and 1918 would be permanent. They misperceived the momentum of end-of-the-war "normalization." They exaggerated the neutrality of the war state vis-à-vis class and partial interests. They overstated the ease with which the common good could be perceived and its agents held to account. In the confidence of 1917, however, they had recognized little of this. Searching, like Randolph Bourne in 1914, for an alternative to their nation's excessively individualized way of life, most progressives had come into the war eager, as H. G. Wells had put it for them, to see what the Great State could do when pulled together into efficient, common action.

But for some American progressives the war and the postwar reconstruction fervor provided an unexpected lesson in class relations. Particularly among those closest to transatlantic politics, it taught a new skepticism about consolidated power and a new appreciation for smaller-scale, even class-related democratic arenas. From the smashup of their idealized Germany, they learned to be more shy of the big, centralized European states. The wartime vision of a coordinated, unified economy, liberated from the distortions of private greed and partial interest, remained; but so did a new wariness about state authority as concentrated as many progressives had hoped it would be in 1917 and 1918. Into the New Deal era, some would look to the labor movement to democratize the economic structures the markets had made. Others would hunt up whatever lay at the end of the cooperative way. And still others would see what answers might be found in smaller places on the European periphery.

8

Rural Reconstruction

Cooperative Farming

The agenda of social politics began with the new. Along the edges of modernity, where the economic transformations cut most deeply, social politics' proponents organized their forces, traded salves and redresses, and worried over the problems of control. Old forms of poverty never interested progressives as much as the new domain of wage labor, old forms of trade as much as the outward rush of market commodification, old forms of production as much as the new world of concentrated force and massed economic power. The diffuse and tradition-bound populations of the great rural hinterlands did not, in the first instance, draw their attention at all.

No one brought the plight of the peasantry to the Verein für Sozialpolitik's organizing conference in 1872, nor farmers' grievances to the organizing meeting of the American Economic Association thirteen years later. In Paris in 1900, the shadow that industrial wage labor cast over the social economy pavilion was massive and unmistakable; to find the economic and social disruptions of rural life within its labyrinth of exhibits took considerably more dedication. The "social question" was the wage-labor question; the *Arbeiterfrage;* the great-city question; the question of combined labor and monopoly capital. The countryside inhabited, at first, another category of mind.

By any demographic reckoning of the age, however, the countryside remained a massive presence well into the twentieth century. Though its people had been draining off for generations like rivulets from a vast leaky population reservoir, village and rural Europe was still a virtual continent of its own. From Ireland across the Scandinavian peninsula, down across the plains of Prussia and central Europe and curving back around through the Mediterranean littoral, agrarian Europe circled the continent's urban and industrial core. As late as 1930, almost half the labor force in Ireland and Italy was engaged in the "primary" sector of the economy: in forestry, fisheries, and, above all, agriculture. In Sweden the comparable figure was 39 percent, in France 36 percent, in Denmark 30 percent, in Germany 29 percent. In the United States, where realms of corn, wheat, and cotton stretched in seemingly endless recess west and south of the Philadelphia–New England–Chicago triangle, it was 22 percent.[1]

Farm populations as large as these carried more than vestigial importance. Agrarian political parties emerged with the extension of suffrage. In a spectrum framed by the issues of the urban, industrial cores, the farmers' parties occupied no stable, predictable place. The keys in which the interests of the countryside could be raised ranged across the political scale from the Populists in the late-nineteenth-century United States to the Junker-dominated Bund der Landwirte in late-nineteenth-century Germany, conservative or radical as party leadership, market forces, and political context molded them. Typically the agrarian parties played the role of political makeweights in a field of stronger players. But where the farmers' political blocs cast their lot with the parties of the working class, their impact on progressive politics could be dramatic. Sweden was a case in point, where the Social Democrats' breakthrough into long-term power was secured by their alliance with the Agrarian Party in 1933. So, by the same token, was the American New Deal, which was sustained in its bold, early years by an electoral combination of northern working-class voters and southern cotton interests.[2]

Economically the countryside still carried weight as well. Danish butter, Swedish timber, New Zealand mutton, and American wheat and cotton all played central roles in their respective export economies. In 1930s France and Germany, agricultural products still made up a fifth of the aggregate national product; in Italy they accounted for more than a quarter; in the United States, despite its huge internal market in manufactured goods and services, they made up one-tenth.[3] The farmers' slogan, "Under all, the land," simplified and moralized the economic point. In agrarian rhetoric, artisans and factory workers, bankers and stock-ticker watchers, artists and preachers all ornamented civilization, but food came first; economically the farmers' land and labor supported it all. The claim was exaggerated, but in economies with farm sectors as large as these, it held a visible measure of truth. Not without cause did so many of the best and brightest young New Dealers flock to the Department of Agriculture in 1933, there to try to unlock the riddle of the farmers' depression, confident that, with the countryside's purchasing power restored, the forces of general economic recovery would spring back into motion.

If the countryside held more importance economically, politically, and demographically than urban progressives sometimes awarded it, it was, by the same token, hardly as static as they sometimes allowed themselves to imagine. The age's great engines of commodification were no less profoundly at work in the countryside than in the great cities and factory towns. Attachment of price to land and the "commodities" produced on it was not, of course, new. The disturbing force was the expanding scope and scale of the agricultural market. As railroad, marketing, and credit networks reached deeper and deeper into the countryside, older, smaller, less competitive trade networks broke apart under the strain. More farm goods began to pass over more distant networks and through the hands of more middlemen and processors, their prices set by more distant, more efficiently organized, and much more highly capitalized players. Rural wage labor followed the thickening paths of transportation and exchange, joining the city and countryside in wage-labor markets that spanned the Atlantic itself. As for the land, it was ground for increasingly complex pyramids of debts and credits, liens and mortgages, and landlord and tenant bargains. The peasantry might still wear their customary wooden clogs, countryfolk everywhere might stoop from hoeing and betray themselves by their country speech, landlords might exact from their cotters and croppers their pound and a half of deference along with their pound of trade, but the outward inertia of the countryside belied its increasing incorporation into a world agricultural market.

Still, in one critical regard, the countryside *was* different from the city dwellers' world. Amid the concentrated forces of the age, farm production remained local, small scale, and individualistic. Not even the biggest Junkers' holdings east of the Elbe River or the bonanza farms of the Red River Valley operated on a scale comparable to that of the key players in the transportation, banking, and manufacturing sectors of the economy. Organization of industrial wage laborers, difficult as it was and hazardous as the strike weapon proved to be, proved vastly easier than the organization of rural folk. One by one, the producers of farm products brought their goods to markets over which they had less and less control and against whose hazards they had increasingly little insulation. Between their diffuse and splintered economic power and that of the agricultural markets' more amply capitalized and better organized players, the distance was stark and economically palpable.

In that standing imbalance, only a trickle of the age's gains in goods and leisure reached peasant or tenant-farmer pockets. The early-twentieth-century agricultural market was a classic marriage of economic efficiency and unpaid social costs: cheap food at the expense of education, health, and ambition among its myriad small producers. Its weakest players—Irish tenants, African-American sharecroppers, Danish farm laborers—formed the largest nation of the exploited, laboring poor in the North Atlantic economy.

In this context, it could not be long before the social question led progressives to the countryside. The Verein für Sozialpolitik added rural economics to its agenda in the 1880s; Richard Ely was training American farm economists by the 1890s. Slowly an international network of rural social reformers took shape beside its urban counterpart. Farmers were not prominent in it; their politics tended to be, like their social organization, local and regional. The brokers of rural social economics between the nations of the North Atlantic economy were more likely to be publicists, philanthropists, farm economists, or educators. Some acquired international reputations, like Friedrich Wilhelm Raffeisen, the Rhineland village mayor who founded the German rural credit cooperative movement, or that conscience of the Irish Protestant gentry, Horace Plunkett, Theodore Roosevelt's favorite agricultural reformer abroad. But, as with the other international networks of policy exchange, it was the rank and file of smaller, more modest players that sustained it.

An example of the type was Wisconsin's Charles McCarthy. McCarthy had been born not on a farm but in Brockton, Massachusetts, where his Irish-born father worked in a shoe factory. Leaving home at age fourteen, he tossed about in the world of urban wage labor, worked his way through Brown University on his mental quickness and his talents at football, and eventually arrived at Richard Ely's door in Madison, Wisconsin, as graduate student and football coach. By 1901 McCarthy had an academic appointment of his own at the University of Wisconsin and a post in the state capital, where he was charged with helping legislators put their ideas into more effectively drafted legislation. The Legislative Reference Library, an engine of progressive legislation, soon justified McCarthy's boast that he had "been the man behind nine tenths of the movements for the betterment of the state."[4]

McCarthy's first European trip was to Germany in 1910 as a member of a special state commission on trade and industrial education, but his vicarious immersion in legislative experiments abroad went back further than that. Visitors to McCarthy's statehouse office were struck by the international range of its pamphlets and model statutes, its "thousands of newspapers written in . . . nearly every language known to the world." When Horace Plunkett passed through Madison in 1911 preaching the gospel of agricultural cooperatives, McCarthy soaked up that new idea like the rest. McCarthy's political idealism, his Irishness, his cosmopolitan political interests, and his expert position in a key farm state all helped kindle an instant mutual friendship between the two men. After arranging to see for himself the results of agricultural reform in Ireland and Denmark in 1913, McCarthy threw himself into the organization of an American farm cooperative movement based on Plunkett's Irish model, dispatching its first organizers to Dublin for training.[5]

The key southerner on McCarthy's general board, Clarence Poe, had found his way into the international rural reform networks by a less circuitous but equally unplanned route. Born on a North Carolina farm, Poe, like McCarthy, struck out early to find another way of making a living. Signing on as an apprentice writer for the *Progressive Farmer*, North Carolina's most important Populist newspaper, he soon bought the paper for his own, and for the next sixty years he used it as a pulpit from which to preach to southern farmers the gospel of agricultural improvement. By 1908 Poe had accumulated enough margin to afford a young man's grand tour through Europe. He set out to see the museums and the poets' birthplaces, but what unexpectedly caught his eye was the careful, intensive cultivation of the European countryside. There were no broken fences or eroded fields to be found in rural England, Poe marveled to his subscribers, no mud-clogged, impassable roads, no culturally entrenched shiftlessness, none of the reckless human agricultural waste that marked the American countryside. Rural France stirred him in the same way: "No clods, no gullies, no weeds, no poor houses and cattle, no scrub hogs, no disgraceful tenant cabins."[6]

No sharecroppers, no blacks, no illiteracy on the massive southern scale, no laziness, no entrapment in cotton and tobacco: Poe's racially and regionally charged point needed little decoding by southern readers. When the disfranchisement of African-American citizens had come before North Carolina voters in 1899, Poe had defended the measure. But there was more to Poe's European-kindled interest in an agriculture without "loose ends or ragged edges" than simply the sight of a countryside free of the peculiar burdens of the American racial system. What Poe saw in Europe helped him bridge the gap between the hot, abstract rhetoric of Populism and the practical, piecemeal style of the expert, agricultural reformer. Two European trips later, in 1912, he knew his destinations like a seasoned social-political traveler: London for a first-hand look at Lloyd George's new social programs, Plunkett's work in Ireland, and the Danish countryside.[7]

Like McCarthy, Poe brought back an enthusiasm for agricultural cooperatives in all their tested European forms. The atheoretical practicality of the European governments also impressed him: their investments in roads and trade education; and their post offices, which not only brought mail to the farmer's doorstep but also carried packages, sold life insurance annuities, and issued savings certificates. The dedicatory statement of his *A Southerner in Europe*—"To All Alert-Minded Southerners Who Find Lessons for Our Time in the History of Other Times, and for Our Country in the Experience of Other Countries"—encapsulated Poe's new political identity.[8]

Southerners like Poe had not been prominent in the early phases of the Atlantic progressive connection. The region's universities had far fewer European connections than those in the North. The city phase of progressive reform had not put down deep roots in the American South. More than other Americans, white southerners had been prone to wrap themselves not only in a general distrust of foreign borrowings but also in the peculiar burdens of their regional history, so as to create a kind of double insulation from the world. The discovery of an unknown continent of practical agricultural reforms struck southern progressives with particular force and propelled them onto the Atlantic stage as municipal streetcars and the insecurities of wage labor had not. With the poverty and backwardness of southern agriculture on their minds, and, still more, the massive drag of that backwardness on the South's general welfare, they strained to read the social-political lessons in the European countryside.

In that endeavor the Americans joined others: Irish progressives trying to track down the exportable lessons of the Danish rural revival, English investigators of Belgian agricultural organization, Indian and Italian rural reformers in Germany. All were in pursuit of the secret of rural revival—of workable means to rebalance the market in agricultural goods in ways less disadvantageous to the country's small producers.

The orthodox economists' answer to the riddle of farm poverty was simple: let the processes of rural depopulation take their course until the surfeit of farm producers, fated to permanent poverty by undercutting each other's margins, shrank to a more advantageous level. The natural endpoints of such a drainage operation were the cities. But already deeply worried about social fractionation in the great cities, most progressives did not welcome the notion of letting the natural flows of population simply take their course. Colonization of surplus small producers on farms in less crowded parts of one's empire was a much more attractive Atlantic-wide solution—but not all nations had an empire suitable for the purposes.[9]

An alternative course was to try to harness the promotionalist powers of the state to the interests of agriculture. Tariff protection and export bounties fell in this category. So did the efforts of state agricultural experts to prod farmers into more commercial modes of production, by teaching them to keep closer accounts, invest more deeply in fertilizer, hybrid seed, and updated machinery, and in effect, trade the identity of a peasant or landlord for that of a businessman on the make. Large producers were the most common beneficiaries of these endeavors, not smallholders or (rarer still) the countryside's wage hands and sharecroppers. All the rival nations played at this game, appropriating measures from each other as they competed vigorously for advantage in the agricultural export trade. But promotionalism was inescapably nationalist in intent, and weak in sustained international consciousness and connections.

It was yet a third set of solutions that dominated the international rural reform networks. The key to this framing of the countryside's weakness lay not in rural overpopulation or precapitalist consciousness; it lay, rather, in the countryside's social and economic atomization. Its talismanic phrase was social "organization." To foster a new level of cooperative, solidaristic consciousness in the countryside, to promote among its splintered, mutually suspicious small producers new institutions of collective endeavor—this was the distinctive note in the debates that swept up the likes of McCarthy and Poe.

As to means, however, there was considerable variation. The most widely shared hopes centered on the promotion of rural cooperatives. Credit cooperatives to provide an alternative to the local landlord or mortgage banker, purchasing cooperatives as a means around the local feed and fertilizer merchant, dairy cooperatives as an alternative to the local commercial creamery, warehousing cooperatives, breeding cooperatives, and marketing cooperatives all had their spokesmen, and in Europe, after half a century's organizational work, their thickly planted associational networks.

Other agricultural progressives vested their hopes in better rural education. Arming the farmer with a firmer knowledge of economics, a broader sense of history and society, a better grasp of the latest technical agricultural methods, or a deeper cooperative spirit was heralded as the foundation of a broader, less isolated rural culture. From cultural revitalization, it was believed, economic revival would surely follow.

Most ambitious of all was the notion of creating new forms of agricultural settlement from the bottom up: rural communities laid out from the first to promote cooperative enterprise and social solidarity. The planned rural settlement idea was to the debates over the revitalization of the countryside what utopian socialism had been to the nineteenth-century debates over wage labor; the difficulty of its realization did not diminish the magnetism of the idea itself.

All these solutions, in dozens of rival forms, circulated among North Atlantic agricultural progressives from the late nineteenth century through the Great Depression of the 1930s. From Raffeisen banks to the Federal Farm Loan Act, from the Irish cultural revival to Wisconsin's cooperative creameries, from reclamation communities in Victoria, Australia, to the state agricultural colonies in central California, from the folk schools of Denmark to their offspring in southern Appalachia, an intricate weave of connections came into being. The internationally minded agricultural progressives never called the whole tune, but into the New Deal their projects carried weight, both intellectually and politically.

What strikes a modern observer as most remarkable about the agricultural progressives was their refusal to accept the countryside as fated either to the inertia of its past or to the onward force of markets and prices. They took it as an article of faith that the countryside was pliant and moldable, its terrific inner motion bendable into consciously chosen channels—not the least because the fate of so much else depended upon it. The countryside's economic revival was the beginning of the matter, but beyond that—whether the hope found its expression in the evangelical fervor of the cooperators or the lay preaching of the folk school principals—lay a sense that new general principles of social organization were waiting to be born. The isolation of each petty possessor in a competition that left all of them poorer was not, to agricultural progressives, simply a peculiarity of the countryside.

It was a mark, as the National Country Life Conference put it in 1919, of the "individualistic tendency and tradition" of the age.[10]

The social pattern of the countryside was the root pattern. To mold it into more "sociable" forms, to infuse it with more intensive "collective social action," was to take hold of a nation's core historical template. The social pattern on the land lay under all. With this, the farmers' slogan took on its distinctive, progressive meaning.

Of all the institutions within the agricultural progressives' bundle of reforms, the one that flourished most vigorously in the Atlantic progressive connection was the cooperative association. Through the Great Depression of the 1930s, cooperatives were a fixture of the debates over rural reconstruction. In the eyes of their partisans, they were a means of reformulating relations of production, a new mode of purchasing, and a template for the reconstruction of moral and economic values themselves. For almost a century, cooperation was corporate capitalism's twin, its shadow, its progressive alternative.

Historically the cooperative association, the investment corporation, and the trade union had, indeed, important elements in common. All three were legal-institutional attempts to move beyond a regime of proprietary, possessive individualism. All three pooled a multitude of small resources into larger, collective strength. The genius of the corporate form, as it turned out, lay in its extraordinary capacity to amass and expand; the genius of the labor union lay, over the long haul, in its ability to obstruct and demand. The genius of the cooperative association—which was also its weakness—lay in its fusion of entrepreneurial and democratic aspirations in ways that, by the orthodoxies of contemporary economic and political science, should barely have been fusable at all.

Cooperation's first publicists were the utopian socialists. It was they, in 1820s and 1830s France and England, who broadcast the possibilities of artisans banding together to ditch their bosses and repossess their labor's value for themselves; of consumers uniting to oust the profiteers and money lenders; of a world reborn from selfish economic exploitation into a "new system of truthful and social commerce." Cooperation's more sober and more lasting institutional form, however, was an invention of the post-Chartist English working class. The modern cooperative store made its first appearance among handloom weavers in Rochdale, England, in the 1840s, gathering its capital out of members' loans, selling goods to its members at reasonable cost, distributing its profits back as membership dividends, and running its business according to its members' collectively deliberated will.[11]

The cooperative store was a corporation turned in on itself, as it were, in which investors, consumers, and managers formed a single, common body. Politically, the cooperative association was a small-scale, simple democracy. In a corporation organized on capital shares, investments voted: one share, one vote. In the cooperative association—as the mid-nineteenth-century English cooperators worked out its principles—members voted: one person, one vote, whether wealth or mere economic competence stood behind it.

So simple a form proved extraordinarily malleable, both functionally and politically. In Britain, the cooperative store sank roots deep in the economy of working-class and lower-middle-class life. Membership in Britain's cooperative stores grew from 350,000 in 1873 to 1.7 million in 1900, to 7.5 million by 1935. Forty-five percent of all English households and 55 percent of all Scottish households belonged to one in the 1930s. To supply the local associations with cheaper goods, the jointly managed Cooperative Wholesale Society moved aggressively into production with its own farms, factories, coal mines, bakeries, North Sea fishing fleet, even a Ceylon plantation for the production of tea.[12]

Different contexts promoted different cooperative forms. In France, cooperators laid particular stress on producers' cooperatives in the small shop and building trades, with the state, at times, as an active patron. In late-nineteenth-century Germany, the most vigorous growth was in cooperative loan associations. Introduced in the late 1840s by Hermann Schulze-Delitzsch, an admirer of English working-class self-help, there were more than a thousand cooperative credit banks in Germany operating within the Schulze-Delitzsch umbrella association in 1892 and many more outside it. Thirteen years later, the capitalization of the empire's cooperative credit unions, taken as a whole, stood at just over half the combined capital of its five largest commercial banks.[13]

So multiform an institution quickly crossed over to the countryside. Friedrich Wilhelm Raffeisen organized his first peasant credit cooperative in the Rhineland in 1864. By the mid-1890s the rural cooperative field was full of rival patrons, including the Prussian state itself, and its expansion across national boundaries was going on apace. Imported from Germany by northern Italian reformers, cooperative people's banks and *casse rurali* quietly transformed the credit structure of village Italy. In Denmark, a meeting ground for both English and German cooperative influences, a still more striking transformation took hold in agricultural production and processing. The first Danish cooperative creamery began its work in 1882; by the eve of the First World War, half the nation's hog raisers and almost 90 percent of its dairy farmers belonged to a cooperative slaughter house or creamery.[14]

In no two European countries did the agricultural cooperatives take the same form. German rural cooperatives tended to pool a multitude of functions under a common, local roof. In Denmark, by contrast, specialization was the rule. By the early twentieth century most Danish farmers belonged to several cooperatives: a dairy cooperative with its mutually owned cream separator, a cooperative slaughterhouse and bacon factory, and perhaps also a breeding stock cooperative, an egg marketing cooperative, a cooperative store, a purchasing cooperative for feed and fertilizer, and one or more export marketing cooperatives. Beginning with an agenda of spiritual and moral revitalization, the Raffeisen cooperatives slowly moved into the encouragement of commercial farming practices. The Danish and Irish cooperatives were aggressive modernizers from the first. When Charles McCarthy saw his first Danish milk cows in 1913, each with a "control" cooperative's posted record of its consumption and output, not roaming at will like American cows but picketed each day to a precisely defined patch of pasture, he thought it a mark of scientific management in action.[15]

Whatever form they took, the cooperatives' role in the economic revival of the European countryside was unmistakable. Denmark was the most dramatic demonstration of the point. Stripped by Prussia of its southern provinces, its grain production devastated by foreign commerce, Denmark had been a nation in crisis in the 1870s—as American southerners, struck by the parallels to their own history, often pointed out. The bottom strata of its peasantry was as poor as any in Europe. By turning from grain to intensive production of high-quality butter, eggs, and bacon for the English export trade, and by pooling their strengths in their myriad, overlapping production cooperatives, Danish small farmers worked their way back by the early twentieth century to a prosperity envied throughout Europe. Eager to hoist Irish farmers up by the same bootstraps, Horace Plunkett's Irish Agricultural Organisation Society was laboring hard to "Denmarkize" the Irish countryside by the early 1890s. To the extent that agriculture's future lay not in the big, tenanted, grain-producing estates of the old regime but in small, more intensively farmed holdings that produced higher-priced, more carefully graded products for the great cities around them, the rapid growth of cooperatives in the European countryside after 1890 was intimately linked to it.[16]

Capable of so many different forms of work, from producing export-grade butter to promoting a new system of "truthful and social commerce," cooperation's political character shifted like a chameleon with context and background. The Rochdale Pioneers had begun as Owenite socialists. Schulze-Delitzsch was an economic liberal of the classic stripe. Raffeisen was a Christian moralist; the French Union Coopérative's Charles Gide was a dissident social economist. During the boom years of cooperative formation from the 1890s through the 1930s, there was hardly a major European social movement without its affiliated cooperative network. In France, factory and mining town owners were among the most active promoters of cooperative retail associations, not the least (as they saw it) to encourage in their workers bourgeois economic virtues. In Italy, the Catholic church moved aggressively into the formation of cooperative credit banks. In the German countryside, Junker conservatives, Raffeisenites, anti-Semites, and state agricultural officials all pressed forward with their own rival cooperatives.[17]

By the end of the nineteenth century, the fastest growing cooperatives were labor union or socialist sponsored. Orthodox Marxists, insistent on the chasm between their own scientific socialism and the woolly utopianism of their forebears, had a hard time seeing anything in the cooperative idea other than the penny-pinching utopia of the petite bourgeoisie. But labor and socialist cooperatives, vigorously promoted by unions and local workers' associations, had outstripped all the rest in members in Belgium and Germany by the eve of the First World War. The cooperative societies were not "socialism," Eduard Bernstein acknowledged in evolutionary socialism's most important manifesto, but they bore "enough of the element of socialism" to be "indispensable levers for the socialist emancipation."[18]

Into the dominant economic and political categories of the day, in short, the cooperatives failed to fit. Cooperation, fiercely opposed by merchant middlemen, commercial creamery operators, and commercial lenders, was not capitalism. With the culture of competitive individualism in ascent around them, the cooperators were profoundly at odds. Even Schulze-Delitzsch required his affiliated credit cooperatives to write the classic laborist slogan into their constitutions: "All for one and one for all."[19] But if cooperation was not capitalism, it was not socialism either. The cooperators preached a vigorous form of self-help, albeit a self-help in which the cooperators mutually lifted themselves up by their combined resources and character.

The result was a movement unstable at both its socialist and capitalist edges. In Belgium, where the workers' cooperatives returned a fraction of their profits straight into the Parti Ouvrier's coffers, the cooperatives functioned as the socialist movement's prime recruiting ground. In wartime Britain, the cooperative movement folded in its lot with the Labour Party. In other circumstances, however, it was the line between the cooperative society and the joint-stock corporation that was unstable. Rooted in social networks of skilled workers, artisans, and established small farmers, the cooperative societies were rarely as interested in the poor and unskilled as in the dream of getting ahead by hauling together on their jointly knotted bootstraps. In the United States, in particular, the rank-and-file cooperators' eagerness for the main chance was to prove extraordinarily keen.

But for all its ambiguities and instabilities, the dissenting, alternative thread in the cooperative idea could never by wholly obscured. The cooperative association was not merely a carefully managed store, creamery, or loan bank. Beatrice Webb saw the cooperatives as the organizing node for a democratic transformation of economic life. French cooperators sang of the "downfall of selfishness." They named their cooperative stores in the same spirit: Union, Famille Nouvelle, Solidarité. To Charles Gide the cooperatives were the next step beyond the reign of self-interest and competition: the "economic system destined to supersede capitalism."[20]

So protean and deeply charged a movement could hardly escape being pulled across the Atlantic. From the National Labor Union of the 1860s through the Knights of Labor in the 1880s, American labor unions had been a node of cooperative ambition. From the Civil War onward, every farmers' organization, too, was caught up for a time in cooperative designs. In the 1870s, in their struggle to break free of the country store dealers, the Grangers moved from cooperative wholesale purchasing arrangements to cooperative farm machinery purchases, and from there, when equipment manufacturers refused to sell to Grange agents, to a heroic effort to design and manufacture a special harvester for Grange members. In the 1880s the Farmers' Alliance was alive with plans for statewide cooperative crop warehousing. Between 1902 and 1910 the Farmers' Union and the American Society of Equity grew on hopes that farmers could pool the majority of an entire crop, hold it against the traders and speculators, and control its final price. Overextending themselves, however, the farmers' cooperatives repeatedly fell prey to the boomers' optimism all around them. The Grangers' bubble burst in the depression of 1873; the Alliancemen skidded off toward the promise of free silver; the Farmers' Union's cotton pool and the Equity Society's tobacco corner both collapsed by 1910. The American weakness was not in vision but in the small-scale, locally based cooperative infrastructure that was changing the European countryside.[21]

On this score the American record through the 1910s was "extraordinarily weak," as the International Cooperative Alliance saw it, and with reason. The foundation of the English cooperative movement, the solidly established cooperative retail store, was practically nonexistent in the United States. Uncounted until the 1930s, membership in American retail cooperatives, measured as a fraction of the nation's population, cannot have been more than one-tenth that of Britain. On the eve of the First World War, cooperative credit societies, which numbered more than 16,000 in prewar Germany, were scarcely to be found in the United States outside New England, where French-Canadian textile workers had brought them across the border, and among Jewish immigrants in New York.[22]

The American countryside repeated this lopsided pattern. In the upper midwestern triangle formed by Minnesota, Wisconsin, and Iowa, a network of grain elevator and dairy cooperatives, built in part on the solidarities of German and Scandinavian immigrants, had begun to reshape the regional rural economy. As much as half the nation's total agricultural cooperative business was done in this region in 1915. In North Carolina a statute of 1915 registering and encouraging rural credit cooperatives had begun to bear a first, thin crop. But beyond the upper Midwest and the fruit growers' cooperatives in central California, stable agricultural cooperatives were as rare as a summer frost. A quarter of the German peasantry is estimated to have belonged to one of the some 15,500 local rural cooperatives on the eve of the First World War; the comparable figure in the United States at the time could not have exceeded 10 percent.[23]

The central role of the cooperative associations in the economic revitalization of European agriculture, and their ambiguous, mediating politics, so like the American progressives' own, created a circumstance ripe for yet another attempt at importation—this time with the policy makers, not the farmers, in the lead. The key intermediary in this transatlantic project was Horace Plunkett. A slight, stubborn, Protestant, Anglo-Irish aristocrat, Plunkett's Atlantic-spanning reputation was extraordinary at its peak. Theodore Roosevelt claimed he would have named Plunkett his secretary of agriculture had it been possible for a foreigner to be so appointed.

Roosevelt's chief conservationist, Gifford Pinchot, was Plunkett's intimate friend and admirer. Clarence Poe printed Plunkett's portrait as the frontispiece to his *How Farmers Co-operate*. An astonishingly large number of American progressives passed through Plunkett House in Dublin during the decade preceding the First World War: Richard Ely; Henry D. Lloyd; Poe; Pinchot; McCarthy; three of the eight members of the U.S. Country Life Commission, which Plunkett himself had been instrumental in creating; the agriculture secretaries of the Roosevelt and Taft administrations; Woodrow Wilson's chief of southern agricultural extension work; and the young Henry A. Wallace, who was to be agriculture secretary himself during the New Deal. Late-nineteenth-century American travelers had shuddered at Ireland's poverty and the beggars who seemed to spring from behind every country hedge. By 1913, in contrast, Walter Lippmann thought Plunkett's Ireland the most stimulating country in Europe; he wrote a friend that fall that he had been reading about nothing else for a month.[24]

The object of this praise was not himself an original architect of cooperative ideas. But Plunkett joined a publicist's indefatigable energies with close ties to the United States and—as time went on—needs of his own for an American connection. Born into one of the largest landholding families in Ireland, he had come home from an Oxford education to the family seat outside Dublin at loose ends for a career. Like many younger sons of wealthy English families, he grasped at the notion of making a fortune in America. From 1879 to 1889 he spent most of each year in the American West, speculating in town lots, punching cows in Wyoming, investing in cattle ranching syndicates, and developing a lasting interest in United States affairs and politics. He was to visit the United States almost annually through the end of his life to check on his investments, to take the rest cure at the Kellogg sanitarium in Battle Creek, Michigan, where Gifford Pinchot was a companion patient, and to spread his ideas for rural revival.[25]

Called home to manage the family estates in 1889, Plunkett turned his interest to agricultural revitalization. Devastated by the famine of the 1840s, Irish agriculture had been pummeled once again in the 1870s and 1880s by the combined effects of intensive international competition and the old Irish problems of minute agricultural holdings, ubiquitous farm tenancy, and violent rent wars. The official government solution was a massive program to subsidize tenants in the purchase of their rented holdings. Plunkett's work took a different direction: promotion of continental-style cooperative organization. By 1894 he had an organization in gear, the

Irish Agricultural Organisation Society. Borrowing from the Danish example and exploiting a new change in cream separation technology, Plunkett's organizers were soon dotting Ireland with cooperative creameries. By the eve of the First World War, half of all Irish milk, markedly improved in price and quality, flowed through cooperative organizations.[26]

Within the skein of tendencies in the cooperative idea, Plunkett spoke most forcefully for efficient business organization. Of the elements of his triadic slogan, "Better farming, better business, better living," the most important, he insisted to his American friends, was better business. Ireland's failings were not cultural, he maintained: "It is only in their economic and business qualities that they are behindhand." For all Plunkett's pushing of the business theme, however, his Irish Agricultural Organisation Society never narrowed its program down to a single note. Though Plunkett deplored "the political obsession of our national life," he claimed his family's traditional parliamentary seat without hesitation and used it to lobby successfully for an Irish Department of Agriculture and Technical Instruction. As that department's head from 1899 to 1907, he launched an ambitious program of government agricultural extension advice, a decade in advance of the Smith-Lever agricultural extension act in the United States. As the Irish Agricultural Organisation Society's secretary and editor of the *Irish Homestead*, he recruited the poet George W. Russell who, under the pen name AE, wrote with mystical intensity of Ireland's coming liberation from poverty, isolation, and "fanatical" concentration on individual family survival—all through the rebirth of rural cooperative institutions. In the United States, all three generations of Iowa Wallaces devoured the *Irish Homestead;* the young Henry Wallace, who grew up under AE's spell, was to bring the poet himself to the U.S. Agriculture Department in the early 1930s to lecture on rural reconstruction. What made the Irish Agricultural Organisation Society such a magnetic symbol of the possibilities of rural revitalization was its fusion of elements: centrifugal cream separators and poetry, mutualism and business principles, expert state assistance and carefully graded butter.[27]

That and Plunkett's skill as a publicist. From the mid-1890s on, Plunkett talked up the Irish Agricultural Organisation Society with every prominent American his persuasive powers could reach. After 1907, when Plunkett's published aspersions against the Catholic clergy cost him his government office and the Irish Agricultural Organisation Society its modest government subventions, his desire for a transatlantic foundation of support grew all the stronger. Plunkett wooed John D. Rockefeller, Jr., particularly hard, trying to lay aside his dislike of Rockefeller's conventional mind, "poky house [and] second-rate cooking," in hopes of capturing some of his millions for Ireland.[28]

Plunkett's most important catch, however, was Theodore Roosevelt. A regular visitor at the White House, where the two aristocrats traded western ranching tales, Plunkett by 1907 had won Roosevelt over to the creation of a blue-ribbon commission on the ills and needs of rural life. Staffed with agricultural college professors and progressive farm journalists, the U.S. Country Life Commission reported in 1909 in favor of "nothing more or less than the gradual rebuilding of a new agriculture and a new rural life." Its key term, appropriated directly from Plunkett, was "organization." In an organizational age, the countryside's crippling weakness was the lack of neighborly cooperation and strong country institutions, the loneliness and "social sterility" of dispersed rural life, the thinness of "organization" of every sort. It was this that drove farm children off the land, weakened the farmers' influence and status, and left them at the mercy of more organized economic players. The Country Life Commission's manifesto represented a conscious break with the agrarian radicalism of the past. To the country life experts the essential villain was not the predatory interests, the railroads with their monopolistic hold on shipment of the farmers' crop, the banks, or Henry George's landlords; with a few conciliatory gestures toward the farmers' "rights," most of the Populist agenda of the past was set aside. The real villain was the absence of sufficient "common feeling," an enfeebled "rural social sense"—the self-defeating individualism of the farmers themselves.[29]

The Country Life Commission report crystallized the emergent profession of rural sociology and solidified its agenda. Over the next two decades, American rural sociologists would try to map country "communities," contrast the density of farmers' associations with those of city folk, and preach the gospel of stronger schools and stronger rural churches.[30] For Roosevelt and for Plunkett, whom Roosevelt persuaded to address a book to Americans glossing the report, the essential need was more specific: a system of farm cooperatives rivaling the density of Europe's. By 1913 Plunkett was working hard on the creation of an American Agricultural Organization Society to promote "a complete reorganization of [American] agriculture upon cooperative lines." Pinchot was to head it, Plunkett noted in his diary, and Wisconsin's Charles McCarthy was to do the work. Within two years Plunkett had talked Andrew Carnegie into supplying the seed money. The first two staff organizers, a Texas farm journalist and an organizer for the

Wisconsin Society of Equity, were sent to Ireland for training in the summer of 1915.[31]

The American Agricultural Organization Society was unabashedly a product of the Atlantic progressive connection. Its marriage of progressive ideals, Carnegie money, and displaced Irish ambition, harnessed to teach the most modern nation in the North Atlantic economy the hard-earned lessons of one of the poorest and most traditional, spoke profoundly to its moment in that exchange. With Atlantic ties, however, came Atlantic liabilities. When the First World War broke over Ireland, inflaming the inner Irish tensions Plunkett had tried so hard to straddle, Plunkett's American organization could not escape the consequences. A moderate unionist in circumstances in which there was less and less middle ground on which to stand, Plunkett found his cooperative creameries attacked from both sides of the erupting Irish civil war. When nationalists finally burned Plunkett's own Dublin house to a shell, he retreated to English exile. Cut off by the war from their movement's commanding figure, Plunkett's American allies moved on to other projects. Pinchot abandoned the task of cooperative organization; McCarthy moved on to the staff directorship of the Commission on Industrial Relations, a post in the wartime Food Administration, and an unsuccessful run for the United States Senate as a progressive Democrat. As progressive admirers of Germany discovered in 1914, the Atlantic connection was double-edged; it both empowered reform politics and made them peculiarly vulnerable.

Plunkett and Ireland had, nevertheless, gone a long way toward injecting cooperation into the core agenda of American progressives. For an important circle of farm experts, the rural problem seemed now not so much a matter of overstocked markets, soil exhaustion, or tenancy as of inadequate social form and collective endeavor. The open question was not whether the agricultural progressives would make a concerted effort at the cooperative idea's promotion in the United States, but whether, in doing so, they could keep cooperative practice from skittering off into the surrounding sea of capitalist and individualistic ambitions.

The first and most critical test took place over farm credits. Credit had always been a raw political sore on the countryside. Far from major banks, at the mercy of the local credit monopolies of merchants and small-town bankers, and often deeply and perennially in debt, farmers harbored a multitude of grievances against the existing credit system. Country interest rates were high, dramatically so in the bank-poor South; long-term amortized mortgages were unknown. Farmers borrowed on two- to five-year terms, promising to return their loans, with interest, in a lump sum on due day. Given the volatility of farm prices and income, it did not always work that way. For many of the American farmers' needs the European farm credit cooperatives were a made-to-order device, if they could be successfully imported across national political and legal differences.

The middleman this time, David Lubin, was a maverick Sacramento merchant who in any other moment in American history, when self-made European expertise mattered less, almost surely would have been written out of the part. Reared in an orthodox Jewish family in New York, he had set out as a teenager to make his fortune in California. With his half-brother, Harris Weinstock, he made a success of a one-price, no-credit dry goods store. Catching an enthusiasm for agriculture on a trip to the Holy Land in the 1880s, the two men added a central California fruit farm to their holdings. Weinstock went into California progressive politics, undertook a round-the-world quest for means to mediate labor disputes, and won a seat on the nine-person U.S. Commission on Industrial Relations for his effort. Lubin's travels also carried him to Europe, but with the conundrum of inadequate farm prices on his mind.[32]

Convinced that only worldwide dissemination of crop and marketing information would allow farmers to match the shipping and financial trusts in the tightening competitive game, Lubin knocked on doors all over Europe until, in the king of Italy, he found a sponsor for a new International Institute of Agriculture. Settling into the institute's headquarters in Rome in 1908, Lubin immersed himself in what a generation of agricultural reform had wrought in Europe. With a pamphlet mill at his disposal, a mailing list of some fifty thousand farm organizations, an inexhaustible stock of Biblical quotations and moral parables, and the confidence of a self-taught economist, he proceeded to bombard his countrymen with what he had found.

Like markets, credit went to the core of the farmers' dilemma; so long as farmers remained land rich and cash poor, it was clear to Lubin, they could never adequately compete with the holders of liquid capital. He read up eagerly on the Raffeisen and Schulze-Delitzsch cooperatives and the Italian credit banks. But what caught Lubin's imagination was a more exotic, Prussian institution, the *Landschaften*. Landowners' associations organized and managed by the Prussian state, the *Landschaften* were essentially mortgage security pools; through them landowners combined the value of their holdings into units large enough to raise their collective bargaining power with private mortgage lenders. By the principles of the cooperative movement's working-class English pioneers, the *Landschaften* were not true cooperative associations. Rooted in the corporatist past, with the state as their managing patron, they made no pretense of internal democracy. But with a salesman's eager conflations, Lubin saw the *Landschaften* as crystallizing the economic miracle that cooperation made possible. Rather than farmers going one by one to beg their loans from local bankers, Lubin imagined American farm-owners' associations floating gilt-edged land mortgage securities in a nationwide investment market, acting with the scope and freedom of share corporations, transforming their static, underlying land values into "dynamic dollars." The *Landschaften* represented the American way in credit, he argued: the farmers' version of "the American merger, the American corporation, the American trust."[33]

Taking his message—that unlimited credit lay, literally, under the farmers' feet—to the Southern Commercial Congress's meeting in Nashville in April 1912, Lubin inspired the delegates to send an investigatory commission to see for themselves the European rural credit systems at work. The result, the American Commission on Agricultural Cooperation and Rural Credit in Europe, was the most extraordinary of the era's institutions of transatlantic policy inspection. Under Lubin's direction, some 120 Americans, almost half of them from the southern states, trooped across Europe in the summer of 1913. Lubin took the commission on an obligatory pilgrimage to Raffeisen's family house near Coblenz. ("Millions of dollars from nothing," the state of Washington's representatives enthused.) Most of their time, however, they spent assembled as a kind of vast grand jury, listening to delegations of state officials and agricultural experts present their testimony—the expertise of Europe all assembled for the judgment of the American common mind.[34]

In the struggle to shape the commission's conclusions, rival players on both sides of the Atlantic scrambled for advantage. William Howard Taft tried to preempt the issue with an official administration report on European rural credit systems, which praised both the Raffeisen cooperatives and the *Landschaften* but saw no need for federal action in the promotion of either. Woodrow Wilson, taking office on the eve of the commission's departure, appointed a small official delegation to travel with it, and then nervously dispatched yet another to cover the same terrain still more soberly and skeptically.[35] Plunkett, who had no love for Lubin, lobbied furiously to extend the investigation's scope beyond the land mortgage issue and to pry its itinerary out of Italy and Germany and into Denmark and Ireland. When the commission finally turned up in Dublin for lectures by AE and Plunkett, Plunkett could not contain his frustration at this "extraordinary body of semi-official—semi-political trippers."[36]

The commission's conclusion, in fact, could not but have pleased Plunkett. The "astonishing" fact of European farming, the majority reported, was its networks of local cooperation. Within two generations the cooperatives had brought about an agricultural prosperity that set on its heels the stereotype of a backward European peasantry. Responsible for one-third to one-half of the European farmers' total commerce, cooperation was "the characteristic way of doing farm business in Western Europe." Though the commission majority was not short on specific proposals, Europe's overriding lesson was one of education. Rural revitalization began by permeating the countryside with the cooperative "spirit," with the ideals of "a social order . . . where the struggle for existence will give way to a brotherhood of workers; where men, dependent on the success of their united efforts for their own prosperity, will instinctively think first of the community and second of themselves."[37]

The commission's minority was small, but its dissent was biting. American farmers, divided by race, religion, habits, and desires, had none of the Europeans' mutuality on which to build. They had not settled down permanently enough, nor close enough to each other, to police each other's character and credit. Unlike European farmers, the Americans were "ambitious, individualistic and desirous of acquiring means and property." They were "traders" by nature, with "an inherent disinclination to shoulder the financial burdens of another." In short, Americans farmers were capitalists; the contrast with Europe, they insisted, could not be more pronounced.[38]

If the character of the American farmer was one of the points at issue in the ensuing debate, another was the relation between cooperative self-help and state assistance. Lubin championed a *Landschaften*-modeled measure that brought the federal government in as the mortgage bonds' guarantor of last resort. The radical farm organizations demanded straight-out government loans, without any of the complex European intermediaries. Woodrow Wilson threatened to veto any bill that smacked of special subsidies for farmers. Plunkett insisted that the cooperative society must be built from the neighborhood up; Lubin that cooperation's genius lay in tapping investment capital at the top.[39]

In this cacophony of principles, the champions of state assistance had the better grasp of European historical experience. Everywhere in Europe, as all the American reports conceded, the agricultural revival had been propelled by a complex mix of collective self-help, philanthropic promotion, and state assistance. Without the state-financed buyout of the Irish landlords, without the German agricultural tariff and state-sponsored central banks, which gave the local credit cooperative associations their needed liquidity, without the semiofficial status of the Irish Agricultural Organisation Society in its early years, the picture the Americans had seen would have been unimaginable. The core of the matter was not in choosing sides but in striking an effective balance.

The Americans' balancing act—a complicated legislative bundle of European borrowings and home-grown inventions—was finally passed with Wilson's belated assent in 1916. Side by side with a system of newly chartered private land banks, the Farm Loan Act established a quasi-public system of regional mortgage banks, to make loans not to farm owners but to farmers' loan associations. Farmers who banded together in loan cooperatives, approving the credit-worthiness of their members and accepting an element of collective risk, were eligible for long-term, amortized, European-style mortgages. The banks, in turn, would convert the mortgages into bonds and market them to private investors. This was Lubin's *Landschaften* system of sorts, top-heavy in federal investment guarantees but recognizable in its origins. But as the Farm Loan Act's drafters envisioned their work, mortgage bonds would only be the beginning of it. Around the mandatory farm loan associations they were confident there would grow, like a crystal around an injected seed, an ever ramifying set of specialized farmers' cooperative associations for short-term credit, marketing, warehousing, and processing. With the European agricultural revival on their minds, the drafters of the Farm Loan Act yoked the farm credit problem and the rural social organization problem into an ingenious whole.[40]

Measured by the eagerness of farmers to take advantage of its provisions, the Farm Loan Act of 1916 was an instant success. Against the critics' predictions that its cooperative machinery would prove a dead letter, some three thousand four hundred farm loan associations sprang up in accordance with the act's incentives. By 1929 the measure had funneled more than a billion dollars into farm loans. But those who doubted the American farmers' commitment to the cooperative ideal had a point. In the disturbed financial climate of the war and amid uncertainty regarding the act's constitutionality, the promise of tapping virtually inexhaustible reserves of private investment capital through the sale of cooperative mortgage bonds evaporated almost at once. Finding little to tempt them in the new mortgage system, private investors put their money elsewhere, leaving the federal treasury to finance the system by default.[41]

At the local level, the distance between the Farm Loan Act's promises and its results was even greater. With their eyes on the interest differential like marketwise traders, farmers proved quite willing to establish the requisite farm loan associations and to cash in their existing private mortgages for cheaper, longer-term public loans. But they had no equivalent interest in democratic management of the loan associations. Many appointed local bankers and businessmen as their association managers. The short-term cooperative credit associations that the bill's promoters had assumed would spin off from the farm loan associations failed to materialize. If the potential for a new rural social order indeed lay dormant in the countryside, a single federal act and a shower of public credits had not been able to bring it forth.

The heyday of the farmers' cooperative movement, in fact, was to come in the 1920s, in an alliance of Republican Party policy makers and entrepreneurial organizers that looked very much like state-subsidized capitalism. The effective organizing engine was not the locally rooted Raffeisen cooperative, the small-scale cooperative creamery, or the village cooperative store, but the large-scale, regional marketing cooperative, pooling farmers' products under a common label and striking a common bargain with shippers and middlemen. Marketing co-ops of this sort were an Atlantic-wide phenomenon; a fifth of Danish butter exports in 1914 flowed through farmers' export associations.[42] But nowhere was the marketing cooperative to flourish more exuberantly or with higher entrepreneurial ambitions than in the United States.

The first farmers to organize successfully in this way were the California fruit growers; by 1917 two-thirds of the state's orange crop was being sold through the California Fruit Growers' Exchange. Encouraged by the postwar Republican administrations, cooperative marketing boomed in the early 1920s. The Agricultural Credits Act of 1923 extended short-term government credits directly to marketing cooperatives. The Capper-Volsted Act of 1922 exempted agricultural cooperatives from antitrust prosecution; the Cooperative Marketing Act of 1926 exempted them from federal business taxes. At the Commerce Department, Herbert Hoover made marketing cooperatives the centerpiece of his agricultural program—partly in an effort to head off pressure for outright price supports, but equally because Hoover saw in them an analogue to the efficient, modern corporation. Just as businesslike organization had created corporate order out of the "extreme individualism" of industrial capitalism's early stages, Hoover argued, businesslike marketing, with modest state encouragement, could do the same for agriculture.[43]

To Hoover's corporatist ideals must be added the American farmers' eagerness to—indeed their boomers' fantasies of—making agricultural cartelization stick. If the antitrust exemption gave the farmers' cooperatives the status of a kind of labor union, the vision the leading cooperative organizers peddled was the dream of monopoly advantage. The most prominent proponent of these ambitions was the legal architect of the California cooperative system and yet another member of the Lubin-Weinstock family connection, Aaron Sapiro. A gifted evangelist, Sapiro spread the gospel of collective control of farm prices from the Texas cotton fields to the tobacco South.

The short-term effects of Sapiro's work were dramatic. At the high point of the marketing cooperatives' boom from 1923 to 1926, virtually half the nation's tobacco crop was marketed through one of two dozen tobacco associations. Although cotton was never so well controlled, 300,000 cotton growers were enlisted in more than a hundred cotton marketing associations at the movement's peak. This was, as Sapiro insisted, business agriculture on big-business scale. Its secret was not local and democratic mutualism but price control. The project was not worth undertaking, Sapiro cautioned, unless there was a good prospect of gaining at least half the total crop and securing that market position through long-term, binding contracts with members. Power in the big cooperatives was tightly centralized at the top. Cooperative agriculture flourished in the United States, in short, by donning the clothes of the big-business trust.[44]

This appropriation of monopoly capitalism's forms and functions was in some ways a now-familiar consequence of timing. Cooperatives in nineteenth-century Europe found their initial footing in sectors of the economy only weakly colonized by commercial interests. The German credit cooperatives built on business unwanted by the commercial banks; in Ireland, the dairy cooperatives took advantage of a technological revolution in creamery production. By the early twentieth century, when the American movement finally began in earnest, the available economic space was much smaller and the contenders much better organized. It was hardly surprising that the tobacco growers' cartel in these circumstances should have so closely mimicked the tobacco processor's oligopoly, or the California fruit and nut growers' cartels the size and market position of the railroads they faced. Weak at the local level, where the merchant townfolk who dominated local politics succeeded in barring agricultural extension agents from encouraging local cooperative undertakings, the cooperatives made their opening at the top.

But if lateness held part of the answer to the top-heavy structure of agricultural cooperation in the United States, the larger part of the answer lay in the ambitions of farmers themselves. Most farmers, in a crunch, were more interested in prices than in association, more eager for market control than the near-at-hand sustained labor of cooperative work. The lines between cooperative and capitalist association proved maddeningly porous in the United States. Cooperative creameries and grain elevators did not automatically limit their membership to farmers; managed—sometimes initiated—by the very middlemen and capital investors they were designed to supplant, many local farm cooperatives were all but impossible to tell from commercial enterprises except for their special privileges under the law.[45] At the local level democratic management was weak; the regional market cooperatives made barely a pretense of being democratic at all. In their most desperate moments, when struggling to keep their members from selling off too early, the crop cartels degenerated into intimidation and violence.

Dreaming not of escaping the price system but of controlling it, most of the big farmers' cooperatives instead fell victim to the market's dynamics. Overreaching their effective market control in 1926, the tobacco associations unraveled, shedding their members by the thousands. By 1927–1928, they had effectively disappeared. The cotton marketing associations' fortunes rode up and down as irregularly as cotton prices themselves; by 1927–1928 their membership had fallen to half its level at the height of "Sapiroism." The smaller scale cooperatives proved better survivors. Where there had been 3,000 agricultural cooperatives in the United States in 1913 there were 11,000 by 1927–28, half still located in the upper Midwest. Collectively they shipped half of all livestock received at Chicago's Union Stock Yards. They produced almost a third of the nation's cheese. Their grain elevators dotted the northern plains states.[46] With their boom-and-bust temptations and in their flashier, more commercial American dress, cooperative associations had made their way into the countryside. In the American heartland they deposited a European idea.

But the same malleability that had made the cooperative association so exportable meant that cooperatives everywhere were an acutely sensitive test of the surrounding political culture. The flexibility of form that had eased the marriage of the cooperative idea to socialist politics in Belgium, to Raffeisen's project of moral uplift in late-nineteenth-century Germany, or to AE's Irish poetry, exposed the cooperative idea in the United States to the commercial ambitions all around it. Transplantation to the United States squeezed out cooperation's anticapitalist impulses and exaggerated its acquisitive ones. The cooperative form was more easily embraced in America than the idea of a social order beyond capitalism. The culture absorbed the catalyst that was to have transformed it.

Island Communities

To some of those who saw agricultural Europe through progressive eyes, the most striking contrast between New and Old World rural life was not to be found in Europe's workaday cooperatives. It lay, rather, in the very patterns of settlement themselves. No Atlantic observer of the American and European countryside failed to note the difference. The European countryside unfolded to the eye as a series of rural hamlets. One moved across intervening fields and pasture from farm village to farm village—each a compact node of crooked streets and peasant dwellings huddled up against a church or marketplace. To that pattern of clustered settlement, the widely separated farmsteads of the American countryside were a striking exception. The spatial design of the European countryside spoke to the eye of bonds and obligations. The American pattern spoke the visual language of individualism: each rural dwelling surrounded by its attached acreage, each farmer the ruler of his private domain.[47]

As always, the eye exaggerated. The nucleated European farm village was as capable of housing a festering nest of enmities, and as capable of quick, violent eruption, as any place in the United States. The separate farmsteads of the American countryside, by contrast, belied the social bonds between them—mutualist connections, on the one hand, made of borrowing, shared work, and Sunday visiting, and coercive ones, on the other, of landlordism and racial control.[48] On both sides of the Atlantic, regional exceptions varied the dominant pattern. There were areas of dispersed rural settlement in Europe and of nucleated settlement in the United States: the four-square village settlements that the Mormons, with godly discipline in mind, planted on the Utah desert; the remnants of once-thriving agricultural villages in New England; the unplanned, clustered settlements of the Appalachian coves and hollows.

Still, taking all these qualifications in mind, the contrast remained. The American countryside possessed towns in good numbers: mercantile nodes boasting a store, crop transport facilities, a source of credit and agricultural supplies, and an aspiring small-town bourgeoisie. But most working farmers did not live in them. Thanks to the dynamics of frontier settlement, cheap and easily transferable land, and the consciously designed policies of the federal homestead acts and the railroads, farmers lived apart. The dominant pattern on the land ran toward separation, distance, and independence. The anomaly of the American countryside, from an Atlantic perspective, was the absence of farmers living within close conversation and day-to-day cooperation—even within hollering distance—of one another.

Early-nineteenth-century Americans accepted the point with pride. To the republican tourists abroad, the nucleated countryside of the ancien régime was a confirming sign of Old World backwardness. Hemmed in by the broad fields of the aristocracy so that priest and manor agent could lord it more heavily over them, the peasants' tightly compacted villages seemed to broadcast the continent's prevailing inequalities of power. The freed slaves in the American South had done their best to escape their own version of that rural pattern after 1865, dragging their cabins out to the fields. The European rural hamlet—"a few miserable two-story houses huddled together on crooked streets," one American carped in the 1890s—all a two- or three-mile walk from the fields its peasants had to work, seemed to many American observers backward and inefficient, undemocratic and absurd.[49]

But in the transvaluation of social and political sensibilities in which the progressives were engaged, rural reformers began to suspect that the American pattern—marching farm by farm over the horizon, in a landscape of formless, Lockean individualism—was the one more deeply mired in the past. The dominant American design on the land was "archaic, unorganized, [and] uncertain," Frederic Howe objected in 1919. "It is unsocial, lonely, poor in all the things that all normal-minded men and women want." The "fatal" defect of the American countryside, the University of North Carolina professor of rural social economics E. C. Branson wrote from southern Germany in 1923, was its "solitary farmsteads," its pervasive "loneliness," its deficiency in true farm "communities." The thinness of the American countryside reinforced the rural folk's economic and political disorganization. Its diffuseness sustained their social weakness. To preach economic cooperation in these circumstances was to whistle against a prairie wind. To truly revitalize the countryside meant finding a new American form for one of the European countryside's most enduring institutions.[50]

The agricultural progressives of the early twentieth century were not the first to preach the need for closer settlement of the land. An archaeology of rural America would turn up all manner of private experiments in more compact rural settlement that blended religious discipline, utopian politics, and real-estate speculation in varying proportions. Progressive advocates of the renucleated countryside inherited these precedents but departed from them. Their planned rural communities were to be secular and scientific, not sacred or utopian. Their aim was to make out of many slender holdings a new margin of collective, democratic strength. And because the health of the countryside so depended on it, the engine of private idealism would not suffice; this time, the state would be the planned rural community's patron.

Most of the American experts on country life thought the ambition of refashioning the physical frame of rural life unrealistic. The overwhelming majority of country folk dismissed it altogether. But through an intricate set of interconnections between water and land politics in the mountain West, arid Australia, the plains of eastern Prussia, and central California, the idea of fashioning a new physical frame for agricultural settlement found its way even into the United States.

The key intermediary for the planned rural settlement idea was an irrigation engineer and self-made community planner, Elwood Mead. A portrait from the early 1920s shows an urbane, paternal figure, not easily distinguishable from a typical 1920s businessman except for his lack of an arm, severed in a trolley accident. Born and raised on his family's farm in southern Indiana, Mead lit out at the first possible moment for college and a career as a civil engineer, landing a post as territorial engineer for Wyoming in the late 1880s. The main job of a western-state engineer, where both land promotion and mining hinged on water supplies, was water rights—a late-nineteenth-century rattlers' nest of competing claims, fantastic ambitions, and outright fraud. Stream bank owners felt free to claim whatever they could imagine as their potential water needs, leapfrogging upstream to outmaneuver one another's water claims and then unloading their speculative irrigation developments on hapless farm purchasers. The system grated deeply on Mead's orderly, work-driven character, and he helped write into the Wyoming state constitution more extensive state water adjudication powers than anywhere else in the West. That work launched Mead's career as an irrigation and public lands policy expert. Lake Mead, impounded behind Hoover Dam, whose construction he oversaw as director of the U.S. Bureau of Reclamation between 1924 and his death in 1936, is his most enduring legacy. Mead's irrigation work, in turn, made him an expert on agricultural settlements. He became the most prominently placed advocate of state-promoted farm villages for America and the godfather of the New Deal resettlement work. But all this required gathering in experience from well beyond the United States.[51]

Australia was Mead's detour. Offered the chairmanship of the Rivers and Water Supply Commission of the state of Victoria in 1907, Mead spent eight years in Australia managing water development in the arid backcountry. The irrigation works he inherited were, as it turned out, an American inspiration of the 1880s. Land was nineteenth-century Australia's most volatile political issue. Ranchers, many of whom had begun as squatters during the early years of the century, dominated the backcountry, while labor radicals fumed with Georgite anger at land monopolization. Eager for models of alternative settlement patterns, a reform state administration had dispatched a commission to California in 1885 to study the gradual displacement of the California sheep ranchers by intensive, irrigated agriculture.

The California irrigation developments the commissioners inspected were private, speculative undertakings. Borrowing the ends but altering the means, the Victoria government translated the idea into an ambitious public works project of dams and trunk canals with which to try to transform the Murray River basin into a region of small farms. Enlistment of state enterprise was in keeping with the tendencies of Australian politics. Short on both settlers and private sources of capital, turn-of-the-century Australians turned to state promotional investment with a readiness matched nowhere else in the English-speaking world. A high tariff wall, a ban on nonwhite immigration, generous public infrastructure investments, progressive labor protection statutes, and publicly promoted land settlement were all ingredients of Australian "settler statism."[52]

The problem when Mead arrived was that the trunk canals ran nowhere, the fields were unwatered, and the state's investment was almost completely unreturned. The ranchers and wheat growers who owned the land abutting the state canals had no interest in developing their holdings for more intensive agriculture; the urban working class, their anger at the land monopolists notwithstanding, had no practical interest in intensive farming. Critics then and since have suggested the prudent thing would have been to write the investment off as an expensive mistake. But Mead had larger ambitions and the power to get others to see his dreams as vividly as if they had dreamed them themselves. Jacking up taxes on landowners who left their land unirrigated, Mead's agency proceeded to buy up sections of their tracts, subdivide them into small parcels, lay out irrigation ditches, erect houses, plant an initial crop, and bring in European settlers to farm it, loaning them a hefty portion of the purchase price and giving them supervision to make sure they managed the land effectively.[53]

Mead's detractors claimed he tried to transplant an incongruous piece of the California landscape on a terrain where intensive fruit and vegetable cultivation could not be made to pay. Mead had, from the first, no love for pastoral Australia; "the grim solitudes of the vast interior," he called it. He saw Australia, as he had seen Wyoming, with a hatred of land speculators that, if it did not amount to single-tax discipleship, came very close to single-tax sentiments, and an eagerness to see land brought to what he called its full, most intensive fruition. But if Mead imported some of his land politics from the American West, he brought to Australia more distant notions as well. He had spent the summer of 1903 in Italy's Po valley, deeply impressed by the Italian smallholders' ability to manage their complex irrigation cooperatives with a minimum of litigious, water-grabbing contentiousness. In 1910 he had made a still more extensive tour of Europe, partly to advertise Australian settlement possibilities among potential immigrants, partly to see what sorts of settler inducements would be necessary to make intensive European farming take hold in the Murray River basin. From Plunkett House to Denmark, he had hunted up European schemes to stem the population tide flowing away from the land. Most impressive of them all, in Mead's mind, was the work of the German Home Colonization Commission, which, in a massive, nationalistic effort to prevent failing estates in eastern Prussia from falling into the hands of Polish purchasers, was buying up large holdings and resettling them with German small farmers, equipping them with seed, houses, tools, and expert help.[54]

The Australian political context, combined with what he had learned in Europe, gave Mead the program he spent the rest of his life propagandizing. The work he had begun in Victoria, he wrote in 1910, "would doubtless be called Socialism gone mad" in the United States. In the Australian context, where the state owned not only the railroads but also refrigerator cars and cold-storage warehouses to ease the farmers' access to their world market, where in the course of a strike that had threatened to close the rail lines for lack of fuel the state simply bought its own coal mine, where the state owned savings banks, forests, and streetcar systems, the public promotion of farm settlement fit in without a wrinkle of contradiction.[55]

Returning to California in 1915 to take a post as professor of rural institutions at the University of California, Mead moved quickly into progressive political circles, bringing his Australian notions of the state with him. Land was, as usual, a key state issue. The state's private land development companies, accustomed to capitalizing on fancy advertising, farmer naïveté, and half-truths about water supplies, were once again in the eye of controversy. In Wisconsin, where land development companies were unloading worthless cutover land on raw immigrant buyers, Richard Ely's circle was laying plans for a state commission to regulate land development enterprises. In California, Mead convinced the businessmen progressives in the state's Commonwealth Club to back a bolder alternative for more orderly development of the Central Valley: demonstration land development projects run, as in Victoria, directly by a state agency. Harris Weinstock engineered Mead's appointment as chair of a new state Commission on Colonization and Rural Credits. After two years of intensive lobbying, the legislature signed on to the land colony idea. With Mead overseeing the work through a blizzard of correspondence from his office in Berkeley, a dairy colony of some 140 families was launched in 1918 in Durham, near Chico. A second, larger farm colony was begun in Delhi, in the San Joaquin Valley, in 1920. If Mead had had his way, there would soon have been at least a half dozen more.[56]

In most respects the state land commission projects recapitulated Mead's Australian schemes, whose success he ballyhooed at every opportunity. The State Land Settlement Board purchased the land, replatted it into ten- to sixty-acre smallholdings, graded and ditched it for irrigation, selected the most promising of applicants for occupancy, staked them to long-term mortgages, and planted an initial crop, all before the settlers took hold of their parcels. In two respects, however, both of which tapped strains deep in American progressive politics, the California undertakings departed from Mead's Murray River work. The first was the concentration of university expertise on the projects. Professors swarmed over both colonies like watchful hens. University of California soil scientists recommended the colony sites, state architects designed the houses and farmsteads, a University of California animal husbandry professor chose the breeding stock, and resident, university-trained farm managers dispensed day-to-day loans and agricultural advice.[57]

Mead's second innovation was a notion of community far more intensely developed than anything that had been tried in Australia. In Victoria, Mead's "closer settlement" schemes had been scattered, infill projects. Delhi and Durham, by contrast, were concentrated nodes of smallholdings designed to demonstrate the cooperative advantages of compactness. The paper plans drawn up for both settlements included community centers on the most up-to-date city planning lines. Durham's was to contain a meeting hall, a school, a swimming pool, tennis courts, and a permanent stock show building; at Delhi, the small farmsteads were to be anchored at each end by a planned village center. While spatially the settlements' anchors were their community centers, economically their essential institution was a compulsory farmers' cooperative association. Seed, machinery, and livestock were purchased through the co-op, milk marketed through it, breeding stock regulated by it, and the farmers' self-government realized through it. Cooperation, university science, Australian "settler socialism," a dose (from Mead and the resident managers) of highly solicitous paternalism, a dash of something like economic democracy, and a form of the community ideal long in the progressive air all went into the design.

It would be hard to overestimate the attention this combination attracted between 1918 and 1921. With the fate of twentieth-century agriculture on their minds, scores of delegations came to see the neat bungalow-dotted farm plots beneath the scattered oaks at Durham, or to visit Delhi's orchards, vineyards, and gardens struggling out of the blowing sands of a scrubby sheep pasture. In Australia, Mead had offered state-planned land settlement as a means of breaking up the big pastoral holdings and making an idle investment in dams and canals pay. In the United States, in a whirlwind of speeches and articles, Mead posed the colonies in different terms: as the answer to a full-blown crisis in rural class relations. The owner-occupied farm of the past, Mead insisted, was being swept away. As the monotony and loneliness of conventional farm life drew farm children into the cities, their families' lands were being gobbled up by well-capitalized speculators at prices the next pioneering generation could no longer afford and leased out to a new peasant tenantry. With farm tenancy rates rising in early-twentieth-century America, Mead's anxieties were lifted onto the shoulders of broader, bigger urgencies.

To this portrait of a refeudalized countryside, Mead added a racist spin. Although his racism ran no deeper than that of many of his fellow Anglo-Californians, who responded to the rumor that Delhi children were attending school with neighboring Japanese-American farm children with a furious, American Legion-sponsored protest, or that of his former Australian coworkers holding the line against Asian immigration, or that of the Germans whose work to reclaim eastern Prussia for German farmers had early caught his eye, it was, nevertheless, strong in its own right. The population drift away from the family farm was an "American" drift; the tenants that landlords were bringing in to fill their place, Mead protested, were Mexicans, Japanese, Chinese, Portuguese, and "Hindoos." The point was made all the more urgent for the Land Settlement Board by the presence of a privately backed Japanese-American agricultural settlement close by the Delhi colony's northern border, with its own hard-working small farmers and its own communitywide cooperative association.[58]

"California is at the frontier of the white man's world," Mead told a San Francisco audience in 1920. African Americans who applied to take up land at Durham and Delhi were shunted elsewhere; Asian Americans, given Delhi's billing as an "All American" community and the American Legion post planted conspicuously in the village center, knew better than to apply. But to put "white" Americans back on the farm would take more than race consciousness. Intensive, irrigated agriculture was the new frontier, Mead insisted, and to make it pay required a union of state direction and cooperative enterprise utterly different from the "unplanned, individualistic rural society of the past." Raw nativism, a cosmopolitan appeal to a worldwide policy tide, utopianism, and alarm all fused together. The California State Land Settlement Board colonies were not mere reclamation experiments; they were the way of the future, models of "a new social fabric," of a "new and better rural civilization."[59]

The war, breaking into Mead's projects, gave all his visions a still broader canvas. The California endeavor had barely been launched in the summer of 1918 when Mead was summoned to Washington, D.C., where anxiety for the economic future of the demobilized soldiers ran high. There Mead helped put his stamp on the only official reconstruction scheme to survive the puncturing of the war collectivist mood. At the Labor Department, Frederic Howe and Louis Post were already deep into plans for a massive postwar public works program, modeled in part on David Lloyd George's, with government-sponsored farm resettlement colonies to soak up the jobless residue. At the Interior Department, Secretary Franklin K. Lane was touting a scheme of government-sponsored soldier settlements on the department's western reclamation projects to absorb the landless, demoralized, and potentially revolutionary army of discharged soldiers. Mead's contribution was to steer Lane away from a notion of land bonuses to be dealt out individually from the unclaimed public land reserve, and into the idea of planned community settlements. Promoted by Howe's and Mead's publicity work, by Lane's lobbying, and by close to a million copies of the Interior Department's pamphlet, *Hey There! Do You Want a Home on a Farm?* the department's soldier resettlement-colony proposal kept a remnant of reconstruction's banner aloft into 1920. The Delhi colony, opened with special benefits for war veterans, was one of the idea's first beneficiaries.[60]

However grandly proposed, a nationwide experiment in state-sponsored, soldier-settled farm villages was not to be. Realization that the uprooted veterans were not the Bolshevist tinder Lane had imagined soon told against the idea. Clarence Poe lined up the *Progressive Farmer* on the farm colony side, but the threat of government-sponsored competition in an already crowded market turned most farmers and their congressional allies against the scheme, all the more vociferously as the bottom fell out of war-inflated farm prices in 1920–21.[61]

Mead's California colonies were particularly poorly armored for the agricultural depression of the early 1920s. Delhi was the weakest point. Built on a site that mandated an expensive system of concrete pipe irrigation and overhead costs that only the immediate sale of its farmsteads could recoup, Delhi opened in the teeth of the price decline. Throughout 1922 and 1923 Mead and Delhi's resident farm manager struggled with the problem of weak purchaser demand, cranked the publicity mills, and sent recruiters east to look for potential buyers, trying by sheer energy and will power to buck the general agricultural collapse. But the land would not sell fast enough with so little prospect of return. When a supplemental bond issue failed narrowly at the polls in 1922, Mead abandoned direct supervision of the California land colonies for consulting assignments in New South Wales and Palestine. Demanding that their loans be forgiven, the Delhi settlers, emboldened by the war veterans in their ranks, took Mead's portrait down from their community hall and hanged it from a tree. When the Delhi settlers were eventually granted special hardship terms, the Durham settlers filed a lawsuit for equivalent concessions. By the end of the decade, the state, back in conservative political hands, had written off both colonies at a loss and was selling out its interest in Mead's "paternalistic" experiment.[62]

The economic difficulties of its flagship demonstration colonies did not, however, exhaust the planned agricultural settlement idea. It was characteristic of the farm village ideal, so tightly did it weave together the strands of progressive politics, that its rationale possessed an exceptional fluidity, that it could be reconstructed around so many shifting needs. If Mead had given a statist, Australian twist to the country life reformers' concerns, if his vision of resocialized agriculture was top-heavy with expert management and advice, if his notion of "putting the government into farming" (as his enemies called it) entailed costs and risks in excess of what the public's representatives were willing to accept, if his sense of individualistic agriculture at its wit's end raised hackles among farmers, the Mead colonies, trailing their foreign pedigree so conspicuously, nevertheless gathered up too many of the threads in the progressives' imagination to be altogether abandoned.

Defeat, accordingly, sent the planned rural community idea in search of a more propitious occasion. For a while Mead hoped the Bureau of Reclamation would take up the work. Blocked on that front, he struck up yet another set of converts among southern progressives. One of them, the maverick land developer Hugh MacRae, had been drumming up interest since the early 1920s in a privately financed, ruralized "American Letchworth" to be built in rings of intensively cultivated, ten- to twenty-acre farmsteads in eastern North Carolina. With an advisory committee that glittered with prominent progressives (Poe, Pinchot, Lane, Kenyon Butterfield of the Country Life Commission, Albert Shaw, Ray Stannard Baker, and Mead himself among them), with a site plan by Raymond Unwin's closest American friend, John Nolen, and a platform blaming the flight from farm to city on the country's failure to meet the modern "craving for social and intellectual companionship," MacRae's Farm City project distilled yet another variant of the progressive dream of somehow reshaping the backward, atomistic countryside.[63]

What Mead offered the southern progressives who discovered him in the late 1920s was potential access to Reclamation Bureau funds and a ready-made solution still waiting for the right need and political opportunity. The alliance settled on a bill to establish a planned rural demonstration community, along Durham and Delhi lines, on a tract of reclaimed land in every southern state. The group that Mead and MacRae assembled to boost the proposal was knee-deep in southern land and railroad investors, who were eager to boost the market price of their cutover pineland holdings. But to the country life reformers in the alliance, the bottom line of the scheme was "human reclamation." Mired in isolation and ignorance, "the farmers of the South . . . live as no other farmers in the world live," University of North Carolina rural sociologist E. C. Branson wrote in explaining the planned settlement colony's newest rationale. No mere increase in schools or farm agents would change that, only practically demonstrated alternative settlement models. Thus, out of a scheme to recoup public irrigation works expenses that had then become an answer to a crisis in rural class relations and, briefly, a device to absorb a demobilized army, Mead's southern backers drew a device to shame and educate southern farmers out of their inefficient, individualistic ways.[64]

Flexibility is the key distinction between borrowable and context-fixed policies, between the extractable and that which is so wedded to its political and social environment as to be inextricably fixed to it. In conventional cases the flexibility lies in means and form; in others, however, where the form captures the imagination, the moveable part is the rationale. The expert-planned, cooperative farm village, gathering as it did so many of the contrasts and anxieties in the air, moved as a floating answer from problem to problem into the early 1930s. It could not be realized; but neither, on the eve of the New Deal, would it go away.

Vis-à-vis those who traced the countryside's weakness to the splintered, individuated organization of its economy and those who traced it to the dispersed and isolated settlement pattern on the land, there remained a third alternative. The farmers' fundamental weakness might be, at bottom, one of mind and values. The atomization of the countryside, the "lack of organization and cohesion" that left the small farmer prey to the better organized interests around him, the suspicion of cooperative enterprise that made him all the more susceptible to those who would cash in on his economic fantasies, might all be better traced, perhaps, to mores and culture.[65]

At a certain level, the point was irrefutable. The cooperatives ran or fell by their members' ability to forge an ethos larger than possessive individualism. There was not a movement for rural reconstruction, from the Raffeisen cooperatives to Mead's California farm colonies, that did not make room for a strong, didactic effort in this direction. But if, under all, the way of the land was ultimately set by culture, then the place to start was with the schools.

The problem was knowing what to teach that did not intensify the handicaps of the countryside. Literacy and technical agricultural education clearly held rewards for country folk. Tenants who could reckon gained no automatic immunity from the crooked arithmetic of their merchant-landlords, but they stood a better bargaining chance. Technologically up-to-date farm cooperatives held far better cards in the agricultural market than those that merely pooled the poverty and inefficiency around them. The rub lay in finding a form of education that, in pulling farm children into the heady streams of book learning and town life, did not spur the most ambitious to bolt the countryside all the sooner. The cities had only to nod and beckon, AE wrote, and all over the world country folk fled to them—all the faster as newspapers, books, and consolidated schools brought home the contrast between the mental stimulation of the one and the intellectual narrowness of the other.[66] How could rural schools awaken the mind without accelerating the exodus of the brightest young country folk—without leaving, in the end, the slow and the dull to inherit the earth?

For those who wrestled with the horns of this dilemma, the most important country in the North Atlantic economy was Denmark. A number of American progressives had sought out Denmark before the war, Poe and McCarthy among them. In the course of a career that took him from a Tennessee farm to the office of U.S. commissioner of education, Philander P. Claxton had chanced on a Danish folk high school in 1896 and become an active promoter of folk schools for the American South. Booker T. Washington had pronounced Denmark the only bright spot in prewar rural Europe. But the absence of a Plunkett to act as Denmark's intermediary and the pull of the continent's bigger nations both worked against prewar Denmark. The Institute of Educational Travel's Civic and Social Tour of Europe in 1914 allotted Denmark three days, sandwiching in its credit and creamery cooperatives with its castles and museums, its old-age pension scheme, its model housing, and its model garbage disposal techniques. The American Commission on Agricultural Cooperation and Rural Credit in 1913 dismissed Denmark with an optional side excursion.[67]

In the war's reconstruction of national reputations, however, Denmark enjoyed a dramatic rise in the esteem of American progressives. Ireland in the early 1920s was consumed in civil war; Germany was economically prostrate. In the post-1919 disillusionment with the top-heavy war state at home, smallness emerged for American progressives as having new advantages. Frederic Howe, one of prewar Germany's keenest progressive admirers, had transferred his longings to Denmark by 1920. Cooperative Denmark, as Howe saw it, was a commonwealth with virtually none of the usual trappings and pretensions of state power: a nation "concerned solely with the intensive development of her own territory and the promotion of the well-being of her three million people." That in itself made it, Howe thought, "quite the most valuable political exhibit in the modern world." Josephine Goldmark in the mid 1930s was to write about Danish social policy in the same way. "Why should anyone want to go to Russia when one can go to Denmark?" her brother-in-law Louis Brandeis was heard by New Dealers to remark. Wholly removed from "the vortex of European politics," as an American observer put it in 1927, Denmark was, for the moment, at the crossroads of the progressives' world.[68]

By 1923 E. C. Branson could report that Denmark was "over-run" by foreign investigators. In the course of two months in the Danish countryside, he had met educators from Japan, Vienna, Berlin, Canada, the Hampton Institute, and the Appalachian social settlements, to say nothing of a trainload of English dairy farmers and a conference full of social workers, all trying to learn the secrets of the Danish agricultural revival. "Denmark is being examined by students of this sort more thoroughly at this moment than any other country of the world," he was convinced.

> They are farmers and farm organization officials, college professors and teachers of every grade and rank, graduate students digging doctorate dissertations out of life itself and not out of dust bins, legislative committees and commissions, congressmen and field investigators from the agricultural department at Washington, members of the English parliament and details from the Home Office, settlement workers, social secretaries, public welfare officers, research students representing the social-work foundations of America, authors assembling material for books on Denmark, Scandinavian-American scholarship students, and so on and on.

They were "all using Denmark as a field laboratory in political science and social economics, swapping addresses, exchanging letters of introduction."[69]

The American-Scandinavian Foundation, organized to promote mutual exchanges between the Scandinavian countries and the United States, granted special traveling fellowships for the study of Danish cooperative agriculture, Danish industrial organization, and the Danish folk high schools. Chris Christensen, who was to become the U.S. Agriculture Department's first director of the division of cooperative marketing, held one of them; Olive Campbell, founder of the first Danish-modeled American folk school, held another. So did the young African-American sociologist E. Franklin Frazier, though in deference to American racial sensibilities the foundation pulled his name from its publicity release.[70]

Highest on the minds of most of Denmark's progressive visitors were its farm cooperatives. Howe was sure the cooperatives had been the key to the Danish rural revival. Branson, for whom the contrast between the Danish farmers' standard of living and hard-scrabble North Carolina poverty "literally kept my brain in a blaze" during his weeks in Denmark, came to the same conclusion. The Farm City promoter Hugh MacRae confessed he was "almost appalled by the possibilities" of Danish cooperative agriculture.

From the other side of the South's racial divide, E. Franklin Frazier came back from his nine months of intensive study to champion the formation of small-scale farm cooperatives throughout the black South, as islands of self-made economic democracy in a racially hostile sea.[71]

Fewer Americans noticed the hand of the land-reforming state in the Danish rural revival. Worried about rural political restiveness in the poorest and most exploited sector of the rural economy, the government in 1899 had inaugurated a program of subsidized state loans to enable marginal farm tenants to purchase smallholdings of their own. The government's purposes were not wholly altruistic. Most purchases made under the act ran to barely seven or eight acres, large enough to anchor their owners to the countryside but too small, by design, to enable them to withdraw from the pool of agricultural wage labor that the larger farm owners required. Nonetheless the smallholdings act—extended, liberalized, and finally pushed by a smallholder-socialist alliance into a tool for the breakup of some of the largest estates—contributed to a dramatic drop in Danish farm tenancy. In 1850, 42 percent of Danish farm operators had been tenants. By the end of the First World War, though the smallholders remained a visibly separate social and political group on the Danish countryside, only 10 percent were now tenants.[72]

Alarmed as they were by their own country's farm tenancy rate, which had risen from 26 percent to 38 percent between 1880 and 1920, American progressives might have been expected to broadcast the Danish smallholdings legislation. But land reform was constitutionally difficult, expensive, and, in the South, mined by racial politics. Branson, though a member of the North Carolina State Commission on Farm Tenancy and State-Aid to Farm Ownership, barely noticed Danish land reform. Even Howe, who deluded himself into thinking of Danish agriculturists as a single class with a common interest, did not recommend it.

If American progressives systematically downplayed the hand of the state in Danish social politics, the problems familiar from London or Manchester barely crossed their consciousness in Denmark at all. There were far more wage earners in Denmark, more periodic unemployment crises, more socialists, and more conflict than an American reader of the reports from progressive Denmark could ever have imagined. Danish workers had staged a general strike in 1920. In 1924, contemporaneous with the first Labour Party government in Britain, Danish socialists had formed their first, short-lived government. But American progressives did not go to Denmark to see labor and capital at war, or Danish politics in action. They went to Denmark with an agrarian commonwealth on their minds. They could barely begin to see Denmark except in terms of their own countryside—"without having North Carolina in the tail of one's eye," as Branson put it—and they wrapped their impressions tightly around the spool they brought with them.[73]

If the socialists and the state tended to skitter out of the Americans' focus, however, Denmark's folk schools riveted it. In the folk schools progressive Americans found the answer to what statistical enumeration of the range of Danish rural cooperative undertakings only made enigmatic: how the transition from peasant to cooperative commonwealth had come about. The folk school story was one many Danes liked to tell themselves. Older than the cooperatives, the folk schools had taken hold in the 1860s, in the aftershocks of German invasion. By the 1870s some three thousand young men and women were enrolled each year; by the late 1920s it was guessed that almost a third of the Danish farm population had, as young adults, passed through them.

In practical terms, a folk school was a gathering of young country adults between the ages of nineteen and twenty-five, men and women in separate sessions, drawn from their farms and villages for a single season in residence. In pedagogical terms, the folk schools' mission was cultural revival. Few of them taught the book-learned, commercial farming of the American agricultural colleges. Most of them taught with virtually no books at all and with neither grades nor examinations. Instead, their curricula mixed Danish cultural nationalism, through talks on Danish literature and history, with the experience of cooperative group living, all reinforced with singing, group games, and inspirational lectures by the teachers. The folk schools' founding philosopher, Nikolai Frederik Severin Grundtvig, had been himself a key figure in the endeavor to extricate Scandinavian vernacular literature from the scorn of salon aristocrats. The folk schools were to the Danish agricultural revival what the poet-reformer AE tried to be for the Irish agricultural revival—the spiritual adjunct to, if not the spiritual motor for, the day-to-day business of practical cooperation.[74]

Within that frame the folk schools varied widely. Americans tended to visit the most established: Roskilde, an easy hour's travel from Copenhagen, or Askov, the training school for folk school teachers, where the white-collared students and collegiate setting reminded Americans of home. Beyond these two were many more that rose and fell according to the individual vision and charisma of their principals *(Forstaender)*, most of whom owned their schools outright. Some gave special place to gymnastics, others to religion. There were special folk schools for smallholders; there was a socialist-sponsored school for young urban workers and another, with an international student body, for the promotion of international peace. In one fashion or another, however, the experience of cooperative living and the inspirational "living word" of the teachers was central to them all. Nationalistic yet highly varied, private and yet subsidized by state tuition assistance, the folk schools mixed public and private energies as freely as the Danish rural cooperatives, whose cultural adjunct they were.

Readily open to visitors, even those whose Danish was not up to the task, and far easier to observe than the farmers' maze of cooperative connections, the Danish folk schools quickly caught the eye of progressive American travelers. Philander Claxton dispatched a team of special investigators from the Bureau of Education to take the folk schools' measure. Booker T. Washington, eliding the gulf between the Danish curriculum and the trade school training of his own Tuskegee Institute, hitched his project to their prestige. Hampton Institute's *Southern Workman* ran some of the earliest reports on the folk schools, E. Franklin Frazier's among them.[75] In the 1920s, progressive educators formed another node of admiring visitors.[76] Matched to the educationalist strain in the American progressive imagination, the Danish folk school principals preached a message their American visitors wanted to hear: that if the prerequisite for effective agricultural revival was cooperation, the prerequisite for cooperation was education—not learning that stripped country folk of their rooted attachments but education for cultural revitalization.

Inevitably, some Americans tried to take home what they had observed and establish it on native ground. The effort most faithful to the Danish model was launched in Wisconsin by Chris Christensen, an American-Scandinavian Foundation fellowship recipient and Agriculture Department expert on agricultural cooperation, now dean of the University of Wisconsin's Agricultural College. As Christensen redesigned it in 1932, the Wisconsin short course for farmers brought young farm men in their twenties to Madison for a four-month immersion in the things their isolation denied them: lectures on history, art, sociology, and economics, together with singing, public speaking, and sports. They wrote poetry, and under the inspiration of John Steuart Curry, were encouraged to paint. John Barton, who had gone from a Missouri farm to Yale Divinity School to a position on the faculty of the international folk high school in Elsinore, Denmark, was brought in to lecture on Danish land reform and social movements. The class in cooperative organization was compulsory.[77]

But as deeply attractive as the Danish folk schools were—with their energetic young farmers hanging eagerly on their teachers' "living word"—they were not an easy institution to transplant. The problem was the problem of the folk. In one sense, the issue was a false one, an error in translation. The more accurate rendering of the Danish *Folkehøjskoler* was "people's high schools." The additional anthropological burden that the word "folk" carried in the 1920s and 1930s was not, in a literal sense, necessary. Still, folk schools without strong threads of common ways and culture, without a living, collective tradition on which to build, were impossible to imagine.

But in the extraordinary cultural heterogeneity of the United States, its countryside a patchwork of rival immigrant and racial subcultures, where was the curricular content of an American version of the folk schools to be found? Where could one find the folk songs and sagas and traditional dances, the literature and history that young country men and women would recognize as unproblematically theirs? Even the Wisconsin countryside, with its farm families barely a generation or two from Germany, Poland, Sweden, or Finland, posed a challenge in this regard. In the face of this difficulty, it was hardly surprising that the mainstream adult education movement in the United States should run so strongly toward information and technical skills—not toward group identity but toward more effective individual competence.

There was, however, a region that seemed to many observers to meet the cultural criteria for a Danish-inspired rural revival, and that was Appalachia—or, as it was then commonly called, the southern highlands. The ambitions of southern admirers of the folk schools gravitated there quickly. Racially more homogeneous than the rest of the South, far less schooled, farther from the acids of commerce and modernity, the mountain South was an obvious site for experiments in adult education. In the late nineteenth century, outsiders to the southern mountains had written off the region's culture as isolated and degenerate, a backwater of feuding, moonshining, and illiteracy. By the early years of the twentieth century, however, ballad and craft collectors had begun to seek out Appalachia for skills and cultural remnants long discarded elsewhere: songs with a touch of Elizabethan culture to them, old country dances, traditional quilting and woodcarving patterns. Here, in the threads of a culture older than commercial capitalism, was the stuff out of which a revitalization movement might perhaps be made.[78]

The initiators of the highland folk school movement were active players in this revaluation of southern mountain culture. Olive Campbell was a pioneering ballad collector, one of several song collectors who had begun to scour the mountain coves looking for country folk who still knew mountain music as it had been played before the mail-order banjo had gotten hold of it. Her husband, John Campbell, had come south from Andover Theological Seminary in Massachusetts in the 1890s to teach in the region's missionary-sponsored colleges and academies. In 1908 he convinced the new Russell Sage Foundation to add a Southern Highlands Division—balancing off its urban, industrial projects with a survey of social life at the other end of the scale of economic development. Between 1908 and 1919, Campbell was the division's one-man staff, seeking to bring the social survey techniques perfected in London and Pittsburgh to the region's needs and resources, and to refocus the work of its outside tutelary agencies.

If a living connection with history was the region's strength, "extreme individualism," as John Campbell saw it, was the mountain South's weakness. Moonshining, feuding, and violence were its regional manifestations, but the larger cultural burden was not Appalachia's alone. "Individualism is the great American fault, and in the mountaineer, the surviving original American, individualism is raised to the highest power," Campbell wrote in 1916; in the region, as in the nation at large, "cooperation . . . is what we so much need." As the Campbells' ambitions shifted from traditional educational work to a program focused, somehow, on culture and cooperation, it is not surprising that the Danish example should have caught their imagination. Claxton first told them of the folk school idea. They were booked for a trip to Denmark and were already trying to raise funds for a folk school of their own in the southern highlands when the war broke out.[79]

It was Olive Campbell, after her husband's death in 1919, who put their joint project into practice. With the aid of an American-Scandinavian Foundation fellowship, she spent fourteen months in Scandinavia in 1922 and 1923, most of it as an acutely attentive observer of the Danish folk schools, with a side trip to seek out AE in Ireland. By 1925 she had raised funds to purchase a farmstead near Brasstown in the hills of western North Carolina as the site of the John C. Campbell Folk School. For the first several years it took in no students, concentrating instead on the development of a local cooperative creamery, cooperative chicken hatchery, and cooperative purchasing association and credit union among the neighboring farmers. On Saturday nights the school invited farmers in for lectures, agricultural discussions, and singing. When the first students arrived in the late 1920s, the curriculum consisted of history and literature, folk dances, singing games, gymnastics, work on the school's demonstration farm, and revived mountain crafts.

To stem the drift of mountain folk into the cities, whose effects Olive Campbell deeply distrusted; to revitalize mountain folkways rather than educate young highlanders out of them, all the while rechanneling the self-destructive individualism of mountain culture into cooperative forms—these were the Campbell Folk School's ambitions. Compared with the typical rural school, drumming book learning into the heads of its pupils, or even to the work of the Pine Mountain Settlement in eastern Kentucky, where visitors noted how clean and neat the resident students were, how well they knew the use of napkins, how much they behaved "just like the well brought up children of gentle-folk," Campbell's break with the traditions of missionary uplift was striking. There were no examinations or credits at the Campbell Folk School; after an experiment or two, she scrapped Danish-style lectures for discussions, whose topics went round the world and then came back again to the business of mountain farming. She raised money for a fund to help graduates of the school purchase small, neighboring dairy farms. Through the Conference of Southern Mountain Workers, she helped encourage the region's craft revival. "School" was "a misleading term" for the work she had undertaken, she readily admitted. Through a mix of more intelligent farming, handicraft production, and cooperative enterprises, she hoped to fashion a pattern for the highlands' economic and cultural renewal.[80]

None of this, however, quite resolved the problem of the folk—as an issue both in Campbell's mind and in the contested mores of Appalachia itself. Square dances were native enough, but their association with drinking and rowdiness made them anathema to many mountain church folk; the banjo and its newfangled "hillbilly" music set the teeth on edge of those looking for a living, archaic culture; at the centers of the mountain crafts revival, outside experts censored bad design and farmed out models of the good, all in the name of more authentic folk art. The folk schools' powers of cultural revitalization depended on their ability to tap a deep, preconscious strain of collective identity. When that strain failed, what was to be done?

In the face of this discord, Campbell could not fully resist the temptation to sidestep the problem by leaning all the harder on her imported, Danish borrowings. Early on she had brought over two young Danish teachers to manage the school's animals and the creamery. The gymnastics taught at the school were Danish gymnastics. Danish songs mixed with Campbell's beloved native Appalachian ballads, Danish dances (discreetly renamed "games") with home-grown folk dances.

The problem of excessive literalism had been always a standing one in the transatlantic progressive connection. The trick of vision that had allowed American city planners to see Paris's étoiles and triumphal arches in their own city streets, or municipal ownership partisans to imagine Glasgow streetcars buzzing down Chicago's elevated tracks, or Elwood Mead to envision Po Valley vineyards in the Delhi sands, could not be kept out of Campbell's North Carolina hills. Between the transformative and imitative impulses within the Atlantic progressive connection the American folk school pioneers struggled particularly hard for balance.

The Campbell School's most famous rival in the folk school movement, the Highlander Folk School, seized the more radical way past the issues encapsulated in the idea of the folk. Alarmist billboards in the 1950s South blew up a photo of Martin Luther King, Jr., seated in a Highlander classroom—proof, it seemed to white southern segregationists, of King's communist past. In fact, Highlander's origins were no less deeply entangled with Denmark than those of the Campbell School. Highlander's founder, Myles Horton, was himself a product of the Appalachian South, cut with a strong dose of social-gospel Protestantism. Fleeing the region's mills and small factories for Cumberland College and a stint of organizing work for the Young Men's Christian Association, Horton had come back from college to Ozone, Tennessee, one summer to organize Bible study classes. From that summer on, Horton's notes for a long-term "Ozone project," full of self-doubt and confusion about method, grew in ever-thickening masses. He was in search of blueprints when he arrived at Union Theological Seminary in New York City in 1929, where he read John Dewey and where Reinhold Niebuhr took him under his wing, and he was still searching when he landed at the University of Chicago in 1930 to see if he could learn from Robert Park and Hull House how social change happened. "I was trying these ideas out on everybody. Everybody," he later recalled. "I could never get this idea straight . . . Every time I would get it to the place I wanted to use it would get fuzzy." A Lutheran minister Horton met in Chicago told him his Ozone project sounded like the folk schools he had attended in Denmark as a young man. Within a year, Horton had worked his passage to Denmark to see the folk school movement for himself.[81]

His Danish sojourn, as Horton later chose to remember it, was a disappointment, the last stage before he finally broke through what Jane Addams, in similar circumstances, once called the "snare of preparation." Only the Workers' Folk School in Esbjerg caught his interest, he recalled years later. In fact, he had read everything in English on the folk school movement and had taught himself Danish. Armed with Olive Campbell's book and her letters of introduction, he sought out rural folk schools all across Denmark. With every country *Forstander* he met, he tried out his ideas about religion, psychology, and social change, struggling to penetrate the secret of the movement's impact and the essence of its "living word."[82]

All these imported threads converged on Horton's project. Highlander's cofounder, Don West, had, like Horton, spent a year in Denmark, and had written his divinity degree thesis on the application of Danish educational methods to the Appalachian South. When the Highlander Folk School opened in Monteagle, Tennessee, in 1932, folk dancing (both Danish and mountain), piano lessons and folk music, lantern slide talks on West's and Horton's European travels, a women's canning cooperative, and Horton's class on how minds change were all part of its work. Olive Campbell's help was solicited on the organization of cooperative work. The land for the Highlander Folk School was given by Lilian Johnson, a Wellesley- and Cornell-trained historian who had been in attendance at the Southern Commercial Congress in Nashville in 1912 to see the audience swept off its feet by David Lubin's oratory. Inspired herself, Johnson had gone to Rome, immersed herself in the literature of European rural cooperation, drummed up donors for the Commission on Agricultural Cooperation and Rural Credit in Europe, served as the commission's staff assistant, and written much of its report before moving to eastern Tennessee to see if she could herself be the seed around which a local, thriving cooperative movement could grow. Though Monteagle was at the ends of the earth, paths from all over Europe converged on it.[83]

Unlike Campbell's Brasstown, however, Monteagle's farming days were long in the past. Timber and coal interests dominated the county's economy by the early 1930s. And Horton, unlike Campbell, was a socialist. He had been so at least from his Union Seminary days. He brought John Barton from Madison to lecture on cooperatives and Barton's wife, Rebecca, to teach labor literature, but much of the early faculty he recruited from the ranks of Union Seminary students, many of them still more radical than he. At Highlander the mountain songs and square dances blended with courses in labor history and current economic conditions. Asked by a Danish village *Forstander* what he wanted to teach, Horton had replied: "'I shall teach sociology and history in the light of ethical principles (meaning love)." By the time he sat down to write prospective donors, his aim was to develop "a bit of proletarian culture" in the mountain South—an indigenous leadership, locally rooted but no longer ignorant of class and economics, able to help the mountaineers effectively resist the coal and textile industries that were lapping up their cheap, unorganized labor. Among the South's historical resources, he thought, was its resistance to capitalism—"a defense, it is true," he reminded himself, "but nevertheless of some value."[84]

Having started up the school in the teeth of the Depression with so many delicately balanced ambitions, the Highlander staff was quickly caught up in the labor struggles erupting around it. Within a month Horton had been arrested for trying to write up the story of a coal strike in the northern part of the state. The school put its students on picket lines, where some of them were fired upon by factory guards. It undertook to unionize the county's Works Progress Administration workers. In 1937, when the CIO launched a concerted organizing drive in the South, the Highlander Folk School, long active in strike activities, announced that its "total resources" were being devoted to the labor movement.

As its labor commitments grew, however, Highlander's local ties slowly disintegrated. It won a grant for a local cannery cooperative from the Federal Emergency Relief Administration's Self-Help Cooperative Division, and almost immediately lost it when the Chattanooga papers took up the cry that the money would go to "reds and labor organizers." After seven years of intense local organizing, having been red-baited so thoroughly as finally to be a liability to the projects it touched, the faculty decided to withdraw altogether from local politics. From Horton's "Ozone" ambition of creating a node of social change naturalized among southern mountain folk, Highlander became a regional staging ground for the labor left (and later for the civil rights movement)—a Brookwood Labor College, in its own way, in a particularly rustic setting.

Olive Campbell had written Horton early on that it was hard for her "to see how you can develop a real folk school on the basis on which you have begun."[85] Horton's own memories, in time, discounted his Danish borrowings no less completely. In fact, the Danish traces were not hard to find at Highlander. In its emphasis on group cooperative living, in its dances and games, in the mountain songs the Highlander staff and students extracted from their neighbors to make a part of the radical subculture of the 1930s labor left, and, not least, in Horton's own chosen role as its philosophical

Forstander, hunting to the end for the "living word," Highlander's transatlantic connections clung to it, in their own way, as clearly as Campbell's did at Brasstown.

But in the end the secret of yoking local folk cultures and customs to a thoroughgoing movement of social change eluded Horton as much as Campbell. His construction of a CIO encampment in the Tennessee mountains was different from Campbell's reversion to her Danish borrowings. But neither had found a way to bring the folk school's core promise home—not when so much many of the tendencies in the surrounding political culture ran so hard against them.

"There is no doubt that the H.[igh] S.[chools] here were swept to fame by a tide beginning in the early 19 cent[ury] which seems to be the hope made possible by legislation regarding the land," Horton had written in a note to himself while in Denmark. Contemporaneous with the experiments of the early folk school *Forstaender*, an awakening in literature and culture had swept through Denmark and helped carry their work along with it. "Is a school like this possible without a tide or is there a tide in it?" Horton wondered.[86] His question went to the heart of the rural reformers' dilemma. If under the land lay still deeper strata of institutions, expectations, and culture, how could the whole geological structure itself be moved?

In one way or another, all the Europe-inspired rural reformers had pressed against this point. Underneath their talk of *Landschaften* and creamery cooperatives, Danish cows and Australian statism, folk schools and farm villages, the core discourse had been about values as much as market inequalities—and about the United States as much as about the nation's farming heartland. Rural folk, not always to their pleasure, stood for everyone. The excessive individualism of the countryside stood in for a general atomism, which might be the frontier's doing, the work of the barely checked market, or the work of culture itself. The question was the one Horton had worried so doggedly, filling so many notecards with its conundrums and difficulties before finally taking his plunge in the Tennessee mountains: where were the tides of cultural change generated?

The narratives out of which the transatlantic progressive connection was woven—the stories the Danish *Forstaender* told about Grundtvig, AE about Plunkett, Mead about his victories over land monopolists in the Australian outback, or the cooperators about the pioneer English band at Rochdale—all collapsed the problem into biography. But if the tide of historical change was not in persons or institutions but in the culture itself, how could one expect a transplanted device as frail as a folk school or a farmers' cooperative fundamentally to affect its course?

The question was not one of importability. That under the right circumstances institutions could be successfully transferred across national lines was clearly beyond doubt. Corporations and cooperatives had both slipped across the territorial lines of Europe like gypsy migrants. It was possible to say, without bending history past the breaking point, that from the English Owenites to the Schulze-Delitzsch and Raffeisen movements in Germany to the Italian people's banks pioneers a baton of sorts had been passed. Through an idea as exotic as the Prussian *Landschaften* the American farmers' long-standing demands for federal financial aid had come, finally, to political fruition. The tides of culture were not inflexible, just as they were not neatly contained by nation-states.

Boundary crossing itself was not the issue. The root problem the American reconstructors of the countryside faced was that their imported institutions would not stay fixed. Where the imported correctives to the countryside's social weaknesses had held out promises at odds with the surrounding culture of the market, they had been difficult to transplant. Where the institutions had been successfully naturalized, it was by taking on the traits of the market's culture. The big marketing cooperatives of the mid-1920s, with their boomers' zeal and monopoly ambitions, formed the most sobering case in point. When the imported measures could not but be transformed in the very act of adaptation and appropriation, when everything was in motion, how could one find the Archimedean point for the work of change?

That was a quandary the New Dealers would inherit, as they would inherit so many of the other products of the Atlantic progressive exchange. Each of the interwar projects of rural reconstruction was to flow into their capacious agenda. The Irish and Danish cooperatives, Mead's farm villages, the folk school idea, Plunkett's preoccupation with rural "organization" and AE's with the "fanatical . . . isolation and individualism" of rural life, all ended up in the corridors of the New Dealers' Washington, along with a profound, new sensitivity to culture itself.[87] It would be theirs to discover what second chance the temporary suspension of normal politics in the 1930s might bring to the project of reconstructing the particularly atomized economy of the American countryside.

9

The Machine Age

The American Invasion of Europe

Of all the countryside's reformers, the one who ignited the most extravagant expectations in the era between the wars was not Horace Plunkett, or Elwood Mead, or even Aaron Sapiro. It was Henry Ford. Made cheap enough so that every farmer could own a car and a tractor, his machine would revolutionize farm labor, Ford liked to boast. It would eliminate drudgery. It would knit city and country together. It would bring to the masses the array of goods and the freedom of motion that in every other historical era had been the special preserve of elites. What social politics had failed to do, technological change would accomplish. The "new era" was the machine age, and Ford was its prophet.

The new era was as much a public relations coup as an accomplished social fact, but it had important effects on the flow of influence within the Atlantic progressive connection. European social policy framers had been just as adept as their American counterparts at scavenging across national frontiers in the generation before the First World War, but they had places more important and nearer at hand in which to hunt for social-political innovations than the United States. The extraordinary curiosity of the Atlantic-facing American progressives about European social politics was, to the Americans' chagrin, only weakly reciprocated by informed European interest in progressive America. Against the main tide in the prewar social-political connection, a number of European progressives had indeed traversed the Atlantic in the other direction to see what extractable lessons they could find in American schools and playgrounds, juvenile courts and settlement houses, bureaus of labor statistics and standards of living. But the very dynamic of the Atlantic progressive connection in America turned not on its symmetries but on its imbalances—on its participants' sense of distance and lag and on the embarrassments of behindhandedness.

The 1920s marked, in this regard, a critical shift in both fact and consciousness. The rhetoric of leading and lagging nations endured. Others might talk of distinctive national geniuses and incomparable political destinies, but it was the mark of those who shaped the Atlantic progressive connection to see the world as a long line of runners pumping down a common track of progress, some in advance, others straggling in the rear. The 1920s did not fundamentally upset the metaphor of a common race, but on both sides of the Atlantic the decade scrambled and confused the order of the participants.

The first break in the prewar asymmetry came not through the technological and economic transformations that Europeans were soon bundling together as "Fordism," but with the war itself. Into the heart of guidebook Europe the American expeditionary army had rushed in the summer of 1918, not as a junior partner in an entangling foreign alliance but, as the American progressives preferred to see it, in a crusade to rescue civilization itself. "America had the infinite privilege of fulfilling her destiny and saving the world," Woodrow Wilson put the war's moral in a nutshell in late 1919, in the messianic rhetoric that American war propaganda agencies had disseminated wholesale on both sides of the Atlantic. With Wilson mapping out the future of democracy in liberated Europe, with cheering crowds lining his procession through Dover, Paris, and Rome, it was not hard to imagine that the torch of world progress had indeed passed, once more, to the United States.[1]

None felt the war's role reversals more keenly than the progressives who followed the American troops into France as part of a great civilian tail of Red Cross organizers, ex-charity association visitors, and amateur relief workers. Enlisted, for the most part, to help sanitize the war for the American army recruits, the American social workers quickly expanded their work to embrace the needs of war-devastated French civilians. The largest of the French relief enterprises was the American Red Cross's Department of Civil Affairs. Staffed with social work leaders temporarily on loan for the war's duration, it cared for French refugees and repatriates, distributed relief supplies, assisted in the rehabilitation of the civilian war wounded, and ran baby clinics, child health centers, and health and hygiene demonstration courses.[2]

Even as they rushed to aid war-torn France, the American relief workers could not resist the temptation to change it. The most important arena in this regard was the so-called devastated region northeast of Paris, a wilderness of shell holes, blasted trees, twisted and abandoned barbed wire, rubble, and hunger left behind by the German retreat in late 1914. The Marne and Meuse districts were already the territory of British Quaker relief workers. The Somme and Oise became the Americans' project. The first in the field was the Smith College Relief Unit, which undertook the care of fifteen small villages near Noyon in the summer of 1917. Other relief units were organized at Vassar, Barnard, Wellesley, Goucher, and Stanford, amounting in all to a women's moral equivalent of the work of the war's male ambulance volunteers. Settling into their shell-devastated villages, the Smith College women inventoried inhabitants and resources in social survey style, established medical dispensaries, gave out sewing so that the village women might have a tiny stream of income, and distributed emergency food, circumventing the male village officialdom in favor of distribution networks of village women. Distressed by the aimless recreation of French peasant children, they organized American-style play programs and team games.[3]

They behaved, in short, like settlement workers, not the least in their concern for the social disorganization, the "extreme individualism," with which they found themselves embattled. When they dreamed of a permanent legacy for their work, their minds ran toward organization of the faltering French civic sense. As Ruth Gaines of the Smith College Relief Unit imagined it, every reconstructed village would include a new House of the People, built hard by the church in the town's symbolic center, with shower baths, a medical dispensary, club rooms, a library, a consulting nurse for mothers with infants, and a room for civic exhibitions: a civic center in miniature, returned, in improved American form, to Europe.

The Americans' eagerness to reshape France on lines closer to the Europe of their own imagination was made even more graphic in the competition for the reconstruction of Reims. The most important city in the devastated region, Reims was virtually a tabula rasa of rubble at the war's end, more than half its buildings hollowed out or destroyed. The man who presided over the work, George B. Ford, was a veteran of the American settlement house network, the Congestion Committee and the campaign for zoning in New York City, and European travel. After coming to France as head of the American Red Cross Reconstruction Research Service, he stayed on to become a roving French government expert on city planning and, in 1920, to win the design contest for Reims's rebuilding.

Ford's plan was an extraordinary amalgam of the influences that had swept from Paris into American progressive city design. Through the old city's tangle of crooked inner streets, Ford imagined cutting a network of boulevards and étoiles straight out of Haussmann. His sketches swept away the houses and shops that crowded up against the cathedral, blurring, as Ford saw it, the city's mandatory civic focus. He dotted Reims's outskirts with new parks and American-style playgrounds for supervised and socialized play. In the city's four main quarters, in a move that had no analogue in Haussmann's Paris, he penciled in American-style community centers, much as Gaines had envisioned them, with health services, meeting rooms for civic groups, auditoriums, libraries, perhaps even temperance cafeterias. The progressives' yearning for civic unity, the visions of coherence they themselves had picked up in Paris or projected onto the old market squares of village Europe, Ford brought back—more socialized than Europe itself—to Reims's design.[4]

The social workers' European expedition was temporary, but the flood of American consumer goods that began to pour into Europe out of the apparently limitless, mechanized cornucopia of the United States at the war's end was more permanent and had a much more profound effect. European concern at the American commercial invasion of Europe had arisen before the war. German businessmen were talking nervously of the "American danger" as early as 1902. But none of this held a candle to the shift in trade flows after 1918.[5]

The invasion of American goods was most striking in Central Europe, where the war had brought the most smoothly oiled economic machine in prewar Europe to a virtual standstill. Under an Allied food blockade until the peace treaty was signed in mid-1919, steeply taxed for reparations payments, thrown into the maw of hyperinflation in 1922–23, Germany was in economic wreckage in the first half of the twenties. Visitors to Berlin in the early 1920s reported a city near despair, without laughter, strained and hungry. Even the prostitutes who now haunted every major street were said to wear looks of need and desperation. Half of the city was "wallowing in fleshpots," the writer Matthew Josephson thought, while the rest was "half-famished." Sociologist Robert Lynd's more sober eye was fixed by the middle-class Berliners queued up at the free municipal kitchens, their soup pots wrapped up in a newspaper or hidden in a satchel as they struggled to preserve their last vestiges of dignity.[6]

Half a decade later, Berlin seemed to visitors to be bursting with American goods. There was scarcely a store window in central Berlin that did not remind American visitors of the United States, Joseph Wood Krutch wrote in 1928. One could now buy American-style ice cream sodas, Boston baked beans, and "griddle cakes mit syrup" in a new, gleaming, American-style cafeteria on the Kurfürstendamm, and see the results of imported American engineering techniques everywhere. "No other European city that I have ever seen looks so much like New York, and the effort to make it look more so is continuous and conscious," Krutch wrote. There were American plays in the theaters, American news in the papers, American movies in the cinemas, and a ferocious debate over *Amerikanismus* in the bookstalls.[7]

Berlin was a particularly striking case of the commercial Americanization of 1920s Europe, thanks in part to the Dawes Plan loans pouring into Germany after 1924 to ease the reparations burden. But Berlin was hardly alone. There were American-style five-and-ten-cent stores in nearly every British city, Charles Beard reported in early 1929. Under pressure from Woolworth-style *magasins à prix uniques*, French retail cooperatives were scrambling to modernize their methods through professional managers and bolder advertising techniques. American-style advertising was now to be seen everywhere. "Paris is plastered with American signs," Beard wrote. Billboards in Berlin proclaimed the pleasures of American chewing gum; the great Ringstrasse in Vienna blazed with American-style electric advertising. In the cinemas, America was on screens from Stockholm to Turkey. At the high point of the American movie makers' invasion of Europe in 1925, just before retaliatory quotas took hold, 60 percent of all movies shown in Germany, 70 percent in France, and 95 percent in Britain were American made—and all brought with them, larger and more tempting than life, an extraordinary display of American consumer goods.[8]

America "bores its way into European consciousness," Beard wrote. Its jazz, its tempo, its chrome, and its commercialism penetrated the continent. But above all it was as a machine of almost magical efficiency, turning out mass consumer goods at a rate never seen before, that the United States reentered the symbolic universe of European progressives. Where its genius had once crystallized in its democracy, and later in its monopolists and plutocrats, it now crystallized around "Fordism." The term was ubiquitous in 1920s Europe. Ford's business innovations—his construction of a massive, assembly line–driven machine for the production of a standardized motor machine for the masses, together with his boast of paying workers wages high enough that even they could buy one—made a profound impression on European social observers. In Germany alone, Beard noted, the bibliography on efficiency and *Rationalisierung* ran into the hundreds of titles. Henry Ford's autobiography was a best-seller in 1920s Germany; the Frankfurt Social Museum entered the already crowded lists with a symposium pointedly entitled "Ford and Us." The hottest topic at the combined meetings of the International Association for Labor Legislation, the International Association on Unemployment, and the International Committee on Social Insurance held in Vienna in 1927, an American participant reported, was the effects of "Fordism" on labor and society.[9]

To see the land of machine production for themselves, a new cadre of reporters steamed their way across the Atlantic. "Pilgrimages across the Atlantic were made," Gustav Stolper writes; "America, so to speak, was discovered all over again." The Musée Social sent André Siegfried, son of its founder, to take the measure of 1920s America. The International Garden City and Town Planning Federation convened its 1925 meeting in New York City, in the shadow of the city's new skyscrapers. German engineers came by the dozens, and hard on their heels came German trade union and Social Democratic delegations to make their own independent assessments. German reviewers were noting the "flood" of books about America by 1927. Automobiles, city life, factories, department stores, the great Sears and Roebuck mail order mart in Chicago, and always, if one could manage it, the Ford factories in Highland Park and River Rouge, Michigan: these were the destinations on the new American tours.[10]

On one point, everyone agreed. Measured by access to consumer goods, the advantages of American over European wage earners were now beyond doubt. These were urban comparisons; they bypassed the rural, race-divided American South, and about the comparative lot of the continents' poor they made no judgments. But clearly the rough parity between the real earnings of average, unskilled industrial wage earners during the prewar era no longer obtained. Herbert Hoover's boast that "our workers with their average weekly wages can today buy two or even three times more bread and butter than *any* wage earner in Europe" cannot be taken literally. But informed German observers in the mid-1920s put the continental differential in average real wages at not less than two to one.[11]

Consumer goods statistics reinforce the point. In 1932 there were three and a half times as many radio listeners per inhabitant in the United States as in Europe, eight times as many telephone service subscribers, and twenty-six times as many automobiles. Forty percent of the world's industrial production by 1928 now issued from factories and workshops in the United States; Russia excluded, Europe's combined share was 42 percent. "We are the wealthiest people in the world," I. M. Rubinow concluded in the early 1930s: "the wealthiest nation in history."[12]

Beyond recognition of the astonishing material productivity of the United States, the impressions of European progressives fell quickly into disagreement. The unabashed commercialism of 1920s American cities astonished even Londoners and Berliners. "The very goods had tongues. 'Buy me; sell me,'" H. W. Massingham reported. "We don't build houses," a knowledgeable American told Arthur Feiler in Chicago, "but commodities with which we can speculate." Manhattan, the first stop on virtually every European traveler's itinerary, pushed these initial impressions to the limit. Bathed in early morning fog or in the illumination of its electric lights against the twilight, Manhattan's 1920s skyline enchanted. A "fairyland" was the clichéd response. But up close it was all elbows and competition, buildings that "seem[ed] to attack the sky" in their fierce competition for light and prestige, buildings that "spurted" up like hot geysers—hoisting "the powers of finance to 20 or 50 stories," as the architect Erich Mendelsohn put it. "Dollar scrapers," the German urban planner Robert Schmidt called them. "An indescribable chaos of degrading, dreary, scandalous ugliness" was the judgment of *Die Form*'s editor, Walter Curt Behrendt.[13]

What struck critical Europeans most of all in 1920s America was not its commercialism or chaos but its uniformity. Standardization and regimentation ruled. Set against the sharp internal conflicts of the era—the bitter rural-urban cultural battles of the American 1920s, its Klansmen, its labor struggles, and its new, northern racial ghettos—this seems at first glance a puzzlingly misplaced judgment. But to those who encountered for the first time the material culture of standardized parts, it did not seem so. Everyone, it struck them forcefully, dressed the same, donned the same brand-name Arrow shirt collars, accepted the season's dictates of the Sears and Roebuck catalog. "Everywhere one encounters the same objects," Alfred Rühl complained; "everything is a mass product."[14]

The startling profusion of standardized consumer goods, standardized clothing sizes, and mass-advertised dictations of taste accounted for part of this impression. The other part was Prohibition's work. André Siegfried thought the American mind of the 1920s doubly imprisoned by Ford and Calvin, the combination conspiring to draw every ounce of its imagination toward production. Georges Duhamel imagined a wickedly satirical conversation with an American on the mechanical possibilities of hygienically regulating excessive sex. Posing as it did culture against mere machine civilization, spirit against materialism, higher against lower desires, the critique of the standardized and regimented American was particularly congenial to conservative Europeans. But this critique was not confined to them alone. Lujo Brentano took the "standardization of persons" under the regime of mass advertising as a fixed point in the America reports. To critics of Americanization, the land of the machine was the land of machine-made persons, their very desires captive to the psychological engineers' new powers of persuasion.[15]

Orthodox Marxists also dismissed machine-age America, not because the era's material preoccupations were ethically false but because under the direction of its business owners the machine's material promise could not be fulfilled. Sapped and undermined by relentless capital accumulation, burdened with a productive capacity that far outran the economic ability of its working masses to consume, as they saw it "late capitalism" could only stagger toward its inevitable internal collapse. That certainty did not preclude imitation of American production techniques, as Soviet recruitment of American engineers and Lenin's well-known embrace of Taylorism attested. But the compliment of appropriation was carefully bounded. In the aftermath of the war, the young, angry Bertolt Brecht had soaked up everything he could find about America, its gangsters, its slang, its novels, its popular songs, and its big city skyscrapers. But when Brecht's inchoate radicalism of the early 1920s turned into more orthodox Marxist channels after 1926, America became old for him, exhausted and frazzled.[16]

It was not on the right or left edges of European politics that the interest in the material promises of 1920s America was keenest, but on the progressive terrain where radicals, left liberals, and pragmatic social democrats met. Where conservatives saw mechanical regimentation and left-Marxists saw hyperexploitation, capitalism's progressive critics were struck by something else: the machinery of industrial capitalism no longer turned inward toward the extraction of surplus labor but outward toward the needs of the many. The astonishing achievement of America, the *New Statesman*'s correspondent wrote in 1929, was not to be found in its prosperity per se, so easily explained away by accidents of geography and resources. The lasting American achievement was the mental "revolution" inherent in the mass-production economy: the recognition that only a mass purchasing base could sustain prosperity. Where European employers, absorbed in day-to-day cost calculations, skimped on wages and technical investments, American employers poured their profits into new machinery and made a vast, new market out of well-paid workers. They had "flung overboard our old conceptions of capital, profits, and wages," the *New Statesman* reported; they had discovered "that there are no such 'laws' as were laid down by Adam Smith, Ricardo, John Stuart Mill, and even Karl Marx." All these had dissolved in the logic of machine production.[17]

In high wages, efficiency, rationalization, and mass production of consumer goods—in "Fordism," in short—Americans had not only discovered the secret of permanent prosperity. They had also, as Philip Kerr seconded the conviction in the London *Nation*, "solved the elementary problem which is still convulsing Europe." They had invented a mass-production economy without antagonistic class interests, without inherent political warfare, without hard political trade-offs.[18]

Fordism invaded Europe as a progressive idea: future-oriented, flexible, and melioristic. Visiting European businessmen, fearful of the large and risky investments Fordism entailed, tended to tiptoe warily past the applicability of its moral to them. Socialist and trade union delegations to the United States, in contrast, were much more profoundly swept up by the possibilities of Americanism's machine-produced plenty. A sea voyage could not itself expunge the critique of barely checked capitalism in the United States. In progressive and working-class Europe, radical and utopian assessments of the United States met in complicated and often contradictory conjunctures. But at its best, the machine democratized. "None of them had ever seen America," Maria Piscator remembered of her husband's leftist theater group in the 1920s, but they knew that America meant "the objective existence of the land of plenty, its material genius, with its prosperity, its slogans, and the great god—the machine."[19]

Machine civilization in the United States gelled, finally, not only in its consumer goods and economic concepts but also for some radical Europeans as an aesthetic. The fourteen photos of broad-windowed American factories and massive grain elevators that the young industrial designer Walter Gropius had assembled in the leading German design forum in 1913, just before the war, did much to shape the machine-age's symbolic language. As images of stripped-down utilitarian form, free of false fronts and bourgeois ornamentation, they reverberated powerfully through the continent's radical, modernist circles. Le Corbusier picked up the grain elevator photos from Gropius, exaggerating their elemental, geometric forms, to illustrate *Vers une architecture* in 1923. Bruno Taut led off his

Modern Architecture with them. Erich Mendelsohn put Buffalo on his itinerary in 1924 to see the machine age's new icon; long before he landed in New York, he wrote, he had had Buffalo's "silos" on his brain.[20]

The grain elevators of the architecture books, with their spare utilitarian lines, were not America, of course, any more than Fordism or the Sears and Roebuck catalog was America. They were fragments of an America much more complicated than any photographic icon could encompass. European architects in America in the twenties quickly had Gropius's pictures jolted out of their heads. Only in a half-built, skeletal state did the American skyscrapers match the modernist aesthetic of the machine. Finished, in their borrowed historical ornament and their savage competition for prestige and height, they were hardly utilitarian at all. You could buy pattern-book buildings in America in any aesthetic or historical style you chose to pay for, Bruno Taut reported caustically: mock-Tudor houses, mock-Spanish gas stations, Greek columns out of mass-produced cast iron, or tiles weathered (so the advertisement ran) to look "exactly like the roofs of Oxford and Cambridge Colleges." The simple, unadorned machine was not art in 1920s America; the European profession of industrial design had, as yet, barely reached the United States. But the American steel skeletons and bridge girders, grain silos and Fordson tractors, assembly lines and Model Ts, fold-down beds and efficiency kitchens helped give machine civilization a set of powerful symbolic representations.[21]

In all these ways the 1920s marked a rebirth of America in European social-political consciousness and a partial rebalancing of the intellectual traffic between Europe and the United States. The terms, as usual, condensed and simplified. Fordism, the standardization of taste, the functionalist revolution in forms, the democratization of goods—they were all threads pulled out of the American tangle, just as Frederic Howe's or Clarence Poe's Europe had been threads pulled out of Europe's tangles. They joined all the other Americas invading Europe in the interwar years: the Dawes loans, the jazz tunes, the screen idols, and the temperance restaurants for devastated France. The resulting interwar movement of ideas and influences could still hardly be called symmetrical. But when American progressive interest in Europe picked up again after the First World War, the exchange was far less one-sided than before.

Up close, machine-age America looked far less attractive to American progressives in the 1920s than it did to many of those who tried to take Fordism's measure from abroad. The consumer goods revolution was undeniable, albeit much less equitably shared than European progressives sometimes imagined. But the internal social-political machinery of the era fell a long way short of the agenda most of the Atlantic-facing progressives had carried into the war.

On the labor relations front, the most heavily publicized innovation of the decade was the spread of "industrial democracy" systems through many of the largest American industrial firms. A carryover from the grievance-resolution systems imposed during the war, the new employee representation plans were a major break from the autocratic and confrontational management styles of the prewar era. Systems of regularized, factory-level employer-employee negotiation had been a central feature of progressive reconstruction programs across the North Atlantic economy. German socialists wrote them into the law in 1920 in a statute mandating the establishment of works councils virtually across the board in the postwar German economy. The results of American voluntarism never approached that level, but with some of the largest corporations in the lead, the number of workers covered by the new employee representation plans shot up from 391,000 in 1919 to 1.2 million in 1924. The aggregate membership of the nation's labor unions in that year was 3.3 million.[22]

Nowhere else, however, were factory representation systems so closely linked to the project of forestalling union organization as in the United States. Only in the garment trades did the new industrial democracy systems include a place for wage earners' independently organized labor unions. Though called on to advise on wage matters, virtually none of the American works councils had even the theoretical access of their German counterparts to their firms' profit accounts. After 1924, when it was clear that employers had broken the back of the wartime and postwar unionization drive, the organization of new employee representation systems slowed dramatically. Ford's own plants, where the five-dollar day, the open shop, and managerial autocracy ruled, made no pretense of industrial democracy at all.[23]

When it came to everyday security against the risks of wage labor, the contrast between the reputation and the accomplishments of machine-age America was even more pronounced. As the social insurance drive stalled in the statehouses, the largest welfare capitalists and insurance firms moved in to stake out the most desirable parts of the new territory as their own. The most common of the era's new employment benefits were group life insurance and a modest, company-financed retirement pension. Group health insurance, resisted by doctors, was much more rare. Against the most dreaded risk of labor, unemployment, a few employers made dramatic gestures, helped by the first accurate cost accounts of seasonal labor turnover. The Procter and Gamble Company guaranteed the jobs of 5,000 of its lowest-wage employees in a widely noted move in 1923. In the garment industry, notorious for its abrupt seasonal hiring swings, employers and International Ladies' Garment Workers' Union's representatives in Cleveland established a guaranteed minimum number of paid work weeks each season; in Chicago and New York, employers and the Amalgamated Clothing Workers Union set up a structure of jointly financed and jointly managed out-of-work funds.[24]

But in comparison with the European systems of social insurance, which were thickening and deepening in the 1920s toward more systematic and broader coverage, the one-by-one innovations of American welfare capitalists barely changed the overall odds in a wage earner's life. On the eve of the Depression, not more than 1 in 5 wage earners was covered by an employer's group life insurance plan, 1 in 8 by a company retirement pension program, not more than 1 in 20 by group health or accident insurance, and not more than 1 in 100 by unemployment insurance benefits of any sort.[25]

The politics of welfare capitalism showed the same double face. The Republican governments of the 1920s marked no rollback to the laissez-faire ideals of the mid-nineteenth century. The Commerce Department under Herbert Hoover's direction was, to the contrary, a virtual factory of public policy innovation. Streamlining and rationalizing the nation's private economic machinery was Hoover's goal, and he turned formidable energy and ingenuity to it. Commerce Department administrators encouraged standardization of products, regularization of employment, and the swifter flow of economic information. They promoted the farmers' marketing cooperatives to stabilize the volatile agricultural markets. They formulated the first systematic federal policies for countercyclical public works spending. "The American Plan" in politics did not leave out the promotional state.[26]

But this was social politics of a highly attenuated sort. Hoover's dedication to restructuring the market's key institutions was matched by no corresponding interest in shrinking the markets' scope at those places where commodification had worked its sharpest human injuries, or setting tighter legal and constitutional bounds on the markets' work; still less was he interested in building a democratic counterforce to concentrated market power at the top. The "welfare" in welfare capitalism trickled down from the top;

it oozed through the paychecks of workers in the mass-production industries; but its patrons were not the solidaristic and civic associations that had fired the imagination of a Frederic Howe or a Jane Addams. The resulting overall balance did not keep many of the leading progressives from casting their votes for Hoover in 1928, as Jane Addams was herself to do. But neither did it keep the 1920s from unfolding as a series of defeats for the projects on which the Atlantic-facing progressives had staked so many hopes.

Social insurance was a clear-cut casualty of the decade. Publicly administered health insurance was a dead letter after its defeats in California and New York in 1918 and 1919. Even the sharp postwar employment crisis could not get British-style unemployment insurance past the Harding administration's firm resistance. The labor party idea was in disarray after 1924. In a key victory for the progressive women's network, Congress passed an Infancy and Maternity Protection Act in 1921—only to defeat its renewal under the pressure of the doctors' lobbies in 1927. On the constitutional front, the defeats were still more bitter. The National Consumers' League coalition's second try at a federal child labor act, designed to short-cut the laborious work of state-by-state reform, was, like the first, disallowed as unconstitutional. After 1923 the Supreme Court began to vacate state minimum wage statutes as well, dismissing the Goldmark-Brandeis "sociological" briefs in favor of the principle it now insisted was constitutional bedrock: that governments could not legitimately usurp markets to set the price of goods or labor.

In all this there was no missing a new arrogance vis-à-vis social politics abroad. Clarence Darrow wrote bitterly of the era that a "spirit of super-patriotism" reigned. The isolation of the Americans from the International Labor Organization, the League of Nations' agency for international labor standards, became for many progressives an embarrassing symbolic injury. The adjective "American" was now cast all across the field of social politics. Doctors defended entrepreneurial medicine as the "American" way; employers billed their anti–labor union drive as the "American Plan" in industrial and economic relations. "We have builded the America of today on the fundamentals of economic, industrial and political life which made us what we are, and the temple needs no remaking now," President Warren Harding said in explaining why he removed unemployment insurance from the agenda of a White House conference on unemployment in 1921.[27]

In this context of progressive isolation and defeat, it was no wonder that the old tropes and hungers should have been revived. Watching the spectacle of an international labor legislation conference unfold in Washington, D.C., in late 1919 without any Americans officially present, W. L. Chenery thought the United States surely among the "backward" nations. "The old notion that Europe is ancient, idealistic and traditional, while we are practical and businesslike, was completely shattered during my recent trip abroad," Abraham Epstein reported in the mid-1920s after observing the contrast in old-age provisions. Europe gave an American a "sense of tidal things" and a feeling of motion, Paul Kellogg wrote in the wake of the international social work convention in Paris in 1928, in contrast to the "dead sea of disillusionment, prosperity, [and] materialism" at home. By 1923 Lincoln Steffens was once more writing of Europe—all of it, from Lenin's Russia to Mussolini's Italy to Labour Britain—as a vast "experiment station." "America cannot help Europe, but Europe can help enlighten, amuse and lead us, if only we will humbly stop, look, and listen to the struggling peoples there."[28]

Slowly, in keeping with the growing mood, the European pilgrimages resumed, and advertisements for the sociological grand tour began to spring up all over again in the liberal magazines. By the 1930s there were a half dozen agencies in the business of European study-tour arrangements—including, by 1933, the *Survey* itself.[29] Still better organized were the new, privately funded European study fellowships. The American-Scandinavian Foundation's traveling fellowship fund supported a stream of students in both directions. The Oberlaender Trust did the same on a larger scale for American-German relations after 1931. American recipients of the trust's fellowships over the next seven years included Jane Addams (though she was too ill to make the journey), Hull House veteran Alice Hamilton (for a study of German industrial sickness insurance), W. E. B. Du Bois (for a study of German industrial education), the city planner John Nolen, and rafts of American mayors, foresters, experts in public administration, and recreation and public health workers.[30]

The Europe that American progressives found in the twenties was different than before—more Americanized and, in the wake of the war's upheavals, more democratic. Social-democratic and labor parties now formed the major political opposition groups. If they rarely held governmental power, they stood everywhere on its doorstep, and American progressives learned to see more clearly than before their affinities with reform social democracy abroad.

Finally, over progressive politics on both sides of the Atlantic fell the shadow of the revolution in Russia. No one looking for the cutting edge of change in 1920s Europe could ignore the new Soviet experiment. Lillian Wald, John Dewey, W. E. B. Du Bois, Robert La Follette, Sidney Hillman, Rexford Tugwell, Paul Douglas, and Lincoln Steffens all visited the Soviet Union in the 1920s. By 1926 the American Russian Institute was in the business of promoting Russian-American exchanges, with Wald and Dewey among its honorary vice presidents. The magnitude of the Russians' economic development plans, their attempt to build a new society on a wholly different basis than "acquisitiveness," as E. C. Lindeman put it, could not fail to move American progressives, many of whom were quick to read the Americans' once vigorous experimental spirit into the new Russia. But the vast majority of progressives, even those inspired by Soviet idealism, did not choose Russia as their model. Reports from the Soviet Union were the hottest items of international social reportage in the 1920s; they crowded out some of the space prewar Germany and Britain had occupied in American progressives' minds. But the Soviet Union came through in progressive reportage as a raw, undeveloped frontier, barely modern economically, hardly comparable to the United States except in natural wealth and ambition.[31]

The Russian experiment fascinated American progressives, but it did not eclipse the older, more developed Europe, struggling to contain and harness capitalism rather than shatter and transcend it. Once more, Americans went hunting in it for tested means to mitigate the regime of market individualism. But this time, in the more complicated intellectual economy of the 1920s, their eagerness to tap the social-political experience of the European nations passed in mid-ocean the new European fascination with the social possibilities of American machine production. From different convictions of backwardness, progressives on both continents now sought their future in each other. In the ensuing traffic of aspirations and appropriations, the two currents did not often meet. The European influences on American social politics and the American invasion of European economics and culture were largely independent events. But where the influences did join, just before the bottom fell out of Weimar Germany, they created social-political forms whose promise and originality illuminated, for a moment, both sides of the Atlantic.

The field of that encounter was housing. Like automobile production, housing production was one of most striking phenomena of the machine age. In the second half of the 1920s a housing construction boom swept across the North Atlantic economy. In Germany by the late 1920s, new housing units were being built at a rate of more than 300,000 a year, twice the prewar peak. In Britain, where new housing starts had run at 86,000 a year in 1910, they reached 261,000 in 1927–28. In the United States, the average number of new houses built per year in the five years before the war (1912 to 1916) had been 505,000; in the five years before the Depression (1924 to 1928) it was 848,000. In an industry marked by long-term boom and bust cycles, the late 1920s was a boom of unprecedented proportions.[32]

In the United States, the housing boom was a private undertaking. In flats and elevator apartments, duplexes and bungalows, and a suburban riot of historical revival styles, investors in land and construction rebuilt America in the twenties. Employing the public powers of zoning and subdivision platting, they planted the exclusive, middle-class, automobile suburb on the American landscape. In virtually every major American city, aggregate housing densities fell in the twenties, in several cases for the first time since 1870. Home ownership rates inched upward. In 1890 in only six of the twenty-eight "great cities" had the fraction of dwellings owned by those who lived in them been as high as one-third; by 1930, home ownership in twenty-one of those same cities had reached that level.[33]

"To possess one's own home is the hope and ambition of almost every individual in our country," Herbert Hoover told the nation in 1931. At the Commerce Department, he had worked hard to introduce more cost-efficient methods into the highly fractionated construction industry so as to put the price of a modest new house within the range of most Americans. Standardized specifications for construction materials, standardized building codes, and model zoning ordinances all issued from this work. On their own, a handful of well-capitalized firms tried to bring efficiencies of scale and mass-production techniques into housing. But in an industry of small players and high profits, none of these piecemeal efforts to bring the promise of the machine to bear on housing made a dent in costs or supply. In Chicago, historian Gail Radford notes, the price of an entry-level home grew more than twice as fast as the overall cost of living between 1885 and 1925. Housing experts at the end of the 1920s took it as a rule of thumb that a new house costing $4,000 or more was within the reach of only the wealthiest third of American families. In Cleveland in 1932, there had been no new homes constructed below that price in the past five years; in Philadelphia during the same period, the cheapest new construction had been marketed at $3,990. Houses were the most basic "machine" of the 1920s, but in the land of high wages and mass production, they were a luxury good.[34]

In postwar Europe, by contrast, housing ran down double tracks: market housing for the well-to-do and publicly assisted housing for the masses. In Britain, both public and private housing construction boomed simultaneously from the mid-1920s until the Second World War. During the briefer housing spurt in late-1920s Germany, about half the total housing investments came from private sources, half from public. In all, between 1919 and 1933 some six million new dwellings were built in Europe, three million of them outside the framework of the private housing market. In an age that prided itself in the democratization of goods, large-scale production of houses for the masses was a European achievement.[35]

Measured simply by the magnitude of the endeavor, the big story of the postwar years was Britain's. Alongside the 900,000 new commercial housing units built for the white-collar middle class in 1920s Britain, Labour and Conservative governments collaborated to construct 600,000 new working-class dwellings, making tax-financed, publicly initiated housing a key pillar of British social politics. "Council" housing estates they were called, named for the town councils that initiated and administered them; by the end of the decade, they sprouted on the suburban edges of virtually every British city, as if Coketown itself were finally emptying its human contents out into the sun. The largest of the English undertakings had no match anywhere in the North Atlantic economy. At Becontree, outside London's eastern city limits, the London County Council constructed a satellite working-class development of "great city" dimensions, housing 115,000 LCC tenants at its completion in 1934, many of them employed in the neighboring Ford Motor plant. Manchester city authorities talked of rebuilding half the city by the century's end. Flying over England in 1932, Lewis Mumford wrote, an air traveler could see two nations laid out below him: old, Black England, with its "row upon row of dingy roofs piled close together . . . , street upon street without a touch of green," built through "the untrammeled action of the classic laws of supply and demand," and a new, publicly built, Green England of brick and grass, lapping at the edges of the old urban environment and destined, he was sure, soon to overwhelm it.[36]

The British council house of the 1920s was no architectural inspiration either in design or production techniques. Four-square and two-story, neo-Georgian in design, built as double houses or in short rows, scattered like hip-roofed shoeboxes according to Raymond Unwin's loose twelve-to-an-acre formula along miles of meandering suburban streets, they made no pretensions of modernity. Recreation facilities and sites for shops were few; pubs, Becontree's residents complained, were desperately scarce. "It was all houses, houses," George Orwell wrote of the typical council estate, "little red cubes of houses all alike, with privet hedges and asphalt paths leading up to the front door."[37]

The social revolution in British housing was an inner revolution in finances and class standards. Council houses democratized space. With their baths and inside toilets, their kitchens—too small, to be sure, for the likes of families that had traditionally lived next to the cook stove, but much better equipped than before—and with their three bedrooms, giving ordinary families a privacy between adults and children that had hitherto been reserved for the middle class, they elevated at a stroke the standards of British working-class housing. With their front and back garden patches and their setting in the green, council housing was working-class Britons' ticket into the suburban environs that prewar private builders had preempted for the professional and middle classes.

Britain's construction of a new working-class suburbia represented one form of the European housing endeavor; Vienna's municipal tenements embodied a different, explicitly collectivist one. With its city council in the hands of a socialist majority from 1919 through 1934, Vienna was the most important laboratory of municipal socialism in postwar Europe. Faced with the familiar quandary of somehow promoting an economic revolution they had no power directly to effect, Vienna's municipal socialists turned to culture and the environment. German and Austrian socialists had long cultivated a party network of sports and gymnastic clubs, youth groups and discussion clubs, lectures and choral societies—all designed to promote the social personality that the coming reconstruction demanded. In Vienna this inner world of socialism was turned public side out. One arm of Viennese municipal socialism, attendant to maternity and the body, constructed one of the most elaborate public prenatal and child health care systems in all of Europe; the other, in a city even more wretchedly housed than Berlin, took on housing.[38]

Vienna's first housing endeavors were on its urban rim, where returned soldiers and their families, forced out of the city's fiercely overburdened housing market, had set up squatters' colonies in the months after the war. Out of the initial chaos, with the help of city authorities and Quaker relief workers, the homeless formed themselves into market gardening cooperatives and, in time, stable subsistence settlements, later to become an important template for the New Deal subsistence colony program. But the major thrust of Vienna's housing program, after the acquisition of new tax powers in 1923, was the construction of large-scale municipal apartment complexes, big enough to form a world within the world of late-capitalist society. Between 1923 and 1934, when civil war toppled the socialists from power and the victors shelled the largest of the new city housing complexes to force out the holdouts, an average of thirty new municipal apartment buildings went up each year. By 1934, 12 percent of Vienna's population was housed in one.[39]

As housing, Vienna's municipal dwellings offered much to criticize. The standard municipal apartment held barely more than half the interior space of the standard council house in Britain. A kitchen, living room, and a single small sleeping room were the norm, plus a toilet and a tiny entrance hall; very few had baths. Even these standards, however, were well above what the private market had provided in prewar Vienna, where inside plumbing, cross ventilation, gas lighting, and separate sleeping rooms beyond a kitchen and all-purpose *Stube* had been beyond the reach of the working class. Cutting economies close, the Vienna designers poured the margin instead into collective space and public amenities. The larger complexes boasted nurseries and kindergartens, public baths and laundries, meeting rooms, workers' libraries, mothers' clinics, sandlots and playgrounds, cooperative grocery stores and restaurants, perhaps a local health insurance society office, and space for political rallies—all governed by a complex network of social rules and inspection.[40]

The inner revolution in socialist Vienna housing went hand in hand with an external monumentality, boldly enough proclaimed that not even the most casual passerby was in danger of missing it. Where British council housing was spare and (except for its repetition) nonintrusive, the Vienna projects broadcast themselves with statues and strikingly articulated facades, four to six stories high, through which one passed, often through a monumental archway, into the building's inner world. The most famous of the municipal apartment complexes of the 1920s, the Karl Marx Hof, incorporated 1,325 dwellings and stretched for three-fifths of a mile along Heiligenstädterstrasse. There were a half dozen others on almost the same scale, including the Georg Washington Hof.[41]

Vienna public housing was class-based housing. City authorities boasted of constructing workers' housing with house and luxury-goods taxes extracted from the propertied bourgeoisie. Their efforts effectively pinched off private housing investments in Vienna, but nowhere else in the North Atlantic economy did tax-subsidized, working-class housing rent at levels so low that even the families of unskilled workers could afford it. "Every visitor to Europe who had any interest whatsoever in reform, housing, social progress, went as a matter of course to look at the magnificent workers' apartments that Vienna had built," Marquis Childs wrote of the city's work. The English housing expert Elizabeth Denby called Vienna's the "greatest housing achievement of the century."[42]

The most eventful meeting of the machine age and the housing question, however, occurred in Weimar Germany. There, the English garden suburb tradition, the Vienna socialists' commitment to labor solidarity and community design, the modernist aesthetics of the American grain silos, a younger German generation's revolt against bourgeois pretensions, and a socialized variant of American Fordism joined to create some of the best working-class housing in Europe. The moment of this convergence was short. But in the brief springtime of the Weimar Republic, between stabilization of the economy in 1924 and the Depression, the task of creating living machines for the masses was pursued there with a creativity unmatched in the North Atlantic economy.[43]

In Germany, more than elsewhere, the First World War and reconstruction fervor radicalized the younger architects. Bruno Taut, who would design some of the best of Berlin's new housing in the 1920s, spent 1919 to 1921 absorbed in fantastic utopias. When the socialist city council of Magdeburg named him city architect *(Stadtbaurat)* in 1921, he proceeded to paint the town's old facades with a riot of fauvist color. Taut's chief collaborator, Martin Wagner, spent the early 1920s endeavoring to organize Berlin's building trades into craft guilds capable of shedding the capitalist middleman. Working-class housing in Germany was born out of utopian strivings, a reaction against the pretensions of the empire and the prewar bourgeoisie, and a determination to yoke politics and architecture in a common revolution.[44]

The financial occasion for this endeavor arrived with the abrupt end of hyperinflation in 1924 and the introduction of a new tax on landlords' income. The tax, designed to recoup a portion of the unearned gains landlords were expected to reap from the sharp drop in interest rates, was earmarked for the "right to decent housing" that was guaranteed in the Weimar constitution. The result was to give a cadre of architects steeped in the social promise of machine-age modernism a canvas as big as that enjoyed by their traditionalist English counterparts.

Frankfurt, where housing initiatives had been on the progressive agenda since the 1880s, was the first important city to experiment with the new tools of finance and design. Under the direction of *Oberbürgermeister* Ludwig Landmann, a left democrat, and the city's new socialist *Stadtbaurat,* Ernst May, the city plunged into new working-class housing construction from 1925 to 1931—some of it directly built by the city, some through limited dividend companies in which the city was a major stockholder. In neighborhoods designed as community units in May's offices, a startlingly new kind of housing development began to make its appearance in Frankfurt: cubistic, precast concrete houses with sunning decks on their flat roofs, their stucco facades a rainbow of color, set in low rows amid intensely cultivated garden plots.[45]

"Liberated dwellings," their architects called them. Even now when one walks through the workers' housing district laid out near the municipal harbor according to Franz Adickes's original zone plan of 1891, the encounter with the early May houses is striking. One moves from the labor-union-sponsored buildings on Raffeisenstrasse and Schulze-Delitzsch-strasse, where nine or twelve apartments are heaped up under high, four-story gabled or hump-backed roofs, like bourgeois villas blown up to an exaggerated scale, to the row houses constructed by the city after the war, clinging to the threads of bourgeois taste with their arched doorways and shuttered windows, their third stories tucked up in dormers under their heavy, pitched roofs, and then suddenly to May's low, two-story, cubistic row houses along Lassallestrasse, Marxstrasse, and Engelsplatz, their facades stripped of every ornament or disguise.

"Light," "air," and "sun" were the catchwords of the new style. But the liberation of housing from its old forms went beyond an assault on the constraints of the pitched roof and shuttered window. The deeper aim of social modernism was to shatter the nineteenth-century connection between aesthetics and emulation—not to monumentalize shelter, as in Vienna, but to simplify and democratize it.

May's most noted achievements were the satellite developments of Praunheim and Römerstadt, constructed at the end of a new, city-owned streetcar line across the Nidda flood plain from Frankfurt proper. Having worked in Raymond Unwin's Hampstead office for two years before the war, May knew the principles of garden city design. Scrapping Unwin's aesthetic traditionalism for modernist forms, he built a sweeping curve of low row houses and three- to four-story apartment blocks surrounding schools, playing fields, a riverside swimming establishment, cooperative nurseries, laundry facilities, grocery stores and garden plots. Machines in a garden, his buildings were, their brightly colored walls shining down on the old city like a giant billboard for what architecture might be, when married to functionalism and social purpose.

Frankfurt, where some 15,000 municipal houses in the modernist style were put up between 1925 and 1931, was the showpiece of modernist social housing in interwar Germany. In the republic's second showplace city, Berlin, authority and initiative were more democratized than in Frankfurt. There the principal builders of new workers' housing were labor union–based building societies, subsidized by public funds. The biggest of them was Martin Wagner's Gehag. Its Hufeisensiedlung, built to Taut and Wagner's designs between 1925 and 1927, was the city's most famous example of the new social architecture. With its row houses and gardens and great horseshoe curve of apartments, all set off from the encircling capitalist metropolis behind the deep red row of apartment buildings that served the part of a medieval town wall, it was a stunning blend of vernacular, romantic, and modernist forms. Still larger was the Gehag project at the edge of the Berlin city woods at Zehlendorf. There Taut and others built a working-class garden suburb of almost two thousand dwellings in the modernist style, joining its flat-roofed, elementary forms with oversized windows, low densities, gardens, trees, and color. Almost a dozen more planned large-scale developments, or *Grosssiedlungen*, soon appeared at the edges of the old "rental barracks" city. By 1932 almost as many low-cost dwellings had been built in the new, radical style in Berlin as in Frankfurt, 70 percent of them with labor union sponsorship.[46]

Stylistically the new buildings mixed appropriations from Rotterdam architect J. J. P. Oud and Frank Lloyd Wright, from modernist painting and American factory design, and from Le Corbusier and the Bauhaus. Unmatched in skills of self-publicity, Le Corbusier and the Bauhaus dominate the history of 1920s architectural modernism. But they did not give the modernist aesthetic its engine of realization. The Bauhaus was an astonishingly fertile meeting point for the radical aesthetic ideas circulating through 1920s Germany; its exhibition house of 1923 helped set the form of the "liberated dwelling." But the architectural action in Weimar Germany was not in Dessau or even in the small suburban working-class housing project Gropius designed there; it was in the great cities, and the working-class parties and labor unions were its patrons.

To the new architecture's labor-union and public-housing-agency sponsors, modernism was not a style but the kernel of a new social and economic form. To popularize it, May launched a journal in November

1926, *Das neue Frankfurt.* "A new people, a new era must rework the inner and outer world of forms," Ludwig Landmann wrote in its first issue. Housing, architecture, store signs, transportation, furniture, swimming pavilions: all were ripe for redesign. May's assistants worked on functional chairs and bedsteads, lamps, wardrobes, doors, door handles—not simply to create furnishings sized to fit the space restraints of the new dwellings but, still more, to bust up the aesthetics of the prewar bourgeoisie, with its overstuffed chairs, draperies, knickknacks, and disguises. Functionalism was the outer form of a socialized society. Who, Taut asked, would choose "life among ruins of past culture" when a new one beckoned?[47]

The middle-class housing societies reinforced these polarities by clinging to the pitched roofs and small windows they thought matched to their members' status, and by raining down on the new, flat roofed buildings the charge that it was soulless, mechanized, poor people's architecture. Bending to the winds after Hitler's appointment to the chancellorship in 1933, Zehlendorf's planners finished off its last units with pitched, red tile roofs and dull, gray, Nazi stucco. Even in the building boom of the late-1920s, most Weimar cities, scurrying from controversy, had shunned the new aesthetics. The cry of the social modernists, in contrast, was to liberate the house from its impossible load of private ambitions and emulative strivings: to create communities and buildings for a postbourgeois society.

The ingredient that completed this mix of social reconstructionist ambitions was Americanism. The point often caught Americans off guard, for neither public nor social-modernist housing was anywhere to be found in the United States. When the young American Catherine Bauer visited the German architect Erich Mendelsohn in Berlin in 1932, Mendelsohn tipped out his folding Murphy bed to show her, pointedly, its American label. Mendelsohn's gesture was not a casual one. Although American visitors like Louis Pink might see "freak" buildings in May's new rim cities, Germans looking at the stripped-down, often prefabricated functional forms, the machine-influenced lines, the folding beds and standardized kitchens, saw Fordism—and America.[48]

Social modernism's architects had, in fact, been eager conduits for American efficiency techniques from the first. Like Taut and Gropius, many of them had a special place for American industrial architecture in their kit of forms. From 1920 on, Wagner's journal *Soziale Bauwirtschaft* had been full of reports on American engineering techniques. Rotterdam's municipal architect, J. J. P. Oud, talked of his buildings as "dwelling Fords." Wagner and May both visited the United States in the 1920s, hunting among its inflated steel-frame skyscrapers and capitalist excesses for rationalized production techniques and efficient designs. Both May and Taut had been profoundly struck by Christine Frederick's *The New Housekeeping*, translated into German in 1921, which treated the kitchen as an exercise in the scientific management of space and effort. In Frankfurt, May's designers produced a standardized, highly efficient, Pullman-style kitchen for tenants to purchase. Beds in May's developments folded, swung, or rolled with a space-saving ingenuity that mirrored the skill of Ford's engineers in cramming production machinery closer and closer together.[49]

In both Berlin and Frankfurt the modernist architects experimented with the mass-production construction techniques that, in the absence of patrons on the German scale, had continually eluded American investors. Precast concrete slabs, standardized building units, great traveling cranes, and rationalized work tasks were key to the German economies of scale. In aesthetic and social terms, the results were worlds away from American assumptions about shelter and housing. But in the idea of a house as a dwelling machine, a contrivance designed to give its inhabitants space, air, privacy, and community facilities, the Fordist connection, however startling the transformation, was deep and essential. Nothing was less and at the same time more American than Weimar social housing.

The worm below the surface, in Germany as in the United States, was economics. Taut's Hufeisensiedlung entailed land and construction costs that, in the end, priced it beyond the reach of working-class Berliners. May's Römerstadt was affordable only by skilled workers, despite its mass-production economies. After the initial burst of inventive designs from 1925 to 1929, the drive for ever greater economies drew Weimar architects into more spartan formulas. The interior space of publicly financed working-class housing shrank; by May's last major Frankfurt project, at Westhausen in 1930 and 1931, it had come down to Vienna's bare-bones standards. The prevailing scale rose from two to four or five stories. The sweeping curves separating inner from outer social worlds were scrapped for the mathematics of *Zeilenbau:* long, parallel blocks, laid with a ruler according to the one best angle at which, by expert calculation, a house was thought to face the sun. By 1930, with the North Atlantic economy already falling apart, the focus of the German housing effort was on defining the minimums of space and air a family needed: *Existenzminimum.* May and much of his architectural team left Frankfurt that year for the Soviet Union, where, with dozens of instant cities in the making, the future for architecture still seemed open. Wagner protested that further efficiencies were futile in the face of the economic juggernaut. Two years later, overwhelmed by the fiscal crisis, German cities were building virtually nothing but rude rim settlements for the unemployed: minimal houses without inside toilets or accessible transportation.[50]

Even in its *Zeilenbau* phase from 1929 to 1932, however, the new Weimar housing had amenities well beyond those of prewar working-class housing—amenities that even middle-class American purchasers in the new bungalow developments could not count on. However battered by the falling markets, the impulse behind Weimar's fusion of American engineering techniques, modernist aesthetics, and social democratic politics was still visible in its latest phases: to turn the privatized, possession-displaying house outward to its natural and social environment, to unload it of its burden of ornament and status, to socialize its design and its finances, to cheapen its cost until decent housing became as ubiquitous as a Model T Ford. Public housing, the 1980s icon of political and economic despair, began wrapped in utopian hope. In Weimar housing, transformed by its new setting and patrons, a piece of machine-age America took root in Europe. It would be no less complicated a test of politics and patrons to bring it home again.

The Politics of Modernism

As so often before in the Atlantic progressive connection, the visual connections were the first to form. In photos and word pictures, a sense of the magnitude of the European revolution in housing and class standards began to filter back to 1920s America. Edith Elmer Wood was in Europe again as early as 1922, gathering the material she would shape into *Housing Progress in Western Europe*, the decade's most important book in its field. Appointed to Governor Al Smith's New York State Board of Housing in 1926, Louis Pink made his first major undertaking an inspection tour of European housing work from London to Vienna. John Nolen was a regular traveler abroad. Dozens more Americans turned up in Vienna (1926), Paris (1928), and Berlin (1931) for the congresses and postcongress tours of the International Housing and Town Planning Federation, of which Nolen himself was elected president at the Berlin meeting in 1931. When housing heated up as an American political issue in the mid-1930s, the transatlantic traffic picked up accordingly, bringing even the National Association of Real Estate Boards into the game. "Europe is the great sociological and economic laboratory," Nolen repeated the familiar point of conviction in 1927. Where local examples failed, Europe was the critically important repository of information: a rotating exhibit of contrasts, alternatives, possibilities, and embarrassments.[51]

American experts on European housing took it as incontestable that in the democratization of decent housing for the masses, the United States, with its one-legged reliance on commercial building, increasingly lagged behind. "Campaign orators, from force of habit, may continue to talk for some years about the 'American workingman's standard of living' as though it were something vastly superior, but our leadership in that respect has already passed from us," Edith Elmer Wood warned at the outset of the decade. "We have more automobiles, it is true . . . [But] the working people of western Europe all have the eight-hour day. They have health insurance, unemployment insurance, old age pensions . . . Most important of all, in a few years the working people of western Europe will be living, rank and file, in such homes as only the fortunate minority can attain under our hit-or-miss system." At the decade's end, she thought the gap only wider. Everywhere in Europe the "right to a home" was being broached as a social promise, while in America "we are still thanking God that we are not as other men and that we do not interfere with the sacred laws of supply and demand in the matter of providing homes for those who need them."[52]

In most American assessments of European housing in the 1920s, the German experiments in the machine-age democratization of shelter did not cut a very large figure. Pink stopped briefly in Frankfurt in 1927 but skipped Berlin and saved his superlatives for Vienna. Wood, for whom Britain and Holland set the standard in publicly assisted working-class housing, had not bothered to put Germany on her route in 1922 at all. The work of transmitting German social modernism to America fell to a young outsider, as so often before in the Atlantic progressive connection. From her first sketches of Le Corbusier's Paris villas to her emergence as the American Federation of Labor's chief housing lobbyist, Catherine Bauer cut an extraordinary swath through housing's political tangles. In the transatlantic progressive connection, her part was both striking and emblematic.

Art was Bauer's starting point. She had first traveled to Europe, fresh from college in 1926, as a political naïf, to spend a year living the life of an art student and writer on Paris' Left Bank. Insofar as modern meant post-bourgeois, Bauer was saturated with the modern mood of the 1920s: ironic, detached, amused by social mores and the legions of men who fell to her smart, intense, bohemian charm. With an elementary training in architecture and an eye for novelty, Bauer sought out the new, strikingly modernist buildings under construction in late-1920s Paris: expensive avant-garde villas that shockingly admitted their concrete and steel girder underpinnings. Of the leftist, social variant of modernism across the Rhine she had not an inkling in 1926 and 1927.[53]

Nor did she in 1930 when, her job at Harcourt, Brace swept away by the crash, she sailed for Europe again "to look at modern architecture from a purely aesthetic angle." This time Paris could not contain her curiosity. The new showplace of European architectural modernism was now the Werkbund's Weissenhof exhibit, built high on a hill above Stuttgart in 1927, with gleaming modernist villas by Taut, Le Corbusier, and Gropius and, tucked away behind them, a row of Oud's spare, minimalist dwelling-Fords. Bauer hunted it up. A letter from Lewis Mumford introduced her to *Die Form*'s Walter Curt Behrendt in Berlin, and Behrendt's circle introduced her, in turn, to Weimar social modernism. Plunging into this unknown world of politics and forms, Bauer quickly saw that the real architectural event in Europe was the revolution in workers' housing. She enrolled in a short course in the new social architecture at Frankfurt, the only American among the 150 participants who fanned out, Ernst May in the lead, over Römerstadt, Praunheim, and Westhausen. Working hard at her German, she interviewed the leading practitioners of modernist *Siedlungsbau*. As she liked to remember the story, "What I saw in Europe in 1930 was so exciting that it transformed me from an aesthete into a housing reformer."[54]

Coming home, Bauer turned her excitement of discovery into a prize-winning article on May's work for *Fortune* magazine in 1931. Early the next year, she helped organize the first American exhibit of the new European housing designs. Hung as a small annex to the Museum of Modern Art in New York's *Modern Architecture* show, it featured photos of Römerstadt and Oud's work in Rotterdam along with a scale model of one of the early *Zeilenbau* projects. In the summer of 1932, Bauer was back in Europe once more, this time as Lewis Mumford's research assistant, guide, and lover. Mumford, at the peak of his career as a critic of culture and society in America, had a Guggenheim fellowship to study the history of technology and a commission from *Fortune* for a series of articles on European solutions to the housing industry's economic woes. Bauer took on the work of the housing series, assembling its material and formulating a good number of its "convictions" as well. When *Fortune* scrapped Mumford's contract after the first three installments after Bauer and Mumford refused to downplay the imperative of government aid in working-class housing, Bauer found herself left with a mountain of unused research material. Over the next two years she wrestled the mound into a book, *Modern Housing*, which—with its force of argument and its command of European experience—made Bauer, overnight, a housing expert.[55]

Modern Housing was, in effect, an updating of Edith Wood's report on European housing initiatives a decade earlier. With a sharper eye for form and politics than Wood possessed, Bauer set out to guide her readers through the theory and practice of the best European work in low-cost, working-class housing design. Bauer billed it not as a book about Europe, however, but as about basic human standards in shelter. By the time *Modern Housing* came off the presses in 1934, it would have been an exercise in political nostalgia to have done otherwise. She herself had barely seen modernist Weimar housing before its moment was over; by 1932 many of Römerstadt's units were empty, their tenants driven back to the city in an effort to save on transportation costs. Bauer had met Ernst May on the very eve of May's departure for the Soviet Union. By 1934, discouraged by Soviet bureaucracy, May was in exile in Kenya; Taut was in Japan; and Martin Wagner was packing for Turkey. The Karl Marx Hof and Georg Washington Hof in Vienna had fallen into the hands of their arch-critics during the Austrian political upheaval. British Conservatives had turned back once more to slum clearance. In Germany the assault on modernism as the fever sign of "cultural bolshevism" was already under way, and the Nazis were beginning to dot Germany with their own reactionary vision of utopia in pitched roofs and shutters.

Extracting "modern housing" from its political specifics, Bauer emphasized its pure, straightforward functionalism. The "freak" buildings that had startled Louis Pink in Frankfurt represented housing stripped down to its physical and community essentials. "Light, air, spaciousness, the sense of urgent and pleasant use. Sun. Grass. Color. Form." Greenbelts. Low densities. "Community unit" planning. These were housing's true standards. Set against the speculative builders' hawking of facades and pseudohistorical references, even the mathematics of *Zeilenbau* had for Bauer a clarifying and liberating logic. Modern housing meant the socialization of art in neighborhood and community designs; it meant forms dedicated straightforwardly to comfort and use; it meant the reconstruction of architecture not on a foundation of price but on inviolable biological standards.[56]

This was American practicality set to a solution of need so straightforward, she warned American readers, that it would take an effort to recognize it. "The thing which will make it [modern housing] incomprehensible to most Americans," she wrote in 1932,

> is the *positive program of wants*, the direct affirmation and solution of physical and economic and social and esthetic needs. Not, heaven knows, that the American's environment is unimportant to him; but that he has little direct or participating relation with it. He is too abstract to want good architecture. Houses are things to look at, like amusements; or shown off as a possession or a literary symbol of culture; or lived in as a daily reminder of isolated personality in competition against the rest of the world; or merely a place to hang a hat, equipped with the latest gadget for hanging hats. While at least a few Europeans apparently want good houses, effective leisure, health, participation in an orderly society . . . what *do* Americans really want? *Just one more chance, dear Lord, and by God next time I'll get out before the crash.*[57]

"There is no getting around the fact," she wrote more soberly in *Modern Housing*, that the premises underlying modern housing "are not the premises of capitalism, of inviolate private property, of entrenched nationalism, or class distinction, of governments bent on preserving old interests rather than creating new values." Modern housing could not be achieved with patchwork; "it is not 'reform' within the old pattern. It is either an entirely new method of providing an entirely new standard of urban environment, or it is nothing."[58]

If decent working-class housing demanded nothing less than that the industrial machine be set to entirely new purposes, how was the transformation to come about? This was the core issue for all those in the early 1930s who, like Bauer, had begun to imagine that a new "use" economy might be made to grow alongside the Depression-shattered "price" economy of the past. "Utility" moved from the engineering shops in the 1930s into the decade's social-political vocabulary; even Frank Lloyd Wright was talking about his new "Usonian" houses. But if social politics now demanded not merely legislation but the yoking of the productive capacities of the machine to new ends, where was a historical motor capable of producing that change to be found?

This was the question on the mind of Bauer's traveling companion, when, in the summer of 1932, Lewis Mumford followed her lead down the path to Weimar social modernism. The two books Mumford was to make out of that transatlantic encounter, *Technics and Civilization* (1934) and *The Culture of Cities* (1938), count among the most celebrated social-historical critiques of the thirties. Bauer, who took along the latter book as reading for her European trip of 1939, picking away at what now seemed to her the flabby patches in Mumford's politics, worried that he had glossed over the "enormous political-administrative difficulties" in the way of change. Like so many progressives before him, Mumford thought he saw the forces of renewal not in politics but in history itself.[59]

The future of machine-dominated civilization was an old theme for Mumford. Growing up in a German-American household on Manhattan's Upper West Side, he had sought escape from its narrow, petit bourgeois mores in books and authors. He soaked up the English and Irish critics of industrial capitalism: John Ruskin, H. G. Wells, George Bernard Shaw, Ebenezer Howard, AE, and, most important of all, his "master," Patrick Geddes.[60] Like Geddes, Mumford had no affection for the money-centered, coal-begrimed, railroad-centralized, "paleotechnic" nineteenth century that had overrun the "life economy" of the past. Mumford's books of the 1920s had been an archeological exercise, an endeavor to dig out of American history whatever buried cultural resources it might hold against the American machine- and money-dominated present.

The project of finding a meaningful tradition of literature and art in America—of extracting its Melvilles and Frank Lloyd Wrights, the functionalist beauty of its clipper ships and Conestoga wagons, from under the massive shadow of its financiers and moralizers—was just under way in the 1920s and Mumford was a key participant. For the old New England village or the prophetic voice of a Thoreau or Whitman, Mumford was full of praise. But the subsequent course of American history, down into the present "mechanical and metropolitan civilization," had followed a falling line of degradation—into barren utilitarianism, economic and artistic timidity, the standardization of forms, mechanized and dehumanized industrialism. Matthew Josephson remembered Mumford in the late 1920s, handsome and eloquent, denouncing with "blazing conviction" the bankruptcy of machine-dominated civilization. From the breakup of the collective life of the colonial village there had been no turning back; the pioneer's eagerness "to barter all his glorious heritage for gas light and paved streets and starched collars and skyscrapers . . . made the path of a dehumanized industrialism in America as smooth as a concrete road."[61]

Mumford had found Europe no different when he first saw it. His editorial position at the *Dial* having evaporated in the postreconstruction disillusionment of 1920, he had sailed for England for a five-month stint as editor of the journal of Patrick Geddes's Sociological Society. Tramping through London with Geddes's associate Victor Branford, the England he saw was not Arthur Gleason's, still burning with the embers of political reconstruction from below—though Mumford himself attended a Labour Party conference and was proud to have caught a glimpse of the miners union's Robert Smillie. The England he saw through Branford's and Geddes's spectacles was a "nightmare," crushed under the forces of industrialism and land monopoly. There was nothing in Europe's legacy from industrialism, he was sure, that was not "just as disagreeable and desolating as anything we can show in America." If anything was worth seeking out in Europe, he wrote, it was not modern but old: "certain institutions, habits of living, and material monuments which . . . Europe has lost sight of" but whose spirit "still lingers like a faint aroma about the guild-halls and market-halls and cathedrals."[62]

Some of Mumford's strident criticism of the machine age had begun to soften by the end of the 1920s. Geddes had been an ultimate optimist about the tendencies of history. Even in turn-of-the-century New York City, "a pandemonium city" if there ever was one, Geddes wrote, he had thought the signs of the "neotechnic" future were already visible. In the coming world of clean, decentralized, electric power and cooperative mores, the nineteenth century's imbalance would be righted. "Neotechnic" civilization eventually succeeded "paleotechnic" civilization in the neologisms on which Geddes hung history's frame: electricity succeeded coal, biology overrode mechanism.[63]

Mumford, too, was not without utopian ambitions. In the early 1920s he had attached himself to a brilliant group of architects and planners assembled around Charles Whitaker, dedicated to keeping the community planning idea alive in the face of the war housing program's debacle. From this work, a small garden suburb project inspired by Letchworth was established in Queens, New York, and into Sunnyside Gardens Mumford and his family had moved. He was already at work there in 1930 on a new book, "Form and Personality," in which he was trying to construct a clearer balance sheet of machine civilization's gains and losses. Still, it was only in shards and lists and pieces—Howard's garden city idea, John Roebling's Brooklyn Bridge, or Louis Sullivan's office buildings—that Mumford could sense the neotechnic possibilities Geddes had envisioned.[64]

What Mumford saw in Europe in the summer of 1932, at the very last moment before Weimar's promise winked out, gave his balance sheets, at last, a historical dynamic. Hunting up the radical new architecture in Germany, tramping through the modernist *Siedlungen* in Frankfurt and Berlin and the workers' housing complexes in Vienna, haunting the late-medieval facades in old Lübeck, and reading in the library of the Deutches Museum in Munich, he immersed himself in history. He was later to write that his summer's discovery was the cultural strengths of the late-medieval world of wood and water power: history's "eotechnic" phase, which the paleotechnic complex of coal, rails, money, and war had run over so disastrously. But it was in fact the likeness between the "eotechnic" past and the postcapitalist future that he saw breaking in all around him in late-1920s Europe that most profoundly caught his imagination.[65]

The simple, direct, medieval facades that entranced him in Lübeck and the new social modernist *Siedlungsbau* took on an unexpected kinship. With its starkly mechanistic aspect, so different from the traditionalist designs of Mumford's Sunnyside Gardens collaborators, social modernist architecture had adopted the "vernacular of the machine," but not as the American skyscraper builders had employed it. Here was architecture, Mumford wrote, rooted in a "mode of thinking [which was] rational, co-operative, practical, non-invidious"—architecture dedicated to "a maximum of use and a minimum of mere pretense and show and romantic wishfulness," the machine dedicated not to private, pecuniary display but to cooperative and common ends.[66]

No one in Germany in the summer of 1932 could miss the signs of the republic's fragility. There were Brownshirts everywhere in Germany by the end of that summer, Mumford later recognized. The crash had brought public works projects to a halt. Still, "on any realistic scale of values, America is the poor country and Germany is the rich one," he wrote. It was not in "backward" Russia or in "advanced" America, but in the social democratic housing built in Germany between 1924 and 1930 that "one had a glimpse of what the new world might be once class distinctions and pecuniary values were supplanted by a functional economy." "The machine is again for the European an instrument of human purpose," he wrote, in summing up the summer's lesson. The precapitalist past and the postcapitalist, modernist future came round into a social-political whole.[67]

It would be too much to suggest that Mumford's prophetic social anticipations of the 1930s were formed in his summer's encounter with Weimar modernism. The economic underpinning of neotechnic civilization was something Mumford had been calling "basic communism" since 1930—a reorientation of the economy from profit to use and a concentration of its resources on the production of basic life goods.[68] But to shape the future, nothing helps more than to have already seen it. In works that leaned as hard on visual as on analytical politics, it was Mumford's architectonic sense of history's tendencies that gave his books of the 1930s their prophetic power. "A new world has come into existence; but it exists only in fragments," he had written soon after returning from his European summer. The logic of the machine itself was beginning to pull history forward.[69]

By the time *The Culture of Cities* appeared in 1938, Mumford was able to include a raft of illustrations of what neotechnic civilization might look like: the Tennessee Valley Authority's spillways, the Welwyn and Sunnyside garden city experiments, glass-walled factories in Detroit and department stores in Prague, a Christine Frederick–inspired kitchen and a starkly modernist Oud-designed church, gracefully simple dwelling machines from Switzerland and Japan. The first New Deal public housing projects received a page of photos; the New Deal demonstration suburb in Greenbelt, Maryland, with its European-inspired, modernist forms, got another.[70]

Mumford was to take them all out in 1961 when he rewrote the book, in a vastly more pessimistic mood, as *The City in History*. The earlier book, with its "cheerful expectations and confident hopes," he thought now "something of a museum piece." His Weimar-imbibed optimism, his 1930s enthusiasm for modernism's elemental forms—"generic, equalized, standardized, communal"—and, not the least, the eotechnic-paleotechnic-neotechnic sequence itself all seemed to him, in retrospect, mistaken.[71]

But in 1938 it seemed otherwise. In a book that leaned hard on its illustrations, Mumford's culminating page of plates was given to Frankfurt's Römerstadt. As in the plates in Bauer's *Modern Housing*, May's spare geometric forms arced through a green expanse of parks and allotment plots; machine and garden were once more made one. But for Mumford, shelter was only the least of it. Here were not houses so much as anticipations of history. Here, Mumford wrote, "the needs of the individual and the common life are effectively reconciled." Here were "forms prophetic of a new civilization: a civilization in the same embryonic state that capitalism and mechanism were in the seventeenth century. Our generation faces the alternative of courageously going forward toward this civilization—or of relapsing into barbarism, marked by the muddled timidities of a disintegrating capitalism, and that neurotic substitute for an integrated order, fascism . . . Forward!"[72]

If the future already lay in history's wallet, the social-political task was to call its impending forms into being. Into that task Mumford entered boldly. With his connections to reformist architectural circles and his open access to the *New Republic*, Mumford waded into the politics of housing in the early 1930s. Together with Bauer and the Sunnyside Gardens group, he helped organize a series of exhibitions of the best new European working-class housing and planning designs. Their answer to the housing question entailed not merely shelter. "Housing is reform: Siedlungen is new form," Mumford had written in a note to himself in Germany. The solution was to ring the old, dying, "pandemonium" cities with new planned communities, each of ten to fifteen thousand persons, with low densities and generous civic spaces: Howard's garden city idea, not in its early philanthropic form and Unwin's picturesque setting, but modernized and democratized as Ernst May had remade it. At the newly formed Housing Study Guild, Mumford's associates were hard at work on designs and cost calculations to show how it could be done. Had vision and expertise alone made public policy, as progressives had so often believed, the Depression-radicalized garden city circle would have succeeded in making it.[73]

What was missing in Mumford's social politics was an immediate, tangible patron: a social-economic motor for his transatlantic visions that was more capable of the hard work of political-cultural transformation than the rational, non-invidious tendencies of technics themselves. Mumford, with his early enthusiasm for AE and Ralph Waldo Emerson, had no love for the apparatus of the big, central state—nor for Franklin Roosevelt, who was too ready to patch and mend, Mumford thought, than to accept that the machinery of finance capitalism was irrevocably broken. With the New Deal Mumford had soon fallen deeply out of sorts. A brief interest in a labor-based housing movement evaporated.

But the social-political problem went beyond the particulars of Mumford's politics. It had always been a hazard of the Atlantic progressive connection that the mechanism of travel emphasized a kind of visual politics. Drawing its participants to its finished products, it diminished the economic and social processes that had been essential to their creation. It made wholes more visible than parts. Like Howe or Bourne before him, Mumford saw the values of the historical age for which he yearned better than he saw the politics that might bring it into being, and its forms even more clearly than its values. Dotting small-town America with its first social-modernist art and modernist public buildings in the 1930s, the New Dealers were soon to know many of the same tensions.

The conundrum in cultural politics was deep-seated. Mumford urged social reconstruction; at the same time, he despaired of reconstruction within the existing cultural-economic frame. Our communities are "chaotic," he wrote in 1934,

> because capitalism is chaotic; they are socially misplanned and economically disorganized because capitalism is misplanned and disorganized; they do not sustain human values because capitalism puts pecuniary values first . . . If our communities display in their structure mainly the predatory and parasitic aspects of modern society, it is because our civilization as a whole has not been organized economically so as to produce what one may call, with the biologist, a flourishing symbiosis, that is, a cooperative life grouping.[74]

The seeds of cultural regeneration lay in the rebirth of community forms; the rebirth of forms waited on a transformation of values. Discount the utopian, transformative ambitions of the social modernists' "new Berlin" and "new Frankfurt," reduce their work to mere class and interest politics, and one played false to their core project; raise the symbolic level of their work too high, and one made transfer all but impossible. Squeezed between poles like these, the politics of cultural transformation were capable of veering quickly from prophecy to historical pessimism. The retreat of Toledo's Brand Whitlock into European aestheticism in the 1920s and the *New Republic*'s Herbert Croly into philosophy were cases in point. Even Frederic Howe temporarily decamped from politics in the late 1920s to philosophize on a Nantucket farm.

Mumford had not retreated to the position of pessimism yet. His attempt to bring back to America the seeds of the neotechnic future he had sensed in Weimar social modernism had plumbed the possibilities of visual-historical social politics. But anticipation alone could not move the wheels of politics. If functional, democratic modernism was to find a niche in the United States, it would have to have a patron closer at hand than the classless force of history itself.

Catherine Bauer's own reading of Weimar social modernism had shifted by the mid-1930s to an altogether different direction. She had supported herself from 1932 to 1934 with part-time work for Mumford's circle of architects and planners; her photos had formed the backbone of social modernism's first American exhibits. By the time she completed *Modern Housing*, however, Bauer had become convinced that Weimar's root lesson was not in forms or functions but in politics: that modern housing was not the product of historical evolution but of working-class agency, and that only a mass, politically aroused labor movement could break the prevailing frame of shelter economics to make it happen. When John Edelman met Bauer, he assumed she was some sort of "red," a charge she was eventually hauled before Congress to deny. Mumford despaired that she had become a politico and a mere "houser." Whatever the justice of the label, Bauer and Mumford had broken apart over class and politics by 1934, and Bauer was searching hard for the kernel of an effective, labor-based housing movement.[75]

The raw materials for such a movement were not hard to find in Depression America. If the inner social world of labor had been far less intensively cultivated by American labor organizations than by their European counterparts, there were nevertheless a few important exceptions. The most active were the garment workers' unions. Nodes of continental notions of labor solidarity, less captive to the cult of manly independence than other unions, and open to a broader range of social issues, they helped sustain a vigorous inner as well as outer social democratic politics in the early twentieth century. In New York City the Amalgamated Clothing Workers Union ran a labor bank and credit cooperative, an employment exchange, and a joint labor-management unemployment insurance fund. It conducted evening education classes and a summer camp for union children; promoted choral and gymnastic clubs for adults; organized bulk purchases of food and electricity; and distributed ice and milk at cost to union families. By the early 1930s, the union had also constructed the two most important labor-sponsored apartment complexes in the country. The second of them, set in the Lower East Side and designed by a young Hungarian immigrant architect, took its bold, heroic forms and inner social amenities straight from socialist Vienna.[76]

The project of mobilizing materials like these into an American counterpart to the union-based housing associations that had left so striking a mark on 1920s Berlin fell to an alliance of political and aesthetic mavericks, all with connections stretching across the Atlantic. Bauer's point of entry came through Oskar Stonorov, a young, cosmopolitan, Frankfurt-raised architect, who had worked briefly in Le Corbusier's studio before emigrating to the United States in 1929. Trying to drum up contracts by knocking on labor union doors, Stonorov had met the American Federation of Hosiery Workers' John Edelman. A newspaperman raised in an English Tolstoyan community, Edelman, in turn, had moved from war resistance circles into a variety of radical political undertakings, including work as a paid organizer for the La Follette campaign of 1924, before landing a job as the Hosiery Workers' publicist and lobbyist. Edelman first learned of union-sponsored housing through an Amalgamated Clothing Workers' organizer, who had showed him, with a convert's intense conviction, a sheaf of photos of the socialists' housing work in Vienna.[77]

The hosiery workers, some of whom had bought a precarious toehold in Philadelphia's new bungalow suburbs, only to lose it again under the weight of their mortgage indebtedness, supplied the demand and organizational muscle. The union's leadership supplied the project's social democratic politics. Stonorov supplied the link to aesthetic modernism. Stonorov's initial design for the Hosiery Workers' housing, three extremely tall, parallel, ten-story buildings, was a potentially disastrous marriage of Le Corbusier's monumentalism and Gropius's *Existenzminimum* mathematics. But after the design was reshaped in accordance with a systematic survey of union members' housing desires, the completed project approached the best models of Weimar labor housing. Constructed in Philadelphia's textile factory district with one of the first New Deal public-works housing loans, the Carl Mackley Houses incorporated three-story modernist forms, precast concrete construction, windows so undisguisedly foreign that the building authorities initially balked at approving them, and a range of inner amenities unthinkable in commercially supplied working-class housing. The inner courtyards contained a tennis court and small swimming pool; the buildings harbored a cooperative grocery store, meeting rooms, a well-equipped nursery, and below-ground automobile parking; the flat roofs held laundry facilities and children's sandboxes; lectures, political discussions, and art classes flourished in the auditorium. If Römerstadt brought a piece of Ford's America to the Nidda Valley, the Carl Mackley Houses represented an authentic piece of European social modernism brought home.[78]

Well before the first tenants had settled in, Stonorov and Edelman were working hard to leverage the project's precedent into a broad-based, grassroots labor housing movement. Together with Stonorov's Bauhaus-trained partner, Alfred Kastner, Charney Vladeck of the *Jewish Daily Forward*, and William Jeanes, the maverick Quaker philanthropist who became the Mackley Houses' resident manager, they set up an organization they optimistically named the Labor Housing Conference, lodged in a corner of Stonorov's office. It was this that Bauer joined in 1934, as the Labor Housing Conference's theorist, publicist, occasionally paid staff, and lobbyist. By 1935, Bauer and Edelman had successfully wrung an endorsement of a federal public housing program from the AFL's leadership and had shifted their lobbying to the inner congressional circles out of which the Wagner Housing Act was eventually to come. The representative they found to introduce Bauer's draft housing bill had himself grown up in Vienna.[79]

Politicizing "modern" housing gave it a political dynamic and a constituency. It made social modernism's complex of social, economic, and aesthetic ambitions potentially portable across the transatlantic institutional differences. Against those who saw public housing as slum betterment, or poorhouse improvement, or the fulfillment of Ebenezer Howard's community visions, the Labor Housing Conference worked hard to inject the interests of the working class into housing politics—not merely as housing's producers (though this played a major role in the building trades unions' endorsement) but as its ultimate consumers. Their project of labor-sponsored working-class housing, financed through public loans and built with the best efficiencies the machine age could manage, would have fit easily into social democratic politics in most great cities in continental Europe.

Within the context of the Atlantic progressive connection, however, class politics, like culture politics, offered no smooth route to success. To generate a grassroots labor demand for housing was not an overnight task in the best of circumstances; where the labor unions' social infrastructure was as patchy as in the United States, it was slower work still. Attaching that demand to state policy without the aid of a labor-based political party was doubly problematic. Where timing mattered intensely, as it did in the relatively narrow political window the Depression had opened, the transmission machinery was slow. And in the endgame of legislative maneuvering, as we shall see in chapter ten, the process ran the risk of breakdown and crippling, last-minute compromise as better-organized interests muscled in.

In the hard times and organization struggles of the mid-1930s, no other labor unions stepped forward to sponsor working-class housing. By the time the Wagner Housing Act was completed in 1937, the window of public subsidies had closed once more. The best-designed of labor housing demonstrations notwithstanding, modernism was not mobilized in the United States as a working-class project. The dwelling machines of 1930s America were not to be for the machine workers.

In all these ways, inertia restricted the politics of a working-class housing movement in the United States. If one wanted quicksilver speed, however, nothing worked faster than the markets themselves. All they demanded of modernism was that it be stripped down to commodifiable units, its politics forgotten, and its patrons exchanged. Where so much was up for sale, not the least of which was taste, it was hardly surprising that the project would be tried. Commercial modernism, to be sure, was not a distinctly American phenomenon. Art in the service of commodity design had been honed to a craft in the prewar German Werkbund and set out for display in the Paris Exposition internationale des arts décoratifs et industriels modernes in 1925, which set the fashion for the art deco style. Still, nothing matched the speed or thoroughness of modernism's depoliticization in the United States. In Weimar Germany, functionalism had momentarily stuck its thumb in the eye of bourgeois culture. But it was in keeping with the transformative potential within the Atlantic connection that the functionalist aesthetics of radical Weimar first swept into 1930s America not as the form of a new social order but as a tonic for skyscraper builders and the consumer goods industry.[80]

The first hints of the marketing of modernism began to show up in fashionable store windows in the late 1920s. By the beginning of the Depression, a new corps of professional product designers, many of them with ties to design studios in Paris, Germany, and Vienna, were hard at work on ways to make machines appear more machinelike than they had any functional reason to appear: modernist forms for telephones and teakettles, streamlined sheet-metal sheathing designed to boost railroad ridership and refrigerator sales out of their Depression slump, eye-catching store signs in the *Das neue Frankfurt*'s idiom, and store interiors that made Oud's cubes and semicircles into marketable novelties.[81]

The Century of Progress exhibition in Chicago in 1933 and 1934 gave most Americans their first clear look at commercial, Depression-era modernism, and there the alliance between avant-garde form and its eager commercial patrons could not be missed. The Century of Progress exhibition was sited on downtown parkland reclaimed from the lake and the railroads according to Daniel Burnham's designs; two of Burnham's sons sat on the exposition's planning boards. But where the iron-frame buildings of Burnham's Chicago fair of 1893 had been painstakingly covered with beaux arts frosting, this time the mechanical elements were everywhere on conspicuous display. The guidebooks touted the style as "moderne," and one saw it in exhibition buildings whose roofs were suspended from external towers, in buildings with their internal skeletons exposed, in buildings hung from central steel pylons, and in still more massed like functional, flat-roofed building blocks, all painted a riot of colors under the supervision of the Vienna émigré Joseph Urban and lit with neon at night. The General Motors building boasted a working automobile assembly line, Firestone's a complete tire factory. The fair's architects claimed not that the overall effect was beautiful but that it was new—that the modernist architecture served as a dramatic billboard for the companies spending their scarce money for exhibition space. Nothing less daring, the design committee explained, could have drawn the paying crowds that the fair needed.[82]

In a corner of the fair originally planned to hold a complete model town, before Depression cost cutting took hold, a housing section boasted eleven futuristic houses built of steel, glass, precast stone, and masonite, put up by construction product firms. The majority of them were billed as affordable and functional. Their cubistic forms, starkly plain facades, and broad windows would have fit into May's Frankfurt without a remark. Many were prefabricated, their steel sections bolted together like children's blocks for quick assembly. But they were not elements within larger solidarities. They were living machines peculiarly for America: detachable altogether from both place and community.[83]

If motion and novelty were essential to the success of modernism in the commercial markets, the modern also needed to be disencumbered of its social democratic past. To this task those who appointed themselves modernism's official curators in America were quick to turn their hand. Philip Johnson and Henry-Russell Hitchcock, Jr., were not yet thirty when they organized the Museum of Modern Art's pathbreaking exhibit of modern architecture in 1932 and wrote the catalog that defined the "international style." Functionalism, to them, had no part in it, nor did the reattachment of architecture to a life economy of physical and social needs, nor did politics. They opened an annex of the exhibit to Bauer and Mumford for their housing display. In fact, through the 1930s the Museum of Modern Art sustained an attention to the design of social housing unthinkable in a later day. But in Johnson and Hitchcock's codification of the "modern," housing was set aside as irrelevant. The "typical family," on whose needs May's designers had spent so much ingenious thought, they wrote off as a "statistical monster."[84]

It was an extraordinary accomplishment, this brash, young, aesthetic commodification of modernism. The fusion of radical politics and radical forms in which modern architecture had been born was cleansed of its utopian strivings. Modernism's social democratic and labor union patronage was erased from the historical record, though as Sibyl Moholy-Nagy was later to protest, the reputation of virtually every modernist architect rested on publicly financed *Siedlungsbau*. Out of the social ferment of 1920s Europe they extracted a purely aesthetic code—an emphasis on open volumes rather than mass, on regularity rather than axial symmetry, on facades free of applied decoration—the canon, in practice, of the "modern" curtain-wall commercial skyscraper. In one of the most striking transformations in the Atlantic connection, it was in this form that machine-age modernism came home to America.[85]

The future was not yet sewn up with Johnson's and Hitchcock's manifesto of 1932. In comparison with the revolution in shelter that had occurred in Europe, the Museum of Modern Art catalog and the temporary pavilions erected in Chicago were mere transient displays. In Europe by the end of the 1920s, a significant part of a continent had been rebuilt with decent, affordable houses; elements of a new, postbourgeois social aesthetics had been broached; in English brick and German glass and precast concrete, new forms of community had taken shape.

In the American context, however, the borrowed elements threatened from the first to dissociate into fragments. Uprooted from politics and patrons, social modernism broke into a bundle of contradictions. It was the external shell of the postcapitalist future; it was a revolution in class relations brought to bear on shelter; it was a principle of pure form; it was the latest advertising card of capitalism itself. In bits and pieces, the late-Weimar fusion of labor housing politics, machine production techniques, and radical aesthetics found its way into 1930s America. But the elements would not stay put. The Atlantic crossing scrambled and dissolved relations in the very process of extraction and appropriation.

Speed was, as usual, part of the matter. Ideas, politics, and goods moved at profoundly different rates through the Atlantic connection. Under the circumstances, no cluster as complicated as social modernism was easy to hold together. But the more fundamental issue had to do with patrons and politics. It was in the nature of the need to recreate alliances anew for each imported policy that the very process of borrowing destabilized the politics of the social forms and recast them in a dozen variants. In a system where ideas and inventions were so much more movable than patrons and politics, hybrid reassemblages were built in to the very structure of international exchange. Thus the marriage of Fordism with social democratic politics in 1920s Europe; thus the marriage of revolutionary modernism with skyscraper commerce in the United States.

Against these quixotic transformations the importers struggled, hunting for stable foundations for their borrowed forms, seeking to minimize the entropy of the borrowing relationship. Had the bridges that Atlantic progressives made, one by one, been supplemented by party-based connective institutions, these destabilizing tendencies might have been better contained. As it was, patronage was always problematic and transformation always close at hand.

The 1930s was to be, in these regards, the crucial decade for the Atlantic progressive connection. On both sides of the Atlantic the Depression shook and remade existing structures of politics and patronage. It wedged open the institutions of politics as no other event had in twentieth-century American history. Into that breach a flood of pent-up progressive projects were to flow, all trailing their Atlantic connections: Clarence Poe's farm cooperatives, Elwood Mead's planned rural settlements, the American Association for Labor Legislation's plans for social insurance, the civic designs of municipal progressives, the war collectivists' ambitions for economic controls, Mumford's sense of neotechnic civilization rising from the ashes of industrial capitalism, and Bauer's dreams for labor housing. The latter two projects were still in the making in the early 1930s, proof of the as yet unexhausted resources within the Atlantic progressive connection. The question was how, in the Depression-reconfigured structure of politics, the selective, sometimes capricious machinery of transmission and adaptation would sort them all out.

British Workman's Social Insurance Protection Compared with American Workman's

Which umbrella would you prefer on the inevitable "rainy day"?

The Politics of Lag. The American Association for Labor Legislation published this comparison of social insurance protection in Britain and the United States in 1919, when the first American campaign for public health insurance was at its height. All but the industrial accident insurance section of the British worker's umbrella had been the work of the Liberal government between 1908 and 1911. (*American Labor Legislation Review* 9 [March 1919]: 65)

The Working-Class Suburb

(a) London County Council suburban working-class housing at White Hart Lane. Built north of London between 1904 and the First World War, this was suburbia thrown open for working-class Londoners: shelter democratized. (London Metropolitan Archives)

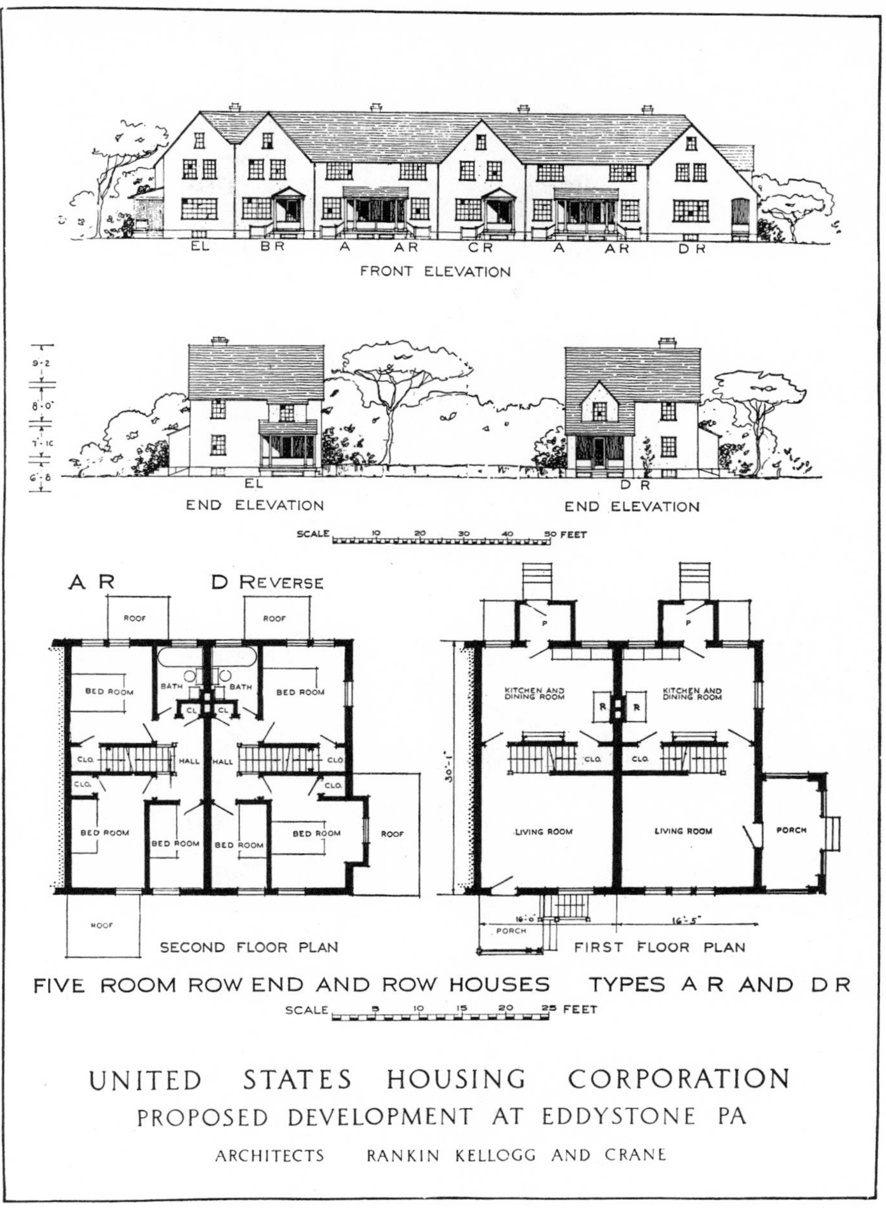

(b) Designs for United States Housing Corporation war workers' housing near Chester, Pennsylvania. (U.S. Department of Labor, Bureau of Industrial Housing and Transportation, *War Emergency Construction (Housing War Workers): Report of the U.S. Housing Corporation*, vol. 2, 1919)

(c) U.S. war workers' housing under construction in Wilmington, Delaware, 1918. (National Archives)

Built in the wartime breach in the normal rules of social politics, American war workers' housing was more generous in standards of interior space than its British prototypes. But the garden suburb scale of the war housing projects and the long, sheltering roofs that the LCC architects had used to bind the units visually together were conscious borrowings.

Streetscapes

(a) The working-class section of Letchworth, England, Ebenezer Howard's pioneer garden city. (First Garden City Heritage Museum, Letchworth Garden City, England)

(b) War workers' rental housing by the United States Housing Corporation in Waterbury, Connecticut, 1918. This reconstruction of an English village lane in an American munitions manufacturing city was a particularly striking manifestation of the international social politics of the war. (National Archives)

The Labor Diaspora

(a) The Karl Marx Hof, Vienna. Built by the city in the late 1920s, this was the most famous example in its day of socialist working-class housing. The monumental wall enclosed an inner world saturated with cooperative and party activities. (Electa archive, Milan, Italy)

(b) The Amalgamated Clothing Workers Union's cooperative apartments on Grand Street in New York City. The garment workers' housing project in the Lower East Side was the most important example of union-sponsored housing in late 1920s America. It echoed not only the architecture of the Vienna projects but also their labor pride and their inner hive of collective endeavors. (Museum of the City of New York)

DAS NEUE FRANKFURT

MONATSSCHRIFT FÜR DIE FRAGEN DER GROSSTADT-GESTALTUNG 1926 - 1927

Machine-Age Social Politics. The cover of the second number of *Das neue Frankfurt* showed Frankfurt's new city-owned working-class housing under construction. The politics were European but, as the photographer took pains to show, the construction techniques were consciously "Fordist" and American: prefabricated, precast concrete slabs, hoisted into place by moving cranes. *(Das neue Frankfurt)*

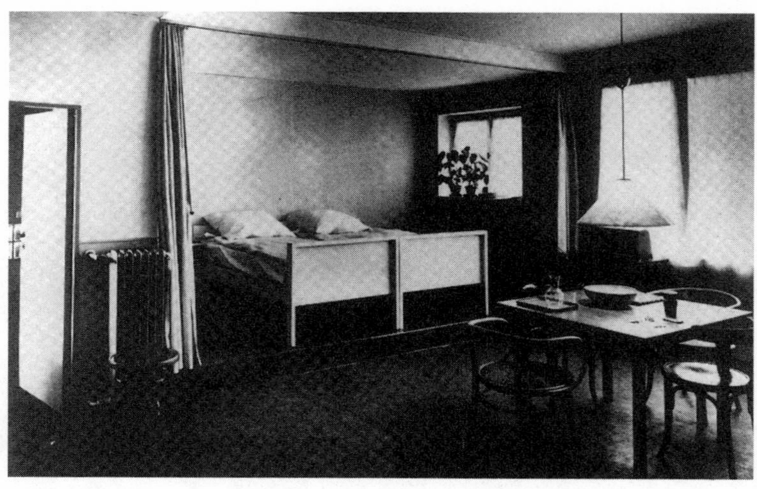

The Politics of Taste

(a) The interior of a living-sleeping room at Römerstadt, Frankfurt's most famous social modernist housing development of the late 1920s. The city architects designed both the buildings and the furniture in a consciously modern style, incorporating ingenious schemes to economize on space, like this moving curtain "wall." *(Das neue Frankfurt)*

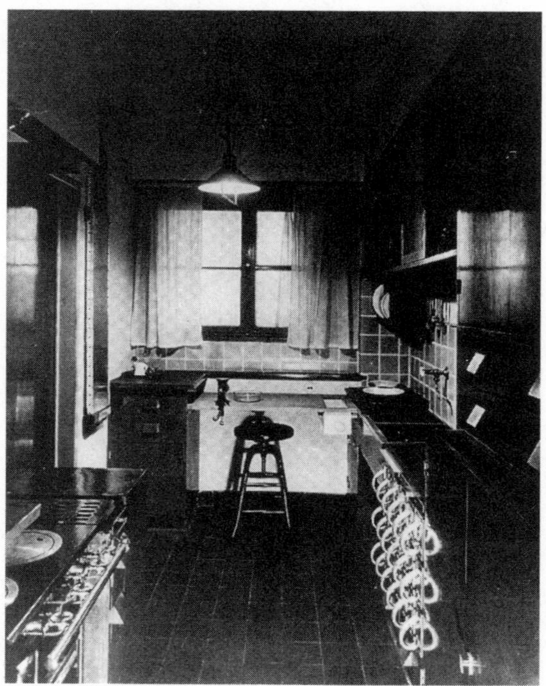

(b) The "Frankfurter kitchen," 1927. Designed by Grete Lihotzky for the city's working-class housing developments, this was the high point of the radical, social modernist style. *(Das neue Frankfurt)*

(c) The model living room in the South Jamaica public housing complex as furnished by the New York Housing Authority in 1940. The space-saving imperatives were no less severe in New York City than in Frankfurt, but the designers took pains not to let them disturb the canons of bourgeois taste. (Museum of the City of New York)

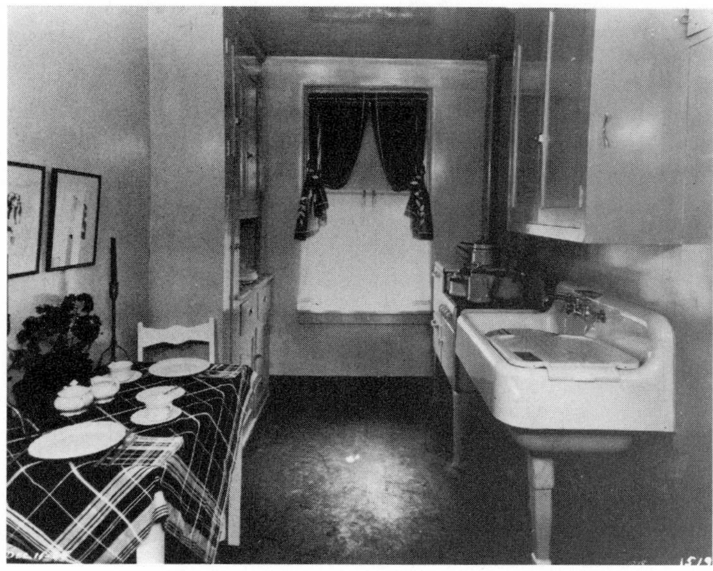

(d) The model kitchen at the South Jamaica public housing project, 1940. In the land of machines, the kitchen was all but immune to the modernist currents around it. (Museum of the City of New York)

Cooperative Economics. The booth of the Workers and Farmers Co-op Company at a Wisconsin county fair in the 1930s. The cooperative ideal spoke, as always, simultaneously to commercial and anticommercial sentiments: "The profits of your co-operative belong to you." (*Survey Graphic* 25 [1936]: 31)

Resettling America

(a) A panel from a traveling exhibit explaining the New Deal Resettlement Administration's rural resettlement work in 1936. At the middle right is the Westmoreland subsistence homestead colony in western Pennsylvania. The photos at the bottom right show farm colony managers and home economics experts at work. (Library of Congress)

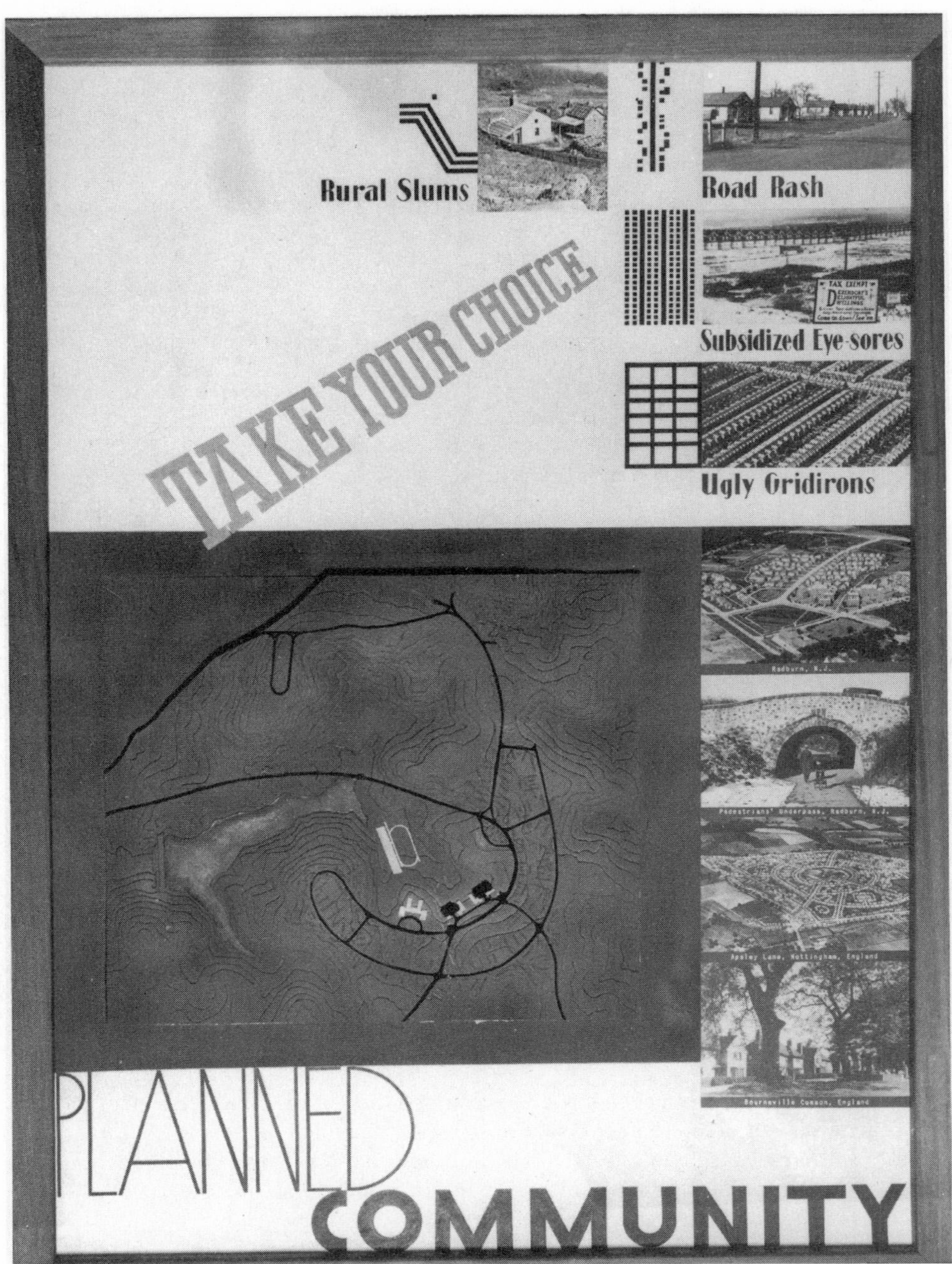

(b) The New Deal's greenbelt suburban program, as advertised by a Resettlement Administration placard, 1935. At the lower left is the site plan for Greenbelt, Maryland. The photos at the bottom right depict two scenes of Radburn, New Jersey, designed by Raymond Unwin's and Ebenezer Howard's American disciples, Henry Wright and Clarence Stein; a new development at Nottingham, England; and the green at George Cadbury's Bournville, England. (Library of Congress)

(c) Franklin Roosevelt at Greenbelt, Maryland, November 1936. In this highly publicized, symbolic endorsement of the greenbelt suburb program, Roosevelt is in the lead car, accompanied by an entourage of officials and, on the right, the site's construction workers. (Library of Congress, reprinted by permission of the Associated Press)

Transatlantic Social Modernism

(a) The Praunheim Siedlung in Frankfurt, Germany, in the late 1920s. *(Das neue Frankfurt)*

(b) An apartment house at the most architecturally radical of the New Deal greenbelt suburbs, Greenbelt, Maryland, in the late 1930s. (Library of Congress)

Solidarity Imagined

(a) An entryway to Harlem River Houses in New York City in the late 1930s. (Museum of the City of New York)

(b) Day nursery at Harlem River Houses. (Museum of the City of New York)

In its community design, this all-black public housing project, built with Public Works Administration financing, epitomized the social-political aspirations that the Atlantic progressive connection brought into the New Deal.

10

New Deal

The Intellectual Economy of Catastrophe

"Aimless experiment, sporadic patchwork, a total indifference to guiding principles or definite goals," Lewis Mumford scolded Franklin Roosevelt's policies in the fall of 1934; there was no logic to the New Deal, he objected, only drift through a sea of "confused and contradictory nostrums." Mumford was in a particularly radical mood that season as the Roosevelt administration moved into its second Depression winter. But his exasperation at the incoherence of the New Deal was a commonplace of the 1930s. Even administration insiders like Rexford Tugwell and Frances Perkins admitted that finding the central tendency in Roosevelt's moves took a kind of lucky divination. The editors of the London *Economist* thought the National Industrial Recovery Act, the centerpiece of the administration's economic recovery hopes in 1933 and 1934, had probably collected "more divergent economic and social theories under the roof of a single enactment than any other piece of legislation known." The outgoing president of the American Political Science Association, Walter Shepard, put his own gloss on the point late in 1934. "The ideology of the New Deal is illogical, inconsistent, and turbid," its program "a mass of undigested and contradictory experiments," he complained. "If there is leadership, it is the leadership of mounting one's horse and dashing off in every direction at once."[1]

To historians since, the New Deal's makeshifts still hang upon it like a cloak of so many incongruous colors as to confound agreement on either its sources or effects. Cutting the New Deal in two, as Rexford Tugwell and others were later to do, so as to separate the "first" New Deal of 1933 and 1934, with its confidence in large-scale economic management, coordination, and planning, from the "second" New Deal of 1935 to 1938, a reversion (so Tugwell complained) to the atomistic, anti–big business policies of Woodrow Wilson's day, does not stand up to close examination. The New Deal divides not into clear phases but, rather, into a maze of divergent tendencies. "Ideologically Roosevelt and the New Deal were a no-man's-land," a recent historian of New Deal economic policies writes: less a program than a free-for-all of competing ideas and interests.[2]

Claims about the New Deal's legacy quickly lead to similar contradictions. The New Deal was a triumph for labor; it was capitalism's ambulance wagon. It was a moment of extraordinary public compassion for the poor and the unemployed; it was shaped by the class and racial prejudices of the white southerners who still dominated the Democratic Party. The New Deal casts its shadow over politics and political argument like no other domestic event of the century. It constitutes the defining moment of twentieth-century American progressive politics. But its logic still eludes us.[3]

How the same event can simultaneously be so defining and so incoherent is the first of the riddles the New Deal presents historians. The second is how such an extraordinary burst of legislative action should have occurred at all. In a land filled with the wreckage of so many earlier social policy designs, the surge of policy energy and initiative in the New Deal remains little short of extraordinary. It reversed overnight the Progressive-era pattern of transatlantic political influences. Not even Henry Ford had riveted European attention as Roosevelt did. Through the Tennessee Valley Authority's model town of Norris, Tennessee, the Resettlement Administration's community projects, the beehives of planning activity in Washington, D.C., and, with luck, an audience with Franklin Roosevelt himself, European progressives now streamed. As Americans had once set off for social-political laboratories in Germany, Denmark, or New Zealand, John Maynard Keynes, William Beveridge, H. G. Wells, Gunnar Myrdal, and others now came to the United States to take the New Deal's measure.

Not all of the New Deal's foreign observers liked what they saw. Appalled by the massive Blue Eagle parades staged to whip up enthusiasm for the National Recovery Administration in 1934, the British Independent Labour Party's Fenner Brockway felt he might as well have been in Nazi Germany. But to most European progressives, the New Deal came as an unexpected beacon in the decade's darkness. There was a "real revolution of ideas . . . sweeping through America," Margaret Bondfield, fresh from a trip across the Atlantic, told her Labour Party colleagues in 1933, reversing the trope Bondfield's American friends had used so often; against the current of events in New Deal America, she thought, the stagnation of political ideas in Britain was an acute embarrassment. Keynes saw in the New Deal the "middle way" American progressives so often looked for in Europe: a "half-way house" between Marxism and laissez-faire. In France, Léon Blum led a socialist-radical government to power in 1936 with a rhetoric of progressive experimentation explicitly derivative of the American New Deal. In Britain, David Lloyd George staged the Liberal Party's quest for renewed power as a "new deal" for Britain. There were three political experiments "upon the success of which the whole course and outlook of the world depends," Lloyd George was sure in the early 1930s: Russian collective planning, Italian corporatism, and the American New Deal—"the American being by far the most important."[4]

So striking a reversal of roles within the Atlantic exchange was an event in itself, but under the rhetorical exaggerations lay a nugget of truth. In no other nation in the North Atlantic economy was the progressive response to the world Depression of the 1930s as vigorous as in New Deal America. Political scientists have long remarked on the point. When they write of American social policy as lurching forward in an "erratic" pattern of fits and starts, stasis and dramatic "policy breakthroughs"—through intermittent "big bangs" rather than the slower, continuous development of other nations—the big bang that clinches the point is the New Deal.[5]

European progressives, by contrast, stumbled through the hard times of the 1930s with considerable difficulty. In Britain, the Labour government of 1929 to 1931 proved helpless in the Depression's grasp. The Conservative-dominated governments that followed were content to muddle through on lines of policy tradition and least resistance. France went through more than twenty governments between 1929 and 1939, in a pattern that ensured that none of them left much permanent effect; Léon Blum's Popular Front government, more long-lived and far more ambitious than most, survived barely a year. In Germany, the object over the years of so many American progressive hopes, both liberals and social democrats were politically extinguished in the Nazi seizure of power. Sweden's Social Democratic coalition, alone among the European progressive governments, steered an innovative and highly successful course through the 1930s. Its combination of a labor-farmer political alliance with an aggressive policy of social investment was a harbinger of the social Keynesianism of the post–World War II era. Still, in sheer volume of legislative initiative, even Sweden does not begin to compare with the record of the New Deal United States. Between 1933 and 1938 the North Atlantic social economy's laggard whirled into extraordinary action. The American tortoise became a hare.[6]

Here, then, is the conundrum the New Deal poses: how to square its energy, in a decade that dealt so cruelly with progressive governments elsewhere, with its monumental confusions. Without intellectual and ideological passion, the New Deal is all but inexplicable, yet virtually every quest for the New Deal's logic seems only to unravel in contradictions. The riddle of the New Deal is how to understand the marriage of such striking success with such massive apparent incoherence.

The conventional historical wisdom stresses the unusual severity of the crisis in America. If political innovation was more vigorous in the United States than elsewhere, the argument runs, it was because the strain on habits and institutions was more intensely felt. Big responses point to big causes and immense social strains. Such is the logic of commonsense functionalism.

That the market collapse of the 1930s bore down with exceptional severity on the United States cannot be doubted. Nowhere else had the interwar boom carried both speculative values and material standards of living so high; nowhere was their collapse more staggering or long lasting. Only in Germany did the Depression hit comparably hard, and in Germany the joblessness crisis, as measured by years of more than 20 percent unemployment, lasted a little more than half as long as in the United States. Construct an index by totaling the estimated national unemployment rates for each of the years between 1930 and 1938 (the last year before war broke out), and one can derive a "cumulative misery" figure for each nation. That figure is 93 for France, 142 for Sweden, 148 for Britain, and 196 for Germany; for the United States, it is 235.[7]

Such a catastrophic breakdown of the economy was a searing and indelible experience. The bread lines and bank runs of the 1930s, the unemployed men at the relief offices and the women scrimping on food and clothing, banks without assets and industries without markets, farmers desperately on the move or stuck with the consequences of thirty-cent wheat and five-cent cotton—all this, traumatic in itself, was doubly unnerving for having fallen in on what had been called an era of limitless prosperity. The more jolting the collapse, the assumption runs, the stronger the ultimate policy-making reaction.

But in the transatlantic pattern of events, severity of circumstances alone turns out to be a markedly weak predictor of political innovation in the 1930s. In Germany and the United States, it is true, dramatic—and dramatically dissimilar—policy shifts went hand in hand with dramatic economic collapse. But in Sweden, innovative policy response conjoined with a crisis far less severe than in either Germany or the United States. In Britain, where the unemployment pattern closely resembled Sweden's, the Labour Party was all but bereft of new ideas. In France, though the Depression's effects there were weakest of all, the Popular Front seethed with plans and programs.[8] Across the North Atlantic economy, levels of innovative response simply cannot be made to correlate in any straightforward way with relative degrees of crisis.

Nor, on reflection, should one expect otherwise. The notion that systematic breakdown is conducive to innovative ideas is largely myth. "That social thought of any sophistication could emerge from an experience as shattering as the depression was itself surprising," Richard Pells writes in the best extant study of 1930s social thought in the United States. "No period of crisis is especially conducive to calm analysis or new concepts; men are much more prone to fall back on inherited and instinctive values in an effort to cope with a totally unprecedented situation."[9] Calm is the moment for reflection on fundamentals; with the seas pouring in over the bow, one reaches numbly and by rote for the bailer.

Crises promote innovation in a different way. Sustained long enough, they can bring the established structure of responses into deep discredit. Almost everywhere, the political parties unlucky enough to preside over the early phases of the Depression—Labour in Britain, Liberals in Sweden, the established parties of every stripe in Germany—suffered dramatic losses in credibility. The same was true in the United States. The New Deal was not, as memory too simply puts it, a response to the Depression, which was already more than three years old by the time Roosevelt took office; it was a response to the failure of the Republicans' recovery program. The New Deal moved into space created by the inability of the Hoover administration to stem the economy's ever-downward slide and the attendant devaluation of the idea of the market's self-adjusting capacity. By eroding the conventional wisdom, extended crises may create room into which innovations may flow.

The paradox of crisis politics is that at the moment when the conventional wisdom unravels, just when new programmatic ideas are most urgently needed, novel ones are hardest to find. The need for well-formulated solutions goes hand in hand with conditions least suited for reflective policy formulation: haste, confusion, the opportunism of expediency, the impossibility of perspective on the onrushing events. One of the most important effects of crises, in consequence, is that they ratchet up the value of policy ideas that are waiting in the wings, already formed though not yet politically enactable.

In modern politics, this phase of a crisis is the social policy experts' moment. Suddenly given a more attentive hearing, they enter the political arena with satchels full of prepared solutions. The fact that those solutions have been constructed and refined prior to the crisis they will be expected to cure does not necessarily devalue them. Rather, in the intellectual economy of catastrophe, their very finishedness, the possibility of taking them directly off the shelf, as it were, gives them special value. Crises lead to a frantic rummaging through the existing stock of policy notions—notions that can be adjusted and refigured for the circumstances, but that carry authority precisely because they possess a pedigree older than the present moment. It is this rapid movement of ready-made ideas into the political center that warps the normal threads of time in crisis politics. The policy ideas pressed into service in the emergency are, as often as not, old, formulated in other circumstances to meet other conditions. They are an eruption of the past into the present.

What gives consequence to this urgent ideational movement, finally, is that crises alter the conditions of the politically possible. In devaluing and delegitimizing certain agendas, they devalue those attached to them. The grid of powers, patrons, interests, and institutions that control political outcomes shifts. This reconfiguration of influence, legitimacy, and veto rights is the doorway through which premade but untried policy steps to center stage. During a far-reaching and extended crisis, a host of policy ideas may crowd through at once.

The New Deal follows this model with exceptional accuracy. Innovation came not with the crash of 1929, even with the moment, in the summer of 1931, when it finally became clear that the economy was not going through a temporary adjustment like that of 1920 to 1922 or 1913 to 1915 but a wrenching collapse on a scale that had not been seen since the 1890s. Only when Hoover's reinvestment policies had run up to their outer limit with desperately little to show for the effort did the authority of the prevailing wisdom unravel. Then, into the vacuum and urgent need of the new administration rushed a legion of proposals-in-waiting. The Civilian Conservation Corps Act, pushed through in the first month of the New Deal, was a reworking of the soldier resettlement plans of 1918 to 1920. The Tennessee Valley Authority (TVA), which came out of the same emergency session, had, in one fashion or another, been before Congress for a decade. The National Recovery Administration was a resuscitation of the wartime economic planning apparatus of 1917 and 1918. And so the list went.

Some of the New Deal's accomplishments had no extensive prehistory. Its Keynesian experiments in the public management of aggregate economic demand were the most important case in point. Hastened by the unexpected recession of 1937–38, the intellectual transformation that would put fiscal policy first had begun to make an important mark on inner New Deal policy debates by the end of the decade.[10] But to a striking degree the New Deal enlisted its ideas and agenda out of the progressive past. Old-age and unemployment insurance, public housing, the National Labor Relations Act, the Fair Labor Standards Act, emergency work relief, rural electrification, banking and securities regulation, holding company legislation, and agricultural reform all had precrisis roots. In style, in urgency, in federal-state relations, and in political alliances there was no missing the administration's new departures. But as a legislative program, it is far more accurate to see the New Deal as a culmination: a great gathering in from the progressive political wings of a generation of proposals and ideas.[11]

Constructed initially for different circumstances, many of those proposals were only weakly related to the recovery of the shattered economy. Some of them, like the old-age insurance taxes instituted in 1935, at a time when any contraction of consumer spending was a hazardous undertaking, ran directly counter to what almost everyone knew to be the needs of the crisis directly at hand. William Beveridge, who spent a gloomy month in the United States late in 1933, came home convinced that there was a reform aspect and a recovery aspect to the New Deal, and that the two worked, to a great extent, at cross purposes to each other.[12]

By now it is trite to note that Beveridge was right. Of all the tasks the New Dealers set for themselves, the one they found most intractable was the task of economic recovery. What they did best was to throw into the breach, with verve and imagination, schemes set in motion years or decades before. The logic of the New Deal is not best to be found by hunting horizontally among its enacted pieces. The New Deal was a great, explosive release of the pent-up agenda of the progressive past; its clearest logic was the vertical logic of history.

In that great release of projects long in the making, an extraordinary number—more than New Dealers at the time were prone to admit, and far more than historians since have chosen to recognize—bore somewhere upon them marks of the Atlantic progressive connection. The point is not a casual one. The problem of New Deal innovation and the problem of transatlantic policy borrowing were joined in two fundamental ways. If there was more progressive innovation in New Deal America than in any other polity within the North Atlantic economy in the 1930s, it was, in the first instance, because the policy backlog was so much larger there. Measures that had gradually worked their way into law elsewhere had been sidetracked so often in the United States as to create an unusually large number of waiting proposals. At the bottom of the Depression, with the authority of conventional business enterprise at its low ebb, the courts under exceptional pressure, ideological convictions in flux, and the field of interests temporarily reformed, some of the central resistances momentarily gave way. Restriction and release: an overly hydraulic metaphor, perhaps, but it is a familiar phenomenon in politics.

Still, the release of a massive logjam entails not only a previous constriction. It also demands the presence of a lot of logs in the stream. Having waited, watchfully, so long on the periphery of European social policy debates, the experts whose moment came in the New Deal had accumulated an exceptionally large store of unfulfilled policy ideas. Their file drawers groaned with pamphlets on German social insurance, London housing, Danish farm revitalization, Australian labor courts, English garden cities, and unemployment measures from around the world. The North Atlantic economy had been for them less a laboratory, as they had optimistically described it, than a swelling cupboard of politically unobtainable projects, stored up in hopes of a shift in the structures of power. In the crisis of the mid-1930s, those borrowed projects were propelled into the political center. In gathering in so much of the progressive agenda, the New Deal gathered in large chunks of European experience as well.

If the transatlantic past was present in the New Deal, so, of course, was the transatlantic present. As in the crisis of the First World War, the Depression triggered among the key players in the North Atlantic economy much common watchfulness of each other's policy moves and a wide array of common responses.

Public economization was a virtually universal response to the onset of the Depression. As tax revenues fell, governments cut their expenditures, struggling to maintain the balanced budgets that orthodox economists and government planners thought were the first step toward renewed economic health. Where governments did not move fast enough to cut expenses, bank creditors forced their hand in what the left, in anger, called a capitalists' "strike." The Labour government in Britain in 1931 and the Popular Front government in France in 1937 were both brought down by the refusal of private creditors to float the loans on which day-to-day government operations depended. More cautious politicians learned to wield the budgetary ax themselves. The last Weimar governments were absorbed with emergency budget cutting; so were the treasury secretaries in both the Hoover and Roosevelt administrations. Roosevelt himself set his first mark on legislation with the Economy Act of March 1933, slashing soldiers' bonuses and government salaries in an effort to bring expenditures in line with crisis-shrunken revenues.[13]

Government manipulation of credits and interest rates was a second general response as the economic crisis wore on. Infusion of emergency government credits into the shattered sectors of the economy was at the heart of Hoover's recovery program; Roosevelt took the institutional centerpiece of Hoover's program and extended it, using the government's credit not only to refinance banks, insurance companies, and railroads from the top of the financial structure down but smaller economic actors from the bottom up. Britain ultimately put its recovery hopes in cheapened credit; so, to a great extent, did the Swedish Keynesians.

No matter how much or how little governments did along these lines, the key economic interests everywhere clamored for more immediate relief: farmers for price supports, labor for work and wages, business for release from marketplace competition. The simplest to satisfy was the business interests' plea for protection from foreign competition. Countries with high tariff and trade barriers raised them still higher in the 1930s; those committed to free trade reversed themselves. The most striking policy turnaround occurred in Britain, long the leading exemplar of free trade, where within a year of the Labour government's fall in 1931 its Conservative-dominated successor was busy building a tariff wall to rival those in protectionist Germany and the United States. Business' desire for exemption from internal market forces was a harder nut to crack. In Germany, Italy, and the United States (during the New Deal's National Recovery Administration phase), governments moved into outright industrial cartelization, dividing up markets and production quotas in an effort to stem the Depression's relentless pressure toward price and profit cutting. Even Britain cartelized outright its sickest industry, coal, and, in more piecemeal fashion, shipbuilding and textiles. Fair-weather capitalists, businessmen everywhere scurried for protection from market pressures during the Depression—into alliances with the state, if necessary.

Even more quickly than businessmen, farmers threw over the market ideal to press for tariff protection, market stabilization, or outright government-administered prices. Agricultural marketing boards with monopoly control over prices and supply were a common makeshift, as were bounties and price guarantees in the most critical crop sectors. In Britain, price and marketing regulations were limited to a few key crops; in France, the government's attempt to maintain a minimum wheat price was short-lived and ineffective. In Sweden, on the other hand, commitment to a system of broad-based, cooperative-administered price supports was key to the farmer-socialist alliance of 1933. In Nazi Germany, the state controlled farm prices and market share allocation virtually across the board. In this sense, the price and production controls of the New Deal's Agricultural Adjustment Act were a chip floating on a much broader international tide.

Labor, for its part, was thrown on the defensive by the economic collapse. As jobs evaporated in the early years of the crisis, depressing union membership and strike activities, union coalitions that had long resisted government adjudication of the terms of collective bargaining turned to the state to broker new pacts between labor, government, and stability-seeking employers. The National Labor Relations Act of 1935, the French Matignon Agreement hammered out in the opening weeks of the Popular Front in 1936, and the Swedish "Basic Agreement" of 1938, though they mixed compulsory and voluntaristic elements in different ways, were all products of a common dynamic.[14]

Still more critical to workers was the restoration of jobs and wages. Among planners, the old labor colony idea had not yet lost its appeal. The German *Randsiedlungen*, government-sponsored shantytowns of semisubsistence workers on the cities' rims; the New Deal's Civilian Conservation Corps camps and subsistence homestead projects; and the French and British subsidies to encourage urban workers to relocate in the countryside or, better yet, in the outer reaches of the empire all flowed from the same desperate hope to drain the wage economy of some of its redundant workers. Wage workers themselves preferred cash in their pockets. British labor unions lobbied doggedly for extension of emergency unemployment insurance payments. In France, the trigger issue was the forty-hour week, a work-spreading demand that helped fuel a firestorm of strikes in May and June of 1936. In Germany, Sweden, and the United States, governments bought off labor's demand for jobs through public works, investing heavily in labor-intensive emergency construction projects—roads, public buildings, and housing—sometimes eschewing labor-saving machinery to make the work go farther.

Governments mixed these ingredients into outcomes as varied as their prior experiences and the balance of interests and politics within them. The United States leaned exceptionally heavily on emergency work relief, nationalizing a familiar city response to the poor in hard times.[15] In Britain the pull of preexisting policy ran in just the opposite direction, closing off repetition of the work relief experiments of 1905 to 1907 to steer policy makers into repeated, emergency amendments to the unemployment insurance act of 1911 in a dogged effort to make the act cover a general economic breakdown it had never been designed to fit. In Sweden, Social Democratic policy making focused on public works employment at prevailing wages. With a much weaker labor component, the New Deal coalition tended toward emergency makeshifts of resuscitation and relief. German social policy, beneath its heavy public works investments, had a violence all its own. Still, the difference was in the mix of policy ingredients; the family resemblances themselves were, from country to country, largely the same.

Behind these common responses lay long-standing transnational networks of ideas and assumptions. Fiscal conservatives throughout the North Atlantic economy shared a commitment to economization, balanced budgets, and currency stability. The "Treasury view," as this was called in Britain, was influential precisely because it incorporated the collective wisdom of economists across a dozen national boundaries: that economic crises had a natural, ultimately self-correcting, deflationary course to run until wages and prices fell back to levels low enough to stimulate renewed investment. Labor organizations, too, had a common program, passed internationally from hand to hand. Reduction of the labor surplus and stimulation of consumer demand were at its core: shorter hours and better wages, more adequate pensions to encourage retirement of older workers from the labor force, longer compulsory schooling to keep more of the young from entering it, public works to reemploy the jobless, and unemployment compensation for those still out of a job. Progressives, for their part, talked of steering the market's forces through "planning." Reform socialists in France and Belgium were as keenly interested in *planisme* as were Liberals like Beveridge; in the United States, the idea of using the planning capacities of the state to construct a more stable concert of interests than market competition itself could achieve was the pivot on which discussion in Roosevelt's inner circle of advisers, the so-called Brains Trust, turned in 1932 and 1933.[16] Circulating through the North Atlantic economy, policy "languages" like these formed the piecemeal demands and emergency measures into larger patterns.

So did the nations' considerable watchfulness of one another's success and failure. Much of the talk of economic planning was inspired by experiments in Mussolini's Italy. Corporatism's reputation was still in its high tide in the early 1930s, even among those repelled by the thuggish side of Italian fascism. Rexford Tugwell, on a quick inspection tour of agricultural policies in Europe in 1934, thought Italy's the only government that was not simply drifting with events. "It's the cleanest, neatest, and most effectively operating piece of social machinery I've ever seen," he confided to his diary; "it makes me envious."[17] Others looked to the Soviet Union's immunity to the surrounding collapse. At the bottom of the economic and political crisis in 1932 and 1933, even Paul Kellogg's *Survey* was plying its social work and social reform audience with Soviet news. Kellogg himself joined the inspection expeditions to the Soviet Union in 1936, traveling a path trodden by progressives on both sides of the Atlantic. Ernst May, as we have seen, abandoned Depression Frankfurt to try his hand at Soviet city design. The Webbs, casting off their last shreds of interest in the United States, were intensely caught up in the Soviet experiment.[18]

Progressive interest in the Soviet Union notwithstanding, the older lines of Atlantic connection remained strong. Britain, despite its mounting economic troubles, still cast a formidable shadow across American policy debates. As the Depression reopened the idea of insurance against the risks of unemployment, a phalanx of American investigators descended on Britain once more to mine its experience for data and arguments. In the fall of 1933, the Rockefeller Foundation brought William Beveridge to the United States to explain the lessons of unemployment insurance to American audiences and, in private, to Roosevelt himself. In an effort to reframe the housing policy debates, the U.S.-based National Association of Housing Officials organized a roving commission of European housing experts, headed by the grand old man of the British war housing and garden city movements, Raymond Unwin. At the Agriculture Department, Henry Wallace brought the poet-philosopher of the Irish rural revival movement, AE, to lecture to an audience of department employees.[19]

Depression Germany was much more enigmatic and troubling. Alice Hamilton, studying industrial health and safety methods in Germany in the summer of 1933, filed a set of early storm warnings on the persecution of the Jews, the destruction of the labor unions, and the demise of the progressive women's movement in Hitler's Germany. But most visitors, she worried, had little inkling of the fear and danger below the surface.[20] As late as 1938, the Oberlaender Trust continued to funnel social policy experts through the familiar stations of German social progress. In 1934, it dispatched a delegation of highly placed American municipal officials to study municipal administration in Germany; in 1935, a delegation to investigate German street cleaning techniques; and in 1936, a delegation of public foresters, including the chief of the U.S. Forest Service himself.[21]

Progressive interest in Scandinavia boomed in the mid-1930s. Frederic Howe, still touting the social-political example of cooperative Denmark, wangled a commission to visit Denmark once more in 1935. Josephine Goldmark mined the familiar Danish social-political stories for yet another account in 1936. Will Alexander, head of the Farm Security Administration, made his own inspection tour of Denmark in 1938. The still bigger draw for progressives both within and beyond the United States was Sweden. Marquis Childs's admiring report on its cooperative movement, *Sweden: The Middle Way*, reached a wide American audience in 1936. Sensing a political issue in that election year, Roosevelt dispatched a high-level inquiry commission to study consumer, credit, and housing cooperatives throughout Europe, with Sweden as its first stop. Two years later, he sent a similar commission to study industrial relations in Sweden and Britain, with Gerard Swope, president of General Electric, among its members.[22]

Still, for all these points of contact, time and circumstances had eroded some of the Atlantic connection's earlier strengths. Few of the key players in the New Deal had been members of the cohort that had awakened, with such surprise, to the idea of a socially progressive Europe in the years before the First World War. Frederic Howe turned sixty-six in 1933; the New Dealers found a place for him as a member of the Consumers' Advisory Board of the National Recovery Administration, as consumers' counsel in Henry Wallace's Agriculture Department, and, after he was "purged" with other social radicals from the Agriculture Department, as special consultant to the president of the Philippines on cooperatives and farm tenancy, but he was too old to influence the course of events. The generation in their fifties played a much more central policy-making part. Isaac Rubinow among the social insurance experts, the *Survey*'s Paul Kellogg, and the American Association for Labor Legislation's John Andrews still brought to bear, from outside the New Deal's core, the cosmopolitan progressive politics of the earlier era. Within the administration, Roosevelt's secretary of labor, Frances Perkins, did the same. Having started out under Florence Kelley's influence as an investigator for the New York Consumers' League, Perkins sustained the cosmopolitan social feminism of the prewar years deep into the 1930s. When the United States government officially joined the International Labor Organization in a long-overdue symbolic gesture of internationalism, the lion's share of the credit was Perkins's.[23]

Weak in labor ties but full of persons with extensive settlement house and Consumers' League connections, Perkins's Labor Department was, in fact, a particularly active site for permeation by the cosmopolitan social progressives. New York senator Robert Wagner's office was another magnet for social progressives, many of whom, like Wagner himself, had extended family connections abroad. Henry Wallace's Agriculture Department had its core of persons who had been awakened by AE, Clarence Poe, or David Lubin. The federal housing agencies, as we shall see, buzzed with persons with European precedents on their mind.[24]

Many of the key New Deal policy drafters, on the other hand, barely knew Europe in its optimistic era. Rexford Tugwell had spent a sabbatical year in France studying agricultural policies in the late 1920s, but he had not found much to inspire him. The cohort still younger than Tugwell, arriving in Washington fresh from college or law school with only the sparest ideological baggage, were too young and too modest of means to have developed significant Atlantic ties at all. Leon Keyserling of Senator Wagner's staff, a key player in the drafting of both the National Labor Relations Act and the United States Housing Act of 1937, was only twenty-five in 1933; Thomas Eliot, one of the principal drafters of the Social Security Act, was twenty-six. By origin, the New Dealers were far more cosmopolitan than their prewar progressive counterparts. There were more Jews and Catholics among them, and more second-generation immigrants with extended family ties to continental Europe. But they themselves brought far less world experience to their work.[25]

Compounding this more distanced relationship to European social politics was Franklin Roosevelt's own attitude toward Europe, which was as mercurial as so many of his other attitudes. Nothing helped a worn-out mind and body more, he thought, than travel. When Harry Hopkins withered under the strain of relief administration, Roosevelt sent him to Europe with a mandate to hunt up material on social insurance and housing; but he quizzed him on his return only on Mussolini's character. When Roosevelt finally faced up to the necessity of firing Hugh Johnson as head of the National Recovery Administration, he did it by suggesting that Johnson undertake an investigatory trip to Europe.[26] He dropped the Inquiry on Cooperative Enterprise when the consumer cooperative idea ran into political turbulence, and buried the report of the commission on Swedish and British industrial relations.

The New Dealers were intellectually too omnivorous to fall in with Herbert Hoover's conviction that the Depression was essentially an external event. Hoover's notion of a unique "American system" momentarily and innocently engulfed by the "malign" economic and political consequences of the Europeans' war was not theirs.[27] They were ready to take ideas and policy lessons wherever they found them. They knew enough about capitalism to recognize its common outlines elsewhere and to respect the common devices of repair and restoration. But there was too little time under the extraordinary pressure of events to develop a strong network of transnational exchange in the 1930s, even if the European experiment with anti-Depression policies had been strong enough to inspire the New Dealers to it.

For all these reasons—the scarcity of clear success stories abroad, the age and experience of the participants, and the immediate needs of the crisis—the Atlantic progressive connection functioned differently in 1930s America than it had before. Spatial connections remained important: travel, the inspection tour, and the fact-finding mission all continued as before. But the vertical connections in time were more important still. Of the products of the Atlantic progressive connection that found their political opening during the New Deal, the great majority were older than the 1930s; they had made their Atlantic crossing years before. Stored up in the progressive lobbying agencies and expert reports, these held the privileged place in the intellectual economy of the catastrophe.

Thus it was no accident that when Roosevelt himself was asked about European parallels to the New Deal, his mind ran back to David Lloyd George's legislative breakthrough of 1909 to 1911. When criticized for the frenetic pace of New Deal legislation, Roosevelt retorted that "Lloyd George a quarter of a century ago put through in two years a greater body of radical reforms than the New Deal has attempted in five." The "liberal" label that Roosevelt drew around his program, in preference to the older term "progressive," was a mark of the same affinity with British Liberal politics in its prewar moment of social-political innovation.[28]

Roosevelt's admirers often pointed out the same parallels. After hearing Roosevelt outline his social security hopes to a delegation of social progressives early in 1934, Paul Kellogg wrote that "we came away feeling that history might be repeating itself; and that just as Lloyd George put over the social insurances in England a quarter of a century ago, so F. D. R. . . . might put such a rounded scheme through the next Congress, and do in a year what might otherwise take a generation." English observers frequently made the connection as well, particularly after the demise of the National Recovery Administration shunted the New Deal back onto tracks more familiar to them. Harold Laski had concluded as early as 1934 that Roosevelt "sought, with a passionate suddenness, to do, as it were overnight, something akin to what the Liberal Government in England had sought to do after 1906."[29]

For British observers, the self-serving element was strong in statements like these. The social insurance issue made the Roosevelt–Lloyd George parallel too neat and colored too many judgments. The critical point is that, in thinking internationally, American and European progressives thought backward in time to draw the lines of connection between 1930s America and an earlier Europe. Instinctively they came back to the rhetoric of historical lag. When Perkins was tapped as secretary of labor in early 1933, she wrote out an ambitious New Deal agenda. "None of it was radical," she recalled telling Roosevelt. "It had all been tried in certain states and foreign countries." As a general characterization of the New Deal, Perkins's claim is not entirely accurate, but neither was it very wrong.[30]

The "European" ingredients came into the New Deal agenda through many different channels and processes. Some of them were revivals of the war collectivism of 1917 and 1918, descendants of the Wilson administration's close and careful watchfulness of the European belligerents. Nowhere, indeed, was the eruption of the past into the present more visible than in the way the New Deal crisis managers reached instinctively for the administrative tools that had seen the nation through the war. The Reconstruction Finance Corporation, centerpiece of Hoover's anti-Depression program before the New Dealers co-opted and enlarged it, was a direct descendent of the War Finance Corporation. The showpiece of New Deal industrial policy in 1933 and 1934, the National Recovery Administration

(NRA), was likewise a revival from wartime, stocked, like the Reconstruction Finance Corporation, with former administrators of the war economy and ballyhooed with techniques explicitly drawn from the war mobilization campaigns. New circumstances made the NRA different from its War Industries Board predecessor. Labor, at a low ebb in early 1933, got not even a symbolic place on the NRA's directing board. In labor's weakness and in the absence of any clear public goal for the NRA beyond business revival itself, the businessmen who staffed it co-opted the NRA even more thoroughly than they had co-opted the War Industries Board. By the time the NRA was declared unconstitutional in 1935, it was functioning essentially as a trade association price- and production-fixing cartel. But even if the road from David Lloyd George's Munitions Ministry to Roosevelt's NRA was paved with unexpected turnings and hasty appropriations, it was nevertheless unmistakable.[31]

Other transatlantic imports were injected into the New Deal by the university experts and social-political pressure groups. The National Employment System Act of 1933 was an explicit adaptation of the British labor exchange system of 1909, a centerpiece of expert progressive unemployment prevention programs on both sides of the Atlantic since the publication of Beveridge's *Unemployment* in 1909. The drafters of the old-age and unemployment insurance sections of the Social Security Act, as we shall see, were steeped in European precedents.

In still other instances, the role of the pretested, European borrowing was catalytic. Blocked itself from enactment, it set persons scrambling to construct preemptive alternatives. The genesis of federal minimum wage legislation, a key Perkins project, was a case in point. The proposals Perkins first set out on the table in 1933 were a close adaptation of the British Trade Boards Act of 1909, a core measure for American social feminists since Florence Kelley had discovered the scheme at an international consumers' league convention in Geneva the year before. Case-by-case administrative judgment was its distinctive marker. Sweated trade by sweated trade, after careful investigation of both employers' profits and employees' living standards, wage minima were to be set by specially appointed trade boards in what amounted to a kind of publicly administered adjudication process. This idea held a key place in the minimum wage bill the administration sent to Congress in 1937. But there it foundered on the opposition of employers (who had no interest in opening their account books to the public), southern economic interests (jealous of their low-wage regional advantage), and the AFL (still confident of the "manlier" course of strikes and bargaining).[32]

The solution to this impasse, brokered by the progressive labor unions, turned minimum wage legislation in the United States down a very different course than Perkins had imagined. Stripped of its investigative flexibility and reframed as a straight wages and hours demand, the minimum wage section of the Fair Labor Standards Act of 1938 entered the statute books as an across-the-board forty-hour maximum work week and forty-cent minimum hourly wage for most industrial trades. The result was a distinctively, and distinctly legalistic, American measure, catalyzed into being by a borrowed European one.

A similar process took place in the field of labor relations. Most of the early New Deal labor relations proposals had looked to joint employer–trade union labor policy and dispute mediation boards to inject a deeper public element into wage bargaining. Proposals of this sort flowed out of memories of the war labor peace of 1917 and 1918 and the reconstruction fervor of 1919, and were mobilized by foreign precedents stretching from the Canadian and British industrial disputes acts of 1907 and 1919 to the economic councils of the Weimar Republic. The National Labor Board of 1933, a tripartite body of labor, management, and public representatives, was set in this mold; Senator Robert Wagner's original labor relations bill of 1934 followed the same basic structure. But in the cauldron of violent and polarized passions that had been the special mark of labor relations in the United States, with employers fiercely resistant to independent union organization and workers just as fiercely determined to capitalize on what they took to be the National Industrial Recovery Act's statutory protection of their organizing rights, the labor relations structures of 1933 and 1934 could not hold. In the impasse, Wagner traded in the corporatist models for the legal-judicial system of explicit fair labor practice rules and expert-administered regulations that has been the distinctive mark of labor relations in the United States ever since—dragging Congress and a reluctant Roosevelt along with him.[33]

In other corners of the New Deal, borrowed and invented ingredients mixed in still different forms. The New Dealers' preoccupation with electric power policy—their crusade against the public utility holding companies; their employment of cheap, publicly produced power from the Tennessee Valley project as a stick with which to beat back the monopoly pricing of private electric utility companies; and their construction of a public rural electrification system—had roots that stretched back to municipal "socialists" in late-nineteenth-century Birmingham, Glasgow, and London, and to the natural monopoly concerns of the insurgent economists before that. The Resettlement Administration was a hive of measures carrying marks of the transatlantic connection somewhere on them: suburban demonstration projects with a lineage reaching back to Letchworth and the British garden city movement, subsistence homesteads with ties to Elwood Mead's Australian imports, cooperatives and tenant purchase plans with links to Ireland and Denmark. The city planning idea cropped up everywhere. The work of the public housing agencies trailed a host of European connections.

On a broader political plane, war- and reconstruction-generated visions of a political alliance of brain and labor, dashed with La Follette's defeat in 1924, took wings again in 1936 as Franklin Roosevelt began to nudge the Democratic Party from its nineteenth-century basis in the white South and urban Catholic North into something much closer to the social democratic parties of Europe. As for the political language of the New Deal, key ingredients of it went back still further, to the rhetorical oppositions that had filled the German lecture halls in the 1870s and 1880s between the active state and the blind forces of the market, between social conscience and (as Henry Wallace put it) "the whole *laissez-faire* doctrine, the Manchester school."[34]

All these Atlantic imports mixed with homegrown measures far less affected by ideas or models from abroad: farm production controls, banking and securities policy, emergency work relief, silver purchase, currency tinkering. The trust busting of 1938 to 1940 was sui generis. So, for obvious reasons, was Roosevelt's ill-fated attempt to bring the Supreme Court under closer presidential control, on which he exhausted so much of his political capital in 1937. Modify and tinker with individual elements on this balance sheet, nonetheless, and the lopsided dominance of measures bearing the marks of the Atlantic progressive connection remains striking. Whether the European measures served as working legislative models, as generalized forms to be remade for American circumstances, or as catalysts for preemptive legislative substitution, their cumulative impact was profound.

The polarity between the appropriated and the homegrown is, of course, false and artificial. No policy measure has a single root, a clear and crystalline origin, by which it can be tagged as either local or foreign goods. The point is a simpler one, that lopping off the story of the New Deal at the borders of the United States is a task that would keep a dozen Procrusteses busy. The New Dealers lived within a world of social policy debate and social policy invention that for two generations had extended far beyond the nation's borders. Those sources had helped stock progressive imaginations with an agenda far larger than any one polity could have constructed in isolation. Seal the United States off from the world beyond its borders, and the New Deal is simply not comprehensible.

First came the crisis: the unsettling of axioms, the sapping and undermining of the ascendant structure of power and authority, the playing out of the existing lines of policy into perceived futility, until the businessmen's talk of a "new era" of permanent, virtually automatic prosperity seemed to too many Americans mere words thrown against the wind. Into the vacuum, into the temporary breach in the notion of a national genius so unique, so providentially blessed, as to make the nation immune from the misfortunes of the Old World, the social policy experts moved, carrying with them their blueprints, their ready-made designs, their waiting agenda. Even they did not always realize how deeply affected their agenda was by the international flow of information and designs throughout the North Atlantic economy and by their years of watching the making of social policy abroad. Consciously or half-consciously, however, they pressed a vast amount of that unfulfilled legacy into the political center.

Even the rhetoric of lag endured. "In five years I think we have caught up twenty years," Roosevelt himself mused, with his mind on British social policy in 1938. "If liberal government continues over another ten years we ought to be contemporary somewhere in the late Nineteen Forties."[35] The polar contrasts and projections, the peripatetic searchings and sociological grand tours, all knotted together in the 1930s. In the New Deal the Atlantic progressive connection reached its culmination.

Of all the New Deal measures, the one that most clearly illustrates the politics of the Atlantic progressive connection in its culminating, crisis moment was Social Security. More than half a century later, the Social Security Act of 1935 bids to be one of the New Deal's longest-running political successes. The National Recovery Administration, the keystone of Roosevelt's economic program, was gone before Roosevelt's first term was out. The 1930s experiment in federal emergency public works was closed down with the Second World War. New Deal housing and farm support measures expanded in the postwar years, only to overwhelmed, at last, by their critics. But the Social Security Act has endured. Indifferently received by labor, whipsawed by Republican critics who made it central to their case against the New Deal, Social Security survived nonetheless, weathering the anti-Roosevelt forces of the late 1930s, the Republican recapture of power in 1952, even the social-political counterrevolution of the 1980s. The "un-American" charge thrown at the act at the time of its passage has been quietly forgotten. Social Security's post-facto success has made it hard to recover how near a thing its inauguration was in the 1930s and how critical were events beyond Depression American in bringing it into being.[36]

Any attempt to explain the Social Security Act as a straightforward response to the economic collapse of the 1930s has a steep, uphill road ahead of it. Social insurance came into the Depression United States trailing twenty years of failed importation efforts. It had no powerful political lobby, grassroots movement, or interest group behind it. Many of its early supporters were tired and discouraged. With its first old-age insurance benefits not scheduled to begin until 1942, it promised no immediate relief from the suffering of the Depression. By draining money from wage earners' pockets at a moment when there was none to spare, its net economic effect was to retard rather than encourage recovery. Its record in Depression Europe was spotty. Social insurance in 1930s America had everything against it, in short, but the Atlantic progressive connection and the political-intellectual dynamics of crisis.

That the risks of unemployment and old-age poverty that the Social Security Act addressed had been profoundly exacerbated by the Depression, of course, hardly needs reemphasis. The everyday pains of the market economy multiplied in the financial collapse. The unemployed haunted the mid-1930s: "shabby men leaning against walls and lamp-posts, and standing on street corners singly or in twos or threes," Louis Adamic reported from Lowell, Massachusetts, in 1930, "pathetic, silent, middle-aged men in torn, frayed overcoats or even without overcoats, broken shoes on their feet (in a town manufacturing shoes!)." The elderly poor kept farther from public sight; but few families did not know firsthand the risks of a gradual descent into lower and more meanly paid work until employers eased the old out of work altogether and forced them back on their children and grandchildren for support. If family experience was not enough, a highly vocal lobby for universal old-age pensions, spearheaded by the California physician Francis Townsend, made headlines out of the issue of old-age poverty. Through its councils of the unemployed, the Communist Party worked hard to do the same for unemployment. The aged and the out of work were not the Depression's only victims, but they were among its most important and most needy.[37]

But if that much was clear, it was not at all clear that what the old and the unemployed needed in the depths of the Depression was a system of risk *insurance*. Even on the European side of the North Atlantic economy, as we have seen, social insurance systems were only part of a complicated repertoire of social-political devices designed to cushion men and women against the risks of the labor market. Policy makers had several systems from which to choose: compulsory, contributory social insurance as first outlined in 1880s Germany; categorical grants to the poor, on the model of the Danish and British old-age pension systems; state subvention of voluntary mutual assistance organizations, still the dominant scheme in the 1920s in France, Belgium, and throughout Scandinavia; employer-administered employee benefits as practiced by model employers everywhere; and, finally—along the line toward which social democratic opinion had been running since the Webbs' attack on Lloyd George's National Insurance Act of 1911—across-the-board social provision of minimum health and income benefits, tax-financed and universally available. When the New Zealand Labour Party wrote its social security act along these lines in 1938, with provisions for medical and maternity care, unemployment assistance, and old-age relief, whose comprehensiveness contrasted sharply with the exemption-riddled, administratively complex U.S. act of 1935, contributory insurance played no role in it at all.[38] The puzzle of the Social Security Act is not why the New Deal Congress should have addressed the economic hazards of unemployment and old age, but why it should have done so through insurance.

To be sure, of the factors running in social insurance's favor, among the strongest was its rapid expansion in 1920s Europe. Sometimes in answer to popular demand, more often in an effort to co-opt and diminish public pressure, systems of social insurance had broadened in the wake of the war. Health, old-age, and accident insurance systems were expanded to cover broader classes of workers and to include their survivors and family dependents. Although state-administered systems of unemployment insurance remained rarer than other forms of risk insurance, they, too, had developed markedly since the British experiment of 1911. In Britain itself, in a rush to satisfy the demands of demobilized soldiers, unemployment insurance coverage had been extended in 1920 from the seven specified cyclical trade sectors of 1911 to embrace industrial wage earners across the board, increasing fivefold the number of covered workers. In Germany, where unemployment insurance had been under discussion since the opening decade of the century, the republic made good on an early promise with a comprehensive unemployment act in 1927.[39]

More striking was the grafting of social insurance systems onto older, differently configured social policies. In Britain in 1925, rather than accede to labor demands for expansion of the old-age pension act of 1908, a Conservative government added a contributory old-age insurance system for wage earners between ages sixty-five and seventy. In France, where popular resistance had quashed an early experiment in compulsory old-age insurance in 1910, the Parliament signed on to comprehensive health and old-age wage earners' insurance in 1928—nationalizing a system the Germans had installed in Alsace-Lorraine before the First World War.[40]

But if social insurance was far more widespread in 1929 than in 1914, it would be a mistake to assume that it had eclipsed the other alternatives. Belgium retained its policy of subsidizing voluntary health insurance mutuals into the Second World War, Sweden into the early 1950s, and Denmark until 1960. In Canada, Australasia, and Britain itself, straight tax-financed pensions remained the linchpin of old-age social policy, not contributory insurance. Even after the German unemployment insurance act of 1927, state-subsidized labor union unemployment benefits remained the European norm.[41]

While social insurance systems grew in 1920s Europe, in the United States social insurance made so little headway during the 1920s that many of its friends had begun to back away toward more politically promising alternatives. The American Association for Labor Legislation, seared by its defeat on the health insurance front, hunkered down in the early 1920s on its old, core issues: improved standards of workmen's compensation, mine and factory safety legislation, and the prevention of occupational diseases.

In 1923 the AALL edged back into more controversial waters by joining forces with a revived movement for state-based pensions for the elderly poor. The alliance for old-age pensions, a coalition of progressive labor federations, fraternal organizations, and university-trained social policy experts, came closer than any of its pre–World War I counterparts to replicating the progressive-labor coalitions familiar in western Europe. Among its prime movers was James Maurer, president of the Pennsylvania State Federation of Labor, a key figure in the Conference for Progressive Political Action, and a labor socialist with broad commitments to workers' education and labor politics. Its administrative energy was provided by Abraham Epstein, a young Russian-born economist who had served as research director for Maurer's state commission on old-age pensions before moving on to direct the old-age pension lobbying efforts of the Fraternal Order of the Eagles.

Epstein, who had an accent thick enough to cut with a hatchet, his friends recalled, was a very different figure than John Andrews or John

Commons, but his path toward policy expertise was the stock one: graduate work in economics, a stint of social policy research, and European contacts. Early on, Epstein struck up a correspondence with the leading social insurance experts in London, Vienna, and in the International Labor Organization offices in Geneva and Montreal. He arranged for himself a year abroad to study social welfare provisions in Russia and western Europe, pouring the fruits of his investigation into the 140-page summary of every public old-age assistance and insurance program in the world that was the climax of his *The Challenge of the Aged* in 1928. But Epstein's labor allies and fraternal employers had no interest in the mandatory wage checkoffs entailed in compulsory old-age insurance. Accommodating themselves to their constituencies and the times, Epstein and the AALL experts went along with the case for simple, British-style, means-tested grants to the elderly poor.[42]

When unemployment came back on the AALL's agenda in the late 1920s, the association's tactical retreat from the social insurance principle was even more clearly pronounced. In Wisconsin Andrews's teacher John Commons had already departed from the idea that temporary unemployment was an insurable, fated risk. To Commons and his students, the key task in unemployment policy was to turn the social costs of frequent layoffs back onto the industries responsible for them. Workmen's compensation was their model: a compensatory levy against businesses for every out-of-work employee they dumped back on society. The Commons proposal was an ingenious invention, half radical, half reactionary depending on which of its facets one fastened on. By raising the cost of boom-and-bust hiring practices, the Commons proposal was designed to force structural changes toward more stable payrolls. At the same time, to protect businesses from limitless penalties, the Wisconsin scheme capped the unemployment liability employers might accrue. During good times, industries would be required to pay into a "reserve" fund to compensate workers they laid off; if, in bad times, the fund should be exhausted, that would be the end of the matter. Regularization of employment was the goal of the Commons proposal, not risk insurance; its focus was on the employers' incentives and pocketbook, not the wage earners' guaranteed minimum.[43]

In the early 1920s, when the idea of employment "reserve" funds was new, Commons had defended the scheme as a direct outgrowth of European experience. By the end of the decade, however, swinging with the rhetorical winds of the "new era," he and his coworkers were touting the idea as "extraordinarily an individualistic and capitalistic scheme"—"poles" apart from European unemployment insurance. When the AALL launched a nationwide campaign for the Commons bill in the winter of 1930–31, it followed suit. In an extraordinary turn on its internationalist past, Andrews's organization now trumpeted the "distinctly American" genius of the plan, which was indebted to no nation's experience but its own.[44]

While the experts hesitated over the social insurance principle or, like Commons, decamped outright, employers resisted it. A handful of employers experienced in company-based group insurance benefits joined the AALL itself, where they gave its key committees a less university-centered and more conservative look than before. For most employers, however, keeping vigilant watch against state incursions into the benefits field was the simpler and more common course. The National Civic Federation and the National Industrial Conference Board both campaigned actively against state social insurance initiatives throughout the early 1930s. So did the major insurance companies, even in fields, like unemployment insurance, that they admitted were commercially unprofitable.

All these factors—the resistance of employers and insurance companies to public incursions into areas they were determined to stake out as their own; the labor legislation experts' retreat toward safer, more "American" ground; and the absence of a popular constituency for contributory social insurance—effectively countered the policy drift toward more systematic systems of social insurance abroad. In a profoundly weary address to the American Association for Labor Legislation in 1930, I. M. Rubinow lamented the need to explain, from the bottom up, the social insurance principles that such an audience would already have understood, without elaboration, fifteen years before. Progressives, he complained, now talked of "workmen's *compensation*, mothers' *pensions*, sick *benefits*, medical *organization*, old age *security*, wage fund *reserves*, and what not." No one now talked of social *insurance*. The comprehensive social insurance agenda of the 1910s had fallen apart into a dozen issues, conceptually and administratively isolated from one another.[45]

If Rubinow exaggerated the dissolution of the prewar social insurance movement, the Depression in itself did little to return it to public favor. To the contrary, where social insurance systems were most systematically elaborated, in Germany and Britain, the economic crisis swept over them like a massive sea. In Britain, acute strains on the unemployment insurance system had begun shortly after the war. The economic contraction of 1920–21 was relatively brief as market crises go, but it was sharp enough to exhaust the unemployment fund established under the 1920 act before it had had a chance to build up an adequate reserve. Under intense pressure not to default on the promised benefits, British policy makers slowly backed into a system of simple, tax-financed, out-of-work relief. The "dole," as it became known, preserved the rhetorical facade of an insurance system, but patched together out of emergency supplements and extensions, it was never one in fact. By 1931, the system's books showed the reserve fund in arrears by 115 million pounds.[46]

British unemployment insurance was, in short, a conservative's nightmare made flesh: a system of politicized entitlements broken free of its initial economic restraints, a Band-Aid on an economy that ran recession-level unemployment rates in every year of the 1920s. To organized labor, on the other hand, out-of-work benefits were a rock from which it would not be moved. Forced into a crisis by London bankers who refused to float new government bonds in the summer of 1931 without substantial cuts in government outlays in general and in the dole in particular, the two-year-old Labour government caviled, compromised, and finally broke apart. British Conservatives succeeded in putting unemployment insurance back on a more modest and stable footing in 1934. But by the mid-1930s few British policy makers still imagined that social insurance alone could avail against a full-blown, cyclical collapse of market values.

In Germany, the unraveling of the interwar unemployment insurance system proceeded even faster than in Britain, and the political fallout proved far more grim. From almost six million recipients in the unemployment insurance system's first winter, in 1927, the number of persons receiving benefits had tripled to almost eighteen million by 1930. Where the British chose to sustain payments and bankrupt the reserve fund, the last Weimar governments exhausted themselves in slashing unemployment benefits—notwithstanding their contractual obligations to workers, whose wage checkoffs had been duly paid into the system fund. Either way, the cardinal principles of insurance went by the boards. By mid-1931 the German government was simply shedding the unemployed as rapidly as possible onto local poor relief funds. After 1933 the National Socialists were content to let the rest of the social insurance system stand, once they had cashiered the principle of democratic self-management in the health insurance mutuals; but the heart of Nazi social politics lay not in the insurance idea but in party-controlled charity funds, raised through mass rallies and thinly disguised business extortion and distributed as local party bosses saw fit. Conceived as a means of easing short-term irregularities in the wage-labor market, unemployment insurance had proved, in short, no match at all for a general crisis of capitalism itself.[47]

Health and old-age insurance systems weathered the Depression better than unemployment insurance. But it did not take any exceptional economic wisdom to see that the institution of a *new* social insurance system—with its long delays and reserve-fund requirements—was economically counterproductive in depression times. Old-age insurance, given its need for exceptionally large long-term reserves, was particularly problematic. Labor unionists, businessmen, and the proto-Keynesians in the Roosevelt administration all warned of the contractionist consequences of any new social insurance wage taxes. The administration's calculation that an unemployment insurance fund instituted in the United States in the early 1920s would have accumulated a surplus large enough to have significantly dampened the investment contraction of 1929 and 1930 was, in the context, beside the point.[48] Burdening the economy with new wage taxes near the bottom of the business cycle's deflationary phase in order to build up long-term social insurance funds for the future would almost certainly delay the moment of economic recovery. When the flood waters lap at one's doorstep, the prudent thing is not to begin to stockpile a long-term supply of sandbags; it is to shore up the levees.

Given all these constraints, it is hardly surprising that the institution of new social insurance systems came virtually to a halt in the early 1930s. Canadian Conservatives pushed through an unemployment insurance act on the New Deal's example in 1935, only to be voted out of office and watch their Liberal successors nullify the measure in the courts.[49] The Swedish unemployment benefits act of 1934 was a belated, subsidarist measure. New Zealand's Social Security Act of 1938 eschewed insurance principles altogether. Only in the United States was there a major push forward in social insurance during the Depression decade. From both a comparativist and a functionalist point of view, in short, the Social Security Act of 1935 can only seem the product of peculiarly misplaced timing.

Public pressure offers no easy answer to the American anomaly. Neither public outcry nor broad-based interest-group coalitions forced the social insurance breakthrough of the 1930s. The key interest groups were indifferent or divided. The AFL had dropped its long-standing objection to contributory social insurance in 1932, but its heart was where it had always been, in higher wages, shorter hours, guaranteed union recognition, and countercyclical public works employment at union wages. Granted a place on the Committee on Economic Security's advisory council, labor's representatives rarely attended and did nothing to affect the legislative outcome.

A handful of leading welfare capitalists—General Electric's Gerard Swope and Eastman Kodak's Marion Folsom most prominent among them—played a much more active role in the act's construction. As their corporate welfare provisions became increasingly difficult to sustain in the early 1930s, some welfare capitalists found themselves attracted to the idea of mandating across-the-board packages of employer-provided risk assurances so as to equalize their own labor costs with those of their competitors. But the great majority of businessmen were deeply, instinctually hostile to compulsory social insurance. The National Association of Manufacturers testified vigorously in opposition to it. The National Industrial Conference Board bent its energies to demonstrating that unemployment was not an insurable risk. Even the welfare capitalists, when the administration's draft bill came out of Frances Perkins's committee, lobbied heavily for special exemptions from it. In a poll of attitudes toward New Deal legislation in 1939 and 1940, only the National Labor Relations Act, the Undistributed Profits Tax, and the Works Progress Administration (WPA) were more unpopular among business executives than the Social Security Act. Given the history of social insurance politics in the United States, even the qualified endorsement of prominent large-scale welfare capitalists was an event of no mean consequence, but it does not begin to approach sufficiency as an explanation for the act itself.[50]

The strongest popular mandates ran toward simple, immediate relief. On that, both left and right agreed. The biggest noise on welfare issues was Townsendism, with its program of old-age pensions for everyone over age sixty—provided they agreed to leave the wage force and did their economic part by spending their pensions as quickly as they received them. The radical left backed a bill that would have guaranteed wages for every worker for as long as he or she was out of work, without either workers' contributions or any pretense of insurance. Conservatives rallied around traditional, means-tested relief; centrists around state pensions for the elderly poor.[51]

Social feminists, for their part, were too well aware how little security wage-based insurance offered women and children to be enthusiastic. During the formative debates over the Social Security Act in the winter of 1934–35, Grace and Edith Abbott's *Social Service Review* kept up a steady drumbeat of dissent from the social insurance idea, buttressing the case with a flurry of quotations from the British left. The Abbotts' ideal was not insurance but straightforward assistance grants on the mothers' pension model—adequate to need, without stigma, work requirements, or wage deductions.[52] European progressives, as the Abbotts knew, were already thinking their way toward universalizing the same principles: tax-financed social provisions unlinked from wage earning, uncomplicated by the complexities of reserve funds and actuarial mathematics, unmediated by the institutions of (male) working-class *mutualité*. Amid all these crisscrossing voices, not even Roosevelt claimed to have heard a public clamor for social insurance.

The breakthrough of social insurance in 1930s America, in short, can be laid to none of the conventional causal motors: economic need, interest group insistence, grassroots political pressure, or the exigencies of the emergency itself. Only within the intellectual economy of catastrophe does the logic of the Social Security Act begin to fall into place. In the moment's hunger for solutions, social insurance came into the crisis premade and pretested, its arguments fully formed and elaborated.

Social insurance was part of the policy agenda of the past. But if, as the Atlantic-facing progressives had so long believed, the world's nations were arrayed in a common line of march, then the very anachronism of social insurance turned in its favor—transforming it into a symbolic marker, a milepost past which, sooner or later, even the laggards must progress. It was this conviction that eased the New Dealers past the otherwise unsettling spectacle of the unraveling of social insurance abroad, past the economic inopportuneness of launching their experiment at the depths of the business cycle, past the counterarguments that there should be no distraction from the urgencies of immediate relief. Its very pastness helped make social insurance compelling.

Franklin Roosevelt himself knew this logic as well as anyone. It is a commonplace to describe Roosevelt as a naïf on issues of labor and capital, his eclectic mental storehouse stocked with barely a shred of economic learning. The list of those who claimed to have been his tutors is yards long. Frances Perkins, his chief adviser on labor affairs first in Albany and then in Washington, was one of them. It was she, she herself liked to remember, who during Roosevelt's years in the New York governor's office between 1929 and 1933 had served as matchmaker between Roosevelt and experts on unemployment relief and employment stabilization. As labor secretary she deserved no small credit for shaping New Deal labor policy along the lines the AALL had outlined as early as 1914: British-style public labor exchanges, public works, employment regularization, and unemployment insurance. But when Rexford Tugwell, another eager tutor, entered the Brains Trust's conversations with Roosevelt in the spring of 1932, he found social insurance was one of the things Roosevelt knew a great deal about, and with expansive conviction. Perkins's concentrated focus on unemployment insurance was not Roosevelt's. What he had in mind was comprehensive risk insurance for everyone: universal insurance against old age, unemployment, ill health, and disability, administered simply and efficiently through the Post Office.[53]

There was no mystery to the provenance of Roosevelt's convictions. New York State had long been the cockpit of the social insurance battles; most of the major clearinghouses of social welfare ideas were headquartered there. Even as blithe a young progressive as Roosevelt could not keep them altogether out of his formative air. To this one must add Roosevelt's instinctual fiscal conservatism, to which the contributory aspects of social insurance were, from the first, congenial. He had been severely disappointed as governor when a special New York commission in 1930 had recommended tax-financed pensions for the elderly poor rather than a self-financing system of contributory old-age insurance.[54] Add, finally, the element of national rivalry that had helped propel social insurance schemes, leapfrog-fashion, toward ever more comprehensiveness, and one has a pretty fair reading of the convictions that Tugwell found fully formed in the campaign summer of 1932. As Lloyd George had boasted in 1911 of beating Germany at Bismarck's game, one cannot miss Roosevelt's desire to go down in history as having trumped them both.

What ultimately put social insurance back on the agenda in early 1930s America, however, was not Roosevelt's ambitions—important as they were—nor even Perkins's. It was the quiet, structural, behind-the-scenes institutionalization of European-acquired social insurance knowledge in the key university economics departments and policy centers. If John Andrews's AALL, scarred by defeat, was in no mood to refight the social insurance battles of the 1910s in the old, bloodied trenches, a rival, largely younger cohort, primed with the best social policy expertise the North Atlantic economy afforded, had fewer inhibitions. There were many examples of the type: William Leiserson, who had gotten his start in 1910 as director of the European investigations of the New York state commission on employers' liability and unemployment relief and now chaired the Ohio Commission on Unemployment Insurance, whose model bill for European-style contributory unemployment insurance in 1932 competed with the Commons plan for expert approval; economists Paul Douglas and Alvin Hansen, key players in the unemployment insurance revival, both of whom had honed their ideas in Europe while on Guggenheim fellowships; Isador Lubin of the Brookings Institution and Robert Wagner's staff, and a key administration adviser on economic issues after 1934; Eveline Burns, who had brought her expertise in wage maintenance policies from the London School of Economics faculty to Columbia University in the late 1920s.[55]

Health insurance ideas found their refuge in the private philanthropic foundations whose public health endeavors had kept them close to issues of medical economics. In the late 1920s the Milbank Memorial Fund had commissioned the one-time chief medical officer of the English Local Government Board, Arthur Newsholme, to conduct an exhaustive, country-by-country survey of the relationship between public and private health efforts that culminated in Newsholme's stirring restatement of the social imperative in medical care, compulsory public health insurance included. Within its own staff, the fund quietly accumulated a key cluster of public health insurance experts, two of whom were to become the primary framers of the health insurance section of the administration's social security proposals in 1934 and 1935.[56] Even I. M. Rubinow returned to the social insurance cause in the late 1920s. On ground that the AALL had once claimed as its own, Abraham Epstein's American Association for Old Age Security broadened its name and program in the early 1930s to embrace all the social insurances. "The [social] insurance crowd has swooped down on [the administration] with a program all ready as to what to do to-day, tomorrow, and the day after," Grace Abbott reported with some dismay in the fall of 1934; "the rest of us talk on rather general principles."[57]

What gave these conduits of European social insurance ideas their political opportunity was, as so often before, an impasse, this one over emergency federal relief. Everyone had recognized that the emergency federal relief payments of the first New Deal winter, 1933–34, were a policy stopgap, an extraordinary, temporary effort to shore up local relief funds that had long passed their point of exhaustion. The emergency federal works program, which somehow found a place for more than four million persons in the New Deal's first year, was a stopgap of the same sort. By February 1934 an astonishing 22 percent of the nation's population was dependent on the three major federal emergency relief agencies.[58] Levels of this sort would have been impossible to sustain, even had the New Dealers themselves not harbored deeply ambivalent feelings about the course into which the crisis had backed them. That first winter was not to be the end of emergency work relief; the WPA was still to come. But most New Dealers, and most especially Roosevelt himself, were uneasy with emergency relief. Harry Hopkins would eventually propose making the WPA part of the permanent New Deal, but Roosevelt could not rid himself of the sense that even work relief was simply another kind of "dole."

By the end of the New Deal's first winter, the New Dealers' mounting questions about their own Band-Aid work suddenly raised the value of whatever structural, longer-run programs the policy makers could construct. As the administration's primary work relief agency, the Civil Works Administration, began to shutter its doors in the spring of 1934, more urgent still was the administration's fear that Congress might be stampeded into a program of straight-out grants or Townsend-style "pensions." In this double pinch, speed was of the essence. When in haste the New Dealers ransacked their cupboards for ready-made, structural alternatives to the clamor for relief, what they found, fully enough formed to make it quickly serviceable, was the progressives' project of social insurance.

Once more the testing ground became Europe, this time less for new ideas than for administrative experience and, above all, rhetorical advantage. Britain, where the collision between the Labour government and the London bankers had put British unemployment policy in the headlines in 1931, was the focal point, and on it both critics and advocates of social insurance descended anew. Lee Frankel, veteran of the Russell Sage Foundation's social insurance investigation of 1908, spent the spring and summer of 1931 in Europe gathering social insurance data on assignment for the Metropolitan Life Insurance Company. Teams of investigators from the National Industrial Conference Board and the Rockefeller-financed Industrial Relations Counselors were sent abroad, the former to prove that unemployment was essentially an uninsurable risk, the latter to demonstrate, in a series of carefully structured monographs, that it was not. Edwin Witte, successor to Charles McCarthy at the Wisconsin Legislative Reference Library, who would soon find himself tapped as head of the Social Security Act's drafting team, undertook a study of European methods of social insurance and relief in 1931. Frances Perkins herself made the trip to Europe the same year at Roosevelt's urging.[59]

The chances that the investigators would find much common ground were small. To the National Industrial Conference Board's team, the critical fact in Britain was the fiscal breakdown of unemployment insurance into a scheme of permanent, expensive, politically driven relief that propped up wages at artificially high levels and undermined the general will to work. Social insurance's partisans, to the contrary, struggled to turn the focus of the argument to the morale of the unemployed. Helen Hall, Lillian Wald's successor at the Henry Street Settlement, set out for England in 1932 with that specifically in mind. Perkins, like Hall, thought the most important lesson to be learned from England was that working-class dignity and self-respect had been far more effectively preserved under the "dole" than under the humiliations and irregularity of American-style charity. The British themselves, Molly Ray Carroll noted, talked casually of "revolution insurance." The point of these journeys was not agreement; the point was, even as their own domestic crisis stared them in the face, how much of the American argument ran through other nations' experiences.[60]

When in the summer of 1934 Roosevelt authorized Perkins to gather together an interdepartmental cadre of experts to draft a comprehensive federal social insurance act, she drew her staff exceptionally heavily from persons with an expert knowledge of the European precedents. "We expected them to be familiar with every experiment in social insurance in every country," Perkins remembered her staff appointments years later. "We expected them to make reasonable, practical choices among patterns tried in different countries. [And] we expected them to remember that this was the United States in the years 1934–1935."[61] In an effort to sidestep the interexpert rivalry over unemployment policy, she snubbed several of the most prominent Atlantic-traveled progressives—Andrews, Rubinow, and Epstein among them. But among the younger, technically trained experts recruited for the work, there was ample enough knowledge of European social insurance practices to shape the results to their borrowed template.

To take charge of drafting the key, unemployment insurance provisions of the act, Perkins appointed a Canadian-American expert on European and American unemployment measures, Bryce Stewart. A former director of the Canadian public employment service, itself modeled closely on the British Labour Exchanges Act of 1909, Stewart had moved to Chicago in the early 1920s to administer the Amalgamated Clothing Workers' new joint union-employer unemployment board, and from there to join Industrial Relations Counselors, where he helped direct investigations of European unemployment insurance. Beveridge's writings had years before converted Stewart to belief in the principle of a comprehensive unemployment policy, including publicly-administered unemployment insurance. The U.S. Labor Department's expert on Perkins's task force, Isador Lubin, had himself just sent to press a highly positive assessment of British unemployment and relief administration.[62]

Leadership of the old-age insurance section of the drafting team went to Barbara Nachtrieb Armstrong, a professor of law at the University of

California, whose *Insuring the Essentials*—an extraordinarily comprehensive digest of European provisions for income maintenance—had been published two years before. "The laggard nation of the western world in the field of socio-economic administration," she had called the United States: "the most backward of all the nations of commercial importance." Perkins was not deeply committed to the old-age section of the committee's work; Thomas Eliot of the Technical Board was virtually certain the old-age insurance section would not survive its congressional opposition. But Armstrong, hard driven and sharp tongued, used her distance from the spotlight on unemployment to draft the only section of the Social Security Act to go to Congress with a workable social insurance scheme actually spelled out. Drafting of the health insurance section went to I. S. Falk and Edgar Sydenstricker, who were on loan for the purposes from the Milbank Memorial Fund.[63]

The staff head of the Committee on Economic Security, Edwin Witte, a Commons protégé brought from the Wisconsin Industrial Commission, was a much less cosmopolitan figure, but he too had made his sociological pilgrimage to Europe. Among the first tasks to which he set his young University of Wisconsin assistant, Wilbur Cohen, was compiling everything Cohen could find about social insurance systems abroad. At one point, for good measure, the committee quietly imported a pair of social insurance experts from the International Labor Organization for advice.[64]

The European-informed experts on the committee's staff did not have the arena all to themselves. In the key working groups they rubbed shoulders with others recruited for their knowledge of commercial insurance or company pension and benefits plans. The influence of this latter group was not unimportant. But the concentration of Europe-based expertise remains striking; in almost any other era, it would have been politically unimaginable. With other nations' experience in the front of their minds, the drafters refit the social insurance idea for the United States.

The shapers of the Social Security Act were in no danger of forgetting that they were making policy for the United States in 1934 and 1935; they were policy constructors, not copyists. The point is more subtle and more important: how much the very definition of social knowledge and expertise in 1930s America had become bound up in the Atlantic progressive connection, and how fully the idea of economic security had taken shape within it.

The experts' moment in the making of social policy is fundamental, but it is transient. Even as the Committee on Economic Security's staff debated and drafted policy behind closed doors, and at breakneck speed, the cruder forces of politics began to dispose of it. Health insurance was the first casualty. When Falk and Sydenstricker bogged down in their drafting, the American Medical Association seized the initiative with a preemptive vote in opposition to any form of public health insurance. Perkins, whose heart did not stray far from the unemployment provisions of the bill, thought a protracted fight over health insurance would kill the rest, and Roosevelt agreed. Though Falk and Sydenstricker labored on with their report, health insurance effectively dropped off the table.[65]

Politics of a different sort overwhelmed the interexpert competition between "reserve" and insurance principles in unemployment benefits. Stewart lobbied for a nationwide unemployment insurance system, with provision for the largest employers to opt out of it with equivalent benefits of their own. Paul Kellogg tried to rally left-wing progressives around the establishment of stringent national standards for state-run plans. But fearful of entangling the act in a contentious dispute over the Commons scheme for unemployment "reserves," and still more fearful of the Supreme Court's looming veto opportunity, Perkins forced the unemployment insurance section of the act into a constitutionally minimalist mold that left virtually all the administrative details to the individual states. Even the term "insurance" was carefully concealed within the bill behind a screen of euphemisms, though only blindfolded Justice herself could have held any doubt about the act's intentions.[66]

To the old-age and unemployment insurance sections of the act, Children's Bureau staffers added subsidies for state mothers' pension systems and, still closer to their heart, some of the key child health provisions that the Republican Congress had let lapse in the late 1920s. To make the whole thing politically palatable, direct grants-in-aid were extended to the states for a number of family welfare and public health programs and, more generously still, for categorical, British-style payments to the elderly poor.

It was the popularity of the last section that ultimately pulled the rest through Congress. The insurance sections, by contrast, ran into much more considerable flack. Conservatives, beating the old corruption drum, worried that the reserves proposed under the old-age insurance section of the act would become simply a gigantic political slush fund. Southerners wielded their potential veto power to slice out every phrase in the act that the courts might have construed as equalizing black and white welfare benefits—and, with the help of Roosevelt's always fiscally cautious secretary of the treasury, to cut workers in agriculture, which was still the core of the southern economy, out of both the old-age and unemployment insurance provisions of the act.

By the time other congressional constituencies had stricken domestic servants and (for the unemployment purposes of the act) small business employees from coverage, the act's targeted population had been contorted into a form unlike anything seen in the prototypes abroad. Social insurance came into 1930s America not as universal, citizenship-based insurance, as Roosevelt had let himself imagine it. Neither was it insurance targeted, like Bismarck's or Lloyd George's, at wage earners, with their special economic insecurities and special political loyalties. Coverage under the Social Security Act of 1935 wound its way across the socioeconomic map like a gerrymandered congressional district, according to the political strength of the affected groups.

The familiar gauntlet of politics, in short, did its work—compromising, amending, crippling, revising. Further from sight but no less effectively, the dominant preexisting institutions did their work as well. The big insurance companies, having themselves come onto the public dole through their Reconstruction Finance Corporation loans in the early 1930s, no longer had the political standing to block social insurance as they had between 1915 and 1919. This time they contented themselves with defeating a European-style provision for supplementary old-age annuities that would have been purchased through the Post Office. But the logic of commercial insurance so pervaded the air in 1930s America (as the friendly societies once had in Britain, and the *Hilfskassen* before that in Germany) that the New Dealers could not escape it. To Roosevelt the difference between relief and insurance was absolute. It was he who insisted that the system of old-age insurance be self-financing, even at the expense of delaying the first benefits under the act until an actuarially sufficient fund could be built up. Only with considerable difficulty was he won over in 1939 to the common European expedient of transition benefits to bring in those who were too close to retirement age to make significant contributions. It was Roosevelt, too, who rejected an imitation of the British move, in 1934, to integrate social insurance with relief, dovetailing the systems designed to keep workers from falling into poverty with the systems designed to sustain them should the safety net fail to work. "Sound insurance finances" occupied a deeply fixed place in Roosevelt's mind; it was when Britain and Germany had departed from it, he was sure, that their unemployment benefits systems had unraveled.[67]

More deeply than they knew, the technical drafters of the Social Security Act also absorbed assumptions from the commercial models all around them. In Britain the flat-rate principle of the turn-of-the-century old-age pensions campaign still carried weight. German social insurance grouped its beneficiaries into a few broad wage classes. In the United States, in contrast, the Social Security Board, like a well-run insurance company or employer-administered pension plan, was expected to peg each person's benefits precisely to his or her individual earnings record in a discreet, individualized account. The editors of the London *Economist* thought the idea of individually tracked lifetime accounts so extraordinarily expensive and administratively top heavy that it could not conceivably survive, but their judgment underestimated the force of preexisting ideas and institutions. Reliant for their risk calculations on experts borrowed from insurance companies and corporate benefits offices, on the defensive in pressing social insurance into the breach where public opinion would have chosen a simpler system of tax-financed relief, and deeply nervous about the ability of their work to survive constitutional scrutiny, the drafters of the old-age insurance section of the Social Security Act took refuge in the commercial principles around them.[68]

New Deal social insurance took the form not of a broad contract between social groups but of myriad private contracts between individuals and the state. Unlike most models abroad, no general tax funds supplemented the system's employer and employee taxes, despite Epstein's and Kellogg's urging on the matter. Of the intermediary social institutions in 1930s America—labor unions, churches, fraternal societies, and the rest—only employers were recognized by the Social Security Act. The garment trades' joint labor-management boards were set aside as a false start. There was to be no devolution of responsibility onto smaller, more democratic agencies, no recognition of intermediate solidarities, no clumping of persons together. When Epstein and others objected that social insurance and commercial insurance were instruments for fundamentally different purposes, they might as well have been shouting upwind.[69]

Still, for all these compromises and limitations, 1935 brought a social insurance variant, unmistakable in its European progeny, past the obstacles that had so long blocked its importation into the American polity. Epstein, never an easy compromiser, hoped the Supreme Court would set it aside and let the experts, under less drastic pressures of time and politics, see if they could get it right. But if it is a mistake to ignore the profound remoldings through which social insurance passed in its Atlantic crossing, it would be a still greater mistake to ignore the ways in which the Atlantic connection had shaped and empowered it. The Social Security Act was not an answer to the economic insecurity of the Depression. Its social insurance provisions did virtually nothing for the third of the nation that was hungry, ragged, and ill-housed, on whose behalf Roosevelt would campaign in 1936. Social insurance had everything against it in the 1930s except the piled up logjam of the past, the behind-the-scenes institutionalization of social-political expertise, and, most important, the weight of other nations' precedents.

What the social insurance revival in the 1930s showed was that in cases in which the social policy experts could do their initial drafting work in relative political isolation, or piggyback their imports on other, more popular measures, crisis itself could ease a borrowed social-political measure across national differences in customs, law, and politics. It should not diminish the experts' work to recognize that the problems the act addressed were problems of other times and contexts. The New Deal was full of such things; it was an overstocked warehouse of reform proposals tumbling into the political center. Where the crisis's need for speed gave them space in which to work, the New Deal was the cosmopolitan progressives' moment. It was their opportunity to match their years of observation, their sense of behindhandedness, and their fact-crammed digests of international precedents to a brief sense in the public at large—if only a crisis-born hint and suspicion—that the United States might not be, after all, in the lead in progress's race.

Solidarity Imagined

The New Dealers did not often enjoy the distance from day-to-day politics that the basic framing of the Social Security Act had granted them. The larger collective and community visions they inherited from the progressive past could not be realized in the expert work of a technical committee. Constructed much closer to the public eye and to the gauntlet lines of interest-group politics, none of their community designs survived with the longevity of the Social Security Act. But one misreads the New Deal if one seeks its meaning only in the pages of statute books. The New Dealers had their own style of visual social politics, their own imagined forms of solidarity—their own community and cooperative visions no less intense than those of the prewar and 1920s progressives, not the least because they were, in so many respects, extensions of them.

The affinity between the community ideals of the early-twentieth-century progressives and their New Deal successors has not always been well acknowledged. It is a commonplace to describe the 1930s progressive imagination as national not local, economic and political not moral or sociological. As capital's wings spread, so did the field of progressive politics. For the old, uphill task of bringing each state legislature, model bill by model bill, up to the standards of enlightened social-political practice, the New Dealers had little remaining patience. Nationalizing the "general welfare" clause of the Constitution, firing off new federal agencies like alphabetic Roman candles, they rode as hard as Congress and the courts would permit over the carefully defended barriers between the general powers of the states and the restricted and enumerated powers of the federal government. In a land where, in 1906, H. G. Wells had thought a sense of the state so weak as barely to exist at all, the New Dealers produced a quantum growth in the scope of central governance.

With a political canvas as large as the nation itself, the New Dealers no longer focused their political imagination on the great cities, as Howe and Ely's generation had. Pieces of the progressives' urban agenda, to be sure, endured into the 1930s. In a few cities, municipalizers took advantage of the business collapse to draw private, Depression-weakened transit lines into public hands. In New York City, Mayor Fiorello La Guardia engineered the consolidation of the city's financially exhausted subway lines into a single public system, realizing the ambitions municipal ownership campaigners had first broached forty years before. In Washington, D.C., the New Dealers gave Daniel Burnham's 1902 city plan a second wind in a spate of vista and monument building. But not even Frederic Howe himself still thought of cities, now shaken to their fiscal core by the Depression, as free-standing laboratories of democracy—or, even less, that the nation's political destiny might hinge (as it had once seemed) on streetcars and municipal lighting plants, convergent boulevards and civic centers. The most profitable of the urban utility monopolies had long since burst their city boundaries, faster than the municipalizers could follow, to establish themselves as regional electric power grids or national holding companies. Urban progressive politics was hardly played out in the 1930s, but the cities, awash in crises of relief and employment, no longer served as the key experiment stations for social politics.

The solidarities that caught the New Dealers' imagination most vividly were smaller in scale than the great cities and stronger in face-to-face relations than the nation or even the "people" to whom the New Dealers often appealed. Although it was in the nature of the new federal agencies to collect power, jockeying with each other in a running struggle over authority and appropriations that took all of Roosevelt's negotiating skill to hold in check, in looking back on the New Deal from the bureaucratic and administrative state that it, half inadvertently, helped to create, it is hard not to be struck by the decentralist elements in the New Deal political imagination. Under the Agricultural Adjustment Act, local farmers' associations voted on acreage controls, setting production quotas, as it were, for the great commons of wheat and cotton. Soil conservation and grazing districts were run by the vote of local growers and ranchers; labor representation issues were put to a referendum of each work site's wage earners. Local cooperatives distributed power under the rural electrification program; cooperative associations marketed agricultural goods in the Resettlement Administration's farm communities; cooperatives essayed to bridge the gap between the huge new power dams the Tennessee Valley Authority was laying across the region's watercourses and the valley's local folk. Early New Deal public housing developments were hives of associational activity.

These community and cooperative projects were not mere emergency shelters against the decade's storms. To their architects they were templates of a better social order than price and property alone could devise. "Hard-headed, 'anti-utopian,' the New Dealers nonetheless had their Heavenly City," William Leuchtenburg wrote acutely, years ago:

> the greenbelt town, clean, green, and white, with children playing in light, airy, spacious schools; the government project at Longview, Washington, with small houses, each of different design, colored roofs, and gardens of flowers and vegetables; the Mormon villages of Utah that M. L. Wilson kept in his mind's eye—immaculate farmsteads on broad, rectangular streets; most of all, the Tennessee Valley, with its model town of Norris, the tall transmission towers, the white dams, the glistening wire strands, the valley where "a vision of villages and clean small factories has been growing in the minds of thoughtful men."[70]

That the New Dealers should have ventured so deeply into projects of community design when there was so much more pressing emergency work to be done, so many values to prop up and private investments to be sustained, dismayed their critics. But here, too, the dynamics of the crisis worked to warp the normal threads of time, pulling the progressive agenda out of its Atlantic-connected past into the exigencies of the present. The wartime planned village program, cut off so abruptly in 1919, was resuscitated for a new life; dreams of the socialized countryside were given a second wind; the cooperative way, as Horace Plunkett and the Danish dairy farmers had once embodied it, was pressed again toward center stage; the democratic revolution in housing standards was propelled, at last, across the Atlantic; Weimar social modernism gained a toehold, of sorts, in New Deal America; even Elwood Mead's farm community projects were lifted, Phoenix-like, out of the California sands.

Within and outside the administration ranks, all these designs were mined with controversy. The right denounced them as blueprints for outright communism; many New Deal centrists, for whom repair of the faltering engine of capitalism was the Depression's one necessity, thought them romantic folly. But even tough-minded New Dealers, convinced that the culture of laissez-faire individualism had played itself out to its endgame, found it hard not to hope that out of the Depression would come not merely economic recovery but a new set of social and solidaristic forms, less anarchic and individualistic than in the past, more stable than the boom-and-bust patterns of the past, less driven by private property's prerogatives—more like, in short, the "organic" European villages that, set in polar fashion against the landscape of American individualism, had haunted the progressives' imagination so long.

The Social Security Act's drafters labored on a relatively precise piece of social machinery; the New Deal's community builders hoped to reshape a social ethos. The former did their work quickly and, for the most part, in camera; for the latter there was no escape from the snares of either politics or publicity. Against these odds, however, they tried to create a landscape beyond individualism. No other administration before or since has ever taken that task so seriously. In urban housing projects, model suburbs, and remote farm villages, the New Dealers dotted 1930s America with the images of solidarity in their political mind's eye. In the process, they gathered in another piece of the Atlantic progressive connection.

A key, early site for the New Dealers' social blueprints, as for progressives before them, was the countryside. The urbanity of the New Dealers notwithstanding, the administration had come into office with a much clearer sense of agricultural than of economic policy. On Inauguration Day, Roosevelt's advisers still had barely a shred of an industrial policy ready. The National Industrial Recovery Act was put together at breakneck speed, late in the administration's first emergency session, largely to head off legislation the New Dealers thought worse. With organized labor, even after

1936, Roosevelt's and Perkins's relations were always strained and complex. Agriculture, by contrast, had been on Roosevelt's mind for more than a decade.[71]

The notion that the front lines of 1930s policy might lie in agriculture was not just Roosevelt's personal conceit, not just part of the seriousness with which he took his work as a scientific gentleman farmer or one of the ways in which he tied himself instinctively to his cousin Theodore Roosevelt's rural life movement. The brightest and most ambitious of the Brains Trusters, Columbia University economist Rexford Tugwell, was an expert on business economics, but when allowed to write his own ticket in 1933, he chose an assistant secretaryship in the Agriculture Department. With one in five Americans still directly dependent on the farm economy, there seemed to many of Roosevelt's key early advisers no quicker or surer road back to prosperity than through the economic revival of the countryside.[72]

To that end the New Dealers set about, from 1933 onward, to funnel money into the farm economy as rapidly as they could find administrative and constitutional means to do so. In quick order the federal farm loan machinery of the previous two decades was dramatically expanded in scope. In exchange for production controls, the government bought up millions of dollars of acreage and livestock production rights to try to stem the downward slide of prices in the leading agricultural commodities. Though the Agricultural Adjustment Act had to be reworked twice before the decade was over, the New Dealers did their price-bolstering work well. For another fifty years, parity and prices were to remain the hardpan of the post–New Deal agricultural order.[73]

Yet if a long-term regime of price and production controls was what the New Dealers got, it would be a serious mistake of retrospection to suppose that it was what they most wanted. No one in 1933 outside the farm lobbies imagined a permanent policy of price supports that would put farmers on the "dole" for most of the rest of the century. Like emergency work relief, price supports and production controls were designed to be a temporary expedient until the New Dealers could find means to bring rural society and markets into lasting balance.

For some, the key structural need was to drain the rural economy of its most marginal producers, emptying its economically redundant population into the urban wage economy, where something other than the permanent poverty of marginal agriculture and overstocked markets might offer them a new chance. Tugwell, the most outspoken structuralist in the Agriculture

Department from 1933 to 1935, thought the planned resettlement of at least a half million persons was none too small. Matching population to the economically sustainable capacities of the land was the first desideratum of agricultural planning. The second was matching the nation's rural lands more closely with their viable economic uses than the private land market—with its boomer's overconfidence, reckless overtaxing of the soil, gullible buyers, and disastrous price collapses—could achieve. A key tool here was zoning, plucked from the urban planners' tool kit of the 1920s for broader national uses. A start in the direction of rural zoning had been made in Wisconsin in 1929 with an act restricting land promoters from marketing as farms cutover land so poor that only poverty could grow on it. More ambitious agricultural economists talked of a national inventory of land resources, reserving each parcel (in the rhetoric urban zoners had made famous) for its best and highest use, and retiring the least productive to publicly owned grass and forest reserves.

As deeply as the inefficiencies of small-scale, hard-scrabble farming struck the New Deal agricultural structuralists, however, none was ready to turn the countryside over to large-scale agribusiness if means could be found to let modest country folk hang on. Cooperation fell into place in this set of ideas as a tool of microefficiency: a way in which local communities of small farm owners or tenants might pull themselves out of poverty by democratizing efficiencies of scale. None of this talk of restructuring the atomized agricultural market was popular among the business farmers who controlled the major farm lobbies. But to those New Dealers who prided themselves on deep thinking, land retirement, rural replanning, a deliberate rebalancing of city and country populations, and stronger forms of social and economic cooperation among the farmers who remained were not diversions or sideshows; they were the main thing.[74]

None of the key architects of the New Deal's long-range agricultural program initially had their minds on Europe—or on the past. Tugwell, who had seen the traditional Russian *mir* through Veblenite eyes in 1927, thought the long walk from its clustered farmhouses to its widely scattered fields absurdly inefficient. Milburn L. Wilson, architect of the Agricultural Adjustment Act's acreage reduction mechanism, had read AE, but he modeled his answer to the expected overflow from the land on the carefully ordered Mormon towns of rural Utah, where opportunities for part-time wage work joined with small farm plots sufficient to produce most of a family's food. When Tugwell thought of the resettled rural folk's economic destination, it was the city wage economy. But where so many frustrated blueprints for small-scale cooperative community design still hovered in the wings of progressive politics—drawn from Horace Plunkett or from Clarence Poe, from Raymond Unwin or Ebenezer Howard, from the Danish cooperatives or the California state land settlements—it should not be surprising that, in the crisis, some tumbled into being.[75]

Grassroots political talk had, in fact, been full of community and cooperative notions since the outset of the crisis. Barter cooperatives, as cash and wages evaporated, were particularly commonplace; reading letters sent to the *New Republic*'s editors, George Soule was struck by how large a place they played in the popular mind in the early 1930s. Another common suggestion was the encouragement of subsistence settlements on the cities' rims—*Randsiedlungen*, the Germans called them—where, in the shadow of the shrunken wage economy, unemployed urban workers could keep their families afloat through part-time employment and subsistence gardening. In the early years of the Depression, Roosevelt had let his mind run in that direction. Clarence Pickett of the American Friends Service Committee, whose community development labors among out-of-work miners in the Appalachian coal valleys were to catch Eleanor Roosevelt's eye, took his model from the Quaker-assisted subsistence homesteads set up on Vienna's outskirts in the aftermath of the war. Southern progressives, still hunting for exits from the region's rural poverty, brought back the planned cooperative farm-community idea they had imbibed from Elwood Mead; Hugh MacRae of the failed Farm City project was, among others, vigorously pleading its case in early 1932.[76]

Into the early New Deal agencies these suggestions flowed. Under an authorization slipped into the National Industrial Recovery Act by Alabama senator John Bankhead, brother of one of Mead's key southern boosters, the Interior Department established a Division of Subsistence Homesteads in the summer of 1933, with M. L. Wilson as its head and Pickett as its assistant administrator. Among its first grant recipients were Pickett's "stranded" miners' settlements in West Virginia and a revived version of MacRae's Farm City project in North Carolina. The Federal Emergency Relief Administration set up a Division of Self-Help Cooperatives and, for rural distress, a Division of Rural Rehabilitation and Stranded Populations—the latter of which soon had a handful of planned cooperative farm colonies in gear. In form and rationale, the early New Deal planned community work was anything but tidy. By the time Tugwell's new Resettlement Administration absorbed all these early ventures in the summer of 1935, the New Deal was acting as landlord for urban workers moving out toward the country, for farm workers moving in toward the city, and for others moving nowhere at all; for small communities of unemployed miners whose pits had been boarded shut, for unemployed city wage earners trying to start anew as part-time subsistence farmers, for migrant crop workers desperate for a decent camp, and for tenant farmers and small farm owners trying to make a new start on a government farm.[77]

That out of this early, eclectic confusion Elwood Mead's farm village designs would emerge as the dominant template for the agency's resettlement work no one expected in 1933. Tugwell, who had persuaded Roosevelt to hive off long-term agricultural planning into an agency separate from the Agriculture Department so as to insulate it from the day-to-day pressures of the farm lobbies, had his eye on larger structures. From the midwestern cutover region, the Appalachian highlands, the desertified Great Plains, and elsewhere, the Resettlement Administration's land utilization division set about to purchase some ten million acres for the public domain. The Rural Rehabilitation Division undertook to try to hold in place—by loans, lessons in account keeping, and generous quantities of advice—thousands of country folk temporarily caught in the market's pincers. But with the cities overflowing with their own unemployed, something had to be done for those pushed off the land by dust, gullies, broken mortgages, or federal land purchase agents.[78]

In this pinch, Mead's proposals came into their own, trailing their scientism, their community and cooperative ideals, and their Australian and European connections. Mead's project had its well-placed southern supporters. It offered a politically essential gesture toward the needs of the marginal and the displaced. Its intellectual start-up costs had been paid off in full years before. Stripped of its connection with irrigation and land reclamation, it reemerged as the germ of a less atomized farm economy, less vulnerable to the market's instabilities. By the summer of 1937, with the former farm manager of the Delhi, California, land colony at the head of the agency's resettlement work, the Resettlement Administration was operating, or had under construction, fifty-eight planned, government farm colonies, three quarters of them in the South.[79]

Speed being of the essence, most of Mead's devices were taken over virtually intact: small plots and prebuilt houses, long-term lease and purchase arrangements rather than fee simple ownership, careful supervision, and an elaborate network of cooperative devices. A paid farm manager administered each resettlement project, equipped, as Mead's had been, with loan funds, efficiency notions, and strong doses of authority and advice. On the largest projects, a resident home economist taught women's classes, distributed pressure cookers and nutritional information, and checked up on housekeeping. In three instances and for target populations thought to bring the least skill to the operation, Resettlement Administration planners experimented with outright collective farms, putting former sharecroppers and migrants to work as agricultural wage hands. But the modal government farm colony was a community of leaseholders held together by a carefully spun web of cooperative associations. Cooperatives ran the colonies' stores, warehouses, breeding barns, repair shops, cotton gins, and grist mills, and marketed their members' crops. Health cooperatives contracted with local doctors for prepaid group medical care. Umbrella cooperative associations operated each colony's community center and served as its local government.[80]

The administration's political enemies, quick to see red, lambasted the resettlement colonies as beachheads of Soviet agriculture. In fact, with 4,441 government colony farmers at work by 1937, the New Deal rural settlements formed, as yet, only the narrowest strip of sand. The Resettlement Administration's rehabilitation loan program, by comparison, enrolled half a million farmers. But with their compact, European-style land-use patterns and intensive farming techniques, their schools and community centers, their cooperative enterprises, and their collective and democratic aspirations, the farm settlements made suddenly tangible a generation of aspirations for alternatives to the private, dispersed, frontier pattern on the land.

The second focus of the Resettlement Administration's community-building work was its model suburbs, and here, too, the Atlantic progressive connection played a central part. When the agency's Suburban Resettlement Division was organized in 1935, Tugwell himself had not much more in mind than a set of catchment basins within commuting distance of urban wage markets to hold the planned rural influx. This time it was the veterans of the war workers' villages of 1918 and the English garden city movement who moved into the breach, carrying their community designs with them. Three of the division's nine chief consultants had worked on the war housing projects or the reconstruction committees that had spun off immediately from them; at least five had made a pilgrimage to Letchworth. Catherine Bauer and the Housing Study Guild's Henry Churchill were sought out early for advice; so were Clarence Stein, Henry Wright, and Frederick

Bigger, who, with Lewis Mumford and others, had spent much of the 1920s enlisted in Ebenezer Howard's garden city cause; so was Unwin's close American friend John Nolen, along with two younger planners, Tracy Augur and Jacob Crane, who had gotten their start in Nolen's planning office. To the need for quickly realizable designs they brought their unrealized agenda, ready-made. The sixty greenbelt town projects Tugwell originally envisioned failed to materialize. But before a court challenge brought a loss of nerve, the Resettlement Administration had launched three working-class satellite suburbs, bringing into New Deal America the best the international garden city movement had to offer.[81]

None of the resettlement suburbs was a precise copy of its European progenitors. Letchworth had been an experiment in largely middle-class, not working-class, housing—a limited-dividend investment, not a government project; Hampstead was a philanthropy. Architecturally, each of the American projects marched to a different drummer. At the most visually radical of the projects, in Greenbelt, Maryland, rows of startlingly geometric two-story townhouses arced across a ridge in the borrowed aesthetic of Weimar social modernism. Greendale, Wisconsin's planners, with a conscious aversion to foreign designs, chose a town center patterned on eighteenth-century Williamsburg and small, free-standing houses of a simple vernacular design.[82] But beneath the competing facades, the European influences ran deep. Not even the designers of British council housing had hewed as closely as the greenbelt suburbs' planners to Ebenezer Howard's single-tax precepts. The land beneath each greenbelt town was to be collectively owned so that there could be no unearned, speculative increments, no chaotic growth, no standing clash between private and public economic advantage.

To make sure the public element could not be missed, each of the three greenbelt suburbs was built around a town center. Greenbelt's housed a school which doubled as the town's recreation center, meeting rooms for the town's clubs and the community church, a library, and a community theater, now called the "Utopian." Generous bands of public, recreational space ran through each settlement. Doctors' care in all three suburbs was provided through a health cooperative, loans through a credit cooperative, groceries through a cooperative general store. With their young, working-class and lower-middle class families, small dwellings, and generous public facilities, the greenbelt suburbs turned inside out the customary class relationships of the commercial suburbs. Across the community center's walls in Greenbelt, Maryland, illustrated by relief sculptures of men and women farming, laboring, and deliberating together, ran the opening sentence of the federal Constitution: "We the people . . ."[83]

Ringing each of the settlements, finally, just as Howard had prescribed, was a broad green buffer. For these greenbelts the planners never found a viable economic use, though they talked about cooperative farms, small industrial parks, and the need to bring town and country products into a closer, more balanced relationship. But symbolically there was no mistaking the greenbelts' meaning: to shelter the encircled towns (as town walls had once protected their medieval predecessors, Clarence Stein thought), marking them off from the conventional, commercial boom town, with its streets stretched out toward the four points of the compass as far as speculative fancy would carry them; sealing these oases of New Deal solidarity from the whims and planless forces of the capitalist land market just outside.[84]

Nowhere else in the 1930s North Atlantic economy was there anything to match these investments in models of the democratic community, visualized and constructable. From their bold suburban extension plans of the 1920s, British council house builders turned back inward to slum clearance in the 1930s; not until the New Towns Act of 1946 did Howard's satellite city idea finally get a public trial in Britain. On the reclaimed Pontine Marches, Italian Fascists undertook a handful of new town projects in the 1930s. In Germany, where the Nazis had rallied loyalists by railing against the "un-German" social-modernist housing of the Weimar era, the National Socialists invested in a number of counterdemonstration community projects for party members. Ostentatiously reactionary in their steeply pitched tile roofs and half-timbered facades, and in their breakup of the row house into free standing single-family cottages, they were built as antibodies to the "cultural bolshevism" of the social modernists. But once that statement had been made, the National Socialists reverted to the architecture that truly moved them: massive, imperial arenas for the militarized party faithful. In France and Scandinavia, the Depression state had other imperatives than model village building. Only in American was the pent-up political agenda that was released in the 1930s so full of collective, already-imagined community designs.[85]

Where planning formed the outer shell of the New Dealers' community visions, the cooperative association formed their socioeconomic heart. At Greendale the flag of the International Cooperative Association hung from the rafters of the town cooperative store. The Tennessee Valley Authority actively promoted small-scale cooperatives, particularly under the aegis of its first chairman, Arthur Morgan. Two of the authority's first cooperative loans went to the Campbell Folk School's cannery and dairy co-ops. Morgan's arch rival on the TVA board, David Lilienthal, despised the TVA's handicraft cooperatives as economic anachronisms yet actively promoted local utility cooperatives for retail distribution of the authority's electric power. The Resettlement Administration farm colony managers fanned the co-op idea with missionary zeal, conducting night classes in the principles of cooperative economics. Laboratories in more intensive civic life, the New Deal communities were also to be laboratories in small-scale democratic economics.[86]

In 1936 it looked, indeed, as if the cooperatives' hour was finally about to strike. That was the year in which Marquis Childs's *Sweden: The Middle Way* took off as a political best-seller. As a report from a foreign promised land, Childs's genre was as old as Henry Lloyd and Frederic Howe. Part of Childs's ability to reinvigorate the form lay in his inspired subtitle, which spoke volumes to those who, fearing themselves caught between uncontrolled capital and the totalizing state, felt the pincers of history closing in. The other part lay in Childs's ability to package Sweden's social politics into a simple, extractable element, importable across differences in institutions and culture.

It was in the nature of the genre to underplay politics, and Childs barely touched on them. Sweden's Social Democratic government did not deeply interest him. Sweden's long-standing backwardness in social insurance provisions played little part in Childs's account. A late industrializer, a follower nation in socioeconomic policy making, Sweden in the 1930s was playing as conscious a game of catch-up as were the New Dealers. But of the economic revisionism of the "social Keynesians" in Ernst Wigforss's Finance Ministry Childs knew next to nothing. For Childs the middle way did not run through the government offices in Stockholm; it ran through Sweden's cooperative societies.[87]

In Britain, Childs admitted, the cooperatives commanded a much larger share of the consumer market than in Sweden. But where the British cooperators' vision was circumscribed by a shopkeeper's mentality, the Swedish cooperatives, as Childs relayed the story, had taken on monopoly capitalism and begun to best it on its own ground. When the European electric lamp cartel had refused to budge on prices, the Swedish cooperative umbrella association had constructed its own light bulb factory and beaten prices back in line. Rather than accept the rubber trust's price for galoshes, the Swedish cooperators had gone into galoshes manufacturing on their own. In flour, oleomargine, and fertilizer production, the story was the same. Still other cooperative associations were dotting Sweden with new low-cost housing complexes; 15 percent of Stockholm's population already lived in one, some of which, like the famed *Kollektivhus*, had facilities far beyond those of any housing in the United States.

The cooperatives had not tried to extinguish capitalism in Sweden, Childs reported. Their achievement had to been to make capitalism "work" by "subjugating" its rawest and most destabilizing characteristics. By halting capital accumulation short of its last, monopoly phase, by staying the processes of relentless accumulation, the cooperatives had served to "check the very tendencies by which capitalism tends to destroy itself." Balance was the key. "If anywhere in modern life a balance has been struck" between individualist and collectivist extremes, Childs wrote, he was sure it was in Sweden. There one found "stability, order, sanity . . . a certain wholeness, a certain health, that is rare in the present period." In phrases like this, the distinctive language of the Atlantic progressive connection returned once more, harnessed to the cooperative way.[88]

By the fall of 1936, amid a flurry of talk about holding in check the year's rising consumer prices, an official presidential fact-finding commission was once more on its way from the United States to Europe, to see if cooperative economics could be made to work in the United States. Roosevelt told reporters that Childs's book had made him "tremendously" interested in Sweden. His critics were to call the Inquiry on Cooperative Enterprise in Europe an election ploy, and, as in every earlier inquiry commission, politics ran deep in it. Having dispatched the commission early in the campaign season, Roosevelt made sure its report was postponed until the election was past. When the farm lobbies objected to the neglect of their interests, Roosevelt added two farm bloc members. When women objected that their needs as consumers had been ignored, Emily Bates, who was active in Midwest consumer cooperative circles, was added—so late that she barely caught up with the others in Europe.[89]

About the commission's core members, however, Roosevelt could have had no doubt. Jacob Baker, one of Harry Hopkins's principal lieutenants in the Works Progress Administration, had spent the early years of the Depression administering a cooperative barter and labor exchange in New York City. Rumor had it that when the expected federal agency for the promotion of consumer cooperatives was created, Baker would head it. Leland Olds, once a labor press journalist and now a member of the New

York State Power Authority staff, had been worrying about the "disease of individualism" in language half religious, half political for a long time. When AE had been recruited for an American lecture tour in 1930–31, Olds had been tapped to manage it. He had worked with Baker to organize barter exchanges in the early years of the Depression. The commission had not been gone a month before Olds was writing home that Sweden was "a more truly organic society than anything we conceive of in America—except in our dreams." The third original member, Charles Stuart, was a mining engineer who had been active in promoting trade with the Soviet Union. Robin Hood of the farm marketing co-ops' National Cooperative Council and Clifford Gregory of the *Prairie Farmer* were thought to be skeptics, but Bates was an acknowledged partisan.[90]

From the cooperative inquiry commission to the farm colonies, these interlaced streams of cooperative and community politics rose to a crest in 1936 and 1937. With a staff of 16,000, the Resettlement Administration was now the seventh largest civilian agency in Washington. Wallace and Tugwell made a well-publicized swing through the administration's southern farm colonies in November 1936. On a single Sunday the month before, 20,000 Milwaukeeans had come out to see the street layout and foundations at Greendale; over the next year, they were to be followed by another 600,000 visitors. Others descended on the TVA model town of Norris, hard by the towering, concrete face of the Norris public power dam. Matthew Josephson thought Norris was "the prettiest town . . . in all America." Coming on it was "as if we had arrived in a new world, a new age placed fifty years in the future." In the spring of 1936, the progressive Boston merchant Edward A. Filene announced the organization of a million-dollar Consumer Distribution Corporation to promote the organization of consumer cooperatives. There were already eight times as many cooperative stores in 1936 as experts had counted a decade earlier and, by 1938, twenty times as many cooperative credit unions. "The cooperative way of life must pervade the community," Henry Wallace wrote, summing up these intertwined ambitions in the book he sent to press in 1936.[91]

Woven through all these strands, finally, was a project for adult education as bold as the Denmark's folk school undertaking. Some of the impetus behind the New Deal educational program came simply from a desire to make an advantageous response to the employment crisis. Putting unemployed teachers to work in adult-education classes made more economic sense to the administration's work-relief planners than setting teachers to road work or street sweeping. But the New Dealers' commitment to adult civic education, drawing on the models of the English workers' education movement and the Danish folk schools, went far beyond the labor market circumstances.

The TVA sponsored "people's colleges" for the discussion of public issues. The WPA ran "public affairs" classes. At the Office of Education, John W. Studebaker promoted a nationwide program of public affairs "forums," local town meetings for open discussion of the headline issues of the day. Henry Wallace led a series on the agricultural crisis, the Hungarian economist Karl Polanyi a series on contemporary Europe, and Harvard University's Thomas Nixon Carver a series on "Re-examination of the Foundations of Our Economic System." The U.S. Housing Authority sponsored civic affairs forums for public housing tenants. A unit of the Federal Emergency Relief Administration conducted workers' education classes. The unit's chief, Hilda Worthington Smith of the Bryn Mawr Summer School for Workers, had spent a sabbatical year in the mid-1920s studying workers' education programs in Germany, England, Sweden, and Denmark. Her Bryn Mawr sponsor, Carey Thomas, had herself brought the college's workers' education project home from Ruskin College, Oxford, in the early 1920s. Out of these strands and the emergency labor problem, the New Dealers constructed, virtually overnight, an adult civic education program of unprecedented scope in America.[92]

Town meetings were the model for New Deal social and civic education, not the lectures of the Danish folk school *Forstaender* or the intensive group study of Albert Mansbridge's Workers' Educational Association in Britain. But the goal of constructing cooperative social groups was no less central to the American project. Forum leaders for the TVA warmed up their audiences with group games and group singing. Teachers in the Federal Emergency Relief Administration's workers' education program were trained in labor songs and folk dancing. At the Resettlement Administration, Charles Seeger's music program sponsored resident music teachers at the larger farm colonies, to find out what music "the people have in them already" and help them use that shared cultural foundation to move from "rugged individualism" (as one of Seeger's musicians put it) to "group action." The first two songs the division printed up were the old Grangers' song, "The Farmer Is the Man Who Feeds Them All," and "Cooperation Is Our Aim."[93]

In hindsight, to be sure, all these projects, from the farm colonies to the civic forums, fell short of the economic democracy they professed. The TVA ran a line of racial segregation through its hiring practices and services that was not much less stark than that in other southern institutions. The Resettlement Administration built farm projects for both black and white Americans, but none in which the two might mix as equals; the greenbelt towns were for whites only. The prevailing relations of class and power, like those of race, set their mark down hard on the New Deal community projects. Studebaker's civic forums grew more tightly controlled and organized as the decade went on; the Civilian Conservation Corps' educational program never escaped the heavy hand of its military managers. In the farm colonies, the resident managers' authority was far too great and the economic knowledge of the farm project colonists much too weak. The farm cooperatives' ambitions routinely exceeded their resources; their management stayed, by and large, in the farm managers' hip pockets. The greenbelt suburbs came closer to the democratic ideal, but even they could not escape the economic and constitutional pressures toward the centralization of power. The desire to buy up land before speculators jacked up its price had led the planners to do their initial work in secrecy, even from local authorities whose cooperation they needed. In the end, in the default of any constitutionally acceptable title owner other than the federal government, the greenbelt towns never did own themselves.[94]

Together these were serious flaws. Still, measured against the prevailing standards around them, the New Deal community planners had reason to think they had resisted at least as much as they had acquiesced. The community they imagined—an island of rational planning within a world of economic chance, its civic life abuzz with committees and town meetings, its cooperatives as thickly planted as Denmark's, its private and public affairs held in a new, more even balance within an economy less growth and bust driven, less fiercely individualistic than before—drew hard on a generation of blocked progressive ambitions. Realized in bits and pieces elsewhere, it did not seem unrealizable in America in 1936.

The urban phase of New Deal community building was slower to emerge than the New Deal's rural projects, and it was worked on a canvas still more crowded with well-organized interests. But here, too, the dynamics of Atlantic progressive politics controlled the basic structure of events, from the agenda-setting role of a cadre of experts steeped in European precedents to the sudden, crisis-facilitated breakthrough of their premade policy proposals into the sphere of the politically enactable, to the play of the heavy commercial interests in the endgame of the legislative process.

The focus of this phase of the New Dealers' civic ambitions was housing. "I see one-third of a nation ill-housed, ill-clad, ill-nourished," Roosevelt was to say in 1937.[95] In fact, in the early years of the New Deal, enlistment of the state in a major effort to change the prevailing standards of working-class housing had not been on the administration's mind at all. Roosevelt himself had to be enlisted, with effort, to the idea. As in the case of Social Security and agricultural reconstruction, public housing was an undertaking shaken out of the New Deal's social-political past by the dynamics of crisis politics.

Poor housing conditions themselves were not the critical causal motor. That urban shelter was often miserable, as the housing reformers had long insisted, goes without saying. That the Depression worsened the housing crisis, however, is a more complicated matter. Rent money, to be sure, disappeared with the collapse of jobs and the overnight evaporation of savings. Hoovervilles of the unemployed and homeless sprouted in every one of the nation's cities: in vacant lots, along the rail yards, and under overpasses—wherever the authorities turned a tolerant eye. As new housing construction ceased, the "filtering up" of working-class families into the vacated shelter of the middle class—never a reliable process to begin with—broke down. Substandard housing grew older and worse. At the same time, sheer crowding had eased considerably since Mary Kingsbury Simkhovitch's Congestion Committee had begun its work a quarter century earlier. Even as new construction ground to a halt in the Depression, the pause in net farm-to-city migration, together with the virtual cessation of foreign immigration, went a long way toward offsetting the pressure on the existing housing stock. The housing crisis of the 1930s was not a crisis in shelter per se, but in income: a crisis not in rooms and structures but in wages, rents, and mortgages.[96]

To many of those at the New Deal's center, the credit markets were, from the outset, the sum and substance of the matter. The administration's first move on the housing front, the Home Owners' Loan Act of 1933, was to bail out the bankrupt mortgage loan system with easier refinancing terms. A follow-up measure, the National Housing Act of 1934, endeavored to unlock private investments in housing construction by extending government loan insurance over a broad array of mortgages. Both measures were in the well-worn traditions of the promotional state, putting the shoulder of government aid behind the temporarily balked machinery of private markets. Propping up middle-class homeowners and—still more—the banks and construction industries that served them, they carried clear recovery potential.

That the New Dealers should have added to this a program of low-cost housing *construction* was another matter. But here, as in so many other aspects of the New Deal, 1930s social politics was a product of its past. For forty years, American progressives had debated the merits of state and quasi-state housing for the urban working class in the context of housing policies across the Atlantic. From the orphaned experiment in model working-class housing at Lowell, Massachusetts, in 1917, from the British-inspired emergency war housing program of 1918, from Edith Wood's and Catherine Bauer's reports of European social housing progress, and from three decades of debate in the international housing congresses, lines of unfulfilled reform converged on the 1930s. Lawrence Veiller might still oppose publicly assisted housing as "foreign to the genius of the American people," but by the 1930s his National Housing Association had shriveled around its one-issue program into a mere paper projection of Veiller himself.[97] Like the New Deal's greenbelt towns and farm villages, public housing was an eruption of the progressive past into the political possibilities of the Depression.

As in other cases of New Deal policy initiation, the experts had completed the basic outlines of a progressive housing policy well before the crisis began. The aim would be to build for the broad strata of urban, working-class families whose incomes fell just below the commercial builders' market. To the housing reformers it was self-evident that publicly assisted housing should raise the standards of shelter and community facilities to which wage-earning families could aspire; it would build not housing, merely, but neighborhoods and solidarities. That it would combine the best of European innovations they took for granted.

The key ingredients in the experts' program of the early 1930s were the limited-dividend and cooperative housing associations of the European continent, assisted by cheap, long-term public credits. This was the policy Edith Elmer Wood had brought back from Europe in 1922. This was the financial motor behind the social democratic housing that had fired Bauer's imagination in Weimar Germany, as it was for the housing cooperatives that were to inspire Marquis Childs in Sweden. Under the prodding of New York City housing progressives, Governor Al Smith had successfully steered a weakened version of the same device through the New York state legislature in 1926, granting tax exemptions (but not low-cost state credits) to nonprofit and limited-dividend builders of decent low-cost shelter. Among the first projects to take advantage of the act had been the Amalgamated Clothing Workers' apartment cooperatives.[98]

Among those who had lobbied for the New York statute, the most prominent was Greenwich House's Mary Simkhovitch, who had headed the New York City Congestion Committee twenty years before. Since her days as a graduate student in economics in Berlin in the 1890s, Simkhovitch had knit together in her own person an extraordinary number of the interlocking threads of American social politics. She had been one of Florence Kelley's key allies at the National Consumers' League, a campaigner for public baths and parks in lower Manhattan, a board member of Abraham Epstein's American Association for Old Age Security, and, since 1931, head of a lobbying group optimistically named the National Public Housing Conference. She had been a Progressive Party member in 1912, a war collectivist in 1917, a signer of the Committee of 48's "Call" in 1919, and a Roosevelt supporter in 1932. In the emergency mood of the administration's first hundred days, Simkhovitch was able to convince Senator Robert Wagner to add to the National Industrial Recovery Act the social housing program that housing reformers had long since settled on: long-term, subsidized credits to municipalities and limited-dividend housing associations that undertook to construct decent low-cost housing.[99]

Through the rest of the 1930s the initiative in public housing policy would come, like Simkhovitch's intervention in 1933, from outside the administration's core. Roosevelt was elusive and noncommittal. The first of the housing bills drafted in Senator Wagner's office was written by Simkhovitch's National Public Housing Conference, which also lined up the expert witnesses for the Senate committee hearings. Public housing was a classic case of extragovernmentally framed social policy that squeezed through the momentary political opportunity the crisis created.[100]

In the public housing endeavor, the Atlantic connections were formative. The most active of the municipal housing authorities organized under the National Industrial Recovery Act, the New York City Housing Authority of 1934, was a case in point. Of its first five board members, three had substantive connections abroad: Louis Pink, the settlement house–linked lawyer who, as a member of the New York State Housing Board, had sought out publicly assisted housing undertakings in Europe for their importable lessons in 1927; Charney Vladeck of the *Jewish Daily Forward*, a long-time municipal socialist and labor-housing advocate; and Simkhovitch herself. The authority's chief architect was Frederick Ackerman, whose dispatches from England had made the British Munitions Ministry's housing work news in the wartime United States.[101]

To stoke broader public interest, the National Association of Housing

Officials arranged to bring a three-person International Housing Commission to the United States in the summer of 1934. Headed by Raymond Unwin, the commission undertook a seven-week, fourteen-city lecture and inspection tour, capped by a conference of the nation's leading housing reformers that in October issued an American call for construction of low-cost, publicly assisted housing. The signers of the conference statement, written largely by Unwin himself, included most of the nation's leading housing reformers: Ackerman, Simkhovitch, and Langdon Post of the New York City Housing Authority; Edith Elmer Wood; Catherine Bauer, Oskar Stonorov, and John Edelman of the Labor Housing Conference; John Nolen and Jacob Crane from the city planning associations; Henry Wright and Albert Mayer from Lewis Mumford's circle; Tracy Augur and Earle Draper from the TVA; Robert Kohn of the war housing program of 1918; even the manager of the National Housing Association's 1914 tour of England, John Ihlder. Coleman Woodbury, who coordinated the Unwin tour and its concluding conference, had cut his teeth on housing issues in England as a Rhodes Scholar in 1926 and 1927.[102]

The leaders of Simkhovitch's National Public Housing Conference were all seasoned European observers. To drum up constituent support, its executive secretary, Helen Alfred, conducted annual European housing study tours from 1936 to 1938, timed to coincide with the meetings of the International Housing and Town Planning Federation.[103] The Labor Housing Conference, as we have seen, was no less thick with European influences.

A particularly striking example of the Atlantic route from housing amateur to housing expert was the New Deal career of Atlanta's Charles Palmer. A Republican businessman and real estate promoter, Palmer was first drawn to the public housing idea by the commissions to be earned in assembling public-housing land parcels. In 1933 and 1934 he had engineered two early Public Works Administration (PWA) slum clearance and rehousing projects, one for whites, one for blacks, in downtown Atlanta. Emerging from that experience bitten with the low-cost housing idea, he set off not for the slums of Charleston or Birmingham, Alabama, or New York, but for two months' intensive study of public housing in Europe. From Naples to Vienna, Moscow, Berlin, and London he progressed, returning with a stump speech and a homemade film, *The World War against Slums*. He took his speech and film wherever he could get a foot in the door: to builders' conferences, to housing reform gatherings, and to New Deal Washington, where he showed his film to Henry Wallace at the Agriculture Department, to Harry Hopkins at the Federal Emergency Relief Administration, to the PWA's Housing Division staff, to Perkins and Ickes at a large gathering at the Interior Department, and finally, through Eleanor Roosevelt's mediation, to FDR himself at a White House dinner in early 1937.[104] With a program patched together out of boundless faith in American business enterprise and a fiscal scheme drawn unabashedly from "red" Vienna, Palmer was an odd figure on the housing circuit. But he was hardly the only housing advocate whose program came home, as it were, in a transatlantic suitcase. The same could be said of Louis Pink; of Nathan Straus, the Macy's heir whom Roosevelt was to name the first head of the United States Housing Authority in 1937; of Edith Wood a generation earlier; and, of course, of Catherine Bauer.[105]

When the housing reformers turned their lobbying efforts to Washington, D.C., their connections and influences came with them. Robert Wagner, the Simkhovitch group's key sponsor in Congress, was a regular visitor to Europe, where he retained close family ties; as housing moved to the fore in 1936, he devoted much of that summer's European trip to housing study. The Labor Housing Conference's point man in Congress, Henry Ellenbogen, had been born in Vienna and knew its great socialist housing projects. Of the fourteen experts Wagner convened to vet the Wagner-Ellenbogen housing bill in early 1936, a least seven had had firsthand, often extensive, exposure to housing programs in Europe. To shepherd the finished product through the congressional battles of 1936 and 1937, Wagner tapped two of them: Coleman Woodbury and, with her labor connections, Catherine Bauer. In time, as homegrown experience in low-cost public housing accumulated, the value of European expertise would diminish. But in the movement of public housing from idea to potentially enactable measure, it was practical knowledge that counted; in practice that meant familiarity with the social-political laboratory that was Europe.[106]

The European reference points jostled with American ones in a complicated counterpoint of oppositions. The housing exhibition arranged by the New York City Housing Authority at the Museum of Modern Art in the fall of 1934 began by focusing the visitor's eye on domestic conditions. The exhibition's walls were hung with photographic exposés of the city's slums; its centerpiece was a life-size reconstruction of a dark, cramped, "old-law" New York City tenement apartment. But a viable social politics cannot be mobilized on negativities alone. When misery has no socially imaginable alternative, it has no political place to go. Past the grim representations of their own American present, then, exhibit organizers led visitors toward an already-made alternative future, culminating in the photos Bauer, Mumford, and others had brought back from Europe. "Realizations Abroad," the section was titled: "Why Doesn't the American Worker Live Here?" How could American slum dwellers know what decent housing might be? Albert Mayer asked in the *Nation* in 1934, in a rhetorical question that underscored the dynamics of juxtapositional Atlantic politics: "How could they . . . for they have not traveled in Germany and Holland and England."[107]

In all these ways and down all these tracks, it was the Atlantic progressive connection that brought something more than lenders' and mortgagors' bailouts into the early New Deal. Public housing was an offshoot of European social politics, set on the Depression agenda by progressives who had built their expertise by standing, as it were, on their European counterparts' shoulders. In transit, however, there was inevitably transformation.

The least anticipated sticking point was administration. The issue had seemed relatively settled in 1933. Beyond Austria and Britain, the heavy administrative work in European working-class housing construction had been done by limited-dividend housing companies—philanthropic, labor-based, or cooperative. This device fit into American traditions of governance far better than the top-heavy machinery of the British system. It was flexible and voluntaristic; it was well tested; it matched the solidarities that the New Dealers imagined. In a simpler world, it should have worked in the United States, too.

The same crisis dynamic that momentarily pried apart the political structure so as to put public credits for low-cost housing construction on the agenda, however, placed a terrific premium on speed. And speed was the limited-dividend program's undoing. Under the National Industrial Recovery Act, the PWA's Housing Division opened its door to applicants. The Hosiery Workers' Mackley Houses was one of the first and best. But out of the other five hundred or so applications the division's examiners received, only twenty proposals were found to be worthy of financing, of which a mere seven were ultimately built. The most vigorous petitioners were small-scale speculative builders who were more than happy, when profits of any sort were as scarce as two-dollar bills, to convert their enterprises temporarily into limited-dividend corporations. Beyond these, the pickings were embarrassingly thin. The big insurance companies, some of which had found model housing an attractive investment in the late 1920s, were skittish and unwilling; the major philanthropies were strapped for capital; the state social insurance funds, which had played such a major role in low-cost model housing finance in turn-of-the-century Germany, were nonexistent.

As for the cooperative and trade union groups that had been at the core of low-cost housing construction in Weimar Germany and elsewhere, the vacuum in the United States was too large to be filled overnight. The active, voluntary, not-for-profit association, so highly praised in America, was barely to be found there—not, at any rate, in the hard times of the 1930s, not quickly enough, and not as concerned housing.[108]

With critics crying to see men back at work in late 1933, the Public Works Administration shifted abruptly from subsidarist principles to a centralized program of direct low-cost housing construction along the lines of the war workers' housing program of 1918. Harold Ickes was eager for centralized control. The Housing Division's head, Robert Kohn, had served as chief of housing construction for the war-time Emergency Fleet Corporation. Down the grooves of past policy experience, once more, emergency policy making rolled.

The PWA Housing Division did heroic work over its three-year span from 1934 to 1937. It built low-scale housing, in clusters and neighborhood groups, with standards of space and amenities far better than surrounding working-class housing and with community facilities unknown in commercial apartment construction. Many included the clinics, laundries, and public rooms that had been the mark of good working-class housing in Europe for a decade. The all-black Harlem River Houses boasted an on-site nursery school, access to city tennis and handball courts, a community newspaper, a tenants' association, and community meeting rooms in which WPA teachers conducted dramatics and dance classes and ran an afternoon day-care program for schoolchildren. Lewis Mumford called Harlem River Houses the closest approximation to housing's ideal one could find in New York City in 1938. This was *Siedlungsbau*, American style: not mere shelter building but the construction of working-class communities. As such, urban public housing joined the greenbelt towns and farm villages, the cooperatives and the civic forums as representations of a world within reach, beyond sheer price and profit.[109]

All of this, however, was emergency work in 1936 and 1937. The Resettlement Administration was an administrative makeshift, based on executive order rather than congressional legislation. The PWA's Housing Division was an extrapolation of the emergency public works mandate of the Roosevelt administration's first hundred days. Neither had, as yet, a firm constitutional or political base. In the process of moving from makeshift to permanence, the interest groups would have their moment.

The most vulnerable of the community undertakings were the resettlement projects. Bypassing the agricultural agent–commercial farmer nexus, Rexford Tugwell had done his best to insulate the Resettlement Administration from the established farm lobbies. He staffed the agency with outsiders not subject to the normal claims of politics: he drew his deputy director, Will Alexander, from the presidency of Dillard University, two of his division directors from his own Columbia University economics department, and a third division head from the rural sociology faculty at North Carolina State University. But partly because Tugwell himself had too active and controversial a tongue, and more because the field of the Resettlement Administration's work was too deeply mined with preestablished investments and fixed political positions, insularity from politics was not in the cards. It was in the very nature of the civic designs of the New Deal that their framers' work could not long be held in secret, that their missteps, their cost overruns, their warts and deficiencies would become immediate grist for journalists, politicians, and the most threatened interest groups.

By 1936 Roosevelt's critics were already making political hay out of the Resettlement Administration's work, its "Tugwell towns," its "communist" notions of agriculture, its impracticalities, its "foreign" ideas. The government suburbs were, to Roosevelt's critics, symbols of New Deal collectivism gone mad: Moscows in Maryland, "The First Communist Towns in America," as a headline in the *Chicago American* put it. By May 1936, James Farley was warning Roosevelt that the "two main points of the greatest attack by the Republicans will be WPA and Tugwell." With the election safely weathered in December 1936, and after a face-saving visit by the president himself to Greenbelt, Maryland, Tugwell bowed out of government. But his resignation did not much change the political circumstances.[110]

Interest groups and ideology both weighed against the New Deal's community and cooperative endeavors; everywhere the planners turned there were claimants with territory to protect. Private builders and land developers had seen red from the start in the government-built suburbs. Before 1936 was out they had obtained a court ruling declaring the fourth planned greenbelt town, slated for New Jersey, to be beyond the federal government's "general welfare" bounds. Rather than challenge the ruling, the administration slogged on with the other three and scuttled its plans for more. Doctors saw in the Resettlement Administration's health cooperatives the threat of government-run medicine. Retail merchants, already up in arms over chain-store competition, saw in the specter of government-assisted retail cooperatives yet another rival for their shrunken trade. With his advisers warning him of a lower-middle-class, shopkeepers' revolt on the part of "millions of small businessmen," Roosevelt pocketed the report of the Inquiry on Cooperative Enterprise and quietly let talk of Sweden drop.[111]

As for the farmers, though ready enough to embrace the promotional state when it proposed to extend them cheap credits or buy out their crops at an advantageous price, the best organized of them wanted nothing to do with an experiment in social reconstruction that might put rural America's bottom rail on top. The welfare of tenant farmers and sharecroppers under the Agricultural Adjustment Act had brought right- and left-wing New Dealers into a sharp, angry struggle in early 1935 that cost the tenants' most outspoken advocates in the Agriculture Department their jobs. Over the Resettlement Administration's policy of advancing its southern farm colony tenants money to pay their poll taxes, the conservative howl of protest was intense. In a deeply depressed market, commercial farmers were no friends of additional, government-sponsored competitors.[112]

To these objections, the established farm cooperatives offered no substantial counterweight; the large milk producers' cooperatives had already deserted the New Deal coalition in 1936 over the dairymen's objections to production controls. The chameleonlike social politics of cooperation played itself out in the tension between the administration and the established farm cooperatives. In Europe, even when cooperative movements had made formal or tacit alliances with labor-based social democratic parties, they had all maintained a wary eye on the state. The Inquiry on Cooperative Enterprise looked in vain for a European authority to recommend that governments should deliberately set out to foster a movement that, from England's Rochdale band forward, had wrapped itself in a narrative—more one-sided than the facts might well have admitted—of cooperation's stateless, organic growth. "Cooperation can grow in the main spontaneously only, from its own soil and roots," even Leland Olds of the cooperative inquiry soon concluded. But where the European cooperative movements walked a narrow line between opposition to big capitalism and wariness of the state, the farm marketing cooperatives in the United States barely hesitated. "Farmers' cooperatives are not anti-capitalistic," Robin Hood of the cooperative inquiry had told a farmers' gathering in early 1936: "The farmer is a capitalist . . . in the true sense of the word." Between the big farm marketing cooperatives of the 1930s and the interests of the commercial farm lobbies in the United States, an expert observer might find a line, but it was eggshell thin.[113]

Compounding interest-group objections were ideological controversies. A half a century and more of agricultural tenancy had done nothing to quench the equation of manhood with ownership of a freestanding house and solely owned farm. Many of the farm colony settlers looked on their government tenancies as temporary, as a time when they might hope to lay away a little cash against the moment when they could move off and buy a farm of their own. Many southern progressives were of the same mind; by early 1935 Alabama's John Bankhead, whose amendment to the National Industrial Recovery Act had set the first subsistence communities in motion, was lobbying hard for a program to help tenant farmers up the "agricultural ladder" to individual farm proprietorship. "Farm ownership?" Tugwell remarked in early 1937, in one of those statements that kept him in political hot water: "Yes, some day for some, under the right conditions, at their own choice and with a clear view of its costs and after they have demonstrated their ability to rise. But now, most importantly for many, treatment of disease, better diet for children, a mule, some seed and fertilizer, clothes to lift the shame of going ragged to town, some hope for the future, a friendly hand in every farm and home crisis." But Tugwell was out of the government by 1937. "The mind of the country . . . is on the individual farms," his successor, Will Alexander, acknowledged. "The psychology runs toward individual farms."[114]

Ownership was the more American way in farming; but it was yet one more mark of the times that, to promote it, the agricultural progressives brought in European borrowings all over again. This time the leverage point was the Irish and Danish land reform measures. At the hearings on the first Bankhead farm tenancy bill, Henry Wallace retold the story of Gladstone's Irish land purchase program as he has seen its results from Plunkett House in 1912. Clarence Poe, at the head a new National Committee on Small Farm Ownership, recommended the Irish and Danish land reform examples. L. C. Gray, who was soon to be tapped to direct the staff of the President's Committee on Farm Tenancy, testified that "the United States is virtually the only civilized nation of consequence that has not set up some system to correct the evils of tenantry." There was nothing "new" or "untried" in land reform, he assured the Senate committee. Citing the same Irish and Danish precedents, Roosevelt gave the program his endorsement just before the 1936 election.[115]

By September 1937 the Resettlement Administration had been replaced by a new government entity, the Farm Security Administration (FSA), designed to absorb the old agency's operations but with a mandate to give the yeoman ideal a second chance. Like the Resettlement Administration, the Farm Security Administration's chief work was to administer rehabilitation loans for farm families in distress. But $50 million a year was set aside to boost more rural folk into the ranks of small farm owners. With that money the FSA was authorized to buy farms, regrade the land against erosion, repair the houses and barns, and sell the farms on long-term loans to tenants and sharecroppers who local county committees thought might stand an especially good chance of making a go of farm ownership. Representatives of the radical Southern Tenant Farmers' Union objected that the program had shunted aside the cooperative farm colony idea for faith in "an economic anachronism, foredoomed to failure." Gardner Jackson, among the victims of the Agriculture Department purge of 1935, told Congress that the times needed "a new type of farm organization" that "must perforce be a communal or village farm economy." The progressive Southern Policy Association made the same point.[116]

In fact, the two ideals were not altogether antagonistic. If the Irish and Danish examples showed anything, it was that small farmers in a world of large-scale capital could not go it alone, without a supporting network of cooperative, mutual-aid, and educational associations—the cooperative creameries, folk schools, credit cooperatives, and the rest, to which Plunkett and the Danish rural life reformers had bent their organizational energies so hard. Quietly the Farm Security Administration planners tried to knit the necessary pieces together. Among hard-pressed tenants and small farmers, FSA staffers promoted the organization of small-scale cooperatives, discussion groups, and cooperative medical-care contracts. Against the right of government-aided tenant purchasers to sell their new land at will, thereby dumping the public's investment back into the speculative land market, the agricultural progressives won an important symbolic victory. Even the farm colonies persisted, though a rider to the Bankhead act stipulated that no more new ones be established.[117]

But the scale of the FSA's efforts was too small to build the political constituency that might have sustained the New Deal's community and cooperative enterprises. Even the Farm Security Administration's tenant purchase allocations barely made a dent in a growth rate of 40,000 new agricultural tenants a year. By the time Congress closed down the FSA altogether in 1947, it had managed to move 47,000 tenant families, disproportionately white and disproportionately better off to start with, into farm ownership. At that rate, Edward Banfield calculated, the elimination of farm tenancy was 400 years in the future.[118] The emptying out of the South's sharecropping millions was to be left to the postwar, market-led exodus of persons and poverty into the northern cities. Oddities in a regime of private property, the New Deal community ventures were abandoned one by one. The last remnants of Elwood Mead's farm colony idea were folded up in 1948. That same year a commercial development firm purchased Norris, Tennessee. The greenbelt suburbs were sold off between 1950 and 1954.

Out of a patchwork of borrowings, the New Deal community planners had set out to see if they could create an alternative to the private markets in land and agriculture, the isolated farm, the speculator-built suburb, the fee-simple owner. The intellectual economy of catastrophe gave them what normal times had not. In the uncertainties of the early 1930s their premade plans, their cooperative ventures, their versions of the "organic" villages and small cities that had so long caught the imaginations of American progressives in Europe, all found their moment. One can still find vestiges of their work, tucked away in today's much more smug and insular America. But these constructions of specific contexts and dynamics were not destined to last. In the face of hostile publicity and top-heavy solicitude, they did not have the resources to survive the exceptional conditions of their inception.

The endgame in housing was more complicated. In the effort to establish federally assisted low-cost housing on a permanent basis, the European-inspired progressives came first. Both Simkhovitch's National Public Housing Conference and Bauer's Labor Housing Conference put housing bills before Congress in 1935—the latter, in a turnabout in the fall of that year, with American Federation of Labor support. After the bills had been welded into one in Senator Robert Wagner's office, a unified public housing measure cleared the Senate in 1936. The next year, sensing passage was imminent, the administration finally came aboard, although with a rationale yet different than either Simkhovitch's or Bauer's. As news of the British economic recovery had begun to filter into Washington in 1935 and 1936, a number of New Dealers had begun to note the relationship between Britain's economic upturn and its sustained public investments in workers' housing. Herbert Morrison, head of the Labourite London County Council, brought the message to Washington in early 1936, where Robert Wagner and others picked it up. Within the administration's ranks, a cadre of proto-Keynesians was beginning to coalesce, convinced that recovery came down, finally, to simple aggregate national spending. Following that line of reasoning, a big public housing program held many attractions. The 1936 hearings on the Wagner-Ellenbogen bill were full of this sort of talk, both from experts knowledgeable about Britain and from labor union witnesses.[119]

Around a permanent low-cost public housing program all these arguments coalesced. Publicly funded housing for the masses was a health and sanitation measure; it was the node around which a democratic workers' and consumers' housing movement might grow; it was a way to set unemployed men to work; it was a pump priming measure for the economy as a whole. The surplus of not altogether compatible rationales behind the social housing idea was typical of social politics. The open question was not coherence; it was what would happen once the measure emerged from the experts' drafting conferences into the field of everyday, interest-group politics.

Some of the housing bill's opponents wanted outright rejection. The Wagner measure "is going to be the beginning of the end of private ownership of real estate," the president of the Bronx Taxpayers' League had testified at the bill's Senate hearings in 1936. The key opposition groups, the U.S. Chamber of Commerce, the U.S. Building and Loan League, the National Association of Real Estate Boards, and the National Retail Lumber Dealers' Association, had been rallying their constituencies on the issue for months. But as passage of a federal housing bill began to seem likely in 1937, they took their stand on the only line that truly mattered to them. Government housing for the poorest segment of the nation was acceptable so long as the rest of the housing market was clearly walled off from encroachment. That meant housing for the most poorly housed—slum reconstruction for existing slum residents.[120]

Simkhovitch and the National Public Housing Conference were not altogether unsympathetic to a housing program focused on the slums. To the social work and settlement house wing of the public housing movement, it seemed obvious that public housing should set down its roots where housing standards were at their worst and the population to be rehoused was closest at hand.[121] Bauer's circle, to the contrary, saw inner-city reconstruction as an economic trap. Slum land purchases were the slum landlord's godsend. Slum rebuilding meant propping up the existing structure of values by buying up substandard property from the very owners who had let it go to ruin. It meant saddling social housing with staggeringly high land costs and crippling physical constraints. It meant an end to the hope of setting new standards in working-class housing design. It meant defeat for the social-democratic idea in housing.[122]

At every stop on his 1934 lecture tour, Raymond Unwin had made the same point: a successful public housing program could not begin with the slums. Public housing needed to build a solid political constituency in the working class, he cautioned, before tackling the thorny issues of condemnation prices and site values that slum rebuilding posed. Everywhere in Europe, Unwin maintained, publicly assisted housing had made its successful start not with the poor but with the working class, including the steadily employed, skilled workers in the middle-income triad. Brought to the United States in 1937 to spread the lesson of British public housing work, Richard Reiss made much the same point; it was "entirely wrong" to begin with slum clearance.[123]

But the Atlantic tides were already shifting fast toward other outcomes. Only Britain and Sweden had sustained heavy public investments in low-cost housing construction into the mid-1930s. The distinctive tools of Swedish low-cost housing policy—extensive municipal land purchases and construction by cooperative housing societies—were politically out of the question in 1930s America. With the Viennese and German experiments in ruins, American attention turned all the more intensely on England. Charles Palmer had traversed all of Europe in search of low-cost housing ideas in 1934, but by his second trip, in 1936, he was sure that all he needed would be found in England. Nathan Straus in 1935 barely bothered to put any other country on his agenda. In the default of cooperative and limited-dividend builders, it was already clear that the administrative machinery of British public housing was going to have to carry the task in the United States.[124]

In this context, the shift in British housing policy back to slum clearance in the mid-1930s carried exceptional weight on the American side of the Atlantic. Politically the slums were a Conservative project. Sensing that Britain's suburban building task was now largely complete, the short-lived Labour government of the early Depression years had added new subsidies for inner-city rebuilding. In 1933, however, its Conservative-dominated successor ended all other housing subsidies, leaving the entire weight of the British program on slum clearance and rehabilitation. With considerable fanfare, the government promised to eliminate the slums within five years time. Plans for the razing and rebuilding of a half million dwelling units were advanced. In a carryover from the 1919 act, local authorities were authorized to condemn and purchase decayed slum properties at their underlying land values alone—without any additional compensation for the building itself or for the landlord's loss of rent. That the success of the British attack on the slums might be inseparably linked to its aggressive treatment of slum owners' investments was hardly mentioned in the representations made for the British policy turn in Congress—though Unwin, among others, went to pains to point it out. Slum clearance and rebuilding had the endorsement of the real estate interests; by the mid 1930s it had, unexpectedly, the cachet of transatlantic example as well.[125]

With the deck already stacked toward slum rehousing, the cards held by the courts—always the special handicap of American progressives—carried all the more value. The courts had not balked at the New Deal's first moves in housing. Injection of public money into private mortgages and mortgage guarantees had cleared the courts without particular difficulty. The element of social and economic redistribution in promotionalist policies had always been relatively easy to disguise. But in narrowing the range of commodified things, social politics inevitably intensified questions of ownership. In parts of the judicial system, the claim that governmental housing construction was not a "public use" was still good law in 1937. The most effective counterargument, enunciated most clearly by the New York Court of Appeals in 1936—that public housing conferred a public safety benefit as part of general attack on the crime- and disease-breeding social environment of the slum—was hardly a ringing endorsement of a public housing program as broad as the working class itself.[126]

Both wings of the housing reform movement resisted the endgame of amendments from the House and Senate floor. But with European precedent now stacked against a broad housing program and the constitutional issues hanging in uncertain balance, the real estate lobbies, building and loan associations, and chambers of commerce quickly whittled the Wagner bill down to its least objectionable denominator: cheap public housing for the poor. The power of the new U.S. Housing Authority to build demonstration projects was stripped away. The limited-dividend and cooperative housing associations so dear to Bauer were eliminated from the act. Only local housing authorities could tap the new federal housing credits. They were to build only for the "lowest income group"—the "lowest of the low income group," Senator David Walsh insisted in debate—within a cost ceiling of $5,000 per unit. The PWA's average cost in the urban Northeast had been slightly more than $7,500.[127]

No matter that even in the housing construction boom of the 1920s private builders had not effectively built for any but the top income third.[128] The aim of the construction interests was not to preserve their existing market from state competition but to preempt one they did not and, under the current economic conditions, could not fill. Lest a growing stock of new houses should cut into the value of old ones, municipal housing authorities were required to buy up and demolish a slum dwelling for each new unit they built. Rejecting the English experience with compensation, the slumlords' price was left, without much doubt about the outcome, to the courts.

The Housing Act of 1937 was "modeled on the most successful public housing experience in the world, that of England," the U.S. Housing Authority's first director, Nathan Straus, was to write two years later, and in an important sense Straus was right. More than most New Deal measures, the Housing Act drew not only on lessons of the European past but also on current European events. Shuttling across the Atlantic, 1930s housing reformers acted out the roles and relationships that for two generations had been characteristic of the transatlantic progressive connection. The language of a common social policy race came as second nature to them. "The only question in our country should be," Charles Palmer had pleaded in the Senate committee hearings in 1937, "how quickly can we begin to catch up with the rest of the world?"[129]

As Depression Americans lined up eagerly for access to the new housing projects, the question had, on the face of it, an easy, affirmative answer. The first projects built under the 1937 act were besieged with applicants: 16,000 families applied for the Queensbridge project in New York City, 62,000 for 2,500 units at the Red Hook project in Brooklyn. Bauer moved into the U.S. Housing Authority as director of its Division of Research and Information in 1937, confident that its mandate would grow broader, not thinner, with time. Expansion was a common enough phenomenon in social provision; the Social Security amendments of 1939 and 1950 were to be an important case in point. Minimizing the battles lost in Congress, Bauer wrote that the Housing Act had come out of Congress "battle-scarred but still in fairly workable shape." Into the late 1940s, housing reformers were certain that a second tier of publicly assisted housing would be built for the middle income third of the nation, through limited-dividend and cooperative housing associations.[130]

But between public policy for the poor and public policy for the working class, the distance, however narrow statistically, was politically immense: ideologically mined and politically hazardous to traverse. Beginning with the nonpoor, Social Security's constituency gradually broadened out over time. Beginning with the poor, public housing in the United States was never successfully to extricate itself from its origins. Squeezed between slum land values and congressionally imposed cost and income limits, Bauer's hope to establish, outside the commercial market, new standards in working-class housing and community design proved beyond reach. There were to be no gleaming Römerstadts in America, no sweeping horseshoes of Taut housing with union backing, no more Mackley Houses, no Swedish housing cooperatives, not even a sprawling, British sea of decent, low-cost, suburban, working-class shelter. When the U.S. Building and Loan League crowed to its members in 1937 that there was to be no "broad, unlimited" housing program under the United States Housing Act, its reading of the signs was not misplaced.[131]

By the early 1940s, Bauer herself was already worried about the "fatal charity smell" that clung to American-style public housing. Height and scale had been pushed too high, architectural cost cutting had resulted in structures too grim and interior spaces reduced to the bottom lines of *Existenzminimum.* The rules of eligibility had been made too rigid, management too paternalistic, the contact points between the housing program and the groups that needed housing too few and sterile. "Our worst obstacle all along to getting popular support for public housing has been the social-work-crime-and-disease smell which we couldn't help when we got started in the thirties," she wrote. The breakout from lowest-income housing to working-class housing required more political resources than American housing progressives proved able to muster. What Congress had established, as it would turn out, was another sort of poorhouse. There was a kind of savage irony in the fact that many of the earliest examples were clothed in the brave, new, now tragically deflated aesthetic of Weimar modernism.[132]

New Deal public housing was a triumph of Atlantic social politics and, at the same time, a reminder of the obstacles and limits within that relationship. The European examples gave the project of decommodifying a sliver of the housing market its political impetus in America. Once more the arena of social politics stretched out across the North Atlantic world. But American public housing was a European borrowing transformed in the very politics of appropriation. It was an effort to catch up to European standards that shuttled the Americans, once more, off on exceptionalist tracks. It was a distinctly American product born within a system of influences and rivalries, adaptations and transformations that, for the moment, still bound North Atlantic social politics inextricably together. Indeed, it would be fair to say the same of the New Deal itself.

Through all these channels, and past all these obstacles and transformations, the dammed-up contents of the transatlantic progressive connection were swept into the New Deal. Never again in the twentieth century would the agenda of American politics be so deeply stocked with imported policy ideas as it was in the 1930s. And yet, between act and word a rift widened in the 1930s. Even as the New Dealers set into the statute books a raft of foreign borrowings, even as they edged the liberal wing of their party toward the politics of European-style social democracy, they wore their cosmopolitanism more hesitantly than progressives before them. They were more apt to veil their foreign reference points behind doubts and disguises.

Some of the evasions of the 1930s were Roosevelt's doing—master that he was of the art of coalition building through indistinctness. Still more were a tactical response to the rhetoric of the New Deal's opponents. Ever since doctors and insurance companies had shown how effectively the economics of medical care could be swept behind a spiked helmet and a "made in Germany" charge, there could be no doubt of cosmopolitan progressive politics' vulnerability to the objection that its schemes were unpatriotic, foreign to the distinctive genius of American politics. "We talk so much in terms of comparison with what has happened in Norway, Sweden, Great Britain, and elsewhere," Congressman Everett Dirksen complained in the public housing hearings in 1937. "I think that we ought to forget about their experiences . . . If we are going to have a housing program, we ought to forget what is going on in the old country and try to resolve it in a characteristically modern, American manner."[133]

Amid the arsenal of arguments thrown against the progressives—that their schemes were inefficient and ineffectual, that they weakened the springs of moral and economic action, that they whetted the appetite of a leviathan state—the un-American charge had not always been the most prominent. By the 1930s, however, that cry was everywhere. Just what "the peculiar genius of the American people" might be, Royal Meeker complained in 1934, "I have never been able to discover, . . . but it is always referred to."[134]

Rexford Tugwell, with his imagination full of sweeping reforms and a summer's trip to the Soviet Union in his professorial past, was a particular magnet for the un-American charge. The Farm Security Administration was lambasted by its critics for its "collectivist" fantasies, its "social experiments," and its "foreign" assumptions; Congress's chief FSA critic complained in 1944 that it had been, from the first, "an experiment station of un-American ideas." The greenbelt towns were un-American. So was the "dole" un-American. Public housing was un-American. Unemployment insurance was not the American way. Public housing was un-American. The New Deal itself was un-American. "If there are any items in the march of European collectivism that the New Deal has not imitated," Herbert Hoover groused in 1936, "it must have been an oversight." Isaac Rubinow was moved to protest wearily in 1934: "We Americans, most of us anyway, hold these truths to be self-evident, that we are the greatest, richest nation and people in the world and by implication the wisest as well; that we are entrusted with the special historic mission to teach the old and effete world and not to learn from it."[135]

Despite the onslaught, many American progressives retained the cosmopolitan faith. Rubinow thought the "great caution in quoting European experience, European ways of meeting problems as an example to follow" was a mistake. Abraham Epstein, testifying at the unemployment insurance hearings, could not be budged from retelling, at length, the story of England's attack on poverty. Pilgrimages abroad continued. Edith Wood attended the international housing congress in Stockholm in the summer of 1939. With a Guggenheim fellowship to study housing in Sweden and the U.S.S.R., Catherine Bauer was in Europe that same summer, though an automobile accident in London caused her to miss the Stockholm conference and she was in the Soviet Union only a week before the outbreak of World War II forced her home. To draw in the lessons of the "civilized world," improving and reworking them for American conditions—this remained an explicit goal for many 1930s progressives.[136]

But under the barrage of un-American charges, others beat a tactical retreat. One of the first to show the way had been John Commons at the University of Wisconsin, which was one of the key laboratories for cosmopolitan progressive politics. Commons himself had never had deep European ties; he had missed out on graduate study in Germany, one of the few prominent social economists of his generation to have done so. His junket through Britain with the National Civic Federation's commission on municipal ownership in 1906 had struck him as a monumental waste of time. Still, he had been one of Richard Ely's star students and, like his teacher, a Christian socialist in the 1890s. He had fought the municipal ownership fight; he had declared himself a "solidarist." The American Association for

Labor Legislation, stocked as it was with German-trained social economists, had tapped him as its executive secretary. On his own at the University of Wisconsin, Commons had routinely sent his students foraging through foreign statute books for administrative models and devices. At one point he had engaged fifty undergraduates to chart the labor laws of all the world's countries, hanging the results in large sheets around his seminar room.[137]

In the wake of the First World War, however, the gravity of Commons's interests began to shift. Splitting with the La Follette progressives over their "softness" toward Germany, he began to talk more about incentives to harness business instincts than about direct control. By the late 1920s he had not only reworked the principles of unemployment compensation on these lines but had also begun to insist, more and more vociferously, that his was a distinctly "American" plan that "totally reversed" the principles of its European competitors. In the search for political efficacy, the nativist polarities had begun to come home.[138]

The American Association for Labor Legislation was a still more striking case of a progressive pressure group turning on its past. The most important organizational carrier of cosmopolitan progressive politics in the prewar years, the AALL had always worn its transatlantic face openly. The rhetoric of lags and contrasts was first nature to it. It had waged its health insurance campaign in those terms. Its widely circulated cartoon of 1918 juxtaposed a British worker, secure under a broad umbrella of protective social insurances, with an American worker, possessed only of a nearly bare frame, the umbrella overhead all holes except for the thin protection of industrial accident insurance. Even in the health insurance campaign's defeat, the AALL had clung to the cosmopolitan style. When the International Labor Organization's Albert Thomas embarked on a speaking tour of the United States in the early 1920s, the *American Labor Legislation Review* tipped his photo into every issue. When critics attacked the British dole, the *Review* enlisted the Labour Party's Margaret Bondfield to make the rebuttal. Its special issue on unemployment in September 1930 featured articles by Bondfield and Mary Gilson on the British unemployment insurance system, Mollie Ray Carroll on the German unemployment insurance law, and an endorsement by Albert Thomas himself.[139]

Deeply shaken by the "tide of extreme reaction" in which health insurance had foundered, however, John Andrews had been rethinking the AALL's tactics for some years. In its December 1930 issue, the association's *American Labor Legislation Review* suddenly abandoned its carefully cultivated European connection to crusade for a distinctly "American Plan" on the unemployment front, with the Wisconsin bill as its centerpiece. For the next five years, Andrews pitched a line in social reform as stridently Americanist as Gompers in his day had managed. There was no point wasting time with foreign comparisons or "extended inquiries abroad into the operation of systems foreign to American experience," he wrote. Not until passage of the Social Security Act did the *Review* finally let down the barriers and allow Europe to seep back into its pages.[140]

Not all of the AALL's retreat to native ground can be explained as merely tactical; but in the fall of 1930, with the German unemployment insurance system staggering under its load of jobless claimants and the news reports full of unemployment insurance's distress in Britain, there could be no doubt that the rhetoric of international juxtaposition was more full of hazards than ever before. Unemployment insurance "did not originate in America, nor was it conceived by an American mind," the National Association of Manufacturers' president was preaching in the winter of 1930–31. At the House of Representatives hearings on unemployment relief in 1934, it was unemployment insurance's critics who were most eager to talk about Europe. With European precedents at a discount in the 1930s, with the antiprogressive forces revving up the un-Americanism machine for a new run, it was expedient to fold the movement's cosmopolitan wing, drop its European reference points, and struggle for the rhetorical advantage of the American way.[141]

For most 1930s progressives, however, tactical abandonment was less common than flip-flops and ambivalence. The Social Security debates were a good illustration. The early leaflets put out by the Committee on Economic Security made no bones of the European roots of Social Security. Social insurance was "not a new idea." "Even the small and so-called 'backward'" nations of Europe had it. "*We Pride Ourselves on Being Progressive but in Social Security Legislation We Are at Least 25 Years Behind the Times,*" another Committee on Economic Security pamphlet declared. Harry Hopkins reiterated the point in a radio broadcast in March 1935: there were no "untried principles" in the Social Security Act. Instructed by the president to find measures that had stood the test of experience, he said, "We did that. We studied the experience of Europe which runs back fifty years. And right now I want to point out that European plans are not being recommended for America." The content of the last sentence turned on specifics only an expert could fully appreciate, but its presence was significant. To draw upon the world's experience and to appear to remain immune from it: both were politically essential.[142]

The same dynamics shaped the greenbelt projects' publicity. An early pamphlet by the Suburban Resettlement Division had juxtaposed photos of Bournville and Welwyn Garden City, May's Römerstadt, and Taut's Zehlendorf against American slums, tenants' shacks, and eroded fields, bread lines of American workers, and acres of monotonous, speculator-built American housing. To make the point clear for all, a graph showed the number of houses built with state aid in Germany, Britain, France, Holland, and (lagging far in the rear) the United States. When Tugwell took the greenbelt city case to an Ohio citizens' meeting in 1936, he began by talking about Ebenezer Howard. But then denial followed quickly. The greenbelt town planners were not really planning at all, he went on to explain, much less drawing on other nations' ideas. They were merely "taking the plans which have been drawn for us" in the towns and villages of New England and the Ohio Valley. The New Deal was a catching up to international standards; it had nothing to do with Europe at all. It was heir to the world's experience; it was as native and natural as the land itself. Even the official publicity wore a Janus face.[143]

Nineteen thirty-six was a better year in this regard than 1939. As the promise of Europe crumbled once more into war, many American progressives found it all the more necessary to place a native tradition behind lessons learned abroad. Even as cosmopolitan an intellectual as Lewis Mumford felt the temptation. In the last year of the 1930s, Mumford collaborated on a movie setting of his *The Culture of Cities.* Set to a score by Aaron Copland, *The City* put in cinematic imagery the great U-curve of history that Mumford had worked out at the decade's beginning. From an eotechnic harmony of water, wood, and village, the film plunged viewers into a paleotechnic hell of coal and iron. Downward still history ran, into the fevers of the megalopolis itself until, as a car spins crazily over a cliff, finance capitalism comes at last to wreck, and a neotechnic balance slowly begins to return. *The City* reiterated Mumford's *The Culture of Cities* in every respect but one; this time Mumford lopped off Europe. From the high Middle Ages, the eotechnic age was transported centuries ahead to late-eighteenth-century Shirley Center, Massachusetts. From there the historical descent led not through England's "black country," as before, but through Pittsburgh and New York. As glimpses into the neotechnic future, Mumford gave film viewers Hoover Dam and the Tennessee Valley

Authority, the gentle vistas of Connecticut's Merritt Parkway (when it was still new and uncrowded), and finally the New Deal town of Greenbelt, Maryland. Römerstadt was an abandoned memory.[144]

There was every reason by 1939 to deny the false spring of Weimar social democracy, to slip into its place a firmer set of native referents. Years afterward Mumford would insist that the New England village had been, all along, the source of his 1930s utopianism. Others, too, would let their memories shift in the same direction, pushing the internationalism of 1930s social politics into smaller and smaller recesses, redrawing 1930s politics as a distinctly American movement. As memory it was wrong, but as prognosis it was not entirely off the mark. Battered by events abroad and opponents at home, the transatlantic progressive connection was under palpable strain. The New Deal was the climax of that connection. It hinted at a quite different future.

11

London, 1942

The Plan to Abolish Want

In the history of the North Atlantic economy, the First World War was an interruption, the Second World War a watershed. On every level it altered the Atlantic world's social and intellectual landscapes. Out of the furnace of World War II came a dramatically altered balance of regional economic forces, dramatically enlarged expectations of state responsibilities, new social-political ambitions, and a new, elaborately articulated tracery of Atlantic connections. In the United States the Second World War marked a triumph of cosmopolitan political consciousness. No one expected that it would also mark the closing of the Americans' Atlantic social-political era.

Among the contrasts across the watershed of the Second World War, the construction of the modern era's welfare states was particularly dramatic. On the near side of that departure, where this story has unfolded, lie sixty-odd years of social-political patchwork: a socioeconomic injustice corrected here, a social good de-commodified there, a handful of particularly acute risks insured, the market amended piece by piece at some of the places where it pinched most tightly and where a workable corrective could be successfully imagined or borrowed from elsewhere. On the other side of the Second World War lie the much more tightly elaborated "welfare states" of our own day, with their permanent staffs of social experts, their commitment to continuous economic management, their more systematic provisions, and their much more broadly targeted populations, everywhere including the middle classes.

The contrast between piecemeal and systematic social politics is, of course, imperfect. The safety nets of the post–World War II welfare states still fail many of those who tumble into them; the capacity of the welfare states' administrative structures to deliver social goods efficiently and fairly may slip; the markets' public regulators may wink an eye, or doze off altogether in the arms of those they are charged with regulating; the ability of the state economic managers to steer their national economies past the economic cycles' hazards may give way; the coherence of the system may be (and usually is) exaggerated. In the mixed economies of modern welfare states, as in the patchwork social economies before them, public agencies do not do all the nation's social-political work. Employers, labor unions, churches, charities, and cooperatives still shoulder major burdens.

Facets of welfare state politics likewise remain intensely controversial. The recipients of particular social provisions may be stigmatized or scapegoated, their assistance severely reduced or eliminated altogether—and this is all the more likely if they are poor or racially marked to begin with. Tax-payer revolts and privatization crusades may erupt, with a Thatcher or a Reagan to articulate and effect them. Still, as sharply contested as the politics of welfare states may be, and fight as their constituents do over who should receive their benefits and protections and who should pay for them, the continuous presence of the state in steering and taming the market economy is, at a deeper level, broadly accepted. As stabilizer, regulator, social goods provider, and ensurer of a modicum of social justice, the state is taken for granted.[1]

The transition from patchwork to system took place within a broad array of political regimes—the policy makers borrowing and competing across their differences, as usual. The first of the twentieth-century welfare states was the one the British Labour Party forged in a rush between 1945 and 1950. Out of a bundle of preexisting progressive ideas, the collectivist experience of the war, and a radical, reconstructionist, victory mood, the Labour government swept the piecemeal accumulations of three generations of social politics into something approaching ideological and practical coherence. In Sweden after 1948 the same work was done more gradually, without the goad of dramatic wartime sacrifices, under Social Democratic auspices. In West Germany, the postwar "social market" state was a construct of a centrist political regime, harried from the left by those who thought the real point of action lay in the ownership of the banks and key industries. Elsewhere, in still different political contexts, other variants took shape. The "welfare state," a phrase Arthur Schlesinger, Jr., thought was barely months old in the fall of 1949, was within another decade the North Atlantic economy's norm.[2]

In this general movement toward wider and more systematic social provisions, the United States was an active participant. The end of the New Deal regime in 1953 brought no wholesale reversal in social politics, however deeply many in the Republican Party desired it. Slowly the surviving elements of the emergency policy making of the Depression were moved to a more permanent status, their coverage expanded, their promises enlarged, their administration made more systematic. The most glaring exclusions of the Social Security Act were remedied. Into the breach where they feared the breakthrough of a national health care system, large-scale employers collaborated with industrial unionists in shoving a system of employment-based health insurance, privately administered but subject to collective bargaining and mediation. Farmers and suburban home owners hung on to their Depression-era subsidies. In the cities, urban "renewal" projects proliferated. Out of the structures and expectations set in motion in the prewar years there emerged, even in America, a kind of welfare state.

More dramatically still, the war internationalized American politics. It pulled the Americans out into the world and held them there as the hot war of 1939 to 1945 bled into the cold war of 1947 to 1989, precipitating an investment in global management without precedent in American history. There were American policy makers everywhere after 1945—inspecting, administering, financing, and pacifying. There were more Americans in motion, more international conferences and agencies, more foreign reportage and foreign data exchanged than at any previous moment in history. The geopolitical marginalization of the United States on the hither edge of the world's power centers was, by the end of the 1940s, a thing of the past. Ray Stannard Baker's "geocentricity" was gone beyond recovery.

On the surface, all these factors seemed to bode well for the North Atlantic progressive connection. Linked together more deeply with other nations than ever before, the United States seemed to many veterans of prewar progressive politics ripe for a period of continuous and regularized engagement with the half-idealized, half-distrusted social-political world beyond its shores. Certainly at no time before in its history had the United States been more *like* the Old World nations—with its new peacetime standing army, its geopolitical ambitions, its expanded state apparatus, its politically mobilized labor movement, and its cosmopolitan intellectuals gathered from all over shattered Europe.[3]

But the promised culmination was not to be. Postwar Americans found themselves suddenly *in* the world, but politically they were not *of* it. Their Atlantic connections proliferated, but these did not function as before. Far more foreign news reached the United States, but domestically it now mattered less. Reports of other nations' social policies piled up in American research libraries, but they no longer moved the wheels of politics. Between the welfare state regimes in Europe and the United States, relationships became more and more attenuated. The entrance of the United States onto the international political stage was also an exit; the advent of the "American century" was also a closure. At the very moment when one might have predicted its success, the North Atlantic progressive connection unraveled.

Endings are never less complicated than beginnings. Closure of the transatlantic age in American social politics was a complex affair, full of false starts, abandoned opportunities, and ironic turns. As a window on the postwar culmination that turned out to be no culmination at all but a return of the old exceptionalism, however, there is no better vantage point than London in 1942, where the construction of the first of the postwar welfare states began.

It was a much grimmer year, this third year of the second global war, than 1900, where our story began. No one put on a fair in 1942; had anyone done so, there were no ladies with parasols now to stroll through it, no William Tolmans to organize its materials on ingeniously hinged boards and cabinets, no Patrick Geddeses to synthesize its tendencies around a master trope of progress, no international gatherings for earnest discussion of the "social question." London itself was much a much grimmer city, too, than it had been forty-two years earlier. Battered and hollowed out by the furious German bomber raids of 1940 and 1941, its people forced into a bare-bones regime of shortages and food rationing, the recent military victories in North Africa hardly a consolation for almost thirty straight months of disasters and retreat, the city was a far cry from John Burns's and Sidney Webb's turn-of-the-century showplace swelling with municipalist ambitions.

Out of this setting burst, nonetheless, in the last months of 1942, a social-political blueprint of instant, transnational importance. A Report to the Inter-Departmental Committee on Social Insurance and Allied Services it was officially titled, though the name that stuck, in honor of its author, was the Beveridge Plan. Of all the welfare state programs and platforms that were to follow, none was to match its influence or the electricity of its reception. Reaching back into the progressive past to map the postwar progressive promise, its status as a foundational document of welfare state politics fell to it almost instantly.

The Beveridge Plan was intensely discussed throughout the North Atlantic economy, including the United States. Virtually everyone, for a moment, seemed to want to catch hold of its political coattails. But though Americans in the North Atlantic progressive network were keenly attentive, they were not listening in the same way as before. In the journals that had followed British progressive politics so long, that had leaped with hope at *Labour and the New Social Order*, one cannot miss the intrusion of a new tone of critical superiority. Like progressives before them, progressives in 1940's America hankered for their future. But Beveridge did not hold it for them—nor did Europe. In European history, 1942 stands at the juncture between the old and new eras in social politics. In the history of the United States, it marks a moment of closure, when American history was set adrift once more on its own cherished, providential tide.

Beveridge's report on the social insurances in 1942 was a twice-made document—first by William Beveridge, and all over again by the public that invested it, in the hard and discouraging third year of the war, with such palpable political hope. Beveridge himself had not wanted to write it. An expert on manpower questions since the demonstrations of the London unemployed had pulled him out of Toynbee Hall's uplift work into the politics of unemployment in 1904, he had rejected invitations to sit on official committees on old-age and health insurance on the grounds that they did not fall within his field of expertise. The post he dearly wanted in 1941 and 1942 was the directorship of wartime labor allocation policy. Beveridge was not even a particularly advanced thinker on social policy questions. Roosevelt's New Deal had not impressed him in 1933: it was "trying all the wrong medicines" in its flurry of first-year contradictions, he thought. New Deal work relief he thought a mistake and the National Recovery Administration a particularly grotesque one. He would have preferred less meddling in the "natural" forces of the business cycle, more attention to business's need for lower interest rates and more stable money. In his own British context, Beveridge was a social Liberal, not a Labourite, a centrist not a radical. Among the puzzles of the Beveridge Plan, the London press noted in early 1943, was how a "reformer so sedate had been able to fashion a weapon so sharp, and how a government so timid should have presented materials for its fashioning."[4]

In fact, the Ministry of Labour's purpose in giving Beveridge chairmanship of an interdepartmental inquiry on the coordination of social insurance benefits had been primarily to get Beveridge out its hair, to safely remove him from day-to-day policy making and influence. Accepting his political fate, Beveridge had focused his energies relentlessly on the only outlet open to them. For anyone with as systematic a turn of mind as he, the social insurances presented an extraordinary tangle of questions. Even in Germany the social insurances had developed one by one in hodgepodge fashion and were administratively uncoordinated and logically incomplete. In countries like Britain, which had appropriated them from elsewhere and tacked the imports onto preexisting institutional structures, the confusion in the social insurances was even more pronounced. In 1940s Britain, each of the social insurances was financed differently from the others and covered a different segment of the population. Some of the insurances were designed to replace a fraction of a worker's lost wages; others determined benefits according to need; still others were set by design to pay out at less than subsistence levels. Health insurance under the 1911 act was limited to wage earners, without statutory benefits for family dependents, and administered through the friendly societies at widely differing support levels. Old-age pensions were for the poor and were centrally administered. Unemployment insurance, patched together again in 1934, was its own peculiar bundle of compromises.

Playing his committee like a one-man band, Beveridge moved into this mix of administrative agencies, delivery vehicles, and benefit levels with a single-minded determination to standardize and simplify them. His aim, as others had laid it out before him, was a single, "all-in" system of insurance for everyone against all the major economic risks of a laboring family's working career: sickness, old-age, unemployment, disabling injury, and childbirth. Working these principles into practical specifics was a task of immense detail. As published in November 1942, the Beveridge Report was a mind-taxing compendium of 461 highly detailed numbered paragraphs, together with a brace of appendixes, all filled with the most minute cost calculations and policy recommendations. But it was detail work at the service of a profound simplicity. Out of the existing materials around him, out of long-standing criticisms of the existing social insurances' failings, together with the Webbs' old case for a national subsistence minimum, Beveridge outlined a social insurance structure of enormous moral clarity.

Every working person (or almost everyone, married women being treated not quite equally in Beveridge's scheme) was to pay into the system at the same rate; everyone hitting one of the life's critical risks was to be tided over at the same, subsistence level. One rate, one level of benefits, one socio-economic class as broad as the nation itself. The Beveridge Plan was Bismarck's scheme wrenched out of Bismarck's context of labor control and political repression; it was social insurance universalized, made democratic and egalitarian.[5]

To this reorganization of the social insurances, Beveridge added three essential "assumptions," each as wide-ranging as the body of the report itself. The first was a system of universal, state-financed children's allowances, designed to help families over one of the key moments when the likelihood of precipitation from competence into poverty lay particularly close at hand. The second was to uncouple doctors' services from social insurance and establish medical care as a free public service. The third was systematic central-government economic responsibility for full employment. Like the insurance ideas in the body of the report, none of the ideas behind these assumptions was new. British feminists had been agitating for universal children's allowances since the First World War; Beveridge himself had been titular president of Eleanor Rathbone's Family Endowment Society since 1925. Complaints of inefficiencies and inequities under the health insurance act of 1911 had been widespread for years. As for employment, Beveridge's mind had been focused on the issue since his Toynbee Hall days. When he was eased out of government in 1943, he would turn his full attention to it, convening a private committee for research and policy recommendation, and issuing, ultimately, one of the most important statements of the 1940s on the possibilities of Keynesian economic management for full and stable employment.[6]

All this was vastly more than Churchill's wartime government had expected or was willing to swallow. Endorsed neither by the government nor by the departments represented on Beveridge's committee, his report on the social insurances was printed with only Beveridge as a signatory. This inauspicious launching notwithstanding, the popular response to the Beveridge Plan was sudden and extraordinary. Within a month 100,000 copies had been sold; the final sales figures ran well over half a million. Taking advantage of every turn at the publicity mills he could take, Beveridge threw himself into the report's popularization. "A revolutionary moment in the world's history is a time for revolutions, not for patching," he urged, in rhetoric that mirrored the war's urgency. He lifted his cost calculations out of the everyday with a metaphorical flourish drawn from John Bunyan's *Pilgrim's Progress.* In the road ahead of wartime Britain, where Bunyan's pilgrim had long before faced the giants of Slay-Good, Maul, Diffidence, and Despair, Beveridge now saw five new "Giants on the Road": Want, Disease, Ignorance, Idleness (by which Beveridge meant unemployment), and Squalor (by which he meant the "hideous" unplanned chaos of the distended capitalist city). All could been slain, he insisted, by a nation that put its political will to the task, even the giant Want itself.[7]

Beveridge's packaging helped garner attention, but on its own it did not sell the Beveridge Report. In the people's remaking of the report from a technical document to a postwar promise, the essential point of the Beveridge Plan was the way in which its ethical simplicity caught, reflected, and magnified the popular political temperament of the war. Beveridge's proposals did not promise much more than subsistence-level assistance across life's hard patches, but they promised that much equally to all—without means testing and without intrusive deterrents. In a time that put a premium on unity, the riveting point of the Beveridge Plan was not the level of its benefits but the democratic assumption behind them. It drew on the sense of common risk forged by bombing alerts and rationing—the war-made recognition of the nation as its citizens' common lifeboat in a threatening sea. Beveridge himself had not played hard on the war's perils. He had not even played hard on the idea that social guarantees to men and women, as citizens, were a democratic right. In the document the people made out of Beveridge's cost calculations, metaphors, and efficiencies, both these themes were pushed to the forefront.[8]

Crystalizing these hopes of a better and fairer world after the war, the Beveridge Plan suddenly turned up everywhere. On a mistaken understanding that the report had the government's backing, the Ministry of Information printed up a special cheap edition to tell the troops what they were fighting for. Clandestine abridgments were circulated through the Nazi-occupied countries of Europe. The report was discussed at church group gatherings, labor union rallies, community service organization meetings, and university symposia; endorsements flowed into the government from organizations across the spectrum, from radical union gatherings of Clydeside workers to staid churchmen's conferences. Within two weeks of the report's publication, nine out of ten Britons were already telling pollsters they approved of it. "Beveridge has become almost a common noun in the English language," the *New York Herald Tribune*'s London correspondent reported in 1945. "It stands for hope."[9]

For this popular tide the government's caution was no match. Dipping back into World War I precedents, the government had already appointed a set of reconstruction committees to try to map the social character of the postwar peace. Now, in the wake of the Beveridge Plan, their work was cranked up to a rapid pitch. Even before the war was over, the Conservative-dominated war government had already set much of Beveridge's agenda in motion. A far-reaching democratization of education and a family allowance program (though at a lower level than Beveridge wanted) were passed in 1944 and early 1945; government white papers endorsed a new national health service, countercyclical peacetime spending, and most of Beveridge's social insurance proposals. The town planners were at work again on a broad range of proposals, including still more effective capture of the unearned increment in public improvements and the ringing of even swollen London with a new, broad girdle of green space. With these accomplishments behind them, the Conservatives went to the polls in the summer of 1945 as new-made champions of the Beveridge Plan. So did the Liberal Party, claiming Beveridge, justly, as one of its own. So did Labour, finally letting go its objections to the contributory social insurance idea to bring Beveridgism into its fold.[10]

When the election was over, it was Labour that had captured the aspirations Beveridge had helped unleash. Turning their backs on Churchill's bid for peacetime power, the voters swept in a Labour government—the first to make a significant mark on British politics since the party's founding. In quick order it passed a National Insurance Act along Beveridge's lines, a National Health Service Act decommodifying basic health service ("terminating the custom of buying and selling medical practices," as the new minister of health, Aneurin Bevan, put it), a Town and Country Planning Act with strong recoupment powers, and a plan for massive housing investment. The New Towns Act of 1946 launched the state on the construction of fourteen new greenbelt cities—public realizations of Ebenezer Howard's idea on a still bolder scale than the U.S. Resettlement Administration had attempted. Beveridge himself was soon to move into one of the new towns, as chair of its development corporation. Cashing in on the precedents of prewar municipal "socialism," the Labourites nationalized most of the nation's transport systems and electric power. The socialists in the party could not be denied their day; coal, iron and steel were all nationalized as well.[11]

Conservatives lumped these policies all together as the "road to serfdom": England gone "red" and radical. In truth, most of the ingredients of the Labour program of 1945 to 1950 came not out of the Marxist heritage but the progressive one. Gathering up a backlog of reform projects, the governmental revolution of 1945 was Britain's New Deal, its recapitulation of the dynamics of crisis politics in a Labourite key. Nationalization of the basic industries tapped a core socialist tradition. But in practice the Labour government evinced little interest in central state planning and still less in wresting fundamental economic control from capital. Its most popular measures were those that built upon the social politics of the past, that sought not to abolish capitalism but to assuage its excesses, extracting from it a few key social goods and setting a common floor under a few of its most acute risks.

It would be wrong to suggest that the Beveridge Report was the blueprint for the entire result. But the tie Beveridge's own person made between the social politics of the 1910s and the welfare state of the post-1945 future was important, both symbolically and politically. The Labour government asked him for no advice; the war government had tried to rusticate him; yet his report articulated many of the central moral and political assumptions of the postwar social order. From an Atlantic perspective, finally, it did one critical thing more. It gave the reconstruction mood in wartime and postwar Britain a program. And in crystallizing aspirations into policy, principle, and metaphor, it made them potentially exportable.

Having felt the force of so many British manifestos before, progressive Americans did not escape the effects of the Beveridge Plan whirlwind. Their own Social Security system, every expert recognized, was a makeshift with vastly more holes and incongruities than Britain's. In 1942 none of it was universal. Only old-age insurance was nationally administered, and even it was so regionally skewed, with its exclusions of agricultural and domestic workers, that it barely touched the rural or African-American South. The rest was a patchwork of state-made standards. Of the oldest of the social insurances, health insurance, there were still no American examples, despite yet another try in Congress in 1939. As war materials spending finally achieved the economic recovery that had so long eluded the New Dealers, the giant Want, to a great extent, skulked away in the 1940s. But there was no systematic insurance against his return. The relevance of the Beveridge Plan to contemporary American conditions was, on all these grounds, too close to be mistaken.

Equally in the Beveridge Report's favor was the severely limited scope of postwar planning in the United States in the first years of the war. One of the lessons Roosevelt had learned from Wilson's debacle of 1919 was that he would not run the war as an ideological crusade. This time there was to be no all-out propaganda campaign; no model, centralized war economy; no celebration of emergency "war socialism." As before, the war made private business public. But unwilling to countenance rival centers of control on the scale of the War Industries Board of 1917 and 1918, Roosevelt devolved the management of war production and pricing onto a set of partial, overlapping agencies. He kept the Amalgamated Clothing Workers' Sidney Hillman at his side for the course of the emergency, far closer than Gompers had ever been to Wilson, but there was no symbolic rearrangement of the seats of power to make institutional room for labor.[12]

The old war economy issues recurred, this time to be met with more cautious answers. Faced once again with intense housing needs at the war production plants, the planners, under heavy pressure from real estate interests, opted not for model town construction but for cheap, emergency housing. A short-lived attempt to enlist distinguished architects brought Walter Gropius, *Existenzminimum*'s keenest proponent among the Weimar social modernists, briefly into the wartime housing program, but his spare, ungainly "Aluminum City" project in western Pennsylvania was a public relations disaster. As workers began streaming into the aircraft manufacturing plants in Detroit, Walter Reuther teamed up with Oskar Stonorov to propose an ambitious wartime model city just outside the sprawling Willow Run works, but the Ford Motor Company refused to sell the surrounding land to be developed into a bastion of social unionism.[13]

As for the postwar reconstruction committees at work once again in Britain, Roosevelt wanted none of them. "We must start winning the war . . . before we do much general planning for the future," he admonished his critics on the left. He told Congress in early 1941 that the future must eventually bring the "simple" things at democracy's foundation: broader Social Security coverage, better opportunities for medical care, "security for those who need it," and "jobs for those who can work." But into reconstruction specifics he would not go.[14]

Roosevelt had ample political grounds for caution. For Churchill's Conservative-dominated government, the road to national unity lay through promises of postwar renewal. In Britain, as the official historians of the war put it in the late 1940s, "there existed, so to speak, an implied contract between Government and the people: the people refused none of the sacrifices that the Government demanded from them for the winning of the war; in return, they expected that the Government should show imagination and seriousness in preparing for the restoration and improvement of the nation's well-being when the war had been won. The plans for reconstruction were, therefore, a real part of the war effort." For Roosevelt, stalemated by an anti–New Deal congressional majority that was quick to read every war policy measure (as Robert Taft put it in 1942) as a sub-rosa scheme to "make the country over under the cover of war," the path to national unity, in contrast, lay in shelving the social-reconstructionist rhetoric of the New Deal past, promising generous postwar benefits to the returning soldiers, and leaving the matter at that. Intent on everyday gains, the labor unions raised no striking reconstructionist banners; a brief flurry of talk in the CIO of labor-management codetermination along the lines of the German Social Democrats of 1919 and 1920 quickly evaporated. Not until early 1944, with the promise of a new "economic bill of rights" for everyone, would Roosevelt try to take the old Wilsonian ground and stake out a progressive agenda for the conflict.[15]

In this vacuum of articulated postwar aspirations in the early years of the Americans' war, the Beveridge Report, with its high and relevant promises, was assured of all the more eager attention. The progressive journals were quick to point up its significance. A special American edition quickly sold some 50,000 copies. The National Policy Committee, a wartime coalition of progressive employers, journalists, and labor unionists, devoted its annual dinner meeting in early 1943 to the Beveridge Report. In March Beveridge himself sailed for the United States for a Rockefeller Foundation–sponsored lecture tour. Over the course of three months he delivered more than a hundred speeches, conferred in private with Roosevelt, Frances Perkins, and dozens of other highly placed public and private officials, and basked in the public attention.[16]

Within the Roosevelt cabinet in early 1943 there was deep concern that the administration had been upstaged. Within weeks of the Beveridge Report's publication, Roosevelt was musing to confidantes about going to Congress with "a kind of Beveridge Plan." Even his eternally cautious treasury secretary urged an American counterpart. "Every single person in England is going to be insured," Henry Morgenthau wrote in his diary in late 1942; "they are going to get unemployment insurance; they are going to get sickness insurance, and the whole business." When in early 1943 Roosevelt made public a broad-gauged National Resources Planning Board (NRPB) report on security and public works programs that had been gathering dust since late 1941, when he had sequestered it as untimely, he was happy to have the press bill it as an "American Beveridge Plan." Progressive and conservative commentators alike picked up the comparison. To clinch the point, *Newsweek* offered readers a chart comparing the planning board's suggestions, category by category, with the British scheme. By the spring of 1943, Senator Robert Wagner had introduced yet another "American Beveridge Plan," this one a bill for an integrated system of health and social insurance provisions. In all these ways, the North Atlantic progressive connection did its work once more—slipping the alien noun "Beveridgism" into the American vocabulary; rekindling the old fears of behindhandedness, rivalry, and inadequacy; sweeping up nation-state politics in transnational systems of emulation and exchange.[17]

And yet, this time there was a difference. An early hint was to be found in that bastion of Anglo-American progressive politics, the *New Republic*. Since its founding in 1914, the journal had boasted a long roster of English contributors and connections. At the war's end in 1945, two of its four editors set off almost immediately for London, to take their bearings there, like so many *New Republic* figures before them, on the future. The *New Republic*'s more maverick and leftist rival, the *Nation*, saving its enthusiasm for the Labour electoral victory, had had little to say in the winter of 1942–43 about Beveridge's work. The *New Republic*, by contrast, gave the Beveridge Plan a strong, early endorsement. But by the early spring the editors had transferred their enthusiasm in toto to the National Resources Planning Board report. Touting it as a "Charter for America," they devoted a special supplement to its proposals in April 1943. The NRPB's recommendations went "far beyond the Beveridge report," the editors advised. It was a "better and sounder" plan, Max Lerner wrote, a more American plan, and a more "revolutionary" one. The *Nation*, making the same comparison, agreed.[18]

Exactly what there was in the National Resources Planning Board report to trigger these editorial comparisons is not, at first glance, easy to see. An unwieldy assemblage of proposals coordinated by an English émigré progressive, Eveline Burns, the NRPB report was essentially a review and justification of the key New Deal programs, with special emphasis on WPA work relief and public works employment policies. It had none of the Beveridge Plan's moral and administrative clarity; it offered no cost estimates; on the social insurance front, its suggestions were cautious in the extreme. Roosevelt deposited it at Congress's door without endorsing it. When the Congress left it there, orphaned and undebated, conservative columnists thought it a sign of political good sense.[19]

To the progressive editors, however, comparison of the social insurance provisions of the Beveridge and NRPB reports missed the point altogether.

Beveridgism, in their minds, was not revolutionary at all. With its pinched and meager talk of subsistence minima, it was about salves and crutches. Out of the National Resources Planning Board's mass of suggestions, in contrast, they extracted what they saw as a fundamentally different seed of hope: a promise of work and jobs ample enough to eliminate the old boom-and-bust rhythms of the business cycle. What made the planning board's proposal "thoroughly American" (as the *Nation*'s editors put it), was its emphasis not merely on security but on an economy set permanently at full capacity: "It represents an abrupt break from the defeatist thinking that held us in economic thralldom through the thirties." It meant abandonment of the Depression era's preoccupation with poverty, abandonment of the notion of permanent economic stagnation that had slipped into the subsistence homestead projects, abandonment of all this for the promise of a full-employment, full-production economy stabilized by public emergency work and permanent publics works planning.[20]

Outside the editorial conferences, the same controlling polarity could be heard. What was the point of selling cut-rate tickets on the national bus for the invalid and crippled if the bus itself wouldn't move? G. Hartley Grattan asked of Beveridge's scheme in *Harper's Magazine*. The very premises of the British scheme, it was said, were fixed in scarcity; a truly American alternative would have to be pitched in terms of economic growth. Henry Wallace thought Beveridge's proposals not fundamentally relevant to a "dynamic" economy like that of the United States. Harry Hopkins, pushing for a permanent Works Progress Administration, did not think that Beveridge's scheme could be "the cornerstone of any American program." "Social-security programs, desirable as they are, constitute a minor part of the total stream of purchasing power required to sustain a high level of production and employment," Wallace wrote, returning to the point in 1945. As these polarities intensified, Beveridgism was invested with dingier and dingier trappings of poverty. Beveridge's flat-rate, subsistence-level benefits, his Webbsian talk of guaranteed minima, his democratization of risks—all this ran counter to the promise of a full-employment economy, to the new upward-to-the-stars notion of economic possibility.[21]

Part of what one overhears in these comments is the conceptual revolution in macroeconomics around which the term "Keynesianism" was to form. The idea that the boom-and-bust cycles of the unmanaged market could be overcome by continuous, carefully calibrated public investment was an idea brewing in many pots in the 1930s, from Stockholm to New Deal Washington—though it was Britain's John Maynard Keynes who gave it the deepest theoretical statement and pushed hardest for it on the international circuit.[22] The notion that maintenance of aggregate national spending and demand might be the most important task of governance came into the late-thirties economic debate as a dazzling simplification of social politics. One need not do everything all at once, in the furiously eclectic manner of the early New Deal. One need not worry overly about which goods were in or outside the market, or even where, in this profoundly mixed system, such a line might be drawn. One crucial thing was needed: to keep one's eye on aggregate investment and demand.

In 1938, when they persuaded Roosevelt to try spending his way out of the year's sharp economic relapse, there had been only a handful of proto-Keynesians in Roosevelt's government. The famous meeting between Keynes and Roosevelt four years before had left both men mystified and frustrated. But as the war economy boomed with government purchases, spewing out more goods than any expert had imagined possible, the tenets of "Keynesian" economic management quickly gathered converts. Under the influence of Harvard economist Alvin Hansen, the National Resources Planning Board was soon steeped in the new paradigm. The market economy cornucopia, empty so long, stood ready to deliver once more, now that its workings were properly understood. By 1945, Henry Wallace was promising sixty million jobs, created not by planning or controls but by the magic of sustained and adequate demand. In a symposium on postwar liberalism that brought the threads of the new progressive creed together, Seymour Harris put the moral: "The core of modern economic policy is stabilization of demand."[23]

Between left "social Keynesians" (with their eye on automatic public works and public spending adjustments) and right "commercial Keynesians" (with their much narrower notion of the central government as an interest-rate-conscious central bank) the economic argument was far from closed in the early 1940s. Most businessmen remained profoundly skeptical of the whole enterprise of aggregate economic management. Full-employment promises, *Newsweek*'s business columnist objected, entailed "nothing but economic Fascism"; the *New York Times* editors thought that only "totalitarian" economic management could bring full employment into being. For its pains in putting together a Keynesian program of public investment, Congress closed down the National Resources Planning Board six months after Roosevelt released its report. For their part, Seymour Harris's progressive collaborators were still full of public goals and projects: more Tennessee Valley Authorities; improved health, housing, and education; a public jobs program. As the nation's aggregate public and private spending accounts should require, each of these projects stood ready to absorb the needed additional investment. But social need now came second. Beveridge's Giants on the Roads were only a sideshow. The first imperative was spending itself.[24]

All these newly absorbed convictions flowed into the American readings of the Beveridge report. Their eyes fixed on the frontiers of growth, the prophets of managed aggregate demand could barely disguise their irritation with Beveridge's preoccupation with poverty; for them, the very language of a "national minimum" struck the wrong note. In fact, as the thoroughly Keynesian analysis of Beveridge's own *Full Employment in a Free Society* was quickly to show, the idea of an inherent contradiction between economic growth and economic security was profoundly misplaced from the outset. Beveridge and Keynes were friends and collaborators who borrowed freely of each other's ideas. Between subsistence floors and jobs, between risk assurance and economic growth, there was no inherent contradiction. On the "American" promise of sustained and managed growth that they juxtaposed to Beveridge's, the Americans clearly had no local patent. The Stockholm economists had been "Keynesians" as long as Keynes himself, and considerably longer than Keynes's new American converts. Keynesianism was an idea of just as much international force as Beveridgism in the 1940s; it was hard to find a social-political blueprint or welfare state design in the postwar North Atlantic economy that did not, in one combination or another, absorb them both.

Something more was clearly at work in the American depreciations of the Beveridge Plan—something simpler, cruder, and more lasting in its effects. Europeans might speak the language of Keynesian multipliers and sustained economic growth, but the war that had made Europeans desperately poor had made the United States uniquely rich. No one in 1939 had anticipated the difference in fortunes the war would make. By 1945, however, the economic comparabilities on which the North Atlantic progressive connection had rested were in a shambles. American reports from 1940s Britain focused on the point. Britain was a nation of "desperate shabbiness," the *Nation*'s London reporter wrote in early 1945; "the watchword is still 'austerity,' a word which summarizes with characteristic understatement the whole process of stripping the civilian economy as nearly as possible to the bare bones." A year later England was "still shabby, pockmarked, and underfed." Britain was not "dying," as many reports had it. But limping along, as it was, on rationed food and fuel (bread rationing persisted into 1949 and meat rationing into 1954), and with consumer goods of every sort in acutely short supply, Britain was poor. As for Germany, it was desperately poor, kept alive in the immediate aftermath of the war only by the victors' charity.[25]

There had been sacrifices on the American home front as well: gasoline rationing, "victory gardens" for home-grown food, scrap metal drives, and (for far more Americans than ever before) a federal income tax. But on the whole, the domestic economic sacrifices had not run deep. The Dunkirk lesson of a nation crowded into a frail, common lifeboat was not the Americans' war moral. Partly through the policy makers' design, but still more through the special geographic dispensation that insulated the United States from the ferocious destruction of the war, the great European catastrophe left the Americans rich. The war's lesson on the American home front was one of jobs and full larders—the ability of the capitalist economy, when pressed hard enough and managed well enough, to spit out both guns and butter in extraordinary quantities. Almost half the world's total manufactured goods in 1945 came from the factories of the United States; five years later, half the world's monetary reserves were still located in the U.S. No single nation's economy had ever before so dominated the world as the economy that Europe's catastrophe gave to the United States. At the war's end, the world had for the moment only one major economic player, and that was the United States.[26]

In the face of imbalances on this scale, the older notion of a common economy, a common social question, a social landscape rolling across the North Atlantic world from Berlin to San Francisco, could not endure. Europe was cramped and poor. Its social-political needs were not those of the United States. The aura of defeatism the American progressives hung around Beveridgism, the new gulf in their own minds between growth and "security," and their reembrace of the market economy's promises all flowed from this starting point. Weary of war sacrifices, the British might take Beveridgism as a noun of hope, but to the Americans—even to progressive Americans—it smelled too much of limits and poverty. Economic minima were an Old World problem; the most famous social-political document of the twentieth century was not fundamentally the Americans' affair. In the sea change the war had made, American progressives repossessed hope as their own providential dispensation.

The Phoenix of Exceptionalism

The Beveridge Plan was hardly the first blueprint for the future to founder in the Atlantic crossing. The Atlantic progressive connection had always had its full share of failures, frustrations, missed conjunctures, and broken communications. But an acute reader of the progressive journals could hardly miss the larger pattern at work. It was not simply that the Beveridge Plan was irrelevant to Americans. As a social-political experiment, Britain itself had become irrelevant, as had, for that matter, the western European democracies as well. The overseas models, strained in the 1930s, fell apart in the 1940s. This time there was no putting them back in the old ways again.

The irony of the unraveled connection was that it ended with the Americans more deeply ensconced in European affairs than at any previous moment in their history. Into the prostrate continent in 1945 the American armies came, and in their wake, once more, followed a broad tail of civilian experts to prop up, manage, and Americanize. On West Germany, as if on a tabula rasa, the American occupational government wrote its eighteenth-century notion of checked and balanced powers: a federal governmental structure, an independent judiciary, a bicameral central government of strictly limited powers, and a written constitution. In social legislation the American authorities were much less interested, except to put up roadblocks against economic nationalization and to help restore and rationalize the institutions of German social insurance. In contrast to their counterparts in the British and French military zones of occupied Germany, the Americans left the replanning of German cities to the Germans themselves. But if the American proconsuls acted with restraint, there was no missing the war's upending of prewar relations.[27]

The postwar American economic and cultural invasion of Europe, so long prophesied abroad, was even more striking. The Marshall Plan brought not only billions of American dollars to Europe but also teams of economists, cultural attachés, U.S. Information Agency administrators, and Central Intelligence Agency officials to oversee their investment. Marshall Plan officials sponsored the visits of thousands of French business and labor figures to the United States, wheeling them through itineraries designed to promote American methods in labor relations, consumer marketing, and productivity. Traveling displays of American consumer goods toured provincial French towns; American-sponsored radio brought the details of American automobile production to Austrian households. In chewing gum, movies, advertisements, and Coca-Cola, American goods penetrated day-to-day European life. "America bestrides the world like a colossus," Harold Laski summed up the postwar order. In large ways and small, the continent was, suddenly, America's.[28]

Or almost America's. As hot war gave way to cold war, refiguring the globe as a deadly earnest contest between the United States and the Soviet Union and drawing the United States economically, militarily, and diplomatically into European history more deeply and intimately than ever before, every twist and turn of the continent's politics now suddenly carried geopolitical significance. Never had western Europe been so minutely scrutinized by so many Americans. But they were no longer looking for lessons, for "marching orders" from the older continent's experience, as Paul Kellogg had once put it. As they folded the European democracies into their military-economic protection in the late 1940s, the Americans refigured Europe's importance. In the repolarized circumstances of the cold war, Paris, London, and Berlin were no longer focal points for American imaginations. Europe was the arena of struggle, the client continent, the place between. Even American progressives had a hard time seeing anything abroad other than themselves and their Manichaean opposite, the Soviets.

The lasting consequence of the war and the postwar crises, in short, was not as much a displacement of force as a displacement of mind. American progressives no longer marched toward the future with an eye cocked on their western European competitors. They no longer imagined themselves in a race with the world's other "civilized nations"—still less that they themselves might be found straggling along in the rear. Those very metaphors now seemed part of an impossibly distant, more innocent age. The late twentieth century's terms were sterner, and the special place of the United States within its dispositions unproblematically clear.

Two political grand tours made almost a half century apart illuminate the contrast. Like William Jennings Bryan in 1905, Adlai Stevenson was a defeated Democratic presidential candidate in 1953, hoping to find rest and political rehabilitation through a trip abroad. Both Bryan and Stevenson circumnavigated the world from Tokyo east to London. Both traveled in a blaze of publicity, Bryan with a contract from the Hearst papers, Stevenson surrounded by an entourage of photographers and correspondents from *Look* magazine. Both knew the rhetoric of mission: of western Christianity for Bryan, western freedom for Stevenson. Of the two, Stevenson's background was by far the more cosmopolitan. He had taken his first grand tour at age twelve and made many Atlantic crossings since. But in keeping with the inward-looking globalism of cold-war progressive politics, Stevenson's report was, in its way, much the more provincial.

Bryan's globe was a great, eclectically stocked cupboard, its shelves overflowing with usable and interesting things. Stevenson's was a world shot through with dangers and "ordeals," responsibilities and "burdens," whose every facet pressed the imagination back on the special destiny of the United States. Stevenson's world was no storehouse of usable social-political experience, no world-circling string of foreign "experiment stations." From it no "salad" of progressive ideas, as Henry D. Lloyd had once put it, waited to be made. It was an arena in which the Americans' "test of leadership" could not be evaded, where the "heaviest burden of greatness" waited to be assumed. Bryan in England, elated by the Liberal victory in 1906, was keen to see what answers to the "natural monopoly" issue the British experience might provide. Stevenson's England gave no respite from the special burden of American destiny. The Americans "had saved the world," Winston Churchill told Stevenson—and the triumph had left them, like Atlas, with the globe on their shoulders. In the "ordeal of the mid century," all the questions converged on one: "how shall we [Americans] bear what Providence has assigned us?"[29]

In new-found eloquence and urgency, the rhetoric of a common footrace down the track of progress gave way to talk of exceptionalist gifts, exceptionalist burdens, an exceptionalist "American way of life," and an exceptionalist history all America's own. Historians and political scientists by the early 1950s were deep in studies working out this point.[30] The old comparative policy questions no longer seemed worth asking, so clear were their answers, so starkly different the cards providence had dealt out to the world's players. For most American progressives there were no longer social-political lessons to be learned abroad, or lags to be overcome. The shutters of self-referentiality closed down again as the Americans reconceived themselves as an exception, once more, in world history. The war that had brought Americans deep into European affairs left them, unexpectedly, all alone.

The unraveling of the North Atlantic progressive connection did not bring progressive politics to a halt. The political dynamics already in motion in 1940s America were powerful enough to go a long way further on their own. Between the eagerness of Roosevelt's opponents to shut down the vestiges of the New Deal, and the determination of labor and the progressive Democrats to extend them, there was energy enough in American social politics that the fading of broader, cross-national referents was not immediately noticed. Harry Truman went to the polls in 1948 pledged not only to a hard line vis-à-vis the Russians in Europe but also to a new lease on the New Deal's promises: expansion of Social Security, a New Deal–inspired program of national health insurance, a large-scale housing program, new public power projects, a higher minimum wage, permanent price supports for agriculture, rural electrification extension, and expanded labor bargaining rights. Into Lyndon Johnson's Great Society project and well beyond, these issues would continue to frame social-political debate.[31]

But for the most part, American progressives no longer talked openly of European analogues or connections. At the congressional hearings on housing legislation in the late 1940s, European references were thinned to the vanishing point. At the congressional hearings on medical insurance in 1949, progressive proponents refused to be pinned down in cross-national comparisons. The 1939 hearings on Social Security Act revisions had, in contrast, still been full of European references. J. Douglas Brown, chair of the administration's Advisory Council on Social Security, had filed with his House testimony not only a chart of the world's social insurance provisions but also a copy of the British insurance stamp book, which he hoped would be soon instituted in the United States. At the counterpart Social Security hearings of 1950, the only witness to lean heavily on the Atlantic connection was a disgruntled former Social Security administration employee, Marjorie Shearon, who claimed to have proof that the Roosevelt-Perkins plot to foist Social Security on the United States had first been hatched by a "socialist" cabal at the International Labor Office in Geneva.[32]

Shearon was only a newsletter writer with a particularly vivid imagination. But as the cold war came home in domestic American politics, it handed the keepers of the providential, uncontaminated American way a powerful advantage. When the Social Security Administration picked a sympathetic investigator to report on New Zealand health insurance in 1947, congressional conservatives raised the alarm at this endorsement of "the Moscow party line" on socialized medicine. The labor-progressive lobby for health insurance was attacked as a communist front. Senator Robert Taft, a Republican with no inconsiderable social-political ambitions of his own, charged the framers of the Full-Employment Bill in 1946 with taking their program straight from the Soviet constitution. To those fearful of the social powers of the state, the cold war added a tactical advantage of extraordinary sweep and power; it freighted talk of lags and deficiencies with heightened political danger.[33]

Not all postwar American progressives, of course, fell into exceptionalist step. Historically more international than the world of middle-class reform, the world of labor remained crisscrossed with transnational social-political connections in the postwar era. Cold war geopolitics pulled American labor unionists and their funders in government deep into European labor affairs, not only to replay the bluff and bluster of Samuel Gompers in 1918 and 1919 but also with less expected domestic consequences. The Reuther brothers were key players on the European scene, preaching the gospel of American productionism at every opportunity. "The Pied Piper of Hope," the British *Daily Herald* called Walter Reuther in 1957, on one of his annual trips abroad; he was the evangelist of "the American dream, the dawn of the era . . . of unprecedented abundance." In 1951, in one of the more curious turns of Marshall Plan politics, Victor Reuther helped funnel union funds into a pilot production plant to demonstrate American manufacturing and labor-relations techniques to the skeptical French. But the Reuthers were also key conduits of European-style social unionism, which, with its conscious affinities with social democratic politics abroad and its internal infrastructure of consumer and credit cooperatives, sports and recreation centers, education programs, and political ambitions, found a home, for the moment, in the CIO.[34]

The experts, too, renewed their international ties in the wake of the war. In the machinery of the new United Nations organizations, in the academic exchanges, in international gatherings of experts and policy specialists, ideas continued to be brokered across nation-state boundaries—international monetary policy being one of the most visible examples. The world after 1945 was intellectually smaller and much more tightly interconnected than the world of Ely's and Bryan's generation, access to its information was gained more quickly, and it was much easier to move around in. During flurries of interest in central European corporatist industrial planning, Swedish economic policy, or continental European land-planning techniques, the older dynamics of the Atlantic progressive connection would make a momentary reappearance on the American social-political scene. Even at the height of exceptionalist politics, more international social-political connections were sustained than the public theater of politics displayed.

But with Americans bestride the world and the fortunes of the European social democracies profoundly diminished, with the hazards of cold war politics weighing hard against employment of foreign examples, with a new exceptionalist literature growing fast in historical and political science circles, with the markets working miracles of abundance that seemed, for the moment, uniquely American, the transatlantic progressive connection's ability to shape the agendas of politics no longer had its old force. The key institutions of the North Atlantic progressive connection gave way with age. John Andrews's American Association for Labor Legislation and Abraham Epstein's American Association for Social Security had both closed up shop by the war's end, upon the death of their founders. Kellogg's *Survey* ceased publication in 1952. Mumford and Bauer continued to campaign for their old causes into the early 1950s, but the dominant language in postwar urban politics was that of New York City planning czar Robert Moses, who dismissed Mumford as "an outspoken revolutionary" and scorned foreign ideas "which don't belong here."[35]

The next progressive generation came to its task with none of the earlier cohorts' intense, reflexive feelings about Europe. The renewal of social politics in Europe in the late 1940s and 1950s, spinning off welfare states in a half dozen potentially exportable models, had only a fraction of the impact on American politics of the social-political experiments of the earlier era. When postwar social politics in the United States set off down its own track toward a set of welfare state provisions and compromises peculiar to it, there was no longer a ready, interconnected lobby of persons to raise those peculiarities for public debate, or to ask—outside the rhetorical polarities of an exceptionalist, expansive America and a "dying" (though never quite dead) Europe—where the divergences from other nations' precedents were wise and where they were not.

The North Atlantic progressive connection had had, to be sure, not a few overextended polarities of its own—and not a few illusions. From the 1870s forward, it had never been easy for Americans within that connection to convey their convictions and borrowed enthusiasms except in a language that ran hard toward exaggeration. Their simplifications were often naive and sometimes—as in the case of Germany admirers like Howe or Dawson in 1914—downright embarrassing. They had trafficked in national stereotypes as the only rhetorical tool they knew with which to wedge into their countrymen's consciousness an understanding that the American balance between markets and politics was not inevitable: that things were done differently, and better, elsewhere. The goods they picked up in the social-political bazaars in Paris and elsewhere were not flawless. Their Glasgow streetcars, their Irish creamery cooperatives, their Haussmannized Paris, their Letchworths, and their German ethical economics were never all that Atlantic-facing progressives cracked them up to be. All this, too, was in the nature of their work and, still more, in the deep, provincial resistance it encountered.

The historical importance of the transatlantic phase of American progressive politics lies not in the exaggerated polarities of its rhetoric but in its experienced connections. It marked a moment when, across the countervailing pull of nationhood, the world of capital seemed to many a world akin. For all the "un-American," "made in Prussia" furor that met their work, the Atlantic progressive travelers made other nations' social policy headline news. They sustained not only highly visible structures of international exchange but also a public debate that bound choices in American social politics with choices elsewhere. From one side of the Atlantic to the other, the dynamics of an interrelated social politics could be felt, connecting—always with rivalry and controversy but connecting nonetheless—what the nation-state political structures endeavored to set apart. Even in America, indeed especially in America, the phenomenon could be felt.

In Paris in 1900, the Americans in the North Atlantic progressive connection were still latecomers to a European-centered debate—by turn eager for entry and prideful of their separateness. A half century later, their efforts had done a great deal to transform the agenda of progressive politics in the United States. Strewn as their transatlantic bridges were with failures and unexpected transformations, a good deal had crossed over. Their expanded world of social-political referents and solutions made politics out of mere economic fate. It energized and framed the vocabulary of progressive reform. It infused the crisis politics of the 1930s. But by the end of the 1940s the era was over. Having saved the world, it would not thereafter be easy to imagine that there was still much to learn from it.

Notes · Acknowledgments · Index

Notes

Prologue

1. Ray Stannard Baker, *American Chronicle* (New York: Charles Scribner's Sons, 1945), p. 83.

2. Raymond Grew, "The Comparative Weakness of American History," *Journal of Interdisciplinary History* 16 (1985): 87–101. For a more extended discussion of these issues: Laurence Veysey, "The Autonomy of American History Reconsidered," *American Quarterly* 31 (1979): 455–477; Ian Tyrell, "American Exceptionalism in an Age of International History," *American Historical Review* 96 (1991): 1031–1072; David Thelen, "Of Audiences, Borderlands, and Comparisons: Toward the Internationalization of American History," *Journal of American History* 79 (1992): 432–462; Michael Kammen, "The Problem of American Exceptionalism: A Reconsideration," *American Quarterly* 45 (1993): 1–43; Michael Geyer and Charles Bright, "World History in a Global Age," *American Historical Review* 100 (1995): 1034–1060; Daniel T. Rodgers, "Exceptionalism," in *Imagined Histories*, ed. Anthony Molho and Gordon Wood (Princeton: Princeton University Press, 1998).

For exceptions to the exceptionalist reading of American social politics: Benjamin R. Beede, "Foreign Influences on American Progressivism," *Historian* 45 (1983): 529–549; Peter J. Coleman, *Progressivism and the World of Reform: New Zealand and the Origins of the American Welfare State* (Lawrence: University Press of Kansas, 1987); James T. Kloppenberg, *Uncertain Victory: Social Democracy and Progressivism in European and American Thought, 1870–1920* (New York: Oxford University Press, 1986); Arthur Mann, "British Social Thought and American Reformers of the Progressive Era," *Mississippi Valley Historical Review* 42 (1956): 672–692; Kenneth O. Morgan, "The Future at Work: Anglo-American Progressivism, 1890–

1917," in *Contrast and Connection: Bicentennial Essays in Anglo-American History*, ed. H. C. Allen and Roger Thompson (Athens: Ohio University Press, 1976); Gertrude A. Slichter, "European Backgrounds of American Reform, 1880–1915," Ph.D. diss., University of Illinois, 1960; Melvyn Stokes, "American Progressives and the European Left," *Journal of American Studies* 17 (1983): 5–28.

3. Raymond Grew, "The Case for Comparing Histories," *American Historical Review* 85 (1980): 763–778. Among the best examples: Gøsta Esping-Andersen, *The Three Worlds of Welfare Capitalism* (Princeton: Princeton University Press, 1990); Colleen A. Dunlavy, *Politics and Industrialization: Early Railroads in the United States and Prussia* (Princeton: Princeton University Press, 1994); Peter Flora and Arnold J. Heidenheimer, eds., *The Development of Welfare States in Europe and America* (New Brunswick, N.J.: Transaction Books, 1981); Tony Freyer, *Regulating Big Business: Antitrust in Great Britain and America, 1880–1990* (Cambridge: Cambridge University Press, 1992); Peter Gourevitch, *Politics in Hard Times: Comparative Responses to International Economic Crises* (Ithaca: Cornell University Press, 1986); Arthur J. Heidenheimer, Hugh Heclo, and Carolyn T. Adams, eds., *Comparative Public Policy: The Politics of Social Choice in America, Europe and Japan*, 3rd ed. (New York: St. Martin's Press, 1990); Christopher Leman, *The Collapse of Welfare Reform: Political Institutions, Policy, and the Poor in Canada and the United States* (Cambridge: MIT Press, 1980); Gary Marks, *Unions in Politics: Britain, Germany, and the United States in the Nineteenth and Early Twentieth Centuries* (Princeton: Princeton University Press, 1989); Stefan Berger, *The British Labour Party and the German Social Democrats, 1900–1931* (Oxford: Clarendon Press, 1994); John Myles, *Old Age in the Welfare State: The Political Economy of Public Pensions* (Boston: Little, Brown, 1984); Margaret Weir and Theda Skocpol, "State Structures and the Possibilities for 'Keynesian' Responses to the Great Depression in Sweden, Britain, and the United States," in *Bringing the State Back In*, ed. Peter B. Evans, Dietrich Rueschemeyer, and Theda Skocpol (Cambridge: Cambridge University Press, 1985).

4. Robert Kelley, *The Transatlantic Persuasion: The Liberal-Democratic Mind in the Age of Gladstone* (New York: Knopf, 1969), p. xiv.

5. For other aspects of the relationship between ideas, language, and politics: Daniel T. Rodgers, *Contested Truths: Keywords in American Politics since Independence* (1987; Cambridge: Harvard University Press, 1998) and *The Work Ethic in Industrial America, 1850–1920* (Chicago: University of Chicago Press, 1978).

6. John W. Kingdon, *Agendas, Alternatives, and Public Policies* (Boston: Little, Brown, 1984). In a similar, but more deeply historical vein: Hugh Heclo, *Modern Social Politics in Britain and Sweden: From Relief to Income Maintenance* (New Haven: Yale University Press, 1974).

1. Paris, 1900

1. John E. Findling and Kimberly D. Pelle, eds., *Historical Dictionary of World's Fairs and Expositions, 1851–1988* (Westport, Conn.: Greenwood, 1990), pp. 111; Henri Loyrette, *Gustave Eiffel* (New York: Rizzoli, 1985), pp. 111, 112, 115.

2. Richard D. Mandell, *Paris 1900: The Great World's Fair* (Toronto: University of Toronto Press, 1967).

3. *Letters of Henry Adams (1892–1918)*, ed. Worthington C. Ford (Boston: Houghton Mifflin, 1938), p. 301; Patrick Geddes, "The Closing Exposition—Paris, 1900," *Contemporary Review* 78 (1900): 653–668; Friedrich Naumann, "Pariser Briefe," in Naumann, *Werke* (Cologne: Westdeutscher Verlag, 1964), vol. 6, pp. 378–387; Jane Addams, *My Friend, Julia Lathrop* (1935; reprint ed., New York: Arno Press, 1974), pp. 145–146.

4. Geddes, "The Closing Exposition," p. 655; E. Cummings, "Social Economy at the Paris Exposition," *Quarterly Journal of Economics* 4 (1890): 212–221; Jules Helbronner, *Report on the Social Economy Section of the Universal International Exposition of 1889 at Paris* (Ottawa: Printed by Order of Parliament, 1890).

5. William F. Willoughby, "The Study of Practical Labor Problems in France," *Quarterly Journal of Economics* 13 (1899): 270–291; Leopold Katscher, "The French Museum of Social Science," *Gunton's Magazine* 23 (1902): 488–495; Sanford Elwitt, "Social Reform and Social Order in Late Nineteenth-Century France: The Musée Social and Its Friends," *French Historical Studies* 11 (1980): 431–451; Judith F. Stone, *The Search for Social Peace: Reform Legislation in France, 1890–1914* (Albany: State University of New York Press, 1985), pp. 52–54. The term *économie sociale* originated in the middle years of the nineteenth century as the catchword of Catholic reformers concerned about the disintegrating effects of industrial change on morals, institutions, and family authority; by the 1880s, however, it was diffusing rapidly in currency and meaning. Charles Gide, "The Economic Schools and the Teaching of Political Economy in France," *Political Science Quarterly* 5 (1890): 625–626.

6. *Exposition universelle internationale de 1900, Catalogue général officiel, Vol. 18, Groupe 16: Économie sociale, Hygiëne, Assistance publique* (Paris: Lemercier, n.d.).

7. *Exposition universelle internationale de 1900, Rapports du jury international. Sixième partie: Économie sociale* (Paris: Imprimerie Nationale, 1902), pp. 2–3; Stone, *Search for Social Peace*, p. 37.

8. The best descriptions of the social economy exhibit are to be found in Charles Gide's introduction to the *Rapports du jury* cited above; *L'Exposition de Paris (1900)* (Paris: Librairie Illustrée, n.d.), vol. 3, pp. 303–304; Nicholas P. Gilman, "Social Economics at the Paris Exposition," U.S. Department of Labor, *Bulletin* 6 (1901): 440–489; W. F. Willoughby, "Special Report on Social Economy, Hygiene, and Public Assistance," *Report of the Commissioner-General of the United States to the International Universal Exposition, Paris, 1900*, 55th Cong., 2nd sess., Senate Document 232 (1901).

9. *New York Times*, Sept. 2, 1900, p. 18; *International Exposition, Paris, 1900: Official Catalogue, Exhibition of the German Empire* (Berlin: Imperial Commission, 1900).

10. J. E. S. Hayward, "The Official Philosophy of the Third Republic: Léon Bourgeois and Solidarism," *International Review of Social History* 6 (1961): 19–48; Charles Gide, "L'Idée de solidarité en tant que programme économique," *Revue*

Internationale de Sociologie 1 (1893): 385–400; Léon Bourgeois, *Solidarité* (Paris: Armand Colin, 1896).

11. "The Exposition of 1900," *North American Review* 170 (1900): 475.

12. W. H. Tolman, "Social Economics in the Paris Exposition," *Outlook* 66 (1900): 311–318; Willoughby, "Special Report on Social Economy"; W. E. B. Du Bois, "The American Negro at Paris," *American Monthly Review of Reviews* 22 (1900): 575–577.

13. William H. Tolman, "The League for Social Service," *Arena* 21 (1899): 474; William H. Tolman, *Municipal Reform Movements in the United States* (New York: Fleming H. Revell, 1895); *Social Progress: A Year Book and Encyclopedia of Economic, Industrial, Social, and Religious Statistics*, ed. Josiah Strong, William H. Tolman, and William D. P. Bliss (New York: Baker and Taylor, 1904–1906); American Institute of Social Service, *Social Service: A Descriptive List of Lantern Slides Illustrating Movements for Social and Industrial Betterment* (New York: American Institute of Social Service, 1905).

14. *L'Exposition de Paris*, p. 3; *Rapports du jury*, p. 19–20.

15. Gilman, "Social Economics at the Paris Exposition," p. 465; Gerhard A. Ritter, *Social Welfare in Germany and Britain: Origins and Development*, trans. Kim Traynor (Leamington Spa: Berg, 1986).

16. Robert Hunter, *Socialists at Work* (New York: Macmillan, 1908), chap. 5; Gary P. Steenson, *"Not One Man! Not One Penny!" German Social Democracy, 1863–1914* (Pittsburgh: University of Pittsburgh Press, 1981); Émile Vandervelde, *Socialism versus the State*, trans. Charles H. Kerr (Chicago: Charles H. Kerr, 1919), pp. 124, 20.

17. Albert S. Lindemann, *A History of European Socialism* (New Haven: Yale University Press, 1983), chap. 4; Peter Gay, *The Dilemma of Democratic Socialism: Eduard Bernstein's Challenge to Marx* (New York: Columbia University Press, 1952). Jaurès is quoted in Hunter, *Socialists at Work*, p. 74.

18. William E. Forbaugh, "The Shaping of the American Labor Movement," *Harvard Law Review* 102 (1989): 1109–1257; Gerald Friedman, "Worker Militancy and Its Consequences: Political Responses to Labor Unrest in the United States, 1877–1914," *International Labor and Working-Class History* 40 (1991): 5–17; James E. Cronin and Peter Weiler, "Working-Class Interests and the Politics of Social Democratic Reform in Britain, 1900–1940," *ibid.* 40 (1991): 47–66.

19. Congrès international des oeuvres et institutions féminines, tenu au Palais de Congrès de l'Exposition universelle de 1900, *Compte rendu des travaux* (Paris: Charles Blot, 1902).

20. Seth Koven and Sonya Michel, "Womanly Duties: Maternalist Policies and the Origins of Welfare States in France, Germany, Great Britain, and the United States, 1880–1920," *American Historical Review* 95 (1990): 1076–1108; Linda Gordon, ed., *Women, the State, and Welfare* (Madison: University of Wisconsin Press, 1990); Kathleen D. McCarthy, ed., *Lady Bountiful Revisited: Women, Philanthropy, and Power* (New Brunswick, N.J.: Rutgers University Press, 1990); Gisela Bock and

Pat Thane, eds., *Maternity and Gender Policies: Women and the Rise of the European Welfare States, 1880s–1950s* (London: Routledge, 1991); Miriam Cohen and Michael Hanagan, eds., "The Politics of Gender and the Making of the Welfare State, 1900–1940," *Journal of Social History* 24 (1991), 469–484; Robyn Muncy, *Creating a Female Dominion in American Reform, 1890–1935* (New York: Oxford University Press, 1991); Ian Tyrrell, *Woman's World/Woman's Empire: The Women's Christian Temperance Union in International Perspective, 1880–1930* (Chapel Hill: University of North Carolina Press, 1991); Theda Skocpol, *Protecting Soldiers and Mothers: The Political Origins of Social Policy in the United States* (Cambridge: Harvard University Press, 1992); Seth Koven and Sonya Michel, eds., *Mothers of a New World: Maternalist Politics and the Origin of Welfare States* (New York: Routledge, 1993); Alisa Klaus, *Every Child a Lion: The Origins of Maternal and Infant Health Policy in the United States and France, 1890–1920* (Ithaca: Cornell University Press, 1993); Susan Pedersen, *Family, Dependence, and the Origins of the Welfare State: Britain and France, 1914–1945* (Cambridge: Cambridge University Press, 1993); Linda Gordon, *Pitied But Not Entitled: Single Mothers and the History of Welfare, 1850–1935* (New York: Free Press, 1994); Gwendolyn Mink, *The Wages of Motherhood: Inequality in the Welfare State, 1917–1942* (Ithaca: Cornell University Press, 1995); Molly Ladd-Taylor, *Mother-Work: Women, Child Welfare, and the State, 1890–1930* (Urbana: University of Illinois Press, 1994); Ulla Wikander, Alice Kessler-Harris, and Jane Lewis, eds., *Protecting Women: Labor Legislation in Europe, the United States, and Australia, 1880–1920* (Urbana: University of Illinois Press, 1995).

21. For a general overview of these debates: Asa Briggs, "The Welfare State in Historical Perspective," *Archives Européennes de Sociologie* 2 (1961): 221–258; Jill Quadagno, "Theories of the Welfare State," *Annual Reviews in Sociology* 13 (1987): 109–128; Gerhard A. Ritter, "Entstehung und Entwicklung des Socialstaates in Vergleichender Perspektive," *Historische Zeitschrift* 243 (1986): 1–90; Skocpol, *Protecting Soldiers and Mothers*, "Introduction"; and the essays in Francis G. Castles, ed., *The Comparative History of Public Policy* (Cambridge: Polity Press, 1989).

22. Among the best work in this vein: Robert Bremner, *From the Depths: The Discovery of Poverty in the United States* (New York: New York University Press, 1956); Roy Lubove, *The Struggle for Social Security, 1900–1935* (Cambridge: Harvard University Press, 1968); James T. Patterson, *America's Struggle against Poverty, 1900–1980* (Cambridge: Harvard University Press, 1981).

23. Harold L. Wilensky, *The Welfare State and Equality: Structural and Ideological Roots of Public Expenditures* (Berkeley: University of California Press, 1975); Peter Flora and Arnold J. Heidenheimer, eds., *The Development of Welfare States in Europe and America* (New Brunswick, N.J.: Transaction Books, 1981). For criticism: Douglas E. Ashford, "The Whig Interpretation of the Welfare State," *Journal of Policy History* 1 (1989): 24–43; Francis G. Castles and R. D. McKinlay, "Public Welfare Provision, Scandinavia, and the Sheer Futility of the Sociological Approach to Politics," *British Journal of Political Science* 9 (1979): 157–172; John H. Goldthorpe, "The End of Convergence: Corporatist and Dualist Tendencies in

Modern Western Societies," in *New Approaches to Economic Life*, ed. Bryan Roberts et al. (Manchester, England: Manchester University Press, 1985); Jens Alber, *Vom Armenhaus zum Wohlfahrtsstaat: Analysen zur Entwicklung der Sozialversicherung in Westeuropa* (Frankfurt: Campus, 1982).

24. Gøsta Esping-Andersen, *Politics against Markets: The Social Democratic Road to Power* (Princeton: Princeton University Press, 1985); J. Rogers Hollingsworth and Robert A. Hanneman, "Working-Class Power and the Political Economy of Western Capitalist Societies," *Comparative Social Research* 5 (1982): 61–80; Ira Katznelson, "Considerations on Social Democracy in the United States," *Comparative Politics* 11 (1978): 77–99; John Myles, *Old Age in the Welfare State: The Political Economy of Public Pensions* (Boston: Little, Brown, 1984); Frances Fox Piven and Richard A. Cloward, *The New Class War: Reagan's Attack on the Welfare State and Its Consequences*, rev. ed. (New York: Pantheon, 1985). On the limits of the "social democratic" interpretation of social policy: Henry Pelling, "The Working Class and the Origins of the Welfare State," in his *Popular Politics and Society in Late Victorian Britain* (London: Macmillan, 1968), and Pat Thane, "The Working Class and State 'Welfare' in Britain, 1880–1914," *Historical Journal* 27 (1984): 877–900.

25. Hans-Ulrich Wehler, *The German Empire, 1871–1918*, trans. Kim Traynor (Leamington Spa: Berg, 1985); J. Craig Jenkins and Barbara G. Brents, "Social Protest, Hegemonic Competition, and Social Reform: A Political Struggle Interpretation of the Origins of the American Welfare State," *American Sociological Review* 54 (1989): 891–909; Jill S. Quadagno, "Welfare Capitalism and the Social Security Act of 1935," *American Sociological Review* 49 (1984): 632–647; Colin Gordon, *New Deals: Business, Labor, and Politics in America, 1920–1935* (Cambridge: Cambridge University Press, 1994). For criticism and qualification: Thomas Nipperdey, "Wehlers 'Kaiserreich': Eine kritische Auseinandersetzung," *Geschichte und Gesellschaft* 1 (1975): 539–560; Allan Mitchell, "Bonapartism as a Model for Bismarckian Politics," *Journal of Modern History* 49 (1977): 181–209; Joseph Melling, "Welfare Capitalism and the Origins of Welfare States: British Industry, Workplace Welfare and Social Reform, c. 1870–1914," *Social History* 17 (1992): 453–478; Edward Berkowitz and Kim McQuaid, *Creating the Welfare State: The Political Economy of Twentieth-Century Reform*, 2nd ed. (New York: Praeger, 1988); Edwin Amenta and Sunita Parikh, "Capitalists Did Not Want the Social Security Act: A Critique of the 'Capitalist Dominance' Thesis," *American Sociological Review* 56 (1991): 124–129; and, more generally, Fred Block, *Revising State Theory: Essays in Politics and Postindustrialism* (Philadelphia: Temple University Press, 1987); Claus Offe, *Contradictions of the Welfare State* (Cambridge: MIT Press, 1984); Theda Skocpol, "Political Response to Capitalist Crisis: Neo-Marxist Theories of the State and the Case of the New Deal," *Politics and Society* 10 (1980): 155–201.

26. Peter B. Evans, Dietrich Rueschemeyer, and Theda Skocpol, eds., *Bringing the State Back In* (Cambridge: Cambridge University Press, 1985); Skocpol, *Protecting Soldiers and Mothers;* Theda Skocpol and John Ikenberry, "The Political Formation of the American Welfare State in Historical and Comparative Perspective,"

Comparative Social Research 6 (1983): 87–148; Weir and Skocpol, "State Structures and the Possibilities for 'Keynesian' Responses"; Christopher Leman, *The Collapse of Welfare Reform: Political Institutions, Policy, and the Poor in Canada and the United States* (Cambridge: MIT Press, 1980); Roger Davidson and Rodney Lowe, "Bureaucracy and Innovation in British Welfare Policy, 1870–1945," in *The Emergence of the Welfare State in Britain and Germany, 1850–1950*, ed. W. J. Mommsen (London: Croom Helm, 1981).

27. Heide Gerstenberger, "The Poor and the Respectable Worker: On the Introduction of Social Insurance in Germany," *Labour History* 48 (1985): 69–85; Eric Gorham, "The Ambiguous Practices of the Civilian Conservation Corps," *Social History* 17 (1992): 231–249; Linda Gordon, "What Does Welfare Regulate?" *Social Research* 55 (1988): 609–630; Barbara J. Nelson, "The Origins of the Two-Channel Welfare State: Workmen's Compensation and Mothers' Aid," in Gordon, ed., *Women, the State, and Welfare*. For criticism: Robert van Krieken, "The Poverty of Social Control: Explaining Power in the Historical Sociology of the Welfare State," *Sociological Review* 39 (1991): 1–25.

28. Hugh Heclo, *Modern Social Politics in Britain and Sweden: From Relief to Income Maintenance* (New Haven: Yale University Press, 1974), p. 305.

29. William W. Bremer, *Depression Winters: New York Social Workers and the New Deal* (Philadelphia: Temple University Press, 1984), pp. 8–10; John M. Glenn, et al., *The Russell Sage Foundation, 1907–1946* (New York: Russell Sage Foundation, 1947).

30. Kathryn Kish Sklar, "Historical Foundations of Women's Power in the Creation of the American Welfare State, 1830–1930," in *Mothers of a New World*, ed. Koven and Michel, p. 49; Henry Pelling, *The Labour Governments, 1945–51* (New York: St. Martin's Press, 1984), pp. 117–118.

31. *Schriften des Vereins für Sozialpolitik: Band 1–187, 1873–1932* (Munich: Duncker und Humblot, 1933).

32. Gøsta Esping-Andersen, *The Three Worlds of Welfare Capitalism* (Princeton: Princeton University Press, 1990), chap. 2.

33. William F. Willoughby Papers, William and Mary College, box 3, folders 18, 22; Francis G. Peabody, *The Social Museum as an Instrument of University Teaching* (Cambridge: Harvard University, 1908); Philip Boardman, *The Worlds of Patrick Geddes* (London: Routledge and Kegan Paul, 1978); Rüdiger vom Bruch, "Bürgerliche Sozialreform und Gewerkschaften im späten Kaiserreich: Die Gesellschaft für Soziale Reform (GSR) 1901–1914," *Internationale wissenschaftliche Korrespondenz zur Geschichte der deutschen Arbeiterbewegung* 15 (1979): 593; Howard Woodhead, "The First German Municipal Exposition," *American Journal of Sociology* 9 (1904): 433–458, 612–630, 812–830, and 10 (1904): 47–63; John R. Commons, *Myself: The Autobiography of John R. Commons* (1934; Madison: University of Wisconsin Press, 1963), pp. 129–130.

34. Jack L. Walker, "The Diffusion of Innovations among the American States," *American Political Science Review* 63 (1969): 880–899; David Collier and Richard E.

Messick, "Prerequisites versus Diffusion: Testing Alternative Explanations of Social Security Adoption," *American Political Science Review* 69 (1975): 1299–1315; Stein Kuhnle, "The Beginnings of the Nordic Welfare States: Similarities and Differences," *Acta Sociologica* 21 supplement (1978): 9–35; Stein Kuhnle, "International Modeling, States, and Statistics: Scandinavian Social Security Solutions in the 1890s," in *States, Social Knowledge, and the Origins of Modern Social Policies*, ed. Dietrich Rueschemeyer and Theda Skocpol (Princeton: Princeton University Press, 1996).

2. *The Atlantic World*

1. Quoted in Birdsey G. Northrop, *Education Abroad, and Other Papers* (New York: A. S. Barnes, 1873), p. 15.

2. J. Hector St. John de Crèvecoeur, *Letters from an American Farmer* (1782; reprint ed., Garden City: Dolphin Books, n.d.), pp. 46, 48. More generally: C. Vann Woodward, *The Old World's New World* (New York: Oxford University Press, 1991); Jack P. Greene, *The Intellectual Construction of America: Exceptionalism and Identity from 1492 to 1800* (Chapel Hill: University of North Carolina Press, 1993).

3. Francois Bédarida, *A Social History of England, 1851–1975* (London: Methuen, 1979), p. 30.

4. E. H. Kossmann, *The Low Countries, 1780–1940* (Oxford: Clarendon Press, 1978), p. 373; Klaus Misgeld et al., eds., *Creating Social Democracy: A Century of the Social Democratic Labor Party in Sweden* (University Park: Pennsylvania State University Press, 1992), p. xviii. More generally: Theodore S. Hamerow, *The Birth of a New Europe: State and Society in the Nineteenth Century* (Chapel Hill: University of North Carolina Press, 1983), chap. 12; Arno J. Mayer, *The Persistence of the Old Regime: Europe to the Great War* (New York: Pantheon, 1981).

5. William H. Dawson, *The Evolution of Modern Germany* (London: Unwin, 1908), pp. 435–436; Neal Blewett, "The Franchise in the United Kingdom, 1885–1918," *Past and Present* 32 (1965): 27–56; Bédarida, *Social History of England*, p. 130.

6. Henry Pelling, *America and the British Left: From Bright to Bevan* (New York: New York University Press, 1957), p. 18; H. M. Hyndman, "Lights and Shades of American Politics," *Fortnightly Review* 35 (1881): 340–357; James Bryce, *The American Commonwealth* (London: Macmillan, 1889), p. 475. See also David P. Crook, *American Democracy in English Politics, 1815–1850* (Oxford: Clarendon Press, 1965); John L. Snell, "The World of German Democracy, 1789–1914," *Historian* 31 (1969): 521–538; R. Laurence Moore, *European Socialists and the American Promised Land* (New York: Oxford University Press, 1970).

7. Gilbert Haven, *The Pilgrim's Wallet; or, Scraps of Travel Gathered in England, France, and Germany* (New York: Hurd and Houghton, 1866), pp. 13, 15, 261.

8. Ibid., pp. 283, 431, 477.

9. Theodore Child, *Summer Holidays: Travelling Notes in Europe* (New York: Harper and Brothers, 1889), p. 190; George H. Calvert, *Scenes and Thoughts in*

Europe. Second Series, new ed. (Boston: Little, Brown, 1863), p. 15; W. E. B. Du Bois, "Germany, 1894–1916," W. E. B. Du Bois Papers (microfilm ed.), University of Massachusetts at Amherst Library.

10. Northrop, *Education Abroad*, pp. 8, 7, 12.

11. Ray Stannard Baker, *Seen in Germany* (New York: McClure, Phillips, 1901), p. 7; Booker T. Washington, *The Man Farthest Down: A Record of Observation and Study in Europe* (Garden City, N.Y.: Doubleday, Page, 1912); Fred H. Matthews, *Quest for an American Sociology: Robert E. Park and the Chicago School* (Montreal: McGill–Queen's University Press, 1977), p. 66.

12. Samuel Gompers, *Labor in Europe and America* (New York: Harper and Brothers, 1910), pp. 286–287.

13. William F. Willoughby to Alice Willoughby, June 4, 1891, William F. Willoughby Papers, Swem Library, College of William and Mary; *The Letters of Lincoln Steffens*, ed. Ella Winter and Granville Hicks (New York: Harcourt, Brace, 1938), vol. 1, p. 7; E. A. Ross, "Turning Towards Nirvana," *Arena* 4 (1891): 736. Christopher Mulvey gives a brilliant description of the aesthetic mood in *Anglo-American Landscapes: A Study of Nineteenth-Century Anglo-American Travel Literature* (Cambridge: Cambridge University Press, 1983).

14. Frederick L. Olmsted, *Walks and Talks of an American Farmer in England* (1859; reprint ed., Ann Arbor: University of Michigan Press, 1967), pp. 58, 60, 69–70.

15. Peter J. Hamilton, *Rambles in Historic Lands* (New York: G. P. Putnam's Sons, 1893), p. 293; Allen F. Davis, *American Heroine: The Life and Legend of Jane Addams* (New York: Oxford University Press, 1973), p. 33; *The Making of a Feminist: Early Journals and Letters of M. Carey Thomas*, ed. Marjorie H. Dobkin (Kent, Ohio: Kent State University Press, 1979), p. 249.

16. John Frey, *An American Molder in Europe* (Cincinnati: n.p., 1910), pp. 63, 55–57; Mulvey, *Anglo-American Landscapes*, p. 111; Oliver Wendell Holmes, *Our Hundred Days in Europe* (Boston: Houghton Mifflin, 1888), p. 29; May Kenny, *Well Trodden Paths: A Diary* (Atlanta: Autocrat, 1896), pp. 198, 202, 205, 210.

17. Mulvey, *Anglo-American Landscapes*, p. 130; Lewis Henry Morgan, *Extracts from the Travel Journal of Lewis H. Morgan*, ed. Leslie A. White (Rochester, N.Y.: Rochester Historical Society, 1937), p. 350; Frey, *American Molder*, pp. 143–144, 148.

18. Quoted in Pelling, *America and the British Left*, p. 65.

19. Charles Booth to Antonia Mary Booth, September 1, 1904, Charles Booth Papers, University of London Library; Samuel Barnett, diary of a round-the-world tour, 1890–1891, July 3, 1890, Samuel Barnett Papers, Greater London Record Office and History Library; Ramsay MacDonald, draft of an unpublished book on America (PRO 30/69/116), chap. 5, pp. 5–6, Ramsay MacDonald Papers, Public Record Office, London, reproduced by permission of the executrix of the late Malcolm MacDonald; H. G. Wells, *The Future in America: A Search after Realities* (New York: Harper and Brothers, 1906), p. 61.

20. Arthur Shadwell, *Industrial Efficiency: A Comparative Study of Industrial Life in England, Germany, and America* (London: Longmans, Green, 1906), vol. 1, pp. 293, 299, 16; vol. 2, pp. 344, 451.

21. Barnett, diary, July 7, 1890; MacDonald, unpublished book on America, chap. 21, p. 8; John Burns, "American Perils," *Independent* 57 (1904): 1475.

22. David Landes, *Unbound Prometheus: Technological Change and Industrial Development in Western Europe, 1750 to the Present* (Cambridge: Cambridge University Press, 1969); E. J. Hobsbawm, *The Age of Capital, 1848–1875* (New York: Scribner's, 1975); Michael Ferber, *The Social Vision of William Blake* (Princeton: Princeton University Press, 1985), chap. 6. The figures in this paragraph are taken from Hamerow, *Birth of a New Europe*, p. 12; Chris Cook and John Paxton, *European Political Facts, 1848–1918* (New York: Facts on File, 1978), pp. 238–246; B. R. Mitchell, *European Historical Statistics, 1750–1975*, 2nd rev. ed. (New York: Facts on File, 1980), pp. 455–456; Derek H. Aldcroft, *The Development of British Industry and Foreign Competition, 1875–1914* (London: George Allen and Unwin, 1968), p. 121; and (for the United States) U.S. Bureau of the Census, *Historical Statistics of the United States, Colonial Times to 1970* (Washington, D.C., 1975).

23. Sidney Pollard, *Peaceful Conquest: The Industrialization of Europe, 1760–1970* (New York: Oxford University Press, 1981). On Glasgow: W. T. Ellis, *A Summer Jaunt of One Hundred Days in Europe* (Owensboro, Ky.: Inquirer Publishing Co., 1885), p. 34. On the English "great cities": Chris Cook and Brendan Keith, *British Historical Facts, 1830–1900* (London: Macmillan, 1975), pp. 234–236.

24. E. A. Wrigley, *Industrial Growth and Population Change: A Regional Study of the Coalfield Areas of North-West Europe in the Later Nineteenth Century* (Cambridge: Cambridge University Press, 1961).

25. Shadwell, *Industrial Efficiency*, vol. 1, chap. 2; Paul Göhre, *Three Months in a Workshop: A Practical Study* (London: Swan Sonnenschein, 1895).

26. Shadwell, *Industrial Efficiency*, vol. 1, pp. 256, 327; Samuel Barnett, diary, June 16, 1890; *The Letters of Sidney and Beatrice Webb*, ed. Norman MacKenzie (Cambridge: Cambridge University Press, 1978), vol. 2, p. 67.

27. U.S. Bureau of the Census, *Historical Statistics*, pp. 693–694; Cook and Paxton, *European Political Facts*, pp. 245–246; Hamerow, *Birth of a New Europe*, p. 12. On the "Americanization" scare: David E. Novack and Matthew Simon, "Commercial Responses to the American Export Invasion, 1871–1914: An Essay in Attitudinal History," *Explorations in Entrepreneurial History* 3 (1966): 121–147; William T. Stead, *The Americanization of the World; or, The Trend of the Twentieth Century* (London: Horace Markley, 1902), esp. pp. 342–380.

28. Andrew Lees, *Cities Perceived: Urban Society in European and American Thought, 1820–1940* (Manchester, England: Manchester University Press, 1985); Paul S. Boyer, *Urban Masses and Moral Order in America, 1820–1920* (Cambridge: Harvard University Press, 1978); H. J. Dyos and Michael Wolff, eds. *The Victorian City: Images and Realities* (London: Routledge and Kegan Paul, 1973).

29. Brian Ladd, *Urban Planning and Civic Order in Germany, 1860–1914* (Cam-

bridge: Harvard University Press, 1990), p. 14; R. D. Anderson, *France, 1870–1914: Politics and Society* (London: Routledge and Kegan Paul, 1977), p. 31; Peter Flora, ed., *State, Economy, and Society in Western Europe 1815–1975: A Data Handbook* (Frankfurt: Campus, 1987), vol. 2, pp. 279, 281, 266; U.S. Bureau of the Census, *Historical Statistics of the United States*, p. 11; Adna F. Weber, *The Growth of Cities in the Nineteenth Century* (Ithaca: Cornell University Press, 1899), pp. 39, 182. The *Millionenstädte* of 1890 were London, Paris, Berlin, Vienna, New York, Chicago, and Philadelphia.

30. Mitchell, *European Historical Statistics*, pp. 455–456.

31. Hamerow, *Birth of a New Europe*, chap. 2; Gøsta Esping-Andersen, *Politics against Markets: The Social-Democratic Road to Power* (Princeton: Princeton University Press, 1985), p. 49.

32. Edward R. Tannenbaum, *1900: The Generation before the Great War* (Garden City, N.Y.: Doubleday, 1976), p. 21; Richard Dennis, *English Industrial Cities of the Nineteenth Century: A Social Geography* (Cambridge: Cambridge University Press, 1984), p. 34; Elaine G. Spencer, *Management and Labor in Imperial Germany: Ruhr Industrialists as Employers, 1896–1914* (New Brunswick, N.J.: Rutgers University Press, 1984), p. 44; Pollard, *Peaceful Conquest*, p. 153; S. H. F. Hickey, *Workers in Imperial Germany: The Miners of the Ruhr* (Oxford: Clarendon Press, 1985), chap. 1. More generally: Dirk Hoerder, ed., *Labor Migration in the Atlantic Economies: The European and North American Working Classes during the Period of Industrialization* (Westport, Conn.: Greenwood, 1985); Dirk Hoerder and Horst Rössler, eds., *Distant Magnets: Expectations and Realities in the Immigrant Experience, 1840–1930* (New York: Holmes and Meier, 1993); Leslie Page Moch, *Moving Europeans: Migration in Western Europe since 1650* (Bloomington: Indiana University Press, 1992).

33. Thomas L. Haskell, *The Emergence of Professional Social Science: The American Social Science Association and the Nineteenth-Century Crisis of Authority* (Urbana: University of Illinois Press, 1977).

34. José Harris, *William Beveridge: A Biography* (Oxford: Clarendon Press, 1977), pp. 86–88; Frederic C. Howe, *The Confessions of a Reformer* (New York: Charles Scribner's Sons, 1925); Sanford Elwitt, *The Third Republic Defended: Bourgeois Reform in France, 1880–1914* (Baton Rouge: Louisiana State University Press, 1986); Willard Wolfe, *From Radicalism to Socialism: Men and Ideas in the Formation of Fabian Socialist Doctrines, 1881–1889* (New Haven: Yale University Press, 1975); Rüdiger vom Bruch, "Bürgerliche Sozialreform im deutschen Kaiserreich," in *Weder Kommunismus noch Kapitalismus: Bürgerliche Sozialreform in Deutschland vom Vormärz bis zur Ära Adenauer*, ed. Rüdiger vom Bruch (Munich: Beck, 1985).

35. James T. Kloppenberg, *Uncertain Victory: Social Democracy and Progressivism in European and American Thought, 1870–1920* (New York: Oxford University Press, 1986), p. 300; Daniel T. Rodgers, "In Search of Progressivism," *Reviews in American History* 10 (1982): 127 n. 1. The exception was France, where the term *progressiste*, ideologically up for grabs in the 1890s, ended up on the right in the party spectrum.

36. On the transatlantic dimensions of this mid-nineteenth-century political

faith: Robert Kelley, *The Transatlantic Persuasion: The Liberal-Democratic Mind in the Age of Gladstone* (New York: Knopf, 1969); David D. Hall, "The Victorian Connection," *American Quarterly* 27 (1975): 561–574.

37. Wells, *Future in America*, p. 248; Laurence Goldman, "The Social Science Association, 1857–1886: A Context for Mid-Victorian Liberalism," *English Historical Review* 101 (1986): 131.

38. Gerhard A. Ritter, *Social Welfare in Germany and Britain: Origins and Development* (Leamington Spa: Berg, 1986); Judith F. Stone, *The Search for Social Peace: Reform Legislation in France, 1890–1914* (Albany: State University of New York Press, 1985).

39. W. B. Sutch, *The Quest for Security in New Zealand* (Oxford: Oxford University Press, 1966); Francis G. Castles, *The Working Class and Welfare: Reflections on the Political Development of the Welfare State in Australia and New Zealand, 1890–1980* (Wellington, New Zealand: Allen and Unwin, 1985).

40. Peter J. Coleman, *Progressivism and the World of Reform: New Zealand and the Origins of the American Welfare State* (Lawrence: University Press of Kansas, 1987), p. 57; Henry D. Lloyd, *Newest England: Notes of a Democratic Traveller in New Zealand, with Some Australian Comparisons* (New York: Doubleday, Page, 1900), p. 1; *Letters of Sidney and Beatrice Webb*, vol. 2, p. 89.

41. Bentley B. Gilbert, *The Evolution of National Insurance in Great Britain: The Origins of the Welfare State* (London: Michael Joseph, 1966); J. R. Hay, *The Origins of the Liberal Welfare Reforms, 1906–1914* (London: Macmillan, 1975); Pat Thane, ed., *The Origins of British Social Policy* (London: Croom Helm, 1978); Stone, *Search for Social Peace*.

42. *The Letters of Theodore Roosevelt*, ed. Elting E. Morison (Cambridge: Harvard University Press, 1951–1954), vol. 7, pp. 398, 406; Walter Weyl, diary entry for Dec. 15, 1912, Walter Weyl Papers, Rutgers University; William Allen White, *The Autobiography of William Allen White* (New York: Macmillan, 1946), p. 410.

43. Henry Pelling, "The Knights of Labor in Britain, 1880–1901," *Economic History Review*, 2nd ser., 9 (1956): 313–331; Stefan Berger, *The British Labour Party and the German Social Democrats, 1900–1931* (Oxford: Clarendon Press, 1994); Cook and Paxton, *European Political Facts*, pp. 115–137; E. J. Hobsbawm, *The Age of Empire, 1875–1914* (New York: Vintage Books, 1989), p. 98.

44. Friedhelm Boll, "International Strike Waves: A Critical Assessment," in *The Development of Trade Unionism in Great Britain and Germany, 1880–1914*, ed. Wolfgang J. Mommsen and Hans-Gerhard Husung (London: George Allen and Unwin, 1985); Leopold Haimson and Charles Tilly, eds., *Strikes, Wars, and Revolutions in an International Perspective: Strike Waves in the Late Nineteenth and Early Twentieth Centuries* (Cambridge: Cambridge University Press, 1989).

45. Boll, "International Strike Waves," p. 84; George Sayers Bain and Robert Price, *Profiles of Union Growth: A Comparative Statistical Portrait of Eight Countries* (Oxford: Basil Blackwell, 1980), p. 88.

46. *Les congrès internationaux de 1681 à 1899: Liste complète* (Brussels: Union of

International Associations, 1960); *Les congrès internationaux de 1900 à 1919: Liste complète* (Brussels: Union of International Associations, 1964).

47. Jürgen Reulecke, "English Social Policy around the Middle of the Nineteenth Century as Seen by German Social Reformers," in *The Emergence of the Welfare State in Britain and Germany, 1850–1950*, ed. W. J. Mommsen (London: Croom Helm, 1981); Lujo Brentano, *Die Arbeitergilden der Gegenwart* (Leipzig: Duncker and Humblot, 1872); J. M. Baernreither, *English Associations of Working Men* (London: Swann Sonnenschein, 1893); Hans Eduard von Berlepsch-Valendas, *Die Gartenstadtbewegung in England: Ihre Entwicklung und ihr jetziger Stand* (Munich: Oldenbourg, 1911); Werner Picht, *Toynbee Hall and the English Settlement Movement* (London: G. Bell and Sons, 1914). For France: Léon Bourgeois, "L'Organisation internationale de la prévoyance sociale," in his *La politique de la prévoyance sociale*, vol. 2: *L'Action* (Paris: Bibliothèque Charpentier, 1919).

48. Günter Hollenberg, *Englisches Interesse am Kaiserreich: Die Attraktivität Preussen-Deutschlands für konservative und liberale Kreise in Grossbrittannien, 1860–1914* (Wiesbaden: Franz Steiner, 1974); J. R. Hay, "The British Business Community, Social Insurance, and the German Empire," in Mommsen, ed., *Emergence of the Welfare State;* Roy Hay, "Employers and Social Policy in Britain: The Evolution of Welfare Legislation, 1905–1914," *Social History* 4 (1977): 435–455; Henry S. Lunn, *Municipal Lessons from Southern Germany* (London: T. Fisher Unwin, 1908); Gainsborough Commission, *Life and Labour in Germany* (London: Simpkin, Marshall, Hamilton, Kent, 1906); W. J. Ashley, *The Progress of the German Working Classes in the Last Quarter of a Century* (London: Longmans, Green, 1904). Cf. Paul M. Kennedy, *The Rise of the Anglo-German Antagonism, 1860–1914* (London: George Allen and Unwin, 1980).

49. B. Seebohm Rowntree, *Land and Labour: Lessons from Belgium* (London: Macmillan, 1910); *Schriften des Vereins für Sozialpolitik*, 1873–1932; Bibliothèque du Musée Social, *Le Musée Social* (Paris, 1908); *Annales du Musée Social*, 1902–1914.

50. Keith Sinclair, *William Pember Reeves: New Zealand Fabian* (Oxford: Clarendon Press, 1965); James Sheehan, *The Career of Lujo Brentano: A Study of Liberalism and Social Reform in Imperial Germany* (Chicago: University of Chicago Press, 1966); Peter Gay, *The Dilemma of Democratic Socialism: Eduard Bernstein's Challenge to Marx* (New York: Columbia University Press, 1952); Hugo Lindemann, *Städteverwaltung und Munizipal-Sozialismus in England* (Stuttgart: Dick, 1897).

51. Hollenberg, *Englisches Interesse am Kaiserreich*, pp. 230–242. William H. Dawson's books on Germany: *German Socialism and Ferdinand Lassalle* (London: Swan Sonnenschein, 1888); *Bismarck and State Socialism: An Exposition of the Social and Economic Legislation of Germany since 1870* (London: Swan Sonnenschein, 1890); *Germany and the Germans* (London: Chapman and Hall, 1894); *German Life in Town and Country* (New York: G. P. Putnam's Sons, 1901); *Protection in Germany* (London: P. S. King and Sons, 1904); *The German Workman: A Study in National Efficiency* (New York: Charles Scribner's Sons, 1906); *The Evolution of Modern Germany* (London: Unwin, 1908); *The Vagrancy Problem: The Case for Measures of Re-*

straint for Tramps, Loafers, and Unemployables (London: P. S. King and Sons, 1910); *Social Insurance in Germany, 1883–1911* (London: Unwin, 1913); *Industrial Germany* (London: Collins, 1913); *Municipal Life and Government in Germany* (London: Longmans, Green, 1914).

52. James Leiby, *Carroll Wright and Labor Reform: The Origin of Labor Statistics* (Cambridge: Harvard University Press, 1960); U.S. Bureau of Labor, *Bulletin* (1895–1912) and U.S. Bureau of Labor Statistics, *Bulletin* (1912–). As an example of the early standards-of-living investigations: Lee Meriwether, *A Tramp Trip: How to See Europe on Fifty Cents a Day* (New York: Harper and Brothers, 1886).

53. Willoughby Papers, folders 18, 21, 22; William F. Willoughby, *Workingmen's Insurance* (New York: Thomas Y. Crowell, 1898); *John Graham Brooks: A Memorial* (Boston: n.p., 1940); *Elgin Ralston Lovell Gould* (privately printed, 1916); *Walter Weyl: An Appreciation* (privately printed, 1922).

54. Joseph O. Baylen, "A Victorian's 'Crusade' in Chicago, 1893–1894," *Journal of American History* 51 (1964): 418–434; William Dwight Porter Bliss, *Dictionary of American Biography*, ed. Allen Johnson and Dumas Malone (New York: Scribner's, 1928–1958), vol. 2, pp. 377–378; Charles R. Henderson, "The German Inner Mission," *American Journal of Sociology* 1 (1896): 581–595, 674–684, and 2 (1896): 58–73. More generally, Peter D'A. Jones, *The Christian Socialist Revival, 1877–1914: Religion, Class, and Social Conscience in Late-Victorian England* (Princeton: Princeton University Press, 1968).

Encouraged by the publication of *Rerum Novarum*, Leo XIII's papal encyclical on the "social question" of 1891, an international social Catholicism developed quickly as well. But in the United States, where anti-Catholic sentiment ran hard in the late nineteenth and early twentieth centuries, its influence never matched that of its Protestant rival.

55. Robert C. Reinders, "Toynbee Hall and the American Settlement Movement," *Social Service Review* 56 (1982): 39–54; Standish Meacham, *Toynbee Hall and Social Reform, 1880–1914: The Search for Community* (New Haven: Yale University Press, 1987); Visitors' Book, Toynbee Hall Papers, Greater London Record Office.

56. Lillian Wald, *Windows on Henry Street* (Boston: Little, Brown, 1934); Edith Abbott, "Grace Abbott and Hull House, 1908–21," *Social Service Review* 24 (1950): 380; Howard E. Wilson, *Mary McDowell, Neighbor* (Chicago: University of Chicago Press, 1928), p. 211; Graham Taylor, *Pioneering on Social Frontiers* (Chicago: University of Chicago Press, 1930), chap. 14.

57. Eleanor H. Woods, *Robert A. Woods, Champion of Democracy* (Boston: Houghton Mifflin, 1929), p. 36; Robert A. Woods, *English Social Movements* (New York: Charles Scribner's Sons, 1891), pp. 24, 265.

58. David A. Shannon, ed., *Beatrice Webb's American Diary, 1898* (Madison: University of Wisconsin Press, 1963). The work of the Fabian Society lecturers in the United States can be followed in the *Fabian News*.

59. *Letters of Sidney and Beatrice Webb*, vol. 2, p. 61; Herbert Burrows and John A. Hobson, eds., *William Clarke: A Collection of His Writings* (London: Swan Sonnen-

schein, 1908); Graham Wallas Papers, British Library of Political and Economic Science, London School of Economics; Thomas P. Jenkin, "The American Fabian Movement," *Western Political Quarterly* 1 (1948): 113–123; Mary Earhart, *Frances Willard: From Prayers to Politics* (Chicago: University of Chicago Press, 1944), p. 241. There are lists of American members and correspondents in the Fabian Society Papers, Nuffield College, Oxford University.

60. *Recueil des travaux du congrès d'assistance publique et de bienfaisance privée, 1900* (Paris, 1900), vol. 1, p. lxxxvii; Congrès international pour la protection légale des travailleurs, 1900, *Compte rendu analytique des sèances* (Paris, 1901); American Association for Labor Legislation, *Unemployment: A Problem of Industry* (New York, 1914), p. 5; International Housing Congress, *Bericht über den IX. Internationalen Wohnungskongress, Wien, 1910* (Vienna, 1911).

61. William Jennings Bryan, *The Old World and Its Ways* (St. Louis: Thompson, 1907).

62. Ray S. Baker, *Seen in Germany* (New York: McClure, Phillips, 1901), first published in part in *McClure's Magazine*, Sept. 1900–Jan. 1901; Charles Edward Russell, *The Uprising of the Many* (New York: Doubleday, Page, 1907), first published in *Everybody's Magazine*, Nov. 1905–Jan. 1907; Benjamin O. Flower, *Progressive Men, Women, and Movements of the Past Twenty-Five Years* (Boston: New Arena, 1914), chap. 14. The quotations are from Charles Edward Russell, "Socialistic Government of London," *Cosmopolitan* 40 (1906): 368; Charles Edward Russell, "Soldiers of the Common Good," *Everybody's Magazine* 16 (1907): 16.

63. Henry D. Lloyd: *Labor Copartnership: Notes of a Visit to Co-operative Workshops, Factories and Farms in Great Britain and Ireland* (New York: Harper and Brothers, 1898); *A Country without Strikes: A Visit to the Compulsory Abritration Court of New Zealand* (New York: Doubleday, Page, 1900); *Newest England: Notes of a Democratic Traveller in New Zealand, with some Australian Comparisons* (New York: Doubleday, Page, 1900); *A Sovereign People: A Study of Swiss Democracy* (New York: Doubleday, Page, 1907). The last, unfinished at Lloyd's death, was completed by his friend J. A. Hobson, the "new Liberal" British economist. The quoted passages are from Caro Lloyd, *Henry Demarest Lloyd, 1847–1903* (New York: G. P. Putnam's Sons, 1912), vol. 1, pp. 306–307, and vol. 2, pp. 181, 96.

64. Frederic C. Howe, *The Confessions of a Reformer* (1925; reprint ed., Kent, Ohio: Kent State University Press, 1988), p. 236.

65. National Civic Federation, Commission on Public Ownership and Operation, *Municipal and Private Operation of Public Utilities* (New York: National Civic Federation, 1907); U.S. Congress, House Committee on the Judiciary, *Employers' Liability and Workmen's Compensation*, Hearings on H.R. 20487, 62nd Cong., 2nd sess., 1913, pp. 61, 64; Ferdinand C. Schwedtman and James A. Emery, *Accident Prevention and Relief: An Investigation of the Subject in Europe with Special Attention to England and Germany together with Recommendations for Action in the United States* (New York: National Association of Manufacturers, 1911); Henry Bruere, Columbia University Oral History Collection; George M. Price, "A Government Tobacco

Factory in Vienna," *Survey* 31 (1914): 439–440; George M. Price, "Unearthing Cellar Bakeries in the Capitals of Europe," ibid., p. 615; George M. Price, "How Europe Protects Bleach Workers—How New York Does It," *Survey* 32 (1914): 58; George M. Price, "Impressions of Women's Work Abroad," ibid., p. 413; Raymond B. Fosdick, *European Police Systems* (New York: Century, 1915); Katharine Coman, *Unemployment Insurance: A Summary of European Systems* (New York: Progressive National Service, 1915); *Agricultural Cooperation and Rural Credit in Europe: Information and Evidence*, 63rd Cong., 1st sess., Senate Doc. 214 (1912); *The Autobiography of Lincoln Steffens* (New York: Literary Guild, 1931), pp. 648–653.

66. *Survey* 25 (1911): 880; *American City* 6 (1912): 611, 687; Institute of Educational Travel, "Civic and Social Tour in Europe" brochure, John Nolen Papers box 4, Cornell University. For an early, half-mocking account of the "sociological tour" of Europe, see William H. Allen, "In Poor Man's England," *Chautauquan* 41 (1905): 264–270.

67. "Losing Our Scorn for 'Abroad,'" *Nation* 99 (July 23, 1914): 94.

68. Elwood P. Lawrence, *Henry George in the British Isles* (East Lansing: Michigan State University Press, 1957); Karl Marx and Frederick Engels, *Letters to Americans, 1848–1895: A Selection* (New York: International Publishers, 1953), p. 164; Chuschichi Tsuzuki, *The Life of Eleanor Marx, 1855–1898: A Socialist Tragedy* (Oxford: Clarendon Press, 1967), chap. 6; Sidney Webb, "Henry George and Socialism," *Church Reformer* (Jan. 1889), copy in the Passfield Papers, British Library of Political and Economic Science, London School of Economics.

69. Fabian Society, *What to Read: A List of Books for Social Reformers* (London: Fabian Society, 1896); Fabian Society, *More Books to Read on Social and Economic Subjects*, Fabian Tract no. 129 (London: Fabian Society, 1906); Fabian Society, *What to Read on Social and Economic Subjects* (London: Fabian Society, 1920).

70. Kenneth Morgan, "The Future at Work: Anglo-American Progressivism, 1890–1917," in *Contrast and Connection: Bicentennial Essays in Anglo-American History*, ed. H. C. Allen and Roger Thompson (Athens: Ohio University Press, 1976), p. 251.

71. Alfred Zimmern, *The Greek Commonwealth: Politics and Economics in Fifth-Century Athens* (Oxford: Clarendon Press, 1911); Alfred Zimmern to his mother, Oct. 20, Oct. 24, Dec. 5, 1911, and to Elsie Zimmern, Jan. 10, 1912, Alfred Zimmern Papers, Bodleian Library, Oxford.

72. Alfred Zimmern to his father, Feb. 11, 1912, and to his mother, March 20, 1912, Zimmern Papers.

73. E. R. Pease in *Fabian News* 13 (July 1903): 27. Clynes is quoted in Pelling, *America and the British Left*, p. 91.

74. Lloyd, *Henry Demarest Lloyd*, vol. 2, p. 185.

75. Charles McCarthy, *The Wisconsin Idea* (New York: Macmillan, 1912), pp. 297–298; "The Government as Landlord," *Arena* 33 (1905): 325.

76. Charles R. Henderson, "To Help the Helpless Child: What the Nations of Europe are Doing for the Abandoned, the Orphaned, the Indigent, and the Anti-

Social," *World's Work* 24 (1912): 627; Brand Whitlock, "The City and Civilization," *Scribner's Magazine* 52 (1912): 625; *Survey* 29 (1912): 50.

77. Benjamin P. De Witt, *The Progressive Movement: A Non-Partisan, Comprehensive Discussion of Current Tendencies in American Politics* (1915; reprint ed., Seattle: University of Washington Press, 1968), p. 24; Paul U. Kellogg, "The Industrial Platform of the New Party," *Survey* 28 (1912): 670.

78. Walter Weyl, *The New Democracy: An Essay on Certain Political and Economic Tendencies in the United States* (New York: Macmillan, 1912), pp. 2, 20.

3. Twilight of Laissez-Faire

1. Richard T. Ely, "The American Economic Association, 1885–1909," *Publications of the American Economic Association*, 3rd ser., 11 (1910): 77; Richard T. Ely, *Ground under Our Feet: An Autobiography* (New York: Macmillan, 1938), pp. 145–146.

2. Even the best historians of late-nineteenth-century American social thought, intent on demonstrating the distinctively "American" aspects of their story, have left the German university connection acknowledged but largely unexplored. Dorothy Ross, *The Origins of American Social Science* (Cambridge: Cambridge University Press, 1991); Dorothy Ross, "Socialism and American Liberalism: Academic Social Thought in the 1880s," *Perspectives in American History* 11 (1977–1978): 5–79; Mary O. Furner, *Advocacy and Objectivity: A Crisis in the Professionalization of American Social Science, 1865–1905* (Lexington: University Press of Kentucky, 1975); Benjamin G. Rader, *The Academic Mind and Reform: The Influence of Richard T. Ely in American Life* (Lexington: University Press of Kentucky, 1966); Sidney Fine, *Laissez Faire and the General-Welfare State: A Study of Conflict in American Thought, 1865–1901* (Ann Arbor: University of Michigan Press, 1956), all model studies in their different ways, share this defect. For exceptions, see Jurgen Herbst, *The German Historical School in American Scholarship: A Study in the Transfer of Culture* (Ithaca: Cornell University Press, 1965) and, though it exaggerates its point, Joseph Dorfman, "The Role of the German Historical School in American Economic Thought," *American Economic Review* 45, no. 2 (1955): 17–28.

3. The debate is summarized in Arthur J. Taylor, *Laissez-Faire and State Intervention in Nineteenth-Century Britain* (London: Macmillan, 1972); Gordon H. Scott, "The Ideology of Laissez-Faire," in *The Classical Economists and Economic Policy*, ed. A. W. Coats (London: Methuen, 1971); John Roach, *Social Reform in England, 1780–1880* (New York: St. Martin's Press, 1978); P. W. J. Bartrip, "State Intervention in Mid-Nineteenth Century Britain: Fact or Fiction?" *Journal of British Studies* 23 (1983): 63–83.

4. Adam Smith, *An Inquiry into the Nature and Causes of the Wealth of Nations*, ed. Edward Cannan (Chicago: University of Chicago Press, 1976), vol. 2, p. 208; Harold Perkin, *The Origins of Modern English Society, 1780–1880* (London: Routledge and Kegan Paul, 1969), p. 186; John Graham Brooks, Scrapbook, 1884–1885,

John Graham Brooks Papers, Schlesinger Library, Radcliffe College, Harvard University.

5. Perkin, *Origins*, p. 324; Alfred Marshall, "The Old Generation of Economists and the New," in *Memorials of Alfred Marshall*, ed. A. C. Pigou (London: Macmillan, 1925), p. 296; John Stuart Mill, *Principles of Political Economy: The Collected Works of John Stuart Mill*, ed. F. E. L. Priestley (Toronto: University of Toronto Press, 1963–1991), vol. 3, p. 945.

6. Colleen A. Dunlavy, *Politics and Industrialization: Early Railroads in the United States and Prussia* (Princeton: Princeton University Press, 1994); Louis Hartz, *Economic Policy and Democratic Thought: Pennsylvania, 1776–1860* (Cambridge: Harvard University Press, 1948); Oscar and Mary F. Handlin, *Commonwealth: A Study of the Role of Government in the American Economy: Massachusetts, 1774–1861* (New York: New York University Press, 1947); Richard L. McCormick, "The Party Period and Public Policy: An Explanatory Hypothesis," *Journal of American History* 66 (1979): 279–298.

7. William J. Novak, *The People's Welfare: Law and Regulation in Nineteenth-Century America* (Chapel Hill: University of North Carolina Press, 1996). For attempts to describe the ensuing legislative balance: William R. Brock, *Investigation and Responsibility: Public Responsibility in the United States, 1865–1900* (Cambridge: Cambridge University Press, 1984); Morton Keller, *Affairs of State: Public Life in Late Nineteenth Century America* (Cambridge: Harvard University Press, 1977); James Bryce, *The American Commonwealth* (1888; reprint ed., New York: G. P. Putnam's Sons, 1959), esp. pt. 5, chap. 2: "Laissez Faire."

8. Ely, *Ground under Our Feet*, p. 35; Richard A. Swanson, "Edmund J. James, 1855–1925: A 'Conservative Progressive' in American Higher Education," Ph.D. diss., University of Illinois, 1966; Millicent Garrett Fawcett, *Political Economy for Beginners*, 4th ed. (London: Macmillan, 1876), p. v. On mid-nineteenth-century academic economics generally: Ross, *Origins of American Social Science*, chap. 2; Furner, *Advocacy and Objectivity*, chap. 2; Robert L. Church, "Economists as Experts: The Rise of an Academic Profession in the United States, 1879–1920," in *The University in Society*, ed. Lawrence Stone, vol. 2 (Princeton: Princeton University Press, 1974).

9. Albert Shaw, "The American State and the American Man," *Contemporary Review* 51 (1887): 696; Francis A. Walker, "Recent Progress of Political Economy in the United States," *Publications of the American Economic Association* 4 (1889): 254.

10. Charles Gide, "The Economic Schools and the Teaching of Political Economy in France," *Political Science Quarterly* 5 (1890): 603–635.

11. James J. Sheehan, *German History, 1770–1866* (Oxford: Clarendon Press, 1989), p. 734; Keith Tribe, *Governing Economy: The Reformation of German Economic Discourse, 1750–1840* (Cambridge: Cambridge University Press, 1988); Donald G. Rohr, *The Origins of Social Liberalism in Germany* (Chicago: University of Chicago Press, 1963); Gustav Schmoller, "Die Arbeiterfrage," *Preussische Jahrbücher* 14 (1864): 421.

12. Gustav Schmoller, "Rede zur Eröffnung der Besprechung über die sociale Frage in Eisenach, den 6. Oktober 1872," in his *Social- und Gewerbepolitik der Gegenwart: Reden und Aufsätze* (Leipzig: Duncker and Humblot, 1890), p. 1; Franz Boese, *Geschichte des Vereins für Sozialpolitik, 1872–1932* (Berlin: Duncker and Humblot, 1939), p. 248.

13. Heinrich von Treitschke, "Der Socialismus und seine Gönner," *Preussische Jahrbücher* 34 (1874): 248–301; Gustav Schmoller, "Ueber einige Grundfragen des Rechts und der Volkswirthschaft," *Jahrbücher für Nationalökonomie und Statistik* 23 (1874): 225–349, and 24 (1875): 81–119; Henry W. Farnam, "Antritts Vorlesung," Farnam Family Papers, Manuscripts and Archives, Yale University Library.

Kathedersozialisten is customarily translated as "socialists of the chair" or (more accurately) "lectern socialists," but "professorial socialists" comes much closer to the point.

14. Gide, "Economic Schools," pp. 628–634; Charles Gide, "L'École économique francaise dans se rapports avec l'École anglaise et l'École allemande," in *Die Entwicklung der deutschen Volkwirtschaftslehre im neunzehnten Jahrhundert: Gustav Schmoller zur siebenzigsten Wiederkehr seines Geburtstages* (Leipzig: Duncker and Humblot, 1908); Judith Stone, *The Search for Social Peace: Reform Legislation in France, 1890–1914* (Albany: State University of New York Press, 1985), chap. 2.

15. Gerard M. Koot, *English Historical Economics, 1870–1926: The Rise of Economic History and Neomercantalism* (Cambridge: Cambridge University Press, 1987); Ellen Frankel Paul, *Moral Revolution and Economic Science: The Demise of Laissez-Faire in Nineteenth-Century British Political Economy* (Westport, Conn.: Greenwood Press, 1979); A. W. Coats, "Sociological Aspects of British Economic Thought (c. 1880–1930)," *Journal of Political Economy* 75 (1967): 706–729; H. S. Foxwell, "The Economic Movement in England," *Quarterly Journal of Economics* 2 (1887): 84–103; W. Cunningham, "Why Had Roscher So Little Influence in England?" *Annals of the American Academy of Political and Social Science* 5 (1894): 317–334.

16. For example: E. L. Godkin, "Political Economy in Germany," *Nation* 19 (1872): 293–294; E. L. Godkin, "The New German Political Economy," ibid. 21 (1875): 161–162; J. M. Hart, "Political Economy in Germany," ibid., 295–296.

17. The phrase was Albert Shaw's in "The American State," p. 697.

18. Ely, *Ground under Our Feet*, pp. 36–63; Richard T. Ely et al., "Memorial to Former President Simon N. Patten," American Economic Association, *Papers and Proceedings of the 35th Annual Meeting* (1923), pp. 259, 276–277.

19. Ellen Nore, *Charles A. Beard: An Intellectual Biography* (Carbondale: Southern Illinois University Press, 1983), chap. 2; John Braeman, "Charles A. Beard: The English Experience," *Journal of American Studies* 15 (1989): 165–189; Charles A. Beard, "Ruskin and the Babble of Tongues," *New Republic* 87 (1936): 370–372; Lela B. Costin, *Two Sisters for Social Justice: A Biography of Grace and Edith Abbott* (Urbana: University of Illinois Press, 1983); Leo S. Rowe, "Instruction in French Universities," *Annals of the American Academy of Political and Social Science* 2 (1892): 62–85. Among those who spent a semester in Paris were E. R. A. Seligman, Frank J. Good-

now, Roland P. Falkner, John H. Gray, Emily Balch, Henry R. Seager, Leo S. Rowe, Walter Weyl, and Frank A. Fetter. But almost all of these sojourns were side affairs in a German-dominated course of study.

20. James Morgan Hart, *German Universities: A Narrative of Personal Experience* (New York: G. P. Putnam's Sons, 1874); Laurence R. Veysey, *The Emergence of the American University* (Chicago: University of Chicago Press, 1965), pp. 130–131; Carl Diehl, *Americans and German Scholarship, 1770–1870* (New Haven: Yale University Press, 1978). For estimates of enrolled American students: Johannes Conrad, *The German Universities of the Last Fifty Years* (Glasgow: David Bryce and Son, 1885), p. 41; George Weisz, *The Emergence of Modern Universities in France, 1863–1914* (Princeton: Princeton University Press, 1983), p. 262.

21. Jack C. Myles, "German Historicism and American Economics: A Study of the Influence of the German Historical School on Economic Thought," Ph.D. diss., Princeton University, 1956, pp. 98–118; Henry W. Farnam, "Deutsch-amerikanische Beziehungen in der Volkswirtschaftslehre," in *Die Entwicklung der deutschen Volkswirtschaftslehre.*

22. Samuel McCune Lindsay Papers, Columbia University; Mary Kingsbury Simkhovitch, *Neighborhood: My Story of Greenwich House* (New York: W. W. Norton, 1938), chap. 3; Mercedes M. Randall, *Improper Bostonian: Emily Greene Balch* (New York: Twayne, 1964), pp. 88–101.

23. Florence Kelley, *Notes of Sixty Years: The Autobiography of Florence Kelley*, ed. Kathryn Kish Sklar (Chicago: Charles H. Kerr, 1986), pp. 61–74; M. Carey Thomas, *The Making of a Feminist: Early Journals and Letters of M. Carey Thomas*, ed. Marjorie H. Dobkin (Kent, Ohio: Kent State University Press, 1979), chap. 2; Alice Hamilton, *Exploring the Dangerous Trades: The Autobiography of Alice Hamilton, M.D.* (Boston: Little, Brown, 1943), pp. 44–45, 47.

24. The original officers of the American Economic Association were Francis A. Walker, president; Henry C. Adams (Berlin, Heidelberg, 1878 to 1880), first vice president; Edmund J. James (Halle, Berlin, Leipzig, 1875 to 1877), second vice president; John B. Clark (Heidelberg, Leipzig, 1873 to 1875), third vice president; Richard T. Ely (Halle, Heidelberg, Berlin, 1877 to 1880), secretary; E. R. A. Seligman (Berlin, Heidelberg, Paris, 1879 to 1881), treasurer. The responses to Farnam's poll are collected in folder 3239, box 248, Farnam Family Papers, (hereinafter referred to as Farnam Survey).

25. Richard T. Ely, "American Economic Association," p. 68; Thomas, *Making of a Feminist*, chap. 2.

26. W. E. B. Du Bois to [illegible], Feb. 23, 1894, W. E. B. Du Bois Papers (microfilm ed.), University of Massachusetts at Amherst Library; W. E. B. Du Bois, *The Autobiography of W. E. B. Du Bois: A Soliloquy on Viewing My Life from the Last Decade of Its First Century* (New York: International Publishers, 1968), chap. 10; Samuel M. Lindsay to his parents, 1889 to 1894, Lindsay Papers.

27. *The Letters of Lincoln Steffens*, ed. Ella Winter and Granville Hicks (New York: Harcourt, Brace, 1938), vol. 1, p. 9.

28. Neil Coughlan, *Young John Dewey: An Essay in American Intellectual History* (Chicago: University of Chicago Press, 1975), pp. 124–130; Garrett Droppers in the Farnam Survey.

29. Henry C. Adams to his mother, Dec. 1, 1878, Henry Carter Adams Papers, Michigan Historical Collections, Bentley Historical Library, University of Michigan; Mary Kingsbury Simkhovitch, *Neighborhood*, chap. 3; Samuel M. Lindsay to his parents, Nov. 1, 1892, Lindsay Papers; *The Correspondence of W. E. B. Du Bois*, ed. Herbert Aptheker (Amherst: University of Massachusetts Press, 1973), vol. 1, p. 23; Kelley, *Autobiography*, pp. 61–77.

30. W. E. B. Du Bois, "The Present Condition of Germany" [c. 1893], unpublished manuscript in the Du Bois Papers, pp. 8, 17.

31. Fritz Ringer, *The Decline of the German Mandarins: The German Academic Community, 1890–1933* (Cambridge: Harvard University Press, 1969).

32. Myles, "German Historicism and American Economics," pp. 112–118; Henry W. Farnam, "Summary" of questionnaire results, Farnam Survey. Johannes Conrad at Halle taught almost as many American students, but "if the truth must be said," Vladimir Simkhovitch remembered, "I don't believe that Conrad ever influenced anybody's thought." Simkhovitch in the Farnam Survey.

33. Richard T. Ely, *Hard Times: The Way In and the Way Out* (New York: Macmillan, 1931), p. 111; Adolph Wagner, "Ueber englische und deutsche Nationalökonomie," *Preussische Jahrbücher* 73 (1893): 414. On Wagner: Kenneth D. Barkin, "Conflict and Concord in Wilhelmian Social Thought," *Central European History* 5 (1972): 55–71; Kenneth D. Barkin, *The Controversy over German Industrialization, 1890–1902* (Chicago: University of Chicago Press, 1970), chap. 4; and, most essentially, Heinrich Rubner, ed., *Adolph Wagner: Briefe, Dokumente, Augenzeugenberichte, 1851–1917* (Berlin: Duncker and Humblot, 1978).

34. Rubner, *Adolph Wagner*, pp. 91, 188–119; Adolph Wagner, *Rede über die sociale Frage* (Berlin: Wiegaandt and Grieben, 1872), p. 4. On the socialists' reciprocal interest in Wagner's ideas: Vernon L. Lidtke, "German Social Democracy and German State Socialism, 1876–1884," *International Review of Social History* 9 (1964): 202–225.

35. Rubner, *Adolph Wagner*, p. 120; Wagner, *Rede über die sociale Frage; Economic Journal* 26 (1916): 131; Garrett Droppers in the Farnam Survey.

36. Adolph Wagner, "Finanzwissenschaft und Staatsocialismus," *Zeitschrift für die gesamte Staatswissenschaft* 43 (1887): 37–122; Adolph Wagner, "The Rights and Wrongs of Socialism," *Fortnightly Review* 81 (1907): 682–694; William H. Dawson, *Bismarck and State Socialism: An Exposition of the Social and Economic Legislation of Germany since 1870* (1890; reprint ed., New York: Fertig, 1973), chap. 1; Wagner, *Rede über die sociale Frage*, pp. 4–5.

37. Rubner, *Adolph Wagner*, p. 172; Adolph Wagner, *Die Kartellierung der Gross-*

industrie und ihr Einfluss auf die Arbeiter (Essen: Christlichen Gerwerkschaftskartells Essen, 1906).

38. Asher, "Professors as Propagandists"; M. Epstein, "Gustave Schmoller," *Economic Journal* 27 (1917): 435–438. The *Jahrbuch für Gesetzgebung, Verwaltung und Volkswirtschaft im Deutschen Reich*, whose editorship Schmoller assumed in 1881, had been rebaptized as *Schmollers Jahrbuch* by 1913.

39. Henry Rogers Seager, "Economics at Berlin and Vienna," *Journal of Political Economy* 1 (1893): 236–262. See also Simkhovitch in the Farnam Survey; F. W. Taussig, "Schmoller on Protection and Free Trade," *Quarterly Journal of Economics* 19 (1905): 501–511.

40. Rüdiger vom Bruch, "Bürgerliche Sozialreform im deutschen Kaiserreich," in *Weder Kommunismus noch Kapitalismus: Bürgerliche Sozialreform in Deutschland vom Vormärz bis zur Ära Adenauer*, ed. Rüdiger vom Bruch (Munich: Beck, 1985), p. 85; Rüdiger vom Bruch, "Bürgerliche Sozialreform und Gewerkschaften in späten deutschen Kaiserreich: Die Gesellschaft für Soziale Reform (GSR) 1901–1914," *IWK (Internationale wissenschaftliche Korrespondenz zur Geschichte der deutschen Arbeiterbewegung)* 15 (1979): 588–589.

41. Vom Bruch, "Bürgerliche Sozialreform," pp. 72–82, 122–130; Dieter Lindenlaub, *Richtungskämpfe im Verein für Sozialpolitik. Vierteljahrschrift für Social- und Wirtschaftsgeschichte*, Beihefte 52–53 (Wiesbaden, 1967). For contemporary accounts of the Verein für Sozialpolitik: Gustav Cohn, "The History and Present State of Political Economy in Germany," *Fortnightly Review* 20 (1873): 337–350; Eugen von Philippovich, "The Verein für Socialpolitik," *Quarterly Journal of Economics* 5 (1891): 220–237; Lujo Brentano, *Mein Leben im Kampf um die soziale Entwicklung Deutschlands* (Jena: Eugen Diederich, 1931).

42. Boese, *Geschichte des Vereins für Sozialpolitik*, p. 241; "Vacation Course of the Verein für Social Politik," *Annals of the American Academy of Political and Social Science* 7 (1896): 69–73; *Schriften des Vereins für Sozialpolitik* (1873–1932).

43. Gustav Schmoller, "Die sociale Frage und der preussische Staat," in his *Social- und Gewerbepolitik der Gegenwart*, p. 62; Schmoller, "Rede zur Eröffnung der Besprechung über die sociale Frage," ibid., p. 9; Gustav Schmoller, "Das Verhältnis der Kartelle zum Staate," *Jahrbuch für Gesetzgebung, Verwaltung und Volkswirtschaft im Deutschen Reich* 29 (1905): 1550–1597. Cf. Jane Caplan, "'The Imaginary Universality of Particular Interests': The 'Tradition' of the Civil Service in German History," *Social History* 4 (1979): 299–317.

44. E. Benjamin Andrews and Emily Balch in the Farnam Survey; Edmund J. James, "The State as an Economic Factor," *Science* 7 (1886): 488; Edmund J. James, "State Interference," *Chautauquan* 8 (1888): 534–536. Even Arthur Hadley, the most orthodox of the German-trained generation, was moved to write home that there were "more sides to some of these questions than Billy [William Graham] Sumner would have us believe." Morris Hadley, *Arthur Twining Hadley* (New Haven: Yale University Press, 1948), p. 32.

45. Franklin H. Dixon in the Farnam Survey. Schmoller himself thought that

only by reinstituting monarchy could the United States stave off class rule, first by the propertied, then the propertiless. Lindenlaub, *Richtungskämpfe im Verein für Sozialpolitik*, p. 243n.

46. W. E. B. Du Bois, "Some Impressions of Europe" [c. 1894], p. 9, Du Bois Papers; Samuel M. Lindsay to his parents, July 12, 1891, Lindsay Papers; Richard T. Ely, "Administration of the City of Berlin," *Nation* 34 (March 23, 1882): 246.

47. "Feisei" [Edmund J. James], "Prince Bismarck," *The American* (Philadelphia), Aug. 16, 1884, pp. 295–296; E. R. A. Seligman to his parents, Oct. 3, 1879, E. R. A. Seligman Papers, Rare Book and Manuscript Library, Columbia University; Richard T. Ely, "Bismarck's Plan for Insuring German Laborers," *International Review* 12 (1882): 504–520; John H. Gray, "The German Act against Socialism," *Quarterly Journal of Economics* 4 (1890): 324. James's authorship of "Prince Bismarck" is identified in the *Annals of American Political and Social Science* 7 (1896): 84.

48. Mary Kingsbury Simkhovitch, *Neighborhood*, p. 52; Henry C. Adams, "Shall We Muzzle the Anarchists?" *Forum* 1 (1886): 453.

49. Joseph Dorfman, "Introduction" to Henry C. Adams, *The Relation of the State to Industrial Action and Economics and Jurisprudence: Two Essays* (reprint ed., New York: Columbia University Press, 1954); Ross, "Socialism and American Liberalism"; A. W. Coats, "Henry Carter Adams: A Case Study in the Emergence of the Social Sciences in the United States, 1850–1900," *Journal of American Studies* 2 (1968): 177–197.

50. Henry C. Adams, Berlin Diary, 1878–1879, pp. 9, 15, 25–26, Adams Papers.

51. Simon Patten, "The Reconstruction of Economic Theory," *Annals of the American Academy of Social and Political Science* 44 supplement (1912): 1; Henry C. Adams, Berlin Diary, 1878–1879, pp. 11–12.

52. Rader, *Academic Mind and Reform*, p. 30; Richard T. Ely, "On Methods of Teaching Political Economy," in *Methods of Teaching History*, ed. G. Stanley Hall, 2nd ed. (Boston: Ginn, Heath, 1885); Richard T. Ely, "Political Economy in Germany in 1882," *Johns Hopkins University Circulars* 3 (1882): 28; Henry C. Adams, *Outline of Lectures upon Political Economy* (Baltimore: n.p., 1881).

53. Rader, *Academic Mind and Reform*, p. 29; Marvin Gettleman, ed., *The Johns Hopkins University Seminary of History and Politics, 1877–1912* (New York: Garland, 1987–), vol. 1.

54. Albion Small, "Some Contributions to the History of Sociology," *American Journal of Sociology* 30 (1924): 303; Richard T. Ely, "The Past and the Present of Political Economy," *Johns Hopkins University Studies in Historical and Political Science* 2 (1884): 202.

55. Herbert B. Adams, "University Extension in America," *Forum* 11 (1891): 510–523; Richard T. Ely, *French and German Socialism in Modern Times* (New York: Harper and Brothers, 1883); Richard T. Ely, *Recent American Socialism* (Baltimore: Johns Hopkins University, 1885); Richard T. Ely, *The Labor Movement in America* (New York: Thomas Y. Crowell, 1886); Richard T. Ely, "Socialism," *Andover Review* 5 (1886): 156; Richard T. Ely, "Address before the Annual Meeting of the American

Federation of Labor," *Christian Union* 37 (Feb. 9, 1888): 170–171; Edmund J. James, "Socialists and Anarchists in the United States," *Our Day* 1 (1888): 81–94; George E. McNeill, ed., *The Labor Movement: The Problem of To-Day* (1887; reprint ed., New York: A. M. Kelley, 1971), chaps. 1–3; Henry C. Adams, "The 'Labor Problem,'" *Scientific American* 22 (1886): 8862.

56. E. R. A. Seligman, "Owen and the Christian Socialists," *Political Science Quarterly* 1 (1886): 206–249; Richard T. Ely, "Christian Socialism in England," *Christian Union* 31 (May 28, 1885): 7–8, (June 4, 1885): 7–8, and (June 11, 1885): 7–8; Ely, *French and German Socialism*, chap. 16. On Seligman, see his autobiographical sketch: E. R. A. Seligman, "Edwin R. Seligman," in *Die Volkswirtschaftslehre der Gegenwart im Selbsdarstellungen*, ed. Felix Meiner (Leipzig: F. Meiner, 1929), vol. 2, pp. 117–160.

57. Ross, "Socialism and American Liberalism," pp. 40–41.

58. Samuel A. Barnett, "Practicable Socialism," *Nineteenth Century* 13 (1883): 554–60; Donald Read, *England, 1868–1914: The Age of Urban Democracy* (London: Longman, 1979), pp. 302–303.

59. Ely, "Past and Present of Political Economy," p. 201n; Seligman, "Owen and the Christian Socialists," p. 207. Cf. Ross, "Socialism and American Liberalism."

60. Ely, "Past and Present of Political Economy," p. 191n; Ely, *Recent American Socialism*, p. 73; Edmund J. James, "The State as an Economic Factor," *Science* 7 (1886): 485; Henry C. Adams, "Economics and Jurisprudence," *Science* 8 (July 2, 1886): 16; Richard T. Ely, *Problems of To-Day: A Discussion of Protective Tariffs, Taxation, and Monopolies* (new ed., New York: Thomas Y. Crowell, 1890), p. 233.

61. For example: Richard T. Ely, "Land, Labor and Taxation," *Independent* 39 (Dec. 1, 1887–Jan. 5, 1888).

62. "The American Economic Association, 1885–1909," *Publications of the American Economic Association*, 3rd ser., 11 (1910): 50–51, 107–111; "Memorial to Simon N. Patten," *American Economic Review* 13 supplement (1923): 260–261.

63. Richard T. Ely, "Report of the Organization of the American Economic Association," *Publications of the American Economic Association* 1 (1886): 1–32.

64. Joseph Dorfman, "The Seligman Correspondence," *Political Science Quarterly* 56 (1941): 281; Richard T. Ely, "The American Economic Association, 1885–1909," *Publications of the American Economic Association*, 3rd ser., 11 (1910): 71–73; ibid. 3 (1888): 222–223. On the AEA's eagerness for sympathetic lay members: Richard T. Ely, "The American Economic Association," *Independent* 39 (1887): 681; Church, "Economists as Experts," p. 591.

65. E. R. A. Seligman, "Changes in the Tenets of Political Economy with Time," *Science* 7 (1886): 375–381; E. J. James, "The State as an Economic Factor," ibid., pp. 485–488; Richard T. Ely, "Ethics and Economics," ibid., pp. 529–533 (emphasis added); Henry C. Adams, "Economics and Jurisprudence," ibid. 8 (1886): 15–19; Richmond Mayo Smith, "Methods of Investigation in Political Economy," ibid., pp. 80–87.

66. Arthur T. Hadley, "Economic Laws and Methods," ibid., pp. 46–48.

67. William E. Barns, ed., *The Labor Problem: Plain Questions and Practical Answers* (New York: Harper and Brothers, 1886), p. 62; Adams, "Labor Problem," p. 8861; E. J. James, "Recent Land Legislation in England," *Science* 6 (1885): 455–456; Seligman, "Changes in the Tenets of Political Economy," p. 382.

68. James B. Angell to Henry C. Adams, March 26, 1887, Adams Papers.

69. Dorfman, "Introduction" to Adams, *Relation of the State of Industrial Action*, p. 16; James B. Angell to Henry C. Adams, March 19, 1886, and Henry C. Adams to James B. Angell, March 25, 1886, Adams Papers.

70. The incident is described in Furner, *Advocacy and Objectivity*, pp. 127–142, who emphasizes the effects of the anarchist scare in May 1886, and Dorfman, "Introduction." Adams's speech and Thurston's response were published in the *Scientific American Supplement* 22 (1886): 8861–8863, 8877–8880.

71. For the Cornell trustees: C. H. Hull to Henry C. Adams, Sept. 19, 1886, Adams Papers. Adams's letter of retraction to Angell is reprinted in Dorfman, "Introduction," pp. 37–42.

72. Furner, *Advocacy and Objectivity;* Steven A. Sass, *The Pragmatic Imagination: A History of the Wharton School, 1881–1981* (Philadelphia: University of Pennsylvania Press, 1982), p. 85; *Publications of the American Economic Association* 2 (1887): 228–295, 495–581, and 3 (1888): 44–46, 54–56.

73. Henry C. Adams, *Principles That Should Control the Interference of the States in Industries: A Paper Read before the Constitution Club of the City of New York* (New York, 1886). A revised version was published as Henry C. Adams, "Relation of the State to Industrial Action," *Publications of the American Economic Association* 1 (1887): 465–549.

74. "Modern Industrial Organization and Its Dangers," *Independent* 38 (1886): 1109; Adams, "Relation of the State to Industrial Action," pp. 540–549. The passage was not in Adams's original paper.

75. E. R. A. Seligman, review of Adams, "Relation of the State to Industrial Action," in *Political Science Quarterly* 2 (1887): 353; Richard T. Ely, "Social Studies, Second Series," *Harper's New Monthly Magazine* 74 (1887): 970–977, and 75 (1887): 71–79, 259–266; Richard T. Ely, "Natural Monopolies and Local Taxation," in Ely, *Problems of To-day;* Richard T. Ely, "A Program of Labor Reform," *Century* 39 (1890): 938–951; Richard T. Ely, *An Introduction to Political Economy* (New York: Chautauqua Press, 1889), p. 243; Edmund J. James, "The Relation of the Modern Municipality to the Gas Supply," *Publications of the American Economic Association* 1 (1886), nos. 2–3. For the shift in Ely's thought, compare Richard T. Ely, "Social Studies," *Harper's New Monthly Magazine* 73 (1886): 250–257, 450–457, 571–578.

76. Sass, *Pragmatic Imagination*, pp. 75–77; *Annals of the American Academy of Political and Social Science* (1890–). In 1890, when its German roots were most pronounced, the opening two numbers of the *Annals* listed every political-economy and public-law course offered the preceding year in the German, Austrian, and Italian universities.

77. Emory R. Johnson, *Life of a University Professor: An Autobiography* (Philadel-

phia: n.p., 1943); Sass, *Pragmatic Imagination*, p. 72; Adna F. Weber and B. H. Meyer in the Farnam Survey; B. H. Meyer, "The Administration of Prussian Railroads," *Arena* 10 (1897): 389–343; B. H. Meyer, "Government Regulation of Railway Rates," *Journal of Political Economy* 14 (1906): 86–106; Frederic C. Howe, *Wisconsin: An Experiment in Democracy* (New York: Charles Scribner's Sons, 1912), esp. chap. 3. See, more generally, Church, "Economists as Experts."

78. E. R. A. Seligman, "The Theory of Progressive Taxation," *Publications of the American Economic Association* 8 (1893): 52–54; Frank L. Tolman, "The Study of Sociology in Institutions of Learning in the United States," *American Journal of Sociology* 8 (1902–1903): 85–121, 251–272, 531–558; Rader, *Academic Mind and Reform.*

79. Roger Davidson and Rodney Lowe, "Bureaucracy and Innovation in British Welfare Policy, 1870–1945," in *The Emergence of the Welfare State in Britain and Germany, 1850–1950*, ed. W. J. Mommsen (London: Croom, Helm, 1981); Mary O. Furner and Barry Supple, eds., *The State and Economic Knowledge: The American and British Experiences* (Cambridge: Cambridge University Press, 1990).

80. Lindenlaub, *Richtungskämpfe im Verein für Sozialpolitik*, p. 142; Wolfgang J. Mommsen, *Max Weber and German Politics, 1890–1920* (Chicago: University of Chicago Press, 1984), p. 76; and, more generally, Dietrich Rueschemeyer and Theda Skocpol, eds., *States, Social Knowledge and the Origins of Modern Social Policies* (Princeton: Princeton University Press, 1996).

81. U.S. Congress, Senate Committee on Education and Labor, *Report upon the Relations between Labor and Capital* (Washington, D.C., 1885); U.S. Industrial Commission, *Reports* (Washington, D.C., 1900–1902); U.S. Commission on Industrial Relations, *Final Report* (Washington, D.C., 1915); William J. Barber, ed., *Breaking the Academic Mould: Economists and American Higher Learning in the Nineteenth Century* (Middletown, Conn.: Wesleyan University Press, 1988), pp. 335–336; Rader, *Academic Mind and Reform*, p. 181.

82. A. F. Weber, "American Economists of To-day," *New England Magazine*, n.s. 21 (1899): 261.

4. *The Self-Owned City*

1. Friedrich Engels, *The Condition of the Working Class in England* (1892; Chicago: Academy Chicago, 1984), p. 58. On the city in progressive imaginations: Gareth Stedman Jones, *Outcast London: A Study in the Relationship between Classes in Victorian Society* (Oxford: Clarendon Press, 1971); Paul Boyer, *Urban Masses and Moral Order in America, 1820–1920* (Cambridge: Harvard University Press, 1978); Andrew Lees, *Cities Perceived: Urban Society in European and American Thought, 1820–1940* (Manchester, England: Manchester University Press, 1985); H. J. Dyos and Michael Wolff, eds., *The Victorian City: Images and Realities* (London: Routledge and Kegan Paul, 1973).

2. Jack London, *The People of the Abyss* (New York: Macmillan, 1903), chap. 1.

3. Sam Bass Warner, Jr., *The Private City: Philadelphia in Three Periods of Its Growth* (Philadelphia: University of Pennsylvania Press, 1968).

4. Anthony S. Wohl, *Endangered Lives: Public Health in Victorian Britain* (Cambridge: Harvard University Press, 1983); Anthony Sutcliffe, "The Growth of Public Intervention in the British Urban Environment during the Nineteenth Century: A Structural Approach," in *The Structure of Nineteenth Century Cities*, ed. James H. Johnson and Colin G. Pooley (London: Croom Helm, 1982).

5. Malcolm Falkus, "The Development of Municipal Trading in the Nineteenth Century," *Business History* 19 (1977): 136–137.

6. Jon C. Teaford, *The Unheralded Triumph: City Government in America, 1870–1900* (Baltimore: Johns Hopkins University Press, 1984), p. 273.

7. Wolfgang Schivelbusch, *Disenchanted Night: The Industrialization of Light in the Nineteenth Century* (Berkeley: University of California Press, 1988); Thomas P. Hughes, *Networks of Power: Electrification in Western Society, 1880–1930* (Baltimore: Johns Hopkins University Press, 1983); John P. McKay, *Tramways and Trolleys: The Rise of Urban Mass Transport in Europe* (Princeton: Princeton University Press, 1976).

8. Milo R. Maltbie, "A Tale of Two Cities: Water Supply in London and Philadelphia," *Municipal Affairs* 3 (1899): 191–224.

9. Christopher Armstrong and H. V. Nelles, *Monopoly's Moment: The Organization and Regulation of Canadian Utilities, 1830–1930* (Philadelphia: Temple University Press, 1986), chap. 5.

10. Richard J. Evans, *Death in Hamburg: Society and Politics in the Cholera Years, 1830–1910* (Oxford: Clarendon Press, 1987), pp. 151–161.

11. Harold J. Laski, W. Ivor Jennings, and William A. Robson, *A Century of Municipal Progress, 1835–1935* (London: George Allen and Unwin, 1935), p. 316; Frederic C. Howe, *The British City: The Beginnings of Democracy* (New York: Scribner's, 1907), p. 71.

12. David Glassberg, "The Design of Reform: The Public Bath Movement in America," *American Studies* 20 (1979): 7; Marilyn Thornton Williams, *Washing "The Great Unwashed": Public Baths in Urban America, 1840–1920* (Columbus: Ohio State University Press, 1991), p. 8. For the German analogue: Brian K. Ladd, "Public Baths and Civic Improvement in Nineteenth-Century German Cities," *Journal of Urban History* 14 (1988): 372–393.

13. Jon Peterson, "The Impact of Sanitary Reform upon American Urban Planners, 1840–1890," *Journal of Social History* 13 (1979): 83–103.

14. Alan Mayne, *The Imagined Slum: Newspaper Representation in Three Cities, 1870–1914* (Leicester: Leicester University Press, 1993).

15. Ibid., chap. 4; Derek Fraser, *Power and Authority in the Victorian City* (New York: St. Martin's Press, 1979), chap. 4; E. P. Hennock, *Fit and Proper Persons: Ideal and Reality in Nineteenth-Century Urban Government* (Montreal: McGill–Queen's University Press, 1973); Asa Briggs, *Victorian Cities* (1963; Berkeley: University of California Press, 1993), chap. 5.

16. Julian Ralph, "The Best Governed City in the World," *Harper's New Monthly Magazine* 81 (1890): 99–111; George F. Parker, "An Object-Lesson in Municipal Government," *Century* 53 (1896): 71–89. On the Corporation Street scheme: Mayne, *Imagined Slum*, chap. 4.

17. Hennock, *Fit and Proper Persons*, p. 56; National Civic Federation, Commission on Public Ownership and Operation, *Municipal and Private Operation of Public Utilities* (New York: National Civic Federation, 1907), vol. 1, p. 52; Mayne, *Imagined Slum*, p. 61. Tawney is quoted in P. J. Waller, *Town, City and Nation: England, 1850–1914* (New York: Oxford University Press, 1983), p. 312.

18. Joseph Chamberlain, "Favorable Aspects of State Socialism," *North American Review* 152 (1891): 547.

19. J. R. Kellett, "Municipal Socialism, Enterprise and Trading in the Victorian City," *Urban History Yearbook, 1978* (Leicester: Leicester University Press, 1978); Falkus, "The Development of Municipal Trading in the Nineteenth Century."

20. Hamish Fraser, "Municipal Socialism and Social Policy in the Victorian City," in *The Victorian City: A Reader in British Urban History, 1820–1914*, ed. R. J. Morris and Richard Rodger (London: Longman, 1993); S. G. Checkland, *The Upas Tree: Glasgow, 1875–1975* (Glasgow: University of Glasgow Press, 1976); Bernard Aspinwall, *Portable Utopia: Glasgow and the United States, 1820–1920* (Aberdeen: Aberdeen University Press, 1984).

21. Wolfgang R. Krabbe, "Munizipalsozialismus und der Interventionsstaat: Die Ausbreitung der städtischen Leistungsverwaltung im Kaisserreich," *Geschichte in Wissenschaft und Unterricht* 30 (1979): 265–284; Wolfgang R. Krabbe, "Die Entfaltung der kommunalen Leistungsverwaltung in deutschen Städten des späten 19. Jahrhunderts," in *Urbanisierung im 19. und 20. Jahrhundert: Historische und geographische Aspekte*, ed. Hans Jürgen Teuteberg (Cologne: Böhlau, 1983); Hans-Dieter Brunckhorst, *Kommunalisierung im 19. Jahrhundert, dargestellt am Beispiel der Gaswirtschaft in Deutschland* (Munich: Tuduv, 1978); William H. Dawson, *Municipal Life and Government in Germany* (London: Longmans, Green, 1914), chap. 9.

22. L. S. Rowe, "Municipal Ownership and Operation of Street Railways in Germany," *Annals of the American Academy of Political and Social Science* 27 (1906): 47–65; Edward W. Bemis, ed. *Municipal Monopolies: A Collection of Papers by American Economists and Specialists* (New York: Thomas Y. Crowell, 1899), pp. 562–565.

23. "The Progress of the World," *American Monthly Review of Reviews* 25 (1902): 259.

24. On Frankfurt: Franz Adickes and G. O. Beutler, *Die sozialen Aufgaben der deutschen Städte* (Leipzig: Duncker und Humblot, 1903); *Franz Adickes: Sein Leben und sein Werk* (Frankfurt: Englert und Schlosser, 1929). On Düsseldorf: Frederic C. Howe, *European Cities at Work* (New York: Charles Scribner's Sons, 1913), chap. 3. More generally: Howard Woodhead, "The First German Municipal Exposition," *American Journal of Sociology* 9 (1904): 413–458, 612–630, 812–831, and 10 (1904) 47–63.

25. Chamberlain, "Favorable Aspects of State Socialism," p. 538; Hamish Fraser,

"Labour and the Changing City," in *Perspectives of the Scottish City*, ed. George Gordon (Aberdeen: Aberdeen University Press, 1985).

26. Albert Shaw, *Municipal Government in Great Britain* (New York: Century, 1895), p. 45; Martin J. Wiener, *Between Two Worlds: The Political Thought of Graham Wallas* (Oxford: Clarendon Press, 1971), p. 40.

Big businessmen did not always call the tune in municipal trading. For a culturally conservative, anti-Semitic, *Kleinbürger* variation on municipal ownership politics: John W. Boyer, *Culture and Political Crisis in Vienna: Christian Socialism in Power, 1897–1918* (Chicago: University of Chicago Press, 1995), chap. 1.

27. Dawson, *Municipal Life and Government in Germany*, chap. 2; Evans, *Death in Hamburg*, p. 546; John D. Rolling, "Liberals, Socialists, and City Government in Imperial Germany: The Case of Frankfurt am Main, 1900–1918," Ph.D. diss., University of Wisconsin—Madison, 1979, p. 50; Edmund J. James, "The City Council of Berlin," *American Journal of Sociology* 6 (1900): 412; Albert Shaw, *Municipal Government in Continental Europe* (New York: Century, 1895), p. 308.

28. James J. Sheehan, *German Liberalism in the Nineteenth Century* (Chicago: University of Chicago Press, 1978), p. 230; James J. Sheehan, "Liberalism and the City in Nineteenth-Century Germany," *Past and Present* 51 (1971): 116–137.

29. Fraser, "Labour and the Changing City," p. 160.

30. Rudolf G. Huber, *Sozialer Wandel und politische Konflikte in einer südhessischen Industriestadt: Kommunalpolitik der SPD in Offenbach, 1898–1914* (Darmstadt: Hessische Historische Komission, 1985), introduction; George Steinmetz, *Regulating the Social: The Welfare State and Local Politics in Imperial Germany* (Princeton: Princeton University Press, 1993), pp. 194–195; Adickes, *Soziale Aufgaben*, pp. 78–81.

31. Joan W. Scott, "Mayors versus Police Chiefs: Socialist Municipalities Confront the French State," in *French Cities in the Nineteenth Century*, ed. John M. Merriman (New York: Holmes and Meier, 1981); Samuel P. Orth, *Socialism and Democracy in Europe* (London: Williams and Norgate, 1913), pp. 113–114; Roger Magraw, *France, 1814–1915: The Bourgeois Century* (London: Fontana, 1983), p. 300.

32. C. K. Yearley, "The 'Provincial Party' and the Megalopolises: London, Paris, and New York, 1850–1910," *Comparative Studies in Society and History* 15 (1975): 51–88.

33. Andrew Saint, ed., *Politics and the People of London: The London County Council, 1889–1965* (London: Hambledon Press, 1989); Susan D. Pennybacker, *A Vision for London, 1889–1914: Labour, Everyday Life, and the LCC Experiment* (London: Routledge, 1995); Paul Thompson, *Socialists, Liberals, and Labour: The Struggle for London, 1885–1914* (London: Routledge and Kegan Paul, 1967). For the impression of London progressive politics on outsiders: Charles Edward Russell, "Socialistic Government of London," *Cosmopolitan Magazine* 40 (1906): 367–376; Hugo Lindemann, *Städteverwaltung und Munizipal-Sozialismus in England* (Stuttgart: Siek, 1897).

34. Susan Pennybacker, "'The Millennium by Return of Post': Reconsidering London Progressivism, 1889–1907," in *Metropolis—London: Historians and Repre-*

sentations since 1800, ed. David Feldman and Gareth Stedman Jones (London: Routledge, 1989); John Burns, "Towards a Commune," *Nineteenth Century* 40 (1906): 367–376. Burns is quoted in John Davis, "The Progressive Council, 1889–1907" in Saint, ed., *Politics and People of London*, p. 35.

35. A. M. McBriar, *Fabian Socialism and English Politics, 1884–1918* (Cambridge: Cambridge University Press, 1962), chap. 9; Sidney Webb, *The London Programme* (London: Swan Sonnenschein, 1891); *Fabian Municipal Programme: Second Series* (London: Fabian Society, 1899–1900).

36. Avner Offer, *Property and Politics, 1870–1914: Landownership, Law, Ideology and Urban Development in England* (Cambridge: Cambridge University Press, 1981), chap. 15.

37. Offer, *Property and Politics*, p. 305; Sidney Webb, "Socialism in England," *Publications of the American Economic Association* 4 (1889): 65.

38. Falkus, "Development of Municipal Trading," p. 136; Trevor I. Williams, *History of the British Gas Industry* (Oxford: Oxford University Press, 1981), p. 27; Howe, *European Cities at Work*, p. 113.

39. Milton S. Heath, *Constructive Liberalism: The Role of the State in Economic Development in Georgia to 1860* (Cambridge: Harvard University Press, 1954), p. 289; Louis Hartz, *Economic Policy and Democratic Thought: Pennsylvania, 1776–1860* (Cambridge: Harvard University Press, 1948), p. 88; Morton Keller, *Affairs of State: Public Life in Late Nineteenth Century America* (Cambridge: Harvard University Press, 1977), p. 167; Colleen A. Dunlavy, *Politics and Industrialization: Early Railroads in the United States and Prussia* (Princeton: Princeton University Press, 1994).

40. Stanley K. Schultz and Clay McShane, "To Engineer the Metropolis: Sewers, Sanitation, and City Planning in Late-Nineteenth-Century America," *Journal of American History* 65 (1978): 389–411; Letty Anderson, "Hard Choices: Supplying Water to New England Towns," *Journal of Interdisciplinary History* 15 (1984): 211–234; National Civic Federation, *Municipal and Private Operation of Public Utilities*, vol. 1, p. 127; Bemis, *Municipal Monopolies*, p. 59.

41. For informed comparisons of public services in U.S. and European cities: Teaford, *Unheralded Triumph;* chaps. 8–9; Martin V. Melosi, *Garbage in the Cities: Refuse, Reform, and the Environment, 1880–1980* (College Station: Texas A & M University Press, 1981); Milo R. Maltbie, *Municipal Functions: A Study of the Development, Scope and Tendency of Municipal Socialism* (New York: Reform Club Committee on Municipal Administration, 1898); Harvey N. Shepard, "Municipal Housekeeping in Europe and America," *American City* 6 (1912): 709–713.

42. Richard T. Ely, "Social Observations in Germany," *Congregationalist* 77 (1892): 206, 214; Richard T. Ely, "The Needs of the City," in his *Problems of To-day: A Discussion of Protective Tariffs, Taxation, and Monopolies*, new ed. (New York: Thomas Y. Crowell, 1890), pp. 229–247.

43. Edmund J. James, "The Relation of the Modern Municipality to the Gas

Supply," *Publications of the American Economic Association* 1 (1886), nos. 2–3; [Edmund J. James], "The Gas Question in England," *Nation* 42 (1886): 71–72; *American Journal of Sociology* 5 (1900): 826–828; Edmund J. James, "Street Railway Policy in Berlin," *Annals of the American Academy of Political and Social Science* 15 (1900): 437–440; *Journal of Political Economy* 9 (1901): 260–271; Chicago, Street Railway Commission, *Report to the City Council of the City of Chicago* (Chicago, 1900).

44. Lloyd J. Graybar, *Albert Shaw of the* Review of Reviews: *An Intellectual Biography* (Lexington: University Press of Kentucky, 1974).

45. Albert Shaw to William T. Stead, Nov. 29, 1894, Albert Shaw Papers, Manuscripts and Archives Division, New York Public Library, The Astor, Lenox, and Tilden Foundations.

46. Albert Shaw, "The Municipal Problem and Greater New York," *Atlantic Monthly* 79 (1897): 748; Shaw, *Municipal Government in Continental Europe*, p. 305.

47. Albert Shaw, "London Polytechnics and People's Palaces," *Century* 40 (1890): 164: Shaw, *Municipal Government in Continental Europe*, pp. 323, 327; Shaw, *Municipal Government in Great Britain*, p. 7.

48. Shaw, *Municipal Government in Great Britain*, p. 2; Albert Shaw, "Municipal Problems of New York and London," *Review of Reviews: American Edition* 5 (1892): 282.

49. "An Object Lesson in Municipal Government," *Century* 39 (1890): 792; "The Key to Municipal Reform," ibid., 42 (1891): 953–954; Harry Pratt Judson, review of *Municipal Government in Great Britain* in *Dial* 18 (Mar. 1, 1895): 147–149.

50. David C. Hammack, *Power and Society: Greater New York at the Turn of the Century* (New York: Russell Sage Foundation, 1982), pp. 243–251.

51. Melvin G. Holli, *Reform in Detroit: Hazen S. Pingree and Urban Politics* (New York: Oxford University Press, 1969), p. 159; George E. Mowry, *The California Progressives* (Chicago: Quadrangle Books, 1963), pp. 23–24; *The Aegis* [University of Wisconsin], Joint Debate Number, 7 (Mar. 3, 1893); Ely, "Needs of the City," p. 245.

52. Geoffrey Blodgett, *The Gentle Reformers: Massachusetts Democrats in the Cleveland Era* (Cambridge: Harvard University Press, 1966), pt. 2; Josiah Quincy, "The Development of American Cities," *Arena* 17 (1897): 529–537.

53. Blodgett, *Gentle Reformers*, p. 255; J. W. Martin, "The Trend in American Cities," *Contemporary Review* 76 (1899): 858; *The Letters of Sidney and Beatrice Webb*, ed. Norman MacKenzie (Cambridge: Cambridge University Press, 1978), vol. 2, pp. 64, 74; Norman and Jeanne MacKenzie, *The Fabians* (New York: Simon and Schuster, 1977), p. 257.

54. Richard T. Ely, *The Coming City* (New York: Thomas Y. Crowell, 1902), p. 94; *Municipal Affairs* 2 (1898): 533–534; J. W. Martin, " A Cure for City Corruption," *Harper's New Monthly Magazine* 99 (1899): 641–646; John W. Martin, "How London Was Saved," *Forum* 31 (1901): 318–327; William Tolman, "Public Baths, or the Gospel of Cleanliness," *Yale Review* 6 (1897): 50–62.

55. Roy E. Littlefield III, *William Randolph Hearst: His Role in American Progressivism* (Lanham, Md.: University Press of America, 1980), esp. chap. 3; Martin, "Trend in American Cities," pp. 856–867.

56. Hammack, *Power and Society;* Augustus Cerillo, Jr., *Reform in New York City: A Study of Urban Progressivism* (New York: Garland, 1991); Williams, *Washing "The Great Unwashed,"* chap. 3.

57. Maltbie, *Municipal Functions*, first published as *Municipal Affairs* vol. 2, no. 4 (1898).

58. Gerald Kurland, *Seth Low: The Reformer in an Urban and Industrial Age* (New York: Twayne, 1971); *The City for the People! Campaign Book of the Citizens' Union, Sept.–Oct. 1897* (New York, 1897); *The City for the People! Campaign Book of the Citizens' Union*, 2nd ed. (New York, 1901); J. W. Martin, "A Constructive Program: What the Low Administration Should Do," *Municipal Affairs* 5 (1901): 641–663; John DeWitt Warner, "Municipal Betterment in the New York City Elections," ibid., 633–634. The *Times* is quoted in Hammack, *Power and Society*, p. 152.

59. Holli, *Reform in Detroit;* Hoyt Landon Warner, *Progressivism in Ohio, 1897–1917* (Columbus: Ohio State University Press, 1964); Tom L. Johnson, *My Story*, ed. Elizabeth J. Hauser (1911; Kent, Ohio: Kent State University Press, 1993); C. H. Cramer, *Newton D. Baker: A Biography* (Cleveland: World, 1961), chap. 3.

60. Brand Whitlock to John D. Barrie, Feb. 26, 1913, Brand Whitlock Papers, Library of Congress; Brand Whitlock, "The City and Civilization," *Scribner's Magazine* 52 (1912): 625; Allan Nevins, ed., *The Letters and Journals of Brand Whitlock* (New York: Appleton-Century, 1936), vol. 1, p. 165.

61. Frederic C. Howe, *The Confessions of a Reformer* (New York: Scribner's, 1925), p. 5; Roy Lubove, "Frederic C. Howe and the Quest for Community in America," *Historian* 39 (1977): 270–291.

62. Howe's books were *The City: The Hope of Democracy* (New York: Scribner's, 1905); *The British City: The Beginnings of Democracy* (New York: Scribner's, 1907); *European Cities at Work* (New York: Scribner's, 1913); *The Modern City and Its Problems* (New York: Scribner's, 1915); *Socialized Germany* (New York: Scribner's, 1915).

63. Frederic C. Howe, "The Peaceful Revolution," *Outlook* 94 (1910): 116; Howe, *European Cities at Work*, pp. 318, 326.

64. Frederic C. Howe, "The German and the American City," *Scribner's Magazine* 49 (1911): 492; Howe, *European Cities at Work*, pp. 267, x, 352.

65. Howe, *European Cities at Work*, p. 248.

66. Sylvester Baxter, "Berlin: A Study of Municipal Government in Germany," *Bulletin of the Essex Institute* 21 (1889): 74; [Richard T. Ely], "Administration of the City of Berlin," *Nation* 34 (1882): 246; Robert C. Brooks, "City Government by Taxpapers: The Three-Class Election System in Prussian Cities," *Municipal Affairs* 3 (1899): 396–433; Robert C. Brooks, "Political Clubs in Prussian Cities," ibid. 4 (1900): 375–384; Robert C. Brooks, "Berlin without an *Oberbürgermeister*," *Annals of the American Academy of Political and Social Science* 14 (1889): 94–98; Brand Whit-

lock, "With All Its Great Public Service Glasgow Has Its Vice and Poverty," *Toledo Bee*, Dec. 9, 1912.

67. William D. Foulke, "A German City Worthy of Emulation," *American City* 6 (1912): 412.

68. Howe, *European Cities at Work*, p. 243.

69. Samuel M. Jones, "The New Patriotism: A Golden Rule Government for Cities," *Municipal Affairs* 3 (1899): 455–461; Leo S. Rowe, *Problems of City Government* (New York: D. Appleton, 1908), pp. 40–42. Cf. Roy Lubove, "The Twentieth Century City: The Progressive as Municipal Reformer," *Mid-America* 41 (1959): 199.

70. For example, Maureen A. Flanagan, "Gender and Urban Political Reform: The City Club and the Women's City Club of Chicago in the Progressive Era," *American Historical Review* 95 (1990): 1032–1050.

71. Milo Maltbie, "Glasgow's Municipal Tramways," *Municipal Affairs* 4 (1900): 41; Howe, *European Cities at Work*, p. viii.

72. *The Papers of Woodrow Wilson*, ed. Arthur S. Link (Princeton: Princeton University Press, 1966–1994), vol. 25, p. 259; *The Letters of Lincoln Steffens*, ed. Ella Winter and Granville Hicks (New York: Harcourt, Brace, 1938), vol. 1, p. 252.

73. Rowe, *Problems of City Government*, chap. 11.

74. Robert D. Weber, "Rationalizers and Reformers: Chicago Local Transportation in the Nineteenth Century," Ph.D. diss., University of Wisconsin—Madison, 1971; Charles W. Cheape, *Moving the Masses: Urban Public Transit in New York, Boston, and Philadelphia, 1880–1912* (Cambridge: Harvard University Press, 1980).

75. David P. Thelen, *The New Citizenship: Origins of Progressivism in Wisconsin, 1885–1900* (Columbia: University of Missouri Press, 1972), esp. chap. 11; Cheape, *Moving the Masses*, p. 212.

76. "Public Ownership of Telegraphs, Tramways, Gasworks, Etc.," *Independent* 49 (1897): 578.

77. Hammack, *Power and Society*, chap. 8.

78. Clifton Hood, *722 Miles: The Building of the Subways and How They Transformed New York* (New York: Simon and Schuster, 1993), quotation from p. 123.

79. Forrest McDonald, "Samuel Insull and the Movement for State Utility Regulatory Commissions," *Business History Review* 32 (1958): 245–246.

80. Weber, "Rationalizers and Reformers," pp. 41–42.

81. Richard E. Becker, "Edward Dunne, Reform Mayor of Chicago, 1905–1907," Ph.D. diss., University of Chicago, 1971; John D. Buenker, "Edward F. Dunne: The Limits of Municipal Reform," in *The Mayors: The Chicago Political Tradition*, ed. Paul M. Green and Melvin G. Holli (Carbondale: Southern Illinois University Press, 1987); Delos F. Wilcox, *The Great Cities in America: Their Problems and Their Government* (New York: Macmillan, 1910), pp. 228–235; Paul Barrett, *The Automobile and Urban Transit: The Formation of Public Policy in Chicago, 1900–1930* (Philadelphia: Temple University Press, 1983).

82. William Jennings Bryan, *The Old World and Its Ways* (St. Louis: Thompson,

1907), chap. 40; Irwin Yellowitz, *Labor and the Progressive Movement in New York State, 1897–1916* (Ithaca: Cornell University Press, 1965), chap. 9; Everett W. Burdett, "Municipal Ownership in Great Britain," *Journal of Political Economy* 14 (1906): 257.

83. Lincoln Steffens, *The Shame of the Cities* (New York: McClure, Phillips, 1904).

84. John R. Commons, *Myself: The Autobiography of John R. Commons* (Madison: University of Wisconsin Press, 1964), pp. 111–120.

85. National Civic Federation, *Municipal and Private Operation;* John R. Commons, "Public Ownership and the Civic Federation," *Independent* 63 (1907): 264–266.

86. Louis D. Brandeis, "How Boston Solved the Gas Problem," *American Review of Reviews* 36 (1907): 594–598.

87. John R. Commons, "The Wisconsin Public Utilities Law," *American Monthly Review of Reviews* 36 (1907): 22–24; Bruce W. Dearstyne, "Regulation in the Progressive Era: The New York Public Service Commission," *New York History* 58 (1977): 331–347; Milo R. Maltbie, "The Fruits of Public Regulation in New York," *Annals of the American Academy of Political and Social Science* 37 (1911): 170–190; Morton Keller, *Regulating a New Economy: Public Policy and Economic Change in America* (Cambridge: Harvard University Press, 1990), pp. 59–60.

88. McDonald, "Samuel Insull," p. 248; Carl V. Harris, *Political Power in Birmingham, 1871–1921* (Knoxville: University of Tennessee Press, 1977), chap. 11; Mansel G. Blackford, "Businessmen and the Regulation of Railroads and Public Utilities in California during the Progressive Era," *Business History Review* 44 (1970): 307–319.

89. Delos Wilcox, "Effects of State Regulation upon the Municipal Ownership Movement," *Annals of the American Academy of Political and Social Science* 53 (1914): 73.

90. David Nord, "The Experts versus the Experts: Conflicting Philosophies of Municipal Utility Regulation in the Progressive Era," *Wisconsin Magazine of History* 58 (1975): 219–236; Clyde L. King, "Municipal Ownership versus Regulation," *New Republic* 1 (Nov. 28, 1914): 12–14; Delos Wilcox, "The Crisis in Public Service Regulation in New York," *National Municipal Review* 4 (1915): 547–563; Delos Wilcox, "Experts, Ethics, and Public Policy in Public Utilities," *National Municipal Review* 6 (1917): 472–485; "Proceedings of the Conference of American Mayors on Public Policies as to Municipal Utilities," pt. IV: "Municipal Ownership and Operations," *Annals of the American Academy of Political and Social Science* 57 (Jan. 1915); Joy E. Morgan and Edna D. Bullock, eds. *Selected Articles on Municipal Ownership: Debaters' Handbook Series*, 2nd ed. (New York: H. W. Wilson, 1914); National Civic Federation, *Shall the Government Own and Operate the Railroads, the Telegraph and Telephone System? Shall the Municipalities Own Their Utilities?* (New York: National Civic Federation, 1915); Eugene M. Tobin, *Organize or Perish: America's Independent Progressives, 1913–1933* (New York: Greenwood, 1986), chap. 2.

91. Charles A. Beard, *American City Government: A Survey of Newer Tendencies* (New York: Century, 1912), pp. 229–230; Sally M. Miller, "Casting a Wide Net: The Milwaukee Movement to 1920," in *Socialism in the Heartland: The Midwestern Experience, 1900–1925*, ed. Donald T. Critchlow (Notre Dame, Ind.: University of Notre Dame Press, 1986); Douglas E. Booth, "Municipal Socialism and City Government Reform: The Milwaukee Experience, 1910–1940," *Journal of Urban History* 12 (1985): 51–74; Frederic C. Howe, "Milwaukee, a Socialist City," *Outlook* 95 (1910): 411–421.

92. Carl D. Thompson, *Public Ownership: A Survey of Public Enterprises, Municipal, State, and Federal, in the United States and Elsewhere* (New York: Thomas Y. Crowell, 1925); Martin G. Glaeser, *Outlines of Public Utility Economics* (New York: Macmillan, 1927). On the trends in transit ownership: Stanley Mallach, "The Origins and Decline of Urban Mass Transportation in the United States, 1890–1930," *Urbanism Past and Present* 8 (1979): 1–17; James A. Dunn, Jr., *Miles to Go: European and American Transportation Policies* (Cambridge: MIT Press, 1981).

93. Massachusetts, Special Committee Appointed to Investigate the Relations between Cities and Towns and Street Railway Companies, *Report* (Boston, 1898), p. 16; "Street Railways: Boston and Glasgow," *Outlook* 82 (1906): 765–766; Douglas Ward, "A Comparative Historical Geography of Streetcar Suburbs in Boston, Massachusetts, and Leeds, England, 1850–1920," *Annals of the Association of American Geographers* 54 (1964): 477–489.

94. Oscar L. Pound, *A Treatise on the Law of Public Utilities Operating in Cities and Towns* (Indianapolis: Bobbs-Merrill, 1913); Dexter Merriam Keezer and Stacy May, *The Public Control of Business* (New York: Harper and Brothers, 1930).

95. "Interview with [James] Dalrymple," *Street Railway Journal* 26 (1905), 222–224; "The Dalrymple Report," ibid. 27 (1906), 422–427.

96. Martin J. Schiesl, *The Politics of Efficiency: Municipal Administration and Reform in America, 1880–1920* (Berkeley: University of California Press, 1977); Clifton K. Yearley, *The Money Machines: The Breakdown and Reform of Governmental and Party Finance in the North, 1860–1920* (Albany: State University of New York Press, 1970). For a particularly acute reading of unreformed city government: Daniel Czitrom, "Underworlds and Underdogs: Big Tim Sullivan and Metropolitan Politics in New York, 1889–1913," *Journal of American History* 78 (1991): 536–558.

97. Arthur Shadwell, *Industrial Efficiency: A Comparative Study of Industrial Life in England, Germany, and America* (London: Longmans, Green, 1906), vol. 1, p. 12; Hennock, *Fit and Proper Persons*, p. 297.

98. Balthasar H. Meyer, "Central Utilities Commissions and Home Rule," *American Political Science Review* 5 (1911): 378.

99. Frederic C. Howe, "The Case for Municipal Ownership," and the ensuing discussion, *Publications of the American Economic Association*, 3rd ser., 7 (1906): 113–132; Richard T. Ely, *Ground under Our Feet: An Autobiography* (New York: Macmillan, 1938), pp. 251–265.

100. Charles Edward Russell, *Bare Hands and Stone Walls: Some Recollections of a Side-Line Reformer* (New York: Scribner's, 1933), pp. 97–103.

101. Victor S. Clark, *The Labour Movement in Australia: A Study in Social-Democracy* (New York: Henry Holt, 1906), p. 45.

5. *Civic Ambitions*

1. Frederic C. Howe, *The Confessions of a Reformer* (New York: Charles Scribner's Sons, 1925), pp. 113–114.

2. H. G. Wells, *The Future in America: A Search after Realities* (New York: Harper and Brothers, 1906), p. 39; Charles Booth to Mary Booth, Aug. 27, 1904, Charles Booth Papers, University of London Library.

3. M. J. Daunton, "American Cities," in *Housing the Workers, 1850–1914: A Comparative Perspective*, ed. M. J. Daunton (Leicester: Leicester University Press, 1990), p. 275.

4. Milo R. Maltbie, *Civic Art in Northern Europe: A Report to the Art Commission of the City of New York* (New York, 1903); *The Letters of Lincoln Steffens*, ed. Ella Winter and Granville Hicks (New York: Harcourt, Brace, 1938), vol. 1, p. 218. On the Russell Sage Foundation: John F. McClymer, *War and Welfare: Social Engineering in America, 1890–1925* (Westport, Conn.: Greenwood Press, 1980), chap. 3.

5. Anthony Sutcliffe, *Towards the Planned City: Germany, Britain, the United States, and France, 1780–1914* (Oxford: Basil Blackwell, 1981), chap. 6.

6. Frederic C. Howe, "The German and the American City," *Scribner's Magazine* 49 (1911): 492; Frederic C. Howe, *European Cities at Work* (New York: Charles Scribner's Sons, 1913), p. 346; Walter Weyl, "From Chaos to City," pp. 2, 7, Walter Weyl Papers, Rutgers University; L. S. Rowe, *Problems of City Government* (New York: D. Appleton, 1908), p. 60.

7. Howe, *European Cities*, p. 361; Frederic C. Howe, "The Remaking of the American City," *Harper's Magazine* 127 (1913): 186.

8. Raymond Unwin, "American Town Planning," *Garden Cities and Town Planning*, n.s. 1 (Aug. 1911): 162–165. On American city plans: John W. Reps, *The Making of Urban America: A History of City Planning in the United States* (Princeton: Princeton University Press, 1965); Mel Scott, *American City Planning since 1890* (Berkeley: University of California Press, 1969); Richard E. Foglesong, *Planning the Capitalist City: The Colonial Era to the 1920s* (Princeton: Princeton University Press, 1986).

9. David H. Pinkney, *Napoleon III and the Rebuilding of Paris* (Princeton: Princeton University Press, 1958); David P. Jordan, *Transforming Paris: The Life and Labors of Baron Haussmann* (New York: Free Press, 1995); Anthony Sutcliffe, *The Autumn of Central Paris: The Defeat of Town Planning, 1850–1970* (London: Edward Arnold, 1970); Anthony Sutcliffe, "Architecture and Civic Design in Nineteenth Century Paris," in *Growth and Transformation of the Modern City*, ed. Ingrid Hammarström and Thomas Hall (Stockholm: Swedish Council for Building Research,

1979); Thomas Hall, *Planung europäischer Hauptstädte: Zur Entwicklung des Städtebaus im 19. Jahrhundert* (Stockholm: Almquist and Wiksell, 1986), pp. 47–68; Ann-Louise Shapiro, *Housing the Poor of Paris, 1850–1902* (Madison: University of Wisconsin Press, 1985). For Morgan's impressions of Paris: *Extracts from the European Travel Journal of Lewis H. Morgan* (Rochester, N.Y.: Rochester Historical Society, 1937), p. 360.

10. Lewis Mumford, *The Culture of Cities* (New York: Harcourt, Brace, 1938), p. 98.

11. Albert Shaw, *Municipal Government in Continental Europe* (New York: Century, 1895), p. 7; Brand Whitlock, "Paris Offers Inspiration to City Builders," *Toledo Bee*, Dec. 12, 1912.

12. Anthony Sutcliffe, "Environmental Control and Planning in European Capitals, 1850–1914: London, Paris, Berlin," in *Growth and Transformation of the Modern City*, ed. Hammarström and Hall; Hall, *Planung europäischer Hauptstädte*, pp. 116–129; Gareth Stedman Jones, *Outcast London: A Study in the Relationship between Classes in Victorian Society* (New York: Oxford University Press, 1971), p. 169.

13. Jon A. Peterson, "The City Beautiful Movement: Forgotten Origins and Lost Meanings," *Journal of Urban History* 2 (1976): 415–434; David Schuyler, *The New Urban Landscape: The Redefinition of City Form in Nineteenth-Century America* (Baltimore: Johns Hopkins University Press, 1986), chap. 10; Michelle H. Bogart, *Public Sculpture and the Civic Ideal in New York City, 1890–1930* (Chicago: University of Chicago Press, 1989); Charles Mulford Robinson, *The Improvement of Cities and Towns; or, The Practical Basis of Civic Aesthetics* (New York: G. P. Putnam's Sons, 1901); Charles Mulford Robinson, *Modern Civic Art; or, The City Made Beautiful* (New York: G. P. Putnam's Sons, 1903).

14. Thomas S. Hines, *Burnham of Chicago: Architect and Planner* (New York: Oxford University Press, 1974), chap. 4.

15. Hines, *Burnham*, chap. 7; Charles Moore, ed., *The Improvement of the Park System of the District of Columbia*, 57th Cong., 1st sess., Senate Report 166 (1902).

16. Thomas S. Hines, "The Paradox of 'Progressive' Architecture: Urban Planning and Building in Tom Johnson's Cleveland," *American Quarterly* 25 (1973): 426–448; Howe, *Confessions of a Reformer*, pp. 80–82; Frederic C. Howe, "The Cleveland Group Plan," *Charities and the Commons* 19 (1908): 1548; Daniel H. Burnham, *Report on a Plan for San Francisco* (San Francisco, 1905).

17. Commercial Club of Chicago, *Plan of Chicago by Daniel H. Burnham and Edward H. Bennett*, ed. Charles Moore (Chicago: Commercial Club, 1909).

18. Walter D. Moody, *Wacker's Manual of the Plan of Chicago: Municipal Economy: Especially Prepared for Study in the Schools of Chicago* (Chicago, 1913), introduction; Thomas J. Schlereth, "Planning and Progressivism: *Wacker's Manual of the Plan of Chicago*," in *Ideas in America's Cultures: From Republic to Mass Society*, ed. Hamilton Cravens (Ames: Iowa State University Press, 1982), p. 174, n. 4; Foglesong, *Planning the Capitalist City*, pp. 210–211.

19. Commercial Club, *Plan of Chicago*, pp. 4, 14, 117, plate cxxx.

20. John L. Hancock, "John Nolen and the American City Planning Movement," Ph.D. diss., University of Pennsylvania, 1964, p. 294; American Institute of Architects, Committee on Town Planning, *City Planning Progress in the United States, 1917*, ed. George B. Ford (Washington, D.C.: Journal of the American Institute of Architects, n.d.).

21. New York City, Improvement Commission, *Report* (New York, 1907); Harvey A. Kantor, "The City Beautiful in New York," *New York Historical Society Quarterly* 57 (1973): 149–171.

22. Flavel Shurtleff, *Carrying Out the City Plan: The Practical Application of American Law in the Execution of City Plans* (New York: Survey Associates, 1914), chap. 3; William H. Wilson, *The City Beautiful Movement in Kansas City* (Columbia: University of Missouri Press, 1964). On Reading: Hancock, "John Nolen," chap. 6. On the conflict between property rights and Burnham's ambitions in San Francisco: Judd Kahn, *Imperial San Francisco: Politics and Planning in an American City, 1897–1906* (Lincoln: University of Nebraska Press, 1979).

23. Lutz Niethammer and Franz Brüggemeier, "Wie wohnten Arbeiter im Kaisserreich?" *Archiv für Sozialgeschichte* 16 (1976): 61–134; Eugen Jaeger, *Grundriss der Wohnungsfrage und Wohnungspolitik* (Munich: Volksverein-Verlag, 1911); Rudolf Eberstadt, *Handbuch des Wohnungswesens und der Wohnungsfrage*, 3rd ed. (Jena: Gustav Fischer, 1917).

24. Eberstadt, *Handbuch*, p. 6; Niethammer, "Wie wohnten Arbeiter?" pp. 91, 90; Emil Klar, "Die Entwicklung des Wohnungswesen von 1870/1914," in *Das Wohnungswesen der Stadt Frankfurt A. M.*, ed. W. Nobisch (Frankfurt: Stadt Frankfurt/Main, 1930), p. 58.

25. Quoted in Anthony Sutcliffe, ed., *Metropolis, 1890–1940* (London: Mansell, 1984), p. 21.

26. Edward T. Hartman, "Berlin and the Garden Cities," *Charities and the Commons* 19 (1908): 1470–1471; Madge C. Jenison, "The Tenement of Berlin," *Harper's Monthly Magazine* 118 (1909): 359–369.

27. Eberstadt, *Handbuch*, p. 6; Hsi-Huey Liang, "Lower-Class Immigrants in Wilhelmine Berlin," *Central European History* 3 (1970): 107, 105. For close-up descriptions of the *Mietskasernen:* Johann F. Geist and Klaus Kürvers, *Das Berliner Mietshaus, 1862–1945* (Munich: Prestel, 1984); *Berlin und seine Bauten: IV Wohngebäude, Band B. Wohnungsbau: Mehrfamilienhäuser* (Berlin: Wilhelm Ernst, 1974).

28. Nicholas Bullock and James Read, *The Movement for Housing Reform in Germany and France, 1840–1914* (Cambridge: Cambridge University Press, 1985), pt. 1; Dorothea Berger-Thimme, *Wohnungsfrage und Sozialstaat: Untersuchungen zu den Anfängen staatlicher Wohnungspolitik in Deutschland (1873–1918)* (Frankfurt: Peter Lang, 1976); Deutsche Verein für Wohnungsreform, *30 Jahre Wohnungsreform 1898–1928* (Berlin, 1928).

29. Jaeger, *Grundriss der Wohnungsfrage*, pp. 143–145; Hugo Lindemann, "Ar-

beiterschaft und Gartenstadt," in Deutsche Gartenstadt-Gesellschaft, *Deutsche Gartenstadtbewegung* (Berlin, 1911).

30. For an overview of these techniques: Sutcliffe, *Towards the Planned City*, chap. 2; Bullock and Read, *Movement for Housing Reform*, chap. 7; Brian Ladd, *Urban Planning and Civic Order in Germany, 1860–1914* (Cambridge: Harvard University Press, 1990).

31. Jaeger, *Grundriss der Wohungsfrage*, p. 77; Bullock and Read, *Movement for Housing Reform*, p. 183; Richard T. Ely, "Ulm on the Danube," *Survey* 31 (1913): 253–258; Thomas C. Horsfall, *The Improvement of the Dwellings and Surroundings of the People: The Example of Germany*, 2nd ed. (Manchester England: University of Manchester Press, 1905), pp. 36–42.

32. Franz Adickes, "Zusammenlegung städtischer Grundstücke und Zonenenteignung," *Handwörterbuch der Staatswissenschaften*, ed. J. Conrad et al. (Jena: Gustav Fischer, 1890–1894), vol. 6, pp. 918–923.

33. Robert C. Brooks, "The German Imperial Tax on the Unearned Increment," *Quarterly Journal of Economics* 24 (1911): 682–709.

34. Franz Adickes, "Stadterweiterung," *Handwörterbuch der Staatswissenschaften*, vol. 5, pp. 847–851; Ladd, *Urban Planning*, chap. 6; Thomas H. Logan, "The Invention of Zoning in the Emerging Planning Profession of Late-Nineteenth-Century Germany," Ph.D. diss., University of North Carolina at Chapel Hill, 1972.

35. Frank B. Williams, "Some Aspects of City-Planning Administration in Europe," *Journal of the American Institute of Planners* 3 (1915): 260–264; Bullock and Read, *Movement for Housing Reform*, p. 178; Ladd, *Urban Planning*, pp. 165–170.

36. John Burnett, *A Social History of Housing, 1815–1985*, 2nd ed. (London: Methuen, 1986); M. J. Daunton, *House and Home in the Victorian City: Working-Class Housing, 1850–1914* (London: Edward Arnold, 1983).

37. Walter L. Creese, *The Search for Environment: The Garden City, Before and After* (New Haven: Yale University Press, 1966), chap. 5.

38. Stanley Buder, "Ebenezer Howard: The Genesis of a Town Planning Movement," *Journal of the American Institute of Planners* 35 (1969): 390–398; Michael Simpson, *Thomas Adams and the Modern Planning Movement: Britain, Canada, and the United States, 1900–1940* (London: Mansell, 1985), chap. 2; Creese, *Search for Environment*, chap. 9; Weyl, "From Chaos to City," pp. 2–3.

39. Creese, *Search for Environment*, chap. 10.

40. Horsfall, *Improvement of the Dwellings and Surroundings of the People;* Gordon Cherry, *The Politics of Town Planning* (New York: Longman, 1982); Sutcliffe, *Towards the Planned City*, chap 3.

41. National Conference on City Planning, *Proceedings* (1915): 157–160.

42. Harvey A. Kantor, "Benjamin Marsh and the Fight over Population Congestion," *Journal of the American Institute of Planners* 40 (1974): 422–429; Mary Kingsbury Simkhovitch, *Neighborhood: My Story of Greenwich House* (New York: W. W. Norton, 1938), pp. 160–161.

43. Benjamin C. Marsh, "The Eighth International Housing Congress," *Charities and the Commons* 18 (1907): 555–570; Benjamin C. Marsh, "The Congestion Exhibit in Brooklyn," ibid. 20 (1908): 209–211; John Martin, "The Exhibit of Congestion Interpreted," ibid., 27–39.

44. Benjamin C. Marsh, *An Introduction to City Planning: Democracy's Challenge to the American City* (New York: published by the author, 1909); U.S. Congress, Senate Committee on the District of Columbia, *City Planning*, 61 Cong., 2nd sess., Senate Document 422 (1910).

45. "The City Plan," ed. Charles M. Robinson, special issue, *Charities and the Commons* 19 (Feb. 1908); "Housing and Town Planning," special issue, *Annals of the American Academy of Political and Social Science* 51 (Jan. 1914).

46. Committee on Congestion of Population in New York, *The True Story of the Worst Congestion in Any Civilized City* (New York, n.d.); Florence Kelley, "Congestion and Sweated Labor," *Charities and the Commons* 20 (1908): 48–50; Eleventh New York State Conference of Charities and Corrections, *Proceedings, 1910* (Albany, 1911), pp. 114–151.

47. Edward E. Pratt, *Industrial Causes of Congestion of Population in New York City*, Columbia University Studies in History, Economics, and Public Law, vol. 43, no. 1 (New York: Columbia University, 1911); New York City, Commission on Congestion of Population, *Report* (New York, 1911); Grosvenor Atterbury, "Model Towns in America," *Scribner's Magazine* 52 (1912): 21.

48. Marsh, "City Planning in Justice to the Working Population"; Benjamin C. Marsh, "Taxation and the Improvement of Living Conditions in American Cities," *Survey* 24 (1910): 605–609; Benjamin C. Marsh, *Taxation of Land Values in American Cities: The Next Step in Exterminating Poverty* (New York: n.p., 1911).

49. Seymour I. Toll, *Zoned America* (New York: Grossman, 1969), chaps. 5–6.

50. New York City, Heights of Buildings Commission, *Report* (New York, 1913); International City and Regional Planning Conference, *Planning Problems of Town, City, and Region* (Baltimore, 1925), pp. 499–500; Frank B. Williams, *The Law of City Planning and Zoning* (New York: Macmillan, 1922); *Journal of the American Institute of Architects* 1 (1913): 449–451.

51. "Day of Skyscrapers Is Passing, He Said," *New York Times*, Mar. 30, 1913. On the history of the skyscraper: Thomas Bender and William R. Taylor, "Culture and Architecture: Some Aesthetic Tensions in the Shaping of Modern New York City," in *Visions of the Modern City*, ed. William Sharpe and Leonard Wallock, new ed. (Baltimore: Johns Hopkins University Press, 1987); Mona Domosh, *Invented Cities: The Creation of Landscape in Nineteenth-Century New York and Boston* (New Haven: Yale University Press, 1996), chap. 3.

52. Frank B. Williams, "Restricted Districts and Industrial Districts in German Cities," in *Housing Problems in America: Proceedings of the Third National Housing Conference, 1913* (New York: National Housing Association, 1913), pp. 54–62; New York City, Board of Estimate and Approval, Committee on the City Plan, *Final Report of the Commission on Building Districts* (New York, 1916).

53. Frank B. Williams, "Public Control of Private Real Estate," in *City Planning: A Series of Papers Presenting the Essential Elements of a City Plan*, ed. John Nolen (New York: D. Appleton, 1916), p. 81.

54. *Survey* 45 (1920): 167.

55. Anthony S. Wohl, *The Eternal Slum: Housing and Social Policy in Victorian London* (London: Edward Arnold, 1977), chaps. 10–11; John N. Tarn, *Five Percent Philanthropy: An Account of Housing in Urban Areas between 1840 and 1914* (Cambridge: Cambridge University Press, 1973); C. F. G. Masterman, ed., *The Heart of the Empire: Discussions of Problems of Modern City Life in England* (1901; Brighton: Harvester, 1973), p. 16.

56. Ian H. Adams, *The Making of Urban Scotland* (Montreal: McGill–Queen's University Press, 1978), p. 167; Burnett, *Social History of Housing*, pp. 184–185; Cherry, *Politics of Town Planning*, pp. 15–17.

57. Wohl, *Eternal Slum*, chaps. 10–11; Mark Swenarton, *Homes Fit for Heroes: The Politics and Architecture of Early State Housing in Britain* (London: Heinemann, 1981), chap. 2; Susan Beattie, *A Revolution in London Housing: LCC Housing Architects and Their Work, 1893–1914* (London: Greater London Council, 1980); London County Council, *Housing of the Working Classes in London* (London, 1913).

58. Wohl, *Eternal Slum*, pp. 362–367.

59. Burnett, *Social History of Housing*, p. 181; Adams, *Making of Urban Scotland*, p. 167.

60. Patricia van den Eeckhout, "Belgium," and Michel Lescure, "France," in *Housing Strategies in Europe, 1880–1930*, ed. Colin G. Pooley (Leicester: Leicester University Press, 1992); Bullock and Read, *Movement for Housing Reform*, chaps. 24–26. The quotation is from ibid., p. 479.

61. Bullock and Read, *Movement for Housing Reform*, pp. 230–248, 133–137.

62. Walter Steitz and Wolfgang R. Krabbe, "Kommunale Wohnungspolitik deutscher Grossstädte, 1871–1914," in *Homo Habitans: Zur Socialgeschichte des ländlichen and städtischen Wohnens in der Neuzeit*, ed. Hans Jürgen Teuteberg (Münster: F. Coppenrath, 1985); *Zum 25 Jährigen Bestehen der Aktienbaugesellschaft für kleine Wohnungen, Frankfurt A.M., 1890–1915* (Frankfurt, 1915); Bullock and Read, *Movement for Housing Reform*, p. 244.

63. Bullock and Read, *Movement for Housing Reform*, p. 239.

64. Ibid., p. 241; Jaeger, *Grundriss der Wohnungsfrage*, pp. 80–82.

65. U.S. Commissioner of Labor, *Eighth Special Report: The Housing of the Working People* (Washington, D.C., 1895); William H. Tolman, "The Progress of Improved Housing during the Last Five Years in the United States," International Housing Congress, *Bericht über den IX. Internationalen Wohnungskongress, Wien, 1910* (Vienna, 1911), pp. 1062–1073; Richard Plunz, *A History of Housing in New York City: Dwelling Type and Social Change in the American Metropolis* (New York: Columbia University Press, 1990), chap. 5; "Government Aid to Home Ownership and Housing of Working People in Foreign Countries," U.S. Bureau of Labor Statistics, *Bulletin* no. 158 (1914). On the French *loi Siegfried* of 1894: William F.

Willoughby, "The Modern Movement for the Housing of the Working Classes in France," *Yale Review* 8 (1899): 233–255; Carol Aronovici, "Housing Reform in France," *Journal of the American Institute of Architects* 3 (Jan. 1915): 32–36.

66. John Ihlder, Diary of European Trip, 1914, and "The Homes of English Workmen," John Ihlder Papers, Franklin Delano Roosevelt Library, Hyde Park, N.Y.; John Ihlder, "Financing English Housing," *American City* 13 (Oct. 1915): 291; John Ihlder, "English Housing through American Eyes," *Survey* 33 (1914): 108–109.

67. Emily Dinwiddie, "Management of Wage-Earners' Dwellings in England," *American City* 13 (Aug. 1915): 93–99; Edward M. Bassett, "Distribution of Population in Cities," ibid. 13 (July 1915): 7–8; Thomas Adams, "English Housing from American Points of View," ibid. 13 (Aug. 1915): 99–100.

68. Roy Lubove, *The Progressives and the Slums: Tenement House Reform in New York City, 1890–1917* (Pittsburgh: University of Pittsburgh Press, 1962); Lawrence Veiller, *Housing Reform: A Hand-Book for Practical Use in American Cities* (New York: Charities Publication Committee, 1910), pp. 193–195.

69. Lawrence Veiller, "The Housing Problem in American Cities," *Annals of the American Academy of Political and Social Science* 25 (1905): 248–272; Lawrence Veiller, "A Program of Housing Reform," *Proceedings of the Academy of Political Science, New York* 2 (1912): 241–248; Lawrence Veiller, "Protecting Residential Districts," *Proceedings of the National Conference on City Planning, Toronto, 1914*, pp. 92–111; Lawrence Veiller, "Housing Reform through Legislation," *Annals of the American Academy of Political and Social Science* 51 (1914): 68–77. The quoted sentence is from the last, p. 76.

Robert de Forest of the New York State Tenement House Commission put the group's point tersely at the International Housing Congress in Vienna in 1910: "There is no municipal housing in the United States of America. There should be no municipal housing in the United States of America." Robert W. de Forest, "Municipal Housing in the United States of America," International Housing Congress, *Bericht über den IX. Internationalen Wohnungskongress, Wien, 1910*, p. 257.

70. Carol Aronovici, "Housing and the Housing Problem," *Annals of the American Academy of Political and Social Science* 51 (1914): 1–7; Carol Aronovici, "The Architecture of the Garden City," *Journal of the American Institute of Architects* 2 (Mar. 1914): 151.

71. Robinson, *Modern Civic Art*, chap. 13; George B. Ford, "The Relation of the 'Social' to the 'Architectural' in Housing and Town Planning," *Proceedings of the Second National Conference on City Planning, 1910* (Boston, 1910), p. 81; Unwin, "American Town Planning"; Thomas Adams, "Garden Cities and Town Planning in America," *Garden Cities and Town Planning*, n.s. 1 (Aug. 1911): 165–173, and (Sept. 1911): 196–198; Peter Marcuse, "Housing in Early City Planning," *Journal of Urban History* 6 (1980): 153–176.

72. U.S. President's Homes Commission, *Report*, 60th Cong., 2nd sess., Senate Document 644 (1909).

73. Massachusetts Homestead Commission, *First Annual Report, 1913* (Boston, 1914), p. 20; Massachusetts Homestead Commission, "Homesteads for Workingmen," *Massachusetts Labor Bulletin* no. 88 (Jan. 1912), p. 44.

74. Massachusetts Homestead Commission, "Homesteads for Workingmen," p. 3; Arthur C. Comey, "Copartnership for Housing in America," *Annals of the American Academy of Political and Social Science* 51 (1914): 140–147; Arthur C. Comey, "Plans for an American Garden Suburb," *American City* 11 (July 1914): 35–36; Roy Lubove, *Community Planning in the 1920s: The Contribution of the Regional Planning Association of America* (Pittsburgh: University of Pittsburgh Press, 1963), chap. 1.

75. Wayne Attoe and Mark Latus, "The First Public Housing: Sewer Socialism's Garden City for Milwaukee," *Journal of Popular Culture* 10 (1976): 142–149.

76. Edith Elmer Wood, "Housing in My Time," p. 3, Edith Elmer Wood Papers, Avery Architectural and Fine Arts Library, Columbia University. The figures are from Stephen Merritt, *State Housing in Britain* (London: Routledge and Kegan Paul, 1979), pp. 331–332n; Bullock and Read, *Movement for Housing Reform*, pp. 247, 244; Michel Lescure, "France," in Pooley, ed., *Housing Strategies in Europe*, p. 232.

77. Quoted in Toll, *Zoned America*, pp. 149, 181.

78. Bullock and Read, *Movement for Housing Reform*, chap. 3; Robert G. Barrows, "Beyond the Tenement: Patterns of American Urban Housing, 1870–1930," *Journal of Urban History* 9 (1983): 395–420.

79. "Day of Skyscrapers Is Passing," p. 11; Ihlder, "Homes of English Workingmen," p. 2.

80. Barrows, "Beyond the Tenement," pp. 409, 414; Martin J. Daunton, "Cities of Homes and Cities of Tenements: British and American Comparisons, 1870–1914," *Journal of Urban History* 14 (1988): 283–319; Michael Doucet and John Weaver, *Housing the North American City* (Montreal: McGill–Queen's University Press, 1991).

81. Robert W. de Forest and Lawrence Veiller, eds., *The Tenement House Problem* (New York: Macmillan, 1903). By 1917 civic groups in more than thirty cities had followed suit with surveys of local housing conditions. Allen Eaton and Shelby M. Harrison, *A Bibliography of Social Surveys* (New York: Rusell Sage Foundation, 1930), pp. 161–173.

82. W. D. P. Bliss, "The Garden Cities Association of America," *Garden City*, n.s. 2 (1907): 268–269; Joseph L. Arnold, *The New Deal in the Suburbs: A History of the Greenbelt Town Program, 1935–1954* (Columbus: Ohio State University Press, 1971), pp. 6–7.

83. Massachusetts Homestead Commission, *Fourth Annual Report, 1916* (Boston, 1917).

84. Adams, "Garden Cities and Town Planning in America," p. 168.

85. Thomas M. Cooley, *A Treatise on the Constitutional Limitations Which Rest upon the Legislative Power of the States of the American Union*, 8th ed., with additions

by Walter Carrington (Boston: Little, Brown, 1927), chaps. 14–15; Breck P. McAllister, "Public Purpose in Taxation," *California Law Review* 18 (1930): 137–148, 241–254; Philip Nichols, Jr., "The Meaning of Public Use in the Law of Eminent Domain," *Boston University Law Review* 20 (1940): 615–641.

86. Ernst Freund, *The Police Power, Public Policy, and Constitutional Rights* (Chicago: Callaghan, 1904).

87. Massachusetts General Court, Committee on Eminent Domain, *Report, 1903: European Land Taking for Public Purposes* (Boston, 1903); City of New York, Committee on Taxation, *Excess Condemnation: A Report* (New York, 1915); Robert E. Cushman, *Excess Condemnation* (New York: D. Appleton, 1917); Edward M. Bassett, "Some Problems in Excess Condemnation," *City Planning* 9 (July 1933): 114–120.

88. *Wineburgh Advertising Co. v. Murphy*, 88 N.Y. 126 (1909); Wilbur Larremore, "Public Aesthetics," *Harvard Law Review* 20 (1906): 35–45; Edward M. Bassett, "Constitutional Limitations on City Planning Powers," National Conference on City Planning, *Proceedings* (1917), p. 205.

89. Shurtleff, *Carrying Out the City Plan*, pp. 3–4.

90. Ibid., pp. 92–93; Williams, *Law of City Planning*, pp. 30–39; Theodora K. Hubbard and Henry V. Hubbard, *Our Cities, To-day and To-morrow: A Survey of Planning and Zoning Progress in the United States* (Cambridge: Harvard University Press, 1929), chap. 10.

91. *Tenement House Dept. v. Moeschen*, 179 N.Y. 325 (1904); J. A. Yelling, *Slums and Slum Clearance in Victorian London* (London: Allen and Unwin, 1986), pp. 80–82.

92. Opinion of the Justices, 211 Mass. 624 (1912); Myres S. McDougal and Addison A. Muller, "Public Purpose in Public Housing: An Anachronism Reburied," *Yale Law Journal* 52 (1942): 42–73; Charles Abrams, *The Future of Housing* (New York: Harper and Brothers, 1946), chap. 15.

93. Donald A. Kruekeberg, ed., *The American Planner: Biographies and Recollections* (New York: Methuen, 1983), p. 16; *Euclid v. Ambler Realty Co.*, 272 U.S. (1926), esp. 371–373; Veiller at the National Conference on City Planning, *Proceedings*, (1918), p. 33.

94. *Ambler Realty Co. v. Village of Euclid*, 297 Fed. (1924) 307; *Euclid v. Ambler Realty Co.*, 272 U.S. (1926), 365. The *Euclid* brief is reprinted in Alfred Bettman, *City and Regional Planning Papers* (Cambridge: Harvard University Press, 1946), pp. 157–193.

95. Edward T. Hartmann, "The Massachusetts Civic Conference," *American City* 2 (Jan. 1910): 30.

96. *The Letters of Sidney and Beatrice Webb*, ed. Norman MacKenzie (Cambridge: Cambridge University Press, 1978), vol. 2, p. 64; Wells, *The Future in America*, pp. 244–245, 248, 74.

6. *The Wage Earners' Risks*

1. *Reports of the United States Commissioners to the Universal Exposition of 1889 at Paris* (Washington, D.C., 1890), vol. 1, p. 260; *Exposition universelle internationale de 1900, Catalogue général officiel*, vol. 18: *Économie sociale, Hygiène, Assistance publique* (Paris: Lemercier, n.d.); *Recueil des travaux du congrès international d'assistance publique et de beinfaisance privée* (Paris, 1900), vol. 1, p. lxxxvii.

2. Peter Mandler, ed., *The Uses of Charity: The Poor on Relief in the Nineteenth-Century Metropolis* (Philadelphia: University of Pennsylvania Press, 1990).

3. John H. Weiss, "Origins of the French Welfare State: Poor Relief in the Third Republic, 1871–1914," *French Historical Studies* 13 (1983): 47–78.

4. Gertrude Himmelfarb, *The Idea of Poverty: England in the Early Industrial Age* (New York: Knopf, 1984); Gertrude Himmelfarb, *Poverty and Compassion: The Moral Imagination of the Late Victorians* (New York: Knopf, 1991); David Thompson, "Welfare and the Historians," in *The World We Have Gained: Histories of Population and Social Structure*, ed. Lloyd Bonfield, Richard M. Smith, and Keith Wrightson (Oxford: Basil Blackwell, 1986); Karel Williams, *From Pauperism to Poverty* (London: Routledge and Kegan Paul, 1981); M. A. Crowther, *The Workhouse System, 1834–1929: The History of an English Social Institution* (Athens: University of Georgia Press, 1981); Felix Driver, *Power and Pauperism: The Workhouse System, 1834–1884* (Cambridge: Cambridge University Press, 1993). The figures are from Michael E. Rose, *The Relief of Poverty, 1834–1914*, 2nd ed. (London: Macmillan, 1982), p. 50.

5. Michael B. Katz, *In the Shadow of the Poorhouse: A Social History of Welfare in America* (New York: Basic Books, 1986); Edith Abbott, *Public Assistance: American Principles and Policies* (1940; New York: Russell and Russell, 1966); Glen C. Altschuler and Jon M. Saltzgaber, "The Limits of Responsibility: Social Welfare and Local Government in Seneca County, New York, 1860–1875," *Journal of Social History* 21 (1988): 515–537.

6. E. Münsterberg, "Principles of Public Charity and Private Philanthropy in Germany," *American Journal of Sociology* 2 (1897): 589–605, 680–698; Francis G. Peabody, "How Should a City Care for Its Poor?" *Forum* 14 (1892): 474–491; Christoph Sachsse and Florian Tennstedt, *Geschichte der Armenfürsorge in Deutschland: Vom Spätmittelalter bis zum Ersten Weltkrieg* (Stuttgart: W. Kohlhammer, 1980), chap. 2; Heide Gerstenberger, "The Poor and the Respectable Worker: On the Introduction of Social Insurance in Germany," *Labour History* 48 (1985): 69–85.

7. Michael E. Rose, "The Crisis of Poor Relief in England, 1860–1890," in *The Emergence of the Welfare State in Britain and Germany, 1850–1950*, ed. W. J. Mommsen (London: George Allen and Unwin, 1981), pp. 56, 55; Katz, *Shadow of the Poorhouse*, chap. 2; Raymond A. Mohl, "The Abolition of Public Outdoor Relief, 1870–1900: A Critique of the Piven and Cloward Thesis," in *Social Welfare or Social Control? Some Historical Reflections on 'Regulating the Poor,'* ed. Walter I. Trattner (Knoxville: University of Tennessee Press, 1983).

8. Leah H. Feder, *Unemployment Relief in Periods of Depression: A Study of Relief Methods Adopted in Certain American Cities, 1857 through 1922* (New York: Russell Sage Foundation, 1936); Alexander Keyssar, *Out of Work: The First Century of Unemployment in Massachusetts* (Cambridge: Cambridge University Press, 1986); Carlos C. Closson, Jr., "The Unemployed in American Cities," *Quarterly Journal of Economics* 8 (1894): 168–217.

9. Sidney and Beatrice Webb, *The Prevention of Destitution* (London: Longmans, Green, 1912), p. 293; Sidney and Beatrice Webb, *The Break-Up of the Poor Law: Being Part One of the Minority Report of the Poor Law Commission* (London: Longmans, Green, 1909), p. 516.

10. Charles Booth, *Life and Labour of the People in London* (London: Macmillan, 1892–1897), vol. 1, pp. 162–171.

11. Francis G. Peabody, "The German Labor-Colonies for Tramps," *Forum* 12 (1892): 751–761; J. H. Gore, "The Poor Colonies of Holland," *Chautauquan* 22 (1896): 581–586.

12. José Harris, *William Beveridge: A Biography* (Oxford: Clarendon Press, 1977), p. 123; Sidney Webb, "The Problem of Unemployment in the United Kingdom, with a Remedy by Organization and Training," *Annals of the American Academy of Political and Social Science* 33 (1909): 420–439; Sidney and Beatrice Webb, eds., *The Public Organisation of the Labour Market: Being Part Two of the Minority Report of the Poor Law Commission* (London: Longmans, Green, 1909). See also José Harris, *Unemployment and Politics: A Study in English Social Policy, 1886–1914* (Oxford: Oxford University Press, 1972); Kenneth D. Brown, *Labour and Unemployment, 1900–1914* (Newton Abbot, England: David and Charles, 1971); Percy Alden and Edward E. Hayward, *The Unemployable and Unemployed* (London: Headley Brooks, 1908); F. Herbert Stead, "Progress with the Unemployed in England," *Charities and the Commons* 15 (1906): 579–582.

13. A. F. Van Schelle, "A City of Vagabonds," *American Journal of Sociology* 16 (1910): 1–20; William H. Dawson, *The Vagrancy Problem: The Case for Measures for Restraint for Tramps, Loafers, and Unemployables* (London: P. S. King, 1910).

14. Francis G. Peabody, "Colonization as a Remedy for City Poverty," *Forum* 17 (1894): 57, 61; John Graham Brooks, "The Future Problem of Charity and Unemployment," *Annals of the American Academy of Political and Social Science* 5 (1894): 266.

15. Edmond Kelly, *The Elimination of the Tramp* (New York: G. P. Putnam's Sons, 1908); Edmond Kelly, "Unemployment in England," *Independent* 65 (1908): 1108–1110; Paul T. Ringenbach, *Tramps and Reformers, 1873–1916: The Discovery of Unemployment in New York* (Westport, Conn.: Greenwood Press, 1973), pp. 125–128; Jane Addams, "Solving the Problem of the Unemployed," *Ladies' Home Journal* 30 (Sept. 1913): 23.

16. Gerhard Ritter, *Social Welfare in Germany and Britain: Origins and Development* (Leamington Spa, England: Berg, 1986); Deltev Zöllner, "Germany," in *The Evolution of Social Insurance, 1881–1981: Studies of Germany, France, Great Britain,*

Austria, and Switzerland, ed. Peter A. Köhler and Hans F. Zacher (London: St. Martin's Press, 1982).

17. Yves Saint-Jours, "France," in *Evolution of Social Insurance*, ed. Köhler and Zacher, pp. 104–105; William F. Willoughby, *Workingmen's Insurance* (New York: Thomas Y. Crowell, 1898), chap. 4.

18. Bentley B. Gilbert, *The Evolution of National Insurance in Great Britain: The Origins of the Welfare State* (London: Michael Joseph, 1966), pp. 165–180; Paul Johnson, *Saving and Spending: The Working-Class Economy in Britain, 1870–1939* (Oxford: Clarendon Press, 1985), chap. 3; P. H. J. H. Gosden, *Self-Help: Voluntary Associations in the Nineteenth Century* (London: B. T. Batsford, 1973), chaps. 2–4.

19. Gilbert, *Evolution of National Insurance*, p. 320; Johnson, *Saving and Spending*, table 2.1.

20. I. M. Rubinow, *Social Insurance* (New York: Henry Holt, 1913), p. 225.

21. B. H. Meyer, "Fraternal Insurance in the United States," *Annals of the American Academy of Political and Social Science* 17(1901): 260–286; Margaret F. Byington, *Homestead: The Households of a Mill Town* (1910; Pittsburgh: Pittsburgh University Press, 1974), p. 113; W. E. B. Du Bois, *The Philadelphia Negro: A Social Study* (Philadelphia: University of Pennsylvania, 1899), pp. 221–225; Charles R. Henderson, *Industrial Insurance in the United States* (Chicago: University of Chicago Press, 1909), pp. 314–316; Hace S. Tishler, *Self-Reliance and Social Security, 1870–1917* (Port Washington, N.Y.: Kennikat Press, 1971), p. 96. Jane Addams is quoted in Henderson, *Industrial Insurance*, p. 82.

22. Edward Cummings, "Report of the Connecticut Labor Bureau," *Quarterly Journal of Economics* 7 (1893): 480–487; B. Seebohm Rowntree, *Poverty: A Study of Town Life*, new ed. (London: Longmans, Green, 1922), pp. 415–424; California Social Insurance Commission, *Report* (Sacramento, 1917), p. 89; Massachusetts Special Commission on Social Insurance, *Report* (Boston, 1917), pp. 184–191.

23. Rubinow, *Social Insurance*, pp. 418, 294, 420. More generally: Viviana A. R. Zelizer, *Morals and Markets: The Development of Life Insurance in the United States* (New York: Columbia University Press, 1979).

24. On women's informal alternatives: Laura Balbo, "Crazy Quilts: Rethinking the Welfare State Debate from a Woman's Point of View," in *Women and the State: The Shifting Boundaries of Public and Private*, ed. Anne Showstack Sassoon (London: Hutchinson, 1987).

25. "Ueber Älters- und Invalidenkassen für Arbeiter," *Schriften des Vereins für Sozialpolitik* 5 (1874); Gustav Schmoller, "Vier Briefe über Bismarcks socialpolitische und volkswirtschaftliche Stellung und Bedeutung," in Gustav Schmoller, *Charakterbilder* (Munich: Duncker and Humblot, 1913); Lujo Brentano, *Die Arbeitterversicherung gemäss der heutigen Wirtschaftsordnung* (Leipzig: Duncker and Humblot, 1879).

26. Ritter, *Social Welfare in Germany and Britain;* Daniel Levine, *Poverty and Society: The Growth of the American Welfare State in International Comparison* (New

Brunswick, N.J.: Rutgers University Press, 1988), chaps. 3–5; Gaston V. Rimlinger, *Welfare Policy and Industrialization in Europe, America, and Russia* (New York: Wiley, 1971), chap. 4.

27. Hans Rothfels, *Theodor Lohmann und die Kampfjahre der staatlichen Sozialpolitik (1871–1905)* (Berlin: C. S. Mittler and Sohn, 1927), chap. 3; Walter Vogel, *Bismarcks Arbeiterversicherung: Ihre Entstehung im Kräftespiel der Zeit* (Braunschweig: Georg Westermann, 1951), esp. p. 151.

28. Germany, Imperial Insurance Office, *The German Workmen's Insurance as a Social Institution* (Berlin, 1904), vol. 1, p. 26.

29. Jürgen Tampke, "Bismarck's Social Legislation: A Genuine Breakthrough?" in Mommsen, ed., *The Emergence of the Welfare State;* Volker Hentschel, *Geschichte der deutschen Sozialpolitik (1880–1980): Soziale Sicherung und kollectives Arbeitsrecht* (Frankfurt: Suhrkamp, 1983), chap. 2. A transitional benefit was extended to wage earners who had already reached age seventy.

30. Gerhard A. Ritter, *Staat, Arbeiterschaft und Arbeiterbewegung in Deutschland, vom Vormärz bis zum Ende der Weimarer Republik* (Bonn: J. H. W. Dietz, 1980); Daniel Levine, "Social Democrats, Socialism, and Social Insurance: Germany and Denmark, 1918–1935," *Comparative Social Research* 6 (1983): 67–86.

31. Elmer Roberts, "Experiments in Germany with Unemployment Insurance," *Scribner's Magazine* 49 (1911): 116–120; William H. Dawson, *The German Workman: A Study in National Efficiency* (New York: Charles Scribner's Sons, 1906), chaps. 1, 3; and, more broadly, John A. Garraty, *Unemployment in History: Economic Thought and Public Policy* (New York: Harper and Row, 1978).

32. Paul Louis, *L'Ouvrier devant l'état: Histoire comparée des lois du travail dans les deux mondes* (Paris: Félix Alcan, 1904).

33. Paul Pic, *Les assurances sociales en France et a l'étranger* (Paris: Félix Alcan, 1913); Léon Bourgeois, *La politique de la prévoyance sociale: L'Action* (Paris: Charpentier, 1919); Allan Mitchell, *The Divided Path: The German Influence on Social Reform in France after 1870* (Chapel Hill: University of North Carolina Press, 1991); Judith F. Stone, *The Search for Social Peace: Reform Legislation in France, 1890–1914* (Albany: State University of New York Press, 1985), pp. 102–122.

34. Susan Pedersen, *Family, Dependence, and the Origins of the Welfare State: Britain and France, 1914–1945* (New York: Cambridge University Press, 1993), chap. 1; Rachel G. Fuchs, "Morality and Poverty: Public Welfare for Mothers in Paris, 1870–1900," *French History* 2 (1988): 288–311; Rachel G. Fuchs, "France in Comparative Perspective," in *Gender and the Politics of Social Reform in France, 1870–1914*, ed. Elinor A. Accampo and Rachel G. Fuchs (Baltimore: Johns Hopkins University Press, 1995); Philip Nord, "The Welfare State in France," *French Historical Studies* 18 (1994): 821–838.

35. Katharine Coman, "Twenty Years of Old Age Pensions in Denmark," *Survey* 31 (1914): 463–465; Levine, *Poverty and Society*, chaps. 6–7; Peter Baldwin, *The Politics of Social Solidarity: Class Bases of the European Welfare State, 1875–1975* (Cambridge: Cambridge University Press, 1990), chap. 1; Henry Demarest Lloyd, *Newest*

England: Notes of a Democratic Traveller in New Zealand, with Some Australian Comparisons (New York: Doubleday, Page, 1900), chap. 14.

36. For brief, lucid summaries of these events: Derek Fraser, *The Evolution of the British Welfare State: A History of Social Policy since the Industrial Revolution* (London: Macmillan, 1973); J. R. Hay, *The Origins of the Liberal Welfare Reforms, 1906–1914* (London: Macmillan, 1975).

37. Williams, *From Pauperism to Poverty*, p. 206.

38. Charles Booth, P*auperism, a Picture, and the Endowment of Old Age, an Argument* (London: Macmillan, 1892).

39. Pat Thane, "Non-Contributory versus Insurance Pensions, 1878–1908," in *The Origins of British Social Policy*, ed. Pat Thane (London: Croom Helm, 1978), esp. pp. 103–104; Gilbert *Evolution of National Insurance*, chap. 4; Hugh Heclo, *Modern Social Politics in Britain and Sweden: From Relief to Income Maintenance* (New Haven: Yale University Press, 1974), chap. 4. Lloyd George is quoted in ibid., p. 176.

40. Edith Abbott, *Democracy and Social Progress in England* (Chicago: University of Chicago Press, 1918), pp. 9–13.

41. E. P. Hennock, *British Social Reform and German Precedents: The Case of Social Insurance, 1880–1914* (New York: Oxford University Press, 1987), pp. 171, 141. For the concept of a policy "impasse," I am indebted to this fine cross-national study.

42. J. R. Hay, "The British Business Community: Social Insurance and the German Example," in Mommsen, ed., *Emergence of the Welfare State.*

43. Harris, *William Beveridge*, p. 50; Hennock, *British Social Reform*, p. 136; William H. Beveridge, *Unemployment: A Problem of Industry* (London: Longmans, Green, 1909).

44. Hennock, *British Social Reform*, pp. 149–150; Gilbert, *Evolution of National Insurance*, pp. 251, 253.

45. Hennock, *British Social Reform*, p. 177. For his comparisons with German social insurance provisions, Lloyd George had relied on William Dawson's calculations.

46. Gilbert, *Evolution of National Insurance*, chaps. 6–7.

47. National Civic Federation, Social Insurance Department, *Report of the Committee on Preliminary Foreign Inquiry* (New York: National Civic Federation, 1914), pp. 22, 28.

48. Heclo, *Modern Social Politics*, pp. 85–90; Beatrice Webb, *Our Partnership* (1948; Cambridge: Cambridge University Press, 1975), pp. 475–476; Sidney Webb and Beatrice Webb, *The Prevention of Destitution* (London: Longmans, Green, 1912); Ritter, *Social Welfare*, p. 91.

49. Gilbert, *Evolution of National Insurance*, p. 273.

50. John Graham Brooks, *The Social Unrest: Studies in Labor and Socialist Movements* (New York: Macmillan, 1903), p. 46. Arthur Shadwell, *Industrial Efficiency: A Comparative Study of Industrial Life in England, Germany, and America* (London: Longmans, Green, 1906) vol. 2, chap. 5.

51. Circular letter of the Executive Committee of the American Association for

Labor Legislation, May 1906, Farnam Family Papers, Manuscripts and Archives, Yale University Library; Circular letter to John P. Frey, March 27, 1908, Papers of the American Association for Labor Legislation, New York State School of Industrial Relations, Cornell University. For general sketches of the AALL's work: Theda Skocpol, *Protecting Soldiers and Mothers: The Political Origins of Social Policy in the United States* (Cambridge: Harvard University Press, 1992), chap. 3; David Moss, *Socializing Security: Progressive-Era Economists and the Origins of American Social Policy* (Cambridge: Harvard University Press, 1996).

52. Maud Nathan, *The Story of an Epoch-Making Movement* (Garden City, N.Y.: Doubleday, Page, 1926).

53. Florence Kelley, *Some Ethical Gains through Legislation* (New York: Macmillan, 1905); Walter I. Trattner, *Crusade for the Children: A History of the National Child Labor Committee and Child Labor Reform in America* (Chicago: Quadrangle, 1970).

54. National Consumers' League, *Sixth Annual Report* (New York, 1905).

55. Felix Frankfurter and Josephine Goldmark, *Women in Industry* (New York: National Consumers' League, 1907); Josephine Goldmark, *Fatigue and Efficiency: A Study in Industry* (New York: Charities Publication Committee, 1912); Felix Frankfurter and Josephine Goldmark, *The Case for the Shorter Work Day* (New York: National Consumers' League, 1916).

56. John A. Ryan, *A Living Wage* (New York: Macmillan, 1906); Diane Kirkby, *Alice Henry: The Power of Pen and Voice: The Life of an Australian-American Labor Reformer* (Cambridge: Cambridge University Press, 1991).

57. Florence Kelley, "Thirty Years of the Consumers' League," *Survey* 63 (1929): 210–212; Elizabeth Glendower Evans, "A Case for Minimum Wage Boards," ibid. 31 (1914): 497–498; Irene Osgood Andrews, *Minimum Wage Legislation: Appendix III of the Third Report of the New York State Factory Investigating Commission* (Albany, 1914); and, more generally, Vivien Hart, *Bound by Our Constitution: Women, Workers, and the Minimum Wage* (Princeton: Princeton University Press, 1994); Peter J. Coleman, *Progressivism and the World of Reform: New Zealand and the Origins of the American Welfare State* (Lawrence: University Press of Kansas, 1987), chap. 5.

58. Elizabeth Brandeis, "Labor Legislation," in John R. Commons et al., *History of Labor in the United States, 1896–1932* (New York: Macmillan, 1918–1935), vol. 3, pp. 458–460, 409; Felix Frankfurter and Josephine Goldmark, *Oregon Minimum Wage Cases: Brief for Defendants in Error upon Re-Argument* (New York: National Consumers' League, 1916).

59. Florence Kelley, "Minimum-Wage Laws," *Journal of Political Economy* 20 (1912): 999–1010; Florence Kelley, "Minimum Wage Legislation," *Survey* 30 (1913): 9–10.

60. Brian Gratton, "Social Workers and Old Age Pensions," *Social Service Review* 57 (1983): 402–415; *Survey* 35 (1915): 197.

61. Skocpol, *Protecting Soldiers and Mothers*, pt. 2. In this otherwise closely and convincingly argued book, Skocpol's suggestion that the Union veterans' benefit

system comprised a "precocious social spending regime" misperceives the relationship between promotionalist state spending and social politics. In a system tipped heavily not toward the working class or toward the poor (southern, black, and post-1865 immigrant) but, rather, toward small-town and rural northerners, the effective cousinhood of the veterans' pension acts was not to social economics—"precocious" or otherwise—but to Republican tariff and western land policies.

In the same vein: Ann Shola Orloff and Theda Skocpol, "Why Not Equal Protection? Explaining the Politics of Public Spending in Britain, 1890–1911, and the United States, 1880s–1920," *American Sociological Review* 49 (1984): 726–750; Ann Shola Orloff, "The Political Origins of America's Belated Welfare State," in *The Politics of Social Policy in the United States*, ed. Margaret Weir, Ann Shola Orloff, and Theda Skocpol (Princeton: Princeton University Press, 1988); Ann Shola Orloff, *The Politics of Pensions: A Comparative Analysis of Britain, Canada, and the United States, 1880–1940* (Madison: University of Wisconsin Press, 1993).

On the size of the veterans' pension system: Maris A. Vinovskis, "Have Social Historians Lost the Civil War? Some Preliminary Demographic Speculations," *Journal of American History* 76 (1989): 34–58; Henderson, *Industrial Insurance*, p. 274.

62. Massachusetts Special Commission on Social Insurance, *Report;* Massachusetts Commission on Old Age Pensions, Annuities and Insurance, *Report* (Boston, 1910), pp. 314, 308; Frank J. Goodnow, *Social Reform and the Constitution* (New York: Macmillan, 1911), pp. 330–317; Susan Sterrett, "Constitutionalism and Social Spending: Pennsylvania's Old Age Pensions in the 1920s," *Studies in American Political Development* 4 (1990): 231–247.

63. Skocpol, *Protecting Soldiers and Mothers*, pt. 3; Linda Gordon, *Pitied But Not Entitled: Single Mothers and the History of Welfare* (New York: Free Press, 1994), chaps. 1–2; Mark H. Leff, "Consensus for Reform: The Mothers' Pension Movement in the Progressive Era," *Social Service Review* 47 (1973): 397–417; Barbara J. Nelson, "The Origins of the Two-Channel Welfare State: Workmen's Compensation and Mothers' Aid," in *Women, the State, and Welfare*, ed. Linda Gordon (Madison: University of Wisconsin Press, 1990).

64. Jane Jenson, "Representations of Gender: Policies to 'Protect' Women Workers and Infants in France and the United States before 1914," in ibid. On the return influence of the American mothers' pension movement on Britain: Pedersen, *Family, Dependence, and the Origins of the Welfare State*, chap. 3.

65. U.S. Commissioner of Labor, *Fourth Special Report: Compulsory Insurance in Germany* (Washington, D.C., 1893); William F. Willoughby, *Workingmen's Insurance* (New York: Thomas Y. Crowell, 1898); U.S. Commissioner of Labor, *Twenty-third Annual Report: Workmen's Insurance and Benefit Funds in the United States* (Washington, D.C., 1909); U.S. Commissioner of Labor, *Twenty-fourth Annual Report: Workmen's Insurance and Compensation Systems in Europe* (Washington, D.C., 1911).

66. Willoughby, *Workingmen's Insurance*, "Conclusion"; Louis D. Brandeis,

"Why Not Savings-Bank Life Insurance for Wage-Earners?" *American Monthly Review of Reviews* 35 (1907): 337–339; Wisconsin Senate Committee on the Practicability of Government and State Insurance, *Report* (Madison, 1907); California Social Insurance Commission, *Report*, pp. 253–254.

67. Willoughby, *Workingmen's Insurance*, p. 112; Henry W. Farnam, "Some Fundamental Distinctions in Labor Legislation," *Publications of the American Economic Association*, 3rd ser., 10 (1900): 104–118; Henry W. Farnam, "The Psychology of German Workmen's Insurance," *Yale Review* 13 (1904): 98–113; U.S. Industrial Commission, *Final Report* (Washington, D.C., 1902).

68. Minnesota Employees' Compensation Commission, *Report* (St. Paul, 1911), pp. 124–128; Donald B. Johnson, ed., *National Party Platforms* (Urbana: University of Illinois Press, 1973), pp. 127–128, 140–142, 163–166; U.S. Congress, House Committee on Labor, *Commission to Study Social Insurance and Unemployment: Hearings on H. J. Res. 159*, 64th Cong., 1st sess., 1916, House Report 914; Morris Hillquit, "Socialism and Social Insurance," National Conference of Social Work, *Proceedings* (1917), pp. 525–528.

69. J. Lee Kreader, "Isaac Max Rubinow: Pioneering Specialist in Social Insurance," *Social Service Review* 50 (1976): 402–425; I. M. Rubinow, "Compulsory State Insurance of Workingmen," *Annals of the American Academy of Political and Social Science* 24 (1904): 331–358; I. M. Rubinow, "Civic Lessons from Europe: Compulsory Insurance," *Chautauquan* 41 (1905): 48–59; Rubinow, *Social Insurance*.

70. I. M. Rubinow, *Was Marx Wrong?* (New York: Marx Institute of America, 1914). The quotations are from I. M. Rubinow, "Sickness Insurance," *American Labor Legislation Review* 3 (1913): 162, and I. M. Rubinow, "Labor Insurance," *Journal of Political Economy* 12 (1904): 362.

71. Walter I. Trattner, ed., *Biographical Dictionary of Social Welfare in America* (Westport, Conn.: Greenwood, 1986), pp. 371–374; *Survey* 34 (1915): 55–56; Steven J. Diner, *A City and Its Universities: Public Policy in Chicago, 1892–1919* (Chapel Hill: University of North Carolina Press, 1980), pp. 31–33.

72. Charles R. Henderson, "Annual Meeting of the German Union for Poor Relief and Charity," *Charities* 7 (1901): 292; Charles R. Henderson, "Workingmen's Insurance," *The World To-day* 10 (1906): 145–148; Charles R. Henderson, *Industrial Insurance in the United States* (Chicago: University of Chicago Press, 1909); Charles R. Henderson, "The Logic of Social Insurance," *Annals of the American Academy of Political and Social Science* 33 (1909): 269; Charles R. Henderson, "The German Social Policy," *Chautauquan* 52 (1908): 397.

73. "Workingmen's Insurance and Old Age Pensions," National Conference of Charities and Corrections, *Proceedings* (1906), pp. 452–457; John Graham Brooks, "Report on German Workingmen's Insurance," ibid. (1905), pp. 452–457, and comment by Florence Kelley, pp. 577–578; Henry R. Seager, "Outline of a Program of Social Legislation with Special Reference to Wage-Earners," American Association for Labor Legislation, *Proceedings* (1907), pp. 85–103; Henry Rogers Seager, *Social Insurance: A Program of Social Reform* (New York: Macmillan, 1910).

74. Gordon, *Pitied But Not Entitled*, chap. 6.

75. Katz, *Shadow of the Poor House*, pp. 191–192.

76. Seager, *Social Insurance*, p. 25.

77. Quoted in Robert Asher, "Workmen's Compensation in the United States, 1880–1935," Ph.D. diss., University of Minnesota, 1971, p. 70.

78. Lawrence M. Friedman and Jack Ladinsky, "Social Change and the Law of Industrial Accidents," *Columbia Law Review* 67 (1967): 50–82. The figures are from Crystal Eastman, *Work-Accidents and the Law* (New York: Charities Publication Committee, 1910), pp. 121–122; Edward D. Berkowitz and Kim McQuaid, *Creating the Welfare State: The Political Economy of Twentieth-Century Reform*, 2nd ed. (New York: Praeger, 1980), pp. 33–41.

79. Emory R. Johnson, "Railway Departments for the Relief and Insurance of Employees," *Annals of the American Academy of Political and Social Science* 7 (1895): 424–468; Robert Asher, "The Limits of Big Business Paternalism: Relief for Injured Workers in the Years before Workmen's Compensation," in *Dying for Work: Workers' Safety and Health in Twentieth-Century America*, ed. David Rosner and Gerald Markowitz (Bloomington: Indiana University Press, 1987).

80. Adna F. Weber, "Employer's Liability and Accident Insurance," *Political Science Quarterly* 17 (1902): 256–283. On the history of the European statutes: Hennock, *British Social Reform*, pt. 1; Anson Rabinbach, "Social Knowledge, Social Risk, and the Politics of Industrial Acccidents in Germany and France," in *States, Social Knowledge, and the Origins of Modern Social Politics*, ed. Dietrich Rueschemeyer and Theda Skocpol (Princeton: Princeton University Press, 1996).

81. *The Works of Theodore Roosevelt*, memorial edition (New York: Charles Scribner's Sons, 1923–1926), vol. 17, p. 591.

82. James Weinstein, *The Corporate Ideal in the Liberal State, 1900–1918* (Boston: Beacon Press, 1968), chap. 2; Roy Lubove, *The Struggle for Social Security, 1900–1935* (Cambridge: Harvard University Press, 1968), chap. 3; Robert Asher, "Business and Workers' Welfare in the Progressive Era: Workmen's Compensation Reform in Massachusetts, 1880–1911," *Business History Review* 43 (1969): 452–475; Robert Asher, "The 1911 Wisconsin Workmen's Compensation Law: A Study in Conservative Labor Reform," *Wisconsin Magazine of History* 57 (1973–1974): 123–140; Robert Asher, "Radicalism and Reform: State Insurance of Workmen's Compensation in Minnesota, 1910–1933," *Labor History* 14 (1973): 19–41; Joseph F. Tripp, "An Instance of Labor and Business Cooperation: Workmen's Compensation in Washington State," ibid. 17 (1976): 530–550; Joseph L. Castrovinci, "Prelude to Welfare Capitalism: The Role of Business in the Enactment of Workmen's Compensation Legislation in Illinois, 1905–1912," *Social Service Review* 50 (1976): 80–102.

83. New York Commission on Employers' Liability, *First Report* (Albany, 1910), pp. 20–25; "Compensation for Industrial Accidents and Their Prevention," *National Civic Federation Review* 3 (July 1, 1991): 2; National Civic Federation, Eleventh Annual Meeting, *Proceedings* (1911), pp. 169–184; Marguerite Green, *The Na-*

tional Civic Federation and the American Labor Movement, 1900–1925 (Washington, D.C.: Catholic University of America Press, 1956), pp. 250–251.

84. For Dawson's and Frankel's conclusions: Atlantic City Conference on Workmen's Compensation Acts, July 29–31, 1909, *Report* (n.p., 1909), pp. 231–261; Lee K. Frankel, "Popularizing Insurance Knowledge in Germany," *Charities and the Commons* 21 (1908): 368–369; Lee K. Frankel and Miles M. Dawson, *Workingmen's Insurance in Europe* (New York: Charities Publication Committee, 1910); Miles M. Dawson, "The System Best Adapted to the United States," *Annals of the American Academy of Political and Social Science* 3 (1911): 175–183; U.S. Congress, House Committee on the Judiciary, *Employers' Liability and Workmen's Compensation: Hearings on H.R. 20487*, 62nd Cong., 2nd sess., 1913, vol. 2, pp. 57–121, 270–287, 590–609. The quotation is from Tishler, *Self-Reliance and Social Security*, p. 182.

85. Conference of Commissions for Industrial Accidents, *Proceedings, 1910* (Boston, 1910), pp. 163–164; Minnesota Employees' Compensation Commission, *Report;* Ferd C. Schwedtman and James A. Emery, *Accident Prevention and Relief: An Investigation of the Subject in Europe, with Special Attention to England and Germany, Together with Recommendations for Action in the United States* (New York: National Association of Manufacturers, 1911); "After the Common Law—What?" *Survey* 2 (1912): 249.

86. E. H. Downey, *Workmen's Compensation* (New York: Macmillan, 1924).

87. Patrick D. Reagan, "The Ideology of Social Harmony and Efficiency: Workmen's Compensation in Ohio, 1904–1919," *Ohio History* 90 (1981): 317–331; H. R. Mengert, "The Ohio Workmen's Compensation Law," *Ohio Archeological and Historical Publications* 29 (1920): 1–48; James H. Boyd, "Workmen's Compensation of Insurance or Workmen and Their Dependents against the Loss of Wages Arising out of Industrial Accidents," *American Journal of Sociology* 17 (1912): 540–545.

88. Coleman, *Progressivism and the World of Reform*, p. 85; Robert F. Wesser, "Conflict and Compromise: The Workmen's Compensation Movement in New York, 1890s–1913," *Labor History* 12 (1971): 345–372; Asher, "Workmen's Compensation," chap. 14; Irwin Yellowitz, *Labor and the Progressive Movement in New York State* (Ithaca: Cornell University Press, 1965), pp. 113–118.

89. Brandeis, "Labor Legislation," pp. 564–609; Lubove, *Struggle for Social Security*, p. 215.

90. National Conference on Workmen's Compensation for Industrial Accidents, *Proceedings of the Third National Conference*, Chicago, June 10–11, 1910 (Princeton, 1910), p. 15; Atlantic City Conference on Workmen's Compensation Acts, 1909, *Report.*

91. *Letters of Louis D. Brandeis*, ed. Melvin I. Urofsky and David W. Levy (Albany: State University of New York Press, 1972), vol. 2, pp. 176, 212; Louis D. Brandeis, "The Road to Social Efficiency," *Outlook* 98 (1911): 292–294; Theodore Roosevelt, *Address before the Convention of the National Progressive Party in Chicago, August 1912* (n.p., 1912); Johnson, *National Party Platforms*, p. 177; Allen F. Davis, *Spearheads for Reform: The Social Settlements and the Progressive Movement, 1890–1914* (New York: Oxford University Press, 1967), pp. 195–197.

92. Yellowitz, *Labor and the Progressive Movement*, pp. 107–118; Tishler, *Self-Reliance and Social Security*, p. 160. The tactics of the AALL can be followed in American Association for Labor Legislation, *Proceedings of the Annual Meeting* (1907–1909) and its *American Labor Legislation Review* (1911–1942).

93. I. M. Rubinow, "First American Conference on Social Insurance," *Survey* 30 (1913): 478–480.

94. John B. Andrews, "A Practical Program for the Prevention of Unemployment in America," *American Labor Legislation Review* 5 (1914): 171–192; New York City, Mayor's Committee on Unemployment, *Report* (New York, 1916); William M. Leiserson, "The Problem of Unemployment Today," *Political Science Quarterly* 31 (1916): 1.

See also Irwin Yellowitz, "The Origins of Unemployment Reform in the United States," *Labor History* 9 (1968): 338–360; Daniel Nelson, *Unemployment Insurance: The American Experience, 1915–1935* (Madison: University of Wisconsin Press, 1969), chap. 1.

95. Ronald L. Numbers, *Almost Persuaded: American Physicians and Compulsory Health Insurance, 1912–1920* (Baltimore: Johns Hopkins University Press, 1978), p. 25; "Health Insurance: Tentative Draft of an Act," *American Labor Legislation Review* 6 (1916): 239–268; Henry R. Seager, "Plan for a Health Insurance Act," ibid. 7 (1916): 20–25.

96. Numbers, *Almost Persuaded;* Lubove, *Struggle for Social Security*, chap. 4; Arthur J. Viseltear, "Compulsory Health Insurance in California, 1915–1918," *Journal of the History of Medicine* 24 (1969): 151–182; Paul Starr, "Transformation in Defeat: The Changing Objectives of National Health Insurance, 1915–1980," in *Compulsory Health Insurance: The Continuing American Debate*, ed. Ronald L. Numbers (Westport, Conn.: Greenwood Press, 1982); California Social Insurance Commission, *Report;* Massachusetts Special Commission on Social Insurance, *Report.*

97. American Association for Labor Legislation, "Comparative Table of Annual Membership and Receipts, Jan. 9, 1914," Farnam Papers. On the French section of the international association: Stone, *Search for Social Peace*, pp. 51–52. On the German section: Rüdiger vom Bruch, "Bürgerliche Sozialreform und Gewerkschaften im späten deutschen Kaiserreich: Die Gesellschaft für Soziale Reform (GSR) 1901–1914," *Internationale wissenschaftliche Korrespondenz zur Geschichte der deutschen Arbeiterbewegung* 15 (1979): 581–610.

98. California Social Insurance Commission, *Report*, pp. 280–283; Edward T. Devine, *Misery and Its Causes* (1909; New York: Macmillan 1913), pp. 247–248; Edward T. Devine, "Pensions for Mothers," *Survey* 30 (1913): 457.

99. For example: Rimlinger, *Welfare Policy;* Tishler, *Self-Reliance and Social Security;* Lubove, *The Struggle for Social Security.*

100. Massachusetts Commission on Old Age Pensions, Annuities and Insurance, *Report*, p. 337; Lubove, *Struggle for Social Security*, p. 84; Insurance Economics Society of America, *Bulletin no. 2: Social Insurance* (Detroit, 1916?), p. 4; Rimlinger, *Welfare Policy*, p. 75; National Civic Federation, *Report of the Committee on Prelimi-*

nary Foreign Inquiry, p. 64. See also Gary Land, "American Images of British Compulsory Health Insurance," in Numbers, ed., *Compulsory Health Insurance.*

101. "The Lloyd-George Insurance Scheme," *Independent* 70 (1911): 1282; Roosevelt, *Address before the Convention of the National Progressive Party*, p. 10; Rubinow, "Sickness Insurance," p. 166.

102. Viseltear, "Compulsory Health Insurance," p. 162; Numbers, *Almost Persuaded*, chap. 7.

103. Samuel Gompers, "Industrial Insurance and Compensation in Germany and Elsewhere," *American Federationist* 17 (1910): 595–596; Samuel Gompers, "'Intellectuals,' Please Note," ibid. 23 (1916): 198–199; Samuel Gompers, "Trade Union Health Insurance," ibid., pp. 1072–1074; U.S. Congress, House Committee on Labor, *Commission to Study Social Insurance.*

104. National Civic Federation, *Report of the Committee on Preliminary Foreign Inquiry*, p. 95; Asher, "Workmen's Compensation," p. 80, n. 41.

105. Tishler, *Self-Reliance and Social Security*, p. 179; National Civic Federation, *Report of the Committee on Preliminary Foreign Inquiry;* Green, *National Civic Federation*, chaps. 6, 9.

106. On the extent of employers' health and pension benefits: California Social Insurance Commission, *Report*, pp. 102–115; Rubinow, *Social Insurance*, pp. 393–396; National Industrial Conference Board, *The Present Status of Mutual Benefit Associations* (New York: National Industrial Conference Board, 1931).

107. Claudia Heuerkamp, "Ärtze und Professionalisierung in Deutschland: Überlegungen zum Wandel des Artzberufs im 19. Jahrhundert," *Geschichte und Gesellschaft* 67 (1980): 366–381; George Rosen, "Contract or Lodge Practice and Its Influence on Medical Attitudes to Health Insurance," *American Journal of Public Health* 67 (1977): 374–378.

108. Burton J. Hendrick, *The Story of Life Insurance* (New York: McClure, Phillips, 1907). The quotation is from Lubove, *Struggle for Social Security*, p. 86.

109. John F. Dryden, *Industrial Insurance: Past and Present* (Newark, N.J.: Prudential Insurance Co. of America, 1912), p. 10.

110. Marquis James, *The Metropolitan Life: A Study in Business Growth* (New York: Viking, 1947), esp. chap. 10; Frederick L. Hoffman to Forrest F. Dryden, Dec. 14, 1916, Frederick L. Hoffman Papers, Rare Book and Manuscript Library, Columbia University. See also Edward T. Devine, "A Revolution in Industrial Insurance," *Charities* 21 (1909): 959–960; Lee K. Frankel, "Industrial Insurance," National Conference of Charities and Corrections, *Proceedings* (1909), pp. 369–380; Charles R. Henderson, "Improvements in Industrial Insurance," *American Journal of Sociology* 15 (1910): 478–450; Louis I. Dublin, *A Family of Thirty Million: The Story of the Metropolitan Life Insurance Company* (New York: Metropolitan Life Insurance Co., 1943).

111. Ella Hoffman Rigney, "Frederick L. Hoffman," Hoffman Papers; Frederick L. Hoffman to Forrest F. Dryden, Feb. 11, 1913, Hoffman Papers.

112. Frederick L. Hoffman to Forrest F. Dryden, Aug. 4 through Dec. 3, 1912, Hoffman Papers.

113. Frederick L. Hoffman to Forrest F. Dryden, Feb. 19, 1913, Jan. 15, 1914, Sept. 22, 1916, Hoffman Papers.

114. For example Frederick L. Hoffman, *Facts and Fallacies of Compulsory Health Insurance* (Newark, N.J.: Prudential Press, 1917); Frederick L. Hoffman, *Autocracy and Paternalism vs. Democracy and Liberty* (New York: n.p., 1918); Frederick L. Hoffman, *More Facts and Fallacies of Compulsory Health Insurance* (Newark, N.J.: Prudential Press, 1920). The quotations are from Numbers, *Almost Persuaded*, pp. 61–62, 78.

7. *War Collectivism*

1. Paul U. Kellogg to Keir Hardie and others, July 23, 1913, Paul U. Kellogg Papers, Social Welfare History Archives, University of Minnesota.

2. Clarke A. Chambers, *Paul U. Kellogg and the* Survey: *Voices for Social Welfare and Social Justice* (Minneapolis: University of Minnesota Press, 1971); Paul U. Kellogg to Frederic C. Howe, Jan. 9, 1926, Survey Associates Papers, Social Welfare History Archives, University of Minnesota.

3. Paul U. Kellogg to his mother, July 6 to Aug. 19, 1908, Kellogg Papers.

4. J. A. Hobson, *Problems of a New World* (New York: Macmillan, 1922), p. 3.

5. *Les congrès internationaux de 1900 a 1919: Liste complète* (Brussels: Union of International Associations, 1964).

6. "Losing Our Scorn for 'Abroad,'" *Nation* 99 (1914): 94–95; Ronald Steel, *Walter Lippmann and the American Century* (Boston: Little, Brown, 1980), pp. 66–73; National Civic Federation, Social Insurance Department, *Report of the Committee on Preliminary Foreign Inquiry* (New York: National Civic Federation, 1914); Institute of Educational Travel, *Civic and Social Tour in Europe in 1914 (1) Municipal Problems and Civic Progress (2) Social Problems and Social Solutions (3) Labor Problems and Industrial Betterment* (New York, n.d.), in the John Nolen Papers, Cornell University; Charles Booth to George Booth, July 9, 1914, Charles Booth Papers, University of London.

7. Bruce Clayton, *Forgotten Prophet: The Life of Randolph Bourne* (Baton Rouge: Louisiana State University Press, 1984); Randolph Bourne, "Impressions of Europe, 1913–1914," in *The History of a Literary Radical and Other Papers*, ed. Van Wyck Brooks (New York: S. A. Russell, 1956), p. 98.

8. Randolph Bourne, "The Social Order in an American Town," *Atlantic Monthly* 111 (1913): 227–236; Van Wyck Brooks, *An Autobiography* (New York: E. P. Dutton, 1965), p. 138.

9. *The Letters of Randolph Bourne: A Comprehensive Edition*, ed. Eric J. Sandeen (Troy, N.Y.: Whitson, 1981), pp. 152, 173, 160, 200; Clayton, *Forgotten Prophet*, pp. 100, 99.

10. *Letters of Randolph Bourne*, p. 200.

11. Randolph Bourne, "An Experiment in Coöperative Living," *Atlantic Monthly* 113 (1914): 831, 823. See also Randolph S. Bourne, "An Hour in Chartres," ibid. 114 (1914): 214–217.

12. *Letters of Randolph Bourne*, p. 241; Randolph S. Bourne, "Berlin in War Time," *Travel* 24 (Nov. 1914): 9ff.

13. *Letters of Randolph Bourne*, pp. 263, 262; Randolph S. Bourne, "American Use for German Ideals," *New Republic* 4 (1915): 117–119; Bourne, "Impressions of Europe," pp. 98–99; Randolph S. Bourne, "Our Unplanned Cities," *New Republic* 3 (1915): 202–203; Randolph S. Bourne, "A Glance at German 'Kultur,'" *Lippincott's Magazine* 95 (Feb. 1915): 27.

14. Bourne, "A Glance at German 'Kultur,'" p. 25.

15. Bourne, "Impressions of Europe," p. 77.

16. "Mental Unpreparedness," *New Republic* 4 (1915): 143; On these themes John A. Thompson, *Reformers and War: American Progressive Publicists and the First World War* (Cambridge: Cambridge University Press, 1987), is a subtle and deeply informed guide.

17. Clayton, *Forgotten Prophet*, p. 116. Baker is quoted in Thompson, *Reformers and War*, p. 89.

18. John Haynes Holmes, "War and the Social Movement," *Survey* 32 (1914): 629–630. In the same vein: Katharine Coman, "What Will the War Mean for Social Insurance in Europe?" ibid. 33 (1914): 74–75.

19. Oswald Garrison Villard, "The Two Germanys," *American Review of Reviews* 50 (1914): 334–336; Oswald Garrison Villard, *Germany Embattled: An American Interpretation* (New York: Charles Scribner's Sons, 1915); "Germanism, Good and Bad," *Independent* 79 (1914): 396–397; William H. Dawson, *What Is Wrong with Germany?* (London: Longmans, Green, 1915).

20. A. Evelyn Newman, "Three Days in Berlin," *Survey* 34 (1915): 226–227; John Jay Chapman, ed., *Deutschland Über Alles; or, Germany Speaks* (New York: G. P. Putnam's Sons, 1914), pp. 37–42.

21. Carol S. Gruber, *Mars and Minerva: World War I and the Uses of the Higher Learning in America* (Baton Rouge: Louisiana State University Press, 1975), esp. p. 72; Simon N. Patten, *Culture and War* (New York: B. W. Huebsch, 1916), pp. 4, 25; Simon N. Patten, "Responsibility for the War," *New Republic* 1 (1914): 21–22; Simon N. Patten, "The German Way of Thinking," *Forum* 54 (1915): 18–26; Henry W. Farnam, *The German Tragedy* (New York: National Security League, 1917); Albion W. Small, "Americans in the World-Crisis," *American Journal of Sociology* 23 (1917): 145–173; Walter E. Weyl, *American World Policies* (New York: Macmillan, 1917), p. 6.

22. "Social Panegyric of Germany," *New Republic* 4 (1915): 343–344; Frederic C. Howe, *Why War?* (New York: Charles Scribner's Sons, 1916). See also Weyl, *American World Policies;* Charles E. Russell, "Who Made This War?" *Pearson's Magazine* 32 (1914): 513–525.

23. Thompson, *Reformers and War*, p. 91; Theodore Roosevelt, *Fear God and Take Your Own Part* (New York: George H. Doran, 1916), p. 41; Allan L. Benson, "How Germany Does It," *Pearson's Magazine* 34 (1915): 329, 331; "U.S. Should Study German State Socialism," *New York Times Magazine*, Sept. 12, 1915, pp. 16–17.

24. Charles Forcey, *The Crossroads of Liberalism: Croly, Weyl, Lippmann, and the Progressive Era, 1900–1925* (New York: Oxford University Press, 1961), pp. 229–231; *Survey* 34 (1915): 1–2; Thompson, *Reformers and War*, p. 108. See also "Retribution," *New Republic* 3 (1915): 215–218; Charles E. Russell, "Why England Falls Down," *Pearson's Magazine* 34 (Aug. 1915): 210–219; Edith Abbott, *Democracy and Social Progress in England* (Chicago: University of Chicago Press, 1918).

25. Alice Lewisohn, "England under the Eaves of War," *Survey* 36 (1916): 161–162; Madeleine Doty, *Short Rations: An American Woman in Germany, 1915 . . . 1916* (New York: Century, 1917), p. 55.

26. William English Walling, "Capitalistic 'Socialism,'" *International Socialist Review* 12 (1911): 303–308; William English Walling, "Government Ownership," ibid. 12 (1912): 652–654; William English Walling, *Socialism As It Is: A Survey of the World-Wide Revolutionary Movement* (New York: Macmillan, 1912); William English Walling, "German State Socialism," *Intercollegiate Socialist* 4 (Dec.–Jan. 1915–16): 10–13.

27. William English Walling, *Progressivism—and After* (New York, Macmillan, 1914), p. viii; William English Walling, *The Socialists and the War* (New York: Henry Holt, 1915), chap. 31; William English Walling, "War—Socialism?" *Intercollegiate Socialist* 4 (Feb.–Mar. 1916): 36–37; "Socialists and the Problems of the War," ibid. 5 (Apr.–May 1917): 7–28; William English Walling, "Internationalism and Government Ownership," *The Public* 21 (Jan. 11, 1918): 49. For a socialist's less exaggerated passage through the war collectivism debates: Harry W. Laidler, "The Conference Speakers," *Intercollegiate Socialist* 5 (Oct.–Nov. 1916): 22–23; Harry W. Laidler, "War Collectivism and Wealth Conscription," ibid. 5 (April–May 1917): 4–7.

28. "The Landslide into Collectivism," *New Republic* 2 (1915): 249–250; "Preparedness—A Trojan Horse," ibid. 5 (1915): 6.

29. "Republican Resurrection," ibid. 9 (1916): 173; Walter Lippmann, *Early Writings*, ed. Arthur Schlesinger, Jr. (New York: Liveright, 1970), pp. 148–149.

30. Christopher Lasch, *The New Radicalism in America (1889–1963): The Intellectual as a Social Type* (New York: Knopf, 1965), chap. 6.

31. Thompson, *Reformers and War*, pp. 212, 213; Gruber, *Mars and Minerva*, pp. 92–93; Frederic C. Howe, "Immigration after the War," *Scribner's Magazine* 58 (1915): 636.

32. Randolph Bourne, "A War Diary," *Seven Arts* 2 (1917): 537.

33. Quoted in John F. McClymer, *War and Welfare: Social Engineering in America, 1880–1925* (Westport, Conn.: Greenwood Press, 1980), p. 170.

34. Richard M. Titmuss, "War and Social Policy," in his *Essays on "The Welfare State,"* ed. Brian Abel-Smith, 3rd ed. (London: George Allen and Unwin, 1976).

35. On the war economies: Gerd Hardach, *The First World War, 1914–1918* (London: Allen Lane, 1977); Arthur Marwick, *War and Social Change: A Comparative Study of Britain, France, Germany, Russia, and the United States* (London: Macmillan, 1974), chap. 3; Susan H. Armitage, *The Politics of Decontrol of Industry: Britain and the United States* (London: Weidenfeld and Nicolson, 1969); Kathleen Burk, ed.,

War and the State: The Transformation of British Government, 1914–1919 (London: George Allen and Unwin, 1982); Arthur Marwick, *The Deluge: British Society and the First World War* (Boston: Little, Brown, 1965); Bernard Waites, *A Class Society at War: England, 1914–1918* (Leamington Spa: Berg, 1987); Chris Wrigley, "The First World War and State Intervention in Industrial Relations, 1914–18," in *A History of British Industrial Relations*, vol. 2: *1914–1939*, ed. Chris Wrigley (Brighton, England: Harvester, 1987); John F. Godfrey, *Capitalism at War: Industrial Policy and Bureaucracy in France, 1914–1918* (Leamington Spa: Berg, 1987); Gerald D. Feldman, *Army, Industry, and Labor in Germany, 1914–1918* (Princeton: Princeton University Press, 1966); Robert D. Cuff, *The War Industries Board: Business-Government Relations during World War I* (Baltimore: Johns Hopkins University Press, 1973); David M. Kennedy, *Over Here: The First World War and American Society* (New York: Oxford University Press, 1980). The arms production quotas are from Gerd Hardach, "Industrial Mobilization in 1914–1918: Production, Planning, and Ideology," in *The French Home Front, 1914–1918*, ed. Patrick Fridenson (Providence, R.I.: Berg, 1992), pp. 60, 63.

36. John N. Horne, *Labour at War: France and Britain, 1914–1918* (Oxford: Clarendon Press, 1991); James E. Cronin, "Labor Insurgency and Class Formation: Comparative Perspectives on the Crisis of 1917–1920 in Europe," and David Montgomery, "New Tendencies in Union Struggles and Strategies in Europe and the United States, 1916–1922," both in *Work, Community, and Power: The Experience of Labor in Europe and America, 1900–1925*, ed. James E. Cronin and Carmen Sirianni (Philadelphia: Temple University Press, 1983). The unionization figures are from Gary Marks, *Unions in Politics: Britain, Germany, and the United States in the Nineteenth and Early Twentieth Centuries* (Princeton: Princeton University Press, 1989), p. 114, and Horne, *Labour at War*, appendix 3.

37. On gender in the war: Susan Pedersen, "Gender, Welfare, and Citizenship in Britain during the Great War," *American Historical Review* 95 (1990): 983–1006; Margaret Randolph Higonnet et al., eds., *Behind the Lines: Gender and the Two World Wars* (New Haven: Yale University Press, 1987).

38. Holmes, "War and the Social Movement," p. 630.

39. Julia Lathrop, "The Military and Naval Insurance Act," *Nation* 106 (1918): 157–158. More generally: Allen F. Davis, "Welfare, Reform and World War I," *American Quarterly* 19 (1967): 516–533.

40. R. H. Tawney, "The Abolition of Economic Controls, 1918–1921," in *History and Society: Essays by R. H. Tawney*, ed. J. M. Winter (London: Routledge and Kegan Paul, 1978), p. 136.

41. *British Industrial Experience During the War*, 65th Cong., 1st sess., Senate Document 114 (1918); Howard L. Gray, *War Time Control of Industry: The Experience of England* (New York: Macmillan, 1918); Ordway Tead, "The American Labor Situation in War-Time," *Century* 95 (1918): 354–359; Mary E. McDowell, "In the Stockyards District," *American Journal of Sociology* 23 (1917): 59–61. See also Sidney Webb, "British Experience for Americans," *Atlantic Monthly* 120 (1917): 14–21, 1162–1166.

42. On the war housing program: Roy Lubove, "Homes and 'A Few Well Placed Fruit Trees': An Object Lesson in Federal Housing," *Social Research* 27 (1960): 469–486; William J. O'Toole, "A Prototype of Public Housing Policy: The USHC," *Journal of the American Institute of Planners* 34 (1968): 140–152.

43. John Ihlder, "How the War Came to Chester," *Survey* 40 (1918): 243–251.

44. Mark Swenarton, *Homes Fit for Heroes: The Politics and Architecture of Early State Housing in Britain* (London: Heinemann, 1981), chap. 3; Simon Pepper and Mark Swenarton, "Home Front: Garden Suburbs for Munitions Workers, 1915–18," *Architectural Review* 163 (1978): 366–375; Great Britain, Ministry of Munitions, *History of the Ministry of Munitions*, vol. 5, pt. 5: *Provision for the Housing of Munitions Workers* (London, 1921).

45. Charles H. Whitaker, "The Rejected Stone," an unpublished autobiographical account in the Avery Architectural and Fine Arts Library, Columbia University; Ewart G. Culpin, "The Remarkable Application of Town-Planning Principles to the War-Time Necessities of England," *Journal of the American Institute of Architects* 5 (1917): 157–159; "The War—The Machine—the Man!" ibid., 421–422.

46. Frederick L. Ackerman, "The Significance of England's Program of Building Workingmen's Housing," ibid., pp. 540, 539, 563.

47. Frederick L. Ackerman, "What Is a House? IV," *Journal of the American Institute of Architects* 5 (1917): 591–639; Frederick L. Ackerman, notes for a lecture in Newark, 1918, as quoted in an unpublished paper, "The Politics of Design," by Randy Garber, School of Architecture, University of Wisconsin—Madison.

48. Charles H. Whitaker et al., "What Is a House?" *Journal of the American Institute of Architects* 5 (1917): 481–485, 541–546, 591–639; 6 (1918): 14–18, 58–67. The series was reprinted as Charles H. Whitaker, Frederick L. Ackerman, Richard S. Childs, and Edith Elmer Wood, *The Housing Problem in War and in Peace* (Washington, D.C.: American Institute of Architects, 1918). See also Sidney Webb, "Wake Up! Architects of America!" *Journal of the American Institute of Architects* 6 (1918): 8–12.

49. Whitaker et al., *Housing Problem*, p. 21. See also Frederick L. Ackerman, "War-Time Housing: England's Most Urgent Civic Lesson for America," *American City* 18 (1918): 97–100; Richard S. Childs, "The New Garden Cities of England," *Outlook* 118 (1918): 364–366.

50. Edith Elmer Wood, "Housing in My Time," p. 5, Edith Elmer Wood Papers, Avery Architectural and Fine Arts Library, Columbia University.

51. Richard S. Childs, "The Government's Model Villages," *Survey* 41 (1919): 584–592; Frederick Law Olmsted, "Lessons from Housing Developments of the United States Housing Corporation," *Monthly Labor Review* 8 (May 1919): 27–38; U.S. Department of Labor, Bureau of Industrial Housing and Transportation, *Report of the United States Housing Corporation: War Emergency Construction (Housing War Workers)*, ed. James Ford and Henry V. Hubbard (Washington, D.C., 1919–20); U.S. Shipping Board, Emergency Fleet Corporation, Passenger Transportation and Housing Division, *Housing the Shipbuilders* (Philadelphia, 1920). I am indebted to Randy Garber for first pointing out the differences in design.

52. George Edgar Vincent, "Housing and Reconstruction," National Housing Association, *Housing Problems in America: Proceedings of the Seventh National Conference on Housing* (Boston, 1918), pp. 43, 47, 49.

53. Quoted in Bentley B. Gilbert, *British Social Policy, 1914–1939* (Ithaca: Cornell University Press, 1970), p. 5.

54. Paul Barton Johnson, *Land Fit for Heroes: The Planning of British Reconstruction, 1916–1919* (Chicago: University of Chicago Press, 1968); Philip Abrams, "The Failure of Social Reform: 1918–1920," *Past and Present* 24 (1963): 43–64. The quoted passages are from Marwick, *The Deluge*, p. 240; Meyer Bloomfield, *Management and Men: A Record of New Steps in Industrial Relations* (New York: Century, 1919), p. 303; William H. Dawson, ed., *After-War Problems* (New York: Macmillan, 1917), p. 10.

55. Arthur Gleason, *What the Workers Want: A Study of British Labor* (New York: Harcourt, Brace and Howe, 1920); Horne, *Labour at War*, chaps. 7–8; J. M. Winter, *Socialism and the Challenge of War: Ideas and Politics in Britain, 1912–1918* (London: Routledge and Kegan Paul, 1974), esp. p. 134; G. D. H. Cole, *Guild Socialism Re-Stated* (London: Leonard Parsons, 1920).

56. *Towards a New World: Being the Reconstruction Programme of the British Labor Party* . . . . (Wyoming, N.Y.: W. R. Browne, 1918), especially p. 9.

57. Ibid., pp. 9, 11, 27, 31.

58. "Resolutions on Reconstruction of the British Labour Party," *Survey* 40 (1918): 500–504.

59. Tony Adams, "The Formation of the Co-operative Party Reconsidered," *International Review of Social History* 32 (1987): 48–68.

60. Mary Heaton Vorse, *A Footnote to Folly: Reminiscences of Mary Heaton Vorse* (New York: Farrar and Rinehart, 1935), p. 170.

61. Walter Weyl, "In the King's Robing Room," *New Republic* 19 (1919): 389–393; "National Industrial Conference, Great Britain," United States Bureau of Labor, *Monthly Labor Review* 8 (1919): 1330–1334; Rodney Lowe, "The Failure of Consensus in Britain: The National Industrial Conference, 1919–1921," *Historical Journal* 21 (1978): 649–675.

62. Swenarton, *Homes Fit for Heroes*, p. 78.

63. Arthur Greenwood, "The Nationalization Movement in Great Britain," *Atlantic Monthly* 125 (1920): 406–411.

64. Armitage, *Politics of Decontrol;* Tawney, "Abolition of Economic Controls"; Rodney Lowe, "The Government and Industrial Relations, 1914–39," in Wrigley, ed., *History of British Industrial Relations.*

65. Dawson, *After-War Problems*, p. 7; Lowe, "Government and Industrial Relations," p. 193.

66. J. A. Hobson, "Representative Government in British Industry," *New Republic* 12 (1917): 130–132; "Towards Industrial Democracy," ibid., p. 122; Ordway Tead, "National Organization by Industries: I. England," ibid. 18 (1919): 48–51; Bloomfield, *Management and Men;* National Industrial Conference Board, *Experi-*

ence with Works Councils in the United States, Research Report no. 50 (New York, 1922); Montgomery, "New Tendencies in Union Struggles," pp. 103–109. The Whitley committee reports were reprinted as appendixes to Bloomfield, *Management and Men*.

67. "Labour and the New Social Order," *New Republic* 14 (1918), pt. 2, p. 2; "Resolutions on Reconstruction of the British Labour Party," *Survey* 40 (1918): 500–504; *Survey* 41 (1918): 225; John M. Blum, *Joe Tumulty and the Wilson Era* (Boston: Houghton Mifflin, 1951), p. 150; *The Papers of Woodrow Wilson*, ed. Arthur S. Link (Princeton: Princeton University Press, 1966–1994), vol. 47, pp. 84, 253–254; George E. Mowry, *The California Progressives* (Berkeley: University of California Press, 1951), p. 297; and, more generally, Stanley Shapiro, "The Great War and Reform: Liberals and Labor, 1917–19," *Labor History* 12 (1971): 323–344. The *New Statesman* is quoted in the last, p. 329n.

68. Clayton, *Forgotten Progressive*, p. 118; Mowry, *California Progressives*, p. 297.

69. *New Republic* 17 (1918): 60; *Survey* 41 (1918): 183; Durant is quoted in Shapiro, "Great War and Reform," p. 342.

70. *Papers of Woodrow Wilson*, vol. 53, pp. 278, 282, 279.

71. Stanley Shapiro, "The Twilight of Reform: Advanced Progressives after the Armistice," *Historian* 33 (1971): 349–364, esp. p. 351; Stanley Shapiro, "Hand and Brain: The Farmer-Labor Party of 1920," Ph.D. diss., University of California, Berkeley, 1967, p. 42; U.S. Council of National Defense, Reconstruction Research Division, *Readjustment and Reconstruction Information*, vol. 2: *Readjustment and Reconstruction Activities in the States* (Washington, D.C., 1920); Lewis Mumford, *Findings and Keepings: Analects for an Autobiography* (New York: Harcourt Brace Jovanovich, 1975), p. 124; *New Republic* 17 (1918): 61.

72. Arthur Gleason to Paul U. Kellogg, July 8, 1919, Survey Associates Papers. The Survey Associates Papers is the best source for the progressive itineraries of 1919. See also Mary McDowell, "'Fear Not to Sow Because of the Birds': Some Impressions of England," *Survey* 41 (1919): 779–780; National Civic Federation, *Second Report of the Committee on Foreign Inquiry* (New York: National Civic Federation, 1920).

73. "Report of Government Commission of Employers to Study Labor Conditions in Europe," U.S. Bureau of Labor Statistics, *Monthly Labor Review* 8 (1919): 1327–28; National Civic Federation, Commission on Foreign Inquiry, *The Labor Situation in Great Britain and France* (New York: E. P. Dutton, 1919); National Industrial Conference Board, European Commission, *Problems of Labor and Industry in Great Britain, France, and Italy*, special report no. 6 (Boston, 1919), pp. 395, 18.

74. "American Labor Politics," *New Republic* 15 (1918): 250.

75. Arthur P. Kellogg, "Shall Social Agencies Unite for Reconstruction?" *Survey* 41 (1918): 316; "Social Reconstruction Program of the National Catholic War Council," U.S. Bureau of Labor Statistics, *Monthly Labor Review* 8 (1919): 1594–1602; Federal Council of the Churches of Christ in America, Commission on the Church and Social Service, *The Church and Social Reconstruction* (New York, 1919);

Harry F. Ward, *The New Social Order: Principles and Programs* (New York: Macmillan, 1919); "We Must Hold the Ground," *Survey* 41 (1918): 266; Hiram Johnson, "What Should the New Congress Do?" *Everybody's Magazine* 40 (Mar. 1919): 28; and, more generally, Estella T. Weeks, *Reconstruction Programs* (New York: Woman's Press, 1919).

76. Blum, *Joe Tumulty*, pp. 150, 306–309; Robert Cuff, "Harry Garfield, the Fuel Administration, and the Search for a Cooperative Order during World War I," *American Quarterly* 30 (1978): 39–53; Albert S. Burleson, "Why We Should Keep the Wires," *Forum* 61 (1919): 152–161.

77. Melvyn Dubofsky, "Abortive Reform: The Wilson Administration and Organized Labor, 1913–1920," in Cronin and Sirianni, eds., *Work, Community and Power*.

78. Harry W. Laidler, "Washington and the Coming Reconstruction," *Intercollegiate Socialist* 7 (Dec. 1918–Jan. 1919): 9. In the same vein: "What Should the New Congress Do?" *Everybody's Magazine* 40 (Mar. 1919): 27 ff.; "After Peace—?" ibid. (May 1919): 58 ff. and (Apr. 1919): 56 ff.

79. Burl Noggle, *Into the Twenties: The United States from Armistice to Normalcy* (Urbana: University of Illinois Press, 1974).

80. U.S. Bureau of Labor Statistics, *Monthly Labor Review* 9 (1919): 1368–1372; John Brophy, *A Miner's Life* (Madison: University of Wisconsin Press, 1964), chaps. 12–13; Glenn E. Plumb and William G. Roylance, *Industrial Democracy: A Plan for Its Achievement* (New York: B. W. Huebsch, 1923).

81. U.S. Bureau of Labor Statistics, *Monthly Labor Review* 9 (1919): 1342–1351; National Industrial Conference Board, *Vital Issues at the Industrial Conference*, special report no. 5 (Boston, 1919); Industrial Conference, *Preliminary Statement* (Washington, D.C., 1919); Haggai Hurvitz, "Ideology and Industrial Conflict: President Wilson's First Industrial Conference of October 1919," *Labor History* 18 (1977): 509–524.

82. Industrial Conference, *Report* (Washington, D.C., 1920).

83. William L. Huggins, *Labor and Democracy* (New York: Macmillan, 1922), p. 43.

84. Allen M. Wakstein, "The Origins of the Open-Shop Movement, 1919–1920," *Journal of American History* 51 (1964): 460–475.

85. Lloyd George is quoted in Lowe, "Government and Industrial Relations," p. 79.

86. New York Legislature, Joint Legislative Committee Investigating Seditious Activities, *Revolutionary Radicalism: Its History, Purpose, and Tactics with an Exposition and Discussion of the Steps being Taken and Required to Curb It* (Albany, 1920); Shapiro, "Hand and Brain," p. 135n; Thompson, *Reformers and War*, p. 260.

87. Ronald L. Numbers, *Almost Persuaded: American Physicians and Compulsory Health Insurance, 1912–1920* (Baltimore: Johns Hopkins University Press, 1978), chaps. 8–9; *For Your Information*, American Association for Labor Legislation circular, Dec. 1919, American Association for Labor Legislation Papers, Cornell University; John B. Andrews, "Introductory Note," *American Labor Legislation Review* 10 (1920): 113.

88. "British and American Labor," *New Republic* 14 (1918): 71.

89. Marvin Swartz, *The Union for Democratic Control in British Politics during the First World War* (Oxford: Clarendon Press, 1971); Alfred F. Havighurst, *Radical Journalist: H. W. Massingham* (Cambridge: Cambridge University Press, 1974).

90. Michael Wreszin, *Oswald Garrison Villard: Pacifist at War* (Bloomington: Indiana University Press, 1965); Oswald Garrison Villard, *Fighting Years: Memoirs of a Liberal Editor* (New York: Harcourt, 1939), p. 391.

91. Paul U. Kellogg, "Two-Edged: Sword or Ploughshare," *Survey Graphic* 29 (1940): 242 ff.; Paul U. Kellogg, "The British Labor Offensive," *Survey* 39 (1918): 585–588; Paul U. Kellogg, "American Labor Out of It," ibid., pp. 617–626; Paul U. Kellogg to Felix Frankfurter, Mar. 11, 1918, Survey Associates Papers; Ray Stannard Baker to Polk, Sept. 12, 1918, Ray Stannard Baker Papers, Library of Congress.

92. Paul U. Kellogg, Samuel Gompers, and William English Walling, *Addresses on the British Labor Party's Program of Reconstruction after the War and the Stockholm Conference, Delivered at a Meeting of the National Civic Federation, New York City, March 16, 1918* (New York, 1918), p. 9; Paul U. Kellogg to Charles W. Eliot, Apr. 13, 1918, Survey Associates Papers.

93. Helen Hayes Gleason, "A.G.: An Appreciation," in *The Book of Arthur Gleason* (New York: William Morrow, 1929); Arthur Gleason and Helen Hayes Gleason, *Golden Lads* (New York: Century, 1916); Arthur Gleason, *Our Part in the Great War* (New York: Frederick A. Stokes, 1917); Arthur Gleason, *Inside the British Isles* (New York: Century, 1917).

94. Gleason, *Inside the British Isles*, pp. 17–18.

95. Arthur Gleason and Paul U. Kellogg, "The England They've Been Fighting For," *Survey* 41 (1918): 243–249; Paul U. Kellogg and Arthur Gleason, *British Labor and the War: Reconstructors for a New World* (New York: Boni and Liveright, 1919).

96. Arthur Gleason to Paul U. Kellogg, July 4, 1919, Survey Associates Papers.

97. Gleason, *What the Workers Want;* Arthur Gleason to Paul U. Kellogg, July 7, 1919, Survey Associates Papers; Arthur Gleason to Bruno Lasker, May 17, 1919, ibid.

98. Ray Stannard Baker, "My Mission in Europe, 1918–1919," pp. 98, 94, Baker Papers; Margaret T. Hodgen, *Workers' Education in England and the United States* (London: Kegan Paul, Trench, Trubner, 1925). On the four pillars of the British Labour Party: Paul Blanshard, *An Outline of the British Labor Movement* (New York: George H. Doran, 1923); Sherwood Eddy, *The New World of Labor* (New York: George H. Doran, 1923).

99. Kellogg et al., *Addresses on the British Labor Party's Program of Reconstruction; Survey* 39 (1918): 688; Samuel Gompers, *Seventy Years of Life and Labor: An Autobiography* (New York: E. P. Dutton, 1925), vol. 2, p. 406.

100. W. A. Appleton, *What We Want and Where We Are: Facts Not Phrases* (New York: George H. Doran, 1922); Kenneth E. Hendrickson, Jr., "The Pro-War Socialists, the Social Democratic League and the Ill-Fated Drive for Industrial De-

mocracy in America, 1917–1920," *Labor History* 11 (1970): 304–322; Kent Kreuter and Gretchen Kreuter, *An American Dissenter: The Life of Algie Martin Simons* (Lexington: University of Kentucky Press, 1969); Henry Pelling, *America and the British Left: From Bright to Bevan* (New York: New York University Press, 1957), chap. 7, esp. pp. 125–126.

101. Frederic C. Howe, *The Confessions of a Reformer* (New York: Scribner, 1925), chap. 32; Eugene M. Tobin, *Organize or Perish: America's Independent Progressives, 1913–1933* (Westport, Conn.: Greenwood, 1986), p. 132.

102. *The Book of Arthur Gleason;* Arthur Gleason, "The Implications of Direct Action," *Freeman* 1 (Apr. 17, 1920): 85–87; Arthur Gleason, *Workers' Education: American and Foreign Experiments* (New York: Bureau of Industrial Research, 1921); Arthur Gleason, "Workers' Education," *New Republic* 26 (1921): 236; Richard J. Altenbaugh, *Education for Struggle: The American Labor Colleges of the 1920s and 1930s* (Philadelphia: Temple University Press, 1990). Gleason was working on child labor issues and on a novel when he died in 1923.

103. Shapiro, "Hand and Brain," p. 33.

104. "Revolution or Reconstruction? A Call to Americans," *Survey* 41 (1919): 882; Shapiro, "Twilight of Reform," p. 359.

105. Charles Merz, "Enter: The Labor Party," *New Republic* (1919): 54.

106. Shapiro, "Hand and Brain"; Tobin, *Organize or Perish*, chap. 5; Dudley Field Malone, "The Birth of the Third Party," *Freeman* 1 (1920): 467–468; Amos Pinchot, "Government by Evasion," ibid. 1 (1920): 538–541.

107. Kenneth Campbell MacKay, *The Progressive Movement of 1924* (1947; reprint ed., New York: Octagon Books, 1972).

108. Harry W. Laidler, "The Collapse of War-Time Collectivism," *American Labor Year Book, 1919–1920* (New York: Rand School of Social Science, 1920), p. 26.

8. Rural Reconstruction

1. Gerold Ambrosius and William H. Hubbard, *A Social and Economic History of Twentieth-Century Europe* (Cambridge: Harvard University Press, 1989), table 2.1; U.S. Bureau of the Census, *Historical Statistics of the United States: Colonial Times to 1970* (Washington, D.C., 1975), p. 139.

2. Kenneth Barkin, "A Case Study in Comparative History: Populism in Germany and America," in *The State of American History*, ed. Herbert J. Bass (Chicago: Quadrangle, 1970); Peter Gourevitch, *Politics in Hard Times: Comparative Responses to International Economic Crises* (Ithaca: Cornell University Press, 1986).

3. B. R. Mitchell, *European Historical Statistics, 1750–1975*, 2nd ed. (New York: Facts on File, 1980), pp. 849, 852; U.S. Bureau of the Census, *Historical Statistics of the United States*, p. 232.

4. Undated autobiographical sketch (c. 1918), Charles McCarthy Papers, Wisconsin State Historical Society, Madison; Edward A. Fitzpatrick, *McCarthy of*

Wisconsin (New York: Columbia University Press, 1944); Charles McCarthy to Walter Hines Page, Feb. 24, 1909, McCarthy Papers.

5. "Dr. McCarthy Is Man of Ideas and Human Encyclopedia," *Sunday State Journal,* Dec. 8, 1912, clipping in the McCarthy Papers.

6. Clarence Poe, *My First Eighty Years* (Chapel Hill: University of North Carolina Press, 1963); Joseph A. Coté, "Clarence Hamilton Poe: The Farmers' Voice, 1899–1964," *Agricultural History* 53 (1979): 30–41. The quotation is from Clarence Poe, *A Southerner in Europe: Being Chiefly Some Old World Lessons for New World Needs as Set Forth in Fourteen Letters of Foreign Travel* (Raleigh, N.C.: Mutual Publishing Co., 1908), p. 74.

7. Clarence H. Poe, "Suffrage Restriction in the South: Its Causes and Consequences" *North American Review* 175 (1902): 534–543; Poe, *A Southerner in Europe,* p. 78.

8. Clarence Poe, *Where Half the World Is Waking Up: The Old and New in Japan, China, the Philippines, and India* (Garden City, N.Y.: Doubleday, Page, 1911); Clarence Poe, *How Farmers Co-operate and Double Profits: First Hand Reports on all the Leading Forms of Rural Co-operation in the United States and Europe—Stories That Show How Farmers Can Co-operate by Showing How They Have Done It and Are Doing It* (New York: Orange Judd, 1915); Clarence Poe, "Lloyd George's England," *World's Work* 23 (1912): 100–111.

9. Kent Fedorowich, *Unfit for Heroes: Reconstruction and Soldier Settlement in the Empire between the Wars* (Manchester, England: Manchester University Press, 1995).

10. American Country Life Association, *Proceedings of the First National Country Life Conference, 1919* (Ithaca: American Country Life Association, 1919), pp. 20–21.

11. Ellen Furlough, *Consumer Cooperation in France: The Politics of Consumption, 1834–1930* (Ithaca: Cornell University Press, 1991), especially p. 24; Sidney Pollard, "Nineteenth-Century Cooperation: From Community Building to Shopkeeping," in *Essays in Labour History,* ed. Asa Briggs and John Saville (London: Macmillan, 1960).

12. G. D. H. Cole, *A Century of Co-operation* (Manchester, England: Co-operative Union, 1944), pp. 371–372, 385; Marquis Childs, *Sweden: The Middle Way* (New Haven: Yale University Press, 1936), p. 16; Clark Kerr, "Measuring the Cooperatives," *Survey Graphic* 26 (Mar. 1937): 140; George Sayers Bain and Robert Price, *Profiles of Union Growth: A Comparative Statistical Portrait of Eight Countries* (Oxford: Basil Blackwell, 1980), p. 37. See also P. H. J. H. Gosden, *Self-Help: Voluntary Associations in the Nineteenth Century* (London: B. T. Batsford, 1973), and Paul Johnson, *Saving and Spending: The Working-Class Economy in Britain, 1870–1939* (Oxford: Clarendon Press, 1985), chap. 5.

13. *Report of the Commissioner General for the United States to the International Universal Exposition, Paris, 1900,* 55th Cong., 2nd sess., Senate Document 232 (1901), vol. 5, pp. 651–652; Kerr, "Measuring the Cooperatives"; Henry W. Wolff, *People's Banks: A Record of Social and Economic Success* (London: Longmans, Green,

1893), chap. 3; Brett Fairbairn, "History from the Ecological Perspective: Gaia Theory and the Problem of Cooperatives in Turn-of-the-Century Germany," *American Historical Review* 99 (1994): 1203–1239, esp. p. 1234.

14. Wolff, *People's Banks;* Harald Faber, *Co-operation in Danish Agriculture* (London: Longmans, Green 1918), pp. 65, 42.

15. M. L. Darling, *Some Aspects of Co-operation in Germany, Italy, and Ireland* (Lahore, India, 1922), p. 6; Faber, *Co-operation in Danish Agriculture;* David Peal, "Self-Help and the State: Rural Cooperatives in Imperial Germany," *Central European History* 21 (1988); 244–266; Charles McCarthy, "The Cost of Living and the Remedy," Speech to the City Club of Chicago, Nov. 28, 1916, McCarthy Papers.

16. Cyril Ehrlich, "Sir Horace Plunkett and Agricultural Reform," in *Irish Population, Economy, and Society*, ed. J. M. Goldstrom and L. A. Clarkson (Oxford: Clarendon Press, 1981), p. 272.

17. Fairbairn, "History from the Ecological Perspective"; Furlough, *Consumer Cooperation in France.*

18. Eduard Bernstein, *Evolutionary Socialism: A Criticism and Affirmation* (London: Independent Labour Party, 1909), p. 187.

19. Fairbairn, "History from the Ecological Perspective," p. 1219.

20. Furlough, *Consumer Cooperation in France*, pp. 96, 88; Johnson, *Saving and Spending*, p. 129.

21. Dana Frank, *Purchasing Power: Consumer Organizing, Gender, and the Seattle Labor Movement, 1919–1929* (Cambridge: Cambridge University Press, 1994); Joseph G. Knapp, *The Rise of American Cooperative Enterprise, 1620–1920* (Danville, Ill.: Interstate Printers and Publishers, 1969).

22. International Co-operative Alliance, *Year-Book of International Co-operation*, 2nd year (London: International Co-operative Alliance, 1913), pp. 133–134; Edson L. Whitney, "Cooperative Credit Societies (Credit Unions) in America and in Foreign Countries," U.S. Bureau of Labor Statistics, *Bulletin* no. 314 (1922); Myron T. Herrick and R. Ingalls, *How to Finance the Farmer: Private Enterprise—Not State Aid* (Cleveland: Ohio State Committee on Rural Credits and Cooperation, 1915); Shelly Tenenbaum, *A Credit to Their Community: Jewish Loan Societies in the United States, 1880–1945* (Detroit: Wayne State University Press, 1993). Urban building and loan societies, on the other hand, flourished in the United States; they had 2.8 million members in 1914.

23. R. H. Elsworth, "Agricultural Cooperative Associations, Marketing and Purchasing, 1925," U.S. Department of Agriculture, *Technical Bulletin* no. 40 (1928); Lewis C. Gray, *Introduction to Agricultural Economics* (New York: Macmillan, 1924), chap. 26; Henry C. Taylor, *Outlines of Agricultural Economics* (New York: Macmillan, 1925), chap. 34; E. C. Branson, "Co-operative Credit Unions in North Carolina," *Southern Workman* 49 (1920): 461–473. The estimate for Germany is from Peter Stearns, *European Society in Upheaval: Social History since 1800* (New York: Macmillan, 1967), p. 232.

24. Plunkett's American contacts can be traced through his diaries and corre-

spondence in the Horace Plunkett Papers, The Plunkett Foundation for Cooperative Studies, Oxford, England. On the Wallace connection: Russell Lord, *The Wallaces of Iowa* (Boston: Houghton Mifflin, 1947). For a late-nineteenth-century view of Irish rural poverty: W. T. Ellis, *A Summer Jaunt of One Hundred Days in Europe* (Owensboro, Ky.: Inquirer Publishing Co., 1885), p. 9. On Lippmann: John Morton Blum, ed. *Public Philosopher: Selected Letters of Walter Lippmann* (New York: Ticknor and Fields, 1985), pp. 15–16.

25. Trevor West, *Horace Plunkett: Co-operation and Politics: An Irish Biography* (Washington, D.C.: Catholic University of America, 1986); Ehrlich, "Sir Horace Plunkett and Agricultural Reform."

26. Cormac Ó Gráda, "The Beginnings of the Irish Creamery System, 1880–1914," *Economic History Review* 30 (1977): 284–305; Patrick Bolger, *The Irish Co-operative Movement: Its History and Development* (Dublin: Institute of Public Administration, 1977). On the Irish credit cooperatives: Timothy W. Guinnane, "Culture and Cooperation: Credit Cooperatives in Late Nineteenth Century Germany," unpublished paper presented to the Davis Seminar in Historical Studies, Princeton University, Sept. 30, 1994.

27. Horace Plunkett, *Ireland in the New Century* (1904; Dublin: Irish Academic Press, 1982); George W. Russell (AE), *The National Being: Some Thoughts on an Irish Polity*, popular ed. (Dublin: Maunsel, 1918); George W. Russell (AE), *Co-operation and Nationality: A Guide for Rural Reformers from This to the Next Generation* (Dublin: Maunsel, 1912). The quotations are from Horace Plunkett, "The Improvement of Rural Conditions," *Southern Workman* 37 (1908): 80, and Plunkett, *Ireland in the New Century*, p. 62.

28. Horace Plunkett Diaries, Dec. 21, 1909, Plunkett Papers.

29. U.S. Country Life Commission, *Report*, 60th Cong., 2nd sess., Senate Document 705 (1909), esp. pp. 17, 50; Liberty Hyde Bailey, *The Country-Life Movement in the United States* (1911; New York: Macmillan, 1920), p. 97.

30. Kenyon L. Butterfield, *Chapters in Rural Progress* (Chicago: University of Chicago Press, 1908); John M. Gillette, *Constructive Rural Sociology* (New York: Sturgis and Walton, 1913); Carl C. Taylor, *Rural Sociology: A Study of Rural Problems* (New York: Harper and Brothers, 1926); Edmund de S. Brunner et al., *American Agricultural Villages* (New York: George H. Doran, 1927); Charles J. Galpin, *Rural Social Problems* (New York: Century, 1924); Charles J. Galpin, *My Drift into Rural Sociology* (Baton Rouge: Louisiana State University Press, 1938). For critical accounts of the country life movement: David B. Danbom, *The Resisted Revolution: Urban America and the Industrialization of Agriculture, 1900–1930* (Ames: Iowa State University Press, 1979); Mary Neth, *Preserving the Family Farm: Women, Community, and the Foundations of Agribusiness in the Midwest, 1900–1940* (Baltimore: Johns Hopkins University Press, 1995).

31. Horace Plunkett, *The Rural Life Problem of the United States: Notes of an Irish Observer* (New York: Macmillan, 1910); *Marketing and Farm Credits: A Collection of Papers Read at the Third Annual Sessions of the National Conference on Marketing and*

Farm Credits, 1916 (Madison, Wis.; National Conference on Marketing and Farm Credits, 1916), p. 17; Horace Plunkett Diaries, Mar. 2, 1913, Plunkett Papers; Charles McCarthy to Gifford Pinchot, Apr. 11, 1913, Plunkett Papers. On the American Agricultural Organization Society: Charles A. Lyman, "An American Estimate of Agricultural Co-operation in Ireland," *Better Business: A Quarterly Journal of Agricultural and Industrial Cooperation* (Jan. 1916): 121–131.

32. Olivia Rossetti Agresti, *David Lubin: A Study in Practical Idealism* (Boston: Little, Brown, 1922); Harris Weinstock, *Report on the Labor Laws and Labor Conditions of Foreign Countries in Relation to Strikes and Lockouts* (Sacramento, 1910); Grace Larsen, "A Progressive in Agriculture: Harris Weinstock," *Agricultural History* 32 (1958): 187–193.

33. David Lubin *Adaptation of the European Cooperative Credit System to Meet the Needs of the American Farmer*, 62nd Cong., 2nd sess., Senate Document 855 (1919), esp. pp. 4, 6; David Lubin, *"The Way Out of the Rut": European Cooperative Rural Credit Systems*, 62nd Cong., 3rd sess., Senate Document 966 (1912); David Lubin, *The* Landschaften *System of Rural Credits*, 63rd Cong., 1st sess. Senate Document 123 (1913).

34. Southern Commercial Congress, *American Commission for the Study of the Application of the Co-operative System to Agricultural Production, Distribution, and Finances in European Countries*, 62nd Cong., 3rd sess., Senate Document 1071 (1913); *Agricultural Cooperation and Rural Credit in Europe: Information and Evidence*, 63rd Cong., 1st sess., Senate Document 214 (1913); David Lubin, *Frederick William Raffeisen: An Address*, 63rd Cong., 1st sess., Senate Document 114 (1913). The quotation is from Ralph Metcalf and Clark G. Black, *Rural Credit Cooperation and Agricultural Organization in Europe* (Olympia, Wash., 1915), chap. 8.

35. Myron T. Herrick, *Preliminary Report on Land and Agricultural Credit in Europe*, 62nd Cong., 3rd sess., Senate Document 967 (1912); Thomas Nixon Carver, *Recollections of an Unplanned Life* (Los Angeles: Ritchie, 1949), chap. 16.

36. George W. Russell (AE), *The Rural Community: An Address to the American Commission of Agricultural Inquiry* (Dublin, 1913); Horace Plunkett to Gifford Pinchot, Feb. 26, 1913, and Horace Plunkett Diaries, Dec. 7, 1913, Plunkett Papers; Horace Plunkett to Gifford Pinchot, July 16, 1913, McCarthy Papers.

37. *Agricultural Cooperation and Rural Credit in Europe*, pt. 1, pp. 9, 18, 10.

38. Ibid., pt. 2, pp. 8–9. For those of this mind, the answer was straightforward: a system of commercial banks empowered to make long-term loans on farm land. See, for example, Duncan U. Fletcher, "A National Rural Banking System," 63rd Cong., 1st sess., Senate Document 158 (1913).

39. U.S. Congress, *Rural Credits: Joint Hearings before the Subcommittee of the Committees on Banking and Currency of the Senate and the House of Representatives Charged with the Investigation of Rural Credit*, 63rd Cong., 2nd sess. (1914); Knapp, *Rise of American Cooperative Enterprise*, chap. 7.

40. U.S. Congress, Senate Committee on Banking and Currency, *Rural Credits: Report to Accompany S. 2986*, 64th Cong., 1st sess., Senate Report 144 (1916); Her-

bert Quick, "The Rural Credit Firing Squad," *Saturday Evening Post* 188 (Apr. 25, 1916): 29ff. The text of the act is reprinted in A. C. Wiprud, *The Federal Farm-Loan System in Operation* (New York: Harper and Brothers, 1921), pp. 111–182.

41. Grant S. Youman, "Rural Credits," 64th Cong., 1st sess., Senate Document 349 (1916); Wiprud, *Federal Farm-Loan System;* Earl S. Sparks, *History and Theory of Agricultural Credit in the United States* (New York: Thomas Y. Crowell, 1932).

42. Faber, *Co-operation in Danish Agriculture*, p. 84.

43. Morton Keller, *Regulating a New Economy: Public Policy and Economic Change in America, 1900–1933* (Cambridge: Harvard University Press, 1990), p. 154; John Hanna, "Co-operative Associations and the Public," *Michigan Law Review* 29 (1930): 148–190; David E. Hamilton, *From New Day to New Deal: American Farm Policy from Hoover to Roosevelt, 1928–1933* (Chapel Hill: University of North Carolina Press, 1991).

44. Aaron Sapiro, "Principles in California Cooperatives" (1921), in *Agricultural Thought in the Twentieth Century*, ed. George McGovern (Indianapolis: Bobbs-Merrill, 1967), pp. 94–103; E. C. Lindeman, "Sapiro, the Spectacular," *New Republic* 50 (1927): 216–219; R. H. Elsworth, "Agricultural Cooperative Associations, Marketing and Purchasing, 1925," U.S. Department of Agriculture, *Technical Bulletin* no. 4 (1928); R. H. Elsworth, "Cooperative Marketing and Purchasing, 1920–1930," U.S. Department of Agriculture, *Circular* no. 121 (1930).

45. G. Harold Powell, *Coöperation in Agriculture* (New York: Macmillan, 1913); *Agricultural Cooperation and Rural Credit in Europe*, pt. 1; *Marketing and Farm Credits, 1915*, pp. 25–39.

46. Elsworth, "Agricultural Cooperative Associations"; Elsworth, "Cooperative Marketing and Purchasing."

47. Walter A. Terpenning, *Village and Open-Country Neighborhoods* (New York: Century, 1931).

48. Neth, *Preserving the Family Farm*, esp. chap. 2.

49. Lee Meriwether, *A Tramp Trip: How to See Europe on Fifty Cents a Day* (1893; New York: Harper and Brothers, 1903), p. 138.

50. Frederic C. Howe, *The Land and the Soldier* (New York: Charles Scribner's Sons, 1919), p. 17; E. C. Branson, *Farm Life Abroad: Field Letters from Germany, Denmark, and France* (Chapel Hill: University of North Carolina Press, 1924), p. 44–45, 10–11.

51. Robert Kluger, "Elwood Mead: Irrigation Engineer and Social Planner," Ph.D. diss., University of Arizona, 1970; Paul K. Conkin, "The Vision of Elwood Mead," *Agricultural History* 34 (1960): 88–97; Elwood Mead, *Irrigation Institutions: A Discussion of the Economic and Legal Questions Created by the Growth of Irrigated Agriculture in the West* (New York: Macmillan, 1903). On water politics more generally: Donald J. Pisani, "Reclamation and Social Engineering in the Progressive Era," *Agricultural History* 57 (1983): 47–63; Donald Worster, *Rivers of Empire: Water, Aridity, and the Growth of the American West* (New York: Pantheon, 1985).

52. Bruce R. Davidson, *European Farming in Australia: An Economic History of*

Australian Farming (Amsterdam: Elsevier, 1981); Gordon Taylor, "Closer Settlement in Victoria," *Economic Record* 12 (1936): 57–70; Francis G. Castles, *The Working Class and Welfare: Reflections on the Political Development of the Welfare State in Australia and New Zealand, 1890–1980* (Wellington: Allen and Unwin, 1985).

53. Elwood Mead, *Helping Men Own Farms: A Practical Discussion of Government Aid in Land Settlement* (New York: Macmillan, 1920), chaps. 3–6; U.S. Congress, Senate Committee on Irrigation and Reclamation, *Creation of Organized Rural Communities to Demonstrate Methods of Reclamation and Benefits of Planned Rural Development: Hearings on S. 2015*, 70th Cong., 1st sess., 1928, pp. 3–23; Elwood Mead, "Government Direction in Land Settlement," *American Economic Review* 8, supplement (1918): 89–94.

54. Elwood Mead, "The Conquest of Arid Australia," n.d., Elwood Mead Papers, Bancroft Library, University of California at Berkeley; Elwood Mead, "Irrigated Australia," n.d., Mead Papers; Elwood Mead, "Irrigation in Northern Italy, Part 1," U.S. Department of Agriculture, Office of Experiment Stations, *Bulletin* no. 144 (1904); California Commission on Land Colonization and Rural Credits, *Report* (Sacramento, 1916), pp. 63, 71–72; Rudolf Lerch, "Internal Colonization in Germany: A Problem in Rural Land Utilization," *Annals of the American Academy of Political and Social Science* 150 (1930): 273–287.

55. Elwood Mead, "Irrigation in Australia," *Independent* 96 (1910): 762; Elwood Mead, "What Our Government Ought to Be and Ought to Do," *Metropolitan Magazine* (1917), copy in the Mead Papers.

56. Richard T. Ely, "Private Colonization of the Land," *American Economic Review* 8 (1918), 522–548; "Land Settlement in California," Commonwealth Club of California, *Transactions* 11, no. 8 (1916); "The Land Settlement Bill of 1917," ibid., 12, no. 1 (1917): 1–66; California Commission on Land Colonization, *Report.*

57. Mead, *Helping Men Own Farms;* California State Land Settlement Board, *Report*, Sept. 30, 1920; California Department of Public Land, Division of Land Settlement, *Information for Intending Settlers Regarding the Delhi State Land Settlement* (n.p., n.d.); Vernon M. Cady, "A Western Experiment in Land Settlement," *Survey* 40 (1918): 684–687. There were also smaller lots, tiny one- to two-acre house and garden allotments for those Mead hoped to attract to work as hired farm laborers.

58. Elwood Mead, "Community Farming," *New Republic* 41 (1925): 327–332; Valerie J. Matsumoto, *Farming the Home Place: A Japanese American Community in California, 1919–1982* (Ithaca: Cornell University Press, 1993).

59. Elwood Mead, "Social Needs of Farm Life," address delivered in San Francisco, 1920, Mead Papers; "The Japanese Land Question in California," *Annals of the American Academy of Political and Social Science* 93 (Jan. 1921): 51–55; Secretary, Division of Land Settlement, to L. W. Manson, June 24, 1922, Mead Papers; Elwood Mead to Winfred Stein, Feb. 8, 1922, Mead Papers; Elwood Mead, "Farm Settlements on a New Plan," *American Review of Reviews* 59 (1919): 271–272; Mead, *Helping Men Own Farms*, pp. 141, 197.

60. Bill G. Reid, "Franklin K. Lane's Idea for Veterans' Colonization, 1918–1921," *Pacific Historical Review* 33 (1964): 447–461; Keith W. Olson, *Biography of a Progressive: Franklin K. Lane, 1864–1921* (Westport, Conn.: Greenwood Press, 1979); Alvin Johnson, "Land for the Returned Soldier," *New Republic* 16 (1918): 218–220; Howe, *The Land and the Soldier.*

61. Bill G. Reid, "Agrarian Opposition to Franklin K. Lane's Proposal for Soldier Settlement, 1918–1921," *Agricultural History* 41 (1967): 167–179.

62. California Department of Agriculture, Division of Land Settlement, *Final Report,* June 30, 1931.

63. Charles S. Bird to Lawrence Veiller, Apr. 14, 1920, and *The Farm Cities Corporation of America: No. 1—April, 1921,* both in the "Farm Cities" file, John Nolen Papers, Cornell University; Alvin Johnson, *Pioneer's Progress: An Autobiography* (New York: Viking, 1952), pp. 289–304; Paul K. Conkin, *Tomorrow a New World: The New Deal Community Program* (Ithaca: Cornell University Press, 1959), chap. 12.

64. U.S. Congress, Senate Committee on Irrigation and Reclamation, *Creation of Organized Rural Communities to Demonstrate Methods of Reclamation and Benefits of Planned Rural Development: Hearings on S. 2015,* 70th Cong., 1st sess., 1928; U.S. Congress, Senate Committee on Irrigation and Reclamation, *Creation of Organized Rural Communities to Demonstrate the Benefits of Planned Settlement: Hearings on S. 412,* 71st Cong, 1st sess., 1929, esp. p. 3; Southern Reclamation Congress, *Proceedings,* 70th Cong., 1st sess., Senate Document 45 (1928).

65. The quoted phrase is from Bailey, *Country-Life Movement,* p. 97.

66. Russell, *Co-operation and Nationality,* p. 6.

67. Charles L. Lewis, *Philander Priestley Claxton: Crusader for Public Education* (Knoxville: University of Tennessee Press, 1948); Booker T. Washington, *The Man Farthest Down: A Record of Observation and Study in Europe* (Garden City, N.Y.: Doubleday, Page, 1912), chap. 17; Institute of Educational Travel, *Civic and Social Tour in Europe in 1914* (New York, 1914), copy in the Nolen Papers.

68. Frederic C. Howe, *Denmark: A Cooperative Commonwealth* (New York: Harcourt, Brace, 1921), esp. pp. viii, iii; Josephine Goldmark, *Democracy in Denmark* (Washington, D.C.: National Home Library Foundation, 1936); William E. Leuchtenburg, *Franklin D. Roosevelt and the New Deal, 1932–1940* (New York: Harper and Row, 1963), p. 345; Thomas H. Eliot, *Recollections of the New Deal: When the People Mattered* (Boston: Northeastern University Press, 1992), p. 27; Edgar W. Knight, *Among the Danes* (Chapel Hill: University of North Carolina Press, 1927), p. viii.

69. Branson, *Farm Life Abroad,* p. 154.

70. Henry Goddard Leach, "Now It Can Be Told," *American-Scandinavian Review* 12 (1924): 99–107; Anthony M. Platt, *E. Franklin Frazier Reconsidered* (New Brunswick, N.J.: Rutgers University Press, 1991), p. 56.

71. Branson, *Farm Life Abroad,* p. 113; Hugh MacRae to John Nolen, Jan. 9, 1924, Nolen Papers; Platt, *E. Franklin Frazier,* pp. 56–59.

72. Howe, *Denmark*, chap. 13; W. Glyn Jones, *Denmark* (New York: Praeger, 1970), pp. 134–135; K. J. Kristensen, "Public Guidance in Rural Land Utilization in Denmark," *Annals of the American Academy of Political and Social Science* 150 (1930): 230–237; U.S. Bureau of the Census, *Historical Statistics of the United States*, p. 465.

73. Branson, *Farm Life Abroad*, p. 108.

74. Harold W. Foght, *Rural Denmark and Its Schools* (New York: Macmillan, 1915); Olive Dame Campbell, *The Danish Folk School: Its Influence in the Life of Denmark and the North* (New York: Macmillan, 1928).

75. L. L. Friend, "The Folk High Schools of Denmark," U.S. Bureau of Education, *Bulletin* no. 5 (1914); Harold W. Foght, "The Danish Folk High Schools," ibid., no. 22 (1914); Martin Hegland, "The Danish People's High Schools," ibid., no. 45 (1915); Booker T. Washington, *My Larger Education* (Garden City, N.Y.: Doubleday, Page, 1911), chap. 11; Gertrude Austin, "Danish Schools for Adults," *Southern Workman* 51 (1911): 624–635; E. Franklin Frazier, "The Folk High School at Roskilde" and "Danish People's High Schools in America," ibid. 51 (1922): 325–328, 425–430.

76. Joseph K. Hart, *Light from the North: The Danish Folk High Schools and Their Meanings for America* (New York: Henry Holt, 1927).

77. Frederic C. Howe, "Wisconsin Folk High School," *School Life* 23 (Sept. 1937): 26–27; John Rector Barton Papers, Wisconsin State Historical Society, Madison.

78. Henry D. Shapiro, *Appalachia on Our Mind: The Southern Mountains and Mountaineers in the American Consciousness, 1870–1920* (Chapel Hill: University of North Carolina Press, 1978); David E. Whisnant, *All That Is Native and Fine: The Politics of Culture in an American Region* (Chapel Hill: University of North Carolina Press, 1983).

79. John C. Campbell, *The Southern Highlander and His Homeland* (New York: Russell Sage Foundation, 1921). The quoted lines are from Shapiro, *Appalachia on Our Mind*, p. 239.

80. Whisnant, *All That Is Native and Fine*, chap. 2; Olive D. Campbell "Adult Education as a Means of Vitalizing and Enriching American Rural Life" and "Adjustment to Rural Industrial Change with Special Reference to Mountain Areas," National Education Association, *Proceedings* 67 (1929): 301–304 and 484–488; Olive Dame Campbell, "I Sing behind the Plough," *Journal of Adult Education* 2 (1930): 248–259, esp. 253. On the Pine Mountain Settlement: Whisnant, *All That Is Native and Fine*, p. 123.

81. John M. Glen, *Highlander: No Ordinary School, 1932–1962* (Lexington: University Press of Kentucky, 1988); Myles Horton with Judith Kohl and Herbert Kohl, *The Long Haul: An Autobiography* (New York: Doubleday, 1990); untitled interview with Myles Horton, 1959, Highlander Research and Education Center Papers, Wisconsin State Historical Society, Madison, esp. pp. 6–8.

82. Myles Horton, Danish notebook, Highlander Papers.

83. "Present Activities and Plans of the Highlander Folk School" (1933); "Sum-

mer School Report and Summary of Reports of Other Educational Activities, Sept. 1933–1934"; "Report of Community and School Activities, '33 3/4–'34"; Lilian W. Johnson, "Beginnings of the Cooperative Movement in the United States," typescript, n.d.—all in the Highlander Papers.

84. "A Report for the Year 1936," Highlander Papers; Myles Horton, "Roskilde Workers School, Forstander Gammelgaard, 11/23/31," Highlander Papers; Myles Horton, "The Highlander Folk School," *The Social Frontier* 2 (Jan. 1936): 117–118; Myles Horton, "Mountain Men," Highlander Papers.

85. Olive Campbell to Myles Horton, Apr. 6, 1933, Highlander Papers.

86. Myles Horton, undated fragment in the Highlander Papers.

87. Russell, *National Being*, p. 24.

9. *The Machine Age*

1. Arthur S. Link, ed., *The Papers of Woodrow Wilson* (Princeton: Princeton University Press, 1966–1994), vol. 63, p. 469.

2. Walter Trattner, *Homer Folks: Pioneer in Social Welfare* (New York: Columbia University Press, 1968), chap. 10.

3. Ruth Gaines, *A Village in Picardy* (New York: E. P. Dutton, 1918); Ruth Gaines, *Helping France: The Red Cross in the Devastated Area* (New York: E. P. Dutton, 1919); Ruth Gaines, *Ladies of Grécourt: The Smith College Relief Unit in the Somme* (New York: E. P. Dutton, 1920); Beulah E. Kennard, "American Games in France," *Survey* 44 (1920): 482–484.

4. George B. Ford, *Out of the Ruins* (New York: Century, 1919); George B. Ford, "Civic Progress in Devastated France," *Survey* 46 (1921): 173–180; William L. Chenery, "American Rebuilder of Martyred Rheims," *New York Times Book Review and Magazine*, July 11, 1920, pp. 5 ff; "Das amerikanische Project für Rheims," *Der Städtebau* 28 (1921): 21 and table 9–10.

5. William C. Dreher, "A Letter from Germany," *Atlantic Monthly* 89 (1902): 401; Frank Costigliola, *Awkward Dominion: American Political, Economic, and Cultural Relations with Europe, 1919–1933* (Ithaca: Cornell University Press, 1984), chaps. 5–6.

6. Bruno Lasker, "Snapshots in Berlin," *Survey* 46 (1921): 647–648; Lothrop Stoddard, "Berlin and Vienna: Likenesses and Contrasts," *Scribner's Magazine* 74 (1923): 651–655; Matthew Josephson, *Life among the Surrealists: A Memoir* (New York: Holt, Rinehart, and Winston, 1962), p. 194; Robert S. Lynd, "Papier Geld," *Survey* 51 (1923): 138–141.

7. Joseph Wood Krutch, "Berlin Goes American," *Nation* 126 (1928): 565.

8. Charles A. Beard, "The American Invasion of Europe," *Harper's Magazine* 158 (1929): 471; Ellen Furlough, "Selling the American Way in Interwar France: Prix Uniques and the Salons des Arts Ménagers," *Journal of Social History* 26 (1993): 491–519; Costigliola, *Awkward Dominion*, p. 176.

9. Beard, "American Invasion of Europe," pp. 472, 478; Mary Nolan, *Visions of*

Modernity: American Business and the Modernization of Germany (New York: Oxford University Press, 1994), chap. 3; Victoria de Grazia, "The Exception Proves the Rule: The American Example in the Recasting of Social Strategies in Europe between the Wars," in *Why Is There No Socialism in the United States?* ed. Jean Heffer and Jeanine Rovet (Paris: École des hautes études en sciences sociales, 1989); Otto T. Mallery, "Notes on Vienna Conference for Social Progress," *American Labor Legislation Review* 17 (1927): 278–283.

10. Earl R. Beck, *Germany Rediscovers America* (Tallahassee: Florida State University Press, 1968), p. 17; Gustav Stolper, Karl Häuser, and Knut Borchardt, *The German Economy, 1870 to the Present* (New York: Harcourt, Brace, and World, 1967), p. 97; André Siegfried, *America Comes of Age: A French Analysis* (New York: Harcourt, Brace, 1927); *Planning Problems of Town, City, and Region: Papers and Discussions at the International City and Regional Planning Conference, New York City, 1925* (Baltimore, 1925); Nolan, *Visions of Modernity*, chap. 2.

11. Peter R. Shergold, *Working-Class Life: The 'American Standard' in Comparative Perspective, 1899–1913* (Pittsburgh: University of Pittsburgh Press, 1982); Arthur Feiler, *America Seen through German Eyes* (New York: New Republic, 1928), pp. 88–89. Hoover is quoted in William E. Leuchtenburg, *The FDR Years: On Roosevelt and His Legacy* (New York: Columbia University Press, 1995), p. 284, italics added. German trade union delegations put the wage differential still higher, at four to one. Nolan, *Visions of Modernity*, pp. 66–67.

12. Detlev J. Peukert, *The Weimar Republic: The Crisis of Classical Modernity* (London: Allen Lane, 1991), p. 174; Gerold Ambrosius and William H. Hubbard, *A Social and Economic History of Twentieth-Century Europe* (Cambridge: Harvard University Press, 1989), table 3.10; I. M. Rubinow, *The Quest for Security* (New York: Henry Holt, 1934), p. 318.

13. H. W. Massingham, "Impressions of America" (1919), in *H. W. M.: A Selection from the Writings of H. W. Massingham*, ed. H. J. Massingham (London: Jonathan Cape, 1925), p. 298; Feiler, *America Seen through German Eyes*, pp. 23, 32; Alfred Agache, "City Planning in the United States," *City Planning* 6 (1930): 266; Erich Mendelsohn, *Amerika: Bilderbuch eines Architekten* (Berlin: Mosse, 1926), p. vi; C. B. Purdom, "The International Conference at New York," *Garden Cities and Town-Planning* 15 (Aug. 1925): 197–198; Walter Curt Behrendt, *Städtebau und Wohnungswesen in den Vereinigten Staaten: Bericht über eine Studienreise* (Berlin: Guido Hackebeil, 1927), p. 16.

14. Nolan, *Visions of Modernity*, p. 110.

15. Siegfried, *America Comes of Age;* Georges Duhamel, *America the Menace: Scenes from the Life of the Future* (Boston: Houghton Mifflin, 1931); Lujo Brentano, "Amerika-Europa," *Gesellschaft* 3 (1926): 193–121.

16. Patty Lee Parmalee, *Brecht's America* (Columbus, Ohio: Miami University Press, 1981).

17. Sisley Huddleston, "American's New Industrial Doctrines," *New Statesman* 34 (1929): 385–386.

18. Philip Kerr, "Can We Learn from America?" *Nation and Athenaeum* (London) 40 (1926): 76–77.

19. Nolan, *Visions of Modernity*, pt. 1; Costigliola, *Awkward Dominion*, pp. 179–180.

20. Reyner Banham, *A Concrete Atlantis: U.S. Industrial Buildings and European Modern Architecture, 1900–1925* (Cambridge: MIT Press, 1986); Le Corbusier, *Towards a New Architecture* (London: John Rodker, 1931), pp. 21–31; Bruno Taut, *Modern Architecture* (London: Studio, 1930); Mendelsohn, *Amerika*, pp. 36–43; Erich Mendelsohn, *Briefe eines Architekten* (Munich: Prestel, 1961), p. 67.

21. Taut, *Modern Architecture*, p. 211.

22. Joseph A. McCartin, "'An American Feeling': Workers, Managers, and the Struggle over Industrial Democracy in the World War I Era," in *Industrial Democracy in America: The Ambiguous Promise*, ed. Nelson Lichtenstein and Howell John Harris (Cambridge: Cambridge University Press, 1993); National Industrial Conference Board, *The Growth of Works Councils in the United States*, Special Report no. 32 (New York, 1925), p. 5.

23. Irving Bernstein, *The Lean Years: A History of the American Worker, 1920–1933* (1960; Baltimore: Penguin, 1966), pp. 156–74; John R. Commons, *Industrial Government* (New York: Macmillan, 1921), chap. 2.

24. Daniel Nelson, *Unemployment Insurance: The American Experience, 1915–1935* (Madison: University of Wisconsin Press, 1969), pp. 57–58, 79–103; Paul H. Douglas, "American Plans of Unemployment Insurance," *Survey* 65 (1931): 484–486.

25. Contemporaries estimated that 5.8 million employees were covered under company group life insurance plans in 1928, 3.75 million under company pension plans in 1929, 1.2 million under group accident and health insurance plans in 1933, and not more than 11,000 under company-provided unemployment compensation in 1928. Employees on the nation's nonfarm and nongovernmental payrolls in 1929 numbered 28.2 million. Berstein, *Lean Years*, pp. 181, 184; National Industrial Conference Board, *Recent Developments in Group Insurance* (New York, 1934), p. 25; U.S. Bureau of the Census, *Historical Statistics of the United States: Colonial Times to 1970* (Washington, D.C., 1975), p. 137.

26. William J. Barber, *From the New Era to the New Deal: Herbert Hoover and American Economic Policy, 1921–1933* (Cambridge: Cambridge University Press, 1985); Ellis Hawley, ed., *Herbert Hoover as Secretary of Commerce: Studies in New Era Thought and Practice* (Iowa City: University of Iowa Press, 1981).

27. Clarence Darrow in "Where are the Pre-War Radicals?" *Survey* 55 (1926): 566; William L. Chenery, "Unemployment at Washington," ibid. 47 (1921): 42.

28. W. L. Chenery, "The Cinema of Conferences," *Survey* 43 (1919): 242; Abraham Epstein, "Brief Report of Findings Abroad" (1925), Abraham Epstein Papers, New York State School of Industrial and Labor Relations, Cornell University; Lincoln Steffens, "How Europe Can Help America," *Century* 106 (1923): 535; Paul

Kellogg to Charles Renold, Jan. 7, 1929, Survey Associates Papers, Social Welfare History Archives, University of Minnesota.

29. These can best be followed in both the advertisements and the regular "Traveler's Notebook" column in the *Survey*, launched in Feburary 1929. On the inauguration of the *Survey*'s own Travel Department: *Survey Graphic* 22 (1933): 241.

30. Hanns Gramm, *The Oberlaender Trust, 1931–1953* (Philadelphia: Carl Schurz Memorial Foundation, 1956); Oberlaender Trust file, John Nolen Papers, Cornell University.

31. Lewis Feuer, "American Travelers to the Soviet Union, 1917–32: The Formation of a Component of New Deal Ideology," *American Quarterly* 14 (1962): 119–149, esp. p. 128; Christopher Lasch, *The American Liberals and the Russian Revolution* (New York: Columbia University Press, 1961); Peter G. Filene, *Americans and the Soviet Experiment, 1917–1933* (Cambridge: Harvard University Press, 1967); American Russian Institute, *Are You Interested in Russia?* (New York, n.d.), copy in the Nolen Papers.

32. Colin G. Pooley, ed., *Housing Strategies in Europe, 1880–1930* (Leicester: Leicester University Press, 1992), pp. 248, 245, 82; U.S. Bureau of the Census, *Historical Statistics*, p. 640.

33. Robert G. Barrows, "Beyond the Tenement: Patterns of American Urban Housing, 1870–1930," *Journal of Urban History* 9 (1983): 409, 416.

34. Kenneth T. Jackson, *The Crabgrass Frontier: The Suburbanization of the United States* (New York: Oxford University Press, 1985), p. 173; Gail Radford, *Modern Housing for America: Policy Struggles in the New Deal Era* (Chicago: University of Chicago Press), pp. 51–53, 20–26; the editors of *Fortune*, *Housing America* (New York: Harcourt, Brace, 1932), p. 23; *President's Conference on Home Building and Home Ownership*, vol. 4: *Home Ownership, Income, and Types of Dwellings* (Washington, D.C., 1932), pp. 70–73.

35. Pooley, *Housing Strategies in Europe*, p. 82; Dan P. Silverman, "A Pledge Unredeemed: The Housing Crisis in Weimar Germany," *Central European History* 3 (1970): 112–139; Catherine Bauer, *Modern Housing* (Boston: Houghton Mifflin, 1934), pp. 127–128.

36. John Burnett, *A Social History of Housing, 1815–1970* (Newton Abbot, England: David and Charles, 1978), chap. 8; London County Council, Housing and Public Health Committee, *London Housing* (London, 1937), pp. 154–167; E. D. Simon and J. Inman, *The Rebuilding of Manchester* (London: Longmans, Green, 1935); Lewis Mumford, "England's Two Million Houses, New," *Fortune* 6 (Nov. 1932): 32, 33.

37. Elizabeth Denby, *Europe Re-Housed* (New York: Norton, 1938); George Orwell, *Coming up for Air* (1939; New York: Harbrace, n.d.), p. 236.

38. Robert Danneberg, *Vienna under Socialist Rule* (London: Labour Party, 1928); Helmut Gruber, *Red Vienna: Experiment in Working-Class Culture, 1919–1934* (New York: Oxford University Press, 1991); Peter Marcuse, "The Housing Policy of

Social Democracy: Determinants and Consequences," in *The Austrian Socialist Experiment: Social Democracy and Austro-marxism, 1918–1934*, ed. Anson Rabinbach (Boulder, Colo.: Westview Press, 1985).

39. Charles O. Hardy, *The Housing Program of the City of Vienna* (Washington, D.C.: Brookings Institution, 1934).

40. "Vienna," undated manuscript in the Catherine Bauer Wurster Papers, Bancroft Library, University of California, Berkeley; Hardy, *Housing Program of Vienna*, chap. 1; Richard Seider, "Housing Policy, Social Welfare, and Family Life in 'Red Vienna,' 1919–1934," *Oral History* 13 (Autumn 1985): 35–48.

41. *Der Karl Marx Hof* (n.d.), pamphlet in the Catherine Bauer Wurster Papers; Manfredo Tafuri, ed., *Vienna Rossa: La politica residenziale nella Vienna socialista, 1919–1933* (Milan: Electa, 1980).

42. Marquis Childs, *Sweden: The Middle Way* (New Haven: Yale University Press, 1936), p. 164; Denby, *Europe Re-Housed*, p. 253.

43. Barbara M. Lane, *Architecture and Politics in Germany, 1918–1945* (Cambridge: Harvard University Press, 1968), chap. 4; Norbert Huse, *"Neues Bauen" 1918 bis 1933: Moderne Architektur in der Weimarer Republik* (Munich: Heinz Moos, 1975).

44. Kurt Junghanns, *Bruno Taut, 1880–1938* (Berlin: Henschelverlag, 1970); *Bruno Taut, 1880–1938: Ausstellung der Akademie der Künste* (Berlin: Akademie der Künste, 1980); *Martin Wagner* (Berlin: Akademie der Künste, 1985).

45. Nicholas Bullock, "Die neue Wohnkultur und der Wohnungsbau in Frankfurt am Main, 1925–1931," *Archiv für Frankfurts Geschichte und Kunst* 57 (1980): 187–207; Justus Buekschmitt, *Ernst May* (Stuttgart: Alexander Koch, 1963); John R. Mullin, "City Planning in Frankfurt, Germany, 1925–1932: A Study in Practical Utopianism," *Journal of Urban History* 4 (1977): 3–28; Ernst May, *Die Frankfurter Wohnungspolitik* (Frankfurt: International Housing Association, 1929); W. Nobisch, *Das Wohnungswesen der Stadt Frankfurt a. M.* (Frankfurt, 1930); Emil Klar, ed., *Vier Jahrzehnte Wohnungsbau: Denkschrift zum vierzigjährigen Bestehen der Aktienbaugesellschaft für kleine Wohnungen in Frankfurt am Main, 1890–1930* (Frankfurt: Aktienbaugesellschaft für kleine Wohnungen, 1930); Douglas Haskell, "'New Mayland,'" *Nation* 134 (1932): 292–293.

46. Klaus-Peter Kloss, *Siedlungen der 20er Jahren* (Berlin: Haude and Spener, 1982); *Berlin und seine Bauten, IV: Wohnungsbau, Band A: Die Entwicklung der Wohngebiete* (Berlin: Wilhelm Ernst, 1970). Beyond Frankfurt and Berlin, the new style was less common in working-class housing. Dresden, Nuremberg, and Hannover held out consistently against it. But by 1932 there were publicly sponsored, modernist working-class housing developments in most large German cities. Lane, *Architecture and Politics*, pp. 103–104, 124.

47. Ludwig Landmann, "Zum Geleit," *Das neue Frankfurt* 1 (1926): 1–2; Taut, *Modern Architecture*, p. 3. See also Fritz Weichert, "Zeitwende—Kunstwende," *Das neue Frankfurt* 1 (1926): 15–24. Martin Wagner launched a parallel journal, *Das neue Berlin*, in 1929.

48. Catherine Bauer Wurster, "The Social Front of Modern Architecture in the 1930s," *Journal of the Society of Architectural Historians* 24 (Mar. 1965): 51; Louis Pink, *The New Day in Housing* (New York: John Day, 1928), p. 49; Catherine Bauer, "The Americanization of Europe," *New Republic* 67 (1931): 153–154.

49. J. J. P. Oud, "The 213 House," *Creative Art* 8 (1931): 174–175; Susan Henderson, "A Revolution in Woman's Sphere: Grete Lihotzky and the Frankfurt Kitchen," in *Architecture and Feminism*, ed. Debra Coleman et al. (Princeton: Architectural Press, 1996). May visited the United States in 1925, just before assuming his Frankfurt position, to attend the International City and Regional Planning Conference in New York City. Wagner made two trips to study American building methods, in 1924 and 1929. In 1984, May's chief designer, Ferdinand Kramer, still possessed his copy of Christine Frederick's *New Housekeeping*.

50. At Römerstadt, most of the dwellings held seventy-five square meters of usable floor space; the smallest apartments had forty-eight square meters. At Westhausen the apartments came in either forty-one- or forty-seven-square-meter units. The Vienna norm was forty to forty-eight square meters. Ernst May, "Grundlagen der Frankfurter Wohnungsbaupolitik," *Das neue Frankfurt* 2 (1928): 126; Ernst May, "Fünf Jahre Wohnungsbautätigkeit in Frankfurt am Main," ibid. 4 (1930): 57. See also Internationale Kongresse für Neues Bauen, *Die Wohnung für Existenzminimum* (Frankfurt: Englert and Schlosser, 1930).

51. Edith Elmer Wood, *Housing Progress in Western Europe* (New York: E. P. Dutton, 1923); Pink, *New Day in Housing;* Herbert Undeen Nelson and Marion Lawrence Nelson, *New Homes in Old Countries* (Chicago: National Association of Real Estate Boards, 1937); John L. Hancock, "John Nolen and the American City Planning Movement," Ph.D. diss., University of Pennsylvania, 1964, p. 433.

52. Wood, *Housing Progress in Western Europe*, pp. 186–187; Edith Elmer Wood, *Recent Trends in American Housing* (New York: Macmillan, 1931), pp. 283–284. See also Arthur Comey, "European Impressions," *City Planning* 3 (Jan. 1927): 55–60.

53. Mary S. Cole, "Catherine Bauer and the Public Housing Movement, 1926–1937," Ph.D. diss., George Washington University, 1975; Radford, *Modern Housing for America*, chap. 3; "Housing's White Knight," *Architectural Forum* 84 (Mar. 1946): 116 ff.; Notebook, 1926–1927, Catherine Bauer Wurster Papers; Catherine Bauer, "Machine-Age Mansions for Ultra-Moderns," *New York Times Magazine*, Apr. 15, 1928, pp. 10 ff.

54. *Architectural Record* 79 (May 1936): 341; Catherine Bauer Wurster, "The Social Front of Modern Architecture," p. 48.

55. Catherine Bauer, "Art in Industry," *Fortune* 3 (May 1931): 94–110; Museum of Modern Art, *Modern Architecture: International Exhibition* (New York: Museum of Modern Art, 1932), pp. 179–199. The *Fortune* articles were published as Lewis Mumford, "England's Two Million Houses, New," *Fortune Magazine* 6 (Nov. 1932): 32 ff.; Lewis Mumford, "Machines for Living," ibid. 7 (Feb. 1933): 78–88; and Lewis Mumford, "Taxes into Houses," ibid. 7 (May 1933): 48 ff.

56. Bauer, *Modern Housing*, esp. pt. 4; Catherine Bauer, "Are Good Houses Un-American?" *New Republic* 70 (1932): 74.

57. Bauer, "Are Good Houses Un-American?" p. 74.

58. Bauer, *Modern Housing*, pp. 136, 247.

59. Lewis Mumford, *Technics and Civilization* (New York: Harcourt, Brace, 1934): Lewis Mumford, *The Culture of Cities* (New York: Harcourt, Brace, 1938); Catherine Bauer to Lewis Mumford, Aug. 7, 1939, Catherine Bauer Wurster Papers.

60. Lewis Mumford's best, though hardly unopinionated, biographer was himself: *Findings and Keepings: Analects for an Autobiography* (New York: Harcourt Brace Jovanovich, 1975); *My Works and Days: A Personal Chronicle* (New York: Harcourt Brace Jovanovich, 1979); *Sketches from Life: The Autobiography of Lewis Mumford: The Early Years* (New York: Dial Press, 1982); "A New York Adolescence," *New Yorker* 13 (Dec. 4, 1937): 86–94; Lewis Mumford, "Lewis Mumford," *Portraits and Self-Portraits*, ed. Georges Schreiber (Boston: Houghton Mifflin, 1936). See also Donald L. Miller, *Lewis Mumford: A Life* (New York: Weidenfeld and Nicolson, 1989); Thomas P. Hughes and Agatha C. Hughes, eds., *Lewis Mumford: Public Intellectual* (New York: Oxford University Press, 1990); and Elmer S. Newman, *Lewis Mumford: A Bibliography, 1914–1970* (New York: Harcourt Brace Jovanovich, 1971).

61. Lewis Mumford, *Sticks and Stones: A Study of American Architecture and Civilization* (New York: Boni and Liveright, 1924); Lewis Mumford, *The Golden Day: A Study of American Experience and Culture* (New York: Horace Liveright, 1926), esp. pp. 80, 73; Lewis Mumford, *Herman Melville* (New York: Harcourt, Brace, 1929); Lewis Mumford, *The Brown Decades: A Study of the Arts in America, 1865–1895* (New York: Harcourt, Brace, 1931); Lewis Mumford, "American Condescension and European Superiority," *Scribner's Magazine* 87 (1930): 526–527; Matthew Josephson, *Infidel in the Temple: A Memoir of the Nineteen-Thirties* (New York: Knopf, 1967), pp. 8–10.

62. Mumford, *My Works and Days*, chap. 5; Lewis Mumford, "Americanized Europe," *Freeman* 6 (1922): 254.

63. Patrick Geddes, *Cities in Evolution: An Introduction to the Town Planning Movement and to the Study of Civics* (London: Williams and Norgate, 1915); Patrick Geddes, "Cities Exhibition," in Geddes, *Cities in Evolution*, new and revised ed. (New York: Oxford University Press, 1950). On Geddes's reaction to New York City: Philip Boardman, *The Worlds of Patrick Geddes: Biologist, Town-planner, Re-educator, Peace-warrior* (London: Routledge and Kegan Paul, 1978), p. 169.

64. Lewis Mumford, "Houses—Sunnyside Up," *Nation* 120 (1925): 115–116; Roy Lubove, *Community Planning in the 1920's: The Contribution of the Regional Planning Association of America* (Pittsburgh: University of Pittsburgh Press, 1963); Lewis Mumford, "The Drama of the Machines," *Scribner's Magazine* 88 (1930): 150–161; Lewis Mumford, draft manuscript, "Form and Personality" (c. 1930), Lewis Mumford Papers, Special Collections, University of Pennsylvania Library.

65. Lewis Mumford to James Henderson, Jan. 7, 1934, Mumford Papers.

66. Lewis Mumford, "North Sea Architecture," *Yale Review* 22 (1933): 515, 521; Mumford, "Machines for Living," p. 84.

67. Lewis Mumford, *Values for Survival* (New York: Harcourt, Brace, 1946), p. 243; Lewis Mumford, "Notes on Germany," *New Republic* 72 (1932): 281; Mumford, "North Sea Architecture," pp. 521, 524.

68. Lewis Mumford, "What I Believe," *Forum* 84 (1930): 263–268; Lewis Mumford, "In Our Stars: The World Fifty Years from Now," ibid. 88 (1932): 338–342; Mumford, *Technics and Civilization*, pp. 400–406.

69. Lewis Mumford, draft manuscript, "Form and Civilization" (1933), p. 1, Mumford Papers.

70. For the "Neotechnic Phase," as Mumford called the emerging stage of history in 1934, he had substituted the "Biotechnic Order" by 1938—modifying the concept but not fundamentally changing it. For simplicity's sake, I have employed the 1934 term throughout.

71. Lewis Mumford, *The City in History* (New York: Harcourt, Brace and World, 1961); Lewis Mumford, "An Appraisal of Lewis Mumford's 'Technics and Civilization' (1934)," *Daedalus* 88 (1959): 532, 534. See also his pessimistic rewriting of *Technics and Civilization:* Lewis Mumford, *The Myth of the Machine* (New York: Harcourt Brace Jovanovich, 1967, 1970), and his second thoughts on modernism: Lewis Mumford, "Monumentalism, Symbolism and Style" (1949), reprinted in his *The Human Prospect*, ed. Harry T. Moore and Karl W. Deutsch (Boston: Beacon Press, 1955).

72. Mumford, *Culture of Cities*, plate 32, ellipsis in the original.

73. Lewis Mumford, "Break the Housing Blockade!" *New Republic* 75 (May 17, 1933): 8–11; "The Planned Community," *Architectural Forum* 58 (1933): 253–274; Albert Mayer, Lewis Mumford and Henry Wright, *New Homes for a New Deal* (New York: New Republic, 1934); Lewis Mumford, "The Social Imperatives of Housing," in *America Can't Have Housing*, ed. Carol Aronovici (New York: Museum of Modern Art, 1934); Lewis Mumford, Travel Note, June 5, 1932, Mumford Papers.

The Housing Study Guild's moving spirit, Henry Wright, had himself made a four-month pilgrimage to Germany in 1932 and 1933, and had come back a convert to modernism. Henry S. Churchill, "Henry Wright," *Journal of the American Institute of Planners* 26 (1960): 293–301.

74. Mumford, "Social Imperatives of Housing," p. 16.

75. John W. Edelman, *Labor Lobbyist: The Autobiography of John W. Edelman*, ed. Joseph Carter (Indianapolis: Bobbs-Merrill, 1974), pp. 109–110.

76. Steven Fraser, *Labor Will Rule: Sidney Hillman and the Rise of American Labor* (New York: Free Press, 1991), chap. 8; Richard Plunz, *A History of Housing in New York City: Dwelling Type and Social Change in the American Metropolis* (New York: Columbia University Press, 1990), pp. 151–163.

77. Edelman, *Labor Lobbyist*, chap. 8.

78. Frederick Gutheim, "The Social Architecture of Oskar Stonorov," *L'Ar-*

chitettura 18 (June 1972): 76 ff.; Eric J. Sandeen, "The Design of Public Housing in the New Deal: Oskar Stonorov and the Carl Mackley Houses," *American Quarterly* 27 (1985): 645–667; Albert Mayer, "A Critique of the Hosiery Workers Housing Development in Philadelphia," *Architecture* 71 (1935): 189–194; Radford, *Modern Housing for America*, chap. 5.

79. Catherine Bauer, "Housing: Paper Plans or a Workers' Movement?" in Aronovici, ed., *America Can't Have Housing;* Catherine Bauer, "Now, at Last: Housing," *New Republic* 92 (1937): 119–121.

80. Joan Campbell, *The German Werkbund: The Politics of Reform in the Applied Arts* (Princeton: Princeton University Press, 1978).

81. Richard Guy Wilson, Dianne H. Pilgrim, and Dickran Tashjian, *The Machine Age in America, 1918–1941* (New York: Brooklyn Museum, 1986); Jeffrey L. Meikle, *Twentieth-Century Limited: Industrial Design in America, 1925–1939* (Philadelphia: Temple University Press, 1979).

82. John E. Findling, *Chicago's Great World's Fairs* (Manchester, England: Manchester University Press, 1994); Forrest Crissey, "Why the Century of Progress Architecture? An Interview with Allen D. Albert," *Saturday Evening Post* 205 (June 10, 1933): 16 ff.; *Official View Book: A Century of Progress Exposition* (Chicago: Reuben H. Donnelly, 1933).

83. Findling, *Chicago's Great World's Fairs*, pp. 108–111; *Century of Progress: Official Guide Book of the Fair, 1933* (Chicago: Century of Progress, 1933), pp. 67–72; Dorothy Raley, ed., *A Century of Progress: Homes and Furnishings* (Chicago: M. A. Ring, 1934).

84. Museum of Modern Art, *Modern Architecture;* Henry-Russell Hitchcock, Jr., and Philip Johnson, *The International Style: Architecture since 1922* (New York: W. W. Norton, 1932).

85. Sibyl Moholy-Nagy, "The Diaspora," *Journal of the Society of Architectural Historians* 24 (March 1965): 24–26.

10. New Deal

1. Lewis Mumford, review of Horace M. Kallen's *A Free Society*, in *New Republic* 80 (1934): 223; editors of the *Economist*, *The New Deal: An Analysis and Appraisal* (New York: Knopf, 1937), p. 46; Walter J. Shepard, "Democracy in Transition," *American Political Science Review* 29 (1935): 11.

2. Rexford G. Tugwell, *The Democratic Roosevelt* (Garden City, N.Y.: Doubleday, 1957); Albert U. Romasco, *The Politics of Recovery: Roosevelt's New Deal* (New York: Oxford University Press, 1983), p. 5.

3. For good, recent assessments of the interpretive debate: Steve Fraser and Gary Gerstle, eds., *The Rise and Fall of the New Deal Order, 1930–1980* (Princeton: Princeton University Press, 1989); Kenneth Finegold and Theda Skocpol, *State and Party in America's New Deal* (Madison: University of Wisconsin Press, 1995).

4. John Dizikes, *Britain, Roosevelt, and the New Deal: British Opinion, 1932–1938*

(New York: Garland, 1979), pp. 166, 95; Henry Pelling, *America and the British Left: From Bright to Bevan* (New York: New York University Press, 1957), p. 136; Joel Colton, *Léon Blum: Humanist in Politics* (New York: Knopf, 1966). More generally: William E. Leuchtenburg, "The Great Depression," in *The Comparative Approach to American History*, ed. C. Vann Woodward (New York: Basic Books, 1968); William E. Leuchtenburg, "The 'Europeanization' of America, 1929–1950," in his *The FDR Years: On Roosevelt and His Legacy* (New York: Columbia University Press, 1995).

5. Edwin Amenta and Theda Skocpol, "Taking Exception: Explaining the Distinctiveness of American Public Policies in the Last Century," in *The Comparative History of Public Policy*, ed. Francis G. Castles (Oxford: Polity Press, 1989), p. 292; Christopher Leman, "Patterns of Policy Development: Social Security in the United States and Canada," *Public Policy* 25 (1977): 261–291; Theda Skocpol and John Ikenberry, "The Political Formation of the American Welfare State in Historical and Comparative Perspective," *Comparative Social Research* 6 (1983): 90.

6. Margaret Weir and Theda Skocpol, "State Structures and the Possibilities for 'Keynesian' Responses to the Great Depression in Sweden, Britain, and the United States," in *Bringing the State Back In*, ed. Peter B. Evans et al. (Cambridge: Cambridge University Press, 1985); Peter Gourevitch, *Politics in Hard Times: Comparative Responses to International Economic Crises* (Ithaca: Cornell University Press, 1986), chap. 4.

7. The underlying data are taken from Peter D. Stachura, ed., *Unemployment and the Great Depression in Weimar Germany* (Basingstoke, England: Macmillan, 1986). Because they are based on different measures, the nation's unemployment rates for this period are not precisely comparable, but the relative orders of magnitude are not in doubt.

8. Gøsta Esping-Andersen, "The Making of a Social Democratic Welfare State," in *Creating Social Democracy: A Century of the Social Democratic Labor Party in Sweden*, ed. Klaus Misgeld et al. (University Park: Pennsylvania State University Press, 1992); Robert Skidelsky, *Politicians and the Slump: The Labour Government of 1929–31* (London: Macmillan, 1967); Ross McKibbin, "The Economic Policy of the Second Labour Government, 1929–31," *Past and Present* 68 (1975): 95–123; Julian Jackson, *The Popular Front in France: Defending Democracy, 1934–38* (Cambridge: Cambridge University Press, 1988).

9. Richard H. Pells, *Radical Visions and American Dreams: Culture and Social Thought in the Depression Years* (New York: Harper and Row, 1973), p. 97. Cf. Nelson Polsby, *Political Innovation in America: The Politics of Policy Initiation* (New Haven: Yale University Press, 1984), esp. pp. 167–172.

10. Alan Brinkley, *The End of Reform: New Deal Liberalism in Recession and War* (New York: Knopf, 1995).

11. Not all progressives rallied to the New Deal, as Otis Graham showed long ago; some were tired out by age, others upset by the contrast in moral-political styles. The continuity of proposals and the continuity of persons were inevitably

two different things. Otis L. Graham, Jr., *An Encore for Reform: The Old Progressives and the New Deal* (New York: Oxford University Press, 1967).

12. William H. Beveridge, "Some Aspects of the American Recovery Programme," *Economica*, n.s. 1 (Feb. 1934): 1–12; William Beveridge, "Observations in America," radio address, Dec. 1 and 4, 1933, William Beveridge Papers, British Library of Political and Economic Science, London School of Economics.

13. The comparisons in this and the following paragraphs draw on the following studies: Gerold Ambrosius and William H. Hubbard, *A Social and Economic History of Twentieth-Century Europe* (Cambridge: Harvard University Press, 1989); John A. Garraty, "The New Deal, National Socialism, and the Great Depression," *American Historical Review* 78 (1973): 907–944; John A. Garraty, *The Great Depression* (San Diego: Harcourt Brace Jovanovich, 1986); John A. Garraty, *Unemployment in History: Economic Thought and Public Policy* (New York: Harper and Row, 1978), chap. 10; Charles S. Maier, "The Economics of Fascism and Nazism," in his *In Search of Stability: Explorations in Historical Political Economy* (Cambridge: Cambridge University Press, 1987); Gourevitch, *Politics in Hard Times;* Daniel Levine, *Poverty and Society: The Growth of the American Welfare State in International Comparison* (New Brunswick, N.J.: Rutgers University Press, 1988); James T. Patterson, "Comparative Welfare History: Britain and the United States, 1930–1945," in *The Roosevelt New Deal: A Program Assessment Fifty Years After*, ed. Wilbur J. Cohen (Austin: Lyndon Baines Johnson School of Public Affairs, 1986); Herman van der Wee, ed., *The Great Depression Revisited: Essays on the Economics of the Thirties* (The Hague: Nijhoff, 1972); Weir and Skocpol, "State Structures." For contemporary comparative assessments: Karl Brandt, "Recent Agricultural Policies in Germany, Great Britain, and the United States," *Social Research* 3 (1936): 167–201; Emil Lengyuel, *The New Deal in Europe* (New York: Funk and Wagnalls, 1934), esp. pp. 292–302.

On Depression Britain: Sean Glynn and John Oxborrow: *Interwar Britain: A Social and Economic History* (New York: Barnes and Noble, 1976); Sidney Pollard, *The Development of the British Economy, 1914–1990*, 4th ed. (London: Edward Arnold, 1992). On Depression Germany: R. J. Overy, *The Nazi Economic Recovery, 1932–1938* (London: Macmillan, 1982); Richard Overy, "Unemployment in the Third Reich," *Business History* 29 (1987): 253–281; Harold James, "Innovation and Conservatism in Economic Recovery: The Alleged 'Nazi Recovery' of the 1930s," in *Reevaluating the Third Reich*, ed. Thomas Childers and Jane Caplan (New York: Holmes and Meier, 1993).

14. In this regard, the German departure from the Depression norm was fundamental. Supressing independent labor unionization and cashiering the works councils established under the 1920 constitution, the National Socialists reconstituted employers as *Betriebsführer*, authorities unchallenged except from above by the party and the state.

15. William W. Bremer, "Along the 'American Way': The New Deal's Work

Relief Programs for the Unemployed," *Journal of American History* 66 (1975): 636–652.

16. Julian Jackson, *The Politics of Depression in France, 1932–1936* (Cambridge: Cambridge University Press, 1985), chap. 7; John Stevenson, *British Society, 1914–45* (London: Allen Lane, 1984), pp. 326–329; Otis L. Graham, Jr., *Toward a Planned Society: From Roosevelt to Nixon* (New York: Oxford University Press, 1976), chap. 1.

17. John P. Diggins, *Mussolini and Fascism: The View from America* (Princeton: Princeton University Press, 1972); *The Diary of Rexford G. Tugwell: The New Deal, 1932–1935*, ed. Michael Vincent Namorato (New York: Greenwood Press, 1992), p. 139.

18. Sidney and Beatrice Webb, *Soviet Communism: A New Civilization?* (London: Longmans, Green, 1935).

19. William H. Beveridge, "Visit to the U.S.A., 1933," Beveridge Papers; National Association of Housing Officials, *A Housing Program for the United States* (Chicago: National Association of Housing Officials, 1934); Russell Lord, *The Wallaces of Iowa* (Boston: Houghton Mifflin, 1947), p. 383.

20. Alice Hamilton, "Below the Surface," *Survey Graphic* 22 (1933): 449 ff., "Sound and Fury in Germany," ibid., 549 ff., and "Women's Place in Germany," ibid. 23 (1934): 26 ff.

21. Hanns Gramm, *The Oberlaender Trust, 1931–1953* (Philadelphia: Carl Schurz Memorial Foundation, 1956); *American–German Review* (1934–1938).

22. Frederic C. Howe, "The Most Complete Agricultural Recovery in History," *Annals of the American Academy of Political and Social Science* 172 (Mar. 1934): 122–129; Frederic C. Howe, *Denmark: The Coöperative Way* (New York: Coward-McCann, 1936); Josephine Goldmark and A. H. Hollman, *Democracy in Denmark* (Washington, D.C.: National Home Library Foundation, 1936); U.S. Congress, House Committee on Agriculture, *Amending the Bankhead-Jones Farm Tenant Act: Hearing on S. 1836*, 76th Cong., 3rd sess., 1940, pp. 32–38; Marquis Childs, *Sweden: The Middle Way* (New Haven: Yale University Press, 1936); Merle Curti, "Sweden in the American Social Mind of the 1930s," in *The Immigration of Ideas: Studies in the North Atlantic Community*, ed. J. Iverne Dowie and J. Thomas Tredway (Rock Island, Ill.: Augustana Historical Society, 1968); U.S. Commission on Industrial Relations in Great Britain and Sweden, *Report* (Washington, D.C., 1938).

23. Roy Lubove, "Frederic C. Howe and the Quest for Community in America," *Historian* 39 (1977): 270–291; Frances Perkins, *The Roosevelt I Knew* (New York: Viking, 1946), esp. chap. 26.

24. Susan Ware, *Beyond Suffrage: Women in the New Deal* (Cambridge: Harvard University Press, 1981); J. Joseph Huthmacher, *Senator Robert F. Wagner and the Rise of Urban Liberalism* (New York: Atheneum, 1968); Richard S. Kirkendall, *Social Scientists and Farm Politics in the Age of Roosevelt* (Columbia: University of Missouri Press, 1966).

25. Rexford G. Tugwell, "The Agricultural Policy of France," *Political Science Quarterly* 45 (1930): 214–230, 405–428, 527–547; Rexford G. Tugwell, *To the Lesser*

Heights of Morningside: A Memoir (Philadelphia: University of Pennsylvania Press, 1982); Thomas H. Eliot, *Recollections of the New Deal: When the People Mattered* (Boston: Northeastern University Press, 1992); Katie Louchheim, ed., *The Making of the New Deal: The Insiders Speak* (Cambridge: Harvard University Press, 1983). On the more diverse backgrounds of the social welfare experts of the 1930s: Linda Gordon, "Social Insurance and Public Assistance: The Influence of Gender in Welfare Thought in the United States, 1890–1935," *American Historical Review* 97 (1992): 19–54.

26. Diggins, *Mussolini and Fascism*, p. 280; Ellis W. Hawley, *The New Deal and the Problem of Monopoly* (Princeton: Princeton University Press, 1966), p. 106.

27. Albert U. Romasco, *The Poverty of Abundance: Hoover, the Nation, the Depression* (New York: Oxford University Press, 1965), pp. 183, 185.

28. Anne O'Hare McCormick, "As He Sees Himself," *New York Times Magazine*, Sept. 16, 1938, p. 2; Ronald D. Rotunda, *The Politics of Language: Liberalism as Word and Symbol* (Iowa City: University of Iowa Press, 1986).

29. Clarke A. Chambers, *Paul U. Kellogg and the* Survey: *Voices for Social Welfare and Social Justice* (Minneapolis: University of Minnesota Press, 1971), p. 156; Harold J. Laski, "The Roosevelt Experiment," *Atlantic Monthly* 153 (Feb. 1934): 151; William E. Leuchtenburg, *Franklin D. Roosevelt and the New Deal, 1932–1940* (New York: Harper and Row, 1963), p. 166.

30. Perkins, *Roosevelt*, p. 151.

31. William E. Leuchtenburg, "The New Deal and the Analogue of War," in *Change and Continuity in Twentieth-Century America*, ed. John Braeman, Robert H. Bremner, and Everett Walters (Columbus: Ohio State University Press, 1964); James S. Olson, *Saving Capitalism: The Reconstruction Finance Corporation and the New Deal, 1933–1940* (Princeton: Princeton University Press, 1988); Hawley, *New Deal and the Problem of Monopoly*.

32. Perkins, *Roosevelt*, chap. 21; John S. Forsythe, "Legislative History of the Fair Labor Standards Act," *Law and Contemporary Problems* 6 (1939): 464–490; Vivien Hart, *Bound by Our Constitution: Women, Workers, and the Minimum Wage* (Princeton: Princeton University Press, 1994), chap. 8.

33. David Brody, "Workplace Contractualism: A Historical Comparative Analysis," in his *In Labor's Cause: Main Themes on the History of the American Worker* (New York: Oxford University Press, 1993); Melvyn Dubofsky, *The State and Labor in Modern America* (Chapel Hill: University of North Carolina Press, 1994), chap. 5; Christopher L. Tomlins, *The State and the Unions: Labor Relations, Law, and the Organized Labor Movement in America, 1880–1960* (Cambridge: Cambridge University Press, 1985).

34. Maurizio Vaudagna, "The New Deal and European Social Democracy in Comparative Perspective," in *Why Is There No Socialism in the United States?* ed. Jean Heffer and Jeanine Rovet (Paris: École des hautes études en sciences sociales, 1988); Henry A. Wallace, *Democracy Reborn* (New York: Reynal and Hitchcock, 1944), p. 100.

35. McCormick, "As He Sees Himself," p. 2.

36. There are many good historical accounts of the making of the Social Security Act—though none treats its transatlantic dimensions adequately: Edward D. Berkowitz, *America's Welfare State: From Roosevelt to Reagan* (Baltimore: Johns Hopkins University Press, 1991); Clark A. Chambers, ""Social Reform, Social Work, and Social Security: A Subject Revisited," in *The Quest for Security: Papers on the Origins and the Future of the American Social Insurance System*, ed. John N. Schacht (Iowa City: Center for the Study of the Recent History of the United States, 1982); Mark H. Leff, "Historical Perspectives on Old Age Insurance: The State of the Art and the Art of the State," in *Social Security after Fifty: Successes and Failures*, ed. Edward D. Berkowitz (Westport, Conn.: Greenwood Press, 1987); Mark H. Leff, "Taxing the 'Forgotten Man': The Politics of Social Security Finance in the New Deal," *Journal of American History* 70 (1983): 359–381; Jill Quadagno, *The Transformation of Old Age Security: Class and Politics in the American Welfare State* (Chicago: University of Chicago Press, 1988); and the contemporary account by the director of the Committee on Economic Security's technical staff, Edwin E. Witte, *The Development of the Social Security Act* (1936; Madison: University of Wisconsin Press, 1962).

37. Louis Adamic, *My America, 1928–1938* (New York: Harper and Brothers, 1938), p. 268.

38. Raymond Richards, *Closing the Door to Destitution: The Shaping of the Social Security Acts of the United States and New Zealand* (University Park: Pennsylvania State University Press, 1994).

39. I. M. Rubinow, *The Quest for Security* (New York: Henry Holt, 1934), pp. 599–602; Ambrosius and Hubbard, *Social and Economic History of Twentieth-Century Europe*, pp. 121–123; Glynn and Oxborrow, *Interwar Britain*, p. 249.

40. Paul H. Douglas, "The French Social Security Act," *Annals of the American Academy of Political and Social Science* 164 (1932): 210–248.

41. E. C. Buehler, ed., *Compulsory Unemployment Insurance* (New York: H. W. Wilson, 1931), p. 12.

42. Louis Leotta, "Abraham Epstein and the Movement for Old Age Security," *Labor History* 16 (1975): 359–377; Paul H. Douglas, *In the Fullness of Time: The Memoirs of Paul H. Douglas* (New York: Harcourt Brace Jovanovich, 1972), p. 69; Abraham Epstein, *The Challenge of the Aged* (New York: Vanguard, 1928); John B. Andrews, "Old Age Pensions: Their Basis in Social Needs," *American Labor Legislation Review* 19 (1929): 356–358. Epstein's European contacts can be followed in the Abraham Epstein collections at Cornell University and Columbia University.

43. John R. Commons, "Unemployment and Prevention," *American Labor Legislation Review* 12 (1922): 15–30; "Unemployment Prevention Program of the American Association for Labor Legislation," ibid. 13 (1923): 69–71. More generally: Udo Sautter, *Three Cheers for the Unemployed: Government and Unemployment before the New Deal* (Cambridge: Cambridge University Press, 1991); Daniel Nelson, *Unemployment Insurance: The American Experience, 1915–1935* (Madison: University of Wisconsin Press, 1969).

44. John R. Commons, "Unemployment: Compensation and Prevention," *Survey* 47 (1921): 5–9; Elizabeth Brandeis, "Wisconsin Tackles Job Security," ibid. 67 (1931): 296; John R. Commons, "Compensation for Idle Labor in Wisconsin," *American Labor Legislation Review* 22 (1932): 9; John B. Andrews, "Act Now on Unemployment!" ibid. 20 (1930): 339–340.

45. I. M. Rubinow, "Public and Private Interests in Social Insurance," *American Labor Legislation Review* 21 (1931): 181–191 (italics added).

46. Bentley B. Gilbert, *British Social Policy, 1914–1939* (Ithaca: Cornell University Press, 1970), chap. 2; Alan Deacon, "Concession and Coercion: The Politics of Unemployment Insurance in the Twenties," in *Essays in Labour History, 1918–1939*, ed. Asa Briggs and John Saville (London: Croom Helm, 1977); John Stevenson, "The Making of Unemployment Policy, 1931–1935," in *High and Low Politics in Modern Britain*, ed. Michael Bentley and John Stevenson (Oxford: Clarendon Press, 1983); Sidney Checkland, *British Public Policy, 1776–1939: An Economic, Social, and Political Perspective* (Cambridge: Cambridge University Press, 1983), p. 379.

47. Richard J. Evans and Dick Geary, eds., *The German Unemployed: Experiences and Consequences of Mass Unemployment from the Weimar Republic to the Third Reich* (London: Croom Helm, 1987); Thomas E. J. DeWitt, "The Economics and Politics of Welfare in the Third Reich," *Central European History* 11 (1978): 256–278; Aryeh L. Unger, "Propaganda and Welfare in Nazi Germany," *Journal of Social History* 4 (1970): 125–140; Christoph Sachsse and Florian Tennstedt, *Der Wohlfahrtsstaat im Nationalsozialismus: Geschichte der Armenfürsorge in Deutschland*, vol. 3 (Stuttgart: Kohlhammer, 1992).

48. U.S. Congress, Senate Finance Committee, *Economic Security Act: Hearings on S. 1130*, 74th Cong., 1st sess., 1935, pp. 1322, 2.

49. James Struthers, *No Fault of Their Own: Unemployment and the Canadian Welfare State, 1914–1941* (Toronto: University of Toronto Press, 1983); Richards, *Closing the Door to Destitution.*

50. The role of welfare capitalists in the making of the Social Security Act of 1935 is particularly contested historical terrain. See Jill S. Quadagno, "Welfare Capitalism and the Social Security Act of 1935," *American Sociological Review* 49 (1984): 632–647, and its rebuttal by Theda Skocpol and Edwin Amenta, "Did Capitalists Shape Social Security?" ibid. 50 (1985): 572–575; J. Craig Jenkins and Barbara G. Brents, "Social Protest, Hegemonic Competition, and Social Reform: A Political Struggle Interpretation of the American Welfare State," *American Sociological Review* 54 (1989): 891–909; Edwin Amenta and Sunita Parikh, "Capitalists Did Not Want the Social Security Act: A Critique of the 'Capitalist Dominance' Thesis," *American Sociological Review* 56 (1991): 124–129; Colin Gordon, "New Deal, Old Deck: Business and the Origins of Social Security, 1920–1935," *Politics and Society* 19 (1991): 165–207; Colin Gordon, *New Deals: Business, Labor, and Politics in America, 1920–1935* (Cambridge: Cambridge University Press, 1994); and, less polemically, Edward D. Berkowitz, *Creating the Welfare State: The Political Economy of Twentieth-Century Reform* (New York: Praeger, 1980), chap. 6; Sanford M. Jacoby,

"Employers and the Welfare State: The Role of Marion B. Folsom," *Journal of American History* 80 (1993): 525–556. On the *Fortune* polls of 1939 and 1940: Herman A. Kroos, *Executive Thought on Economic Issues, 1920s–1960s* (Garden City, N.Y.: Doubleday, 1970), p. 193.

51. Kenneth Casebeer, "The Workers' Unemployment Insurance Bill: American Social Wage, Labor Organization, and Legal Ideology," in *Labor Law in America: Historical and Critical Essays*, ed. Christopher J. Tomlins and Andrew J. King (Baltimore: Johns Hopkins University Press, 1992); William W. Bremer, *Depression Winters: New York Social Workers and the New Deal* (Philadelphia: Temple University Press, 1984); Judith Ann Trolander, *Settlement Houses and the Great Depression* (Detroit: Wayne State University Press, 1975).

52. [Edith Abbott], "Social Insurance and/or Social Security," *Social Service Review* 8 (1934): 537–540; "How Much Security?" ibid. 9 (1935): 103–104; "The Wagner-Lewis Plan for Unemployment Compensation and the So-Called 'Subsidy System,'" ibid., 104–106; "Federal Grants-in-Aid for Home Relief," ibid. 9 (1935): 757–760; "Farewell to FERA," ibid. 10 (1936): 133–135. On the gendered divisions over social security: Linda Gordon, *Pitied But Not Entitled: Single Mothers and the History of Welfare, 1890–1935* (New York: Free Press, 1994), chap. 9. When the drafting of the act was completed, Grace Abbott swallowed her doubts and lobbied for it.

53. Tugwell, *Democratic Roosevelt*, p. 251; Perkins, *Roosevelt*, pp. 282–283.

54. *The Public Papers and Addresses of Franklin D. Roosevelt*, ed. Samuel I. Rosenman (New York: Random House, 1938–1950), vol. 1, p. 247.

55. J. Michael Eisner, *William Morris Leiserson: A Biography* (Madison: University of Wisconsin Press, 1967); Paul H. Douglas, *Standards of Unemployment Insurance* (Chicago: University of Chicago Press, 1933); Paul H. Douglas, *In the Fullness of Time* (New York: Harcourt Brace Jovanovich, 1972); Alvin Hansen, *Economic Stabilization in an Unbalanced World* (New York: Harcourt, Brace, 1932); Alvin Hansen, Merrill G. Murray, Russell A. Stevenson, and Bryce Stewart, *A Program for Unemployment Insurance and Relief in the United States* (Minneapolis: University of Minnesota Press, 1934); Shirley Jenkins, ed., *Social Security in International Perspective: Essays in Honor of Eveline M. Burns* (New York: Columbia University Press, 1969).

56. Arthur Newsholme, *International Studies on the Relation between the Private and Official Practice of Medicine with Special Reference to the Prevention of Disease* (London: George Allen and Unwin, 1931); Arthur Newsholme, *Medicine and the State: The Relation between the Private and Official Practice of Medicine, with Special Reference to Public Health* (London: George Allen and Unwin, 1932). In 1935, under fierce pressure from some of its board members for sidling up too close to the New Deal, and from doctors for advocating "state medicine," the Milbank Fund lost its nerve, fired its director, and discontinued further research in medical economics. Its activities up to that point can be followed in Clyde V. Kiser, *The Milbank Memorial Fund: Its Leaders and Its Work, 1905–1974* (New York: Milbank Memorial Fund, 1975), and in the papers of its secretary, John A. Kingsbury, in the Library of Congress.

57. American Association for Social Security, *Social Security in the United States,*

1933: A Record of the Sixth National Conference on Old Age and Social Security (New York: American Association for Social Security, 1933), parts 3–4; Grace Abbott to Homer Folks, Oct. 3, 1934, Grace and Edith Abbott Papers, Joseph Regenstein Library, University of Chicago.

58. James T. Patterson, *America's Struggle against Poverty, 1900–1985* (Cambridge: Harvard University Press, 1986), p. 57. On the New Deal's first winter: William R. Brock, *Welfare, Democracy, and the New Deal* (Cambridge: Cambridge University Press, 1988); Bonnie Fox Schwartz, *The Civil Works Administration, 1933–1934: The Business of Emergency Employment in the New Deal* (Princeton: Princeton University Press, 1984).

59. Vaughn Davis Bornet, "Herbert Hoover's Planning for Unemployment and Old Age Insurance Coverage, 1921 to 1933," in Schacht, ed., *Quest for Security*, p. 42; National Industrial Conference Board, *Unemployment Benefits and Insurance* (New York: National Industrial Conference Board, 1931); National Industrial Conference Board, *Unemployment Insurance and Relief in Germany* (New York: National Industrial Conference Board, 1932); Witte, *Development of the Social Security Act*, p. xv; George W. Martin, *Madam Secretary: Frances Perkins* (Boston: Houghton Mifflin, 1976), p. 226.

The most systematic series of investigations was the Industrial Relations Counselors' comparison of compulsory and subsidarist systems of unemployment insurance in the United States and Europe: Bryce M. Stewart, *Unemployment Benefits in the United States* (New York: Industrial Relations Counselors, 1930); Mary Barnett Gilson, *Unemployment Insurance in Great Britain* (New York: Industrial Relations Counselors, 1931); T. G. Spates and G. S. Rabinovitch, *Unemployment Insurance in Switzerland: The Ghent System Nationalized with Compulsory Features* (New York: Industrial Relations Counselors, 1931); Constance A. Kiehel, *Unemployment Insurance in Belgium: A National Development of the Ghent and Liège Systems* (New York: Industrial Relations Counselors, 1932). See also Mary Barnett Gilson, *What's Past Is Prologue: Reflections on My Industrial Experience* (New York: Harper and Brothers, 1940).

60. Charles Morris Mills, "Dole-itis," *Survey* 65 (1931): 487 ff.; Helen Hall, *Unfinished Business in Neighborhood and Nation* (New York: Macmillan, 1971), chap. 6; Helen Hall, "English Dole and American Charity," *Atlantic Monthly* 151 (1933): 538–549; Helen Hall, "Miners Must Eat: The Workings of English Dole and American Charity," ibid. 152 (1933): 153–162; Frances Perkins, "Job Insurance," *American Labor Legislation Review* 23 (1933): 117–120; Frances Perkins, "Toward Security," *Survey Graphic* 23 (1934): 144; Mollie Ray Carroll, "Social Insurance," National Congress of Social Work, *Proceedings* (1934), p. 260.

61. Perkins, *Roosevelt*, p. 286.

62. Struthers, *No Fault of Their Own*, chap. 1; Bryce Stewart, "The Functions of Public Employment Service and Public Works," *American Labor Legislation Review* 13 (1923): 54–63; Bryce M. Stewart, "Some Phases of European Unemployment Insurance Experience," *Proceedings of the American Academy of Political Science* 14

(1932): 493–514; Alvin Hansen et al., *Program for Unemployment Insurance and Relief;* A. C. C. Hill, Jr. and Isador Lubin. *The British Attack on Unemployment* (Washington, D.C.: Brookings Institution, 1934).

63. Barbara Nachtrieb Armstrong, *Insuring the Essentials: Minimum Wage Plus Social Insurance: A Living Wage Program* (New York: Macmillan, 1932), pp. xiv, 13; J. Douglas Brown, *An American Philosophy of Social Security: Evolution and Issues* (Princeton: Princeton University Press, 1972), chap. 1; Eliot, *Recollections of the New Deal*, chap. 5.

64. Theron F. Schlabach, *Edwin E. Witte: Cautious Reformer* (Madison: State Historical Society of Wisconsin, 1969); Louchheim, *Making of the New Deal*, pp. 151–152, 94; Perkins, *Roosevelt*, p. 282.

65. Daniel S. Hirshfield, *The Lost Reform: The Campaign for Compulsory Heath Insurance in the United States from 1932 to 1943* (Cambridge: Harvard University Press, 1970), chap. 2.

66. Witte, *Development of the Social Security Act;* Jerry R. Cates, *Insuring Inequality: Administrative Leadership in Social Security, 1935–54* (Ann Arbor: University of Michigan Press, 1983), pp. 32–33. Within months after the Supreme Court upheld the Social Security Act, the Social Security Board's Bureau of Old-Age Benefits was renamed the Bureau of Federal Old Age Insurance.

67. *Public Papers and Addresses of Franklin D. Roosevelt*, vol. 1, p. 792.

68. Editors of the *Economist*, *New Deal*, chap. 2; Eveline M. Burns, "Social Security in Evolution," *American Economic Review* 34, supplement, pt. 2 (Mar. 1944): 199–211; J. Douglas Brown, "British Precedent and American Old Age Insurance," *American Labor Legislation Review* 27 (1937): 18–33; J. Douglas Brown, "Current Social Insurance Problems," ibid. 28 (1938): 6–8.

On the contrast with European social insurance systems: Karl Pibram, "Social Insurance and Social Security in the United States," *International Labor Review* 36 (1937): 732–771; C. A. Kulp, "European and American Social Security Parallels," *American Labor Legislation Review* 28 (1938): 13–20.

69. Abraham Epstein, "Our Social Insecurity Act," *Harper's Monthly Magazine* 172 (1935): 55–68; Abraham Epstein, "Financing Social Security," *Annals of the American Academy of Political and Social Science* 183 (1936): 212–226.

70. Leuchtenburg, *Franklin D. Roosevelt and the New Deal*, p. 345. The internal quotation is from Rexford Tugwell.

71. Franklin D. Roosevelt, "A New Rural Planning," *Rural Government: Proceedings of the 14th American Country Life Conference, 1931* (Chicago: University of Chicago Press, 1931), pp. 10–17; Rexford Tugwell, "The Preparation of a President," *Western Political Quarterly* 1 (1948): 131–153.

72. Tugwell, *Diary*, pp. 40–41; Tugwell, *To the Lesser Heights*, pp. 241–242.

73. Richard S. Kirkendall, "The New Deal and Agriculture," in *The New Deal: The National Level*, ed. John Braeman, Robert H. Bremner, and David Brody (Columbus: Ohio State University Press, 1975); Theodore Saloutos, *The American*

Farmer and the New Deal (Ames: Iowa State University Press, 1982); Finegold and Skocpol, *State and Party*, pt. 1.

74. M. L. Wilson, "A Land Use Program for the Federal Government," *Journal of Farm Economics* 15 (1933): 217–235; Rexford G. Tugwell, "The Place of Government in a National Land Program," ibid. 16 (1934): 55–69; Lewis C. Gray, *Land Planning* (Chicago: University of Chicago Press, 1936).

75. Rexford Guy Tugwell, "Russian Agriculture," in *Soviet Russia in the Second Decade: A Joint Survey of the Technical Staff of the First American Trade Union Delegations*, ed. Stuart Chase, Robert Dunn, and Rexford Guy Tugwell (New York: John Day, 1928), p. 59; M. L. Wilson, *Farm Relief and the Domestic Allotment Plan* (Minneapolis: University of Minnesota Press, 1933); Milburn L. Wilson, "The Place of Subsistence Homesteads in Our National Economy," *Journal of Farm Economics* 16 (1934): 73–84; M. L. Wilson, "Decentralization of Industry in the New Deal," *Social Forces* 13 (1934–1935): 588–598; Rexford G. Tugwell, "The Resettlement Idea," *Agricultural History* 33 (1959): 159–164.

76. Matthew Josephson, *Infidel in the Temple: A Memoir of the Nineteen-Thirties* (New York: Knopf, 1967), p. 61; Clarence E. Pickett, "Subsistence Homesteading in Europe," n.d., copy in the Nolen Papers; U.S. Congress, House Committee on Labor, *Relief of Distress Due to Unemployment*, 72nd Cong., 1st sess., 1932, pp. 27–32, 43–44.

77. Paul K. Conkin, *Tomorrow a New World: The New Deal Community Program* (Ithaca: Cornell University Press, 1959).

78. Sidney Baldwin, *Poverty and Politics: The Rise and Decline of the Farm Security Administration* (Chapel Hill: University of North Carolina Press, 1968).

79. Conkin, *Tomorrow a New World*, appendix. On the enduring support for the farm village idea among southern progressives: W. T. Couch, "An Agrarian Programme for the South," *American Review* 3 (1934): 313–326; Herman C. Nixon, *Forty Acres and Steel Mules* (Chapel Hill: University of North Carolina Press, 1938).

80. David Holley, *Uncle Sam's Farmers: The New Deal Communities in the Lower Mississippi Valley* (Urbana: University of Illinois Press, 1975), chaps. 8–9.

81. Joseph L. Arnold, *The New Deal in the Suburbs: A History of the Greenbelt Town Program, 1935–1954* (Columbus: Ohio State University Press, 1971); Arnold R. Alanen and Joseph A. Eden, *Main Street Ready-Made: The New Deal Community of Greendale, Wisconsin* (Madison: State Historical Society of Wisconsin, 1987); Conkin, *Tomorrow a New World*, chap. 14. Earle Draper, recruited from designing southern mill villages to work on the TVA model town at Norris, was the only one of the major influences on the suburban division's work who did not have significant European connections. On the interlocking connections of the others: Roy Lubove, *Community Planning in the 1920's: The Contribution of the Regional Planning Association of America* (Pittsburgh: University of Pittsburgh Press, 1963).

82. Elbert Peets, "Washington, Williamsburg, the Century of Progress, and Greendale," in Werner Hegemann, *City Planning—Housing* (New York: Architectural Book Publishing, 1936), vol. 2, chap. 27.

83. Hugh A. Bone, "Greenbelt Faces 1939," *American City* 54 (Feb. 1939): 59–61; Arnold, *New Deal in the Suburbs*, pp. 138–139.

84. Clarence S. Stein, "Greendale and the Future," *American City* 63 (June 1948): 106–109; Rexford G. Tugwell, address to the Regional Planning Commission of Hamilton County, Ohio, Feb. 3, 1936, copy in the Justin Hartzog Papers, Cornell University.

85. Diane Ghirardo, *Building New Communities: New Deal America and Fascist Italy* (Princeton: Princeton University Press, 1989); Barbara Miller Lane, *Architecture and Politics in Germany, 1918–1945* (Cambridge: Harvard University Press, 1968), chaps. 6–8.

86. Alanen and Eden, *Main Street*, p. 61; Arthur E. Morgan, "Bench Marks in the Tennessee Valley, IV: The Road to Prosperity in the TVA," *Survey Graphic* 23 (1934): 548; Roy Talbert, Jr., *FDR's Utopian: Arthur Morgan of the TVA* (Jackson: University Press of Mississippi, 1987), pp. 127, 146.

87. Childs, *Sweden: The Middle Way;* Marquis Childs, "Cooperatives in America," *North American Review* 243 (1937): 217–230. In *This Is Democracy: Collective Bargaining in Scandinavia* (New Haven: Yale University Press, 1938), Childs shifted his emphasis to labor-management relations in Sweden before and after the "basic agreement" of 1938. But Childs's second report from Sweden had only a fraction of the impact of his first.

88. Childs, *Sweden: The Middle Way*, pp. xii, 50, xiv.

89. *The Complete Presidential Press Conferences of Franklin D. Roosevelt* (New York: DaCapo, 1972), vol. 7, p. 295; O. S. Granducci, "The Co-op—A New Bogeyman," *Today Magazine* 7 (Oct. 31, 1936): 6 ff.

90. Leland Olds, undated notebook entry (circa 1931) and Leland Olds to Marion Olds, Aug. 18, 1936, both in the Leland Olds Papers, Franklin D. Roosevelt Library, Hyde Park, N.Y.

91. Baldwin, *Poverty and Politics*, p. 103; Alanen and Eden, *Main Street*, p. 49; Earle S. Draper, "The New TVA Town of Norris, Tennessee," *American City* 48 (Dec. 1933): 67–68; Walter L. Creese, *TVA's Public Planning: The Vision, the Reality* (Knoxville: University of Tennessee Press, 1990), chap. 5; Josephson, *Infidel in the Temple*, pp. 440–441; Henry A. Wallace, *Whose Constitution? An Inquiry into the General Welfare* (1936; Westport, Conn.: Greenwood, 1971), p. 309. On the growth of cooperative associations: "Cooperative Movement in the United States in 1925 (Other than Agricultural)," U.S. Bureau of Labor Statistics, *Bulletin* no. 437 (1927); Cooperative League of the United States of America, *Fourth Yearbook: A Survey of Consumer Cooperation in the United States, 1939* (Minneapolis: Northern States Cooperative League, 1939), pp. 23–25; Joseph G. Knapp, *The Advance of American Cooperative Enterprise, 1920–1945* (Danville, Ill.: Interstate Printers, 1973), pt. 2.

92. Max Bond, "The Training Program of the Tennessee Valley Authority for Negroes," *Journal of Negro Education* 7 (1938): 388; Doak S. Campbell et al., *Educational Activities of the Works Progress Administration*, Works Progress Administration, Advisory Committee on Education, Staff Study 14 (Washington, D.C., 1939),

pp. 45–47, 74–79; John W. Studebaker, *The American Way: Democracy at Work in the Des Moines Forums* (New York: McGraw-Hill, 1935); William Graebner, *The Engineering of Consent: Democracy and Authority in Twentieth-Century America* (Madison: University of Wisconsin Press, 1987), chap. 4; Hilda Worthington Smith, "Opening Vistas in Workers' Education: An Autobiography," unpublished typescript in the Bryn Mawr College Library, 1978; and, more generally, Joseph F. Kett, *The Pursuit of Knowledge Under Difficulties: From Self-Improvement to Adult Education in America, 1750–1990* (Stanford: Stanford University Press, 1994), chap. 11.

93. Maurice Seay, "Adult Education: A Description of the Educational and Training Program of the Tennessee Valley Authority," *Bulletin of the Bureau of School Service* (College of Education, University of Kentucky) 10, no. 4 (1938): 184; Joyce L. Kornbluh, *A New Deal for Workers' Education: The Workers' Service Program* (Urbana: University of Illinois Press, 1987), p. 73; Charles Seeger and Margaret Vailant, "Journal of a Field Representative (1937)," *Ethnomusicology* 24 (1980): 168; Janelle Warren-Findley, "Musicians and Mountaineers: The Resettlement Administration's Music Program in Appalachia, 1935–1937," *Appalachian Journal* 7 (1979–1980): 113; Archie Green, "A Resettlement Administration Song Sheet," *JEMF Quarterly* 11 (1975): 80–87.

94. Nancy L. Grant, *TVA and Black Americans: Planning for the Status Quo* (Philadelphia: Temple University Press, 1990); Harvard Sitkoff, *A New Deal for Blacks: The Emergence of Civil Rights as a National Issue* (New York: Oxford University Press, 1978); Marion Clawson, "Resettlement Experience on Nine Selected Resettlement Projects" [1943], *Agricultural History* 52 (1978): 1–92.

95. *Public Papers of Franklin D. Roosevelt*, vol. 6, p. 5.

96. Robert G. Barrows, "Beyond the Tenement: Patterns of American Urban Housing, 1870–1930," *Journal of Urban History* 9 (1983): 395–420.

97. Lawrence Veiller, "Rehousing the People in the United States of America," International Housing and Town Planning Congress, London, 1935, *Papers and General Reports* (London: International Federation for Housing and Town Planning, 1935), p. 358.

98. Richard Plunz, *A History of Housing in New York City: Dwelling Type and Social Change in the American Metropolis* (New York: Columbia University Press, 1990).

99. Walter J. Trattner, ed., *Biographical Dictionary of Social Welfare in America* (Westport, Conn.: Greenwood Press, 1986), pp. 673–676.

100. *The Secret Diary of Harold L. Ickes* (New York: Simon and Schuster, 1953–1954), vol. 2, p. 218; U.S. Congress, Senate Committee on Education and Labor, *Slum and Low-Rent Public Housing: Hearings on S. 2392*, 74th Cong., 1st sess., 1935.

101. Louis H. Pink, *The New Day in Housing* (New York: John Day, 1928); John Herling, "Vladeck," *Survey Graphic* 29 (1940): 29 ff.

102. Raymond Unwin, "Low-Cost Housing in England and America," *Housing Officials Yearbook, 1935* (Chicago: National Association of Housing Officials, 1935), pp. 51–54; National Association of Housing Officials, *A Housing Program for the*

United States; U.S. Congress, Senate Committee on Education and Labor, *Slum and Low-Rent Public Housing;* Coleman Woodbury, "Between the Housers and the Planners: The Recollections of Coleman Woodbury," in *The American Planner: Biographies and Recollections,* ed. Donald A. Krueckeberg (New York: Methuen, 1983). Unwin was joined on the International Housing Commission by Ernst Kahn of Frankfurt and Alice Samuels of the English Society of Women Housing Estate Managers, but he was the commission's leading figure.

103. *American City* 52 (1937): 109; *Survey Graphic* 27 (1938): 244.

104. Charles F. Palmer, *Adventures of a Slum Fighter* (Atlanta: Tupper and Love, 1955).

105. Pink, *New Day in Housing;* Nathan Straus, *Low Cost Housing Here and Abroad: Report to Mayor La Guardia* (New York: n.p., 1935).

106. Within the group Senator Robert Wagner convened in 1936, the seven housing experts with significant connections abroad were Charles Abrams, Helen Alfred, Catherine Bauer, Bleeker Marquette, Mary Simkhovitch, Edith Elmer Wood, and Coleman Woodbury. Timothy L. McDonnell, *The Wagner Housing Act: A Case Study of the Legislative Process* (Chicago: Loyola University Press, 1957), p. 158. On Ellenbogen: Mary S. Cole, "Catherine Bauer and the Public Housing Movement, 1926–1937," Ph.D. diss., George Washington University, 1975, p. 460. On Wagner: Joseph J. Huthmacher, *Senator Robert F. Wagner and the Rise of Urban Liberalism* (New York: Atheneum, 1968).

107. Carol Aronovici, ed., *America Can't Have Housing* (New York: Museum of Modern Art, 1934); Albert Mayer, "Why the Housing Program Failed," *Nation* 138 (1934): 408.

108. Michael W. Straus and Talbot Wegg, *Housing Comes of Age* (New York: Oxford University Press, 1938).

109. Radford, *Modern Housing for America,* chap. 6; Lewis Mumford, *The Culture of Cities* (New York: Harcourt, Brace, 1938), plate 28.

110. Arnold, *New Deal in the Suburbs,* chap. 11; Bernard Sternsher, *Rexford Tugwell and the New Deal* (New Brunswick, N.J.: Rutgers University Press, 1964), esp. chap. 25. Farley is quoted in Kirkendall, *Social Scientists and Farm Politics,* p. 120.

111. J. V. Fitzgerald to Stephen Early, July 31, 1936, Inquiry on Cooperative Enterprise Papers, Franklin D. Roosevelt Library.

112. David Eugene Conrad, *The Forgotten Farmers: The Story of Sharecroppers in the New Deal* (Urbana: University of Illinois Press, 1965).

113. James L. Guth, "The National Cooperative Council and Farm Relief, 1929–1942," *Agricultural History* 5 (1977): 441–458; Leland Olds to Marion Olds, Feb. 28, 1937, Leland Olds Papers; Granducci, "The Co-op: A New Bogeyman," p. 29. By the time the report finally appeared, Jacob Baker's efforts to achieve a common ground had stripped it of virtually any controversial recommendations. U.S. Inquiry on Cooperative Enterprise, *Report of the Inquiry on Cooperative Enterprise in Europe* (Washington, D.C., 1937).

114. Baldwin, *Poverty and Politics*, p. 163; U.S. Congress, House Committee on Agriculture, *Farm Tenancy: Hearing on H.R. 8*, 75th Cong., 1st sess., 1937, p. 77.

115. U.S. Congress, Senate Committee on Agriculture and Forestry, *To Create the Federal Farm Tenant Homes Corporation: Hearings on S. 1800*, 74th Cong., 1st sess., 1935, pp. 8–9, 74, 20; *Public Papers of Franklin Delano Roosevelt*, vol. 5, p. 373.

116. U.S. President's Committee on Farm Tenancy, *Report* (Washington, D.C., 1937), p. 22; Saloutos, *The American Farmer and the New Deal*, pp. 169, 171–173.

117. Baldwin, *Poverty and Politics*, chap. 7.

118. U.S. Congress, House Committee on Agriculture, *Farm Tenancy*, pp. 46–47; Edward C. Banfield, "Ten Years of the Farm Tenant Purchase Program," *Journal of Farm Economics* 31 (1949): 469.

119. McDonnell, *Wagner Housing Act;* U.S. Congress, Senate Committee on Education and Labor, *United States Housing Act of 1936: Hearings on S. 4424*, 74th Cong., 2nd sess., 1936.

120. U.S. Congress, Senate Committee on Education and Labor, *Slum and Low-Rent Public Housing*, p. 130. The lumber merchants' interest in the issue stemmed from their fear that government housing would be built not of wood but of steel and concrete.

121. Edith Elmer Wood, "A Nation Scrapping Its Slums," *Survey* 67 (1932): 668–669; National Public Housing Conference, *Speeches: The First Washington Conference on Public Housing, 1934* (New York: National Public Housing Conference, 1934); National Public Housing Conference, *Speeches: The Third Washington Conference on Slum Clearance and Low Rent Housing* (Washington, D.C.: National Public Housing Conference, 1936).

122. Catherine Bauer, "'Slum Clearance' or 'Housing,'" *New Republic* 137 (1933): 730–731; Catherine Bauer, *Modern Housing* (Boston: Houghton Mifflin, 1934), esp. pp. 243–247; Lewis Mumford, "Break the Housing Blockade!" *New Republic* 75 (1933): 6–11; Albert Mayer, Lewis Mumford, and Henry Wright, *New Homes for a New Deal* (New York: New Republic, 1934); Carol Aronovici, "The Outlook for Low-Cost Housing in America," in Aronovici, ed., *America Can't Have Housing.*

123. Raymond Unwin, "Low-Cost Housing in England and America," pp. 51–54; Richard L. Reiss, *British and American Housing* (New York: National Public Housing Conference, 1937), p. 102. Frankfurt's Ernst Kahn of the 1934 commission agreed: Ernst Kahn, "Ten Million Homes," *Survey Graphic* 24 (1935): 221 ff.

124. Palmer, *Adventures of a Slum Fighter;* Straus, *Low Cost Housing Here and Abroad.* In the same vein: Ernest M. Fisher and Richard U. Ratcliffe, *European Housing Policy and Practice* (Washington, D.C.: Federal Housing Administration, 1936).

125. Marian Bowley, *Housing and the State, 1919–1944* (London: Allen and Unwin, 1945).

126. *Matter of N.Y. City Housing Authority v. Muller*, 270 N.Y. 333 (1936); Myres S. McDougal and Addison A. Mueller, "Public Purpose in Public Housing: An Anachronism Reburied," *Yale Law Journal* 52 (1942): 48.

127. McDonnell, *Wagner Housing Act*, pp. 336, 49.

128. Edith Elmer Wood, *Recent Trends in American Housing* (New York: Macmillan, 1931), pp. 43–59.

129. Nathan Straus, "Housing: A National Achievement," *Atlantic Monthly* 163 (1939): 204; U.S. Congress, House Committee on Banking and Currency, *To Create a United States Housing Authority: Hearings on H.R. 5033*, 75th Cong, 1st sess., 1937, p. 193.

130. Joel Schwartz, *The New York Approach: Robert Moses, Urban Liberals, and Redevelopment of the Inner City* (Columbus: Ohio State University Press, 1993), p. 46; Catherine Bauer, "Now, at Last: Housing," *New Republic* 92 (1937): 119; "Housing For America: A Ten-Year Program," *Nation* 166 (May 15, 1948): pt. 2.

131. M. B. Schnapper, ed., *Public Housing in America* (New York: H. W. Wilson, 1939), p. 196.

132. Cole, "Catherine Bauer," pp. 648, 658n; Plunz, *History of Housing in New York City*, chap. 7.

133. U.S. Congress, House Committee on Banking and Currency, *To Create a United States Housing Authority*, p. 79.

134. U.S. Congress, House Committee on Ways and Means, *Unemployment Insurance: Hearings on H.R. 7659*, 73rd Cong., 2nd sess., 1934, p. 201.

135. Holley, *Uncle Sam's Farmers*, pp. 270, 272; Leuchtenburg, "The 'Europeanization' of America," p. 295; Rubinow, *The Quest for Security*, p. 254.

136. Rubinow, *The Quest for Security*, p. 254; U.S. Congress, House Committee on Ways and Means, *Unemployment Insurance*, pp. 34–47.

137. John R. Commons, *Myself: The Autobiography of John R. Commons*, reprint ed. (Madison: University of Wisconsin Press, 1964); John R. Commons and John B. Andrews, *Principles of Labor Legislation*, rev. ed. (New York: Harper and Brothers, 1927), pp. 546–547.

138. Commons, "Unemployment: Compensation and Prevention," p. 7; Commons, "Compensation for Idle Labor," p. 8.

139. *Survey* 41 (1918): 2; *American Labor Legislation Review* 12 (1922): 186; ibid. 20 (Sept. 1930).

140. John B. Andrews, "Introductory Note," *American Labor Legislation Review* 10 (1920): 113; John B. Andrews, "Act Now on Unemployment!" ibid. 20 (1930): 340.

141. John E. Edgerton, "Public Unemployment Insurance," in Buehler, ed., *Compulsory Unemployment Insurance*, p. 286.

142. U.S. Committee on Economic Security, *What Is Social Insurance?* (Washington, D.C., 1935); U.S. Committee on Economic Security, *Social Security at Home and Abroad* (Washington, D.C., 1935), p. 2; Harry L. Hopkins et al., *Toward Economic*

Security: A Review of President Roosevelt's Economic Security Program (Washington, D.C.: President's Committee on Economic Security, 1935), p. 2.

143. U.S. Resettlement Administration, *Greenbelt Towns* (Washington, D.C., 1936); Rexford G. Tugwell, address to the Regional Planning Commission of Hamilton County, p. 6

144. *The City*, directed by Ralph Steiner and Willard Van Dyke, 1939.

11. London, 1942

1. Among the many developments of these themes, see especially Gøsta Esping-Andersen, *The Three Worlds of Welfare Capitalism* (Princeton: Princeton University Press, 1990), and Neil Gilbert and Barbara Gilbert, *The Enabling State: Modern Welfare Capitalism in America* (New York: Oxford University Press, 1989).

2. Arthur Schlesinger, Jr., "'The Welfare State,'" *Reporter* 1 (Oct. 11, 1949): 28.

3. Cf. William E. Leuchtenburg, *The FDR Years: On Roosevelt and His Legacy* (New York: Columbia University Press, 1995), chap. 9: "The 'Europeanization' of America, 1929–1950."

4. José Harris, *William Beveridge: A Biography* (Oxford: Clarendon Press, 1977); William Beveridge, "Afterthoughts on the Recovery Program," Oct. 10, 1934, and "Some Aspects of the American Recovery Program," memorandum to the Rockefeller Foundation [1934], in the William Beveridge Papers, British Library of Political and Economic Science, London School of Economics; *Nation* 156 (1943): 95.

5. William Beveridge, *Social Insurance and Allied Services*, American ed. (New York: Macmillan, 1942).

6. Jane Lewis, "Models of Equality for Women: The Case of State Support for Children in Twentieth-Century Britain," in *Maternity and Gender Policies: Women and the Rise of the European Welfare States, 1880s–1950s*, ed. Gisela Bock and Pat Thane (London: Routledge, 1991); Susan Pedersen, *Family, Dependence, and the Origins of the Welfare State: Britain and France, 1914–1945* (Cambridge: Cambridge University Press, 1993), chap. 3; William H. Beveridge, *Full Employment in a Free Society* (New York: W. W. Norton, 1945); José Harris, "Social Planning in War-Time: Some Aspects of the Beveridge Report," in *War and Economic Development*, ed. J. N. Winter (Cambridge: Cambridge University Press, 1975).

7. Beveridge, *Social Insurance*, p. 6; William H. Beveridge, *The Pillars of Security and Other War-Time Essays and Addresses* (New York: Macmillan, 1943).

8. Cf. John Dryzek and Robert E. Goodin, "Risk-Sharing and Social Justice: The Motivational Foundations of the Post-War Welfare State," *British Journal of Political Science* 16 (1986): 1–34; Harold L. Smith, ed., *War and Social Change: British Society in the Second World War* (Manchester, England: Manchester University Press, 1986).

9. Harris, *William Beveridge*, chap. 17; Steven Fielding, Peter Thompson, and Nick Tiratsoo, *"England Arise!" The Labour Party and Popular Politics in 1940s Britain* (Manchester, England: Manchester University Press, 1995), p. 34; Joseph Barnes, "When the Coalition Ends," *Survey Graphic* 34 (1945): 224.

10. F. W. S. Craig, *British General Election Manifestos, 1918–1966* (Chichester, England: Political Reference Publications, 1970).

11. Henry Pelling, *The Labour Governments, 1945–51* (New York: St. Martin's Press, 1984); Kenneth O. Morgan, "Socialism and Social Democracy in the British Labor Party, 1945–1989," *Archiv für Sozialgeschichte* 29 (1989): 297–325.

12. Richard Polenberg, *War and Society: The United States, 1941–1945* (Philadelphia: Lippincott, 1972); Alan Brinkley, *The End of Reform: New Deal Liberalism in Recession and War* (New York: Knopf, 1995), chaps. 8–9; Nelson Lichtenstein, *Labor's War at Home: The CIO in World War II* (Cambridge: Cambridge University Press, 1982); Steven Fraser, *Labor Will Rule: Sidney Hillman and the Rise of American Labor* (New York: Free Press, 1991).

13. "Aluminum City Terrace Housing," *Architectural Forum* 81 (July 1944): 65–76; Nelson Lichtenstein, *The Most Dangerous Man in Detroit: Walter Reuther and the Fate of American Labor* (New York: Basic Books, 1995), p. 172.

14. David Brody, "The New Deal, Labor, and World War II," in Brody, *In Labor's Cause: Main Themes on the History of the American Worker* (New York: Oxford University Press, 1993), p. 178; *The Public Papers and Addresses of Franklin D. Roosevelt*, ed. Samuel I. Rosenman (New York: Random House, 1938–1950), vol. 9, p. 671.

15. Brody, *In Labor's Cause*, pp. 176, 181.

16. National Policy Committee, *Memorandum of the Washington Dinner on the Beveridge Report, Feb. 1943* (Washington, D.C.: National Policy Committee, 1943); Harris, *William Beveridge*, pp. 427–428.

17. Monte M. Poen, *Harry S. Truman versus the Medical Lobby* (Columbia: University of Missouri Press, 1979), pp. 35–36; John W. Jeffries, "Franklin D. Roosevelt and the 'America of Tomorrow,'" in *Power and Responsibility: Case Studies in American Leadership*, ed. David M. Kennedy and Michael E. Parrish (New York: Harcourt Brace Jovanovich, 1986), esp. p. 39; Keith W. Olsen, "The American Beveridge Plan," *Mid-America* 65 (1983): 87–99; "Social Security: What We Have and What's Proposed," *Newsweek*, Mar. 22, 1943, p. 28. On the political fates of the Beveridge and NRPB plans: Edwin Amenta and Theda Skocpol, "Redefining the New Deal: World War II and the Development of Social Provision in the United States," in *The Politics of Social Policy in the United States*, ed. Margaret Weir, Ann Shola Orloff, and Theda Skocpol (Princeton: Princeton University Press, 1988).

18. "A Beveridge Plan for America," *New Republic* 107 (1942): 810–811; Max Lerner, "Charter for a New America: The President's Job-and-Security Plan," ibid. 108 (1943): 369; Bruce Bliven, Max Lerner, and George Soule, "Charter for America," ibid. 108 (1943): 523–542; "A New Bill of Rights," *Nation* 156 (1943): 401–

402. Cf. Theodore Rosenof, "The American Democratic Left Looks at the British Labour Government, 1945–1951," *Historian* 38 (1976): 98–119.

19. U.S. National Resources Planning Board, Committee on Long-Range Work and Relief Policies, *Security, Work, and Relief Policies* (1942; reprint ed., New York: Da Capo Press, 1973); Edwin E. Witte, "American Post-War Social Security Proposals," *American Economic Review* 33 (1943): 825–838. For examples of the conservative reaction: "Cradle to Grave to Pigeonhole," *Time Magazine*, Mar. 22, 1943, p. 13; "Why Don't the Planners Read the Papers?" *Saturday Evening Post*, Apr. 10, 1943, p. 112; "Which Path America?" *New York Times*, Mar. 14, 1943, p. 10E. See also Eveline M. Burns, "The Security Report of the National Resources Planning Board," National Conference of Social Work, *Proceedings* (1943), pp. 370–381.

20. "A New Bill of Rights," *Nation* 156 (1943): 401–402.

21. G. Hartley Grattan, "Beveridge Plans Are Not Enough," *Harper's Magazine* 186 (1943): 376; Jeffries, "Franklin D. Roosevelt and the 'America of Tomorrow,'" p. 44; Henry A. Wallace, "Jobs for All," *New Republic* 112 (1945): 139.

22. Peter A. Hall, ed., *The Political Power of Economic Ideas: Keynesianism across Nations* (Princeton: Princeton University Press, 1989).

23. Brinkley, *End of Reform;* John W. Jeffries, "The 'New' New Deal: FDR and American Liberalism, 1937–1945," *Political Science Quarterly* 105 (1990): 397–418; Henry A. Wallace, *Sixty Million Jobs* (New York: Simon and Schuster, 1945); Seymour E. Harris, ed., *Saving American Capitalism: A Liberal Economic Program* (New York: Knopf, 1948), esp. p. 11.

24. Ira Katznelson, "Rebuilding the American State: Evidence from the 1940s," *Studies in American Political Development* 5 (1991): 301–309; Ralph Robey, "Post War Bureaucratic Utopia: Part II," *Newsweek*, May 10, 1943, p. 62; "Which Path America?" *New York Times*, Mar. 14, 1943, p. 10E.

25. Keith Hutchison, "Britain—Sixth Winter," *Nation* 160 (Jan. 6, 1945): 9; Andrew Roth, "Britain's Greatest Gamble," ibid. 163 (July 6, 1946): 10.

26. John Morton Blum, *V Was for Victory: Politics and American Culture during World War II* (New York: Harcourt Brace Jovanovich, 1976), chap. 3; Geir Lundestad, *The American "Empire" and Other Studies of U.S. Foreign Policy in a Comparative Perspective* (Oxford: Oxford University Press, 1990), p. 40.

27. Lucius D. Clay, *Decision in Germany* (Garden City, N.Y.: Doubleday, 1950), esp. chaps. 21–22; Hans Günter Hockerts, *Sozialpolitische Entscheidungen im Nachkriegsdeutschland: Allierte und deutsche Sozialversicherungspolitik, 1945 bis 1957* (Stuttgart: Klett-Cotta, 1980); Jeffry M. Diefendorf, *In the Wake of War: The Reconstruction of German Cities after World War II* (New York: Oxford University Press, 1993).

28. Richard F. Kuisel, *Seducing the French: The Dilemma of Americanization* (Berkeley: University of California Press, 1993), chap. 4; Reinhold Wagnleitner, *Coca-Colonization and the Cold War: The Cultural Mission of the United States in Austria after the Second World War* (Chapel Hill: University of North Carolina Press,

1994), pp. 125–27; and, more generally, Rob Kroes, Robert W. Rydell, and Doeko F. J. Bosscher, eds., *Cultural Transmissions and Receptions: American Mass Culture in Europe* (Amsterdam: VU University Press, 1993). Laski is quoted in Lundestad, *American "Empire,"* p. 39.

29. *The Papers of Adlai E. Stevenson*, vol. 5: *Visit to Asia, the Middle East, and Europe, March–August 1953*, ed. Walter Johnson (Boston: Little, Brown, 1974), pp. 488–489; Michael H. Prosser, ed., *An Ethic for Survival: Adlai Stevenson Speaks on International Affairs, 1936–65* (New York: William Morrow, 1969), p. 182; William Jennings Bryan, *The Old World and Its Ways* (St. Louis: Thompson, 1907).

30. Daniel T. Rodgers, "Exceptionalism," in *Imagined Histories: American Historians and the Past*, ed. Anthony Molho and Gordon S. Wood (Princeton: Princeton University Press, 1998).

31. Alonzo L. Hamby, *Beyond the New Deal: Harry S. Truman and American Liberalism* (New York: Columbia University Press, 1973); William E. Leuchtenburg, *In the Shadow of FDR: From Harry Truman to Ronald Reagan* (Ithaca: Cornell University Press, 1983).

32. U.S. Congress, Senate Committee on Banking and Currency, *Housing: Hearings on S. 287*, 91st Cong., 1st sess., 1947; idem, *Middle-Income Housing: Hearings on Amendments to S. 2246*, 81st Cong., 2nd sess., 1950; U.S. Congress, Senate Committee on Labor and Public Welfare, Subcommittee on Health Legislation, *National Health Program: Hearings on S. 1106*, 81st Cong., 1st sess., 1949, esp. the testimony of Seymour Harris, pp. 170–172; U.S. Congress, House Committee on Ways and Means, *Social Security: Hearings Relative to the Social Security Amendments of 1939*, 76th Cong., 1st sess., 1939, pp. 1258–1261, 1245; U.S. Congress, Senate Committee on Finance, *Social Security Revision: Hearings on H.R. 6000*, 81st Cong., 2nd sess., 1950, pp. 529–530.

33. Poen, *Harry S. Truman versus the Medical Lobby*, pp. 105, 107, 88; Forest Hackett, "Our Most Dangerous Lobby—II," *Readers' Digest* 51 (Dec. 1947): 63–66.

34. Lichtenstein, *Most Dangerous Man in Detroit*, chap. 15; Nelson Lichtenstein, "Labor in the Truman Era: Origins of the 'Private Welfare State,'" in *The Truman Presidency*, ed. Michael J. Lacey (Cambridge: Cambridge University Press, 1989); Alan Derickson, "Health Security for All? Social Unionism and Universal Health Insurance, 1935–1958," *Journal of American History* 80 (1994): 1333–1356; Beth Stevens, "Labor Unions, Employee Benefits, and the Privatization of the American Welfare States," *Journal of Policy History* 2 (1990): 233–260; Elizabeth A. Fones-Wolf, *Selling Free Enterprise: The Business Assault on Labor and Liberalism, 1945–60* (Urbana: University of Illinois Press, 1994), chap. 4. The quotation is from Lichtenstein, *Most Dangerous Man in Detroit*, pp. 336–337.

35. Robert Moses, "Mr. Moses Dissects the 'Long-Haired Planners,'" *New York Times Magazine*, June 25, 1944, p. 38.

Acknowledgments

This book is the product of many years and many helping hands. The most generous of its patrons have been the institutions whose support provided time away from classroom teaching for research and writing. At an early stage, this project was assisted by a fellowship and research grants from the American Council of Learned Societies and the University of Wisconsin—Madison. Later phases of the research were supported by fellowships from the National Endowment for the Humanities and Princeton University. A Senior Fulbright Lectureship at the University of Frankfurt made the European phase of the research possible. Much of the manuscript was written at the Center for Advanced Study in the Behavioral Sciences, which provided both fellowship assistance and an ideal setting in which to work.

Equally essential has been the assistance of the individuals who have helped this project along its way. Two terrifically talented undergraduate research assistants, Cathy Lager and Joshua Marshall, blazed many of the research trails ahead of me. Ferdinand Kramer shared his memories of Ernst May's projects; Ernst Köhner guided me through Römerstadt. Fred Fox took me in, uninvited, and generously answered my questions in Delhi, California. Across two continents, research librarians and archivists too numerous to name fielded my inquiries, pointed me in fruitful directions, and helped me find the materials on which this study rests.

Others heard these ideas out, read them closely, or argued with them, in the give-and-take that is indespensable to scholarship. Faculty forums at Princeton, Harvard, Stanford, Yale, the Institute of United States Studies at the University of London, the Johann Wolfgang Goethe University at Frankfurt, and the Center for Anglo-American History at Cologne helped sharpen many aspects of this project. Friends and colleagues—Alan Brinkley, Dan Czitrom, Alan Dawley, James Kloppenberg, Arno Mayer, Andy Rabinbach, Dorothy Ross, and John A. Thompson—gave generously of their time to read all or parts of the manuscript and share their critical responses to it. It goes without saying that each one of them would have written this story differently, but the end result is far better for their interventions.

In the final phases of the manuscript, Melissa Chan untangled many knotted footnotes. John Blazejewski assisted with many of the photographs. Julie Ericksen Hagen edited the manuscript with grace and scrupulous care. At Harvard University Press, Aïda Donald gave this book its title, a wise and generous reading, and the care of a talented staff.

Closest to home, my wife, Irene, read the drafts of these pages with her unfailing wisdom, patience, and insight, taking time from her own work to set me straight. My sons, Peter and Dwight, grew up with this project and followed its travels from Madison to Princeton, Frankfurt, and Palo Alto—taking care, all the while, to make sure that the claims of the past were never left uncountered by their wonderfully insistent present. They are readers of life and computer screens rather than history. But they are inheritors of the endeavors recounted here, and as keepers of that legacy—fulfilled and yet to be fulfilled—I give the book to them.

Index